Mathematical Analysis of Machine Learning Algorithms

The mathematical theory of machine learning not only explains current algorithms but can also motivate principled approaches for the future. This self-contained textbook introduces students and researchers of AI to the main mathematical techniques used to analyze machine learning algorithms, with motivations and applications. Topics covered include analysis of supervised learning algorithms in the iid setting, analysis of neural networks (e.g. neural tangent kernel and mean-field analysis), and analysis of machine learning algorithms in the sequential decision setting (e.g. online learning, bandit problems, and reinforcement learning). Students will learn the basic mathematical tools used in the theoretical analysis of these machine learning problems and how to apply them to the analysis of various concrete algorithms.

This textbook is perfect for readers who have some background knowledge of basic machine learning methods, but want to gain sufficient technical knowledge to understand research papers in theoretical machine learning.

TONG ZHANG is Chair Professor of Computer Science and Mathematics at the Hong Kong University of Science and Technology where his research focuses on machine learning, big data, and their applications. A Fellow of the IEEE, the American Statistical Association, and the Institute of Mathematical Statistics, Zhang has served as chair or area chair at major machine learning conferences such as NeurIPS, ICML, and COLT, and he has been an associate editor for several top machine learning publications including *PAMI*, *JMLR*, and *Machine Learning*.

Mathematical Analysis of Machine Learning Algorithms

Tong Zhang
Hong Kong University of Science and Technology

CAMBRIDGE
UNIVERSITY PRESS

Shaftesbury Road, Cambridge CB2 8EA, United Kingdom

One Liberty Plaza, 20th Floor, New York, NY 10006, USA

477 Williamstown Road, Port Melbourne, VIC 3207, Australia

314–321, 3rd Floor, Plot 3, Splendor Forum, Jasola District Centre, New Delhi – 110025, India

103 Penang Road, #05–06/07, Visioncrest Commercial, Singapore 238467

Cambridge University Press is part of Cambridge University Press & Assessment, a department of the University of Cambridge.

We share the University's mission to contribute to society through the pursuit of education, learning and research at the highest international levels of excellence.

www.cambridge.org
Information on this title: www.cambridge.org/9781009098380
DOI: 10.1017/9781009093057

First published 2023

A catalogue record for this publication is available from the British Library.

A Cataloging-in-Publication data record for this book is available from the Library of Congress.

ISBN 978-1-009-09838-0 Hardback

Cambridge University Press & Assessment has no responsibility for the persistence or accuracy of URLs for external or third-party internet websites referred to in this publication and does not guarantee that any content on such websites is, or will remain, accurate or appropriate.

Contents

Preface

Machine learning is a relatively young scientific discipline with the goal of achieving the capability of human decision-making by learning from past experience. It is an interdisciplinary field that requires knowledge of statistics, optimization, engineering, and many innovations in computing. In the past few decades, we have seen rapid development of empirically successful machine learning algorithms, to the degree that machine learning has become an indispensable technology to solve many challenging problems in modern society. In the meantime, the mathematical theory of machine learning has been developed by researchers in computer science, statistics, optimization, and engineering, who are interested in establishing a rigorous mathematical foundation that not only can explain the current algorithms but also can motivate principled approaches for the future. However, many of the existing theoretical results are scattered in the literature. While there are a number of introductory books and survey articles that have tried to cover some of these theoretical results, there isn't any in-depth textbook that is able to provide a comprehensive introduction to standard mathematical tools that have been developed in the literature.

The goal of this book is to present a systematic treatment of the main mathematical techniques that are commonly used to analyze machine learning algorithms in the current literature. Due to the space limitation, the book itself does not explain various machine learning algorithms and their application backgrounds in detail. Therefore it is assumed that readers of the book are already familiar with standard machine learning algorithms such as support vector machines, decision trees, boosting, and neural networks. The readers of the book should also have basic mathematical knowledge of calculus, linear algebra, and probability, as well as sufficient mathematical maturity to follow rigorous theoretical proofs. For such readers, the main purpose of this book is to introduce the modern mathematical techniques that are commonly used to analyze these machine learning algorithms. The selected material is at a level that can provide readers with sufficient technical background and knowledge to read research papers in theoretical machine learning without much difficulty.

The topics selected in the book are intended to cover the most useful and commonly encountered mathematical tools and results at the current research level. Some more specialized topics (such as active learning, semisupervised learning, loss function consistency, differential privacy, to name a few) are omitted, but readers who have learned the technical tools presented in the book should have no difficulty following current research on these topics. The book can be used for a graduate-level course on theoretical machine learning, and it can also serve as a reference for researchers working on theoretical machine learning. While the most fundamental concepts are illustrated in sufficient depth, some other topics of current interest are covered in less detail. Due to the large number of topics, some presentations are relatively concise, and some other topics are presented with a level of abstraction that targets the unification of different special cases that have appeared in the literature. Such abstraction and the concise presentation might lead to some difficulty at a first reading. To alleviate the difficulty, many examples are included to provide concrete interpretations and appropriate context of the theoretical results. Historical remarks are included to give the original sources of the topics covered in the book, as well as extra reading material for readers who are interested in deeper understanding. The exercises provided at the end of each chapter can help the readers to check their mastery of the main concepts. Most exercises require good knowledge of the material, but are not difficult. Moreover, some of the exercises are designed to provide additional information on topics related to, but not directly covered in, the main text.

The book contains two main parts. The first part, from Chapter 1 to Chapter 12, covers analysis of supervised learning algorithms in the iid setting. It starts with the standard exponential tail inequalities for sums of independent variables, and then spends several chapters developing the technical tools for uniform convergence, which is the main mathematical machinery to analyze machine learning algorithms. Key results are established using classical concepts such as covering numbers, VC dimension, and Rademacher complexity. The first part of the book also covers the more recently emerged technique of stability analysis, which can handle specific learning procedures such as stochastic gradient descent. As applications of these basic mathematical tools, analysis of several commonly used machine learning models, including kernel methods, additive models, and neural networks, have also been presented in varying amounts of detail. Finally, the first part concludes with standard lower bound analysis in Chapter 12, which covers the commonly used techniques such as Fano's inequality and Assouad's lemma. Examples on least squares regression and density estimation are also provided.

The second part of the book, starting from Chapter 13, covers the analysis of sequential statistical estimation problems, including online learning, bandit problems, and reinforcement learning. It starts with a generalization of the exponential tail inequalities and uniform convergence analysis from iid random variables to martingales in the sequential setting. It then describes specific algorithms and their analysis in the subsequent chapters on online learning, bandits, and reinforcement learning. Both upper bounds and lower bounds are provided.

The book contains sufficient material for a two-semester graduate-level course, one semester for each part of the book. It can also be used for a one-semester course that covers part of the book. The author has taught graduate courses at the Hong Kong University of Science and Technology based on the contents of the book. Students taking the courses have already learned basic machine learning algorithms, and wish to study further the mathematical tools to analyze these algorithms.

For a one-semester class on the mathematical foundation of machine learning, the following selected materials can be considered: Sections 2.1–2.6 on exponential inequalities, Chapter 3 on uniform convergence, Sections 4.1–4.4 on VC theory, Sections 5.1–5.2 on covering numbers, Sections 6.1–6.4 on Rademacher complexity (covering only the standard Rademacher complexity, while leaving the offset Rademacher complexity as reading material), Sections 8.1–8.3 on model selection, Sections 9.1–9.3 on kernel methods, Sections 10.1–10.3 on additive models, Sections 11.3, 11.4, 11.6, and 11.7 on neural networks, Sections 12.3 and 12.4 on lower bounds, Sections 13.1 and 13.3 on martingales, Sections 14.1–14.4 on online learning, Sections 16.1, 16.2, and 16.6 on bandits, Sections 17.1, 17.3, and 17.4 on contextual bandits, and Sections 18.1–18.3 on reinforcement learning. Lecture slides on these topics are available on the author's website.

The author would like to thank students who read early drafts of the book and provided useful suggestions. In particular, Chutian Huang, Yujia Jin, Yong Lin, Zhefeng Qiao, Yifei Shen, Wei Xiong, and Mengyue Zha provided feedback on parts of the book. I'd also like to thank the editorial staff at Cambridge University Press, Johnathan Fuentes and Katie Leach, for their help and suggestions on the writing of the book. Finally I want to thank my wife Yue for her tremendous support on this undertaking, which has made the writing of the book possible.

1

Introduction

The goal of mathematical analysis of machine learning algorithms is to study the statistical and computational behaviors of methods that are commonly used in machine learning, and to understand their theoretical properties, such as the statistical rate of convergence (usually deriving upper bounds for specific algorithms), the optimality of a statistical method (whether the derived statistical upper bound matches the information theoretical lower bound), and the computational efficiency for various learning models under different assumptions.

This book mainly focuses on the analysis of two common learning models: supervised learning and sequential decision-making problems.

In supervised learning, we train a machine learning model using training data, and then evaluate the model's prediction performance on unseen test data. In this case, we want to investigate the performance of this model on test data.

A mathematical theory for supervised learning answers the following basic questions, where we take the linear model as an example.

- Suppose that we learn a d-dimensional linear classifier with n training data by minimizing the training error. Assume that the training error is 10%. What is the classifier's test error on the (unseen) test data? The test error in this setting is also referred to as the *generalization error*, because it is not observed.
- Can we find a linear classifier that has a test error nearly as small as the optimal linear classifier?
- Can we find a computationally efficient procedure to find a linear classifier with a small test error?

The online learning model is an example of sequential decision-making problems. In online learning, we are interested in the sequential prediction problem, where we train a statistical model using historic data, and then test it on the data in the next time step. We then observe the true outcome after prediction. This process is repeated in a sequential manner. The problem itself is motivated from time series analysis and forecasting problems. We want to know the ability of a learning algorithm to predict future events based on historic observations.

A mathematical theory for online learning needs to answer the following basic questions, where we, again, take the linear model as an example.

- In the online sequential prediction setting. Given a time step t, can we construct an online learning algorithm that predicts nearly as well as the optimal linear classifier up to time step t?

This course develops the mathematical tools to answer these questions.

1.1 Standard Model for Supervised Learning

In supervised learning, we observe an input random variable (feature vector) $X \in \mathbb{R}^d$ that represents the known information, and an output variable (label) Y that represents the unknown information we want to predict. The goal is to predict Y based on X.

As an example, we may want to predict whether an image (represented as input vector X) contains a cat or a dog (label Y).

In practice, the set of prediction rules are derived by parametrized functions $f(w, \cdot) \colon \mathbb{R}^d \to \mathbb{R}^k$, where $w \in \Omega$ is the model parameter that can be learned on the training data. As an example, for the k-class classification problem, where $Y \in \{1, \ldots, k\}$, we predict Y using the following prediction rule given function $f(w, x) = [f_1(w, x), \ldots, f_k(w, x)] \in \mathbb{R}^k$:

$$q(x) = \arg \max_{\ell \in \{1,\ldots,k\}} f_\ell(w, x).$$

The prediction quality is measured by a loss function $L(f(x), y)$: the smaller the loss, the better the prediction accuracy.

The supervised learning approach is to estimate $\hat{w} \in \Omega$ based on observed (labeled) historical data $\mathcal{S}_n = [(X_1, Y_1), \ldots, (X_n, Y_n)]$.

A supervised learning algorithm $\mathcal{A}$ takes a set of training data $\mathcal{S}_n$ as input, and outputs a function $f(\hat{w}, \cdot)$, where $\hat{w} = \mathcal{A}(\mathcal{S}_n) \in \Omega$. The most common algorithm, which we will focus on in this course, is *empirical risk minimization* (ERM):

$$\hat{w} = \arg \min_{w \in \Omega} \sum_{i=1}^{n} L(f(w, X_i), Y_i). \tag{1.1}$$

In the standard theoretical model for analyzing supervised learning problems, we assume that the training data $\{(X_i, Y_i) : i = 1, \ldots, n\}$ are iid (independent and identically distributed), according to an unknown underlying distribution $\mathcal{D}$. The loss of a classifier $\hat{f}(x) = f(\hat{w}, x)$ on the training data is the training error:

$$\text{training-loss}(\hat{w}) = \frac{1}{n} \sum_{i=1}^{n} L(f(\hat{w}, X_i), Y_i).$$

Moreover, we assume that the test data (X, Y) (future unseen data) are also taken from the same distribution $\mathcal{D}$, and we are interested in knowing the generalization error of $\hat{f}$ on the test data, defined as:

$$\text{test-loss}(\hat{w}) = \mathbb{E}_{(X,Y) \sim \mathcal{D}} L(f(\hat{w}, X), Y).$$

Since we only observe the training error of $\hat{f} = f(\hat{w}, \cdot)$, a major goal is to estimate the test error (i.e. generalization error) of $\hat{f}$ based on its training error, referred to as *generalization bound*, which is of the following form. Given $\epsilon \geq 0$, we want to determine $\delta_n(\epsilon)$ so that

$$\Pr\left(\mathbb{E}_{(X,Y)\sim\mathcal{D}}L(f(\hat{w}, X), Y) \geq \frac{1}{n}\sum_{i=1}^{n} L(f(\hat{w}, X_i), Y_i) + \epsilon\right) \leq \delta_n(\epsilon),$$

where the probability is with respect to the randomness over the training data $\mathcal{S}_n$. In general, $\delta_n(\epsilon) \to 0$ as $n \to \infty$.

In the literature, this result is often stated in the following alternative form, where we want to determine a function $\epsilon_n(\delta)$ of δ, so that with probability at least $1 - \delta$ (over the random sampling of the training data $\mathcal{S}_n$):

$$\mathbb{E}_{(X,Y)\sim\mathcal{D}}L(f(\hat{w}, X), Y) \leq \frac{1}{n}\sum_{i=1}^{n} L(f(\hat{w}, X_i), Y_i) + \epsilon_n(\delta). \tag{1.2}$$

We want to show that $\epsilon_n(\delta) \to 0$ as $n \to \infty$.

Another style of theoretical result, often referred to as *oracle inequalities*, is to show that with probability at least $1 - \delta$ (over the random sampling of training data $\mathcal{S}_n$):

$$\mathbb{E}_{(X,Y)\sim\mathcal{D}}L(f(\hat{w}, X), Y) \leq \inf_{w\in\Omega} \mathbb{E}_{(X,Y)\sim\mathcal{D}}L(f(w, X), Y) + \epsilon_n(\delta). \tag{1.3}$$

This shows that the test error achieved by the learning algorithm is nearly as small as that of the optimal test error achieved by $f(w, x)$ with $w \in \Omega$. We say the learning algorithm is consistent if $\epsilon_n(\delta) \to 0$ as $n \to 0$. Moreover, the rate of convergence refers to the rate of $\epsilon_n(\delta)$ converging to zero when $n \to \infty$.

Chapter 2 and Chapter 3 establish the basic mathematical tools in empirical processes for analyzing supervised learning. Chapter 4, Chapter 5, and Chapter 6 further develop the techniques. Chapter 7 considers a different analysis that directly controls the complexity of a learning algorithm using stability. This analysis is gaining popularity due to its ability to work directly with algorithmic procedures such as SGD. Chapter 8 introduces some standard techniques for model selection in the supervised learning setting. Chapter 9 analyzes the kernel methods. Chapter 10 analyzes additive models with a focus on sparsity and boosting. Chapter 11 investigates the analysis of neural networks. Chapter 12 discusses some common techniques and results for establishing statistical lower bounds.

1.2 Online Learning and Sequential Decision-Making

In online learning, we consider observing (X_t, Y_t) one by one in a time sequence from $t = 1, 2, \ldots$. An online algorithm $\mathcal{A}$ learns a model parameter $\hat{w}_t$ at time t based on previously observed data $(X_1, Y_1), \ldots, (X_t, Y_t)$:

$$\hat{w}_t = \mathcal{A}(\{(X_1, Y_1), \ldots, (X_t, Y_t)\}).$$

We then observe the next input vector X_{t+1}, and make prediction $f(\hat{w}_t, X_{t+1})$. After the prediction, we observe Y_{t+1}, and then compute the loss $L(f(\hat{w}_t, X_{t+1}), Y_{t+1})$. The goal of online learning is to minimize the aggregated loss:

$$\sum_{t=0}^{T-1} L(f(\hat{w}_t, X_{t+1}), Y_{t+1}).$$

In the mathematical analysis of online learning algorithms, we are interested in the following inequality, referred to as *regret bound*, where the aggregated loss of an online algorithm is compared to the optimal aggregated loss:

$$\sum_{t=0}^{T-1} L(f(\hat{w}_t, X_{t+1}), Y_{t+1}) \leq \inf_{w \in \Omega} \sum_{t=0}^{T-1} L(f(w, X_{t+1}), Y_{t+1}) + \epsilon_T. \qquad (1.4)$$

The regret ϵ_T, is the extra loss suffered by the learning algorithm, compared to that of the optimal model at time T in retrospect.

As an example, we consider the stock price prediction problem, where the opening price of a certain stock at each trading day is $p_1, p_2, \ldots$. At the beginning of each day t, we observe $p_1, \ldots, p_t$, and want to predict p_{t+1} on day $t+1$, so we use this prediction to trade the stock.

The input X_{t+1} is a d-dimensional real-valued vector in R^d that represents the observed historical information of the stock on day t. The output $Y_{t+1} = \ln(p_{t+1}/p_t)$ will be observed on day $t+1$. We consider a linear model with $f(w, x) = w^\top x$, with $\Omega = \mathbb{R}^d$. The quality is measured by the least squares error:

$$L(f(w, X_{t+1}), Y_{t+1}) = (f(w, X_{t+1}) - Y_{t+1})^2.$$

The learning algorithm can be empirical risk minimization, where

$$\hat{w}_t = \arg\min_{w \in \mathbb{R}^d} \frac{1}{t} \sum_{i=1}^{t} (w^\top X_i - Y_i)^2.$$

In regret analysis, we compare the prediction error

$$\sum_{t=0}^{T-1} (\hat{w}_t^\top X_{t+1} - Y_{t+1})^2$$

to the optimal prediction

$$\inf_{w \in \mathbb{R}^d} \sum_{t=0}^{T-1} (w^\top X_{t+1} - Y_{t+1})^2.$$

Martingale inequalities used in the analysis of sequential decision problems will be introduced in Chapter 13. The online learning model will be studied in Chapter 14 and Chapter 15. The related bandit problem will be investigated in Chapter 16 and Chapter 17. In the bandit problem, we investigate online problems with incomplete information, where Y_t is only partially revealed based on actions of the learning algorithm. The goal is to take an optimal sequence of actions to maximize rewards (or minimize loss). Finally, in Chapter 18, we will introduce some basic techniques to analyze reinforcement learning. The reinforcement learning model can be considered as a generalization of the bandit model, where, at each time step (epoch), multiple actions are taken to interact with the environment. This is still an actively developing field, with major theoretical advances appearing in recent years. We will only cover some basic results that are most closely related to the analysis of bandit problems.

1.3 Computational Consideration

In the ERM method, the model parameter $\hat{w}$ is the solution of an optimization problem. If the optimization problem is convex, then the solution can be efficiently computed. If the optimization problem is nonconvex, then its solution may not be obtained easily.

Theoretically, we separately consider two different types of complexity. One is statistical complexity, where we may ignore the complexity of computation, and try to derive bounds (1.3) and (1.4) even though the computational complexity of the underlying learning algorithm (such as ERM) may be high.

However, in practice, an important consideration is computational complexity, where we are interested in computationally efficient algorithms with good generalization performance or regret bounds. For nonconvex models, this kind of analysis can be rather complex, and usually requires problem specific analyses that are not generally applicable.

A generally studied approach to a nonconvex problem is to use convex approximation (also referred to convex relaxation) to solve the nonconvex problem approximately. The related theoretical question is under what circumstances the solution has statistical generalization performance comparable to that of the nonconvex methods. An example is the sparse learning problem, where the convex formulation with L_1 regularization is used as a proxy to the nonconvex L_0 regularization. In this case, we are interested in establishing the condition under which one can obtain a solution from L_1 regularization that is close to the true sparse model.

The combined analysis of computational and statistical complexity is a major research direction in theoretical machine learning. This book mainly covers the statistical analysis aspect. Nevertheless, the computational complexity will also be considered when practical algorithms are investigated.

1.4 Basic Concepts in Generalization Analysis

The goal of machine learning is to find a function $f(\hat{w}, x)$ that predicts well on unseen data (test data). However, we only observe the prediction accuracy of $f(\hat{w}, x)$ on the training data. In order to achieve high prediction accuracy, we need to balance the following two aspects of learning:

- The prediction function should fit the training data well; that is, achieve a small training error. This requires a more expressive model, with a larger parameter space Ω.

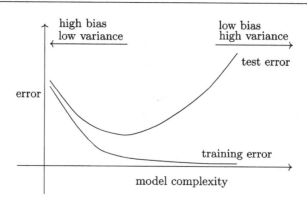

Figure 1.1 Training and test errors versus model complexity

- Performance of prediction function on the test data should match that on the training data. The difference is smaller for a less expressive model with a smaller parameter space Ω.

The gap between training error and test error depends on model complexity, which characterizes how large the model parameter space Ω is. When Ω is too large, the training error becomes smaller, but the difference between training error and test error increases. Therefore, in practice, there is a trade-off in machine learning, and the best prediction performance is achieved with the right balance, often via a tuning parameter in the learning algorithm that characterizes model complexity. The phenomenon is described in Figure 1.1. Such a tuning process is often referred to as hyperparameter optimization.

When the class of prediction functions is too large (or complex), then the difference between training error and test error increases. This leads to the so-called *overfitting* phenomenon. A simple example of overfitting can be described as follows. Let X be a one-dimensional feature uniformly distributed in $[-1, 1]$, with class label $Y = 1$ when $X \geq 0$ and $Y = -1$ when $X < 0$. The optimal classifier can achieve a test error of 0.

Given training data (X_i, Y_i) $(i = 1, \ldots, n)$, and assuming X_i are all different, if we consider a prediction function class that contains all possible functions, then the empirical risk minimization method with the following solution can fit the data perfectly:

$$\hat{f}(X) = \begin{cases} Y_i & \text{if } X = X_i \text{ for some } i, \\ 1 & \text{otherwise.} \end{cases}$$

This model class has high model complexity measured by its *covering number*, which we will study in the book. However, the resulting ERM prediction rule does not make any meaningful prediction when X is not in the training data. This is because, although the training error of 0 is small, it is significantly different from the test error of 0.5.

In contrast, if we let the prediction model contain only one function $\{f(x): f(x) \equiv 0\}$, then, using the tail inequality of independent random variables of Chapter 2, we know that the difference between the training error and the test error will be small when n is large. However, since the training error of ≈ 0.5 is large, the test error is also large.

Let $\mathbf{1}(x \in A)$ be the set indicator function that takes value 1 if $x \in A$, and 0 if $x \notin A$. Assume that we pick the model function class $\{f(w, x): f(w, x) = 2\mathbf{1}(x \geq w) - 1\}$ parametrized by a parameter $w \in R$. Assume also that we find a classifier $f(\hat{w}, x)$ that minimizes the training error. Using techniques in Chapter 3, it can be shown that both training error and test error of this classifier converge to zero when $n \to \infty$. This model class balances the training error and generalization performance. In summary, a key technique of the mathematical theory for machine learning is to estimate the generalization performance (prediction accuracy on unseen data) of learning algorithms, and quantify the degree of overfitting.

Finally it is worth pointing out that the mathematical theory developed for limiting model size and preventing overfitting is the key classical technique to obtain good generalization results in machine learning. However, in recent years, this classical view point has evolved due to the empirical observation in modern neural network models that large models nearly always perform better. For such models, one observes the so-called *benign overfitting* phenomenon, where learning algorithms with appropriate *implicit bias* can still achieve good test performance even if the resulting model completely overfits the noise. This is an active research area that is still developing rapidly. Consequently, the related theoretical results are less mature. We will thus only discuss some theoretical intuitions behind this phenomenon in Section 11.7, but dedicate the main parts of the book to the classical learning theory.

1.5 Historical and Bibliographical Remarks

Machine learning is now considered the key technology for artificial intelligence (AI), which aims to create computing machines that can mimic the problem-solving skills of a human (McCarthy et al., 2006). In recent years, machine learning has become an important scientific research field on its own, and has many applications that have made significant impact in our modern society. The term "machine learning" has often been attributed to Samuel (1959), who defined it as the "field of study that gives computers the ability to learn without being explicitly programmed."

There are two approaches to machine learning (AI): one is to use statistical methods to learn functions from data and past experience, in order to predict future events. This is the approach considered in this book. An alternative approach to AI is symbolic reasoning, which creates a knowledge base, and then uses logic to create rules that can perform inference (Haugeland, 1989). The latter approach explicitly incorporates human knowledge into computer programs, without the need for direct learning from past experiences. Although the symbolic approach showed some promise in the early decades of AI research (Studer et al., 1998), it has major limitations in dealing with uncertainty in real-world applications. For complex problems, the symbolic rules needed to handle difficult situations are often too complex to build and maintain. For this reason, the modern applications of machine learning heavily relied on the statistical approach, although the hybrid of statistic-based machine learning and symbolic AI is still an active research direction.

The mathematical foundation of machine learning has its origin in probability and theoretical statistics. In particular, the theory of empirical processes has been used to analyze the generalization performance of machine learning algorithms. The first part of the book will describe the basic tools of empirical processes that are commonly used in machine learning. Learning in the sequential decision setting is a different paradigm for theoretical analysis, and the key quantity of interests, regret bound, has its origin in theoretical computer science. The techniques used in the analysis are also closely related to stochastic optimization and stochastic processes. Both computational and statistical aspects are considered in some of the procedures while only the statistical aspects are considered for others. The second part of the book will describe the mathematical tools for analyzing learning problems in the sequential decision setting.

2

Basic Probability Inequalities for Sums of Independent Random Variables

In machine learning, the observations contain uncertainty, and to incorporate uncertainty, these observations are modeled as random variables. When we observe many data, a basic quantity of interest is the empirical mean of the observed random variables, which converges to the expectation according to the law of large numbers. We want to upper bound the probability of the event when the empirical mean deviates significantly from the expectation, which is referred to as the tail probability. This chapter studies the basic mathematical tools to estimate tail probabilities by using exponential moment estimates.

Let $X_1, \ldots, X_n$ be n real-valued independent and identically distributed (iid) random variables, with expectation $\mu = \mathbb{E}X_i$. Let

$$\bar{X}_n = \frac{1}{n} \sum_{i=1}^{n} X_i. \tag{2.1}$$

Given $\epsilon > 0$, we are interested in estimating the following tail probabilities:

$$\Pr(\bar{X}_n \geq \mu + \epsilon),$$
$$\Pr(\bar{X}_n \leq \mu - \epsilon).$$

In machine learning, we can regard $\bar{X}_n$ as the training error observed on the training data. The unknown mean μ is the test error that we want to infer from the training error. Therefore in machine learning, these tail inequalities can be interpreted as follows: with high probability, the test error is close to the training error. Such results will be used to derive rigorous statements of generalization error bounds in subsequent chapters.

2.1 Normal Random Variable

The general form of tail inequality for the sum of random variables (with relatively light tails) is exponential in ϵ^2. To motivate this general form, we will consider the case of normal random variables. The bounds can be obtained using simple calculus.

Theorem 2.1 *Let $X_1, \ldots, X_n$ be n iid Gaussian random variables $X_i \sim N(\mu, \sigma^2)$, and let $\bar{X}_n = n^{-1} \sum_{i=1}^{n} X_i$. Then given any $\epsilon > 0$,*

$$0.5 e^{-n(\epsilon + \sigma/\sqrt{n})^2/2\sigma^2} \leq \Pr(\bar{X}_n \geq \mu + \epsilon) \leq 0.5 e^{-n\epsilon^2/2\sigma^2}.$$

Proof We first consider a standard normal random variable $X \sim N(0,1)$, which has probability density function

$$p(x) = \frac{1}{\sqrt{2\pi}} e^{-x^2/2}.$$

Given $\epsilon > 0$, we can upper bound the tail probability $\Pr(X \geq \epsilon)$ as follows:

$$\Pr(X \geq \epsilon) = \int_\epsilon^\infty \frac{1}{\sqrt{2\pi}} e^{-x^2/2} dx$$

$$= \int_0^\infty \frac{1}{\sqrt{2\pi}} e^{-(x+\epsilon)^2/2} dx \leq \int_0^\infty \frac{1}{\sqrt{2\pi}} e^{-(x^2+\epsilon^2)/2} dx$$

$$= 0.5 e^{-\epsilon^2/2}.$$

We also have the following lower bound:

$$\Pr(X \geq \epsilon) = \int_\epsilon^\infty \frac{1}{\sqrt{2\pi}} e^{-x^2/2} dx$$

$$\geq \int_0^1 \frac{1}{\sqrt{2\pi}} e^{-(x+\epsilon)^2/2} dx$$

$$\geq \int_0^1 \frac{1}{\sqrt{2\pi}} e^{-x^2/2} e^{-(2\epsilon+\epsilon^2)/2} dx \geq 0.34 e^{-(2\epsilon+\epsilon^2)/2}$$

$$\geq 0.5 e^{-(\epsilon+1)^2/2}.$$

Therefore we have

$$0.5 e^{-(\epsilon+1)^2/2} \leq \Pr(X \geq \epsilon) \leq 0.5 e^{-\epsilon^2/2}.$$

Since $\sqrt{n}(\bar{X}_n - \mu)/\sigma \sim N(0,1)$, by using

$$\Pr(\bar{X}_n \geq \mu + \epsilon) = \Pr(\sqrt{n}(\bar{X}_n - \mu)/\sigma \geq \sqrt{n}\epsilon/\sigma),$$

we obtain the desired result.   □

We note that the tail probability of a normal random variable decays exponentially fast, and such an inequality is referred to as an *exponential inequality*. This exponential bound is asymptotically tight as $n \to \infty$ in the following sense. For any $\epsilon > 0$, we have

$$\lim_{n\to\infty} \frac{1}{n} \ln \Pr(|\bar{X}_n - \mu| \geq \epsilon) = -\frac{\epsilon^2}{2\sigma^2}.$$

Such a result is also called a large deviation result, which is the regime when the deviation ϵ of the empirical mean from the true mean μ is much larger than the standard deviation $\sigma/\sqrt{n}$ of $\bar{X}_n$ (Deuschel and Stroock, 2001). The analysis of normal random variables can rely on standard calculus. For general random variables with exponentially decaying tail probabilities, we can use the technique of exponential moment to derive similar results. This leads to a general technique to estimate the probability of large deviation of the empirical mean from the true mean.

2.2 Markov's Inequality

A standard technique to estimate the tail inequality of a random variable is the Markov inequality. Let $X_1, \ldots, X_n$ be n real-valued iid random variables (which are not necessarily normal random variables) with mean μ. Let $\bar{X}_n$ be the empirical mean defined in (2.1). We are interested in estimating the tail bound $\Pr(\bar{X}_n \geq \mu + \epsilon)$, and Markov's inequality states as follows.

Theorem 2.2 (Markov's Inequality) *Given any nonnegative function $h(x) \geq 0$, and a set $S \subset \mathbb{R}$, we have*

$$\Pr(\bar{X}_n \in S) \leq \frac{\mathbb{E}\, h(\bar{X}_n)}{\inf_{x \in S} h(x)}.$$

Proof Since $h(x)$ is nonnegative, we have

$$\mathbb{E}\, h(\bar{X}_n) \geq \mathbb{E}_{\bar{X}_n \in S}\, h(\bar{X}_n) \geq \mathbb{E}_{\bar{X}_n \in S}\, h_S = \Pr(\bar{X}_n \in S)\, h_S,$$

where $h_S = \inf_{x \in S} h(x)$. This leads to the desired bound. $\square$

In particular, we may consider the choice of $h(z) = z^2$, which leads to Chebyshev's inequality.

Corollary 2.3 (Chebyshev's Inequality) *We have*

$$\Pr(|\bar{X}_n - \mu| \geq \epsilon) \leq \frac{\mathrm{Var}(X_1)}{n\epsilon^2}. \tag{2.2}$$

Proof Let $h(x) = x^2$, then

$$\mathbb{E}\, h(\bar{X}_n - \mu) = \mathbb{E}(\bar{X}_n - \mu)^2 = \frac{1}{n}\mathrm{Var}(X_1).$$

The desired bound follows from the Markov inequality with $S = \{|\bar{X}_n - \mu| \geq \epsilon\}$. $\square$

Note that Chebyshev's inequality employs $h(z) = z^2$, which leads to a tail inequality that is polynomial in n^{-1} and ϵ. It only requires that the variance of a random variable is bounded. In comparison, the Gaussian tail inequality has a much faster exponential decay. Exponential tail inequality is important for analyzing learning algorithms. In the following, we show that such an inequality can be established for sums of random variables with exponentially decaying tail probabilities.

2.3 Exponential Tail Inequality

In order to obtain exponential tail bounds, we will need to choose $h(z) = e^{\lambda n z}$ in Markov's inequality with some tuning parameter $\lambda \in \mathbb{R}$. Similar to Chebyshev's inequality, which requires that the variance of a random variable is bounded, we assume exponential moment $\mathbb{E}e^{\lambda X_1} < \infty$ for some $\lambda \neq 0$. This requires that the random variable X_i has tail probability that decays exponentially fast. The following definition is helpful in the analysis.

Definition 2.4 Given a random variable X, we may define its logarithmic moment generating function as

$$\Lambda_X(\lambda) = \ln \mathbb{E}e^{\lambda X}.$$

Moreover, given $z \in \mathbb{R}$, the rate function $I_X(z)$ is defined as

$$I_X(z) = \begin{cases} \sup_{\lambda>0} [\lambda z - \Lambda_X(\lambda)] & z > \mu, \\ 0 & z = \mu, \\ \sup_{\lambda<0} [\lambda z - \Lambda_X(\lambda)] & z < \mu, \end{cases}$$

where $\mu = \mathbb{E}[X]$.

This definition can be used to obtain exponential tail bounds for sums of independent variables as follows.

Theorem 2.5 *For any n and $\epsilon > 0$,*

$$\frac{1}{n} \ln \Pr(\bar{X}_n \geq \mu + \epsilon) \leq -I_{X_1}(\mu + \epsilon) = \inf_{\lambda>0} \left[-\lambda(\mu + \epsilon) + \ln \mathbb{E}e^{\lambda X_1} \right],$$

$$\frac{1}{n} \ln \Pr(\bar{X}_n \leq \mu - \epsilon) \leq -I_{X_1}(\mu - \epsilon) = \inf_{\lambda<0} \left[-\lambda(\mu - \epsilon) + \ln \mathbb{E}e^{\lambda X_1} \right].$$

Proof We choose $h(z) = e^{\lambda n z}$ in Theorem 2.2 with $S = \{\bar{X}_n - \mu \geq \epsilon\}$. For $\lambda > 0$, we have

$$\Pr(\bar{X}_n \geq \mu + \epsilon) \leq \frac{\mathbb{E}e^{\lambda n \bar{X}_n}}{e^{\lambda n(\mu+\epsilon)}} = \frac{\mathbb{E}e^{\lambda \sum_{i=1}^n X_i}}{e^{\lambda n(\mu+\epsilon)}}$$

$$= \frac{\mathbb{E} \prod_{i=1}^n e^{\lambda X_i}}{e^{\lambda n(\mu+\epsilon)}} = e^{-\lambda n(\mu+\epsilon)} \left[\mathbb{E}e^{\lambda X_1} \right]^n.$$

The last equation used the independence of X_i as well, as they are identically distributed. Therefore by taking the logarithm, we obtain

$$\ln \Pr(\bar{X}_n \geq \mu + \epsilon) \leq n \left[-\lambda(\mu + \epsilon) + \ln \mathbb{E} \, e^{\lambda X_1} \right].$$

Taking inf over $\lambda > 0$ on the right-hand side, we obtain the first desired bound. Similarly, we can obtain the second bound. ☐

The first inequality of Theorem 2.5 can be rewritten as

$$\Pr(\bar{X}_n \geq \mu + \epsilon) \leq \exp[-nI_{X_1}(\mu + \epsilon)].$$

It shows that the tail probability of the empirical mean decays exponentially fast, if the rate function $I_{X_1}(\cdot)$ is finite. More concrete exponential tail inequalities can be obtained by applying Theorem 2.5 to specific random variables. For example, for Gaussian random variables, we can derive a tail inequality using Theorem 2.5, and compare it to that of Theorem 2.1.

Example 2.6 (Gaussian Random Variable) Assume that $X_i \sim N(\mu, \sigma^2)$, then the exponential moment is

$$\mathbb{E}e^{\lambda(X_1-\mu)} = \int_{-\infty}^{\infty} \frac{1}{\sqrt{2\pi}\sigma}e^{\lambda x}e^{-x^2/2\sigma^2}dx$$

$$= \int_{-\infty}^{\infty} \frac{1}{\sqrt{2\pi}}e^{\lambda^2\sigma^2/2}e^{-(x/\sigma-\lambda\sigma)^2/2}dx/\sigma = e^{\lambda^2\sigma^2/2}.$$

Therefore,

$$I_{X_1}(\mu+\epsilon) = \sup_{\lambda>0}\left[\lambda\epsilon - \ln \mathbb{E}e^{\lambda(X_1-\mu)}\right] = \sup_{\lambda>0}\left[\lambda\epsilon - \frac{\lambda^2\sigma^2}{2}\right] = \frac{\epsilon^2}{2\sigma^2},$$

where the optimal λ is achieved at $\lambda = \epsilon/\sigma^2$. Therefore

$$\Pr(\bar{X}_n \geq \mu+\epsilon) \leq \exp[-nI_{X_1}(\mu+\epsilon)] = \exp\left[\frac{-n\epsilon^2}{2\sigma^2}\right].$$

This leads to the same probability bound as that of Theorem 2.1 up to a constant factor.

This Gaussian example, together with Theorem 2.1, implies that the exponential inequality derived from Theorem 2.5 is asymptotically tight. This result can be generalized to the large deviation inequality for general random variables. In particular, we have the following theorem.

Theorem 2.7 *For all $\epsilon' > \epsilon > 0$,*

$$\varliminf_{n\to\infty}\frac{1}{n}\ln \Pr(\bar{X}_n \geq \mu+\epsilon) \geq -I_{X_1}(\mu+\epsilon').$$

Similarly,

$$\varliminf_{n\to\infty}\frac{1}{n}\ln \Pr(\bar{X}_n \leq \mu-\epsilon) \geq -I_{X_1}(\mu-\epsilon').$$

Proof We only need to prove the first inequality. Consider $\Pr(X_i \leq x)$ as a function of x, and define a random variable X_i' with density at x as

$$d\Pr(X_i' \leq x) = e^{\lambda x - \Lambda_{X_1}(\lambda)}d\Pr(X_i \leq x).$$

This choice implies that

$$\frac{d}{d\lambda}\Lambda_{X_1}(\lambda) = \frac{\int xe^{\lambda x}d\Pr(X_1 \leq x)}{\int e^{\lambda x}d\Pr(X_1 \leq x)} = \mathbb{E}_{X_1'}X_1'.$$

We now take λ such that

$$\lambda = \arg\max_{\lambda'>0}\left[\lambda'(\mu+\epsilon') - \Lambda_{X_1}(\lambda')\right].$$

By setting the derivative to zero, we obtain

$$\mathbb{E}_{X_1'}X_1' = \frac{d}{d\lambda}\Lambda_{X_1}(\lambda) = \mu+\epsilon', \tag{2.3}$$

$$-\lambda(\mu+\epsilon') + \Lambda(\lambda) = -I(\mu+\epsilon'). \tag{2.4}$$

Let $\bar{X}'_n = n^{-1}\sum_{i=1}^n X'_i$. Then, by the law of large numbers, we know that for $\epsilon'' > \epsilon'$, we obtain from (2.3)

$$\lim_{n\to\infty} \Pr(\bar{X}'_n - \mu \in [\epsilon, \epsilon'']) = 1. \qquad (2.5)$$

Since the joint density of $(X'_1, \ldots, X'_n)$ satisfies

$$e^{-\lambda\sum_{i=1}^n x_i + n\Lambda_{X_1}(\lambda)} \prod_i d\Pr(X'_i \leq x_i) = \prod_i d\Pr(X_i \leq x_i), \qquad (2.6)$$

by using $\mathbb{1}(\cdot)$ to denote the set indicator function, we obtain

$$\begin{aligned}
\Pr(\bar{X}_n \geq \mu + \epsilon) &\geq \Pr(\bar{X}_n - \mu \in [\epsilon, \epsilon'']) \\
&= \mathbb{E}_{X_1,\ldots,X_n} \mathbb{1}(\bar{X}_n - \mu \in [\epsilon, \epsilon'']) \\
&= \mathbb{E}_{X'_1,\ldots,X'_n} e^{-\lambda n \bar{X}'_n + n\Lambda(\lambda)} \mathbb{1}(\bar{X}'_n - \mu \in [\epsilon, \epsilon'']) \\
&\geq e^{-\lambda n(\mu+\epsilon'')+n\Lambda(\lambda)} \Pr(\bar{X}'_n - \mu \in [\epsilon, \epsilon'']).
\end{aligned}$$

The first equality used the definition of $\Pr(\cdot)$. The second equality used (2.6). The last inequality used Markov's inequality. Now by taking the logarithm, and dividing by n, we obtain

$$\frac{1}{n}\ln\Pr(\bar{X}_n \geq \mu + \epsilon) \qquad (2.7)$$

$$\geq -\lambda(\mu+\epsilon'') + \Lambda(\lambda) + \frac{1}{n}\ln\Pr(\bar{X}'_n - \mu \in [\epsilon, \epsilon''])$$

$$= -I(\mu+\epsilon') - \lambda(\epsilon''-\epsilon') + \frac{1}{n}\ln\Pr(\bar{X}'_n - \mu \in [\epsilon, \epsilon'']). \qquad (2.8)$$

The equality used (2.4). Now we obtain the desired bound by letting $n \to \infty$, applying (2.5), and letting $\epsilon'' \to \epsilon'$ so that $\lambda(\epsilon'' - \epsilon') \to 0$ (this is true because λ depends only on ϵ'). $\qquad\square$

The combination of Theorem 2.5 and Theorem 2.7 shows that the large deviation tail probability is determined by the rate function. This result is referred to as Cramér's theorem (Cramér, 1938; Deuschel and Stroock, 2001).

For specific cases, one can obtain an estimate of $\Pr(\bar{X}'_n - \mu \in [\epsilon, \epsilon''])$ in (2.8) with finite n at $\epsilon' = \epsilon + 2\sqrt{\mathrm{Var}(X_1)/n}$ and $\epsilon'' = \epsilon + 4\sqrt{\mathrm{Var}(X_1)/n}$. Using Chebyshev's inequality, we expect that $\Pr(\bar{X}'_n - \mu \in [\epsilon, \epsilon''])$ is lower bounded by a constant. This means that as $n \to \infty$, the exponential tail inequality of Theorem 2.5 is generally loose by no more than $O(\sqrt{\mathrm{Var}(X_1)/n})$ in terms of deviation ϵ. A concrete calculation will be presented for bounded random variables in Section 2.5.

Before we investigate concrete examples of random variables, we state the following property of the logarithmic generating function of a random variable, which provides intuitions on its behavior. The proof is left as an exercise.

Proposition 2.8 *Given a random variable with finite variance, we have*

$$\Lambda_X(\lambda)\Big|_{\lambda=0} = 0, \qquad \frac{d\Lambda_X(\lambda)}{d\lambda}\Big|_{\lambda=0} = \mathbb{E}[X], \qquad \frac{d^2\Lambda_X(\lambda)}{d\lambda^2}\Big|_{\lambda=0} = \mathrm{Var}[X].$$

In the application of large deviation bounds, we are mostly interested in the case that deviation ϵ is close to zero. As shown in Example 2.6, the optimal λ we shall choose is $\lambda = O(\epsilon) \approx 0$. It is thus natural to consider the Taylor expansion of the logarithmic moment generating function around $\lambda = 0$. Proposition 2.8 implies that the leading terms of the Taylor expansion are

$$\Lambda_X(\lambda) = \lambda\mu + \frac{\lambda^2}{2}\mathrm{Var}[X] + o(\lambda^2),$$

where $\mu = \mathbb{E}[X]$. The first two terms match that of the normal random variable in Example 2.6. When $\epsilon > 0$ is small, to obtain the rate function

$$I_X(\mu + \epsilon) = \sup_{\lambda > 0}\left[\lambda(\mu + \epsilon) - \lambda\mu - \frac{\lambda^2}{2}\mathrm{Var}[X] - o(\lambda^2)\right],$$

we should set the optimal λ approximately as $\lambda \approx \epsilon/\mathrm{Var}[X]$, and the corresponding rate function becomes

$$I_X(\mu + \epsilon) \approx \frac{\epsilon^2}{2\mathrm{Var}[X]} + o(\epsilon^2).$$

For specific forms of logarithmic moment generation functions, one may obtain more precise bounds of the rate function. In particular, the following general estimate is useful in many applications. This estimate is what we will use throughout the chapter.

Lemma 2.9 *Consider a random variable X so that $\mathbb{E}[X] = \mu$. Assume that there exists $\alpha > 0$ and $\beta \geq 0$ such that for $\lambda \in [0, \beta^{-1})$,*

$$\Lambda_X(\lambda) \leq \lambda\mu + \frac{\alpha\lambda^2}{2(1 - \beta\lambda)}, \tag{2.9}$$

then for $\epsilon > 0$,

$$-I_X(\mu + \epsilon) \leq -\frac{\epsilon^2}{2(\alpha + \beta\epsilon)},$$

$$-I_X\left(\mu + \epsilon + \frac{\beta\epsilon^2}{2\alpha}\right) \leq -\frac{\epsilon^2}{2\alpha}.$$

Proof Note that

$$-I_X(\mu + \epsilon) \leq \inf_{\lambda > 0}\left[-\lambda(\mu + \epsilon) + \lambda\mu + \frac{\alpha\lambda^2}{2(1 - \beta\lambda)}\right].$$

We can take λ at $\bar{\lambda} = \epsilon/(\alpha + \beta\epsilon)$. This implies that $\alpha\bar{\lambda}/(1 - \beta\bar{\lambda}) = \epsilon$. Therefore

$$-I_X(\mu + \epsilon) \leq -\bar{\lambda}\epsilon + \frac{\alpha\bar{\lambda}^2}{2(1 - \beta\bar{\lambda})} = -\frac{\bar{\lambda}\epsilon}{2} = -\frac{\epsilon^2}{2(\alpha + \beta\epsilon)}.$$

Moreover, with the same choice of $\bar{\lambda}$, we have

$$-I_X\left(\mu + \epsilon + \frac{\beta}{2\alpha}\epsilon^2\right) \leq -\bar{\lambda}\epsilon\left(1 + \frac{\beta}{2\alpha}\epsilon\right) + \frac{\alpha\bar{\lambda}^2}{2(1 - \beta\bar{\lambda})} = -\frac{\epsilon^2}{2\alpha}.$$

This proves the second desired bound. □

Lemma 2.9 implies the following generic theorem.

Theorem 2.10 *If X_1 has a logarithmic moment generating function that satisfies (2.9) for $\lambda > 0$, then for all $\epsilon > 0$,*

$$\Pr(\bar{X}_n \geq \mu + \epsilon) \leq \exp\left[\frac{-n\epsilon^2}{2(\alpha + \beta\epsilon)}\right].$$

Moreover, for $t > 0$, we have

$$\Pr\left(\bar{X}_n \geq \mu + \sqrt{\frac{2\alpha t}{n}} + \frac{\beta t}{n}\right) \leq e^{-t}.$$

Proof The first inequality of the theorem follows from the first inequality of Lemma 2.9 and Theorem 2.5. The second inequality of the theorem follows from the second inequality of Lemma 2.9 and Theorem 2.5, with $\epsilon = \sqrt{2\alpha t/n}$. □

2.4 Sub-Gaussian Random Variable

The logarithmic moment generating function of a normal random variable is quadratic in λ. More generally, we may define a sub-Gaussian random variable as a random variable with logarithmic moment generating function dominated by a quadratic function in λ. Such random variables have light tails, which implies that they have a tail probability inequality similar to that of a Gaussian random variable.

Definition 2.11 A sub-Gaussian random variable X has quadratic logarithmic moment generating function for all $\lambda \in \mathbb{R}$:

$$\ln \mathbb{E}e^{\lambda X} \leq \lambda\mu + \frac{\lambda^2}{2}b. \tag{2.10}$$

Using (2.10), we can obtain an upper bound of the rate function for sub-Gaussian random variables, which imply the following tail inequality.

Theorem 2.12 *If X_1 is sub-Gaussian as in (2.10), then for all $t > 0$,*

$$\Pr\left(\bar{X}_n \geq \mu + \sqrt{\frac{2bt}{n}}\right) \leq e^{-t},$$

$$\Pr\left(\bar{X}_n \leq \mu - \sqrt{\frac{2bt}{n}}\right) \leq e^{-t}.$$

Proof The result follows from Theorem 2.10 with $\alpha = b$ and $\beta = 0$. □

Common examples of sub-Gaussian random variables include Gaussian random variables and bounded random variables.

Example 2.13   A Gaussian random variable $X_1 \sim N(\mu, \sigma^2)$ is sub-Gaussian with $b = \sigma^2$.

Example 2.14   Consider a bounded random variable: $X_1 \in [\alpha, \beta]$. Then X_1 is sub-Gaussian with $b = (\beta - \alpha)^2/4$.

The tail probability inequality of Theorem 2.12 can also be expressed in a different form. Consider $\delta \in (0, 1)$ such that $\delta = \exp(-t)$, so we have $t = \ln(1/\delta)$. This means that we can alternatively express the first bound of Theorem 2.12 as follows. With probability at least $1 - \delta$, we have

$$\bar{X}_n < \mu + \sqrt{\frac{2b \ln(1/\delta)}{n}}.$$

This form is often preferred in the theoretical analysis of machine learning algorithms.

2.5 Hoeffding's Inequality

Hoeffding's inequality (Hoeffding, 1963) is an exponential tail inequality for bounded random variables. In the machine learning and computer science literature, it is often referred to as the Chernoff bound.

Lemma 2.15   *Consider a random variable $X \in [0, 1]$ and $\mathbb{E}X = \mu$. We have the following inequality:*

$$\ln \mathbb{E}e^{\lambda X} \leq \ln[(1 - \mu)e^0 + \mu e^\lambda] \leq \lambda \mu + \lambda^2/8.$$

Proof   Let $h_L(\lambda) = \mathbb{E}e^{\lambda X}$ and $h_R(\lambda) = (1 - \mu)e^0 + \mu e^\lambda$. We know that $h_L(0) = h_R(0)$. Moreover, when $\lambda \geq 0$,

$$h'_L(\lambda) = \mathbb{E}X e^{\lambda X} \leq \mathbb{E}X e^\lambda = \mu e^\lambda = h'_R(\lambda),$$

and similarly $h'_L(\lambda) \geq h'_R(\lambda)$ when $\lambda \leq 0$. This proves the first inequality.

Now we let

$$h(\lambda) = \ln[(1 - \mu)e^0 + \mu e^\lambda].$$

It implies that

$$h'(\lambda) = \frac{\mu e^\lambda}{(1 - \mu)e^0 + \mu e^\lambda},$$

and

$$h''(\lambda) = \frac{\mu e^\lambda}{(1 - \mu)e^0 + \mu e^\lambda} - \frac{(\mu e^\lambda)^2}{[(1 - \mu)e^0 + \mu e^\lambda]^2}$$
$$= |h'(\lambda)|(1 - |h'(\lambda)|) \leq 1/4.$$

Using Taylor expansion, we obtain the inequality $h(\lambda) \leq h(0) + \lambda h'(0) + \lambda^2/8$, which proves the second inequality. $\square$

The lemma implies that the maximum logarithmic moment generating function of a random variable X taking values in $[0, 1]$ is achieved by a $\{0, 1\}$-valued Bernoulli random variable with the same mean. Moreover, the random variable X is sub-Gaussian. We can then apply the sub-Gaussian tail inequality in Theorem 2.12 to obtain the following additive form of Chernoff bound.

Theorem 2.16 (Additive Chernoff Bounds)   *Assume that $X_1 \in [0, 1]$. Then for all $\epsilon > 0$,*

$$\Pr(\bar{X}_n \geq \mu + \epsilon) \leq e^{-2n\epsilon^2},$$
$$\Pr(\bar{X}_n \leq \mu - \epsilon) \leq e^{-2n\epsilon^2}.$$

Proof   We simply take $b = 1/4$ and $t = 2n\epsilon^2$ in Theorem 2.12 to obtain the first inequality. The second inequality follows from the equivalence of $\bar{X}_n \leq \mu - \epsilon$ and $-\bar{X}_n \leq -\mu + \epsilon$.   □

In some applications, one may need to employ a more refined form of Chernoff bound, which can be stated as follows.

Theorem 2.17   *Assume that $X_1 \in [0, 1]$. Then for all $\epsilon > 0$, we have*

$$\Pr(\bar{X}_n \geq \mu + \epsilon) \leq e^{-n\mathrm{KL}(\mu+\epsilon\|\mu)},$$
$$\Pr(\bar{X}_n \leq \mu - \epsilon) \leq e^{-n\mathrm{KL}(\mu-\epsilon\|\mu)},$$

where $\mathrm{KL}(z\|\mu)$ is the Kullback–Leibler divergence *(KL-divergence) defined as*

$$\mathrm{KL}(z\|\mu) = z \ln \frac{z}{\mu} + (1 - z) \ln \frac{1 - z}{1 - \mu}.$$

Proof   Consider the case $z = \mu + \epsilon$. We have

$$-I_{X_1}(z) \leq \inf_{\lambda > 0} [-\lambda z + \ln((1 - \mu)e^0 + \mu e^\lambda)].$$

Assume that the optimal value of λ on the right-hand side is achieved at λ_*. By setting the derivative to zero, we obtain the expression

$$z = \frac{\mu e^{\lambda_*}}{(1 - \mu)e^0 + \mu e^{\lambda_*}},$$

which implies that

$$e^{\lambda_*} = \frac{z(1 - \mu)}{\mu(1 - z)}.$$

This implies that $-I_{X_1}(z) \leq -\mathrm{KL}(z\|\mu)$. The case of $z = \mu - \epsilon$ is similar. We can thus obtain the desired bound from Theorem 2.5.   □

In many applications, we will be interested in the situation $\mu \approx 0$. For example, this happens when the classification error is close to zero. In this case, Theorem 2.17 is superior to Theorem 2.16, and the result implies a simplified form stated in the following corollary.

Corollary 2.18 (Multiplicative Chernoff Bounds) *Assume that $X_1 \in [0, 1]$. Then for all $\epsilon > 0$,*

$$\Pr\left(\bar{X}_n \geq (1+\epsilon)\mu\right) \leq \exp\left[\frac{-n\mu\epsilon^2}{2+\epsilon}\right],$$

$$\Pr\left(\bar{X}_n \leq (1-\epsilon)\mu\right) \leq \exp\left[\frac{-n\mu\epsilon^2}{2}\right].$$

Moreover, for $t > 0$, we have

$$\Pr\left(\bar{X}_n \geq \mu + \sqrt{\frac{2\mu t}{n}} + \frac{t}{3n}\right) \leq e^{-t}.$$

Proof The first and the second results can be obtained from Theorem 2.17 and the inequality $\mathrm{KL}(z\|\mu) \geq (z-\mu)^2/\max(2\mu, \mu+z)$ (which is left as an exercise). We then take $z = (1+\epsilon)\mu$ and $z = (1-\epsilon)\mu$, respectively, for the first and the second inequalities.

For the third inequality (which is sharper than the first inequality), we may apply Theorem 2.10. Just observe from Lemma 2.15 that when $\lambda > 0$,

$$\Lambda_{X_1}(\lambda) \leq \ln[(1-\mu)e^0 + \mu e^\lambda]$$

$$\leq \mu(e^\lambda - 1) = \mu\lambda + \mu \sum_{k\geq 2} \frac{\lambda^k}{k!}$$

$$\leq \mu\lambda + \frac{\mu\lambda^2}{2(1-\lambda/3)}.$$

In this derivation, the equality used the Taylor expansion of exponential function. The last inequality used $k! \geq 2 \cdot 3^{k-2}$ and the sum of infinite geometric series. We may take $\alpha = \mu$ and $\beta = 1/3$ in Theorem 2.10 to obtain the desired bound. $\square$

The multiplicative form of Chernoff bound can be expressed alternatively as follows. With probability at least $1 - \delta$,

$$\mu < \bar{X}_n + \sqrt{\frac{2\mu \ln(1/\delta)}{n}}.$$

It implies that for any $\gamma \in (0, 1)$,

$$\bar{X}_n > (1-\gamma)\mu - \frac{\ln(1/\delta)}{2\gamma n}. \tag{2.11}$$

Moreover, with probability at least $1 - \delta$,

$$\bar{X}_n < \mu + \sqrt{\frac{2\mu \ln(1/\delta)}{n}} + \frac{\ln(1/\delta)}{3n}.$$

It implies that for any $\gamma > 0$,

$$\bar{X}_n < (1+\gamma)\mu + \frac{(3+2\gamma)\ln(1/\delta)}{6\gamma n}. \tag{2.12}$$

For Bernoulli random variables with $X_1 \in \{0, 1\}$, the moment generating function achieves equality in Lemma 2.15, and thus the proof of Theorem 2.17 implies that the rate function is given by

$$I_{X_1}(z) = \mathrm{KL}(z||\mu).$$

We can obtain the following lower bound from (2.8), which suggests that the KL formulation of Hoeffding's inequality is quite tight for Bernoulli random variables when n is large.

Corollary 2.19 *Assume that $X_1 \in \{0, 1\}$. Then for all $\epsilon > 0$ that satisfy*

$$\epsilon' = \epsilon + 2\sqrt{(\mu + \epsilon)(1 - (\mu + \epsilon))/n} < 1 - \mu$$

and $n \geq (1 - \mu - \epsilon)/(\mu + \epsilon)$, we have

$$\Pr(\bar{X}_n \geq \mu + \epsilon) \geq 0.25 \, \exp\left[-n\mathrm{KL}(\mu + \epsilon'||\mu) - \sqrt{n}\Delta I\right],$$

where

$$\Delta I = 2\sqrt{(\mu + \epsilon)(1 - \mu - \epsilon)} \ln \frac{(\mu + \epsilon')(1 - \mu)}{(1 - (\mu + \epsilon'))\mu}.$$

Proof In (2.8), we let $\epsilon'' = 2\epsilon' - \epsilon$. Since $X_i' \in \{0, 1\}$ and $\mathbb{E}X_i' = \mu + \epsilon'$, we have $\mathrm{Var}(X_1') = (\mu + \epsilon')(1 - \mu - \epsilon')$. Using Chebyshev's inequality, we obtain

$$\Pr\left(|\bar{X}_n' - (\mu + \epsilon')| \geq \epsilon' - \epsilon\right) \leq \frac{(\mu + \epsilon')(1 - \mu - \epsilon')}{n(\epsilon' - \epsilon)^2}$$

$$= \frac{(\mu + \epsilon')(1 - \mu - \epsilon')}{4(\mu + \epsilon)(1 - (\mu + \epsilon))} \leq \frac{(\mu + \epsilon')}{4(\mu + \epsilon)} = 0.25 + \frac{\epsilon' - \epsilon}{4(\mu + \epsilon)}.$$

Therefore

$$\Pr\left(\bar{X}_n' \in (\mu + \epsilon, \mu + \epsilon'')\right) = 1 - \Pr\left(|\bar{X}_n' - (\mu + \epsilon')| \geq \epsilon' - \epsilon\right)$$

$$\geq 0.75 - \frac{\epsilon' - \epsilon}{4(\mu + \epsilon)} = 0.75 - 0.5\sqrt{\frac{1 - \mu - \epsilon}{n(\mu + \epsilon)}} \geq 0.25.$$

The choice of λ in (2.4) is given by

$$\lambda = \ln \frac{(\mu + \epsilon')(1 - \mu)}{(1 - (\mu + \epsilon'))\mu}.$$

By using these estimates, we can obtain the desired bound from (2.8). □

2.6 Bennett's Inequality

In Bennett's inequality, we assume that the random variable is upper bounded and has a small variance. In this case, one can obtain a more refined estimate of the moment generating function by using the variance of the random variable (Bennett, 1962).

Lemma 2.20 *If $X - \mathbb{E}X \leq b$, then $\forall \lambda \geq 0$:*

$$\ln \mathbb{E}e^{\lambda X} \leq \lambda \mathbb{E}X + \lambda^2 \phi(\lambda b)\mathrm{Var}(X),$$

where $\phi(z) = (e^z - z - 1)/z^2$.

Proof Let $X' = X - \mathbb{E}X$. We have

$$\ln \mathbb{E}e^{\lambda X} = \lambda \mathbb{E}X + \ln \mathbb{E}e^{\lambda X'}$$
$$\leq \lambda \mathbb{E}X + \mathbb{E}e^{\lambda X'} - 1$$
$$= \lambda \mathbb{E}X + \lambda^2 \mathbb{E}\frac{e^{\lambda X'} - \lambda X' - 1}{(\lambda X')^2}(X')^2$$
$$\leq \lambda \mathbb{E}X + \lambda^2 \mathbb{E}\phi(\lambda b)(X')^2,$$

where the first inequality used $\ln z \leq z - 1$; the second inequality follows from the fact that the function $\phi(z)$ is non-decreasing (left as an exercise) and $\lambda X' \leq \lambda b$. $\square$

Lemma 2.20 gives an estimate of the logarithmic moment generating function, which implies the following result from Theorem 2.5.

Theorem 2.21 (Bennett's Inequality) *If $X_1 \leq \mu + b$, for some $b > 0$. Let $\psi(z) = (1 + z)\ln(1 + z) - z$, then $\forall \epsilon > 0$:*

$$\Pr[\bar{X}_n \geq \mu + \epsilon] \leq \exp\left[\frac{-n\mathrm{Var}(X)}{b^2}\psi\left(\frac{\epsilon b}{\mathrm{Var}(X_1)}\right)\right],$$

$$\Pr[\bar{X}_n \geq \mu + \epsilon] \leq \exp\left[\frac{-n\epsilon^2}{2\mathrm{Var}(X_1) + 2\epsilon b/3}\right].$$

Moreover, for $t > 0$,

$$\Pr\left[\bar{X}_n \geq \mu + \sqrt{\frac{2\mathrm{Var}(X_1)t}{n}} + \frac{bt}{3n}\right] \leq e^{-t}.$$

Proof Lemma 2.20 implies that

$$-I_{X_1}(\mu + \epsilon) \leq \inf_{\lambda > 0}\left[-\lambda\epsilon + b^{-2}(e^{\lambda b} - \lambda b - 1)\mathrm{Var}(X_1)\right].$$

We can set the derivative of the objective function on the right-hand side with respect to λ to zero at the minimum solution, and obtain the condition for the optimal λ as follows:

$$-\epsilon + b^{-1}(e^{\lambda b} - 1)\mathrm{Var}(X_1) = 0.$$

This gives the solution $\lambda = b^{-1}\ln(1 + \epsilon b/\mathrm{Var}(X_1))$. Plugging this solution into the objective function, we obtain

$$-I_{X_1}(\mu + \epsilon) \leq -\frac{\mathrm{Var}(X_1)}{b^2}\psi\left(\frac{\epsilon b}{\mathrm{Var}(X_1)}\right).$$

The first inequality of the theorem follows from an application of Theorem 2.5.

Given $\lambda \in (0, 3/b)$, it is easy to verify the following inequality using the Taylor expansion of the exponential function:

$$\Lambda_{X_1}(\lambda) \leq \mu\lambda + b^{-2}\left[e^{\lambda b} - \lambda b - 1\right]\mathrm{Var}(X_1)$$

$$\leq \mu\lambda + \frac{\mathrm{Var}(X_1)\lambda^2}{2}\sum_{m=0}^{\infty}(\lambda b/3)^m = \mu\lambda + \frac{\mathrm{Var}(X_1)\lambda^2}{2(1 - \lambda b/3)}. \qquad (2.13)$$

The second and the third desired bounds follow from direct applications of Theorem 2.10 with $\alpha = \mathrm{Var}(X_1)$ and $\beta = b/3$. $\qquad\square$

Bennett's inequality can be expressed alternatively as follows. Given any $\delta \in (0, 1)$, with probability at least $1 - \delta$, we have

$$\bar{X}_n < \mu + \sqrt{\frac{2\mathrm{Var}(X_1)\ln(1/\delta)}{n}} + \frac{b\ln(1/\delta)}{3n}.$$

If we apply this to the case that $X_i \in [0, 1]$, then using the variance estimation $\mathrm{Var}(X_1) \leq \mu(1 - \mu)$, and $b \leq 1 - \mu$, the bound implies

$$\bar{X}_n < \mu + \sqrt{\frac{2\mu(1 - \mu)\ln(1/\delta)}{n}} + \frac{(1 - \mu)\ln(1/\delta)}{3n}.$$

This is slightly tighter than the corresponding multiplicative Chernoff bound in Corollary 2.18.

Compared to the tail bound for Gaussian random variables, this form of Bennett's inequality has an extra term $b\ln(1/\delta)/(3n)$, which is of higher order $O(1/n)$. Compared to the additive Chernoff bound, Bennett's inequality is superior when $\mathrm{Var}(X_1)$ is small.

2.7 Bernstein's Inequality

In Bernstein's inequality, we obtain results similar to Bennett's inequality, but using a moment condition (Bernstein, 1924) instead of the boundedness condition. There are several different forms of such inequalities, and we only consider one form, which relies on the following moment assumption.

Lemma 2.22 *If X satisfies the following moment condition with $b, V > 0$ for integers $m \geq 2$:*

$$\mathbb{E}[X - c]^m \leq m!(b/3)^{m-2}V/2,$$

where c is arbitrary. Then when $\lambda \in (0, 3/b)$,

$$\ln\mathbb{E}e^{\lambda X} \leq \lambda\mathbb{E}X + \frac{\lambda^2 V}{2(1 - \lambda b/3)}.$$

Proof We have the following estimation of logarithmic moment generating function:

$$\ln \mathbb{E}e^{\lambda X} \le \lambda c + \mathbb{E}e^{\lambda(X-c)} - 1 \le \lambda \mathbb{E}X + 0.5V\lambda^2 \sum_{m=2}(b/3)^{m-2}\lambda^{m-2}$$
$$= \lambda \mathbb{E}X + 0.5\lambda^2 V(1 - \lambda b/3)^{-1}.$$

This implies the desired bound. □

In general, we may take $c = \mathbb{E}[X]$ and $V = \text{Var}[X]$. The following bound is a direct consequence of Theorem 2.10.

Theorem 2.23 (Bernstein's Inequality) *Assume that X_1 satisfies the moment condition in Lemma 2.22. Then for all $\epsilon > 0$,*

$$\Pr[\bar{X}_n \ge \mu + \epsilon] \le \exp\left[\frac{-n\epsilon^2}{2V + 2\epsilon b/3}\right],$$

and for all $t > 0$,

$$\Pr\left[\bar{X}_n \ge \mu + \sqrt{\frac{2Vt}{n}} + \frac{bt}{3n}\right] \le e^{-t}.$$

Proof We simply set $\alpha = V$ and $\beta = b/3$ in Theorem 2.10. □

Similar to Bennett's inequality, Bernstein's inequality can be alternatively expressed as follows. With probability at least $1 - \delta$,

$$\mu < \bar{X}_n + \sqrt{\frac{2V\ln(1/\delta)}{n}} + \frac{b\ln(1/\delta)}{3n},$$

which implies with probability at least $1 - \delta$, the following inequality holds for all $\gamma > 0$:

$$\mu < \bar{X}_n + (\gamma/b)V + \frac{b(3 + 2\gamma)\ln(1/\delta)}{6\gamma n}. \tag{2.14}$$

Example 2.24 If the random variable X is bounded with $|X - \mu| \le b$, then the moment condition of Lemma 2.22 holds with $c = \mu$ and $V = \text{Var}(X)$.

2.8 Nonidentically Distributed Random Variables

If $X_1, \ldots, X_n$ are independent but not identically distributed random variables, then a tail inequality similar to that of Theorem 2.5 holds. Let $\bar{X}_n = n^{-1}\sum_{i=1}^n X_i$, and $\mu = \mathbb{E}\bar{X}_n$, then we have the following bound.

Theorem 2.25 *We have for all $\epsilon > 0$,*

$$\Pr(\bar{X}_n \ge \mu + \epsilon) \le \inf_{\lambda > 0}\left[-\lambda n(\mu + \epsilon) + \sum_{i=1}^n \ln \mathbb{E}e^{\lambda X_i}\right].$$

For sub-Gaussian random variables, we have the following bound.

Corollary 2.26 *If $\{X_i\}$ are independent sub-Gaussian random variables with* $\ln \mathbb{E} e^{\lambda X_i} \leq \lambda \mathbb{E} X_i + 0.5\lambda^2 b_i$, *then for all $\epsilon > 0$,*

$$\Pr(\bar{X}_n \geq \mu + \epsilon) \leq \exp\left[-\frac{n^2\epsilon^2}{2\sum_{i=1}^{n} b_i}\right].$$

The following inequality is a useful application of the aforementioned sub-Gaussian bound for Rademacher average. This bound, also referred to as the Chernoff bound in the literature, is essential for the symmetrization argument of Chapter 4.

Corollary 2.27 *Let $\sigma_i = \{\pm 1\}$ be independent Bernoulli random variables (each takes value ± 1 with equal probability). Let a_i be fixed numbers $(i = 1, \ldots, n)$. Then for all $\epsilon > 0$,*

$$\Pr\left(n^{-1}\sum_{i=1}^{n} \sigma_i a_i \geq \epsilon\right) \leq \exp\left[-\frac{n\epsilon^2}{2n^{-1}\sum_{i=1}^{n} a_i^2}\right].$$

Proof Consider $X_i = \sigma_i a_i$ in Corollary 2.26. We can take $\mu = 0$ and $b_i = a_i^2$ to obtain the desired bound. □

One can also derive a Bennett-style tail probability bound.

Corollary 2.28 *If $X_i - \mathbb{E} X_i \leq b$ for all i, then for all $\epsilon > 0$,*

$$\Pr(\bar{X}_n \geq \mu + \epsilon) \leq \exp\left[-\frac{n^2\epsilon^2}{2\sum_{i=1}^{n}\mathrm{Var}(X_i) + 2nb\epsilon/3}\right].$$

2.9 Tail Inequality for χ^2

Let $X_i \sim N(0, 1)$ be iid normal random variables $(i = 1, \ldots, n)$, then the random variable

$$Z = \sum_{i=1}^{n} X_i^2$$

is distributed according to the chi-square distribution with n degrees of freedom, which is often denoted by χ_n^2.

This random variable plays an important role in the analysis of least squares regression. More generally, we may consider the sum of independent sub-Gaussian random variables, and obtain the following tail inequality from Theorem 2.5.

Theorem 2.29 *Let $\{X_i\}_{i=1}^{n}$ be independent zero-mean sub-Gaussian random variables that satisfy*

$$\ln \mathbb{E}_{X_i} \exp(\lambda X_i) \leq \frac{\lambda^2 b_i}{2},$$

then for $\lambda < 0.5 b_i$, we have

$$\ln \mathbb{E}_{X_i} \exp(\lambda X_i^2) \leq -\frac{1}{2}\ln(1 - 2\lambda b_i).$$

Let $Z = \sum_{i=1}^{n} X_i^2$, then

$$\Pr\left[Z \geq \sum_{i=1}^{n} b_i + 2\sqrt{t\sum_{i=1}^{n} b_i^2 + 2t(\max_i b_i)} \right] \leq e^{-t}$$

and

$$\Pr\left[Z \leq \sum_{i=1}^{n} b_i - 2\sqrt{t\sum_{i=1}^{n} b_i^2} \right] \leq e^{-t}.$$

Proof Let $\xi \sim N(0,1)$, which is independent of X_i. Then for all $\lambda b_i < 0.5$, we have

$$\begin{aligned}
\Lambda_{X_i^2}(\lambda) &= \ln \mathbb{E}_{X_i} \exp(\lambda X_i^2) \\
&= \ln \mathbb{E}_{X_i} \mathbb{E}_{\xi} \exp(\sqrt{2\lambda}\xi X_i) \\
&= \ln \mathbb{E}_{\xi} \mathbb{E}_{X_i} \exp(\sqrt{2\lambda}\xi X_i) \\
&\leq \ln \mathbb{E}_{\xi} \exp(\lambda \xi^2 b_i) \\
&= -\frac{1}{2}\ln(1 - 2\lambda b_i),
\end{aligned}$$

where the inequality used the sub-Gaussian assumption. The second and the last equalities can be obtained using Gaussian integration. This proves the first bound of the theorem.

For $\lambda \geq 0$, we obtain

$$\begin{aligned}
\Lambda_{X_i^2}(\lambda) &\leq -0.5\ln(1 - 2\lambda b_i) \\
&= 0.5\sum_{k=1}^{\infty} \frac{(2\lambda b_i)^k}{k} \\
&\leq \lambda b_i + (\lambda b_i)^2 \sum_{k\geq 0}(2\lambda b_i)^k \\
&= \lambda b_i + \frac{(\lambda b_i)^2}{1 - 2\lambda b_i}.
\end{aligned}$$

The first probability inequality of the theorem follows from Theorem 2.10 with $\mu = n^{-1}\sum_{i=1}^{n} b_i$, $\alpha = (2/n)\sum_{i=1}^{n} b_i^2$, and $\beta = 2\max_i b_i$.

If $\lambda \leq 0$, then

$$\Lambda_{X_i^2}(\lambda) \leq -0.5\ln(1 - 2\lambda b_i) \leq \lambda b_i + \lambda^2 b_i^2.$$

The second probability inequality of the theorem follows from the sub-Gaussian tail inequality of Theorem 2.12 with $\mu = n^{-1}\sum_{i=1}^{n} b_i$ and $b = (2/n)\sum_{i=1}^{n} b_i^2$. $\quad\square$

From Theorem 2.29, we can obtain the following expressions for χ_n^2 tail bound by taking $b_i = 1$. With probability at least $1 - \delta$,

$$Z \leq n + 2\sqrt{n\ln(1/\delta)} + 2\ln(1/\delta),$$

and with probability at least $1 - \delta$,

$$Z \geq n - 2\sqrt{n \ln(1/\delta)}.$$

One may also obtain a tail bound estimate for χ_n^2 distributions using direct integration. We leave it as an exercise.

2.10 Historical and Bibliographical Remarks

Chebyshev's inequality is named after the Russian mathematician Pafnuty Chebyshev, and was known in the nineteenth century. The investigation of exponential tail inequalities for sums of independent random variables occurred in the early twentieth century. Bernstein's inequality was one of the first such results. The large deviation principle was established by Cramér, and was later rediscovered by Chernoff (1952). In the following decade, several important inequalities were obtained, such as Hoeffding's inequality and Bennett's inequality. The tail bounds in Theorem 2.29 for χ^2 random variables was first documented in Laurent and Massart (2000), where they were used to analyze least squares regression problems with Gaussian noise. It was later extended to arbitrary quadratic forms of independent sub-Gaussian random variables by Hsu et al. (2012b).

Exercises

2.1   Assume that $X_1, X_2, \ldots, X_n$ are real-valued iid random variables with density function

$$p(x) = \frac{x^2}{\sqrt{2\pi}} \exp(-x^2/2).$$

Let $\mu = \mathbb{E} X_1$, and $\bar{X}_n = n^{-1} \sum_{i=1}^n X_i$.
- Estimate $\ln \mathbb{E} \exp(\lambda X_1)$
- Estimate $\Pr(\bar{X}_n \geq \mu + \epsilon)$
- Estimate $\Pr(\bar{X}_n \leq \mu - \epsilon)$

2.2   Prove Proposition 2.8.

2.3   Prove the inequality

$$\mathrm{KL}(z \| \mu) \geq \frac{(z - \mu)^2}{\max(z + \mu, 2\mu)},$$

which is needed in the proof of Corollary 2.18.

2.4   Prove that the function $\phi(z) = (e^z - z - 1)/z^2$ is non-decreasing in z.

2.5   Assume that the density function of a distribution $\mathcal{D}$ on $\mathbb{R}$ is $(1-p)U(-1, 1) + pU(-1/p, 1/p)$ for $p \in (0, 0.5)$, where $U(\cdot)$ denotes the density of the uniform distribution. Let $X_1, \ldots, X_n$ be iid samples from $\mathcal{D}$. For $\epsilon > 0$, estimate the probability

$$\Pr\left(\frac{1}{n} \sum_{i=1}^n X_i \geq \epsilon \right)$$

using Bernstein's inequality.

2.6   Write down the density of χ^2 distribution, and use integration to estimate the tail inequalities. Compare the results to those of Theorem 2.29.

2.7   Prove Corollary 2.26 and Corollary 2.28.

3

Uniform Convergence and Generalization Analysis

3.1 Probabilistic Approximately Correct Learning

Probabilistic Approximately Correct (PAC) learning is a mathematical model for analyzing algorithms that can learn Boolean functions (Valiant, 1984) from random examples. This is analogous to supervised learning, except that there is a computational complexity requirement.

In this model, we observe a binary-valued vector $X \in \{0,1\}^d$ as input. A Boolean function f maps a binary vector X to a binary output $Y \in \{0,1\}$. Such a Boolean function is also referred to as a *concept* in the literature. A *concept class* $\mathcal{C}$ is a set of such Boolean functions: $\{0,1\}^d \to \{0,1\}$. In the machine learning literature, a concept is also referred to as a *hypothesis*, and a concept class is also referred to as a *hypothesis space* or *hypothesis class*. In machine learning, $\mathcal{C}$ is also called a *model class*.

Example 3.1 (AND Function Class)   Each member of the AND function class can be written as

$$f(x) = \prod_{j \in J} x_j, \qquad J \subset \{1, \ldots, d\}.$$

Example 3.2 (Decision List)   A decision list is a function of the following form. Let $\{i_1, \ldots, i_d\}$ be a permutation of $\{1, \ldots, d\}$, and let $a_i, b_i \in \{0,1\}$ for $i = 1, \ldots, d+1$. The function $f(x)$ can be computed as follows: if $x_{i_1} = a_1$ then $f(x) = b_1$; else if $x_{i_2} = a_2$ then $f(x) = b_2$, ..., else if $x_{i_d} = a_d$ then $f(x) = b_d$; else $f(x) = b_{d+1}$.

Assume now that there is an unknown true function $f_*(x) \in \mathcal{C}$ that we want to learn. In the PAC learning model, the input X is taken from an unknown distribution $\mathcal{D}$, and there is an oracle $\mathcal{O}$ that can sample from this distribution. Each call to $\mathcal{O}$ returns a sample $X \sim \mathcal{D}$, together with the value $Y = f_*(X)$. The goal of a PAC learner is to learn this function approximately up to an accuracy ϵ with respect to $\mathcal{D}$ by randomly sampling its inputs.

More formally, the (generalization) error of a learned function $f(x)$ is defined as

$$\mathrm{err}_{\mathcal{D}}(f) = \mathbb{E}_{X \sim \mathcal{D}} \mathbb{1}(f(x) \neq f_*(x)).$$

We may call $\mathcal{O}$ n times to form a training data $\mathcal{S}_n = \{(X_i, Y_i)\}_{i=1,\ldots,n} \sim \mathcal{D}^n$. The learner $\mathcal{A}$ takes $\mathcal{S}_n$ and returns a function $\hat{f} \in \mathcal{C}$. Due to the randomness of

$\mathcal{S}_n$, the function $\hat{f}$ is also random. Therefore the quality of the learner should be stated in probabilistic terms.

Definition 3.3 (PAC Learning)   A concept class $\mathcal{C}$ is PAC learnable if there exists a learner $\mathcal{A}$ so that for all $f_* \in \mathcal{C}$, distribution $\mathcal{D}$ on the input, approximation error $\epsilon > 0$ and probability $\delta \in (0, 1)$, the following statement holds. With probability at least $1 - \delta$ over samples from the oracle $\mathcal{O}$ over $\mathcal{D}$, the learner produces a function $\hat{f}$ such that

$$\mathrm{err}_{\mathcal{D}}(\hat{f}) \leq \epsilon,$$

with the computational complexity polynomial in $(\epsilon^{-1}, \delta^{-1}, d)$.

The term *probabilistic approximately correct* means that the statement has a probability of at least $1-\delta$, and the correctness is up to approximation error ϵ. The PAC learning model is similar to the supervised learning framework, except for the additional requirement that the computational complex should be polynomial. One may also extend the basic notation of PAC learning by assuming that the oracle $\mathcal{O}$ may take additional information, so that the learning algorithm can interact with the oracle sequentially.

In Definition 3.3, we assume that the output Y is generated by a function $f_* \in \mathcal{C}$. This is referred to as *realizable* in the learning theory literature, and referred to as a *correctly specified model* (or well-specified) in the statistics literature. In general, one may also extend the definition of PAC learning to nonrealizable situations, where the output Y is not generated by a function $f_* \in \mathcal{C}$. This corresponds to the situation of a misspecified model in statistics. We will only consider the realizable case in this section, but will consider more general situations in subsequent sections.

In the statistical complexity analysis of learning algorithms, the computational complexity requirement is de-emphasized. The analysis will focus on the *sample complexity*, which is the minimum sample size n as a function of $(\epsilon^{-1}, \delta^{-1}, d)$, required to achieve ϵ accuracy with probability $1 - \delta$.

Definition 3.4 (ERM)   Define the training error of $f \in \mathcal{C}$ as

$$\widehat{\mathrm{err}}_{\mathcal{S}_n}(f) = \frac{1}{n} \sum_{i=1}^{n} \mathbb{1}(f(X_i) \neq Y_i).$$

The ERM (empirical risk minimization) method finds a function $\hat{f} \in \mathcal{C}$ that minimizes the training error.

Since by the realizable assumption of PAC learning, $f_* \in \mathcal{C}$ achieves zero training error, the empirical minimizer also finds a function $\hat{f}$ that achieves zero training error. That is,

$$\widehat{\mathrm{err}}_{\mathcal{S}_n}(\hat{f}) = 0.$$

However, there may be more than one function that can achieve zero-error on any given training data. The algorithm simply returns an arbitrarily chosen example of such functions. More generally, we may consider approximate ERM, which returns $\hat{f}$, so that

$$\widehat{\mathrm{err}}_{\mathcal{S}_n}(\hat{f}) \leq \epsilon' \tag{3.1}$$

for some accuracy $\epsilon' > 0$.

Next we show that by using union bound and Hoeffding's inequality, we can obtain a sample complexity bound for PAC learning analysis.

3.2 Analysis of PAC Learning

In the analysis of the ERM learner, we are interested in bounding the difference of the test error $\mathrm{err}_{\mathcal{D}}(\hat{f})$ and the optimal test error $\mathrm{err}_{\mathcal{D}}(f_*)$, using a decomposition. Note that although, in the realizable PAC learning setting, $\mathrm{err}_{\mathcal{D}}(f_*) = 0$, in the more general case considered in later sections, the optimal test error may be nonzero. The following decomposition can be applied both to the realizable PAC learning setting and the more general situation where $\mathrm{err}_{\mathcal{D}}(f_*) \neq 0$.

$$
\begin{aligned}
\mathrm{err}_{\mathcal{D}}&(\hat{f}) - \mathrm{err}_{\mathcal{D}}(f_*) \\
&= \underbrace{[\mathrm{err}_{\mathcal{D}}(\hat{f}) - \widehat{\mathrm{err}}_{\mathcal{S}_n}(\hat{f})]}_{A} + \underbrace{[\widehat{\mathrm{err}}_{\mathcal{S}_n}(\hat{f}) - \widehat{\mathrm{err}}_{\mathcal{S}_n}(f_*)]}_{B} + \underbrace{[\widehat{\mathrm{err}}_{\mathcal{S}_n}(f_*) - \mathrm{err}_{\mathcal{D}}(f_*)]}_{C} \\
&\leq \underbrace{\sup_{f \in \mathcal{F}}[\mathrm{err}_{\mathcal{D}}(f) - \widehat{\mathrm{err}}_{\mathcal{S}_n}(f)]}_{A'} + 0 + \underbrace{[\widehat{\mathrm{err}}_{\mathcal{S}_n}(f_*) - \mathrm{err}_{\mathcal{D}}(f_*)]}_{C} \\
&\leq \underbrace{2 \sup_{f \in \mathcal{F}} |\mathrm{err}_{\mathcal{D}}(f) - \widehat{\mathrm{err}}_{\mathcal{S}_n}(f)|}_{A''}.
\end{aligned}
$$

In decomposition, the key idea is to bound the test error in term of the training error. The inequality $B \leq 0$ follows from the fact that ERM achieves the smallest training error. The inequality $A \leq A'$ follows from $\hat{f} \in \mathcal{F}$. The quantity C can be bounded using the probability inequalities of Chapter 2. The quantity A' or A'' requires that the convergence of empirical mean to the true mean holds for all $f \in \mathcal{F}$. Such a convergence result is referred to as *uniform convergence*, and probability inequalities of Chapter 2 are not immediately applicable.

The key mathematical tool to analyze uniform convergence is the *union bound*, described in Proposition 3.5. In this book, we employ one-sided uniform convergence A', and the quantity C will be analyzed separately. The bounding of C is relatively simple, and it doesn't require uniform convergence because f_* is a fixed function. The one-sided analysis makes it easier to handle probability inequalities that may have different forms in the case of underestimating the true mean versus overestimating the true mean (e.g. this happens with multiplicative Chernoff bounds). However, we note that in the literature, much of the existing analysis considers the two-sided uniform convergence quantity A'' for the sake of simplicity.

Proposition 3.5 (Union Bound) *Consider m events $E_1, \ldots, E_m$. The following probability inequality holds:*

$$\Pr\left(E_1 \cup \cdots \cup E_m\right) \leq \sum_{j=1}^{m} \Pr(E_j).$$

The union bound has an alternative expression, which is often used in the learning theory analysis. If each E_j occurs with probability at least $1 - \delta_j$ for $j = 1, \ldots, m$, then with probability at least $1 - \sum_{j=1}^{m} \delta_j$, all of events $\{E_j\}$ occur simultaneously for $j = 1, \ldots, m$.

In the application of the union bound, we generally assume that the probability $\sum_{j=1}^{m} \Pr(E_j)$ is small. In such cases, Exercise 3.1 implies that when the events $\{E_j : j = 1, \ldots, m\}$ are independent, then the union bound is relatively tight. If $\{E_j\}$ are correlated, then the union bound may not be tight. For example, when they are completely correlated: $E_1 = \cdots = E_m$, then

$$\Pr(E_1 \cup \cdots \cup E_m) = \Pr(E_1) = \frac{1}{m} \sum_{j=1}^{m} \Pr(E_j),$$

which can be significantly smaller than the union bound. Therefore in some theoretical analyses, in order to obtain sharp results from the union bound, we may need to carefully define events so that they are not highly correlated.

We will use the union bound to derive sample complexity bounds for PAC learning using ERM. To simplify the analysis, we will first assume that the concept class $\mathcal{C}$ contains N different functions.

An important observation is that we cannot directly apply the Chernoff bound of Theorem 2.16 to the function $\hat{f}$ learned from the training data $\mathcal{S}_n$, because it is a random function that depends on $\mathcal{S}_n$. Instead, we can apply Theorem 2.16 to each fixed function $f(x) \in \mathcal{C}$, and rely on the union bound to obtain the desired result that holds uniformly for all $f(x) \in \mathcal{C}$ given any sample $\mathcal{S}_n$. Since the bound holds uniformly for all $f(x) \in \mathcal{C}$, it also holds for $\hat{f}$ that depends on $\mathcal{S}_n$.

To illustrate the basic argument, we first apply the additive Chernoff bound of Theorem 2.16 to obtain values for each fixed $f \in \mathcal{C}$:

$$\Pr\left(\mathrm{err}_{\mathcal{D}}(f) \geq \widehat{\mathrm{err}}_{\mathcal{S}_n}(f) + \epsilon\right) \leq \exp(-2n\epsilon^2).$$

Therefore

$$\Pr\left(\sup_{f \in \mathcal{C}} [\mathrm{err}_{\mathcal{D}}(f) - \widehat{\mathrm{err}}_{\mathcal{S}_n}(f)] \geq \epsilon\right)$$

$$= \Pr\left(\exists f \in \mathcal{C} : \mathrm{err}_{\mathcal{D}}(f) \geq \widehat{\mathrm{err}}_{\mathcal{S}_n}(f) + \epsilon\right)$$

$$\leq \sum_{f \in \mathcal{C}} \Pr\left(\mathrm{err}_{\mathcal{D}}(f) \geq \widehat{\mathrm{err}}_{\mathcal{S}_n}(f) + \epsilon\right) \leq N \exp(-2n\epsilon^2).$$

The first inequality used the union bound, and the second inequality used Theorem 2.16. Now by setting $N \exp(-2n\epsilon^2) = \delta$ and solving for ϵ to get

$$\epsilon = \sqrt{\frac{\ln(N/\delta)}{2n}},$$

we obtain the following equivalent statement. With probability at least $1 - \delta$, the following inequality holds for all $f \in \mathcal{C}$:

$$\mathrm{err}_{\mathcal{D}}(f) < \widehat{\mathrm{err}}_{\mathcal{S}_n}(f) + \sqrt{\frac{\ln(N/\delta)}{2n}}.$$

Such a result is called *uniform convergence*, because given an empirical sample $\mathcal{S}_n$, the inequality holds for all $f \in \mathcal{C}$, and thus it also holds for the output $\hat{f}$ of any learning algorithm.

By applying the uniform convergence result to the approximate ERM learner of (3.1), we obtain the following generalization bound. With probability at least $1 - \delta$, the following inequality holds for the ERM PAC learner (3.1) for all $\gamma > 0$:

$$\mathrm{err}_{\mathcal{D}}(\hat{f}) < \epsilon' + \sqrt{\frac{\ln(N/\delta)}{2n}} = (1 + \gamma)\sqrt{\frac{\ln(N/\delta)}{2n}}, \tag{3.2}$$

with

$$\epsilon' = \gamma \sqrt{\frac{\ln(N/\delta)}{2n}}.$$

In the generalization analysis, we are interested in the dependency of the generalization error on the training sample size n. The bound on the right-hand side implies a statistical convergence rate of $O(1/\sqrt{n})$. It can be expressed in another form of sample complexity bound. If we let

$$n \geq \frac{(1 + \gamma)^2 \ln(N/\delta)}{2\epsilon^2},$$

then $\mathrm{err}_{\mathcal{D}}(\hat{f}) < \epsilon$ with probability at least $1 - \delta$. That is, with large probability, the result implies a sample complexity bound of $n = O(1/\epsilon^2)$ to achieve ϵ generalization error.

Next, we show that for the realizable case considered here, we can obtain a better result by applying the union bound, together with the multiplicative form of Chernoff bound in Corollary 2.18.

Theorem 3.6 *Consider a concept class $\mathcal{C}$ with N elements. With probability at least $1 - \delta$, the ERM PAC learner (3.1) with*

$$\epsilon' = \gamma^2 \frac{2\ln(N/\delta)}{n}$$

for some $\gamma > 0$ satisfies

$$\mathrm{err}_{\mathcal{D}}(\hat{f}) \leq (1 + \gamma)^2 \frac{2\ln(N/\delta)}{n}.$$

Proof Given any $f \in \mathcal{C}$, we have from Corollary 2.18 that

$$\Pr\left(\mathrm{err}_{\mathcal{D}}(f) \geq \widehat{\mathrm{err}}_{\mathcal{S}_n}(f) + \epsilon\right) \leq \exp\left(\frac{-n\epsilon^2}{2\mathrm{err}_{\mathcal{D}}(f)}\right).$$

Now by setting $\exp(-n\epsilon^2/2\mathrm{err}_{\mathcal{D}}(f)) = \delta/N$, and solving for ϵ,

$$\epsilon = \sqrt{\frac{2\mathrm{err}_{\mathcal{D}}(f)\ln(N/\delta)}{n}},$$

we obtain the following equivalent statement. With probability at least $1 - \delta/N$,

$$\mathrm{err}_{\mathcal{D}}(f) \leq \widehat{\mathrm{err}}_{\mathcal{S}_n}(f) + \sqrt{\frac{2\mathrm{err}_{\mathcal{D}}(f)\ln(N/\delta)}{n}}.$$

The union bound thus implies the following statement. With probability at least $1 - \delta$, for all $f \in \mathcal{C}$,

$$\mathrm{err}_{\mathcal{D}}(f) \leq \widehat{\mathrm{err}}_{\mathcal{S}_n}(f) + \sqrt{\frac{2\mathrm{err}_{\mathcal{D}}(f)\ln(N/\delta)}{n}}.$$

The above inequality also holds for the ERM PAC learner solution (3.1). We thus obtain

$$\mathrm{err}_{\mathcal{D}}(\hat{f}) \leq \widehat{\mathrm{err}}_{\mathcal{S}_n}(\hat{f}) + \sqrt{\frac{2\mathrm{err}_{\mathcal{D}}(\hat{f})\ln(N/\delta)}{n}}$$

$$\leq \gamma^2 \frac{2\ln(N/\delta)}{n} + \sqrt{\frac{2\mathrm{err}_{\mathcal{D}}(\hat{f})\ln(N/\delta)}{n}}.$$

The second inequality uses the assumption of the theorem on the approximate ERM solution. We can solve the inequality for $\mathrm{err}_{\mathcal{D}}(\hat{f})$ and obtain

$$\mathrm{err}_{\mathcal{D}}(\hat{f}) \leq (\gamma^2 + 0.5 + \sqrt{\gamma^2 + 0.25})\frac{2\ln(N/\delta)}{n},$$

which implies the desired bound because $\gamma^2 + 0.5 + \sqrt{\gamma^2 + 0.25} \leq (1 + \gamma)^2$. $\square$

Note that compared to (3.2), which shows that the generalization error $\mathrm{err}_{\mathcal{D}}(\hat{f})$ decays at a rate of $O(1/\sqrt{n})$, Theorem 3.6 implies that the generalization error decays at a faster rate of $O(1/n)$. This means that the multiplicative Chernoff bound is preferred to the additive Chernoff bound for the realizable case, where Y is generated by $f_*(X)$ for some $f_* \in \mathcal{C}$.

Theorem 3.6 implies the following sample complexity bound. Given $\delta \in (0, 1)$, for all sample size

$$n \geq (1 + \gamma)^2 \frac{2\ln(N/\delta)}{\epsilon},$$

we have $\mathrm{err}_{\mathcal{D}}(\hat{f}) < \epsilon$ with probability at least $1 - \delta$.

The generalization error bound has a logarithmic dependency $\ln N$ on the concept class size N. This logarithmic dependency is important for analyzing machine learning algorithms, and such a dependency requires the exponential tail probability bounds developed in Chapter 2. Since the generalization analysis does not depend on the underlying distribution $\mathcal{D}$, the resulting bound is referred to as a *distribution-free* generalization bound.

Example 3.7 The AND concept class $\mathcal{C}$ is PAC learnable. To show this, we will prove that the ERM (3.1) solution can be obtained in a computationally efficient way with $\epsilon' = 0$. If this is true, then Theorem 3.6 implies that $\mathcal{C}$ is PAC learnable because the number of AND functions cannot be more than $N = 2^d$. Therefore $\ln N \leq d \ln 2$.

In the following, we show that ERM solutions can be efficiently obtained. Given $\mathcal{S}_n = \{(X_1, Y_1), \ldots, (X_n, Y_n)\} \sim \mathcal{D}^n$, we define $\hat{J} = \{j: \quad \forall 1 \leq i \leq n, X_{i,j} \geq Y_i\}$ (where X_{ij} denotes the jth component of the ith training data X_i) and $\hat{f}(x) = \prod_{j \in \hat{J}} x_j$. This choice implies that $\hat{f}(X_i) = Y_i$ when $Y_i = 1$. It can be easily verified that if the true target is $f_*(x) = \prod_{j \in J} x_j$, then $\hat{J} \supset J$. This implies that $\hat{f}(x) \leq f_*(x)$. This implies that $\hat{f}(X_i) = Y_i$ when $Y_i = 0$, and hence $\widehat{\mathrm{err}}_{\mathcal{S}_n}(\hat{f}) = 0$.

3.3 Empirical Process

The analysis of realizable PAC learning can be generalized to deal with general non-binary-valued function classes that may contain an infinite number of functions. It may also be generalized to handle the nonrealizable case where $f_*(x) \notin \mathcal{C}$ or when the observation Y contains noise. For such cases, the corresponding analysis requires the technical tool of *empirical processes*.

To simplify the notations, in the general setting, we may denote the observations as $Z_i = (X_i, Y_i) \in \mathcal{Z} = \mathcal{X} \times \mathcal{Y}$, prediction function as $f(X_i)$ (which is often a vector-valued function) and loss function as $L(f(X_i), Y_i)$. Assume further that $f(x)$ is parametrized by $w \in \Omega$ as $f(w, x)$, and the hypothesis space is $\{f(w, \cdot): w \in \Omega\}$.

Let training data $\mathcal{S}_n = \{Z_i = (X_i, Y_i): i = 1, \ldots, n\}$. In the following, we consider a more general form of ERM, approximate ERM, which satisfies the following inequality for some $\epsilon' > 0$:

$$\frac{1}{n} \sum_{i=1}^{n} L(f(\hat{w}, X_i), Y_i) \leq \inf_{w \in \Omega} \left[\frac{1}{n} \sum_{i=1}^{n} L(f(w, X_i), Y_i) \right] + \epsilon'. \tag{3.3}$$

The quantity $\epsilon' > 0$ indicates how accurately we solve the ERM problem.

We introduce the following simplified notation that will be used throughout the book.

Definition 3.8 We define

$$\phi(w, z) = L(f(w, x), y) - L_*(x, y) \tag{3.4}$$

for $w \in \Omega$ and $z = (x, y) \in \mathcal{Z} = \mathcal{X} \times \mathcal{Y}$, and a pre-chosen $L_*(x, y)$ of $z = (x, y)$ that does not depend on w.

For training data $\mathcal{S}_n = \{Z_i = (X_i, Y_i): i = 1, \ldots, n\}$, we define the training loss for $w \in \Omega$ as

$$\phi(w, \mathcal{S}_n) = \frac{1}{n} \sum_{i=1}^{n} \phi(w, Z_i). \tag{3.5}$$

Moreover, for a distribution $\mathcal{D}$ on $\mathcal{Z}$, we define the test loss for $w \in \Omega$ as

$$\phi(w, \mathcal{D}) = \mathbb{E}_{Z \in \mathcal{D}} \phi(w, Z). \tag{3.6}$$

Since $L_*(x, y)$ does not depend on w, the ERM solution with respect to the loss $L(\cdot)$ is equivalent to the ERM solution with respect to $\phi(w, \cdot)$. Therefore with the simplified notations, the approximate ERM method (3.3) is a special case of the following method:

$$\phi(\hat{w}, \mathcal{S}_n) \leq \inf_{w \in \Omega} \phi(w, \mathcal{S}_n) + \epsilon'. \tag{3.7}$$

In general, we may simply take $L_*(x, y) = 0$ in (3.4). However, for some applications, we may choose a nonzero $L_*(x, y)$ so that

$$L(f(w, x), y) - L_*(x, y)$$

has a small variance. For least squares loss, this can be achieved with $L_*(x, y) = L(f_*(x), y)$, where $f_*(x)$ is the optimal prediction function that minimizes the test loss as shown in Example 3.9. The smaller variance, combined with Bernstein's inequality, implies better generalization bound (see Section 3.6 for more details).

Example 3.9   Consider linear model $f(w, x) = w^\top x$, and let $L(f(w, x), y) = (w^\top x - y)^2$ be the least squares loss. Then with $L_*(x, y) = 0$, we have $\phi(w, z) = (w^\top x - y)^2$ for $z = (x, y)$.

If we further assume that the problem is realizable by linear model, and w_* is the true weight vector: $\mathbb{E}[y|x] = w_*^\top x$. It follows that we may take $L_*(x, y) = (w_*^\top x - y)^2$, and

$$\phi(w, z) = (w^\top x - y)^2 - (w_*^\top x - y)^2,$$

which has a small variance when $w \approx w_*$ because $\lim_{w \to w_*} \phi(w, z) = 0$.

We assume now that training data Z_i are iid samples from an unknown test distribution $\mathcal{D}$. Similar to the PAC learning analysis, we are interested in bounding the test error $\phi(\hat{w}, \mathcal{D})$ in terms of the training error $\phi(\hat{w}, \mathcal{S}_n)$ for the ERM method (3.7).

The family of loss functions forms a function class $\{\phi(w, z): w \in \Omega\}$ indexed by $w \in \Omega$. We call $\{\phi(w, \mathcal{S}_n): w \in \Omega\}$ an *empirical process* indexed by Ω. Similar to the PAC learning analysis in Section 3.2, we need to bound the uniform convergence of training error to test error that holds true for all $w \in \Omega$. This is also referred to as uniform convergence of the empirical process $\{\phi(w, \mathcal{S}_n): w \in \Omega\}$.

Definition 3.10 (Uniform Convergence)   Given a model space Ω and distribution $\mathcal{D}$, let $\mathcal{S}_n \sim \mathcal{D}^n$ be n iid examples sampled from $\mathcal{D}$ on $\mathcal{Z}$. We say that $\phi(w, \mathcal{S}_n)$ $(w \in \Omega)$ converges to $\phi(w, \mathcal{D})$ uniformly in probability if for all $\epsilon > 0$,

$$\lim_{n \to \infty} \Pr \left(\sup_{w \in \Omega} |\phi(w, \mathcal{S}_n) - \phi(w, \mathcal{D})| > \epsilon \right) = 0,$$

where the probability is over iid samples of $\mathcal{S}_n \sim \mathcal{D}^n$.

Uniform convergence is also referred to as the uniform law of large numbers. It says that the law of large numbers holds for all $\hat{w} \in \Omega$ that may depend on the training data $\mathcal{S}_n$. It can thus be applied to the output of any learning algorithm. While two-sided uniform convergence of Definition 3.10 is frequently used in the literature, we will employ one-sided uniform convergence as this is more convenient for multiplicative bounds.

Similar to the analysis of PAC learning, the uniform convergence result can be used to obtain an oracle inequality for the approximate ERM solution as in the following lemma. Note that for a Chernoff-style bound, we may take $\alpha = \alpha' = 1$. However, if we apply multiplicative Chernoff bound, or Bernstein's inequality, then we often choose multiplicative factors $\alpha < 1$ and $\alpha' > 1$.

Lemma 3.11 *Assume that for any $\delta \in (0,1)$, the following uniform convergence result holds with some $\alpha > 0$ (we allow α to depend on $\mathcal{S}_n$). With probability at least $1 - \delta_1$,*

$$\forall w \in \Omega: \ \alpha\phi(w, \mathcal{D}) \leq \phi(w, \mathcal{S}_n) + \epsilon_n(\delta_1, w).$$

Moreover, $\forall w \in \Omega$, the following inequality holds with some $\alpha' > 0$ (we allow α' to depend on $\mathcal{S}_n$). With probability at least $1 - \delta_2$,

$$\phi(w, \mathcal{S}_n) \leq \alpha'\phi(w, \mathcal{D}) + \epsilon_n'(\delta_2, w).$$

Then the following statement holds. With probability at least $1 - \delta_1 - \delta_2$, the approximate ERM method (3.7) satisfies the oracle inequality:

$$\alpha\phi(\hat{w}, \mathcal{D}) \leq \inf_{w \in \Omega} \left[\alpha'\phi(w, \mathcal{D}) + \epsilon_n'(\delta_2, w) \right] + \epsilon' + \epsilon_n(\delta_1, \hat{w}).$$

Proof Consider an arbitrary $w \in \Omega$. We have with probability at least $1 - \delta_1$,

$$\alpha\phi(\hat{w}, \mathcal{D}) \leq \phi(\hat{w}, \mathcal{S}_n) + \epsilon_n(\delta_1, \hat{w})$$
$$\leq \phi(w, \mathcal{S}_n) + \epsilon' + \epsilon_n(\delta_1, \hat{w}), \tag{3.8}$$

where the first inequality is due to uniform convergence, and the second inequality is due to (3.7). Moreover, with probability at least $1 - \delta_2$,

$$\phi(w, \mathcal{S}_n) \leq \alpha'\phi(w, \mathcal{D}) + \epsilon_n'(\delta_2, w). \tag{3.9}$$

Taking the union bound of the two events, we obtain with probability at least $1 - \delta_1 - \delta_2$, both (3.8) and (3.9) hold. It follows that

$$\alpha\phi(\hat{w}, \mathcal{D}) \leq \phi(w, \mathcal{S}_n) + \epsilon' + \epsilon_n(\delta_1, \hat{w})$$
$$\leq \alpha'\phi(w, \mathcal{D}) + \epsilon_n'(\delta_2, w) + \epsilon' + \epsilon_n(\delta_1, \hat{w}).$$

Since w is arbitrary, we let w approach the minimum of the right-hand side, and obtain the desired bound. $\square$

We observe that in Lemma 3.11, the first condition requires one-sided uniform convergence for all $w \in \Omega$. The second condition does not require uniform convergence, but only requires that a tail bound of Chapter 2 holds for all individual $w \in \Omega$. The result here shows that the uniform convergence of empirical processes can be used to derive oracle inequalities for the ERM method.

Example 3.12 We consider the PAC learning example of Theorem 3.6, but assume that $\inf_f \mathrm{err}_{\mathcal{D}}(f) \neq 0$. We have the following uniform convergence result from the proof of Theorem 3.6. With probability $1 - \delta_1$,

$$\forall f \colon \mathrm{err}_{\mathcal{D}}(f) \leq \widehat{\mathrm{err}}_{\mathcal{S}_n}(f) + \sqrt{\frac{2\mathrm{err}_{\mathcal{D}}(f)\ln(N/\delta_1)}{n}} \leq \widehat{\mathrm{err}}_{\mathcal{S}_n}(f) + \gamma \mathrm{err}_{\mathcal{D}}(f) + \frac{\ln(N/\delta_1)}{2\gamma n}.$$

In addition, from (2.12), we have for all f, with probability $1 - \delta_2$,

$$\widehat{\mathrm{err}}_{\mathcal{S}_n}(f) < (1+\gamma)\mathrm{err}_{\mathcal{D}}(f) + \frac{(3+2\gamma)\ln(1/\delta_2)}{6\gamma n}.$$

We can thus take $\alpha = 1 - \gamma$, $\alpha' = 1 + \gamma$, $\epsilon_n = \frac{\ln(N/\delta_1)}{2\gamma n}$, and $\epsilon'_n = \frac{(3+2\gamma)\ln(1/\delta_2)}{6\gamma n}$ in Lemma 3.11. Let $\delta = \delta_1/2 = \delta_2/2$, we obtain the following oracle inequality from Lemma 3.11. With probability at least $1 - \delta$,

$$(1-\gamma)\mathrm{err}_{\mathcal{D}}(\hat{f}) \leq (1+\gamma)\inf_f \mathrm{err}_{\mathcal{D}}(f) + \epsilon' + \frac{\ln(2N/\delta)}{2\gamma n} + \frac{(3+2\gamma)\ln(2/\delta)}{6\gamma n}.$$

Next we will investigate the main technique to derive uniform convergence bounds.

3.4 Covering Number

If Ω is finite, then we can use the union bound to obtain uniform convergence of empirical processes. If Ω is infinite, then we can approximate the function class

$$\mathcal{G} = \{\phi(w, z) \colon w \in \Omega\}$$

using a finite function class. We can then apply union bound to this finite approximation. Different types of approximations lead to different types of covering, which lead to different definitions of covering numbers. This section introduces a simple covering number that is easy to apply.

Definition 3.13 (Lower Bracketing Cover) Given a distribution $\mathcal{D}$, a finite function class $\mathcal{G}(\epsilon) = \{\phi_1(z), \ldots, \phi_N(z)\}$ is an ϵ-lower bracketing cover of $\mathcal{G}$ (with $L_1(\mathcal{D})$ metric) if for all $w \in \Omega$, there exists $j = j(w)$ such that

$$\forall z \colon \phi_j(z) \leq \phi(w, z), \qquad \mathbb{E}_{Z \sim \mathcal{D}}\phi_j(Z) \geq \mathbb{E}_{Z \sim \mathcal{D}}\phi(w, Z) - \epsilon.$$

The ϵ-lower bracketing number of $\mathcal{G}$, denoted by $N_{LB}(\epsilon, \mathcal{G}, L_1(\mathcal{D}))$, is the smallest cardinality of such $\mathcal{G}(\epsilon)$. The quantity $\ln N_{LB}(\epsilon, \mathcal{G}, L_1(\mathcal{D}))$ is referred to as the ϵ-lower bracketing entropy.

We shall mention that the functions $\phi_j(z)$ may not necessarily belong to $\mathcal{G}$. Next we show that the lower bracketing number can be used to obtain uniform convergence bounds for infinite function classes.

Theorem 3.14 Assume that $\phi(w, z) \in [0, 1]$ for all $w \in \Omega$ and $z \in \mathcal{Z}$. Let $\mathcal{G} = \{\phi(w, z) \colon w \in \Omega\}$. Then given $\delta \in (0, 1)$, with probability at least $1 - \delta$, the following inequality holds:

$$\forall w \in \Omega \colon \phi(w, \mathcal{D}) \leq [\phi(w, \mathcal{S}_n) + \epsilon_n(\delta, \mathcal{G}, \mathcal{D})],$$

where

$$\epsilon_n(\delta, \mathcal{G}, \mathcal{D}) = \inf_{\epsilon > 0} \left[\epsilon + \sqrt{\frac{\ln(N_{LB}(\epsilon, \mathcal{G}, L_1(\mathcal{D}))/\delta)}{2n}} \right].$$

Moreover, with probability at least $1 - \delta$, the following inequality holds:

$$\forall \gamma \in (0, 1), \forall w \in \Omega: \ (1 - \gamma)\phi(w, \mathcal{D}) \leq \phi(w, \mathcal{S}_n) + \epsilon_n^{\gamma}(\delta, \mathcal{G}, \mathcal{D}),$$

where

$$\epsilon_n^{\gamma}(\delta, \mathcal{G}, \mathcal{D}) = \inf_{\epsilon > 0} \left[(1 - \gamma)\epsilon + \frac{\ln(N_{LB}(\epsilon, \mathcal{G}, L_1(\mathcal{D}))/\delta)}{2\gamma n} \right].$$

Proof For any $\epsilon > 0$, let $\mathcal{G}(\epsilon) = \{\phi_1(z), \ldots, \phi_N(z)\}$ be an ϵ-lower bracketing cover of $\mathcal{G}$ with $N = N_{LB}(\epsilon, \mathcal{G}, L_1(\mathcal{D}))$. We may assume that $\phi_j(z) \in [0, 1]$ for all j (otherwise, we may set $\phi_j(z)$ to $\min(1, \max(0, \phi_j(z)))$). In the following, we let $j = j(w)$ for simplified notation:

$$\frac{1}{n} \sum_{i=1}^{n} \phi(w, Z_i) - \mathbb{E}_{Z \sim \mathcal{D}} \phi(w, Z) \geq \frac{1}{n} \sum_{i=1}^{n} \phi_j(Z_i) - \mathbb{E}_{Z \sim \mathcal{D}} \phi_j(Z) - \epsilon. \quad (3.10)$$

Let $\epsilon'' = \sqrt{\ln(N/\delta)/2n}$. It follows from the union bound on j that

$$\Pr\left(\exists w \in \Omega: \left[\frac{1}{n} \sum_{i=1}^{n} \phi(w, Z_i) - \mathbb{E}_{Z \sim \mathcal{D}} \phi(w, Z) + \epsilon + \epsilon'' \right] \leq 0 \right)$$

$$\leq \Pr\left(\exists j: \left[\frac{1}{n} \sum_{i=1}^{n} \phi_j(Z_i) - \mathbb{E}_{Z \sim \mathcal{D}} \phi_j(Z) + \epsilon'' \right] \leq 0 \right)$$

$$\leq \sum_{j=1}^{N} \Pr\left(\frac{1}{n} \sum_{i=1}^{n} \phi_j(Z_i) - \mathbb{E}_{Z \sim \mathcal{D}} \phi_j(Z) + \epsilon'' \leq 0 \right)$$

$$\leq N \exp(-2n(\epsilon'')^2) = \delta.$$

The first inequality used (3.10). The second inequality used the union bound. The last inequality used the additive Chernoff bound (Theorem 2.16). This leads to the first desired bound of the theorem.

Moreover, using the multiplicative Chernoff bound (2.11) and the union bound, we obtain the following statement. With probability at least $1 - \delta$, the following inequality holds for all j:

$$(1 - \gamma)\mathbb{E}_{Z \sim \mathcal{D}} \phi_j(Z) \leq \frac{1}{n} \sum_{i=1}^{n} \phi_j(Z_i) + \frac{1}{2\gamma} \frac{\ln(N/\delta)}{n}. \quad (3.11)$$

Therefore for all $w \in \Omega$, let $j = j(w)$. We obtain

$$(1 - \gamma)\mathbb{E}_{Z \sim \mathcal{D}}\phi(w, Z) \leq (1 - \gamma)\mathbb{E}_{Z \sim \mathcal{D}}\phi_j(Z) + (1 - \gamma)\epsilon$$

$$\leq \frac{1}{n}\sum_{i=1}^{n}\phi_j(Z_i) + \frac{1}{2\gamma}\frac{\ln(N/\delta)}{n} + (1 - \gamma)\epsilon$$

$$\leq \frac{1}{n}\sum_{i=1}^{n}\phi(w, Z_i) + \frac{1}{2\gamma}\frac{\ln(N/\delta)}{n} + (1 - \gamma)\epsilon.$$

The first and the third inequalities used the definition of lower bracketing cover. The second inequality used (3.11). This leads to the second desired bound. □

The uniform convergence bounds in Theorem 3.14 imply generalization bounds as follows. We may take $\phi(w, z) = L(f(w, x), y)$ with $L_*(x, y) = 0$ to obtain an oracle inequality for the approximate ERM method (3.3).

Corollary 3.15 *Assume that $\phi(w, z) \in [0, 1]$ for all $w \in \Omega$ and $z \in \mathcal{Z}$. Let $\mathcal{G} = \{\phi(w, z) : w \in \Omega\}$. With probability at least $1 - \delta$, the approximate ERM method (3.7) satisfies the (additive) oracle inequality:*

$$\phi(\hat{w}, \mathcal{D}) \leq \inf_{w \in \Omega} \phi(w, \mathcal{D}) + \epsilon' + \inf_{\epsilon > 0}\left[\epsilon + \sqrt{\frac{2\ln(2N_{LB}(\epsilon, \mathcal{G}, L_1(\mathcal{D}))/\delta)}{n}}\right].$$

Moreover, with probability at least $1 - \delta$, we have the following (multiplicative) oracle inequality for all $\gamma \in (0, 1)$:

$$(1 - \gamma)\phi(\hat{w}, \mathcal{D}) \leq \inf_{w \in \Omega}(1 + \gamma)\phi(w, \mathcal{D}) + \epsilon'$$

$$+ \inf_{\epsilon > 0}\left[(1 - \gamma)\epsilon + \frac{(\gamma + 2)\ln(2N_{LB}(\epsilon, \mathcal{G}, L_1(\mathcal{D}))/\delta)}{2\gamma n}\right].$$

Proof We can set $\alpha = 1$ and take $\epsilon_n(\delta/2, w) = \epsilon_n(\delta/2, \mathcal{G}, \mathcal{D})$, as defined in the first bound of Theorem 3.14. We then use the additive Chernoff bound of Theorem 2.16, and set $\alpha' = 1$ and

$$\epsilon_n'(\delta/2, w) = \sqrt{\frac{\ln(2/\delta)}{2n}} \leq \sqrt{\frac{\ln(2N_{LB}(\epsilon, \mathcal{G}, L_1(\mathcal{D}))/\delta)}{2n}}$$

for an arbitrary $\epsilon > 0$. The conditions of Lemma 3.11 hold. We can then use the above upper bound on $\epsilon_n'(\delta/2, w)$ to simplify the result of Lemma 3.11, and take the minimum over ϵ to obtain the first desired bound of the corollary.

To derive the second desired inequality of the corollary, we can set $\alpha = (1 - \gamma)$ and $\epsilon_n(\delta/2, w) = \epsilon_n^\gamma(\delta/2, \mathcal{G}, \mathcal{D})$, as defined in the second bound of Theorem 3.14. We then use the multiplicative Chernoff bound as in (2.12), and set $\alpha' = 1 + \gamma$ and

$$\epsilon_n'(\delta/2, w) = \frac{(1 + \gamma)\ln(2/\delta)}{2\gamma n} \leq \frac{(1 + \gamma)\ln(2N_{LB}(\epsilon, \mathcal{G}, L_1(\mathcal{D}))/\delta)}{2\gamma n}$$

for an arbitrary $\epsilon > 0$. Now by combining these estimates with the second bound of Theorem 3.14, we can obtain the desired bounds from Lemma 3.11. □

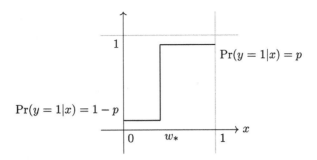

Figure 3.1 Conditional probability $\Pr(y = 1|x)$ as a function of x

3.5 A Simple Example

We consider a one-dimensional classification problem, where the input x is uniformly distributed in $[0, 1]$, and the output $y \in \{\pm 1\}$ is generated according to

$$\Pr(y = 1|x) = \begin{cases} p & \text{if } x \geq w_*, \\ (1 - p) & \text{otherwise} \end{cases} \tag{3.12}$$

for some unknown $w_* \in [0, 1]$ and $p \in (0.5, 1]$. See Figure 3.1.

Since we don't know the true threshold w_*, we can consider a family of classifiers

$$f(w, x) = 2\mathbb{1}(x \geq w) - 1 = \begin{cases} 1 & \text{if } x \geq w, \\ -1 & \text{otherwise,} \end{cases}$$

where $w \in \Omega = [0, 1]$ is the model parameter to be learned from the training data. Here $\mathbb{1}(\cdot)$ is the binary indicator function, which takes value 1 if the condition in $\mathbb{1}(\cdot)$ holds, and value 0 otherwise.

In this example, we consider the following classification error loss function:

$$L(f(x), y) = \mathbb{1}(f(x) \neq y).$$

In this case, the optimal Bayes classifier is $f_*(x) = 2\mathbb{1}(x \geq w_*) - 1$, and the optimal Bayes error is

$$\mathbb{E}_{X,Y} \, L(f(w_*, X), Y) = 1 - p.$$

We will study the generalization performance of empirical risk minimization. Since, for this example, it is easy to find a model parameter $\hat{w}$ to minimize the empirical risk (the solution may not be unique), we will set $\epsilon' = 0$ in (3.3).

Lower bracketing cover

Given any $\epsilon > 0$, we let $w_j = 0 + j\epsilon$ for $j = 1, \ldots, \lceil 1/\epsilon \rceil$. Let

$$\phi_j(z) = \begin{cases} 0 & \text{if } x \in [w_j - \epsilon, w_j], \\ \phi(w_j, z) & \text{otherwise,} \end{cases}$$

where $z = (x, y)$. Note that $\phi_j \notin \mathcal{G}$.

It follows that for any $w \in [0,1]$, if we let w_j be the smallest j such that $w_j \geq w$, then we have $\phi_j(z) = 0 \leq \phi(w, z)$ when $x \in [w_j - \epsilon, w_j]$, and $\phi_j(z) = \phi(w, z)$ otherwise, where $z = (x, y)$. Moreover,

$$\mathbb{E}_{Z \sim \mathcal{D}}[\phi_j(Z) - \phi(w, Z)] = \mathbb{E}_{X \in [w_j - \epsilon, w_j]}[0 - \phi(w, Z)] \geq -\epsilon.$$

This means that $\{\phi_j(z)\}$ is an ϵ-lower bracketing cover of $\mathcal{G}$, and thus

$$N_{LB}(\epsilon, \mathcal{G}, L_1(\mathcal{D})) \leq 1 + \epsilon^{-1}.$$

Oracle inequalities

We have (by picking $\epsilon = 2/n$):

$$\inf_{\epsilon > 0} \left[\epsilon + \sqrt{\frac{2 \ln(2 N_{LB}(\epsilon, \mathcal{G}, L_1(\mathcal{D}))/\delta)}{n}} \right] \leq \frac{2}{n} + \sqrt{\frac{2 \ln((n+2)/\delta)}{n}}.$$

This implies the following additive oracle inequality from Corollary 3.15 with $\phi(w, z) = L(f(w, x), y)$. With probability at least $1 - \delta$,

$$\mathbb{E}_{(X,Y) \sim \mathcal{D}} L(f(\hat{w}, X), Y) \leq (1 - p) + \frac{2}{n} + \sqrt{\frac{2 \ln((n+2)/\delta)}{n}}.$$

In addition, we have (by picking $\epsilon = 2/n$)

$$\inf_{\epsilon > 0} \left[(1 - \gamma)\epsilon + \frac{(\gamma + 2) \ln(2 N_{LB}(\epsilon, \mathcal{G}, L_1(\mathcal{D}))/\delta)}{2\gamma n} \right]$$
$$\leq \frac{2(1 - \gamma)}{n} + \frac{(\gamma + 2) \ln((n+2)/\delta)}{2\gamma n}.$$

This implies the following multiplicative oracle inequality from Corollary 3.15 with $\phi(w, z) = L(f(w, x), y)$. With probability at least $1 - \delta$, for all $\gamma \in (0, 1)$,

$$\mathbb{E}_{(X,Y) \sim \mathcal{D}} L(f(\hat{w}, X), Y) \leq \frac{1 + \gamma}{1 - \gamma}(1 - p) + \frac{2}{n} + \frac{(\gamma + 2) \ln((n+2)/\delta)}{2\gamma(1 - \gamma)n}.$$

The multiplicative bound is superior to the additive bound when the Bayes error is small, such as when $p = 1$. In this case, the multiplicative bound implies a convergence rate of $\ln n/n$ instead of $\sqrt{\ln n/n}$ from the additive form.

3.6 Uniform Bernstein's Inequality

In this section, we show that better bounds can be obtained with Bernstein's inequality under the following condition.

Definition 3.16 (Variance Condition)   Given a function class $\mathcal{G}$, we say it satisfies the variance condition if there exists $c_0, c_1 > 0$ such that for all $\phi(z) \in \mathcal{G}$,

$$\mathrm{Var}_{Z \sim \mathcal{D}}(\phi(Z)) \leq c_0^2 + c_1 \mathbb{E}_{Z \sim \mathcal{D}} \phi(Z), \tag{3.13}$$

where we require that $\mathbb{E}_{Z \sim \mathcal{D}} \phi(Z) \geq -c_0^2/c_1$ for all $\phi \in \mathcal{G}$.

In applications, the following modification of the variance condition is often more convenient to employ:

$$\mathbb{E}_{Z \sim \mathcal{D}}[\phi(Z)^2] \leq c_0^2 + c_1 \mathbb{E}_{Z \sim \mathcal{D}} \phi(Z). \tag{3.14}$$

It is easy to see that (3.14) implies (3.13). If $\phi(Z)$ is bounded, then the two conditions are equivalent.

In general, if the variance condition (3.13) only holds for $c_1 = 0$, then we can only obtain a convergence rate that is $O(1/\sqrt{n})$ at the best. When the variance condition holds for $c_1 > 0$ and $c_0 = 0$, then we may be able to obtain a convergence rate faster than $O(1/\sqrt{n})$ by using Bernstein's inequality. The ability to achieve faster convergence is the main reason to study this condition. The following examples satisfy the variance condition.

Example 3.17 (Bounded Function) Let $\mathcal{G} = \{\phi(\cdot) \colon \forall z, \ \phi(z) \in [0,1]\}$. Then $\mathcal{G}$ satisfies the variance condition (3.14) with $c_0 = 0$ and $c_1 = 1$.

Example 3.18 (Least Squares) Consider the least squares method $L(f(x), y) = (f(x) - y)^2$, with bounded response $L(f(x), y) \leq M^2$ for some $M > 0$. Let $\mathcal{F}$ be a convex function class (i.e. for any $f_1, f_2 \in \mathcal{F}$, and $\alpha \in (0,1)$, $\alpha f_1 + (1-\alpha) f_2 \in \mathcal{F}$), and define the optimal function in $\mathcal{F}$ as follows:

$$f_{\text{opt}} = \arg \min_{f \in \mathcal{F}} \mathbb{E}_{(x,y) \sim \mathcal{D}} L(f(x), y). \tag{3.15}$$

Let $z = (x, y)$, and

$$\mathcal{G} = \{\phi(\cdot) \colon \phi(z) = L(f(x), y) - L(f_{\text{opt}}(x), y), f(x) \in \mathcal{F}\}.$$

Then $\mathcal{G}$ satisfies the variance condition (3.14) with $c_0 = 0$, and $c_1 = 4M^2$. We leave the proof as an exercise.

More generally, assume that $\mathcal{F}$ is a bounded nonconvex function class with $f(x) \in [0, M]$ for all $f \in \mathcal{F}$. If we assume that $y \in [0, M]$, then the variance condition may not hold with f_{opt} in (3.15). However, if we replace f_{opt} by $f_*(x) = \mathbb{E}[Y|X = x]$ in the definition of $\mathcal{G}$ as follows:

$$\mathcal{G} = \{\phi(\cdot) \colon \phi(z) = L(f(x), y) - L(f_*(x), y), f(x) \in \mathcal{F}\},$$

then all functions in $\mathcal{G}$ satisfy the variance condition (3.14) with $c_0 = 0$, and $c_1 = 2M^2$. Note that, in general, f_* may not belong to $\mathcal{F}$. However if the problem is well specified (i.e. $f_*(x) \in \mathcal{F}$), then the variance condition holds with $f_{\text{opt}} = f_*$.

Example 3.19 (Tsybakov's Noise Condition) Consider the binary classification problem on $\mathcal{X} \times \mathcal{Y}$ with $y \in \{0,1\}$. A distribution $\mathcal{D}$ on $\mathcal{X} \times \mathcal{Y}$ satisfies the Tsybakov noise condition if there exists $\beta \in (0,1]$, $c > 0$, and $\epsilon_0 \in (0, 0.5]$, so that

$$\Pr_{X \sim \mathcal{D}} [|\Pr(Y = 1|X) - 0.5| \leq \epsilon] \leq c\epsilon^{\beta/(1-\beta)}$$

for $\epsilon \in [0, \epsilon_0]$.

This condition says that the ambiguous points $\Pr(Y = 1|X) \approx 0.5$ occur with small probability. In particular, if $\beta = 1$, then $|\Pr(Y = 1|X) - 0.5| \geq \epsilon_0$ for all X.

Under the Tsybakov noise condition, for any binary function class $f(w, x)\colon \Omega \times \mathcal{X} \to \{0, 1\}$, the binary classification loss

$$\phi(w, z) = \mathbb{1}(f(w, x) \neq y) - \mathbb{1}(f_*(x) \neq y)$$

satisfies the following generalized variance condition, where $f_*(x) = \mathbb{1}(\Pr(Y = 1|X = x) \geq 0.5)$ is the optimal Bayes classifier. There exists $c_\beta > 0$ so that

$$\mathbb{E}_{Z \sim \mathcal{D}}[\phi(w, Z)^2] \leq c_\beta^{2-\beta}[\mathbb{E}_{Z \sim \mathcal{D}}\phi(w, Z)]^\beta. \tag{3.16}$$

We leave the proof as an exercise. When $\beta = 1$, this is equivalent to (3.14) with $c_0 = 0$. When $\beta < 1$, it also implies the variance condition of (3.14) with

$$c_0 = (1 - \beta)^{0.5}\gamma^{0.5/(1-\beta)}c_\beta, \qquad c_1 = \beta c_\beta \gamma^{-1/\beta},$$

where $\gamma > 0$ is a tuning parameter.

Example 3.20 In the example of Section 3.5, there exist p dependent constants $c_0(p)$ and $c_1(p)$ such that the ϵ lower bracket cover of $\mathcal{G}$ satisfies (3.14) with $c_0^2 = c_0(p)\epsilon$ and $c_1 = c_1(p)$. The proof is left as an exercise.

Under the variance-condition (3.13), we can obtain the following uniform convergence result using Bernstein's inequality. The statement allows unbounded loss function $\phi(w, z)$ because the logarithmic moment generating function estimate in Lemma 2.22 for Bernstein's inequality allows unbounded functions. The condition holds automatically for bounded functions such that $\max \phi(z) - \min \phi(z) \leq b$ for all $\phi \in \mathcal{G}$.

Theorem 3.21 *Assume that for all $\epsilon \in [0, \epsilon_0]$, $\mathcal{G} = \{\phi(w, z)\colon w \in \Omega\}$ has an ϵ-lower bracketing cover $\mathcal{G}(\epsilon)$ with $N_{LB}(\epsilon, \mathcal{G}, L_1(\mathcal{D}))$ members so that $\mathcal{G}(\epsilon)$ satisfies the variance condition (3.13).*

Moreover, assume for all $\phi(z) = \phi(w, z) \in \mathcal{G} \cup \mathcal{G}(\epsilon)$ as a function of $z \in \mathcal{Z}$, the random variable $\phi(z)$ satisfies the conditions of Lemma 2.22 with $V = \mathrm{Var}(\phi(Z))$, and $\mathbb{E}_{Z \sim \mathcal{D}}\phi(Z) \geq 0$. Then $\forall \delta \in (0, 1)$, with probability at least $1 - \delta$, the following inequality holds for all $\gamma \in (0, 1)$ and $w \in \Omega$:

$$(1 - \gamma)\phi(w, \mathcal{D}) \leq \phi(w, \mathcal{S}_n) + \epsilon_n^\gamma(\delta, \mathcal{G}, \mathcal{D}),$$

where

$$\epsilon_n^\gamma(\delta, \mathcal{G}, \mathcal{D}) = \inf_{\epsilon \in [0, \epsilon_0]} \left[(1 - \gamma)\epsilon + c_0 \left(\frac{2\ln(N_{LB}(\epsilon, \mathcal{G}, L_1(\mathcal{D}))/\delta)}{n} \right)^{1/2} \right. \tag{3.17}$$

$$\left. + \frac{(3c_1 + 2\gamma b)\ln(N_{LB}(\epsilon, \mathcal{G}, L_1(\mathcal{D}))/\delta)}{6\gamma n} \right].$$

Proof For any $\epsilon > 0$, let $\mathcal{G}(\epsilon) = \{\phi_1(z), \ldots, \phi_N(z)\}$ be an ϵ-lower bracketing cover of $\mathcal{G}$ with $N = N_{LB}(\epsilon, \mathcal{G}, L_1(\mathcal{D}))$.

Using Bernstein's inequalities and the union bound, we obtain the following statement. With probability at least $1 - \delta$, the following inequality holds for all j:

$$\mathbb{E}_{Z \sim \mathcal{D}} \phi_j(Z) \leq \frac{1}{n} \sum_{i=1}^n \phi_j(Z_i) + \sqrt{\frac{2 \text{Var}_{Z \sim \mathcal{D}} \phi_j(Z) \ln(N/\delta)}{n}} + \frac{b \ln(N/\delta)}{3n}$$

$$\leq \frac{1}{n} \sum_{i=1}^n \phi_j(Z_i) + \sqrt{\frac{2c_0^2 \ln(N/\delta)}{n}} + \sqrt{\frac{2c_1 [\mathbb{E}_{Z \sim \mathcal{D}} \phi_j(Z)] \ln(N/\delta)}{n}} + \frac{b \ln(N/\delta)}{3n}$$

$$\leq \frac{1}{n} \sum_{i=1}^n \phi_j(Z_i) + c_0 \sqrt{\frac{2 \ln(N/\delta)}{n}} + \gamma \mathbb{E}_{Z \sim \mathcal{D}} \phi_j(Z) + \frac{c_1 \ln(N/\delta)}{2\gamma n} + \frac{b \ln(N/\delta)}{3n}.$$

$$(3.18)$$

The derivation of the first inequality used Bernstein's inequality. The derivation of the second inequality used the fact that $\phi_j(z)$ satisfies the variance (3.13), and used the inequality $\sqrt{a + b} \leq \sqrt{a} + \sqrt{b}$ to simplify the result. The derivation of the third inequality used $\sqrt{2ab} \leq \gamma a + (b/2\gamma)$.

Therefore for all $w \in \Omega$, let $j = j(w)$, we obtain

$$(1 - \gamma) \mathbb{E}_{Z \sim \mathcal{D}} \phi(w, Z)$$
$$\leq (1 - \gamma) \mathbb{E}_{Z \sim \mathcal{D}} \phi_j(Z) + (1 - \gamma) \epsilon$$
$$\leq \frac{1}{n} \sum_{i=1}^n \phi_j(Z_i) + c_0 \left(\frac{2 \ln(N/\delta)}{n} \right)^{1/2} + \frac{(3c_1 + 2\gamma b) \ln(N/\delta)}{6\gamma n} + (1 - \gamma) \epsilon$$
$$\leq \frac{1}{n} \sum_{i=1}^n \phi(w, Z_i) + c_0 \left(\frac{2 \ln(N/\delta)}{n} \right)^{1/2} + \frac{(3c_1 + 2\gamma b) \ln(N/\delta)}{6\gamma n} + (1 - \gamma) \epsilon.$$

In this derivation, the first inequality and the third inequality used the definition of lower bracket cover. The second inequality used (3.18). This implies the desired bound. $\square$

Similar to Corollary 3.15, we can obtain from Theorem 3.21 and Lemma 3.11 the following oracle inequality.

Corollary 3.22 *Let $w_* = \arg \min_{w \in \Omega} \mathbb{E}_{(X,Y) \sim \mathcal{D}} L(f(w, X), Y)$, and assume that the conditions of Theorem 3.21 hold with $\phi(w, z) = L(f(w, x), y) - L(f(w_*, x), y)$. Then, with probability at least $1 - \delta$, the approximate ERM method (3.3) satisfies the oracle inequality*

$$\mathbb{E}_{(X,Y) \sim \mathcal{D}} L(f(\hat{w}, X), Y) \leq \mathbb{E}_{(X,Y) \sim \mathcal{D}} L(f(w_*, X), Y) + 2(\epsilon_n^{0.5}(\delta, \mathcal{G}, \mathcal{D}) + \epsilon'),$$

where $\epsilon_n^\gamma(\delta, \mathcal{G}, \mathcal{D})$ is given by (3.17).

Proof Theorem 3.21 implies the following. For all $\delta \in (0, 1)$, with probability at least $1 - \delta$,

$$(1 - \gamma) \phi(\hat{w}, \mathcal{D}) \leq \phi(\hat{w}, \mathcal{S}_n) + \epsilon_n^\gamma(\delta, \mathcal{G}, \mathcal{D}).$$

Since the approximate empirical risk minimizer satisfies

$$\phi(\hat{w}, \mathcal{S}_n) \leq \epsilon',$$

we obtain

$$(1 - \gamma)\phi(\hat{w}, \mathcal{D}) \leq \epsilon' + \epsilon_n^\gamma(\delta, \mathcal{G}, \mathcal{D}).$$

This implies the desired bound with $\gamma = 0.5$.   □

We use the following example to illustrate Corollary 3.22.

Example 3.23   Consider the example of Section 3.5. We consider the modified definition of $\phi(w, z)$,

$$\phi(w, z) = \mathbb{1}(f(w, x) \neq y) - \mathbb{1}(f(w_*, x) \neq y),$$

and the functions $\phi_j'(z) = \phi_j(z) - \mathbb{1}(f(w_*, x) \neq y)$ with $\phi_j(z)$ defined in Section 3.5 form an ϵ-lower bracketing cover of $\{\phi(w, z) : w \in [0, 1]\}$. Example 3.20 implies that, for this cover, the conditions of Theorem 3.21 hold for $\epsilon \leq \epsilon_0$ with $c_0^2 = c_0(p)\epsilon_0$, $c_1 = c_1(p)$. We may also take $b = 2$. By taking $\gamma = 0.5$, $\epsilon = \epsilon_0 = 2/n$, $\epsilon' = 0$, together with $N_{LB}(\epsilon, \mathcal{G}, L_1(\mathcal{D})) \leq (n + 2)/2$, we obtain

$$\epsilon_n^\gamma(\delta/2, \mathcal{G}, \mathcal{D}) = O\left(\frac{\ln(n/\delta)}{n}\right).$$

Note also that $\mathbb{E}_{(X,Y)\sim\mathcal{D}}\,\mathbb{1}(f(w_*, X) \neq Y) = 1 - p$, we obtain from Corollary 3.22 that with probability at least $1 - \delta$,

$$\mathbb{E}_{(X,Y)\sim\mathcal{D}}\mathbb{1}(f(\hat{w}, X) \neq Y) \leq (1 - p) + O\left(\frac{\ln(n/\delta)}{n}\right).$$

This shows the ERM method has generalization error converging to the Bayes error at a rate of $O(\ln n/n)$. This result achieves a better convergence rate than those in Section 3.5 when $p \in (0.5, 1)$. The rate $O(\ln n/n)$ can be improved to $O(1/n)$ using a slightly more refined technique referred to as "peeling." We leave it as an exercise.

Example 3.24   In general, for bounded parametric function classes with d real-valued parameters (such as linear models $f(w, x) = w^\top x$ defined on a compact subset of $\mathbb{R}^d$), we expect the entropy (more details can be found in Section 5.2) to behave as

$$\ln N_{LB}(\epsilon, \mathcal{G}, L_1(\mathcal{D})) = O(d\ln(1/\epsilon)).$$

Assume that the variance condition (3.16) holds. Then it implies (3.14) with appropriate tuning c_0 and c_1. By optimizing the trade-off between c_0 and c_1, it can be shown that the generalization bound in Corollary 3.22 implies a convergence rate of

$$\mathbb{E}_{\mathcal{D}}L(f(\hat{w}, X), Y) \leq \mathbb{E}_{\mathcal{D}}L(f(w_*, X), Y) + O\left(\left(\frac{\ln(n^d/\delta)}{n}\right)^{1/(2-\beta)}\right).$$

Example 3.25 Consider the parametric least squares regression problem with either a convex or a nonconvex but realizable function class $\mathcal{F}$. Example 3.18 implies that the variance condition holds with $f_{\text{opt}}(x) \in \mathcal{F}$. Example 3.24 shows that by using Corollary 3.22, we obtain with probability at least $1 - \delta$,

$$\mathbb{E}_{\mathcal{D}} L(\hat{f}(X), Y) \leq \mathbb{E}_{\mathcal{D}} L(f_{\text{opt}}(X), Y) + O\left(\frac{M^2 \ln(n^d/\delta)}{n}\right),$$

where $\hat{f}$ is the empirical risk minimizer in $\mathcal{F}$ with the least squares loss.

However, if the function class $\mathcal{F}$ is nonconvex, then the variance condition does not hold with respect to f_{opt} when the model is misspecified (i.e. when $f_*(x) = \mathbb{E}[y|x] \notin \mathcal{F}$). This implies a convergence rate of $O(1/\sqrt{n})$ when competing with f_{opt}. In fact, even for problems with two functions, one can obtain a convergence no better than $O(1/\sqrt{n})$ for least squares problem in the worst case. For example, we can assume $f_*(X) = 0$, and assume $Y \sim N(0, 1)$. Consider $\mathcal{F} = \{f_1, f_2\}$, with $f_{\text{opt}}(X) = f_1(X) = -1$ and $f_2(X) = 1 + 1/\sqrt{n}$. Then with n observations, ERM will choose f_2 with constant probability, which implies a test loss that is $\Omega(1/\sqrt{n})$ worse than the optimal function $f_{\text{opt}} = f_1$ (also Proposition 8.12). This suggests the importance of convex function classes for least squares regression.

For nonparametric function classes such as kernel methods, we generally expect the entropy to grow polynomially in $1/\epsilon$ as

$$\ln N_{LB}(\epsilon, \mathcal{G}, L_1(\mathcal{D})) = O(1/\epsilon^q)$$

for some $q > 0$ (see Chapter 5). Another way to view nonparametric models is that the "effective dimension" of nonparametric models depends on the approximation scale ϵ, and it increases as $d \approx 1/\epsilon^q$ when $\epsilon \to 0$.

Example 3.26 Let $\mathcal{G}$ be the class of monotone functions $[0, 1] \to [0, 1]$. Then the low bracketing entropy of $\mathcal{G}$ satisfies $\ln N_{LB}(\epsilon, \mathcal{G}, L_1(\mathcal{D})) = O(1/\epsilon)$.

In the case of nonparametric functions, Corollary 3.22 may not be tight. It can be improved by using a technique called "chaining," which requires the use of $L_2(\mathcal{D})$ bracketing number (see Definition 3.27), instead of the L_1-lower bracketing number considered here. In this book, we will only explain the chaining technique for L_2-empirical covering numbers in Chapter 4. A similar analysis for L_2-bracketing numbers can be found in van der Vaart and Wellner (1996).

3.7 General Bracketing Number

In some applications, we are interested in two-sided uniform convergence, which bounds the error

$$\sup_{w \in \Omega} |\phi(w, \mathcal{S}_n) - \phi(w, \mathcal{D})|.$$

In order to obtain such a uniform convergence result, we may employ two-sided bracketing cover defined as follows.

Definition 3.27 (Bracketing Number) Let $\mathcal{G} = \{\phi(w, \cdot) \colon w \in \Omega\}$ be a real-valued function class, equipped with a pseudometric d. We say

$$\mathcal{G}(\epsilon) = \{[\phi_1^L(z), \phi_1^U(z)], \dots, [\phi_N^L(z), \phi_N^U(z)]\}$$

is an ϵ-bracket of $\mathcal{G}$ under metric d if for all $w \in \Omega$, there exists $j = j(w)$ such that $\forall z$

$$\phi_j^L(z) \leq \phi(w, z) \leq \phi_j^U(z), \qquad d(\phi_j^L, \phi_j^U) \leq \epsilon.$$

The ϵ-bracketing number is the smallest cardinality $N_{[]}(\epsilon, \mathcal{G}, d)$ of such $\mathcal{G}(\epsilon)$. The quantity $\ln N_{[]}(\epsilon, \mathcal{G}, d)$ is called ϵ bracketing entropy.

In particular, given a distribution $\mathcal{D}$ and $p \geq 1$, we define L_p-seminorm in function space as

$$\|f - f'\|_{L_p(\mathcal{D})} = [\mathbb{E}_{Z \sim \mathcal{D}}|f(Z) - f'(Z)|^p]^{1/p}. \tag{3.19}$$

It induces a pseudometric, denoted as $d = L_p(\mathcal{D})$, and the corresponding bracketing number is $N_{[]}(\epsilon, \mathcal{G}, L_p(\mathcal{D}))$.

For $p = \infty$, the $L_\infty(\mathcal{D})$-seminorm is defined as the essential supremum seminorm, which leads to the pseudometric

$$d(f, f') = \inf \{\omega \colon \Pr_{\mathcal{D}}[|f(Z) - f'(Z)| \leq \omega] = 1\}.$$

However, when $p = \infty$, instead of using the L_∞ bracketing number, it is more conventional to use the equivalent notion of L_∞ covering number (see Proposition 4.3).

We have the following relationship of lower bracketing number and bracketing numbers with different norms.

Proposition 3.28 *We have for all $p \geq 1$,*

$$N_{LB}(\epsilon, \mathcal{G}, L_1(\mathcal{D})) \leq N_{[]}(\epsilon, \mathcal{G}, L_1(\mathcal{D})) \leq N_{[]}(\epsilon, \mathcal{G}, L_p(\mathcal{D})).$$

Proposition 3.28 implies that Theorem 3.14 also holds for the $L_p(\mathcal{D})$ bracketing numbers ($p \geq 1$). Under the variance condition, Theorem 3.21 also holds for the $L_p(\mathcal{D})$ bracketing numbers ($p \geq 1$). It follows that Theorem 3.14 and Theorem 3.21 apply for all $N_{[]}(\epsilon, \mathcal{G}, L_p(\mathcal{D}))$ with $p \geq 1$. However, for $p \geq 2$, one may use the chaining technique to derive better uniform convergence bounds than those of Theorem 3.21. We will not develop such refined analysis for bracketing numbers in this book because bracketing numbers are not used as widely as empirical and uniform covering numbers in the machine learning literature. We will thus only derive the consequence of the chaining analysis for L_2-uniform covering numbers in Chapter 4. The analysis for the bracketing numbers, using Bernstein's inequality, will be similar.

We also have the following property of bracketing numbers, which can be used to derive bracketing numbers for compositions of function classes.

Proposition 3.29 *Consider function classes $\mathcal{F}$ and $\mathcal{G}$. For any real number α and β, define the function class*

$$\alpha \mathcal{F} + \beta \mathcal{G} = \{\alpha f(z) + \beta g(z) : f \in \mathcal{F}, g \in \mathcal{G}\},$$

then

$$\ln N_{[]}(|\alpha|\epsilon_1 + |\beta|\epsilon_2, \alpha \mathcal{F} + \beta \mathcal{G}, L_p(\mathcal{D})) \leq \ln N_{[]}(\epsilon_1, \mathcal{F}, L_p(\mathcal{D})) + \ln N_{[]}(\epsilon_2, \mathcal{G}, L_p(\mathcal{D})).$$

Moreover, let $\psi(a) \colon \mathbb{R} \to \mathbb{R}$ be a Lipschitz function: $|\psi(a) - \psi(b)| \leq \gamma|a - b|$. Let $\psi(\mathcal{F}) = \{\psi(f(z)) \colon f \in \mathcal{F}\}$, then

$$\ln N_{[]}(\gamma\epsilon, \psi(\mathcal{F}), L_p(\mathcal{D})) \leq \ln N_{[]}(\epsilon, \mathcal{F}, L_p(\mathcal{D})).$$

3.8 Historical and Bibliographical Remarks

The theory of empirical process was started from the study of the convergence property of empirical distributions of real-valued random variables. In our notation, this corresponds to the choice of function class $\phi(w, z) = \mathbb{1}(z \leq w)$, where $w \in \mathbb{R}$ and $z \in \mathbb{R}$. It was shown in (Cantelli, 1933; Glivenko, 1933) that the uniform law of large numbers hold for this function class. Therefore function classes that satisfy the uniform law of large numbers are also called *Glivenko–Cantelli classes*. Similar to Theorem 3.14, it can be shown (see van der Vaart and Wellner, 1996, chapter 2.4) that $\mathcal{G}$ is a Glivenko–Cantelli class under distribution $\mathcal{D}$ if

$$\forall \epsilon > 0, \quad N_{[]}(\epsilon, \mathcal{G}, L_1(\mathcal{D})) < \infty.$$

One can further prove a functional extension of the central limit theorem for certain empirical processes (Donsker, 1952), and function classes that satisfy such central limit theorems are called *Donsker classes*. It is known (see van der Vaart and Wellner, 1996, chapter 2.5) that $\mathcal{G}$ is a Donsker class if

$$\int_0^\infty \sqrt{\ln N_{[]}(\epsilon, \mathcal{G}, L_2(\mathcal{D}))}\, d\epsilon < \infty.$$

We will not consider central limit theorems in this book, and refer the readers to (van der Vaart and Wellner, 1996) for further readings on empirical processes.

The first use of empirical process to analyze empirical risk minimization is attributed to Vapnik and Chervonenkis (1968, 1971) during the late 1960s. The theory is also referred to as the VC theory, which was described in some recent papers and books by Vapnik (1999, 2013). The modern theory of machine learning covers a much broader range of techniques and problems. The PAC learning framework, introduced by Valiant (1984), incorporated computational constraints into statistical learning. The theoretical study of machine learning algorithm with computational constraints is often referred to as *computational learning theory*.

The variance condition (3.14) and its extension in (3.16) are widely used in the recent learning theory literature to obtain faster than $O(1/\sqrt{n})$ convergence rates for ERM. In particular, for binary classification problems, the condition is implied by the Tsybakov noise condition of Example 3.19 (Mammen and Tsybakov, 1999; Tsybakov, 2004).

Exercises

3.1 Assume that E_j $(j = 1, \ldots, m)$ are independent events. Prove

$$\Pr(E_1 \cup \cdots \cup E_m) \geq \sum_{j=1}^{m} \Pr(E_j) - 0.5 \left(\sum_{j=1}^{m} \Pr(E_j) \right)^2.$$

3.2 Describe a computationally efficient learning algorithm for Decision List, and show that it is PAC learnable.

3.3 In Section 3.4, if we assume that all functions $\phi \in \mathcal{G} \cup \mathcal{G}(\epsilon)$ are sub-Gaussians. That is, there is a constant V so that

$$\ln \mathbb{E}_Z \exp(\lambda \phi(Z)) \leq \lambda \mathbb{E} \phi(Z) + \frac{\lambda^2}{2} V.$$

Derive an oracle inequality for approximate ERM in the form of Corollary 3.1.

3.4 Prove Example 3.18.

3.5 Prove Example 3.19.

3.6 In Example 3.20, compute $c_0(p)$ and $c_1(p)$.

3.7 Consider Example 3.23. We illustrate how to remove the $\ln n$ factor in the resulting generalization bound using the peeling technique, which considers a sequence of local covers. Let $\epsilon_0 = c \ln(4/\delta)/n$ for a sufficiently large constant c. For $\ell = 1, 2, \ldots$, let $\epsilon_\ell = 2^\ell \epsilon_0$, and define $\Omega_\ell = \{w : \phi(w, \mathcal{D}) \in [\epsilon_\ell, \epsilon_{\ell+1}]\}$.

- Show that $\mathcal{G}_\ell = \{\phi(w, z) : w \in \Omega_\ell\}$ has a constant $\epsilon_\ell/4$-bracketing cover.
- Apply Theorem 3.21 to $\mathcal{G}_\ell$ $(\ell \geq 1)$ and show that when c is sufficiently large and $\gamma = 0.5$,

$$\epsilon_n^\gamma(\delta/(\ell(\ell+1)), \mathcal{G}_\ell, \mathcal{D}) < (1 - \gamma)\epsilon_\ell.$$

Show that this implies $\Pr(\forall w \in \Omega_\ell : \phi(w, \mathcal{S}_n) > 0) \geq 1 - \delta/(\ell(\ell+1))$.

- Show that with probability at least $1 - \delta$, the empirical risk minimizer $\hat{w} \notin \Omega_\ell$ for all $\ell \geq 1$. This implies that with probability at least $1 - \delta$, $\phi(\hat{w}, \mathcal{D}) \leq 2\epsilon_0$.

3.8 Prove Example 3.24.

3.9 Consider a modification of the Example in Section 3.5, where we assume that the conditional probability in (3.12) is replaced by

$$\Pr(y = 1|x) = 0.5 + 0.5(x - w_*).$$

Show this example satisfies an appropriate Tsybakov noise condition, and use this condition to derive a variance condition (3.16). Derive the corresponding oracle inequality using Corollary 3.22.

3.10 Prove Example 3.26.

3.11 Prove Proposition 3.29.

4

Empirical Covering Number Analysis and Symmetrization

In the seminal paper of Vapnik and Chervonenkis (1971), a mathematical theory was developed to analyze the generalization performance of binary classification algorithms. This paper influenced the development of computational learning theory, including PAC learning described in Chapter 3. An essential component of the analysis is a bound on the empirical covering number of binary functions (which can be considered as a family of sets) using VC dimension; another essential component is the uniform convergence analysis using empirical covering numbers.

In Chapter 3, we have shown uniform convergence results can be established using lower-bracketing covers, which directly estimate the number of functions over the unknown test distribution. To analyze empirical covering numbers, we need to introduce an additional technique, leading to the analysis of *symmetrized* empirical processes. The symmetrization method is also used in the analysis of Rademacher complexity, which is studied in Chapter 6.

In this chapter, we will consider a version of the symmetrization argument for empirical covering numbers. The key idea is to consider a validation set of size n, and analyze the empirical validation performance on the validation data, with the model trained on the training data of size n. The uniform convergence is with respect to the convergence of training loss to the validation loss under random assignments of pairs of data to training and validation sets. We show that the uniform convergence with respect to the validation data can be used to derive a generalization bound on the test distribution. We note that the method for partitioning a dataset randomly into training and validation subsets is also a technique heavily used in the empirical evaluation of machine learning algorithms. A typical scheme in practice employs random permutation. The permutation argument was also used in the original analysis of Vapnik and Chervonenkis (1971). We will not study the permutation technique, but rather employ the related symmetrization argument instead of permutation because it is also used in the Rademacher complexity analysis (see Chapter 6).

4.1 Metric and Empirical Covering Numbers

We introduce metric covering numbers on a general pseudometric space as follows.

Definition 4.1 Let $(\mathcal{V}, d)$ be a pseudometric space with metric $d(\cdot, \cdot)$. A finite set $\mathcal{G}(\epsilon) \subset \mathcal{V}$ is an ϵ cover (or ϵ net) of $\mathcal{G} \subset \mathcal{V}$ if, for all $\phi \in \mathcal{G}$, there exists

$\phi' \in \mathcal{G}(\epsilon)$ so that $d(\phi', \phi) \le \epsilon$. The ϵ covering number of $\mathcal{G}$ with metric d is the smallest cardinality $N(\epsilon, \mathcal{G}, d)$ of such $\mathcal{G}(\epsilon)$. The number $\ln N(\epsilon, \mathcal{G}, d)$ is called the ϵ-entropy.

For a function class $\mathcal{G}$ with seminorm $L_p(\mathcal{D})$ in (3.19), we denote the corresponding $L_p(\mathcal{D})$covering number as $N(\epsilon, \mathcal{G}, L_p(\mathcal{D}))$. When $1 \le p \le q$, we have

$$N(\epsilon, \mathcal{G}, L_p(\mathcal{D})) \le N(\epsilon, \mathcal{G}, L_q(\mathcal{D})).$$

It is easy to verify the following relationship, which implies that $L_p(\mathcal{D})$ bracketing cover is a stronger requirement than $L_p(\mathcal{D})$ cover.

Proposition 4.2 *The following result holds:*

$$N(\epsilon, \mathcal{G}, L_p(\mathcal{D})) \le N_{[]}(2\epsilon, \mathcal{G}, L_p(\mathcal{D})).$$

Proof Let $\{[\phi_1^L(z), \phi_1^U(z)], \ldots, [\phi_N^L(z), \phi_N^U(z)]\}$ be a 2ϵ $L_p(\mathcal{D})$-bracketing cover of $\mathcal{G}$. Let $\phi_j(z) = (\phi_j^L(z) + \phi_j^U(z))/2$, then $\{\phi_1(z), \ldots, \phi_N(z)\}$ is an ϵ $L_p(\mathcal{D})$-cover of $\mathcal{G}$. □

The following result shows that with $p = \infty$, the reverse of Proposition 4.2 holds. That is, the $L_\infty(\mathcal{D})$ bracketing cover is equivalent to the $L_\infty(\mathcal{D})$ cover. This means that the analysis in Chapter 3, which employs a lower bracketing number, can be applied to the $L_\infty(\mathcal{D})$ covering number as well.

Proposition 4.3 *We have*

$$N_{[]}(\epsilon, \mathcal{G}, L_\infty(\mathcal{D})) = N(\epsilon/2, \mathcal{G}, L_\infty(\mathcal{D})).$$

Proof Let $\{\phi_j\}$ be an $\epsilon/2$ $L_\infty(\mathcal{D})$ cover of $\mathcal{G}$. Let $\phi_j^L = \phi_j - \epsilon/2$ and $\phi_j^U = \phi_j + \epsilon/2$. Then $[\phi_j^L, \phi_j^U]$ forms an ϵ bracketing cover. The reverse is also true, as in Proposition 4.2. □

This result implies that the $L_\infty(\mathcal{D})$ covering number leads to an upper bound of the $L_1(\mathcal{D})$ bracketing number. Consequently, one can obtain uniform convergence result using $L_\infty(\mathcal{D})$ covering numbers as indicated by Theorem 3.14. However, one cannot directly obtain uniform convergence using $L_p(\mathcal{D})$ covering numbers directly with $p < \infty$. In order to do so, one needs to introduce the concept of empirical and uniform covering numbers.

Definition 4.4 (Empirical and Uniform Covering Number) Given an empirical distribution $\mathcal{S}_n = \{Z_1, \ldots, Z_n\}$, we define the pseudometric $d = L_p(\mathcal{S}_n)$ as

$$d(\phi, \phi') = \left[\frac{1}{n} \sum_{i=1}^{n} |\phi(Z_i) - \phi'(Z_i)|^p\right]^{1/p}.$$

The corresponding metric covering number $N(\epsilon, \mathcal{G}, L_p(\mathcal{S}_n))$ is referred to as the empirical L_p covering number. Given n, the largest L_p covering number over empirical distribution $\mathcal{S}_n$ is referred to as the uniform L_p covering number

$$N_p(\epsilon, \mathcal{G}, n) = \sup_{\mathcal{S}_n} N(\epsilon, \mathcal{G}, L_p(\mathcal{S}_n)).$$

Since the $L_p(\mathcal{S}_n)$ pseudometric increases with p, we have the following simple result.

Proposition 4.5 *For $1 \leq p \leq q$, we have*

$$N(\epsilon, \mathcal{G}, L_p(\mathcal{S}_n)) \leq N(\epsilon, \mathcal{G}, L_q(\mathcal{S}_n)),$$

and

$$N_p(\epsilon, \mathcal{G}, n) \leq N_q(\epsilon, \mathcal{G}, n).$$

We will later show that the uniform L_1 covering number can be used to obtain uniform convergence and oracle inequalities. First, we show that it is easy to obtain an estimate of the empirical L_∞ covering number for linear classifiers, which implies a bound on the uniform L_1 covering number.

Example 4.6 Consider $\{0, 1\}$-valued linear classifiers in d dimension of the form $f(w, x) = \mathbb{1}(w^\top x \geq 0)$, where $w \in \Omega = \mathbb{R}^d$ and $\in \mathcal{X} = \mathbb{R}^d$. Let $Y \in \{0, 1\}$, then classification error is $\phi(w, z) = \mathbb{1}(f(w, x) \neq y)$, where $z = (x, y)$. Note that it is difficult to obtain bracketing cover for such problems with arbitrary $\mathcal{D}$. However it is easy to obtain the L_∞ empirical covering number. A general bound of uniform L_∞ covering numbers can be obtained using the concept of VC dimension. One may also use convex optimization to obtain a bound for linear classifiers as

$$N_\infty(\mathcal{G}, \epsilon, n) \leq (2n)^d,$$

with $\epsilon = 0$. See Exercise 4.4.

4.2 Symmetrization

Using the notations in Chapter 3, we let $Z = (X, Y)$. Consider the setting that we observe training data $\mathcal{S}_n = \{Z_1, \ldots, Z_n\}$, drawn independently from $\mathcal{D}$, and a separate validation data $\mathcal{S}'_n = \{Z'_1, \ldots, Z'_n\}$, also drawn independently from $\mathcal{D}$.

Given a function $f(Z)$, we may define the training loss and the validation loss as

$$f(\mathcal{S}_n) = \frac{1}{n} \sum_{Z \in \mathcal{S}_n} f(Z), \quad f(\mathcal{S}'_n) = \frac{1}{n} \sum_{Z \in \mathcal{S}'_n} f(Z)$$

for each partition $(\mathcal{S}_n, \mathcal{S}'_n)$. A natural question is how to bound the validation loss in terms of training loss. Note that such a validation result can be naturally converted into a generalization result with respect to the test distribution $\mathcal{D}$.

In the symmetrization argument, we bound the validation loss using the uniform convergence of symmetrized empirical process, which is defined as follows.

Since the symmetrized empirical process only depends on the empirical data $\mathcal{S}_n$, it can be analyzed using covering numbers on the empirical data.

Definition 4.7 Consider a real-valued function family $\mathcal{F} \colon \mathcal{Z} \to \mathbb{R}$. Consider n iid Bernoulli random variables $\sigma_i \in \{\pm 1\}$, where $\Pr(\sigma_i = 1) = \Pr(\sigma_i = -1) = 0.5$. The symmetrized empirical process is

$$f(\sigma, \mathcal{S}_n) = \frac{1}{n} \sum_{i=1}^n \sigma_i f(Z_i) \qquad f \in \mathcal{F},$$

where the randomness is with respect to both $\mathcal{S}_n = \{Z_i\}$ and $\sigma = \{\sigma_i\}$.

Note that in order to bound the symmetrized empirical process, we only need a covering number result on $\mathcal{S}_n$. Therefore the symmetrization analysis allows us to work with empirical covering numbers. Next, we will show that a bound on the symmetrized empirical process can be used to obtain uniform convergence of the empirical process $\{f(\mathcal{S}_n) \colon f \in \mathcal{F}\}$ to the corresponding result on the validation data. Since one can relate the validation loss of a learning algorithm to its generalization error on the test data, we can use this result to obtain generalization bounds.

The following lemma shows that if we can obtain an upper bound on the symmetrized empirical process $\{f(\sigma, \mathcal{S}_n) \colon f \in \mathcal{F}\}$, and the upper bound satisfies a superadditive property, then we can obtain the uniform convergence of the empirical process $\{f(\mathcal{S}_n) \colon f \in \mathcal{F}\}$ on the training data $\mathcal{S}_n$ to the corresponding result on the validation data $\mathcal{S}'_n$.

Lemma 4.8 (Symmetrization) *Consider a real-valued function family $\mathcal{F} = \{f \colon \mathcal{Z} \to \mathbb{R}\}$. Assume there exists a function $\psi \colon \mathcal{F} \times \mathcal{Z}^n \to \mathbb{R}$ and $\epsilon_n \colon (0,1) \to \mathbb{R}$, so that with probability at least $1 - \delta$,*

$$\forall f \in \mathcal{F}, \quad f(\sigma, \mathcal{S}_n) \leq \psi(f, \mathcal{S}_n) + \epsilon_n(\delta),$$

where the randomness is over both $\mathcal{S}_n \sim \mathcal{D}^n$ and σ. If there exists $\widetilde{\psi}(f, \mathcal{S}_n \cup \mathcal{S}'_n)$ so that the following superadditive inequality holds for all $(\mathcal{S}_n, \mathcal{S}'_n)$

$$\psi(f, \mathcal{S}_n) + \psi(f, \mathcal{S}'_n) \leq \widetilde{\psi}(f, \mathcal{S}_n \cup \mathcal{S}'_n),$$

then with probability at least $1 - \delta$ over independent random data $(\mathcal{S}_n, \mathcal{S}'_n) \sim \mathcal{D}^{2n}$,

$$\forall f \in \mathcal{F}, \quad f(\mathcal{S}'_n) \leq f(\mathcal{S}_n) + \widetilde{\psi}(f, \mathcal{S}_n \cup \mathcal{S}'_n) + 2\epsilon_n(\delta/2).$$

Proof Consider independent random samples $(\mathcal{S}_n, \mathcal{S}'_n) \sim \mathcal{D}^{2n}$. The distribution of $f(\mathcal{S}_n) - f(\mathcal{S}'_n)$ is the same as that of $f(\sigma, \mathcal{S}_n) - f(\sigma, \mathcal{S}'_n)$, and the latter contains additional randomness from Bernoulli random variables σ, drawn independently of $(\mathcal{S}_n, \mathcal{S}'_n)$, as in Definition 4.7. It follows that

$$\Pr\left(\exists f \in \mathcal{F}, f(\mathcal{S}'_n) > f(\mathcal{S}_n) + \widetilde{\psi}(f, \mathcal{S}_n \cup \mathcal{S}'_n) + 2\epsilon_n(\delta/2)\right)$$

$$= \Pr\left(\exists f \in \mathcal{F}, f(\sigma, \mathcal{S}'_n) > f(\sigma, \mathcal{S}_n) + \widetilde{\psi}(f, \mathcal{S}_n \cup \mathcal{S}'_n) + 2\epsilon_n(\delta/2)\right)$$

$$\overset{(a)}{\leq} \Pr\left(\underbrace{\exists f \in \mathcal{F}, f(\sigma, \mathcal{S}'_n) > f(\sigma, \mathcal{S}_n) + (\psi(f, \mathcal{S}_n) + \psi(f, \mathcal{S}'_n)) + 2\epsilon_n(\delta/2)}_{E_0}\right)$$

$$\overset{(b)}{\leq} \Pr\left(\underbrace{\exists f \in \mathcal{F}, f(\sigma, \mathcal{S}'_n) > \psi(f, \mathcal{S}'_n) + \epsilon_n(\delta/2)}_{E_1}\right)$$

$$+ \Pr\left(\underbrace{\exists f \in \mathcal{F}, -f(\sigma, \mathcal{S}_n) > \psi(f, \mathcal{S}_n) + \epsilon_n(\delta/2)}_{E_2}\right)$$

$$= 2\Pr\left(\exists f \in \mathcal{F}, f(\sigma, \mathcal{S}_n) > \psi(f, \mathcal{S}_n) + \epsilon_n(\delta/2)\right) \leq 2(\delta/2).$$

In derivation, the first equation used the fact that $f(\mathcal{S}_n) - f(\mathcal{S}'_n)$ and $f(\sigma, \mathcal{S}_n) - f(\sigma, \mathcal{S}'_n)$ have the same distributions. The (a) used the assumption $\psi(\mathcal{S}_n) + \psi(\mathcal{S}'_n) \leq \widetilde{\psi}(\mathcal{S}_n \cup \mathcal{S}'_n)$; (b) used the union bound, and the fact that if event E_0 holds, then either event E_1 holds or event E_2 holds. The next equation used the symmetry of $-f(\sigma, \mathcal{S}_n)$ and $f(\sigma, \mathcal{S}_n)$, and the last inequality used the assumption of the lemma. The result implies the desired bound. $\square$

Lemma 4.8 shows that the symmetrized empirical process can be used to obtain a uniform convergence result of a properly defined training statistics (e.g. training loss) to validation statistics (e.g. validation loss). The following example illustrates the consequences.

Example 4.9 We may take $\psi = \widetilde{\psi} = 0$ in Lemma 4.8. Assume we have the following bound for the symmetrized empirical process:

$$\forall f \in \mathcal{F}, \quad f(\sigma, \mathcal{S}_n) \leq \epsilon_n(\delta),$$

then with probability at least $1 - \delta$,

$$\forall f \in \mathcal{F}, \quad f(\mathcal{S}'_n) \leq f(\mathcal{S}_n) + 2\epsilon_n(\delta/2).$$

Example 4.10 In Lemma 4.8, we may also take $\gamma \in (0, 1)$. Let

$$\psi(f, \mathcal{S}_n) = \gamma f(\mathcal{S}_n) = \frac{\gamma}{n} \sum_{i=1}^{n} f(Z_i), \qquad \widetilde{\psi}(f, \mathcal{S}_n \cup \mathcal{S}'_n) = \frac{\gamma}{n} \sum_{i=1}^{n} [f(Z_i) + f(Z'_i)].$$

Assume that we have the following bound for the symmetrized empirical process: with probability at least $1 - \delta$,

$$\forall f \in \mathcal{F}, \quad f(\sigma, \mathcal{S}_n) \leq \gamma f(\mathcal{S}_n) + \epsilon_n(\delta),$$

then we obtain with probability at least $1 - \delta$,

$$\forall f \in \mathcal{F}, \quad (1 - \gamma)f(\mathcal{S}'_n) \leq (1 + \gamma)f(\mathcal{S}_n) + 2\epsilon_n(\delta/2).$$

The following result can be used with Lemma 4.8 to obtain the uniform convergence of training statistics to the test statistics (e.g. test loss). The resulting bound can then be used with Lemma 3.11 to obtain oracle inequalities for empirical risk minimization.

Lemma 4.11 *Let $\psi_{\mathrm{trn}}\colon \mathcal{F} \times \mathcal{Z}^n \to \mathbb{R}$, $\psi_{\mathrm{val}}\colon \mathcal{F} \times \mathcal{Z}^n \to \mathbb{R}$, $\psi_{\mathrm{tst}}\colon \mathcal{F} \times \mathcal{D} \to \mathbb{R}$ be appropriately training (where $\mathcal{D}$ denotes probability distributions on $\mathcal{Z}$), validation, and test statistics. Assume that for any $\delta_1 \in (0,1)$, the following uniform convergence result holds. With probability at least $1 - \delta_1$ over randomly drawn training and validation sets $(\mathcal{S}_n, \mathcal{S}_n') \sim \mathcal{D}^{2n}$,*

$$\forall f \in \mathcal{F}\colon\ \psi_{\mathrm{val}}(f, \mathcal{S}_n') \le \psi_{\mathrm{trn}}(f, \mathcal{S}_n) + \epsilon_n^1(\delta_1).$$

Moreover, assume $\forall f \in \mathcal{F}$, we have with probability $1 - \delta_2$ over randomly drawn $\mathcal{S}_n' \sim \mathcal{D}$:

$$\psi_{\mathrm{tst}}(f, \mathcal{D}) \le \psi_{\mathrm{val}}(f, \mathcal{S}_n') + \epsilon_n^2(\delta_2).$$

Then the following uniform convergence statement holds. With probability at least $1 - \delta_1 - \delta_2$,

$$\forall f \in \mathcal{F}\colon\ \psi_{\mathrm{tst}}(f, \mathcal{D}) \le \psi_{\mathrm{trn}}(f, \mathcal{S}_n) + \epsilon_n^1(\delta_1) + \epsilon_n^2(\delta_2).$$

Proof Let $Q(f, \mathcal{S}_n) = \psi_{\mathrm{tst}}(f, \mathcal{D}) - \psi_{\mathrm{trn}}(f, \mathcal{S}_n) - (\epsilon_n^1(\delta_1) + \epsilon_n^2(\delta_2))$, and let E be the event that $\sup_{f \in \mathcal{F}} Q(f, \mathcal{S}_n) \le 0$. We pick $\hat{f}(\mathcal{S}_n) \in \mathcal{F}$ so that if E holds, then we choose an arbitrary $Q(\hat{f}(\mathcal{S}_n), \mathcal{S}_n) \le 0$, and if E does not hold, we choose $\hat{f}(\mathcal{S}_n)$ so that $Q(\hat{f}(\mathcal{S}_n), \mathcal{S}_n) > 0$. We consider sample $(\mathcal{S}_n, \mathcal{S}_n') \sim \mathcal{D}^{2n}$. For simplicity, in the following, we let $\hat{f} = \hat{f}(\mathcal{S}_n)$. The uniform convergence condition of the theorem implies that with probability at least $1 - \delta_1$, the following event holds:

$$E_1\colon\quad \psi_{\mathrm{val}}(\hat{f}, \mathcal{S}_n') \le \psi_{\mathrm{trn}}(\hat{f}, \mathcal{S}_n) + \epsilon_n^1(\delta_1).$$

Note that the validation data $\mathcal{S}_n'$ is independent of the training data $\mathcal{S}_n$. Therefore $\mathcal{S}_n'$ is also independent of $\hat{f}$. Therefore the condition of the theorem implies that with probability at least $1 - \delta_2$, the following event holds:

$$E_2\colon\quad \psi_{\mathrm{tst}}(\hat{f}, \mathcal{D}) \le \psi_{\mathrm{val}}(\hat{f}, \mathcal{S}_n') + \epsilon_n^2(\delta_2).$$

If both events E_1 and E_2 hold, then

$$\psi_{\mathrm{tst}}(\hat{f}, \mathcal{D}) \le \psi_{\mathrm{val}}(\hat{f}, \mathcal{S}_n') + \epsilon_n^2(\delta_2)$$
$$\le \psi_{\mathrm{trn}}(\hat{f}, \mathcal{S}_n) + \epsilon_n^1(\delta_1) + \epsilon_n^2(\delta_2).$$

The definition of $\hat{f}$ implies that E holds. Therefore $\Pr(E) \ge \Pr(E_1 \& E_2) \ge 1 - \delta_1 - \delta_2$. This implies the desired bound. $\square$

In the literature, one can also obtain a different bound by considering the independence relationship between $\hat{f}$ and E_2. We leave the derivation as an exercise.

4.3 Uniform Convergence with Uniform L_1 Covering Number

Using the same notations as Chapter 3, we consider a function class

$$\mathcal{G} = \{\phi(w, z) \colon w \in \Omega\},$$

with $\phi(w, \mathcal{S}_n)$ and $\phi(w, \mathcal{D})$ defined in (3.5) and (3.6). We can obtain the following uniform convergence bounds, which are analogous to the results of Theorem 3.14. Here we simply replace the $L_1(\mathcal{D})$-lower bracketing number with the L_1 uniform covering number. It is also possible to relax the requirement of uniform covering number by assuming the bound holds with large probability. We do not consider such analysis, for simplicity.

Theorem 4.12 *Assume that $\phi(w, z) \in [0, 1]$ for all w and z. Then given $\delta \in (0, 1)$, with probability at least $1 - \delta$, the following inequality holds:*

$$\forall w \in \Omega \colon \phi(w, \mathcal{D}) \leq \phi(w, \mathcal{S}_n) + \epsilon_n(\delta),$$

where

$$\epsilon_n(\delta) = \inf_{\epsilon > 0} \left[2\epsilon + 3\sqrt{\frac{\ln(3N_1(\epsilon, \mathcal{G}, 2n)/\delta)}{2n}} \right].$$

Moreover, for any $\gamma \in (0, 1)$, with probability at least $1 - \delta$, the following inequality holds:

$$\forall w \in \Omega \colon (1 - \gamma)^2 \phi(w, \mathcal{D}) \leq \phi(w, \mathcal{S}_n) + \epsilon_n(\delta),$$

where

$$\epsilon_n(\delta) = \inf_{\epsilon > 0} \left[2\epsilon + \frac{(5 - 4\gamma)\ln(3N_1(\epsilon, \mathcal{G}, n)/\delta)}{2\gamma n} \right].$$

Proof Let $\mathcal{F} = \{f(z) = \phi(w, z) - 0.5 \colon w \in \Omega\}$. Given $\mathcal{S}_n$, we consider an ϵ-$L_1(\mathcal{S}_n)$ cover $\mathcal{F}_\epsilon(\mathcal{S}_n)$ of $\mathcal{F}$, of size no more $N = N_1(\epsilon, \mathcal{G}, n)$. We may assume that $f(Z_i) \in [-0.5, 0.5]$ for $f \in \mathcal{F}_\epsilon(\mathcal{S}_n)$. From Corollary 2.27 (with $a_i = 0.5$) and the union bound, we obtain the following uniform convergence result over $\mathcal{F}_\epsilon(\mathcal{S}_n)$. With probability $1 - \delta$,

$$\forall f \in \mathcal{F}_\epsilon(\mathcal{S}_n) \colon f(\sigma, \mathcal{S}_n) \leq \sqrt{\frac{\ln(N/\delta)}{2n}}.$$

Since for all $f \in \mathcal{F}$, we can find $f' \in \mathcal{F}_\epsilon(\mathcal{S}_n)$ so that $n^{-1} \sum_{Z \in \mathcal{S}_n} |f(Z) - f'(Z)| \leq \epsilon$ for all $Z \in \mathcal{S}_n$. It follows that

$$f(\sigma, \mathcal{S}_n) \leq f'(\sigma, \mathcal{S}_n) + \epsilon \leq \epsilon + \sqrt{\frac{\ln(N/\delta)}{2n}}.$$

Using Lemma 4.8 with $\psi = 0$, this uniform convergence result for the symmetrized empirical process implies the following uniform convergence result. With probability at least $1 - \delta_1$ over $(\mathcal{S}_n, \mathcal{S}'_n) \sim \mathcal{D}^{2n}$,

$$\forall w \in \Omega \colon \underbrace{\phi(w, \mathcal{S}'_n)}_{\psi_{\text{val}}} \le \underbrace{\phi(w, \mathcal{S}_n)}_{\psi_{\text{trn}}} + \underbrace{2\epsilon + \sqrt{\frac{2 \ln(2N/\delta_1)}{n}}}_{\epsilon_n^1(\delta_1)}.$$

The standard additive Chernoff bound implies that for all $w \in \Omega$, with probability at least $1 - \delta_2$,

$$\underbrace{\phi(w, \mathcal{D})}_{\psi_{\text{tst}}} \le \underbrace{\phi(w, \mathcal{S}'_n)}_{\psi_{\text{val}}} + \underbrace{\sqrt{\frac{\ln(1/\delta_2)}{2n}}}_{\epsilon_n^2(\delta_2)}.$$

Therefore in Lemma 4.11, we can take symbols as defined, together with $\delta_1 = 2\delta/3$ and $\delta_2 = \delta/3$ to obtain the desired bound.

Similarly, we consider $\mathcal{F} = \{f(z) = \phi(w, z) \colon w \in \Omega\}$. Given $\mathcal{S}_n$, we consider an ϵ-$L_1(\mathcal{S}_n)$ cover $\mathcal{F}_\epsilon(\mathcal{S}_n)$ of $\mathcal{F}$, of size no more $N = N_1(\epsilon, \mathcal{G}, n)$. We assume that $f(Z_i) \in [0, 1]$ for all $f \in \mathcal{F}_\epsilon(\mathcal{S}_n)$. From Corollary 2.27 and the union bound, we obtain the following uniform convergence result over $\mathcal{F}_\epsilon(\mathcal{S}_n)$. With probability at least $1 - \delta$,

$$\forall f \in \mathcal{F}_\epsilon(\mathcal{S}_n) \colon f(\sigma, \mathcal{S}_n) \le \sqrt{\frac{2 \sum_{Z \in \mathcal{S}_n} f(Z)^2 \ln(N/\delta)}{n^2}}$$

$$\le \gamma' \frac{1}{n} \sum_{Z \in \mathcal{S}_n} f(Z) + \frac{\ln(N/\delta)}{2\gamma' n}.$$

The first inequality used Corollary 2.27. The second inequality used $\sqrt{2ab} \le \gamma' a + b/(2\gamma')$ and $f(Z)^2 \le f(Z)$. Since for all $f \in \mathcal{F}$, we can find $f' \in \mathcal{F}_\epsilon(\mathcal{S}_n)$ so that $\frac{1}{n} \sum_{Z \in \mathcal{S}_n} |f(Z) - f'(Z)| \le \epsilon$. It follows that

$$f(\sigma, \mathcal{S}_n) \le f'(\sigma, \mathcal{S}_n) + \epsilon$$

$$\le \gamma' \frac{1}{n} \sum_{Z \in \mathcal{S}_n} f'(Z) + \frac{\ln(N/\delta)}{2\gamma' n} + \epsilon$$

$$\le \gamma' \frac{1}{n} \sum_{Z \in \mathcal{S}_n} f(Z) + \frac{\ln(N/\delta)}{2\gamma' n} + (1 + \gamma')\epsilon.$$

Now, with $\psi(f, \mathcal{S}_n) = \widetilde{\psi}(f, \mathcal{S}_n) = \gamma' \frac{1}{n} \sum_{Z \in \mathcal{S}_n} f(Z)$, we obtain from Lemma 4.8 the following uniform convergence result. With probability at least $1 - \delta_1$ over $(\mathcal{S}_n, \mathcal{S}'_n) \sim \mathcal{D}^{2n}$,

$$\forall w \in \Omega \colon (1 - \gamma')\phi(w, \mathcal{S}'_n) \le (1 + \gamma')\phi(w, \mathcal{S}_n) + 2(1 + \gamma')\epsilon + \frac{\ln(2N/\delta_1)}{\gamma' n}.$$

Let $\gamma' = \gamma/(2-\gamma)$, then it is easy to check algebraically that $(1-\gamma')/(1+\gamma') = 1-\gamma$ and $1/(\gamma'(1+\gamma')) = (2 - \gamma)^2/(2\gamma)$. We thus obtain

$$\forall w \in \Omega \colon \underbrace{(1 - \gamma)\phi(w, \mathcal{S}'_n)}_{\psi_{\text{val}}} \le \underbrace{\phi(w, \mathcal{S}_n)}_{\psi_{\text{trn}}} + \underbrace{2\epsilon + \frac{(2 - \gamma)^2 \ln(2N/\delta_1)}{2\gamma n}}_{\epsilon_n^1(\delta_1)}. \qquad (4.1)$$

The standard multiplicative Chernoff bound in (2.11) implies that with probability $1 - \delta_2$,

$$\underbrace{(1-\gamma)(1-\gamma)\phi(w, \mathcal{D})}_{\psi_{\mathrm{tst}}} \leq \underbrace{(1-\gamma)\phi(w, \mathcal{S}'_n)}_{\psi_{\mathrm{val}}} + \underbrace{(1-\gamma)\frac{\ln(1/\delta_2)}{2\gamma n}}_{\epsilon_n^2(\delta_2)}.$$

Therefore in Lemma 4.11, we can use symbols as displayed here, together with $\delta_1 = 2\delta/3$ and $\delta_2 = \delta/3$ to obtain the desired bound. $\square$

Using Lemma 3.11, the following oracle inequalities can be obtained from Theorem 4.12. The result is analogous to Corollary 3.15, with a similar proof. We will thus leave the proof as an exercise.

Corollary 4.13 *If $\phi(w, z) \in [0, 1]$. Let $\mathcal{G} = \{\phi(w, z) : w \in \Omega\}$. With probability at least $1 - \delta$, the approximate ERM method (3.3) satisfies the (additive) oracle inequality:*

$$\mathbb{E}_{Z\sim\mathcal{D}}\phi(\hat{w}, Z) \leq \inf_{w\in\Omega} \mathbb{E}_{Z\sim\mathcal{D}}\phi(w, Z) + \epsilon'$$

$$+ \inf_{\epsilon>0}\left[2\epsilon + \sqrt{\frac{8\ln(4N_1(\epsilon, \mathcal{G}, n)/\delta)}{n}}\right].$$

Moreover, we have the following (multiplicative) oracle inequality for all $\gamma \in (0, 1)$: with probability at least $1 - \delta$,

$$(1-\gamma)^2\mathbb{E}_{(X,Y)\sim\mathcal{D}}\phi(\hat{w}, Z) \leq \inf_{w\in\Omega}(1+\gamma)\mathbb{E}_{(X,Y)\sim\mathcal{D}}\phi(w, Z) + \epsilon'$$

$$+ \inf_{\epsilon>0}\left[2\epsilon + \frac{(6-3\gamma)\ln(4N_1(\epsilon, \mathcal{G}, n)/\delta)}{2\gamma n}\right].$$

Example 4.14 Consider the linear classifier example in Example 4.6. Since $\ln N_\infty(\epsilon, \mathcal{G}, n) \leq d\ln(2n)$, it follows that for the ERM method, we have the following oracle inequalities. With probability at least $1 - \delta$,

$$\mathbb{E}_{\mathcal{D}}\mathbf{1}(f(\hat{w}, X) \neq Y) \leq \inf_{w\in\mathbb{R}^d} \mathbb{E}_{\mathcal{D}}\mathbf{1}(f(w, X) \neq Y) + \sqrt{\frac{8(\ln(4/\delta) + d\ln(2n))}{n}}.$$

Moreover, by optimizing the multiplicative bound over γ from the set $\gamma \in \{i/n : i \in [n]\}$, and taking a union bound, we can obtain the following inequality. With probability at least $1 - \delta$,

$$\mathbb{E}_{\mathcal{D}}\mathbf{1}(f(\hat{w}, X) \neq Y) \leq \mathrm{err}_*$$

$$+ C\left[\sqrt{\mathrm{err}_* \frac{\ln(\delta^{-1}) + d\ln(n)}{n}} + \frac{\ln(\delta^{-1}) + d\ln(n)}{n}\right],$$

where C is an absolute constant and

$$\mathrm{err}_* = \inf_{w\in\Omega} \mathbb{E}_{\mathcal{D}}\mathbf{1}(f(w, X) \neq Y).$$

4.4 Vapnik–Chervonenkis Dimension

Let $\mathcal{G} = \{\phi(w, z) \colon w \in \Omega\}$ be a $\{0, 1\}$-valued binary function class of $z \in \mathcal{Z}$ indexed by $w \in \Omega$. Given an arbitrary set of n samples $\mathcal{S}_n = \{Z_1, \ldots, Z_n\} \in \mathcal{Z}^n$, we are interested in the number of functions (uniform L_∞ cover of the function class at $\epsilon = 0$) that $\mathcal{G}(\mathcal{S}_n) = \{[\phi(w, Z_1), \ldots, \phi(w, Z_n)] \colon w \in \Omega\}$ can achieve. We introduce the following definition of Vapnik and Chervonenkis (1971).

Definition 4.15 (VC Dimension) We say that $\mathcal{G}$ shatters $\mathcal{S}_n$ if the number of elements $|\mathcal{G}(\mathcal{S}_n)|$ is 2^n. That is, we can always find $w \in \Omega$ so that $\phi(w, z)$ matches any arbitrary possible choice of $\{0, 1\}^n$ values at the n points. The maximum n such that $\mathcal{G}$ shatters at least one instance of $\mathcal{S}_n \in \mathcal{Z}^n$, denoted by $\mathrm{vc}(G)$, is called the VC dimension of $\mathcal{G}$.

Note that the maximum number of functions in $\mathcal{G}(\mathcal{S}_n)$ is 2^n. If $n > d$, then for any n samples $\mathcal{S}_n$, $\mathcal{G}(\mathcal{S}_n)$ contains fewer than 2^n elements. Surprisingly, if a binary-valued function class $\mathcal{G}$ has VC dimension d, then when $n > d$, the size of set $\mathcal{G}(\mathcal{S}_n)$ can grow only polynomially in n. This gives an $O(d \ln n)$ upper bound on the uniform entropy of the function class $\mathcal{G}$ with a finite VC dimension (see Vapnik and Chervonenkis, 1968, 1971; Sauer, 1972).

Lemma 4.16 (Sauer's Lemma) *If $\mathrm{vc}(\mathcal{G}) = d$, then we have for all $n > 0$ and empirical samples $\mathcal{S}_n = \{Z_1, \ldots, Z_n\} \in \mathcal{Z}^n$,*

$$|\mathcal{G}(\mathcal{S}_n)| \le \sum_{\ell=0}^{d} \binom{n}{\ell} \le \max(2, en/d)^d.$$

Proof First, we prove the statement under the assumption that $|\mathcal{G}(\mathcal{S}_n)|$ is upper bounded by the number of subsets of $\mathcal{S}_n$ (including the empty set) that are shattered by $\mathcal{G}$. Under this assumption, since any subset shattered by $\mathcal{G}$ cannot be larger than d by the definition of VC dimension, and the number of subsets of size ℓ is $\binom{n}{\ell}$, we know that the number of subsets shattered by $\mathcal{G}$ cannot be more than $\sum_{\ell=1}^{d} \binom{n}{\ell}$. When $n \ge d$, we have (see Exercise 4.1)

$$\sum_{\ell=0}^{d} \binom{n}{\ell} \le (en/d)^d. \tag{4.2}$$

When $n \le d$, we have $\sum_{\ell=0}^{d} \binom{n}{\ell} \le 2^d$. This implies the desired result.

In the following, we only need to prove the statement that $|\mathcal{G}(\mathcal{S}_n)|$ is upper bounded by the number of subsets of $\mathcal{S}_n$ that are shattered by $\mathcal{G}$. This can be proved by induction on n. When $n = 1$, one can check that the claim holds trivially.

Now assume that the claim holds for all empirical samples of size no more than $n - 1$. Consider n samples $\{Z_1, \ldots, Z_n\}$. We define

$$\phi(w, \mathcal{S}_k) = [\phi(w, Z_1), \ldots, \phi(w, Z_k)],$$
$$\mathcal{G}_{n-1}(\mathcal{S}_n) = \{[\phi(w, \mathcal{S}_{n-1}), 1] \colon [\phi(w, \mathcal{S}_{n-1}), 0], [\phi(w, \mathcal{S}_{n-1}), 1] \in \mathcal{G}(\mathcal{S}_n)\}.$$

Using the induction hypothesis, we know that $|\mathcal{G}_{n-1}(\mathcal{S}_n)|$ is bounded by the number of shattered subset $\mathcal{S} \subset \mathcal{S}_{n-1}$; for each shattered $\mathcal{S} \subset \mathcal{S}_{n-1}$, $\mathcal{S} \cup \{Z_n\}$ is shattered by $\mathcal{G}(\mathcal{S}_n)$ because both $[\phi(w, \mathcal{S}_{n-1}), 1]$ and $[\phi(w, \mathcal{S}_{n-1}), 0]$ belong to $\mathcal{G}(\mathcal{S}_n)$. Therefore $|\mathcal{G}_{n-1}(\mathcal{S}_n)|$ is no more than the number of shattered subsets of $\mathcal{S}_n$ that contains Z_n.

Moreover, since for $\phi(w, \cdot) \in \mathcal{G}(\mathcal{S}_n) - \mathcal{G}_{n-1}(\mathcal{S}_n)$, $\phi(w, Z_n)$ is uniquely determined by its values at $\mathcal{S}_{n-1}$ (if not, then both $[\phi(w, \mathcal{S}_{n-1}), 0]$ and $[\phi(w, \mathcal{S}_{n-1}), 1]$ can be achieved in $\mathcal{G}(\mathcal{S}_n) - \mathcal{G}_{n-1}(\mathcal{S}_n)$, which is impossible because, by definition, we should have put $[\phi(w, \mathcal{S}_{n-1}), 1]$ in $\mathcal{G}_{n-1}(\mathcal{S}_n)$), it follows that $|\mathcal{G}(\mathcal{S}_n) - \mathcal{G}_{n-1}(\mathcal{S}_n)|$ is no more than $|\mathcal{G}(\mathcal{S}_{n-1})|$. By induction hypothesis, $|\mathcal{G}(\mathcal{S}_{n-1})|$ is no more than the number of shattered subsets of $\mathcal{S}_n$ that does not contain Z_n. By combining these two facts, $|\mathcal{G}(\mathcal{S}_n)|$ is no more than the number of shattered subsets of $\mathcal{S}_n$. □

Sauer's lemma implies the following oracle inequalities for problems with finite VC dimensions. It is a direct consequence of Corollary 4.13.

Theorem 4.17 *Assume $L(\cdot, \cdot) \in \{0, 1\}$ is a binary-valued loss function. Let $\mathcal{G} = \{L(f(w, x), y) : w \in \Omega\}$, with a finite VC dimension $\mathrm{VC}(\mathcal{G}) = d$. Given $n \geq d$, and considering the approximate ERM method (3.3), with probability at least $1 - \delta$,*

$$\mathbb{E}_\mathcal{D} L(f(\hat{w}, X), Y) \leq \inf_{w \in \Omega} \mathbb{E}_\mathcal{D} L(f(w, X), Y)$$
$$+ \epsilon' + \sqrt{\frac{8d\ln(en/d) + 8\ln(4/\delta)}{n}}.$$

Moreover, for all $\gamma \in (0, 1)$, with probability at least $1 - \delta$, the following inequality holds:

$$(1 - \gamma)^2 \mathbb{E}_\mathcal{D} L(f(\hat{w}, X), Y) \leq \inf_{w \in \Omega} (1 + \gamma) \mathbb{E}_\mathcal{D} L(f(w, X), Y)$$
$$+ \epsilon' + \frac{(6 - 3\gamma)(d\ln(en/d) + \ln(4/\delta))}{2\gamma n}.$$

Proposition 4.18 *Consider d-dimensional $\{0, 1\}$-valued linear classifiers of the form $\mathcal{F} = \{f_w(x) = \mathbb{1}(w^\top x \geq 0), w \in \mathbb{R}^d\}$, so we have $\mathrm{VC}(\mathcal{F}) = d$. This implies that d-dimensional linear classifier $\mathcal{G} = \{\mathbb{1}(f_w(X) \neq Y), w \in \mathbb{R}^d\}$ has VC dimension $\mathrm{VC}(\mathcal{G}) = d$.*

Proof Since it is easy to find $n = d$ points shattered by $\mathcal{F}$, we only need to show that any $n = d + 1$ points cannot be shattered by linear functions.

Let the $d + 1$ points be $x_1, \ldots, x_{d+1}$. Then we know that they are linearly dependent. Therefore there exist $d + 1$ real-valued coefficients $a_1, \ldots, a_{d+1}$ that are not all zeros such that $a_1 x_1 + \cdots + a_{d+1} x_{d+1} = 0$, and we can assume that there exists at least one a_j such that $a_j > 0$.

In order to show that $x_1, \ldots, x_{d+1}$ cannot be shattered, we only need to show that there is no $w \in \mathbb{R}^d$ such that

$$\mathbb{1}(w^\top x_i \geq 0) = 0 \quad (a_i > 0); \qquad \mathbb{1}(w^\top x_i \geq 0) = 1 \quad (a_i \leq 0),$$

which implies that a particular set of function value on these points cannot be achieved. We prove this by contradiction. Assume the above function values can be achieved, then $a_i w^\top x_i \le 0$ for all i. Since there is at least one $a_j > 0$, we know that for this j, $a_j w^\top x_j < 0$. Therefore

$$\sum_{i=1}^{d+1} a_i w^\top x_i < 0.$$

However, this is a contradiction to the fact that $a_1 x_1 + \cdots + a_{d+1} x_{d+1} = 0$. $\square$

Note that results of Theorem 4.17 hold uniformly for all distributions $\mathcal{D}$. Therefore concept classes with finite VC dimensions are PAC learnable by ERM if we assume that it is computationally efficient to solve ERM. On the other hand, if the VC dimension of a concept class is infinity, then for any sample size n, there exists a distribution $\mathcal{D}$ with n samples, so that the concept class can achieve all possible binary values of 2^n on $\mathcal{D}$. Therefore on such a distribution, the learning of this concept class cannot be better than random guessing on some training distributions. The following is an example of infinite VC dimension.

Example 4.19 The binary-valued function class $\mathcal{G} = \{\mathbb{1}(\cos(wz) \ge 0) \colon w, z \in \mathbb{R}\}$ has infinite VC dimension.

Given any d, we consider $\{z_j = 16^{-j}\pi \colon j = 1, \ldots, d\}$. Let $w = \sum_{j=1}^{d}(1 - b_j)16^j$, with $b_j \in \{0, 1\}$. It is easy to verify that $\mathbb{1}(\cos(w z_j) \ge 0) = b_j$. It follows that the set can be shattered by $\mathcal{G}$.

4.5 Uniform Convergence with Uniform L_2 Covering Number

In order to apply Lemma 4.8, we need to estimate the uniform convergence of a symmetrized empirical process. We have shown, in Section 4.3, that such a bound can be obtained using the empirical L_1 covering number. In the following, we show that with empirical L_2 covering numbers, one can obtain a more refined result by using an important technique called *chaining*. The improvement is obtained by considering multiple approximation scales instead of a single scale used in Section 4.3 (also in Chapter 3). The resulting formula is often expressed in the so-called entropy integral form, due to Dudley (1984).

While it is possible to work with empirical L_2 covering numbers directly, it is more convenient to apply Rademacher complexity and concentration inequalities, as in Chapter 6. We will thus leave the analysis to Chapter 6, but list its consequence here for comparison with the L_1 covering number analysis presented earlier.

The following result is a direct consequence of the uniform convergence result of Corollary 6.19, oracle inequality of Corollary 6.21, with Rademacher complexity estimated from the L_2 empirical covering number in Theorem 6.25.

Proposition 4.20 *Given a function class $\mathcal{G} \in [0, 1]$, let*

$$\tilde{R}(\mathcal{G}, \mathcal{S}_n) = \inf_{\epsilon_0 \ge 0} \left[4\epsilon_0 + 12 \int_{\epsilon_0}^{\infty} \sqrt{\frac{\ln N(\epsilon', \mathcal{G}, L_2(\mathcal{S}_n))}{n}} d\epsilon' \right],$$

then with probability at least $1 - \delta$, for all $w \in \Omega$,

$$\phi(w, \mathcal{D}) \leq \phi(w, \mathcal{S}_n) + 2\mathbb{E}_{\mathcal{S}_n}[\tilde{R}(\mathcal{G}, \mathcal{S}_n)] + \sqrt{\frac{\ln(1/\delta)}{2n}}.$$

This implies that for the approximate ERM method (3.3), we have with probability at least $1 - \delta$,

$$\phi(\hat{w}, \mathcal{D}) \leq \inf_{w \in \Omega} \phi(w, \mathcal{D}) + \epsilon' + 2\mathbb{E}_{\mathcal{S}_n}[\tilde{R}(\mathcal{G}, \mathcal{S}_n)] + 2\sqrt{\frac{\ln(2/\delta)}{2n}}.$$

In Proposition 4.20, the average integral of L_2 entropy replaces the worst case L_1 entropy of Theorem 4.12. If the uniform L_2 entropy of $\mathcal{G}$ is of the form

$$\ln N_2(\epsilon, \mathcal{G}, n) = O(d \ln(1/\epsilon))$$

as in the case of VC dimension (see Theorem 5.6), then the complexity term

$$\mathbb{E}_{\mathcal{S}_n}[\tilde{R}(\mathcal{G}, \mathcal{S}_n)] = O(1/\sqrt{n}),$$

which removes an $\ln n$ factor from the uniform L_1 entropy analysis in Section 4.3. Moreover, if uniform L_2 entropy of $\mathcal{G}$ is of the form

$$\ln N_2(\epsilon, \mathcal{G}, n) = O(\epsilon^{-q}) \tag{4.3}$$

for some $q < 2$, then the complexity term

$$\mathbb{E}_{\mathcal{S}_n}[\tilde{R}(\mathcal{G}, \mathcal{S}_n)] = O(1/\sqrt{n}).$$

Function classes with uniform L_2 entropy that satisfies (4.3) are Donsker classes for which the central limit theorem holds.

In comparison, if we consider the uniform L_1 covering number analysis of Theorem 4.12, and assume that

$$\ln N_1(\epsilon, \mathcal{G}, n) = O(\epsilon^{-q}),$$

then the complexity term in the additive Chernoff bound is

$$\epsilon_n(\delta) = \inf_{\epsilon > 0} O\left(\epsilon + \sqrt{\epsilon^{-q}/n}\right) = n^{-1/(q+2)},$$

which implies a convergence rate slower than $1/\sqrt{n}$.

It is also possible to obtain fast convergence rate under the variance condition. We will leave such derivation to Section 6.5.

4.6 Uniform Convergence with Uniform L_∞ Covering Number

The L_∞ covering number analysis has been used to study large margin methods where the training loss and the test loss differ. Consider a function class

$\mathcal{F} = \{f(w, x) \colon w \in \Omega\}$ and a test loss $L(f(x), y)$. However, instead of minimizing the test loss directly, we try to minimize a surrogate training loss:

$$\frac{1}{n} \sum_{i=1}^{n} \tilde{L}(f(\hat{w}, X_i), Y_i) \leq \inf_{w \in \Omega} \left[\frac{1}{n} \sum_{i=1}^{n} \tilde{L}(f(w, X_i), Y_i) \right] + \epsilon', \qquad (4.4)$$

where we assume that the surrogate is an upper bound of training loss under small L_∞ perturbation of size $\gamma > 0$:

$$\tilde{L}(f, y) \geq \sup_{|f' - f| \leq \gamma} L(f', y). \qquad (4.5)$$

In this case, one would like to bound the test loss using surrogate training loss. An example for binary classification problem ($y \in \{\pm\}$) is to take the test loss as the binary classification error $L(f(x), y) \leq \mathbb{1}(f(x)y \leq 0)$, and $\tilde{L}(f(x), y) = \mathbb{1}(f(x)y \leq \gamma)$ as the margin error with margin $\gamma > 0$.

The L_∞ covering number can be used to obtain a result similar to Theorem 4.12, with a similar proof.

Theorem 4.21 *Assume that* $\tilde{L}(f(w, x), y), L(f(w, x), y) \in [0, 1]$ *for all* w *and* (x, y), *and both* (4.4) *and* (4.5) *hold. Then given* $\delta \in (0, 1)$, *with probability at least* $1 - \delta$, *the following inequality holds for all* $w \in \Omega$:

$$\mathbb{E}_{(X, Y) \sim \mathcal{D}} L(f(w, X), Y) \leq \frac{1}{n} \sum_{i=1}^{n} \tilde{L}(f(w, X_i), Y_i)$$

$$+ 3 \sqrt{\frac{\ln(3 N_\infty(\gamma/2, \mathcal{F}, 2n)/\delta)}{2n}}.$$

Moreover, with probability at least $1 - \delta$, *the following inequality holds for all* $w \in \Omega$:

$$(1 - \gamma)^2 \mathbb{E}_{(X, Y) \sim \mathcal{D}} L(f(w, X), Y) \leq \frac{1}{n} \sum_{i=1}^{n} \tilde{L}(f(w, X_i), Y_i)$$

$$+ \frac{(5 - 4\gamma) \ln(3 N_\infty(\gamma/2, \mathcal{F}, 2n)/\delta)}{2\gamma n}.$$

Proof Given $\mathcal{S}_n = \{(X_1, Y_1), \ldots, (X_n, Y_n)\}$ and $\mathcal{S}'_n = \{(X_1, Y_1), \ldots, (X_n, Y_n)\}$, we consider a $\gamma/2$-$L_\infty(\mathcal{S}_n)$ cover $\mathcal{F}_{\gamma/2}(\mathcal{S}_n \cup \mathcal{S}'_n)$ of $\mathcal{F}$, of size no more $N = N_\infty(\gamma/2, \mathcal{F}, 2n)$. Let

$$L'(f, y) = \sup_{|f' - f| \leq \gamma/2} L(f', y),$$

then for any f, f' such that $|f - f'| \leq \gamma/2$, we have

$$\tilde{L}(f, y) \geq L'(f', y) \geq L(f, y). \qquad (4.6)$$

We obtain from Corollary 2.27 (with $a_i = 0.5$) the following uniform convergence result over $\mathcal{F}_{\gamma/2}(\mathcal{S}_n \cup \mathcal{S}'_n)$. With probability $1 - \delta$,

$$\forall f \in \mathcal{F}_{\gamma/2}(\mathcal{S}_n \cup \mathcal{S}'_n) : \frac{1}{n} \sum_{i=1}^{n} \sigma_i [L'(f(X_i), Y_i) - 0.5] \leq \sqrt{\frac{\ln(N/\delta)}{2n}}.$$

Lemma 4.8 (which is valid even when $\mathcal{F}$ in the lemma depends on $\mathcal{S}_n \cup \mathcal{S}'_n$) with $\psi = 0$ implies that with probability at least $1 - \delta_1$,

$$\forall f \in \mathcal{F}_{\gamma/2}(\mathcal{S}_n \cup \mathcal{S}'_n) : \frac{1}{n} \sum_{i=1}^{n} L'(f(X'_i), Y'_i) \leq \frac{1}{n} \sum_{i=1}^{n} L'(f(X_i), Y_i) + \sqrt{\frac{2\ln(2N/\delta_1)}{n}}.$$

Since for all $f \in \mathcal{F}$, we can find $f' \in \mathcal{F}_{\gamma/2}(\mathcal{S}_n \cup \mathcal{S}'_n)$ so that $|f(x) - f'(x)| \leq \gamma/2$, it follows that

$$\underbrace{\frac{1}{n} \sum_{i=1}^{n} L(f(X'_i), Y'_i)}_{\psi_{\text{val}}} \leq \frac{1}{n} \sum_{i=1}^{n} L'(f'(X'_i), Y'_i)$$

$$\leq \frac{1}{n} \sum_{i=1}^{n} L'(f'(X_i), Y_i) + \sqrt{\frac{2\ln(2N/\delta)}{n}}$$

$$\leq \underbrace{\frac{1}{n} \sum_{i=1}^{n} \tilde{L}(f(X_i), Y_i)}_{\psi_{\text{trn}}} + \underbrace{\sqrt{\frac{2\ln(2N/\delta_1)}{n}}}_{\epsilon_n^1(\delta_1)}.$$

Note that the first and the last inequalities used (4.6). The standard additive Chernoff bound implies that for all $w \in \Omega$, with probability at least $1 - \delta_2$,

$$\underbrace{\mathbb{E}_{(X,Y) \sim \mathcal{D}} L(f(X), Y)}_{\psi_{\text{tst}}} \leq \underbrace{\frac{1}{n} \sum_{i=1}^{n} L(f(X'_i), Y'_i)}_{\psi_{\text{val}}} + \underbrace{\sqrt{\frac{\ln(1/\delta_2)}{2n}}}_{\epsilon_n^2(\delta_2)}.$$

Therefore in Lemma 4.11, we can take symbols as defined, together with $\delta_1 = 2\delta/3$, and $\delta_2 = \delta/3$, to obtain the desired bound.

Similarly, we obtain from Corollary 2.27 the following uniform convergence result over $\mathcal{F}_{\gamma/2}(\mathcal{S}_n \cup \mathcal{S}'_n)$. With probability $1 - \delta$, $\forall f \in \mathcal{F}_{\gamma/2}(\mathcal{S}_n \cup \mathcal{S}'_n)$,

$$\frac{1}{n} \sum_{i=1}^{n} \sigma_i L'(f(X_i), Y_i) \leq \sqrt{\frac{2 \sum_{i=1}^{n} L'(f(X_i), Y_i)^2 \ln(N/\delta)}{n^2}}$$

$$\leq \gamma' \underbrace{\frac{1}{n} \sum_{i=1}^{n} L'(f(X_i), Y_i)}_{\psi(f, \mathcal{S}_n)} + \frac{\ln(N/\delta)}{2\gamma' n}.$$

Then Lemma 4.8 (which is valid even when $\mathcal{F}$ in the lemma depends on $\mathcal{S}_n \cup \mathcal{S}'_n$) implies the following uniform convergence result. With probability at least $1 - \delta_1$ over $(\mathcal{S}_n, \mathcal{S}'_n) \sim \mathcal{D}^{2n}$,

$$\forall f \in \mathcal{F}_{\gamma/2}(\mathcal{S}_n \cup \mathcal{S}'_n): \quad \frac{1-\gamma'}{n}\sum_{i=1}^n L'(f(X'_i), Y'_i)$$

$$\leq \frac{1+\gamma'}{n}\sum_{i=1}^n L'(f(X_i), Y_i) + \frac{\ln(2N/\delta_1)}{\gamma' n}.$$

Since for all $f \in \mathcal{F}$, we can find $f' \in \mathcal{F}_\epsilon(\mathcal{S}_n)$ so that $|f(x) - f'(x)| \leq \gamma/2$, it follows that

$$\frac{1-\gamma'}{n}\sum_{i=1}^n L(f(X'_i), Y'_i) \leq \frac{1-\gamma'}{n}\sum_{i=1}^n L'(f'(X'_i), Y'_i)$$

$$\leq \frac{1+\gamma'}{n}\sum_{i=1}^n L'(f'(X_i), Y_i) + \frac{\ln(2N/\delta_1)}{\gamma' n}$$

$$\leq \frac{1+\gamma'}{n}\sum_{i=1}^n \tilde{L}(f(X_i), Y_i) + \frac{\ln(2N/\delta_1)}{\gamma' n}.$$

Note that the first and the last inequalities used (4.6). Let $\gamma' = \gamma/(2-\gamma)$, then it is easy to check algebraically that $(1-\gamma')/(1+\gamma') = 1 - \gamma$ and $1/(\gamma'(1+\gamma')) = (2-\gamma)^2/(2\gamma)$. We thus obtain

$$\forall f \in \mathcal{F}: \quad \underbrace{\frac{1-\gamma}{n}\sum_{i=1}^n L(f(X'_i), Y'_i)}_{\psi_{\mathrm{val}}} \leq \underbrace{\frac{1}{n}\sum_{i=1}^n \tilde{L}(f(X_i), Y_i)}_{\psi_{\mathrm{trn}}} + \underbrace{\frac{(2-\gamma)^2 \ln(2N/\delta_1)}{2\gamma n}}_{\epsilon_n^1(\delta_1)}.$$

The standard multiplicative Chernoff bound in (2.11) implies that with probability $1 - \delta_2$,

$$\underbrace{(1-\gamma)(1-\gamma)\mathbb{E}_{(X,Y)\sim\mathcal{D}}L(f(X), Y)}_{\psi_{\mathrm{tst}}} \leq \underbrace{\frac{1-\gamma}{n}\sum_{i=1}^n L(f(X'_i), Y'_i)}_{\psi_{\mathrm{val}}}$$

$$+ \underbrace{(1-\gamma)\frac{\ln(1/\delta_2)}{2\gamma n}}_{\epsilon_n^2(\delta_2)}.$$

Therefore in Lemma 4.11, we can use symbols as displayed, together with $\delta_1 = 2\delta/3$ and $\delta_2 = \delta/3$ to obtain the desired bound. $\qquad\square$

Similar to Corollary 4.13, one may also obtain an oracle inequality from Theorem 4.21, which we will not state here.

Example 4.22 Consider binary classification with classifier $f(w, X) \in \mathbb{R}$ and $Y \in \{\pm 1\}$. The classification loss is

$$L(f(X), Y) = \mathbb{1}(f(X)Y \leq 0),$$

and the margin loss for $\gamma > 0$ is

$$\tilde{L}(f(X), Y) = \mathbb{1}(f(X)Y \leq \gamma).$$

Theorem 4.21 implies that

$$\mathbb{1}(f(X)Y \leq 0) \leq \frac{1}{n} \sum_{i=1}^{n} \mathbb{1}(f(w, X_i)Y_i \leq \gamma) + 3\sqrt{\frac{\ln(3N_\infty(\gamma/2, \mathcal{F}, 2n)/\delta)}{2n}}.$$

Therefore if the function class has a finite L_∞ norm at scale $\gamma/2$, then minimizing the margin loss leads to approximate minimization of training loss. Unlike VC-dimension, the L_∞ cover can be small even for infinite-dimensional systems with proper regularization. For example, if we consider regularized linear function class with

$$\left\{ f(w, x) = w^\top \psi(x) \colon \|w\|_2 \leq A \right\},$$

and assume that $\|\psi(x)\|_2 \leq B$, then Theorem 5.20 implies that

$$\ln N_\infty(\gamma/2, \mathcal{F}, 2n) = O\left(\frac{A^2 B^2 \ln(n + AB/\gamma)}{\gamma^2} \right),$$

which is independent of the dimension of w. In comparison, the VC dimension depends on the dimensionality of w even with regularization. This implies that for high-dimensional problems, maximizing margin leads to more stable generalization performance.

4.7 Historical and Bibliographical Remarks

In Vapnik and Chervonenkis (1968, 1971), the authors developed a theory to use the uniform entropy to analyze empirical processes and the generalization performance of empirical risk minimization. This style of analysis is covered in Section 4.3, and often referred to as the VC theory. The original analysis of Vapnik and Chervonenkis (1968) used a random permutation argument instead of the symmetrization argument employed here. We leave it as Exercise 4.7. The symmetrization argument for the additive version of the Chernoff bound was used by Pollard (1984). However, the treatment here is modified so that it can handle more general situations such as the multiplicative Chernoff bound and Bernstein's inequality. The multiplicative form of Chernoff bound can also be found in Blumer et al. (1989) using the permutation argument. Note that we do not try to optimize constants here. It is possible to obtain better constants using more complex techniques, for example, concentration inequalities in Chapter 6.

Lemma 4.16 was obtained by Vapnik and Chervonenkis (1968, 1971), and independently discovered by Sauer (1972). It is often referred to as Sauer's lemma in the computer science literature. The idea of chaining was invented by Kolmogorov in the 1930s, according to Chentsov (1956), and further developed by Dudley (1967, 1978, 1984). The entropy integral form in Proposition 4.20 is often credited to Dudley.

The L_∞-cover analysis follows the analysis of large margin methods by Schapire et al. (1998), with a slight generalization. Similar analysis has been employed to analyze support vector machines (see Cristianini and Shawe-Taylor, 2000).

Exercises

4.1 Prove that (4.2) holds for $n \geq d$. Hint: consider the upper bound $\sum_{\ell=0}^{d}(d/n)^{\ell-d}\binom{n}{\ell}$.

4.2 Prove that for any nondecreasing convex function $\Phi\colon \mathbb{R}_+ \to \mathbb{R}_+$, the following symmetrization inequality holds:

$$\mathbb{E}\,\Phi\left(\sup_{f\in\mathcal{F}}[f(\mathcal{S}_n) - f(\mathcal{D})]\right) \leq \mathbb{E}\,\Phi\left(2\sup_{f\in\mathcal{F}} f(\sigma, \mathcal{S}_n)\right).$$

4.3 In the proof of Lemma 4.11. Show that $\Pr(E^c \& E_2) \leq \Pr(E_1^c)$. Use this relationship to show that $\Pr(E) \geq 1 - \delta_1/(1-\delta_2)$.

4.4 Prove the result of Example 4.6 using convex optimization.

- Consider $\{X_1, \ldots, X_n\}$. Consider any w, and let $\tilde{w}(J)$ be defined as the unique solution to the following optimization problem for all $J \subset J_n = \{1, \ldots, n\}$:

$$\tilde{w}(w, J) = \arg\min_u \|u\|_2^2$$

$$\text{subject to } \begin{cases} u^\top X_i \geq 0 & \text{if } w^\top X_i \geq 0 \\ u^\top X_i \leq -1 & \text{if } w^\top X_i < 0 \end{cases} \text{ for } i \in J.$$

Show this is a convex optimization problem, with a unique solution determined by J. Write the KKT conditions of the solution.
- Let $\tilde{J}$ be the smallest cardinality of subsets J of J_n such that $\tilde{w}(w, J) = \tilde{w}(w, J_n)$. Show that for all $i \in \tilde{J}$: $\tilde{w}^\top X_i = 0$ if $w^\top X \geq 0$ and $\tilde{w}^\top X_i = -1$ if $w^\top X < 0$. Moreover, $|\tilde{J}| \leq d$.
- Show that there are at most $(2n)^d$ possible choices of $\tilde{J}$, and this implies that the achievable values of $\{\mathbb{1}(w^\top X_i \geq 0)\colon 1 \leq i \leq n\}$ can be no more than $(2n)^d$.

4.5 Prove Corollary 4.13.

4.6 Consider $z \in \mathbb{R}^d$, let $w = [w_1, \ldots, w_d, w_{d+1}, \ldots, w_{2d}]$. Find the VC dimension of the function class

$$f_w(z) = \mathbb{1}(z \in C(w)),$$

where $C(w) = \{z = [z_1, \ldots, z_d]\colon z_j \in [w_j, w_{d+j}]\}$.

4.7 In addition to symmetrization, uniform convergence can be obtained using random permutations, as in Vapnik and Chervonenkis (1971). Consider $\mathcal{F} = \{f\colon \mathcal{Z} \to [0, 1]\}$. Given a dataset $\mathcal{S}_{2n}$, we consider random partitions of $\mathcal{S}_{2n}$ into disjoint training and validation subsets $\mathcal{S}_n \cup \mathcal{S}_n'$ via random permutation of the data, with the first half in $\mathcal{S}_n$, and the second half in $\mathcal{S}_n'$.

- Show that conditioned on $\mathcal{S}_{2n}$, for random permutation, the following inequality holds for all $f \in \mathcal{F}$:

$$\ln \mathbb{E}_{\mathcal{S}_n, \mathcal{S}_n'} \exp(\lambda n f(\mathcal{S}_n)) \leq n \ln \mathbb{E}_{\mathcal{S}_n} \exp(\lambda f(X_1)).$$

Hint: this inequality was proved in Hoeffding (1963).
- Use this inequality to derive a result similar to Theorem 2.5, and then use this result to derive an additive Chernoff bound of the form for all $f \in \mathcal{F}$:

$$\Pr\left(f(\mathcal{S}_n') \leq f(\mathcal{S}_{2n}) + \epsilon(\delta)\right) \geq 1 - \delta.$$

- Derive a uniform convergence result of the form

$$\Pr\left(\forall f \in \mathcal{F}\colon f(\mathcal{S}_n') \leq f(\mathcal{S}_{2n}) + \epsilon(\delta)\right) \geq 1 - \delta$$

using the empirical covering number $N(\epsilon, \mathcal{F}, L_\infty(\mathcal{S}_{2n}))$ of $\mathcal{S}_{2n}$.

- Derive a uniform convergence result of the form

$$\Pr\left(\forall f \in \mathcal{F} \colon f(\mathcal{D}) \leq f(\mathcal{S}_n) + \epsilon(\delta)\right) \geq 1 - \delta$$

using Lemma 4.11.
- Derive an oracle inequality for the empirical risk minimization method, and compare to that of Corollary 4.13.

5

Covering Number Estimates

This chapter derives covering number estimates of certain function classes, including some parametric and nonparametric function classes.

5.1 Packing Number

In many applications, it is more convenient to estimate the packing number of a set, which is a concept closely related to covering number. Given a set $\mathcal{G}$ in a pseudometric space, one can naturally define its metric covering number as in Definition 4.1. Similarly, one can also define its packing number.

Definition 5.1 (Packing Number) Let $(\mathcal{V}, d)$ be a pseudometric space with metric $d(\cdot, \cdot)$. A finite subset $\mathcal{G}(\epsilon) \subset \mathcal{G}$ is an ϵ packing of $\mathcal{G}$ if $d(\phi, \phi') > \epsilon$ for all $\phi, \phi' \in \mathcal{G}(\epsilon)$. The ϵ packing number of $\mathcal{G}$, denoted by $M(\epsilon, \mathcal{G}, d)$, is the largest cardinality of ϵ packing of $\mathcal{G}$.

The following results illustrate the equivalence between covering number and packing number. One advantage of using an ϵ packing of $\mathcal{G}$ instead of an ϵ cover of $\mathcal{G}$ is that all members in the ϵ packing also belong to $\mathcal{G}$. There, if members in $\mathcal{G}$ satisfy certain assumptions such as the variance condition, then members of its ϵ packing also satisfy such assumptions. For this reason, we will use packing numbers instead of covering numbers in some of the theoretical analysis in later chapters.

Theorem 5.2 *For all $\epsilon > 0$, we have*

$$N(\epsilon, \mathcal{G}, d) \leq M(\epsilon, \mathcal{G}, d) \leq N(\epsilon/2, \mathcal{G}, d).$$

Proof Let $\mathcal{G}(\epsilon) = \{\phi_1, \ldots, \phi_M\} \subset \mathcal{G}$ be a maximal ϵ packing of $\mathcal{G}$. Given any $\phi \in \mathcal{G}$, by the definition of maximality, we know that there exists $\phi_j \in \mathcal{G}(\epsilon)$ so that $d(\phi_j, \phi) \leq \epsilon$. This means that $\mathcal{G}(\epsilon)$ is also an ϵ cover of $\mathcal{G}$. Therefore $N(\epsilon, \mathcal{G}, d) \leq M$. This proves the first inequality.

On the other hand, let $\mathcal{G}'(\epsilon/2)$ be an $\epsilon/2$ cover of $\mathcal{G}$. By definition, for any $\phi_j \in \mathcal{G}(\epsilon)$, there exists $\tilde{g}(\phi_j) \in \mathcal{G}'(\epsilon/2)$ such that $d(\tilde{g}(\phi_j), \phi_j) \leq \epsilon/2$. For $j \neq i$, we know that $d(\phi_i, \phi_j) > \epsilon$, and thus triangle inequality implies that

$$d(\tilde{g}(\phi_j), \phi_i) \geq d(\phi_i, \phi_j) - d(\tilde{g}(\phi_j), \phi_j) > \epsilon/2 \geq d(\tilde{g}(\phi_i), \phi_i).$$

Therefore $\tilde{g}(\phi_i) \neq \tilde{g}(\phi_j)$. This implies the map $\phi_j \in \mathcal{G}(\epsilon) \to \tilde{g}(\phi_j) \in \mathcal{G}'(\epsilon/2)$ is one to one. Therefore $|\mathcal{G}(\epsilon)| \leq |\mathcal{G}'(\epsilon/2)|$. This proves the second inequality. □

We have the following well-known estimate of the covering and packing numbers on a finite-dimensional compact set.

Theorem 5.3 *Let $\|\cdot\|$ be a seminorm on $\mathbb{R}^k$. Let $B(r) = \{z \in \mathbb{R}^k : \|z\| \leq r\}$ be the $\|\cdot\|$-ball with radius r. Then*

$$M(\epsilon, B(r), \|\cdot\|) \leq (1 + 2r/\epsilon)^k.$$

Moreover,

$$N(\epsilon, B(r), \|\cdot\|) \geq (r/\epsilon)^k.$$

Proof Let $\{z_1, \ldots, z_M\} \subset B(r)$ be a maximal ϵ packing of $B(r)$. Let $B_j = \{z \in \mathbb{R}^k : \|z - z_j\| \leq \epsilon/2\}$, then $B_j \cap B_k = \emptyset$ for $j \neq k$ and $B_j \subset B(r + \epsilon/2)$ for all j. It follows that

$$\sum_{j=1}^{M} \text{volume}(B_j) = \text{volume}(\cup_{j=1}^{M} B_j) \leq \text{volume}(B(r + \epsilon/2)).$$

Let $v = \text{volume}(B(1))$. Since $\text{volume}(B_j) = (\epsilon/2)^k v$ and $\text{volume}(B(r + \epsilon/2)) = (r + \epsilon/2)^k v$, we have

$$M(\epsilon/2)^k v \leq (r + \epsilon/2)^k v.$$

This implies the first bound.

Let $\{z_1, \ldots, z_N\} \subset \mathbb{R}^k$ be a cover of $B(r)$. If we define $B_j = \{z \in \mathbb{R}^k : \|z - z_j\| \leq \epsilon\}$, then $B(r) \subset \cup_j B_j$. Therefore

$$\text{volume}(B(r)) \leq \text{volume}(\cup_{j=1}^{N} B_j) \leq \sum_{j=1}^{N} \text{volume}(B_j).$$

Let $v = \text{volume}(B(1))$. Since $\text{volume}(B_j) = (\epsilon)^k v$ and $\text{volume}(B(r)) = r^k v$, we have

$$r^k v \leq N \epsilon^k v.$$

This implies the second bound. □

5.2 Lipschitz Function in Finite Dimension

We now consider the following function class

$$\{\phi(w, Z) : w \in \Omega\}, \tag{5.1}$$

where $\Omega \subset \mathbb{R}^k$ is a compact set. The situation where in the model parameter w is finite dimensional is often called a *parametric model*. The following result shows that the bracketing number of parametric model is polynomial in ϵ.

Theorem 5.4 *Consider (5.1). Assume that $\Omega \subset \mathbb{R}^k$ is a compact set so that $\Omega \in B(r)$ with respect to a norm $\|\cdot\|$. Assume for all z, $\phi(w, z)$ is $\gamma(z)$ Lipschitz with respect to w:*

$$|\phi(w, z) - \phi(w', z)| \le \gamma(z)\|w - w'\|.$$

Given $p \ge 1$, let $\gamma_p = (\mathbb{E}_{Z \sim D}|\gamma(Z)|^p)^{1/p}$. Then

$$N_{[]}(2\epsilon, \mathcal{G}, L_p(\mathcal{D})) \le (1 + 2\gamma_p r/\epsilon)^k.$$

Proof Let $\{w_1, \ldots, w_M\}$ be an ϵ/γ_p packing of Ω. Then it is also an ϵ/γ_p cover of Ω. Let $\phi_j^L(z) = \phi(w_j, z) - \gamma(z)\epsilon/\gamma_p$ and $\phi_j^U(z) = \phi(w_j, z) + \gamma(z)\epsilon/\gamma_p$. Then $\{[\phi_j^L, \phi_j^U] : j = 1, \ldots, M\}$ is a 2ϵ $L_p(\mathcal{D})$-bracketing cover. We can now apply Theorem 5.3 to obtain the desired result. □

Note that if we take $p = \infty$, then we obtain the following result on the uniform covering number:

$$N_\infty(\epsilon, \mathcal{G}, n) \le (1 + 2\gamma_\infty r/\epsilon)^k.$$

One may also obtain bracketing numbers for certain smooth nonparametric function classes, with entropy of the form

$$\ln N_{[]}(\epsilon, \mathcal{G}, L_p(\mathcal{D})) = O(\epsilon^{-\beta}).$$

We refer the readers to van der Vaart and Wellner (1996, chapter 2.7) and Nickl and Pötscher (2007) for such examples.

5.3 Empirical L_p Covering Numbers of VC Class

We have obtained empirical L_∞ covering number bounds for VC classes in Section 4.4, and the covering number depends logarithmically on the sample size n. It is also possible to obtain the empirical L_p covering number for VC classes for $p < \infty$, which is independent of n. The estimate of L_2 empirical covering numbers can be directly used with chaining.

Recall that given empirical distribution $\mathcal{S}_n$, the empirical L_p cover is the number of functions needed to cover ϕ_w based on the empirical L_p metric:

$$d_p(\phi, \phi') = \left[\frac{1}{n}\sum_{i=1}^n |\phi(Z_i) - \phi'(Z_i)|^p\right]^{1/p}.$$

We have the following estimate.

Theorem 5.5 *If a binary-valued function class $\mathcal{G} = \{\phi(w, Z) : w \in \Omega\}$ is a VC class, then for $\epsilon \le 1$,*

$$\ln M(\epsilon, \mathcal{G}, L_1(\mathcal{S}_n)) \le 3d + d\ln(\ln(4/\epsilon)/\epsilon).$$

Proof Given $\mathcal{S}_n = \{Z_1, \ldots, Z_n\}$, let $Q = \{\phi_1, \ldots, \phi_m\}$ be a maximal ϵ $L_1(\mathcal{S}_n)$ packing of $\mathcal{G}$. Q is also an L_1 ϵ cover of $\mathcal{G}$. Consider the empirical distribution, denoted by $\mathcal{S}_n$, which puts a probability of $1/n$ on each Z_i. We have for $j \neq k$,

$$\Pr_{Z \sim \mathcal{S}_n} [\phi_j(Z) = \phi_k(Z)] = 1 - \mathbb{E}_{Z \sim \mathcal{S}_n} |\phi_j(Z) - \phi_k(Z)| < 1 - \epsilon.$$

Now consider random sample with replacement from $\mathcal{S}_n$ for T times to obtain samples $\{Z_{i_1}, \ldots, Z_{i_T}\}$. We have

$$\Pr(\{\forall \ell \colon \phi_j(Z_{i_\ell}) = \phi_k(Z_{i_\ell})\}) < (1 - \epsilon)^T \leq e^{-T\epsilon}.$$

That is, with probability larger than $1 - e^{-T\epsilon}$,

$$\exists \ell \colon \phi_j(Z_{i_\ell}) \neq \phi_k(Z_{i_\ell}).$$

Taking the union bound for all $j \neq k$, we have with probability larger than $1 - \binom{m}{2} \cdot e^{-T\epsilon}$, for all $j \neq k$,

$$\exists \ell \colon \phi_j(Z_{i_\ell}) \neq \phi_k(Z_{i_\ell}).$$

If we take $T = \lceil \ln(m^2)/\epsilon \rceil$, then $e^{-T\epsilon} \binom{m}{2} \leq 1$. Then there exist T samples $\{Z_{i_\ell} \colon \ell = 1, \ldots, T\}$ such that $\phi_j \neq \phi_k$ for all $j \neq k$ when restricted to these samples. Since $\mathrm{vc}(G) = d$, we obtain from Sauer's lemma,

$$m \leq \max[2, eT/d]^d \leq \max[2, e(1 + \ln(m^2)/\epsilon)/d]^d.$$

The theorem holds automatically when $m \leq 2^d$. Otherwise,

$$\ln m \leq d \ln(1/\epsilon) + d \ln((e\epsilon/d) + (2e/d) \ln(m)).$$

Let $u = d^{-1} \ln m - \ln(1/\epsilon) - \ln \ln(4/\epsilon)$ and let $\epsilon \leq 1$. We can obtain the following bound by using the upper bound of $\ln m$:

$$u \leq - \ln \ln(4/\epsilon) + \ln((e\epsilon/d) + 2e(u + \ln(1/\epsilon) + \ln \ln(4/\epsilon)))$$
$$\leq \ln \frac{2e(u + 0.5 + \ln(1/\epsilon) + \ln \ln(4/\epsilon))}{\ln(4/\epsilon)}$$
$$\leq \ln(4u + 7),$$

where the last inequality is obtained by taking sup over $\epsilon \in (0, 1]$. By solving this inequality we obtain a bound $u \leq 3$. This implies the desired result. $\qquad \square$

It is possible to prove a slightly stronger result using a refined argument in the proof of Theorem 5.5.

Theorem 5.6 (Haussler, 1995) *Let $\mathcal{G}$ be a binary-valued function class with* $\mathrm{vc}(G) = d$. *Then*

$$\ln M(\epsilon, \mathcal{G}, L_1(\mathcal{S}_n)) \leq 1 + \ln(d + 1) + d \ln(2e/\epsilon).$$

From Exercise 5.3, we have

$$\ln N(\epsilon, \mathcal{G}, L_p(\mathcal{S}_n)) \leq 1 + \ln(d+1) + d\ln(2e/\epsilon^p).$$

If we replace $\mathcal{S}_n$ by any distribution $\mathcal{D}$ over Z, then we still have

$$\ln N(\epsilon, \mathcal{G}, L_p(\mathcal{D})) \leq 1 + \ln(d+1) + d\ln(2e/\epsilon^p),$$

because any $\mathcal{D}$ can be approximated by empirical distribution drawn from $\mathcal{D}$ with sufficiently large n. We thus have the following result.

Corollary 5.7 *If* $\mathrm{vc}(\mathcal{G}) = d$, *then for all distributions* $\mathcal{D}$ *over* Z, *we have*

$$\ln N(\epsilon, \mathcal{G}, L_p(\mathcal{D})) \leq 1 + \ln(d+1) + d\ln(2e/\epsilon^p)$$

for $\epsilon \in (0, 1]$ *and* $p \in [1, \infty)$.

We note that the result of Corollary 5.7 is independent of the underlying distribution. For empirical distribution $\mathcal{S}_n$, the bound is independent of n. Of particular interest is the case of $p = 2$, for which we may apply the chaining technique with the $L_2(\mathcal{S}_n)$ covering number bound of Corollary 5.7. The result (see Example 6.26) removes a $\ln n$ factor, when compared to the result in Theorem 4.17, which employs the original $L_\infty(\mathcal{S}_n)$ VC covering number bound.

5.4 VC Subgraph Class

One may extend the concept of VC dimension to real-valued functions by introducing the definition of a VC subgraph class.

Definition 5.8 A real-valued function class of $z \in \mathcal{Z}$,

$$\mathcal{G} = \{\phi(w, Z) \colon w \in \Omega\},$$

is a VC subgraph class if the binary function class

$$\mathcal{G}_{\mathrm{subgraph}} = \{\mathbb{1}(t < \phi(w, z)) \colon w \in \Omega\}$$

defined on $(z, t) \in \mathcal{Z} \times \mathbb{R}$ is a VC class. The VC dimension (sometimes also called the pseudodimension) of $\mathcal{G}$ is $\mathrm{vc}(\mathcal{G}) = \mathrm{vc}(\mathcal{G}_{\mathrm{sub-graph}})$.

Example 5.9 The d-dimensional linear function of the form $f_w(x) = w^\top x$ is a VC subgraph class of VC dimension $d + 1$. This is because $w^\top x - t$ is a linear function in $d+1$ dimension, and we have shown that it has VC dimension $d + 1$.

Example 5.10 If $\mathcal{F} = \{f(w, x) \colon w \in \Omega\}$ is a VC subgraph class and h is a monotone function, then $h \circ \mathcal{F} = \{h(f(w, x)) \colon w \in \Omega\}$ is a VC subgraph class with $\mathrm{vc}(h \circ \mathcal{F}) \leq \mathrm{vc}(\mathcal{F})$.

Theorem 5.11 *Assume that* $\mathcal{G}$ *is a VC subgraph class, with VC dimension d, and all* $\phi \in \mathcal{G}$ *are bounded:* $\phi(Z) \in [0, 1]$. *Then for any distribution* $\mathcal{D}$ *over* Z, $\epsilon \in (0, 1]$ *and* $p \in [1, \infty)$, *we have*

$$\ln N(\epsilon, \mathcal{G}, L_p(\mathcal{D})) \leq 1 + \ln(d+1) + d\ln(2e/\epsilon^p).$$

Moreover,

$$\ln N_\infty(\epsilon, \mathcal{G}, n) \leq d \ln \max[2, en/(d\epsilon)].$$

Proof Let U be a random variable distributed uniformly over $[0,1]$. Then for all $a \in (0,1)$: $\mathbb{E}_U \mathbf{1}(U \leq a) = a$. Thus for all $\phi, \phi' \in \mathcal{G}$,

$$
\begin{aligned}
\mathbb{E}_\mathcal{D}|\phi(Z) &- \phi'(Z)|^p \\
&= \mathbb{E}_\mathcal{D}|\mathbb{E}_U[\mathbf{1}(U \leq \phi(Z)) - \mathbf{1}(U \leq \phi'(Z))]|^p \\
&\leq \mathbb{E}_\mathcal{D}\mathbb{E}_U|\mathbf{1}(U \leq \phi(Z)) - \mathbf{1}(U \leq \phi'(Z))|^p.
\end{aligned}
$$

The last inequality used the Jensen inequality. Therefore

$$\ln N(\epsilon, \mathcal{G}, L_p(\mathcal{D})) \leq \ln N(\epsilon, \mathcal{G}_{\text{subgraph}}, L_p(\mathcal{D} \times U(0,1))).$$

This leads to the first desired bound.

The second bound can be proved by discretizing U into intervals with thresholds $\min(1, \epsilon(2k+1))$ for $k = 0, 1, \ldots$ with no more than $\lceil (2\epsilon)^{-1} \rceil \leq 1/\epsilon$ thresholds. This gives an ϵ cover of U in Euclidean distance. We can then approximate $\mathbb{E}_U$ by average over the thresholds to get ϵ L_∞ cover with the discretization. Let the set of thresholds be U'. If $\mathcal{D}$ contain n data points, then $\mathcal{D} \times U'$ contains at most $n|U'| \leq n/\epsilon$ points, and one may apply Sauer's lemma to obtain a cover on these points. This implies the second bound. $\qquad\square$

5.5 Convex Hull Class

Convex hull of a function class is frequently encountered in applications, and is related to L_1 regularization. We can define the convex hull of a function class as follows.

Definition 5.12 The convex hull of a function class $\mathcal{F} = \{f(\theta, x) \colon \theta \in \Theta\}$ is defined as

$$\text{CONV}(\mathcal{F}) = \left\{ \sum_{j=1}^m w_j f(\theta_j, x) \colon m > 0, \ \|w\|_1 = 1, \ w_j \geq 0, \ \theta_j \in \Theta \right\}.$$

We also include the closure of the finite sum functions with respect to an appropriate topology in the convex hull.

If $\mathcal{F}$ is finite, then we have the following covering number estimates.

Theorem 5.13 *Consider a finite function class $\mathcal{F} = \{f_1, \ldots, f_d\}$, and assume that for a distribution $\mathcal{D}$ and $p \in [1, p]$, $\sup_{f \in F} \|f\|_{L_p(\mathcal{D})} \leq A$. Then for $\epsilon \leq A$,*

$$\ln M(\epsilon, \text{CONV}(\mathcal{F}), L_p(\mathcal{D})) \leq d \ln(3A/\epsilon).$$

Proof Let $B_1 \in R^d$ be the L_1 ball

$$B_1 = \{q \in R^d \colon \|q\|_1 \leq 1\}.$$

Let $Q = \{q^1, \ldots, q^M\}$ be a maximal ϵ L_1 packing of B_1. Theorem 5.3 implies that $M \leq (3/\epsilon)^d$.

Note that for any $q = [q_1, \ldots, q_d] \in B_1$, let $q^k \in Q$ so that $\|q - q^k\|_1 \leq \epsilon$, then

$$\left[\mathbb{E}_{Z \sim \mathcal{D}} \left| \sum_{j=1}^{d} q_j^k f_j(Z) - \sum_{j=1}^{d} q_j f_j(Z) \right|^p \right]^{1/p} \leq \epsilon A.$$

Therefore $\left\{ \sum_{j=1}^{d} q_j^k f_j : k = 1, \ldots, N \right\}$ is an ϵA L_p cover of $\text{CONV}(F)$. The result follows. $\square$

The result is linear in the dimension d. However, for high-dimensional problems, one would like to obtain a bound that is logarithmic in the dimensionality d. The following result gives such a bound for L_2 cover, but with a polynomial dependency on $1/\epsilon$ instead of logarithmic dependency on $1/\epsilon$.

Theorem 5.14 *Consider any class $\mathcal{F} = \{f_1, \ldots, f_d\}$, and assume that for a distribution $\mathcal{D}$, $\sup_{f \in \mathcal{F}} \|f\|_{L_2(\mathcal{D})} \leq A$. Then*

$$\ln N(\epsilon, \text{CONV}(\mathcal{F}), L_2(\mathcal{D})) \leq \lceil A^2/\epsilon^2 \rceil \ln[e + ed\epsilon^2/A^2].$$

Proof For simplicity, we assume that $A = 1$. Given any $f = \sum_j \alpha_j f_j \in \text{CONV}(\mathcal{F})$, with $\sum_j \alpha_j = 1$ and $\alpha_j \geq 0$, we can regard p_α as a probability measure on $\{1, \ldots, d\}$ with $p_\alpha(j) = \alpha_j$ $(j = 1, \ldots, d)$. Now, let $j_1, \ldots, j_k$ be k iid samples from p_α, then $f = \sum_j \alpha_j f_j = \mathbb{E}_{j_s} f_{j_s}$.

$$\mathbb{E}_{j_1, \ldots, j_k} \left\| \frac{1}{k} \sum_{s=1}^{k} f_{j_s} - f \right\|_{L_2(\mathcal{D})}^2 = \text{Var}_{j_1, \ldots, j_k} \left(\left\| \frac{1}{k} \sum_{s=1}^{k} f_{j_s} \right\|_{L_2(\mathcal{D})} \right)$$

$$= k^{-2} \sum_{s=1}^{k} \text{Var}_{j_s} (\|f_{j_s}\|_{L_2(\mathcal{D})})$$

$$\leq k^{-2} \sum_{s=1}^{k} \mathbb{E}_{j_s} (\|f_{j_s}\|_{L_2(\mathcal{D})}^2) \leq 1/k.$$

It means that there exists $j_1, \ldots, j_s$ such that

$$\left\| \frac{1}{k} \sum_{s=1}^{k} f_{j_s} - f \right\|_{L_2(\mathcal{D})} \leq 1/\sqrt{k}.$$

Now, consider

$$Q_k = \left\{ \frac{1}{k} \sum_{j=1}^{d} n_j f_j : \sum_{j=1}^{d} n_j = k; n_j \geq 0 \right\}.$$

Since $k^{-1} \sum_{s=1}^{k} f_{j_s} \in Q_k$, we know that Q_k is an $1/\sqrt{k}$ cover of $\text{CONV}(\mathcal{F})$. Take $k = \lceil 1/\epsilon^2 \rceil$, we know that Q_k is an ϵ cover. Moreover, since

$$|Q_k| \leq \binom{d + k - 1}{k} \leq e^k (1 + d/k)^k,$$

we obtain the bound in the theorem. $\square$

We can also estimate the L_2 covering number for the convex hull of a parametric function class, such as VC-subgraph class. Specifically, in a parametric function class, the covering number is given by

$$\ln N(\epsilon, \mathcal{F}, L_2(\mathcal{D})) \leq V \ln(c/\epsilon), \tag{5.2}$$

where c is a constant, and V is the dimensionality (such as VC dimension) of the function class $\mathcal{F}$.

The convex hull of (5.2) is referred to as the *VC-hull class*. Its covering number estimate can be obtained as follows.

Theorem 5.15 *Consider a function class $\mathcal{F}$ with covering number given by (5.2) for some $c > 0$ and $V > 0$. Let $A = \sup_{f \in \mathcal{F}} \|f\|_{L_2(\mathcal{D})}$, then we have*

$$\ln N(\epsilon, \mathrm{CONV}(\mathcal{F}), L_2(\mathcal{D})) \leq 10(2c/\epsilon)^{2V/(V+2)} \ln \max[12A/\epsilon, 3 + 3(2c/\epsilon)^V]$$

for all $\epsilon \leq 2c$.

Proof We let $\mathcal{F}_\epsilon$ be an $\epsilon/2$ cover of $\mathcal{F}$ in $L_2(\mathcal{D})$. Then any $\epsilon/2$ cover of $\mathrm{CONV}(\mathcal{F}_\epsilon)$ gives an ϵ cover of $\mathrm{CONV}(\mathcal{F})$.

Moreover, we consider $\mathcal{F}_{\epsilon'}$ as an $\epsilon'/2$ cover of $\mathcal{F}_\epsilon$ for some $\epsilon' \geq \epsilon$, and decompose each $f_j \in \mathcal{F}_\epsilon$ as

$$f = f' + \Delta f,$$

where $f' \in \mathcal{F}_{\epsilon'}$ and $\|\Delta f\|_{L_2(\mathcal{D})} \leq \epsilon'/2$.

Let $\Delta \mathcal{F}_\epsilon = \{\Delta f \colon f \in \mathcal{F}_\epsilon\}$, then using this decomposition, we know that

$$\mathrm{CONV}(\mathcal{F}_\epsilon) \subset \mathrm{CONV}(\Delta \mathcal{F}_\epsilon) + \mathrm{CONV}(\mathcal{F}_{\epsilon'}).$$

It follows that

$$\ln N(\epsilon, \mathrm{CONV}(\mathcal{F}), L_2(\mathcal{D})) \leq \ln N(\epsilon/2, \mathrm{CONV}(\mathcal{F}_\epsilon), L_2(\mathcal{D}))$$
$$\leq \ln N(\epsilon/4, \mathrm{CONV}(\mathcal{F}_{\epsilon'}), L_2(\mathcal{D})) + \ln N(\epsilon/4, \mathrm{CONV}(\Delta \mathcal{F}_\epsilon), L_2(\mathcal{D})).$$

Since

$$|\mathcal{F}_{\epsilon'}| \leq (2c/\epsilon')^V,$$

we have from Theorem 5.13

$$\ln N(\epsilon/4, \mathrm{CONV}(\mathcal{F}_{\epsilon'}), L_2(\mathcal{D})) \leq (2c/\epsilon')^V \ln(12A/\epsilon).$$

Moreover, since

$$|\Delta \mathcal{F}_\epsilon| \leq |\mathcal{F}_\epsilon| \leq (2c/\epsilon)^V,$$

we have from Theorem 5.14 that

$$\ln N(\epsilon/4, \mathrm{CONV}(\Delta \mathcal{F}_\epsilon), L_2(\mathcal{D})) \leq (3\epsilon'/\epsilon)^2 \ln[e + e(2c/\epsilon)^V(\epsilon/\epsilon')].$$

Now let $\epsilon'/2c = (\epsilon/2c)^{2/(V+2)}$, and we have

$$\ln N(\epsilon/4, \mathrm{CONV}(\mathcal{F}_{\epsilon'}), L_2(\mathcal{D})) + \ln N(\epsilon/4, \mathrm{CONV}(\Delta \mathcal{F}_\epsilon), L_2(\mathcal{D}))$$
$$\leq (2c/\epsilon')^V \ln(12A/\epsilon) + (3\epsilon'/\epsilon)^2 \ln[e + e(2c/\epsilon)^V(\epsilon/\epsilon')]$$
$$\leq (2c/\epsilon)^{2V/(V+2)} \ln(12A/\epsilon) + 9(2c/\epsilon)^{2V/(V+2)} \ln[e + e(2c/\epsilon)^V].$$

This proves the theorem. $\square$

Note that for a finite-dimensional class $d = |\mathcal{F}| < \infty$, its VC dimension is no more than $\log_2 d$ because any $\lfloor \log_2 |\mathcal{F}| \rfloor + 1$ points cannot be shattered. It means that we can take $V = \log_2 d$, and obtain a result

$$\ln N(\epsilon, \text{CONV}(\mathcal{F}), L_2(\mathcal{D})) = O\left(\epsilon^{-2\log_2 d/\log_2(4d)} \log_2 d \ln(1/\epsilon)\right),$$

which is slightly better in its dependency of ϵ than that of Theorem 5.14, which has an entropy growth rate of $O(\epsilon^{-2})$.

Using a similar proof technique, but with a more careful analysis, it is possible to get rid of $\ln(1/\epsilon)$ in Theorem 5.15, and obtain the following result. The details can be found in van der Vaart and Wellner (1996).

Theorem 5.16 *Let $A = \sup_{f \in \mathcal{F}} \|f\|_{L_2(\mathcal{D})}$. If $\ln N(\mathcal{F}, \epsilon, L_2(\mathcal{D})) \leq V \ln(cA/\epsilon)$ for some $c \geq 1$ and $V > 0$, then when $\epsilon \leq 1$, we have*

$$\ln N(\text{CONV}(\mathcal{F}), \epsilon, L_2(\mathcal{D})) \leq K(c, V)(A/\epsilon)^{2V/(V+2)}$$

for some $K(c, V)$ that depends on c and V.

The convex hull of a parametric function class has entropy growth rate with a polynomial $(1/\epsilon)^r$ dependency on $1/\epsilon$. Since $r < 2$, the entropy integral

$$\int_0^\infty \sqrt{N(\epsilon, \text{CONV}(\mathcal{F}), L_2(\mathcal{D}))} d\epsilon < \infty.$$

Therefore the convex hull of a parametric function class is a Donsker class, for which the central limit theorem holds for the corresponding empirical process.

Example 5.17 Consider neural networks with $x \in \mathbb{R}^d$. Let $h(z) = 1/(1 + \exp(-z))$ be the sigmoid activation function. Let

$$\mathcal{F} = \{h(\theta^\top x) \colon \theta \in \mathbb{R}^d\} \cup \{-h(\theta^\top x) \colon \theta \in \mathbb{R}^d\}$$

be the function class of one-layer neurons, then $\mathcal{F}$ is a VC subgraph class with $\text{VC}(\mathcal{F}) = d + 1$. Thus it has parametric covering number

$$N(\epsilon, \mathcal{F}, L_2(\mathcal{D})) \leq (c/\epsilon)^{d+1}$$

uniformly for all distributions $\mathcal{D}$. The L_1 regularized two-layer neural network of the form

$$G = \left\{ \sum_{j=1}^m w_j h(\theta_j^\top x) \qquad \|w\|_1 \leq A \right\}$$

has entropy number of

$$\ln N(\epsilon, \mathcal{G}, L_2(\mathcal{D})) = O(\epsilon^{-2(d+1)/(d+3)}).$$

5.6 Regularized Linear Function Classes

In machine learning, one often encounters a linear function class of the form

$$\mathcal{F} = \{f(w, x) = w^\top \psi(x) \colon w \in \Omega, x \in \mathcal{X}\}, \tag{5.3}$$

where $\psi(x)$ is a known feature vector, and we assume both w and $\psi(x)$ can be infinite dimensional. This includes kernel methods, which are studied in Chapter 9.

We have the following theorem, which can be used to estimate the covering numbers for kernel methods. The result is independent of the dimensionality of the problem.

Theorem 5.18 *Let $w = [w_1, w_2, \ldots] \in \mathbb{R}^\infty$ and $\psi(x) = [\psi_1(x), \psi_2(x), \ldots] \in \mathbb{R}^\infty$. Let $\Omega = \{w\colon \|w\|_2 \leq A\}$. Given a distribution $\mathcal{D}$ on $\mathcal{X}$, assume there exists $B_1 \geq B_2 \geq \cdots$ such that*

$$\mathbb{E}_{x \sim \mathcal{D}} \sum_{i \geq j} \psi_i(x)^2 \leq B_j^2.$$

Define

$$\tilde{d}(\epsilon) = \min\{j \geq 0\colon AB_{j+1} \leq \epsilon\}.$$

Then the function class $\mathcal{F}$ of (5.3) satisfies

$$\ln N(\epsilon, \mathcal{F}, L_2(\mathcal{D})) \leq \tilde{d}(\epsilon/2) \ln\left(1 + \frac{4AB_1}{\epsilon}\right).$$

Proof Given $\epsilon > 0$, consider $j = \tilde{d}(\epsilon/2)$ such that $AB_{j+1} \leq \epsilon/2$. Let $\mathcal{F}_1 = \{\sum_{i=1}^j w_i \psi_i(x)\colon w \in \Omega\}$ and $\mathcal{F}_2 = \{\sum_{i>j} w_i \psi_i(x)\colon w \in \Omega\}$. Since $\|f\|_{L_2(\mathcal{D})} \leq \epsilon/2$ for all $f \in \mathcal{F}_2$, we have $N(\epsilon/2, \mathcal{F}, L_2(\mathcal{D})) = 1$. Moreover, Theorem 5.3 implies that

$$\ln N(\epsilon/2, \mathcal{F}_1, L_2(\mathcal{D})) \leq \tilde{d}(\epsilon/2) \ln\left(1 + \frac{4AB_0}{\epsilon}\right).$$

Note that $\mathcal{F} \subset \mathcal{F}_1 + \mathcal{F}_2$. We have $\ln N(\epsilon, \mathcal{F}, L_2(\mathcal{D})) \leq \ln N(\epsilon/2, \mathcal{F}_1, L_2(\mathcal{D})) + \ln N(\epsilon/2, \mathcal{F}_2, L_2(\mathcal{D}))$. This implies the result. $\square$

One may regard $d(\epsilon)$ as the effective dimension of the regularized linear system (5.3) at a scale ϵ. The following example gives a consequence of Theorem 5.18.

Example 5.19 Assume that $B_j = j^{-q}$, then

$$\ln N(\epsilon, \mathcal{F}, L_2(\mathcal{D})) = O\left(\epsilon^{-q} \ln(1/\epsilon)\right).$$

If $B_j = O(c^j)$ for some $c \in (0, 1)$, then

$$\ln N(\epsilon, \mathcal{F}, L_2(\mathcal{D})) = O\left((\ln(1/\epsilon))^2\right).$$

For a general linear function class (5.3) with L_2 regularization $\|w\|_2 \leq A$ and $\|\psi(x)\|_2 \leq B$, we can obtain a bound on $\ln N(\epsilon, \mathcal{F}, L_2(\mathcal{D}))$ using Gaussian complexity estimate and Sudakov minoration (see Theorem 12.4).

Moreover, it is known that the uniform L_∞ covering number of L_2-regularized linear function class can be bounded as follows. The proof can be found in Zhang (2002).

Theorem 5.20 *Assume that $\Omega = \{w\colon \|w\|_2 \leq A\}$ and $\|\psi(x)\|_2 \leq B$, then the function class (5.3) has the following covering number bound:*

$$\ln N(\mathcal{F}, \epsilon, L_\infty(\mathcal{S}_n)) \leq \frac{36A^2B^2}{\epsilon^2} \ln[2\lceil(4AB/\epsilon) + 2\rceil n + 1].$$

It is also possible to obtain uniform L_∞ covering number results under other regularization conditions. Of particular interest is the covering number for L_1-regularization, presented here. The proof can also be found in Zhang (2002).

Theorem 5.21 *Assume that $\Omega = \{w \in \mathbb{R}^d : \|w\|_1 \le A\}$ and $\|\psi(x)\|_\infty \le B$, then the function class (5.3) has the following covering number bound:*

$$\ln N(\mathcal{F}, \epsilon, L_\infty(\mathcal{S}_n)) \le \frac{288A^2B^2(2 + \ln d)}{\epsilon^2} \ln[2\lceil(8AB/\epsilon) + 2\rceil n + 1].$$

The uniform L_∞ cover results in Theorem 5.20 and Theorem 5.21 can be combined with the analysis of Section 4.6 to study large margin methods. They can also be used to study vector-valued prediction problems that were considered in Section 9.4.

5.7 Historical and Bibliographical Remarks

The concepts of covering number and entropy were introduced by Kolmogorov and Tikhomirov (1959). A number of results for smooth function classes were established there. Since then, the tool of covering numbers has been widely used in the theoretical analysis of empirical processes. The volume comparison argument used in the proof of Theorem 5.2 is well known, and can be found in Lorentz (1966). See Pisier (1999) and Edmunds and Triebel (1996) for entropy estimates on Banach and general function spaces. Some estimates of bracketing numbers for smooth function classes can be found in van der Vaart and Wellner (1996, chapter 2.7), van der Vaart (1994), and Nickl and Pötscher (2007). Such estimates can be used as estimates of lower bracketing numbers, which can be used to analyze ERM as in Chapter 3. Additional applications of bracketing numbers in statistical analysis such as the analysis of maximum likelihood estimate can be found in Birgé and Massart (1993); van de Geer (1993, 2000); and Wong and Shen (1995).

In the machine learning literature, the use of uniform covering numbers has become prevalent, largely influenced by the original VC analysis (Vapnik and Chervonenkis, 1971). Note that uniform covering number results similar to bracketing results can be obtained for smooth function classes (Nickl and Pötscher, 2007). Therefore this is not a severe limitation. For VC-classes, the n-independent empirical L_1 covering number bounds have been considered by Dudley (1978) and Haussler (1992). The extension of VC dimension to real-valued VC subgraph class was investigated in Pollard (1984) and Haussler (1992). Additional generalization to *fat-shattering dimension* was proposed in Kearns and Schapire (1994) and Bartlett et al. (1996), which can also be used to obtain bounds of covering numbers. However, due to the complexity of fat-shattering dimension, it is often easier to directly estimate covering numbers using other techniques. Therefore we do not discuss fat-shattering dimension in this chapter. The result in Theorem 5.6 is due to Haussler (1995), where a matching lower bound was also obtained. The covering number estimates of VC-hull class can be found in van der Vaart and Wellner (1996, chapter 2.6) and Carl (1997). Covering number bounds for kernel function classes were studied in Guo et al. (1999); Cucker and Smale (2002); Zhou (2002, 2003); and Kühn (2011). We have only considered a simplified version in Theorem 5.18. Uniform L_∞ covering number bounds for general regularized linear function classes were obtained in Zhang (2002). These bounds are useful in large-margin analysis, and in vector-valued prediction problems.

Exercises

5.1 Consider the function class $\mathcal{F}$ of monotone functions from $\mathbb{R} \to [0, 1]$. Show that for any distribution $\mathcal{D}$ on $\mathbb{R}$,

$$\ln N_{[]}(\epsilon, \mathcal{F}, L_1(\mathcal{D})) \leq \left\lceil \frac{2}{\epsilon} \right\rceil \ln \left\lceil \frac{2}{\epsilon} \right\rceil.$$

Hint: discretize both $\mathbb{R}$ and $[0, 1]$ into regular grids and use piecewise constant approximations.

5.2 For Exercise 5.1, a more involved argument can be used to show that

$$\ln N_{[]}(\epsilon, \mathcal{F}, L_p(\mathcal{D})) \leq \frac{K_p}{\epsilon},$$

where K_p is a constant that depends on p (see van der Vaart and Wellner, 1996, Theorem 2.7.5). Use this result to bound the bracketing numbers of real-valued function class with bounded total variation:

$$\mathcal{F} = \{f \colon V(f) \leq B\}, \quad V(f) = \sup_{x_0 \leq x_1 \leq \cdots \leq x_m} \sum_{i=1}^{m} |f(x_i) - f(x_{i-1})|.$$

5.3 Assume that $\phi(z) \in [0, 1]$ for all $g \in \mathcal{G}$. Show that for $p \geq 1$,

$$\ln N(\epsilon, \mathcal{G}, L_p(\mathcal{D})) \leq \ln N(\epsilon^p, \mathcal{G}, L_1(\mathcal{D})).$$

5.4 Consider the following set in $\mathbb{R}^d$:

$$\Omega = \{x \colon \|x\|_p \leq 1\},$$

where $1 \leq p < 2$. Show that there are constants C_p and r_p such that

$$\ln N(\epsilon, \Omega, \|\cdot\|_2) \leq C_p \epsilon^{-r_p} \ln d.$$

5.5 Consider the set

$$\Omega = \left\{ x = [x_1, x_2, \ldots] \in \mathbb{R}^\infty \colon \sum_{i=1}^{\infty} i \cdot x_i^2 \leq 1 \right\},$$

with metric induced by the L_2-norm $\|x\|_2 = \sqrt{\sum_{i=1}^{\infty} x_i^2}$. Derive an upper bound and a lower bound for $\ln N(\epsilon, \Omega, \|\cdot\|_2)$.

Rademacher Complexity and Concentration Inequalities

In Chapter 3 and Chapter 4, we obtained uniform convergence results using covering numbers and exponential probability inequalities. This chapter considers a different, though closely related, method. In this approach, we first bound the expectation of the supremum of an underlying empirical process using the so-called *Rademacher complexity*, and then use *concentration inequalities* to obtain high probability bounds. This approach simplifies various derivations in generalization analysis.

6.1 Rademacher Complexity

Using the notations from Section 3.3, we are given a function class $\mathcal{G} = \{\phi(w, z) \colon w \in \Omega\}$, and are interested in the uniform convergence of training error

$$\phi(w, \mathcal{S}_n) = \frac{1}{n} \sum_{i=1}^{n} \phi(w, Z_i)$$

on a training data $\mathcal{S}_n = \{Z_1, \ldots, Z_n\} \sim \mathcal{D}^n$, to the test error

$$\phi(w, \mathcal{D}) = \mathbb{E}_{Z \sim \mathcal{D}} \phi(w, Z)$$

on the test data $\mathcal{D}$. In particular, in the general analysis of learning algorithms, we want to estimate the supremum of the associated empirical process

$$\sup_{w \in \Omega} \left[\phi(w, \mathcal{D}) - \phi(w, \mathcal{S}_n) \right].$$

We introduce the following definition, which will be useful in the analysis of this chapter.

Definition 6.1 Given an empirical process $\{\phi(w, \mathcal{S}_n) \colon w \in \Omega\}$, with $\mathcal{S}_n \sim \mathcal{D}^n$, define the expected supremum of this empirical process as

$$\epsilon_n(\mathcal{G}, \mathcal{D}) = \mathbb{E}_{\mathcal{S}_n} \sup_{w \in \Omega} \left[\phi(w, \mathcal{D}) - \phi(w, \mathcal{S}_n) \right],$$

which will be referred to as the *uniform convergence complexity* of the function class $\mathcal{G}$.

The smaller this quantity is, the closer the gap between the training error and the test error, which implies that we have less overfitting. In Chapter 3, we obtained large probability uniform convergence results for empirical processes, and then derived oracle inequalities in large probabilities. In the following, we show that if average convergence can be obtained, then we can derive oracle inequalities in expectation directly.

Theorem 6.2 *Consider* $\phi(w, Z)$ *with* $Z \sim \mathcal{D}$. *Let* $\mathcal{S}_n \sim \mathcal{D}^n$ *be* n *iid samples from* $\mathcal{D}$. *Then the approximate ERM method of* (3.7) *satisfies*

$$\mathbb{E}_{\mathcal{S}_n} \phi(\hat{w}, \mathcal{D}) \leq \inf_{w \in \Omega} \phi(w, \mathcal{D}) + \epsilon' + \epsilon_n(\mathcal{G}, \mathcal{D}).$$

Proof Given any $w \in \Omega$, we have for each instance of training data $\mathcal{S}_n$,

$$\phi(\hat{w}, \mathcal{D}) \leq \phi(\hat{w}, \mathcal{S}_n) + \sup_{w \in \Omega}[\phi(w, \mathcal{D}) - \phi(w, \mathcal{S}_n)]$$
$$\leq \phi(w, \mathcal{S}_n) + \epsilon' + \sup_{w \in \Omega}[\phi(w, \mathcal{D}) - \phi(w, \mathcal{S}_n)].$$

Taking expectation with respect to $\mathcal{S}_n$, and note that w does not depend on $\mathcal{S}_n$, we obtain

$$\mathbb{E}_{\mathcal{S}_n} \phi(\hat{w}, \mathcal{D}) \leq \phi(w, \mathcal{D}) + \epsilon' + \mathbb{E}_{\mathcal{S}_n} \sup_{w \in \Omega}[\phi(w, \mathcal{D}) - \phi(w, \mathcal{S}_n)].$$

This implies the desired bound. $\square$

We are now ready to define Rademacher complexity. While the standard definition is two-sided where the supremum is over the absolute value of the sum, we consider a one-sided bound, which is more convenient for our purpose.

Definition 6.3 Given $\mathcal{S}_n = \{Z_1, \ldots, Z_n\}$, the (one-sided) empirical Rademacher complexity of $\mathcal{G}$ is defined as

$$R(\mathcal{G}, \mathcal{S}_n) = \mathbb{E}_\sigma \sup_{w \in \Omega} \frac{1}{n} \sum_{i=1}^{n} \sigma_i \phi(w, Z_i),$$

where $\sigma_1, \ldots, \sigma_n$ are independent uniform $\{\pm 1\}$-valued Bernoulli random variables. Moreover, the expected Rademacher complexity is

$$R_n(\mathcal{G}, \mathcal{D}) = \mathbb{E}_{\mathcal{S}_n \sim \mathcal{D}^n} R(\mathcal{G}, \mathcal{S}_n).$$

The following result shows that the quantity $\epsilon_n(\mathcal{G}, \mathcal{D})$ can be upper bounded by Rademacher complexity. It follows that an average oracle inequality can be obtained using Rademacher complexity. The proof employs the *symmetrization* technique, which was also used in Chapter 4 to obtain uniform convergence bounds from empirical covering numbers.

Theorem 6.4 *We have*

$$\epsilon_n(\mathcal{G}, \mathcal{D}) \leq 2R_n(\mathcal{G}, \mathcal{D}).$$

Consequently, the approximate ERM method of (3.7) satisfies

$$\mathbb{E}_{\mathcal{S}_n} \phi(\hat{w}, \mathcal{D}) \leq \inf_{w \in \Omega} \phi(w, \mathcal{D}) + \epsilon' + 2R_n(\mathcal{G}, \mathcal{D}).$$

Proof Let $\mathcal{S}'_n = \{Z'_1, \ldots, Z'_n\} \sim \mathcal{D}^n$ be n iid samples from $\mathcal{D}$ that are independent of $\mathcal{S}_n$. We have

$$\epsilon_n(\mathcal{G}, \mathcal{D}) = \mathbb{E}_{\mathcal{S}_n \sim \mathcal{D}^n} \sup_{w \in \Omega} [\phi(w, \mathcal{D}) - \phi(w, \mathcal{S}_n)]$$

$$= \mathbb{E}_{\mathcal{S}_n \sim \mathcal{D}^n} \sup_{w \in \Omega} [\mathbb{E}_{\mathcal{S}'_n \sim \mathcal{D}^n} \phi(w, \mathcal{S}'_n) - \phi(w, \mathcal{S}_n)]$$

$$\leq \mathbb{E}_{(\mathcal{S}_n, \mathcal{S}'_n) \sim \mathcal{D}^{2n}} \sup_{w \in \Omega} [\phi(w, \mathcal{S}'_n) - \phi(w, \mathcal{S}_n)]$$

$$= \mathbb{E}_{(\mathcal{S}_n, \mathcal{S}'_n) \sim \mathcal{D}^{2n}} \mathbb{E}_\sigma \sup_{w \in \Omega} \frac{1}{n} \sum_{i=1}^{n} [\sigma_i \phi(w, Z'_i) - \sigma_i \phi(w, Z_i)]$$

$$\leq \mathbb{E}_{(\mathcal{S}_n, \mathcal{S}'_n) \sim \mathcal{D}^{2n}} [R(\mathcal{G}, \mathcal{S}_n) + R(\mathcal{G}, \mathcal{S}'_n)] = 2R_n(\mathcal{G}, \mathcal{D}).$$

This proves the desired bound. □

One reason to introduce Rademacher complexity is that it can be estimated on the training data. Moreover, for many problems, it is often not difficult to estimate this quantity theoretically. The following example demonstrates this.

Example 6.5 Consider a (binary-valued) VC class $\mathcal{G}$ such that $\text{VC}(\mathcal{G}) = d$. Consider $n \geq d$. Then Sauer's lemma implies that for any $\mathcal{S}_n$, the number of functions of $\phi \in \mathcal{G}$ on $\mathcal{S}_n$ is no more than $(en/d)^d$. We thus obtain (see Theorem 6.23)

$$R(\mathcal{G}, \mathcal{S}_n) \leq \sqrt{\frac{2d \ln(en/d)}{n}}.$$

This implies that the approximate ERM method of (3.7) satisfies

$$\mathbb{E}_{\mathcal{S}_n} \phi(\hat{w}, \mathcal{D}) \leq \inf_{w \in \Omega} \phi(w, \mathcal{D}) + \epsilon' + 2\sqrt{\frac{2d \ln(en/d)}{n}}.$$

A better bound can be obtained using Theorem 5.6 and Theorem 6.25, which removes the $\ln n$ factor. Also see Example 6.26.

6.2 Offset Rademacher Complexity

While the standard Rademacher complexity is suitable for many problems, for regularized empirical risk minimization problems that frequently occur in practice, it can be more convenient to use *offset Rademacher complexity*. In this section, we consider a generalization of the empirical risk minimization method, where we allow the training error to be different from the test error, which frequently occurs in practical applications. A typical example is to include a regularizer in the training loss to stabilize the training process, such as L_2 regularization

$0.5\lambda\|w\|_2^2$. In such case, we consider the following regularized training loss, with a general training set dependent regularizer $h(w, \mathcal{S}_n)$:

$$\phi(w, \mathcal{S}_n) + h(w, \mathcal{S}_n), \qquad \text{where } \phi(w, \mathcal{S}_n) = \frac{1}{n} \sum_{i=1}^{n} \phi(w, Z_i).$$

Here we assume that $h(w, \mathcal{S}_n)$ is a general function that can depend on the training data $\mathcal{S}_n$. By following the notation from Section 3.3, we use $\phi(w, z)$ to denote the loss function at a data point z, and use $\mathcal{S}_n = \{Z_1, \ldots, Z_n\}$ to denote the training data. The test loss is

$$\phi(w, \mathcal{D}) = \mathbb{E}_{Z \sim \mathcal{D}} \phi(w, Z)$$

with respect to the unknown test distribution $\mathcal{D}$. Training data $\mathcal{S}_n$ are iid samples from $\mathcal{D}$.

We consider a function class $\mathcal{G} = \{\phi(w, z) \colon w \in \Omega\}$, and the following approximate regularized ERM method to find $\hat{w}$:

$$[\phi(\hat{w}, \mathcal{S}_n) + h(\hat{w}, \mathcal{S}_n)] \leq \min_{w \in \Omega} [\phi(w, \mathcal{S}_n) + h(w, \mathcal{S}_n)] + \epsilon', \tag{6.1}$$

which is a more general formulation than (3.7). This formulation will become convenient in some of the future analysis. In order to analyze the behavior of this method, we need to analyze the uniform convergence of the regularized training loss to the test loss.

For this purpose, we consider a modified empirical process (to compensate the difference of training error and test error), which we refer to as *offset empirical process*, and study the supremum of this offset empirical process:

$$\sup_{w \in \Omega} [\phi(w, \mathcal{D}) - \phi(w, \mathcal{S}_n) - h(w, \mathcal{S}_n)].$$

It characterizes the degree of (one-sided) uniform convergence of function class $\mathcal{G}$, with a offset function $h(w, \mathcal{S}_n)$. Here we incorporate a known offset function $h(w, \mathcal{S}_n)$ into the training loss, which may depend on the model parameter and training data. In the usual setting of empirical process in Chapter 3 and Chapter 4, one may simply take $h(w, \mathcal{S}_n) = 0$.

Definition 6.6 Consider any known data-dependent offset function $h(w, \mathcal{S}_n)$. Define the uniform convergence complexity of a function class $\mathcal{G}$ with offset h as

$$\epsilon_n^h(\mathcal{G}, \mathcal{D}) = \mathbb{E}_{\mathcal{S}_n \sim \mathcal{D}^n} \sup_{w \in \Omega} [\phi(w, \mathcal{D}) - \phi(w, \mathcal{S}_n) - h(w, \mathcal{S}_n)]. \tag{6.2}$$

This quantity measures the one-sided *expected uniform convergence* of function class $\mathcal{G}$ with offset function $h(w, \mathcal{S}_n)$.

We note that

$$\epsilon_n(\mathcal{G}, \mathcal{D}) = \epsilon_n^h(\mathcal{G}, \mathcal{D}), \qquad \text{with } h = 0.$$

We have the following generalization of Theorem 6.2, with a similar proof.

Theorem 6.7 *Let $\mathcal{S}_n$ be n iid samples from $\mathcal{D}$. Then the approximate ERM method of (6.1) satisfies*

$$\mathbb{E}_{\mathcal{S}_n} \phi(\hat{w}, \mathcal{D}) \leq \inf_{w \in \Omega} [\phi(w, \mathcal{D}) + \mathbb{E}_{\mathcal{S}_n} h(w, \mathcal{S}_n)] + \epsilon' + \epsilon_n^h(\mathcal{G}, \mathcal{D}).$$

Proof Given any $w \in \Omega$, we have for each training data $\mathcal{S}_n$,

$$\phi(\hat{w}, \mathcal{D})$$
$$= [\phi(\hat{w}, \mathcal{S}_n) + h(\hat{w}, \mathcal{S}_n)] + [\phi(\hat{w}, \mathcal{D}) - \phi(\hat{w}, \mathcal{S}_n) - h(\hat{w}, \mathcal{S}_n)]$$
$$\leq [\phi(\hat{w}, \mathcal{S}_n) + h(\hat{w}, \mathcal{S}_n)] + \sup_{w \in \Omega}[\phi(w, \mathcal{D}) - \phi(w, \mathcal{S}_n) - h(w, \mathcal{S}_n)]$$
$$\leq [\phi(w, \mathcal{S}_n) + h(w, \mathcal{S}_n)] + \epsilon' + \sup_{w \in \Omega}[\phi(w, \mathcal{D}) - \phi(w, \mathcal{S}_n) - h(w, \mathcal{S}_n)].$$

In the derivation of the last inequality, we used (6.1). Taking expectation with respect to $\mathcal{S}_n$, and note that w does not depend on $\mathcal{S}_n$, we obtain

$$\mathbb{E}_{\mathcal{S}_n} \phi(\hat{w}, \mathcal{D}) \leq \phi(w, \mathcal{D}) + \mathbb{E}_{\mathcal{S}_n} h(w, \mathcal{S}_n) + \epsilon'$$
$$+ \mathbb{E}_{\mathcal{S}_n} \sup_{w \in \Omega}[\phi(w, \mathcal{D}) - \phi(w, \mathcal{S}_n) - h(w, \mathcal{S}_n)].$$

This implies the desired bound. $\square$

The following example shows that with an appropriately defined offset function, we can obtain generalization result for regularized empirical risk minimization.

Example 6.8 Take $h(w, \mathcal{S}_n) = g(w)$ in (6.1), and let $\phi(w, z) = L(f(w, x), y)$, then Theorem 6.7 implies the following generalization bound for the approximate regularized ERM method in (6.1):

$$\mathbb{E}_{\mathcal{S}_n} \mathbb{E}_{(X,Y) \sim \mathcal{D}} L(f(\hat{w}, X), Y) \leq \inf_{w \in \Omega} \mathbb{E}_{(X,Y) \sim \mathcal{D}} [L(f(\hat{w}, X), Y) + g(w)]$$
$$+ \epsilon' + \epsilon_n^h(\mathcal{G}, \mathcal{D}).$$

From Theorem 6.7, we may also obtain a slightly more general formulation, which is some times useful.

Corollary 6.9 *Consider (6.1), and define*

$$\tilde{h}(w, \mathcal{S}_n) = h(w, \mathcal{S}_n) + h'(w),$$

where $h'(w)$ is an arbitrary function of w. Then

$$\mathbb{E}_{\mathcal{S}_n}[\phi(\hat{w}, \mathcal{D}) - h'(\hat{w})] \leq \inf_{w \in \Omega} [\phi(w, \mathcal{D}) + \mathbb{E}_{\mathcal{S}_n} h(w, \mathcal{S}_n)] + \epsilon' + \epsilon_n^{\tilde{h}}(\mathcal{G}, \mathcal{D}).$$

Proof Let

$$\tilde{\phi}(w, z) = \phi(w, z) - h'(w),$$

then (6.1) remains the same with $\phi(w, z)$ replaced by $\tilde{\phi}(w, z)$, and $h(w, \mathcal{S}_n)$ replaced by $\tilde{h}(w, \mathcal{S}_n)$. We can now apply Theorem 6.7 with $\epsilon_n^h(\mathcal{G}, \mathcal{D})$ replaced by

$$\epsilon_n^{\tilde{h}}(\mathcal{G}, \mathcal{D}) = \mathbb{E}_{\mathcal{S}_n} \sup_{w \in \Omega} [\phi(w, \mathcal{D}) - \phi(w, \mathcal{S}_n) - h(w, \mathcal{S}_n) - h'(w)]$$

to obtain

$$\mathbb{E}_{\mathcal{S}_n} \tilde{\phi}(\hat{w}, \mathcal{D}) \leq \inf_{w \in \Omega} \left[\tilde{\phi}(w, \mathcal{D}) + \mathbb{E}_{\mathcal{S}_n} \tilde{h}(w, \mathcal{S}_n) \right] + \epsilon' + \epsilon_n^{\tilde{h}}(\mathcal{G}, \mathcal{D}).$$

This implies the desired bound. ☐

Example 6.10   One advantage of Corollary 6.9 is that it allows us to introduce an unknown distribution dependent offset term $h'(w)$ into the definition of uniform convergence complexity because the learning algorithm in (6.1) does not depend on $h'(w)$. As a simple example, we may take $h'(w) = \gamma \phi(w, \mathcal{D})$ and obtain

$$(1 - \gamma) \mathbb{E}_{\mathcal{S}_n} \phi(\hat{w}, \mathcal{D}) \leq \inf_{w \in \Omega} [\phi(w, \mathcal{D}) + \mathbb{E}_{\mathcal{S}_n} h(w, \mathcal{S}_n)] + \epsilon' + \epsilon_n^{\tilde{h}}(\mathcal{G}, \mathcal{D}).$$

We are now ready to define (one-sided) offset Rademacher complexity. Note that the offset function in Rademacher complexity is more restrictive than the more general offset function considered in the uniform convergence complexity (6.2). This is because we would like to use symmetrization argument, which works only for this special form of offset function.

Definition 6.11   Consider a function class $\mathcal{G} = \{\phi(w, Z) : w \in \Omega\}$, and let h be an offset function of the following form:

$$h(w, \mathcal{S}_n) = \frac{1}{n} \sum_{i=1}^{n} h(w, Z_i), \quad h(w, z) = h_0(w) + h_1(w, z). \tag{6.3}$$

Given $\mathcal{S}_n = \{Z_1, \ldots, Z_n\}$, the (one-sided) empirical Rademacher complexity of $\mathcal{G}$ with offset h decomposition (6.3) is defined as

$$R^h(\mathcal{G}, \mathcal{S}_n) = \mathbb{E}_\sigma \sup_{w \in \Omega} \left[\frac{1}{n} \sum_{i=1}^{n} \sigma_i [\phi(w, Z_i) + 0.5 h_1(w, Z_i)] - 0.5 h(w, \mathcal{S}_n) \right],$$

where $\sigma_1, \ldots, \sigma_n$ are independent uniform $\{\pm 1\}$-valued Bernoulli random variables. Moreover, the expected Rademacher complexity is

$$R_n^h(\mathcal{G}, \mathcal{D}) = \mathbb{E}_{\mathcal{S}_n \sim \mathcal{D}^n} R^h(\mathcal{G}, \mathcal{S}_n).$$

We note that the standard Rademacher complexity can be regarded as a special case of the offset Rademacher complexity with $h(\cdot) = h_0(\cdot) = h_1(\cdot) = 0$:

$$R(\mathcal{G}, \mathcal{S}_n) = R^0(\mathcal{G}, \mathcal{S}_n), \quad R_n(\mathcal{G}, \mathcal{D}) = R_n^0(\mathcal{G}, \mathcal{D}).$$

It should be pointed out that the decomposition of h in (6.3) may not be unique, and the offset Rademacher complexity relies on the specific decomposition used. As shown in Example 6.10, we allow distribution dependent offset in the definition of uniform convergence complexity. We also allow distribution dependent offset in the definition of offset Rademacher complexity.

The following result shows that for some cases, offset Rademacher complexity can be obtained easily for some function classes.

Example 6.12 Consider a function class $\mathcal{F} = \{f(w, x) = w^\top \psi(x) : w \in \mathbb{R}^d\}$, consisting of linear functions. Let $h(w) = h_0(w) = 0.5\lambda \|w\|_2^2$. Then for any $\mathcal{S}_n$, we have

$$R^h(\mathcal{F}, \mathcal{S}_n) = \mathbb{E}_\sigma \sup_{w \in \mathbb{R}^d} \left[\frac{1}{n} \sum_{i=1}^n \sigma_i w^\top \psi(X_i) - \frac{\lambda}{4}\|w\|_2^2 \right]$$

$$= \frac{1}{\lambda} \mathbb{E}_\sigma \left\| \frac{1}{n} \sum_{i=1}^n \sigma_i \psi(X_i) \right\|_2^2 = \frac{1}{\lambda n^2} \sum_{i=1}^n \|\psi(X_i)\|_2^2.$$

Let $\mathcal{F}_{A,B} = \{\{f(w, x) = w^\top \psi(x) : \|w\|_2 \leq A, \|\psi(x)\|_2 \leq B\}$. Then, for any λ,

$$R(\mathcal{F}_{A,B}, \mathcal{S}_n) \leq R^h(\mathcal{F}, \mathcal{S}_n) + \frac{\lambda}{4}A^2 \leq \frac{B^2}{\lambda n} + \frac{\lambda}{4}A^2.$$

By optimizing over λ, we obtain

$$R(\mathcal{F}_{A,B}, \mathcal{S}_n) \leq AB/\sqrt{n}.$$

The following example illustrates that offset Rademacher complexity can lead to a result analogous to the multiplicative form of the Chernoff bound.

Example 6.13 Consider a (binary-valued) VC class $\mathcal{G}$ such that $\mathrm{vc}(\mathcal{G}) = d$. Consider $n \geq d$, and let $h(f, \mathcal{S}_n) = h_1(f, \mathcal{S}_n) = (\gamma/n) \sum_{i=1}^n f(Z_i)$. Then Sauer's lemma implies that for any $\mathcal{S}_n$, the number of functions of $\phi \in \mathcal{G}$ on $\mathcal{S}_n$ is no more than $(en/d)^d$. We thus obtain (see Theorem 6.23)

$$R^h(\mathcal{G}, \mathcal{S}_n) \leq \frac{(1 + 0.5\gamma)^2 d \ln(en/d)}{\gamma n}.$$

This result can be compared to the standard Rademacher complexity result in Example 6.5, which leads to an additive expected generalization bound.

The following result is a generalization of Theorem 6.4.

Theorem 6.14 *Consider offset function of* (6.3). *We have*

$$\epsilon_n^h(\mathcal{G}, \mathcal{D}) \leq 2R_n^h(\mathcal{G}, \mathcal{D}).$$

Consequently, the approximate regularized ERM method of (6.1) *satisfies*

$$\mathbb{E}_{\mathcal{S}_n} \phi(\hat{w}, \mathcal{D}) \leq \inf_{w \in \Omega} [\phi(w, \mathcal{D}) + \mathbb{E}_{\mathcal{S}_n} h(w, \mathcal{S}_n)] + \epsilon' + 2R_n^h(\mathcal{G}, \mathcal{D}).$$

Proof Let $\mathcal{S}'_n = \{Z'_1, \ldots, Z'_n\} \sim \mathcal{D}^n$ be n iid samples from $\mathcal{D}$ that are independent of $\mathcal{S}_n$. We have

$$\epsilon_n(\mathcal{G}, \mathcal{D}) = \mathbb{E}_{\mathcal{S}_n \sim \mathcal{D}^n} \sup_{w \in \Omega} [\phi(w, \mathcal{D}) - \phi(w, \mathcal{S}_n) - h(w, \mathcal{S}_n)]$$

$$= \mathbb{E}_{\mathcal{S}_n \sim \mathcal{D}^n} \sup_{w \in \Omega} [\mathbb{E}_{\mathcal{S}'_n \sim \mathcal{D}^n} \phi(w, \mathcal{S}'_n) - \phi(w, \mathcal{S}_n) - h(w, \mathcal{S}_n)]$$

$$\leq \mathbb{E}_{(\mathcal{S}_n, \mathcal{S}'_n) \sim \mathcal{D}^{2n}} \sup_{w \in \Omega} [\phi(w, \mathcal{S}'_n) - \phi(w, \mathcal{S}_n) - h(w, \mathcal{S}_n)]$$

$$= \mathbb{E}_{(\mathcal{S}_n, \mathcal{S}'_n) \sim \mathcal{D}^{2n}} \sup_{w \in \Omega} [[\phi(w, \mathcal{S}'_n) + 0.5 h_1(w, \mathcal{S}'_n)] - 0.5 h(w, \mathcal{S}'_n)$$

$$- [\phi(w, \mathcal{S}_n) + 0.5 h_1(w, \mathcal{S}_n)] - 0.5 h(w, \mathcal{S}_n)]$$

$$\overset{(a)}{=} \mathbb{E}_{(\mathcal{S}_n, \mathcal{S}'_n) \sim \mathcal{D}^{2n}} \mathbb{E}_\sigma \sup_{w \in \Omega} \frac{1}{n} \sum_{i=1}^n [\sigma_i(\phi(w, Z'_i) + 0.5 h_1(w, Z'_i)) - 0.5 h(w, \mathcal{S}'_n)$$

$$- \sigma_i(\phi(w, Z_i) + 0.5 h_1(w, Z_i)) - 0.5 h(w, \mathcal{S}_n)]$$

$$\leq \mathbb{E}_{(\mathcal{S}_n, \mathcal{S}'_n) \sim \mathcal{D}^{2n}} \mathbb{E}_\sigma \sup_{w \in \Omega} \frac{1}{n} \sum_{i=1}^n [\sigma_i(\phi(w, Z'_i) + 0.5 h_1(w, Z'_i)) - 0.5 h(w, \mathcal{S}'_n)]$$

$$+ \mathbb{E}_{(\mathcal{S}_n, \mathcal{S}'_n) \sim \mathcal{D}^{2n}} \mathbb{E}_\sigma \sup_{w \in \Omega} \frac{1}{n} \sum_{i=1}^n [-\sigma_i(\phi(w, Z_i) + 0.5 h_1(w, Z_i) - 0.5 h(w, \mathcal{S}_n)]$$

$$= \mathbb{E}_{(\mathcal{S}_n, \mathcal{S}'_n) \sim \mathcal{D}^{2n}} [R^h(\mathcal{G}, \mathcal{S}_n) + R^h(\mathcal{G}, \mathcal{S}'_n)] = 2 R_n^h(\mathcal{G}, \mathcal{D}).$$

In this derivation, (a) used the fact that $\sigma_i(\phi(w, Z'_i) + 0.5 h_1(w, Z'_i)) - \sigma_i(\phi(w, Z_i) + 0.5 h_1(w, Z_i))$ and $(\phi(w, Z'_i) + 0.5 h_1(w, Z'_i)) - (\phi(w, Z_i) + 0.5 h_1(w, Z_i))$ have the same distributions. $\square$

Example 6.15 Using the offset Rademacher complexity estimate for VC class in Example 6.13, we can obtain the following multiplicative form of expected oracle inequality from Theorem 6.14:

$$\mathbb{E}_{\mathcal{S}_n} \phi(\hat{w}, \mathcal{D}) \leq (1 + \gamma) \inf_{w \in \Omega} \phi(w, \mathcal{D}) + \epsilon' + \frac{2(1 + 0.5\gamma)^2 d \ln(en/d)}{\gamma n}.$$

This implies an expected generalization of $O(d \ln n / n)$ when $\inf_{w \in \Omega} \phi(w, \mathcal{D}) = 0$. In comparison, the standard Rademacher complexity leads to a convergence of $O(\sqrt{d \ln n / n})$ in Example 6.5.

6.3 Concentration Inequality

We showed that using Rademacher complexity, we may obtain an oracle inequality in expectation. By using concentration inequality, we can also obtain high-probability uniform convergence and oracle inequality statements.

The simplest concentration inequality is a generalization of the additive Chernoff bound, due to McDiarmid (1989).

Theorem 6.16 (McDiarmid's Inequality) *Consider n independent random variables $X_1, \ldots, X_n$, and a real-valued function $f(X_1, \ldots, X_n)$ that satisfies the following inequality:*

$$\sup_{x_1,\ldots,x_n,x_i'} |f(x_1,\ldots,x_n) - f(x_1,\ldots,x_{i-1},x_i',x_{i+1},\ldots,x_n)| \le c_i$$

for all $1 \le i \le n$. Then for all $\epsilon > 0$,

$$\Pr\left[f(X_1,\ldots,X_n) \ge \mathbb{E}f(X_1,\ldots,X_n) + \epsilon\right] \le \exp\left(\frac{-2\epsilon^2}{\sum_{i=1}^n c_i^2}\right).$$

Similarly,

$$\Pr\left[f(X_1,\ldots,X_n) \le \mathbb{E}f(X_1,\ldots,X_n) - \epsilon\right] \le \exp\left(\frac{-2\epsilon^2}{\sum_{i=1}^n c_i^2}\right).$$

Proof Let $X_k^l = \{X_k,\ldots,X_l\}$. Consider X_1^n, and for some $1 \le k \le n$, we use the simplified notation $\tilde{X}_1^n = \{X_1,\ldots,X_{k-1},\tilde{X}_k,X_{k+1},X_n\}$. Then we have

$$|\mathbb{E}_{X_{k+1}^n} f(X_1^n) - \mathbb{E}_{X_{k+1}^n} f(\tilde{X}_1^n)| \le c_k.$$

We now consider $\mathbb{E}_{X_{k+1}^n} f(X_1^n)$ as a random variable depending on X_k, conditioned on X_1^{k-1}. It follows from derivation of the Chernoff bound that we have the following logarithmic moment generating function estimate (see Example 2.14):

$$\ln \mathbb{E}_{X_k} \exp[\lambda \mathbb{E}_{X_{k+1}^n} f(X_1^n)] \le \lambda \mathbb{E}_{X_k^n} f(X_1^n) + \lambda^2 c_k^2/8.$$

Now we may exponentiate the above inequality, and take expectation with respect to X_1^{k-1} to obtain

$$\mathbb{E}_{X_1^k} \exp[\lambda \mathbb{E}_{X_{k+1}^n} f(X_1^n)] \le \mathbb{E}_{X_1^{k-1}} \exp[\lambda \mathbb{E}_{X_k^n} f(X_1^n) + \lambda^2 c_k^2/8].$$

By taking the logarithm, we obtain

$$\ln \mathbb{E}_{X_1^k} \exp[\lambda \mathbb{E}_{X_{k+1}^n} f(X_1^n)] \le \ln \mathbb{E}_{X_1^{k-1}} \exp[\lambda \mathbb{E}_{X_k^n} f(X_1^n)] + \lambda^2 c_k^2/8.$$

By summing from $k = 1$ to $k = n$, and canceling redundant terms, we obtain

$$\ln \mathbb{E}_{X_1^n} \exp[\lambda f(X_1^n)] \le \lambda \mathbb{E}_{X_1^n} f(X_1^n) + \lambda^2 \sum_{k=1}^n c_k^2/8. \tag{6.4}$$

Let

$$\delta = \Pr\left[f(X_1^n) \ge \mathbb{E}_{X_1^n} f(X_1^n) + \epsilon\right].$$

Using Markov's inequality, we have for all positive λ,

$$\delta \le e^{-\lambda(\mathbb{E}_{X_1^n} f(X_1^n) + \epsilon)} \mathbb{E}_{X_1^n} e^{\lambda f(X_1^n)} \le \exp\left[-\lambda\epsilon + \frac{\lambda^2}{8} \sum_{k=1}^n c_k^2\right].$$

Since $\lambda > 0$ is arbitrary, we conclude that

$$\ln \delta \le \inf_{\lambda \ge 0}\left[\frac{\lambda^2}{8} \sum_{k=1}^n c_k^2 - \lambda\epsilon\right] = -\frac{2\epsilon^2}{\sum_{k=1}^n c_k^2}.$$

This implies the theorem. $\qquad\qquad\qquad\qquad\qquad\qquad\qquad\qquad\qquad\qquad\square$

McDiarmid's inequality is referred to as *concentration inequality* because it states that the sample dependent quantity $f(X_1, \ldots, X_n)$ does not deviate significantly from its expectation $\mathbb{E}f(X_1, \ldots, X_n)$.

Note that if we take

$$f(x_1, \ldots, x_n) = \frac{1}{n}\sum_{i=1}^{n} x_i,$$

and assume that $x_i \in [0, 1]$, then we can take $c_i = 1/n$, which implies the additive Chernoff bound in Theorem 2.16. Therefore, McDiarmid's inequality is a generalization of the additive Chernoff bound.

We can apply Theorem 6.16 to empirical processes and obtain a uniform convergence result. In order to handle offset Rademacher complexity, we introduce the sensitivity of $h(w, \mathcal{S}_n)$ as follows, which measures the maximum change when the data $\mathcal{S}_n$ is modified by no more than one element. Note that the sensitivity is needed in order to apply McDiarmid's inequality.

Definition 6.17 Given a function $h(w, \mathcal{S}_n)$, we define

$$\Delta_n h(w) = \sup\{n \cdot |h(w, \mathcal{S}_n) - h(w, \mathcal{S}'_n)| : |\mathcal{S}_n \cap \mathcal{S}'_n| = n - 1\}.$$

Example 6.18 If the offset function $h(w, \mathcal{S}_n)$ has the decomposition (6.3), then

$$\Delta_n h(w) \leq \sup_{z, z'}[h_1(w, z) - h_1(w, z')].$$

In particular, if $h(w, \mathcal{S}_n) = h_0(w)$, then

$$\Delta_n h(w) = 0.$$

We have the following uniform convergence result using Rademacher complexity.

Corollary 6.19 *Assume that for some $M \geq 0$,*

$$\sup_{w \in \Omega}\left[\sup_{z, z'}[\phi(w, z) - \phi(w, z')] + \Delta_n h(w)\right] \leq M.$$

Then with probability at least $1 - \delta$, for all $w \in \Omega$,

$$\phi(w, \mathcal{D}) \leq \phi(w, \mathcal{S}_n) + h(w, \mathcal{S}_n) + \epsilon_n^h(\mathcal{G}, \mathcal{D}) + M\sqrt{\frac{\ln(1/\delta)}{2n}}.$$

Moreover, assume that the decomposition (6.3) holds, then with probability at least $1 - \delta$, for all $w \in \Omega$,

$$\phi(w, \mathcal{D}) \leq \phi(w, \mathcal{S}_n) + h(w, \mathcal{S}_n) + 2R_n^h(\mathcal{G}, \mathcal{D}) + M\sqrt{\frac{\ln(1/\delta)}{2n}}.$$

Proof Consider $\mathcal{S}_n = \{Z_1, \ldots, Z_n\}$ and $\mathcal{S}'_n = \{Z_1, \ldots, Z_{i-1}, Z'_i, Z_{i+1}, \ldots, Z_n\}$. Let $f(\mathcal{S}_n) = \sup_{w \in \Omega}[\phi(w, \mathcal{D}) - \phi(w, \mathcal{S}_n) - h(w, \mathcal{S}_n)]$. For simplicity, we assume that the sup can be achieved at $\hat{w}$ as

$$\hat{w} = \arg\max_{w \in \Omega}[\phi(w, \mathcal{D}) - \phi(w, \mathcal{S}_n) - h(w, \mathcal{S}_n)].$$

Then

$$\begin{aligned}
f(\mathcal{S}_n) &- f(\mathcal{S}'_n) \\
&= [\phi(\hat{w}, \mathcal{D}) - \phi(\hat{w}, \mathcal{S}_n) - h(\hat{w}, \mathcal{S}_n)] - \sup_{w \in \Omega}[\phi(w, \mathcal{D}) - \phi(w, \mathcal{S}'_n) - h(w, \mathcal{S}'_n)] \\
&\leq [\phi(\hat{w}, \mathcal{D}) - \phi(\hat{w}, \mathcal{S}_n) - h(\hat{w}, \mathcal{S}_n)] - [\phi(\hat{w}, \mathcal{D}) - \phi(\hat{w}, \mathcal{S}'_n) - h(\hat{w}, \mathcal{S}'_n)] \\
&\leq \frac{1}{n}[\phi(\hat{w}, Z'_i) - \phi(\hat{w}, Z_i) + \Delta_n h(\hat{w})] \leq M/n.
\end{aligned}$$

Similarly, $f(\mathcal{S}'_n) - f(\mathcal{S}_n) \leq M/n$. Therefore we may take $c_i = M/n$ in Theorem 6.16, which implies the first desired result. The second bound follows from the estimate $\epsilon_n^h(\mathcal{G}, \mathcal{D}) \leq 2R_n^h(\mathcal{G}, \mathcal{D})$ of Theorem 6.14. $\square$

Example 6.20 If we use the standard Rademacher complexity, then $\Delta_n h(w) = 0$. Corollary 6.19 implies that

$$\phi(w, \mathcal{D}) \leq \phi(w, \mathcal{S}_n) + \epsilon_n(\mathcal{G}, \mathcal{D}) + M\sqrt{\frac{\ln(1/\delta)}{2n}}$$

$$\leq \phi(w, \mathcal{S}_n) + 2R_n(\mathcal{G}, \mathcal{D}) + M\sqrt{\frac{\ln(1/\delta)}{2n}},$$

where $M = \sup_{w \in \Omega} \sup_{z, z'}[\phi(w, z) - \phi(w, z')]$.

Corollary 6.19 implies the following result.

Corollary 6.21 *Assume that for some $M \geq 0$,*

$$\sup_{w \in \Omega}\left[\sup_{z, z'}[\phi(w, z) - \phi(w, z')] + \Delta_n h(w)\right] \leq M.$$

Then the approximate ERM method (6.1) *satisfies the following oracle inequality. With probability at least $1 - \delta - \delta'$,*

$$\phi(\hat{w}, \mathcal{D}) \leq \inf_{w \in \Omega}\left[\phi(w, \mathcal{D}) + \mathbb{E}_{\mathcal{S}_n} h(w, \mathcal{S}_n) + \Delta_n h(w)\sqrt{\frac{\ln(1/\delta')}{2n}}\right]$$

$$+ \epsilon' + \epsilon_n^h(\mathcal{G}, \mathcal{D}) + 2M\sqrt{\frac{\ln(2/\delta)}{2n}}.$$

If $h(\cdot)$ has the decomposition (6.3), *then*

$$\phi(\hat{w}, \mathcal{D}) \leq \inf_{w \in \Omega}\left[\phi(w, \mathcal{D}) + \mathbb{E}_{\mathcal{S}_n} h(w, \mathcal{S}_n) + \Delta_n h(w)\sqrt{\frac{\ln(1/\delta')}{2n}}\right]$$

$$+ \epsilon' + 2R_n^h(\mathcal{G}, \mathcal{D}) + 2M\sqrt{\frac{\ln(2/\delta)}{2n}}.$$

Proof Given any $w \in \Omega$, from the Chernoff bound, we know that with probability $1 - \delta/2$,

$$\phi(w, \mathcal{S}_n) \leq \phi(w, \mathcal{D}) + M\sqrt{\frac{\ln(2/\delta)}{2n}}. \tag{6.5}$$

Moreover, from McDiarmid's inequality, we know that with probability $1 - \delta'$,

$$h(w, \mathcal{S}_n) \leq \mathbb{E}_{\mathcal{S}_n} h(w, \mathcal{S}_n) + \Delta_n h(w)\sqrt{\frac{\ln(1/\delta')}{2n}}. \tag{6.6}$$

Taking the union bound with the inequality of Corollary 6.19 at $\delta/2$, we obtain at probability $1 - \delta - \delta'$,

$$\phi(\hat{w}, \mathcal{D}) \leq \phi(\hat{w}, \mathcal{S}_n) + h(\hat{w}, \mathcal{S}_n) + \epsilon_n^h(\mathcal{G}, \mathcal{D}) + M\sqrt{\frac{\ln(2/\delta)}{2n}}$$

$$\leq \phi(w, \mathcal{S}_n) + h(w, \mathcal{S}_n) + \epsilon' + \epsilon_n^h(\mathcal{G}, \mathcal{D}) + M\sqrt{\frac{\ln(2/\delta)}{2n}}$$

$$\leq \phi(w, \mathcal{D}) + h(w, \mathcal{S}_n) + \epsilon' + \epsilon_n^h(\mathcal{G}, \mathcal{D}) + 2M\sqrt{\frac{\ln(2/\delta)}{2n}}$$

$$\leq \phi(w, \mathcal{D}) + \mathbb{E}_{\mathcal{S}_n} h(w, \mathcal{S}_n) + \Delta_n h(w)\sqrt{\frac{\ln(1/\delta')}{2n}}$$

$$+ \epsilon' + \epsilon_n^h(\mathcal{G}, \mathcal{D}) + 2M\sqrt{\frac{\ln(2/\delta)}{2n}}.$$

In this derivation, the first inequality used Corollary 6.19. The second inequality used (6.1). The third inequality used (6.5). The last inequality used (6.6). This proves the first desired bound. The second desired bound employs Theorem 6.14. $\square$

Example 6.22 If we use standard Rademacher complexity, then $\Delta_n h(w) = 0$. Corollary 6.21 implies that the approximate ERM method (6.1) satisfies the following oracle inequality. With probability at least $1 - \delta$,

$$\phi(\hat{w}, \mathcal{D}) \leq \inf_{w \in \Omega} \phi(w, \mathcal{D}) + \epsilon' + \epsilon_n(\mathcal{G}, \mathcal{D}) + 2M\sqrt{\frac{\ln(2/\delta)}{2n}}$$

$$\leq \inf_{w \in \Omega} \phi(w, \mathcal{D}) + \epsilon' + 2R_n(\mathcal{G}, \mathcal{D}) + 2M\sqrt{\frac{\ln(2/\delta)}{2n}},$$

where $M = \sup_{w \in \Omega} \sup_{z, z'} [\phi(w, z) - \phi(w, z')]$.

The Rademacher complexity analysis (together with McDiarmid's inequality) is convenient to apply. Therefore we will focus on this analysis in later chapters.

However, one drawback of the Rademacher complexity analysis is that it only leads to convergence rates of no better than $O(1/\sqrt{n})$. In order to prove faster convergence rate, we will have to reply on more sophisticated analysis, referred to as *local Rademacher complexity analysis*, which we will discuss in Section 6.5.

6.4 Estimating Rademacher Complexity

This section provides some useful results to estimate Rademacher complexity. We mainly focus on the standard Rademacher complexity. For a finite function class, we have the following simple estimate.

Theorem 6.23 *If $\mathcal{G}$ is a finite function class with $|\mathcal{G}| = N$, then*

$$R(\mathcal{G}, \mathcal{S}_n) \leq \sup_{g \in \mathcal{G}} \|g\|_{L_2(\mathcal{S}_n)} \cdot \sqrt{\frac{2 \ln N}{n}}.$$

If moreover, for all $g \in \mathcal{G}$, $g(z) \in [0, 1]$. Consider the offset decomposition (6.3), and let $h_0(g) = 0$, and $h_1(g, \mathcal{S}_n) = (\gamma/n) \sum_{i=1}^n g(Z_i)$. Then we have

$$R^h(\mathcal{G}, \mathcal{S}_n) \leq \frac{(1 + 0.5\gamma)^2 \ln N}{\gamma n}.$$

Proof Let $B = \sup_{g \in \mathcal{G}} \|g\|_{L_2(\mathcal{S}_n)}$. Then we have for all $\lambda > 0$,

$$R(\mathcal{G}, \mathcal{S}_n) = \mathbb{E}_\sigma \sup_{g \in \mathcal{G}} \frac{1}{n} \sum_{i=1}^n \sigma_i g(Z_i)$$

$$\overset{(a)}{\leq} \mathbb{E}_\sigma \frac{1}{\lambda n} \ln \sum_{g \in \mathcal{G}} \exp\left[\lambda \sum_{i=1}^n \sigma_i g(Z_i)\right]$$

$$\overset{(b)}{\leq} \frac{1}{\lambda n} \ln \mathbb{E}_\sigma \sum_{g \in \mathcal{G}} \exp\left[\lambda \sum_{i=1}^n \sigma_i g(Z_i)\right]$$

$$= \frac{1}{\lambda n} \ln \sum_{g \in \mathcal{G}} \prod_{i=1}^n \mathbb{E}_{\sigma_i} \exp\left[\lambda \sigma_i g(Z_i)\right]$$

$$\overset{(c)}{\leq} \frac{1}{\lambda n} \ln \sum_{g \in \mathcal{G}} \prod_{i=1}^n \exp[\lambda^2 g(Z_i)^2/2] \leq \frac{1}{\lambda n} \ln N \exp[\lambda^2 n B^2/2].$$

In (a), we used soft-max to bound the max operator. In (b), we used Jensen's inequality and the concavity of logarithm. In (c), we used the moment generating function for bounded random variables (see Example 2.14). Now we can obtain the first desired bound by optimizing over $\lambda > 0$.

For the second desired bound, we can obtain by duplicating the previous steps up to step (c) to obtain

$$R^h(\mathcal{G}, \mathcal{S}_n) = \mathbb{E}_\sigma \sup_{g \in \mathcal{G}} \frac{1}{n} \sum_{i=1}^n [\sigma_i(1 + 0.5\gamma)g(Z_i) - 0.5\gamma g(Z_i)]$$

$$\leq \frac{1}{\lambda n} \ln \sum_{g \in \mathcal{G}} \exp\left[\sum_{i=1}^n [\lambda^2(1 + 0.5\gamma)^2 g(Z_i)^2/2 - 0.5\lambda\gamma g(Z_i)]\right].$$

Now set $\lambda = \gamma/(1 + 0.5\gamma)^2$, and we obtain $R^h(\mathcal{G}, \mathcal{S}_n) \leq \frac{1}{\lambda n} \ln \sum_{g \in \mathcal{G}} 1$, which implies the second bound. $\qquad\square$

Example 6.24 Consider $\phi(w, Z) \in [0, 1]$ and $|\mathcal{G}| = N$, with probability $1 - \delta$. We have the following uniform convergence results for all w. If we use the union of Chernoff bound (covering number) method, then

$$\phi(w, \mathcal{D}) \leq \phi(w, \mathcal{S}_n) + \sqrt{\frac{\ln(N/\delta)}{2n}},$$

which implies that

$$\phi(w, \mathcal{D}) \leq \phi(w, \mathcal{S}_n) + \sqrt{\frac{\ln(N)}{2n}} + \sqrt{\frac{\ln(1/\delta)}{2n}}.$$

If we use the Rademacher complexity bound, then we can obtain from Corollary 6.19 (with the Rademacher complexity estimate from Theorem 6.23),

$$\phi(w, \mathcal{D}) \leq \phi(w, \mathcal{S}_n) + 4\sqrt{\frac{\ln(N)}{2n}} + \sqrt{\frac{\ln(1/\delta)}{2n}},$$

which leads to a similar result. We may also obtain multiplicative bound using offset Rademacher complexity from Corollary 6.19 (with offset Rademacher complexity estimate from Theorem 6.23 with $h(w, \mathcal{S}_n) = \gamma\phi(w, \mathcal{S}_n)$) as follows:

$$\phi(w, \mathcal{D}) \leq (1 + \gamma)\phi(w, \mathcal{S}_n) + \frac{2(1 + 0.5\gamma)^2 \ln N}{\gamma n} + (1 + \gamma)\sqrt{\frac{\ln(1/\delta)}{2n}}.$$

While the expected uniform convergence has $O(1/n)$ rate, the concentration term has a slower rate of $O(1/\sqrt{n})$ due to the use of McDiarmid's concentration. This can be addressed using localized analysis in Section 6.5.

The following result shows that Rademacher complexity can be estimated from the empirical L_2 covering number using the chaining technique. The result is expressed in Dudley's entropy integral. The constant can be improved using packing number (see Exercise 6.4).

Theorem 6.25 *We have*

$$R(\mathcal{G}, \mathcal{S}_n) \leq \inf_{\epsilon \geq 0} \left[4\epsilon + 12 \int_\epsilon^\infty \sqrt{\frac{\ln N(\epsilon', \mathcal{G}, L_2(\mathcal{S}_n))}{n}} d\epsilon' \right].$$

Proof Let $B = \sup_{g \in \mathcal{G}} \|g\|_{L_2(\mathcal{S}_n)}$, and let $\epsilon_\ell = 2^{-\ell}B$ for $\ell = 0, 1, \dots$. Let $\mathcal{G}_\ell$ be an ϵ_ℓ cover of $\mathcal{G}$ with metric $L_2(\mathcal{S}_n)$, and $N_\ell = |\mathcal{G}_\ell| = N(\epsilon_\ell, \mathcal{G}, L_2(\mathcal{S}_n))$. We may let $\mathcal{G}_0 = \{0\}$ at scale $\epsilon_0 = B$.

For each $g \in \mathcal{G}$, we consider $g_\ell(g) \in \mathcal{G}_\ell$ so that $\|g - g_\ell(g)\|_{L_2(\mathcal{S}_n)} \leq \epsilon_\ell$. The key idea in chaining is to rewrite $g \in \mathcal{G}$ using the following multi-scale decomposition:

$$g = (g - g_L(g)) + \sum_{\ell=1}^L (g_\ell(g) - g_{\ell-1}(g)).$$

We also have

$$\|g_\ell(g) - g_{\ell-1}(g)\|_{L_2(\mathcal{S}_n)} \leq \|g_\ell(g) - g\|_{L_2(\mathcal{S}_n)} + \|g_{\ell-1}(g) - g\|_{L_2(\mathcal{S}_n)} \leq 3\epsilon_\ell. \quad (6.7)$$

The number of distinct $g_\ell(g) - g_{\ell-1}(g)$ is no more than $N_\ell N_{\ell-1}$. It implies that

$$R(\mathcal{G}, \mathcal{S}_n) = \mathbb{E}_\sigma \sup_{g \in \mathcal{G}} \frac{1}{n} \sum_{i=1}^n \sigma_i \left[(g - g_L(g))(Z_i) + \sum_{\ell=1}^L (g_\ell(g) - g_{\ell-1}(g))(Z_i) \right]$$

$$\leq \mathbb{E}_\sigma \sup_{g \in \mathcal{G}} \frac{1}{n} \sum_{i=1}^n \sigma_i (g - g_L(g))(Z_i) + \sum_{\ell=1}^L \mathbb{E}_\sigma \sup_{g \in \mathcal{G}} \frac{1}{n} \sum_{i=1}^n \sigma_i (g_\ell(g) - g_{\ell-1}(g))(Z_i)$$

$$\stackrel{(a)}{\leq} \epsilon_L + \sum_{\ell=1}^L \sup_{g \in \mathcal{G}} \| g_\ell(g) - g_{\ell-1}(g) \|_{L_2(\mathcal{S}_n)} \sqrt{\frac{2 \ln[N_\ell N_{\ell-1}]}{n}}$$

$$\stackrel{(b)}{\leq} \epsilon_L + 3 \sum_{\ell=1}^L \epsilon_\ell \sqrt{\frac{2 \ln[N_\ell N_{\ell-1}]}{n}}$$

$$\leq \epsilon_L + 12 \sum_{\ell=1}^L (\epsilon_\ell - \epsilon_{\ell+1}) \sqrt{\frac{\ln[N_\ell]}{n}}$$

$$\leq \epsilon_L + 12 \int_{\epsilon_L/2}^\infty \sqrt{\frac{\ln N(\epsilon', \mathcal{G}, L_2(\mathcal{S}_n))}{n}} \, d\epsilon'.$$

The derivation of (a) used Theorem 6.23, and the derivation of (b) used (6.7). The next two inequalities used $N(\epsilon, \mathcal{G}, L_2(\mathcal{S}_n)$ as a nonincreasing function of ϵ. Now given any $\epsilon > 0$, we can choose ϵ_L so that $\epsilon \in [\epsilon_L/4, \epsilon_L/2]$. This leads to the desired result.   □

Example 6.26   From Corollary 5.7, we know that if a binary-valued function class $\mathcal{G}$ (or a VC subgraph class with values in $[0, 1]$) has VC dimension d, then

$$\ln N_2(\epsilon, \mathcal{G}, n) \leq 1 + \ln(d + 1) + d \ln(2e/\epsilon^2).$$

Since $N_2(0.5, \mathcal{G}, n) = 1$, we have

$$12 \int_0^\infty \sqrt{\ln N_2(\epsilon, \mathcal{G}, n)} d\epsilon \leq 12 \int_0^{0.5} \sqrt{1 + \ln(d + 1) + d \ln(2e/\epsilon^2)} d\epsilon \leq 16\sqrt{d}.$$

It follows that

$$R(\mathcal{G}, \mathcal{S}_n) \leq \frac{16\sqrt{d}}{\sqrt{n}}.$$

The constant is not optimal, and in fact a better constant can be obtained using the packing number (see Example 6.4). The result implies the following uniform convergence result: with probability at least $1 - \delta$, for all $w \in \Omega$,

$$\phi(w, \mathcal{D}) \leq \phi(w, \mathcal{S}_n) + \frac{32\sqrt{d}}{\sqrt{n}} + \sqrt{\frac{\ln(1/\delta)}{2n}}.$$

This bound removes a $\ln n$ factor from the additive uniform convergence bound in Theorem 4.17.

Example 6.27 If $\ln N_2(\epsilon, \mathcal{G}, n) \leq 1/\epsilon^q$ for $q \in (0, 2)$, then

$$\int_0^\infty \sqrt{\ln N_2(\epsilon, \mathcal{G}, n)} d\epsilon < \infty.$$

Therefore there exists $C > 0$ such that

$$R(\mathcal{G}, \mathcal{S}_n) \leq \frac{C}{\sqrt{n}}.$$

If $\ln N_2(\epsilon, \mathcal{G}, n) \leq 1/\epsilon^q$ for $q > 2$, then

$$R(\mathcal{G}, \mathcal{S}_n) \leq O\left(\inf_{\epsilon > 0}\left(\epsilon + \frac{\epsilon^{1-q/2}}{\sqrt{n}}\right)\right) = O(n^{-1/q}).$$

This implies a convergence slower than $1/\sqrt{n}$.

One convenient fact about Rademacher average is the following result. Let $\{\phi_i\}$ be a set of functions, each characterized by a Lipschitz constant γ_i. Then the result implies a bound on the Rademacher complexity of the function composition $\phi \circ f$.

Theorem 6.28 *Let $\{\phi_i\}_{i=1}^n$ be functions with Lipschitz constants $\{\gamma_i\}_{i=1}^n$ respectively; that is, $\forall i \in [n]$:*

$$|\phi_i(\theta) - \phi_i(\theta')| \leq \gamma_i|\theta - \theta'|.$$

Then for any real-valued function $h \colon \mathcal{F} \times \mathcal{Z}^n \to \mathbb{R}$, and $\mathcal{S}_n = \{Z_1, \ldots, Z_n\} \subset \mathcal{Z}^n$, we have

$$\mathbb{E}_\sigma \sup_{f \in \mathcal{F}}\left[\sum_{i=1}^n \sigma_i \phi_i(f(Z_i)) - h(f, \mathcal{S}_n)\right] \leq \mathbb{E}_\sigma \sup_{f \in \mathcal{F}}\left[\sum_{i=1}^n \sigma_i \gamma_i f(Z_i) - h(f, \mathcal{S}_n)\right].$$

Proof The result is a direct consequence of the Lemma 6.29, where we simply set $c(w) = -h(w, \mathcal{S}_n)$, $g_i(w) = \phi_i(f(Z_i))$, and $\tilde{g}_i(w) = \gamma_i f(Z_i)$. $\qquad\square$

Lemma 6.29 (Rademacher Comparison Lemma) *Let $\{g_i(w)\}$ and $\{\tilde{g}_i(w)\}$ be sets of functions defined for all w in some domain Ω. If for all i, w, w',*

$$|g_i(w) - g_i(w')| \leq |\tilde{g}_i(w) - \tilde{g}_i(w')|,$$

then for any function $c(w)$,

$$\mathbb{E}_\sigma \sup_{w \in \Omega}\left[c(w) + \sum_{i=1}^n \sigma_i g_i(w)\right] \leq \mathbb{E}_\sigma \sup_{w \in \Omega}\left[c(w) + \sum_{i=1}^n \sigma_i \tilde{g}_i(w)\right].$$

Proof We prove this result by induction. The result holds for $n = 0$. Assume that the result holds for $n = k$, then when $n = k + 1$, we have

$$\mathbb{E}_{\sigma_1,\ldots,\sigma_{k+1}} \sup_w \left[c(w) + \sum_{i=1}^{k+1} \sigma_i g_i(w) \right]$$

$$= \mathbb{E}_{\sigma_1,\ldots,\sigma_k} \sup_{w_1,w_2} \left[\frac{c(w_1) + c(w_2)}{2} + \sum_{i=1}^{k} \sigma_i \frac{g_i(w_1) + g_i(w_2)}{2} \right.$$
$$\left. + \frac{g_{k+1}(w_1) - g_{k+1}(w_2)}{2} \right]$$

$$= \mathbb{E}_{\sigma_1,\ldots,\sigma_k} \sup_{w_1,w_2} \left[\frac{c(w_1) + c(w_2)}{2} + \sum_{i=1}^{k} \sigma_i \frac{g_i(w_1) + g_i(w_2)}{2} \right.$$
$$\left. + \frac{|g_{k+1}(w_1) - g_{k+1}(w_2)|}{2} \right]$$

$$\leq \mathbb{E}_{\sigma_1,\ldots,\sigma_k} \sup_{w_1,w_2} \left[\frac{c(w_1) + c(w_2)}{2} + \sum_{i=1}^{k} \sigma_i \frac{g_i(w_1) + g_i(w_2)}{2} \right.$$
$$\left. + \frac{|\tilde{g}_{k+1}(w_1) - \tilde{g}_{k+1}(w_2)|}{2} \right]$$

$$= \mathbb{E}_{\sigma_1,\ldots,\sigma_k} \sup_{w_1,w_2} \left[\frac{c(w_1) + c(w_2)}{2} + \sum_{i=1}^{k} \sigma_i \frac{g_i(w_1) + g_i(w_2)}{2} \right.$$
$$\left. + \frac{\tilde{g}_{k+1}(w_1) - \tilde{g}_{k+1}(w_2)}{2} \right]$$

$$= \mathbb{E}_{\sigma_1,\ldots,\sigma_k} \mathbb{E}_{\sigma_{k+1}} \sup_w \left[c(w) + \sigma_{k+1} \tilde{g}_{k+1}(w) + \sum_{i=1}^{k} \sigma_i g_i(w) \right]$$

$$\leq \mathbb{E}_{\sigma_1,\ldots,\sigma_k} \mathbb{E}_{\sigma_{k+1}} \sup_w \left[c(w) + \sigma_{k+1} \tilde{g}_{k+1}(w) + \sum_{i=1}^{k} \sigma_i \tilde{g}_i(w) \right].$$

The last inequality follows from the induction hypothesis. $\qquad\square$

The following example shows an application of Theorem 6.28.

Example 6.30 Consider binary classification with $y \in \{\pm 1\}$, and let $\mathcal{F} = \{f(w,x) = w^\top \psi(x)\}$ be the class of linear classifiers. Consider the smoothed classification loss function $L(f(x), y) = \min(1, \max(0, 1 - \gamma f(x)y))$ for some $\gamma > 0$, as in Figure 6.1. Let $\mathcal{G} = \{L(f(w,x), y)\}$. Then $L(f, y)$ is γ Lipschitz in f. Consider the regularizer in Example 6.12 with $h(w) = h_0(w) = 0.5\lambda\|w\|_2^2$ in (6.3). We obtain from Theorem 6.28,

$$R^h(\mathcal{G}, \mathcal{S}_n) \leq \gamma R^{(h/\gamma)}(\mathcal{F}, \mathcal{S}_n),$$

which implies that

$$R^h(\mathcal{G}, \mathcal{S}_n) \leq \frac{\gamma^2}{\lambda n^2} \sum_{i=1}^{n} \|\psi(X_i)\|_2^2.$$

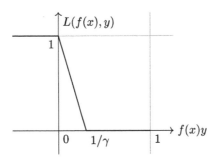

Figure 6.1 Smoothed classification loss

It follows that

$$R_n^h(\mathcal{G}, \mathcal{D}) \leq \frac{\gamma^2}{\lambda n} \mathbb{E}_{X \sim \mathcal{D}} \|\psi(X)\|_2^2.$$

The following result is a direct consequence of Theorem 6.28 and Corollary 6.21.

Theorem 6.31 *Consider real-valued function class $\mathcal{F} = \{f(w, \cdot) : w \in \Omega\}$, and $\mathcal{G} = \{\phi(w, z) = L(f(w, x), y) : w \in \Omega, z = (x, y)\}$. Assume that we have the decomposition in (6.3) with $h_1(w, \mathcal{S}_n) = 0$. Assume that*

$$\sup_{(x,y),(x',y')} |L(f(w, x), y) - L(f(w, x'), y')| \leq M,$$

and $L(f, y)$ is γ-Lipschitz in f:

$$|L(f, y) - L(f', y)| \leq \gamma |f - f'|.$$

Let $\mathcal{S}_n$ be n iid samples from $\mathcal{D}$. With probability at least $1 - \delta$, for all $w \in \Omega$,

$$\mathbb{E}_{\mathcal{D}} L(f(w, X), Y) \leq \frac{1}{n} \sum_{i=1}^{n} L(f(w, X_i), Y_i) + h_0(w)$$

$$+ 2\gamma R_n^{h/\gamma}(\mathcal{F}, \mathcal{D}) + M \sqrt{\frac{\ln(1/\delta)}{2n}}.$$

Moreover, for the approximate regularized ERM method (6.1) with $\phi(w, z) = L(f(w, x), y)$, we have with probability at least $1 - \delta$,

$$\mathbb{E}_{\mathcal{D}} L(f(\hat{w}, X), Y) \leq \inf_{w \in \Omega} \left[\mathbb{E}_{\mathcal{D}} L(f(w, X), Y) + h_0(w) \right]$$

$$+ \epsilon' + 2\gamma R_n^{h/\gamma}(\mathcal{F}, \mathcal{D}) + M \sqrt{\frac{2 \ln(2/\delta)}{n}}.$$

We have the following example for the smoothed classification loss.

Example 6.32 Consider the smoothed classification loss in Example 6.30 with

$$h(w, \mathcal{S}_n) = g(w) = \frac{\lambda}{2} \|w\|_2^2.$$

For the approximate regularized ERM method in (6.1), we have with probability at least $1 - \delta$,

$$\mathbb{E}_{\mathcal{D}} L(f(\hat{w}, X), Y) \leq \inf_{w \in \Omega} \left[\mathbb{E}_{\mathcal{D}} L(f(w, X), Y) + \frac{\lambda}{2} \|w\|_2^2 \right] + \epsilon'$$
$$+ \frac{2\gamma^2}{\lambda n} \mathbb{E}_{X \sim \mathcal{D}} \|\psi(X)\|_2^2 + M \sqrt{\frac{2 \ln(2/\delta)}{n}}.$$

6.5 Local Rademacher Complexity Analysis

The technique to prove McDiarmid's inequality is called the *Martingale method*, and it can derive concentration inequalities with convergence rates of $O(1/\sqrt{n})$. As shown in Example 6.24, it is possible to obtain $O(1/n)$ expected convergence result using offset Rademacher complexity. However, the rate with respect to concentration is still $1/\sqrt{n}$. In order to improve the analysis, we need to establish concentration inequalities with faster convergence rates. It is possible to prove faster convergence rates with the Martingale method by deriving Bernstein-style concentration inequalities. However, more refined forms of Bernstein-style concentration inequalities are needed to analyze empirical processes, and those refined forms are referred to as *Talagrand's concentration inequality* (Talagrand, 1995, 1996b). We state the following version of Talagrand's inequality by Bousquet (2002).

Theorem 6.33 (Bousquet, 2002) *Consider iid random variables $(Z_1, \ldots, Z_n) \sim \mathcal{D}^n$. Let ζ be a real-valued function of $(Z_1, \ldots, Z_n)$. Moreover, for each $k \in [n]$, let ζ_k be a real-valued function of $(Z_1, \ldots, Z_{k-1}, Z_{k+1}, \ldots, Z_n)$ so that*

$$\sum_{k=1}^{n} [\zeta - \zeta_k] \leq \zeta.$$

Assume that for each k, there exists a function ζ_k' of $(Z_1, \ldots, Z_n)$ such that

$$\zeta_k' \leq \zeta - \zeta_k \leq M, \quad \mathbb{E}_{Z_k} \zeta_k' \geq 0, \quad \zeta_k' \leq uM.$$

We have for all $t \geq 0$,

$$\Pr \left[\zeta \geq \mathbb{E}\zeta + \sqrt{2((1+u)M \mathbb{E}\zeta + n\sigma^2)t} + \frac{tM}{3} \right] \leq e^{-t},$$

where $\sigma^2 \geq n^{-1} \sum_{k=1}^{n} \mathbb{E}_{Z_k} (\zeta_k')^2$.

Theorem 6.33 is a Bernstein-style concentration inequality, which can be compared to the additive Chernoff-style concentration inequality of Theorem 6.16. We can apply Theorem 6.33 to empirical processes, and obtain the following counterpart of Corollary 6.19. A similar (two-sided) uniform convergence result can be found in Bousquet (2002).

Corollary 6.34 *Consider a real-valued function class $\mathcal{F} = \{f(z) : \mathcal{Z} \to \mathbb{R}\}$. Let $\mathcal{D}$ be a distribution on $\mathcal{Z}$. Assume that there exists $M, \sigma > 0$, so that $\forall f \in \mathcal{F}$,*

$\sigma^2 \geq \mathrm{Var}_{Z \sim \mathcal{D}}[f(Z)]$, and $\sup_{z' \in \mathcal{Z}}[\mathbb{E}_{Z \sim \mathcal{D}} f(Z) - f(z')] \leq M$. Let $\mathcal{S}_n = \{Z_1, \ldots, Z_n\}$ be n independent random variables from $\mathcal{D}$. Then with probability at least $1 - \delta$ over $\mathcal{S}_n$, for all $f \in \mathcal{F}$,

$$\mathbb{E}_{Z \sim \mathcal{D}} f(Z) - \frac{1}{n} \sum_{i=1}^{n} f(Z_i)$$

$$\leq \epsilon_n(\mathcal{F}, \mathcal{D}) + \sqrt{\frac{(4M\epsilon_n(\mathcal{F}, \mathcal{D}) + 2\sigma^2) \ln(1/\delta)}{n}} + \frac{M \ln(1/\delta)}{3n}$$

$$\leq 2\epsilon_n(\mathcal{F}, \mathcal{D}) + \sqrt{\frac{2\sigma^2 \ln(1/\delta)}{n}} + \frac{4M \ln(1/\delta)}{3n},$$

where $\epsilon_n(\mathcal{F}, \mathcal{D})$ is Definition 6.1.

Proof Let

$$\zeta = \sup_{f \in \mathcal{F}} \left[n\mathbb{E}_{Z \sim \mathcal{D}} f(Z) - \sum_{i=1}^{n} f(Z_n) \right],$$

and

$$\zeta_k = \sup_{f \in \mathcal{F}} \left[(n-1)\mathbb{E}_{Z \sim \mathcal{D}} f(Z) - \sum_{i \neq k} f(Z_i) \right].$$

Assume that ζ_k is achieved at f_k, and ζ at f_0. Then

$$\sum_{k=1}^{n} [\zeta - \zeta_k] \leq \sum_{k=1}^{n} [\mathbb{E}_{Z \sim \mathcal{D}} f_0(Z) - f_0(Z_k)] = \zeta.$$

Let

$$\zeta_k' = \left[n\mathbb{E}_{Z \sim \mathcal{D}} f_k(Z) - \sum_{i=1}^{n} f_k(Z_i) \right] - \zeta_k,$$

then

$$\zeta_k' \leq \zeta - \zeta_k \leq [\mathbb{E}_Z f_0(Z) - f_0(Z_k)] \leq M.$$

Moreover, since Z_k is independent of f_k, we have

$$\mathbb{E}_{Z_k} \zeta_k' = \mathbb{E}_{Z_k} [\mathbb{E}_Z f_k(Z) - f_k(Z_k)] = 0,$$
$$\mathbb{E}_{Z_k} (\zeta_k')^2 = \mathbb{E}_{Z_k} [\mathbb{E}_Z f_k(Z) - f_k(Z_k)]^2 \leq \sigma^2.$$

By taking $u = 1$ in Theorem 6.33, we obtain the first desired bound. The second bound is a consequence of

$$\sqrt{(4M\epsilon_n(\mathcal{F}, \mathcal{D}) + 2\sigma^2) \ln(1/\delta)/n}$$

$$\leq \sqrt{4M\epsilon_n(\mathcal{F}, \mathcal{D}) \ln(1/\delta)/n} + \sqrt{2\sigma^2 \ln(1/\delta)/n}$$

$$\leq \epsilon_n(\mathcal{F}, \mathcal{D}) + M \ln(1/\delta)/n + \sqrt{2\sigma^2 \ln(1/\delta)/n}.$$

The first inequality used $\sqrt{a + b} \leq \sqrt{a} + \sqrt{b}$, and the second inequality used $\sqrt{4ab} \leq a + b$. □

To illustrate its consequences, we introduce the following definition of rate function. In general, we expect the uniform convergence complexity $\epsilon_n(\mathcal{F}^h(r'/\alpha), \mathcal{D})$ to grow sublinearly in r' (see examples later), which implies that the rate function $\bar{r}$ is well defined (see Figure 6.2).

Definition 6.35 Given $\mathcal{D}$ and $\mathcal{F}$, and considering a localization function $h: \mathcal{F} \to \mathbb{R}$ such that $b_0 = \inf_{f \in \mathcal{F}} h(f) > -\infty$, define localized function class $\mathcal{F}^h(b) = \{f \in \mathcal{F} : h(f) \leq b\}$ for all $b > b_0$. For any $\alpha > 0$, the rate function with respect to localization h is defined as

$$\bar{r}_n^h(\alpha, \mathcal{F}, \mathcal{D}) = \sup \left\{ r : r \leq \inf_{r' > \max(r, \alpha b_0)} \epsilon_n \left(\mathcal{F}^h\left(r'/\alpha\right), \mathcal{D} \right) \right\}.$$

We note that the requirement of $r' > \alpha b_0$ in Definition 6.35 is only to make sure that $\mathcal{F}^h(r'/\alpha)$ is always non-empty, and thus $\epsilon_n(\mathcal{F}^h(r'/\alpha), \mathcal{D})$ is well defined.

Example 6.36 In Bartlett et al. (2005), the definition of the localization function is $h(f) = \mathbb{E}_{Z \sim \mathcal{D}}[f(Z)^2]$. The localized function class $\mathcal{F}(b, \mathcal{D})$ is $\{f \in \mathcal{F} : \mathbb{E}[f(Z)^2] \leq b\}$, with $b_0 \geq 0$.

In the analysis of ERM, it is natural to employ the same local function class as in Bartlett et al. (2005); the more general definition given in Definition 6.35 simplifies some calculations of $\bar{r}_n(\alpha, \mathcal{F}, \mathcal{D})$ using the offset uniform convergence complexity, as shown in Proposition 6.40. This leads to a result similar to Example 6.10, which employs offset uniform convergence.

Next we state the following simple property of the rate function.

Proposition 6.37 *The rate function in Definition 6.35 is always nonnegative.*

Proof Note that $\mathcal{F}^h(r'/\alpha) \neq \emptyset$ when $r' > \max(0, \alpha b_0)$. Since $\epsilon_n(\mathcal{F}^h(r'/\alpha), \mathcal{D})$ is always nonnegative, with $r = 0$, we have $r \leq \epsilon_n(\mathcal{F}^h(r'/\alpha), \mathcal{D})$ when $r' > \max(r, \alpha b_0)$. $\qquad \square$

The usefulness of rate function $\bar{r}$ in Definition 6.35 is based on the following result, which shows that ϵ_n can be upper bounded by this quantity.

Proposition 6.38 *For all $\alpha > 0$ and $b > \inf_{f \in \mathcal{F}} h(f)$, we have*

$$\epsilon_n \left(\mathcal{F}^h(b), \mathcal{D} \right) \leq \max \left(\bar{r}_n^h(\alpha, \mathcal{F}, \mathcal{D}), \alpha b \right).$$

Proof Note that $\mathcal{F}^h(b)$ is non-empty. Let $\hat{r} = \bar{r}_n^h(\alpha, \mathcal{F}, \mathcal{D})$. The definition implies that

$$\hat{r} \geq \epsilon_n \left(\mathcal{F}^h(\hat{r}/\alpha), \mathcal{D} \right).$$

If $b \leq \hat{r}/\alpha$, then

$$\epsilon_n(\mathcal{F}^h(b), \mathcal{D}) \leq \epsilon_n\left(\mathcal{F}^h(\hat{r}/\alpha), \mathcal{D}\right) \leq \hat{r} = \bar{r}_n^h(\alpha, \mathcal{F}, \mathcal{D}).$$

Otherwise, let $r' = \alpha b > \hat{r} = \bar{r}_n^h(\alpha, \mathcal{F}, \mathcal{D})$. By the definition of $\bar{r}_n^h(\alpha, \mathcal{F}, \mathcal{D})$, we have

$$\epsilon_n(\mathcal{F}^h(b), \mathcal{D}) = \epsilon_n\left(\mathcal{F}^h(r'/\alpha), \mathcal{D}\right) \leq r' = \alpha b.$$

By combining the two situations, we obtain the desired bound. $\qquad\square$

Example 6.39 Let $h(f) = \mathbb{E}_\mathcal{D}[f(Z)^2]$ and assume that $b_0 = \inf_{f \in \mathcal{F}} h(f) = 0$. If

$$\epsilon_n\left(\mathcal{F}^h(b), \mathcal{D}\right) \leq \frac{\tilde{c}_1}{\sqrt{n}} b^{q/2}$$

for some $0 < q < 1$, then we obtain

$$\bar{r}_n^h(\alpha, \mathcal{F}, \mathcal{D}) \leq \left(\frac{\alpha^{-q} \tilde{c}_1^2}{n}\right)^{1/(2-q)}.$$

As we will see, the convergence rate of ERM under variance condition is determined by $\bar{r}_n^h(\alpha, \mathcal{F}, \mathcal{D})$, and this leads to a rate of convergence faster than $O(1/\sqrt{n})$.

The following result shows that under the variance condition, the rate function can be estimated from the uniform convergence complexity with a properly defined offset function.

Proposition 6.40 *Let $\mathcal{F} = \{\phi(w, Z) \colon w \in \Omega\}$. Consider a localization function $h(w)$ and the corresponding offset function $h'(w, \mathcal{S}_n) = 0.5\alpha h(w)$. Then*

$$\bar{r}_n^h(\alpha, \mathcal{F}, \mathcal{D}) \leq \max\left(2\epsilon_n^{h'}(\mathcal{F}, \mathcal{D}), \alpha \inf_{w \in \Omega} h(w)\right).$$

Proof Let $b_0 = \inf_{w \in \Omega} h(w)$. Consider any $r \geq 0$ such that

$$r \leq \inf_{r' > \max(r, \alpha b_0)} \epsilon_n(\mathcal{F}^h(r'/\alpha), \mathcal{D}).$$

For any $\phi(w, \cdot) \in \mathcal{F}^h(r'/\alpha, \mathcal{D})$, we know by the definition of localized function class that

$$h'(w, \mathcal{S}_n) = 0.5\alpha h(w) \leq 0.5r'.$$

It follows that

$$\epsilon_n(\mathcal{F}^h(r'/\alpha), \mathcal{D}) \leq \epsilon_n^{h'}\left(\mathcal{F}^h(r'/\alpha), \mathcal{D}\right) + 0.5r' \leq \epsilon_n^{h'}(\mathcal{F}, \mathcal{D}) + 0.5r'.$$

This means that for all $r' > \max(r, \alpha b_0)$, the condition

$$r \leq \epsilon_n(\mathcal{F}^h(r'/\alpha), \mathcal{D})$$

implies that

$$r \leq \epsilon_n^{h'}(\mathcal{F}, \mathcal{D}) + 0.5r'.$$

Let $r' \to \max(r, \alpha b_0)$, and we obtain either $r \leq \alpha b_0$, or

$$r \leq \epsilon_n^{h'}(\mathcal{F}, \mathcal{D}) + 0.5r.$$

Therefore

$$r \leq \max\left(2\epsilon_n^{h'}(\mathcal{F}, \mathcal{D}), \alpha b_0\right).$$

This implies the desired bound.   □

By using the concept of rate function, we can obtain the following uniform convergence result from Corollary 6.34, where we assume that the localization function satisfies a variance condition similar to (3.13).

Theorem 6.41 *Consider $\mathcal{F}$, $\mathcal{D}$, and iid samples $\mathcal{S}_n = \{Z_1, \ldots, Z_n\} \sim \mathcal{D}$. Let $f(\mathcal{D}) = \mathbb{E}_{Z \sim \mathcal{D}}[f(Z)]$, and $f(\mathcal{S}_n) = n^{-1}\sum_{i=1}^n f(Z_i)$. Assume that for all $f \in \mathcal{F}$,*

$$\mathrm{Var}_{\mathcal{D}}[f(Z)] \leq c_0^2 + c_1 h(f)$$

for some $c_0, c_1, h(\cdot) \geq 0$. Assume also that $\mathcal{F}$ is bounded: $\sup_{z'}[f(\mathcal{D}) - f(z')] \leq M$ for all $f \in \mathcal{F}$. Then with probability at least $1 - \delta$ over $\mathcal{S}_n$, $\forall f \in \mathcal{F}$ and $\forall \alpha > 0$,

$$f(\mathcal{D}) \leq f(\mathcal{S}_n) + 5\alpha h(f) + 5r_0 + \sqrt{\frac{2c_0^2 \ln(1/\delta)}{n}} + \frac{(3c_1 + 4\alpha M)\ln(1/\delta)}{3\alpha n},$$

where

$$r_0 = \bar{r}_n^h(\alpha, \mathcal{F}, \mathcal{D}) + \alpha \inf_{f \in \mathcal{F}} h(f) + \sqrt{\frac{2c_0^2}{n}} + \frac{(3c_1 + 4\alpha M)}{3\alpha n}$$

$$\leq 2\epsilon_n^{h'}(\alpha, \mathcal{F}, \mathcal{D}) + 2\alpha \inf_{f \in \mathcal{F}} h(f) + \sqrt{\frac{2c_0^2}{n}} + \frac{(3c_1 + 4\alpha M)}{3\alpha n},$$

with $h'(f, \mathcal{S}_n) = 0.5\alpha h(f)$.

Proof The inequality for r_0 is a direct consequence of Proposition 6.40.

We will now use a peeling argument. For $\ell = 1, 2, \ldots$, let $r_\ell = \alpha^{-1}(1.5)^{\ell-1}r_0$. Define $\mathcal{F}_\ell = \{f \in \mathcal{F} : h(f) \leq r_\ell\}$. It follows that

$$\sup_{f \in \mathcal{F}_\ell} \mathrm{Var}_{\mathcal{D}}[f(Z)] \leq c_0^2 + c_1 h(f) \leq c_0^2 + c_1 r_\ell.$$

For each $\ell \geq 1$, let $\delta_\ell = 4\delta/((\ell + 3)(\ell + 4))$. We have with probability $1 - \delta_\ell$,

$\forall f \in \mathcal{F}_\ell$,

$$f(\mathcal{D}) - f(\mathcal{S}_n)$$

$$\leq 2\epsilon_n(\mathcal{F}_\ell, \mathcal{D}) + \sqrt{\frac{2(c_0^2 + c_1 r_\ell)\ln(1/\delta_\ell)}{n}} + \frac{4M\ln(1/\delta_\ell)}{3n}$$

$$\leq 2\bar{r}_n^h(\alpha, \mathcal{F}, \mathcal{D}) + 2\alpha r_\ell + \sqrt{\frac{2(c_0^2 + c_1 r_\ell)\ln(1/\delta_\ell)}{n}} + \frac{4M\ln(1/\delta_\ell)}{3n}$$

$$\leq 2\bar{r}_n^h(\alpha, \mathcal{F}, \mathcal{D}) + 2\alpha r_\ell + \sqrt{\frac{2c_0^2\ln(1/\delta_\ell)}{n}} + \sqrt{\frac{2c_1 r_\ell \ln(1/\delta_\ell)}{n}} + \frac{4M\ln(1/\delta_\ell)}{3n}$$

$$\leq 2\bar{r}_n^h(\alpha, \mathcal{F}, \mathcal{D}) + 2.5\alpha r_\ell + \sqrt{\frac{2c_0^2\ln(1/\delta_\ell)}{n}} + \frac{(3c_1 + 4\alpha M)\ln(1/\delta_\ell)}{3\alpha n}$$

$$\leq 2.5\alpha r_\ell + \sqrt{\frac{2c_0^2\ln(1/\delta)}{n}} + \frac{(3c_1 + 4\alpha M)\ln(1/\delta)}{3\alpha n}$$

$$+ 2\bar{r}_n(\alpha, \mathcal{F}, \mathcal{D}) + \sqrt{\frac{2c_0^2\ln(\frac{(\ell+3)(\ell+4)}{4})}{n}} + \frac{(3c_1 + 4\alpha M)\ln(\frac{(\ell+3)(\ell+4)}{4})}{3\alpha n}$$

$$\overset{(a)}{\leq} 2.5\alpha r_\ell + \sqrt{\frac{2c_0^2\ln(1/\delta)}{n}} + \frac{(3c_1 + 4\alpha M)\ln(1/\delta)}{3\alpha n} + 2r_0 \times (\alpha r_\ell/r_0)^{1/2}$$

$$\leq 3\alpha r_\ell + \sqrt{\frac{2c_0^2\ln(1/\delta)}{n}} + \frac{(3c_1 + 4\alpha M)\ln(1/\delta)}{3\alpha n} + 2r_0.$$

The first inequality used Corollary 6.34. The second inequality used Proposition 6.38 with $r_\ell \geq \alpha^{-1} r_0 > \inf_{f \in \mathcal{F}} h(f) \geq 0$. The third inequality used $\sqrt{a+b} \leq \sqrt{a} + \sqrt{b}$. The fourth inequality used $\sqrt{2ab} \leq 0.5\alpha a + b/\alpha$. The fifth inequality used $\sqrt{a+b} \leq \sqrt{a} + \sqrt{b}$. The last inequality used $2b(\alpha a/b)^{1/2} \leq 0.5\alpha a + 2b$. Inequality (a) used the definition of r_0, and the fact that

$$\max\left(2, \sqrt{\ln\frac{(\ell+3)(\ell+4)}{4}}, \ln\frac{(\ell+3)(\ell+4)}{4}\right) \leq 2(1.2)^{\ell-1} \leq 2(\alpha r_\ell/r_0)^{1/2}.$$

Note that $\sum_{\ell \geq 1} \delta_\ell = \delta$. Taking union bound, we know that the above inequality holds with probability at least $1 - \delta$ for all $\ell \geq 1$ and $f \in \mathcal{F}_\ell$. Given any $f \in \mathcal{F}$, let $\ell(f)$ be the smallest ℓ so that $f \in \mathcal{F}_\ell$. It follows that for this choice of $\ell = \ell(f)$,

$$r_\ell \leq \max(1.5h(f), \alpha^{-1} r_0) \leq 1.5h(f) + \alpha^{-1} r_0.$$

We thus obtain the desired bound. $\qquad\square$

Example 6.42 In Theorem 6.41, we can take $h(f) = 0$, and we can take $c_1, \alpha \to 0$ with $c_1/\alpha \to 0$. Since $\bar{r}_n^0(0, \mathcal{F}, \mathcal{D}) = \epsilon_n(\mathcal{F}, \mathcal{D})$, we obtain

$$f(\mathcal{D}) \leq f(\mathcal{S}_n) + O\left(\epsilon_n(\mathcal{F}, \mathcal{D}) + \sqrt{\frac{2c_0^2 \ln(1/\delta)}{n}} + \frac{M \ln(1/\delta)}{n}\right).$$

If c_0 is small, then this result improves Corollary 6.19 with $h = 0$ since M is replaced by a potentially smaller quantity c_0 in the $O(1/\sqrt{n})$ term.

Example 6.43 In Theorem 6.41, assume that $f(Z) \in [0, 1]$. Then we can take $h(f) = f(\mathcal{D})$ so that the variance condition holds with $c_0 = 0$ and $c_1 = 1$. In such case, we may take α as a constant. This implies the following bound:

$$(1 - 5\alpha)f(\mathcal{D}) \leq f(\mathcal{S}_n) + 5\bar{r}_n^h(\alpha, \mathcal{F}, \mathcal{D}) + O\left(\frac{(1 + \alpha) \ln(1/\delta)}{\alpha n}\right).$$

This leads to a $O(1/n)$ concentration term. This result can be used to improve the concentration of the multiplicative bound in Example 6.24. We leave it as an exercise.

While the Chernoff-style bound of Corollary 6.19 only implies an oracle inequality for ERM with convergence rate no better than $O(1/\sqrt{n})$, the Bennett-style bound in Theorem 6.41 can lead to faster convergence rate. We state the following result, which is a direct consequence of Theorem 6.41.

Corollary 6.44 Let $\phi(w, z) = L(f(w, x), y) - L_*(x, y)$ for an appropriately defined $L_*(x, y)$ so that $\phi(w, \mathcal{D}) \geq 0$. Assume $\sup_w \sup_{z,z'}[\phi(w, z) - \phi(w, z')] \leq M$, and the variance condition (3.13) holds. Consider $h_0(w) \geq 0$, and let $h(w, \mathcal{S}_n) = 5\alpha h_0(w)$. Then for δ such that $\ln(2/\delta) \geq 1$, with probability at least $1 - \delta$, for all $\alpha > 0$, the approximate ERM method (6.1) satisfies

$$(1 - 5\alpha)\phi(\hat{w}, \mathcal{D}) \leq \inf_{w \in \Omega}[(1 + 6\alpha)\phi(w, \mathcal{D}) + 10\alpha h_0(w)] + \epsilon' + 5\bar{r}_n^{h'}(\alpha, \mathcal{G}, \mathcal{D})$$

$$+ 7\sqrt{\frac{2c_0^2 \ln(2/\delta)}{n}} + \frac{(7c_1 + 10\alpha M) \ln(2/\delta)}{\alpha n},$$

where $h'(w) = h_0(w) + \phi(w, \mathcal{D})$ and $\mathcal{G} = \{\phi(w, z) : w \in \Omega\}$. Moreover, with probability at least $1 - \delta$, we have

$$(1 - 5\alpha)\phi(\hat{w}, \mathcal{D}) \leq \inf_{w \in \Omega}[(1 + 11\alpha)\phi(w, \mathcal{D}) + 15\alpha h_0(w)] + \epsilon' + 10\epsilon_n^{0.5\alpha h'}(\mathcal{G}, \mathcal{D})$$

$$+ 7\sqrt{\frac{2c_0^2 \ln(2/\delta)}{n}} + \frac{(7c_1 + 10\alpha M) \ln(2/\delta)}{\alpha n}.$$

Proof For any $w \in \Omega$, we know from Bennett's inequality that with probability

$1 - \delta/2$,

$$\phi(w, \mathcal{S}_n) \le \phi(w, \mathcal{D}) + \sqrt{\frac{2\mathrm{Var}_{Z \sim \mathcal{D}}[\phi(w, Z)] \ln(2/\delta)}{n}} + \frac{M \ln(2/\delta)}{3n}$$

$$\le \phi(w, \mathcal{D}) + \sqrt{\frac{2(c_0^2 + c_1 \phi(w, \mathcal{D})) \ln(2/\delta)}{n}} + \frac{M \ln(2/\delta)}{3n}$$

$$\le \phi(w, \mathcal{D}) + \sqrt{\frac{2c_0^2 \ln(2/\delta)}{n}} + \sqrt{\frac{2c_1 \phi(w, \mathcal{D}) \ln(2/\delta)}{n}} + \frac{M \ln(2/\delta)}{3n}$$

$$\le (1 + 0.5\alpha)\phi(w, \mathcal{D}) + \sqrt{\frac{2c_0^2 \ln(2/\delta)}{n}} + \frac{(3c_1 + \alpha M) \ln(2/\delta)}{3\alpha n}.$$

The first inequality used Bennett's inequality for the sum of independent random variables. The second inequality used the variance condition. The third inequality used $\sqrt{a+b} \le \sqrt{a} + \sqrt{b}$. The last inequality used $\sqrt{2ab} \le 0.5\alpha a + b/\alpha$.

Moreover, from Theorem 6.41 with $h(\phi(w, \cdot)) = h'(w)$, we obtain with probability $1 - \delta/2$:

$$(1 - 5\alpha)\phi(\hat{w}, \mathcal{D}) \le \phi(\hat{w}, \mathcal{S}_n) - 5\alpha\phi(\hat{w}, \mathcal{D}) + 5\alpha h'(\hat{w}) + 5r_0$$

$$+ \sqrt{\frac{2c_0^2 \ln(2/\delta)}{n}} + \frac{(3c_1 + 4\alpha M) \ln(2/\delta)}{3\alpha n}$$

$$= \phi(\hat{w}, \mathcal{S}_n) + 5\alpha h_0(\hat{w}) + 5r_0 + \sqrt{\frac{2c_0^2 \ln(2/\delta)}{n}}$$

$$+ \frac{(3c_1 + 4\alpha M) \ln(2/\delta)}{3\alpha n}$$

$$\le \phi(w, \mathcal{S}_n) + 5\alpha h_0(w) + \epsilon' + 5r_0$$

$$+ \sqrt{\frac{2c_0^2 \ln(2/\delta)}{n}} + \frac{(3c_1 + 4\alpha M) \ln(2/\delta)}{3\alpha n}.$$

The first inequality used Theorem 6.41. The second inequality used (6.1). By taking the union bound of the two inequalities, we obtain with the probability at least $1 - \delta$:

$$(1 - 5\alpha)\phi(\hat{w}, \mathcal{D}) \le [(1 + 0.5\alpha)\phi(w, \mathcal{D}) + 5\alpha h_0(w)] + \epsilon' + 5\bar{r}_n^{h'}(\alpha, \mathcal{G}, \mathcal{D})$$

$$+ 5\alpha[\phi(w, \mathcal{D}) + h_0(w)] + 7\sqrt{\frac{2c_0^2 \ln(2/\delta)}{n}} + \frac{(7c_1 + 10\alpha M) \ln(2/\delta)}{\alpha n},$$

where we used $\ln(2/\delta) \ge 1$ to simplify the result. By taking the inf over $w \in \Omega$ on the right-hand side, we obtain the first bound. By using Proposition 6.40, we obtain

$$5\bar{r}_n^{h'}(\alpha, \mathcal{G}, \mathcal{D}) \le 10\epsilon_n^{0.5\alpha h'}(\mathcal{G}, \mathcal{D}) + 5\alpha[\phi(w, \mathcal{D}) + h_0(w)].$$

Substitute into the previous inequality, and take the inf over $w \in \Omega$ on the right-hand side, we obtain the second bound. $\qquad \square$

We have the following interpretation of Corollary 6.44.

Example 6.45 In Corollary 6.44, we take $L_*(x, y) = L(f(w_*, x), y)$ for some $w_* \in \Omega$, and assume that the variance condition holds with $c_0 = 0$. The rate of convergence is determined by $\bar{r}_n^h(\alpha, \mathcal{G}, \mathcal{D})$, where $h(w) = \phi(w, \mathcal{D})$ (i.e. $h_0(w) = 0$ in Corollary 6.44) and a constant $\alpha = 0.1$.

$$\mathbb{E}_{Z \sim \mathcal{D}} L(f(\hat{w}, X), Y) \leq \mathbb{E}_{Z \sim \mathcal{D}} L(f(w_*, X), Y)$$
$$+ O\left(\epsilon' + \bar{r}_n^h(0.1, \mathcal{G}, \mathcal{D}) + \frac{(c_1 + M)\ln(1/\delta)}{n}\right).$$

Since Example 3.18 implies that least squares regression satisfies the variance condition, this bound holds for least squares regression.

The following result shows that the rate function can be obtained from a uniform upper bound of the Rademacher complexity.

Proposition 6.46 Consider function class $\mathcal{G} = \{\phi(w, z) \colon w \in \Omega\}$ with $h(w) = \phi(w, \mathcal{D})$ and $\inf_{w \in \Omega} h(w) = 0$. Assume that $|\phi(\cdot)| \leq M$ and the variance condition (3.14) holds with $c_0 = 0$. Assume that for any $b > 0$, we have

$$\sup_{\mathcal{S}_n} R\left(\left\{\phi(w, \cdot) \colon \frac{1}{n}\sum_{i=1}^{n} \phi(w, Z_i)^2 \leq b\right\}, \mathcal{S}_n\right) \leq r_n(b),$$

where $r_n(b)$ is a continuous concave function of b. Let $\alpha \leq 0.5 c_1/M$ and

$$b_0 = \sup\{b > 0 \colon b \leq (4c_1/\alpha)r_n(b)\},$$

then $\bar{r}_n^h(\alpha, \mathcal{G}, \mathcal{D}) \leq 0.5\alpha b_0/c_1$.

Proof Consider any $b_0' > b_0$ and let

$$\mathcal{G}_0 = \{\phi(w, \cdot) \colon \phi(w, \mathcal{D}) \leq 0.5 b_0'/c_1\},$$

and define

$$\hat{b}(\mathcal{S}_n) = \sup_{g \in \mathcal{G}_0} \frac{1}{n}\sum_{i=1}^{n} g(Z_i)^2.$$

We have

$$R(\mathcal{G}_0, \mathcal{S}_n) \leq r_n(\hat{b}(\mathcal{S}_n)), \quad R(-\mathcal{G}_0^2, \mathcal{S}_n) \leq 2M r_n(\hat{b}(\mathcal{S}_n)). \tag{6.8}$$

The first inequality used the definition of r_n and the definition of $\hat{b}$. The second inequality used Theorem 6.28 and $|\phi(w_1, z)^2 - \phi(w_2, z)^2| \leq 2M|\phi(w_1, z) - \phi(w_2, z)|$. Let $\tilde{b} = \mathbb{E}_{\mathcal{S}_n} \hat{b}(\mathcal{S}_n)$, then we have

$$\tilde{b} = \mathbb{E}_{\mathcal{S}_n} \hat{b}(\mathcal{S}_n) \leq \epsilon_n(-\mathcal{G}_0^2, \mathcal{D}) + 0.5 b_0'$$
$$\leq 2R_n(-\mathcal{G}_0^2, \mathcal{D}) + 0.5 b_0'$$
$$\leq 4M\mathbb{E}_{\mathcal{S}_n} r_n(\hat{b}(\mathcal{S}_n)) + 0.5 b_0' \leq (2c_1/\alpha)r_n(\tilde{b}) + 0.5 b_0'.$$

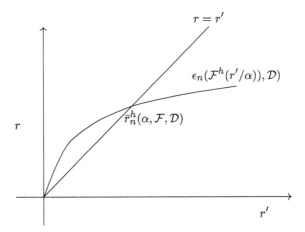

Figure 6.2 Rate function

The first inequality used $\sup_{g \in \mathcal{G}_0} \mathbb{E}_{Z \sim \mathcal{D}} g(Z)^2 \leq 0.5 b'_0$, which follows from the variance condition. The second inequality used Theorem 6.4. The third inequality used (6.8). The last inequality used the concavity of $r_n(\cdot)$ and $4M \leq 2c_1/\alpha$.

From these inequalities, we have either $\tilde{b} < b'_0$, or $\tilde{b} \leq (2c_1/\alpha)r_n(\tilde{b}) + 0.5\tilde{b}$. The latter also implies that $\tilde{b} \leq b_0 < b'_0$ by using the definition of b_0. We thus obtain

$$\epsilon_n(\mathcal{G}_0) \leq 2\mathbb{E}_{\mathcal{S}_n} R(\mathcal{G}_0, \mathcal{S}_n) \leq 2\mathbb{E}_{\mathcal{S}_n} r_n(\hat{b}(\mathcal{S}_n)) \leq 2r_n(\tilde{b}) < (0.5\alpha/c_1)b'_0.$$

The first inequality used Theorem 6.4. The second inequality (6.8). The third inequality used the concavity of $r_n(\cdot)$. The last inequality used $\tilde{b} < b'_0$, $b'_0 > b_0$, and the definition of b_0.

Therefore if we let $r = 0.5(\alpha/c_1)b'_0$, then $\epsilon_n(\mathcal{G}^h(r/\alpha)) = \epsilon_n(\mathcal{G}_0) \leq 2r_n(\tilde{b}) < r$, where $\tilde{b}_0 < 2(c_1/\alpha)r$. The condition that $r_n(\cdot)$ is continuous implies that $\lim_{\Delta r \to 0^+} \epsilon_n(\mathcal{G}^h((r + \Delta r)/\alpha)) < r$. The desired result follows from the definition of $\bar{r}_n^h(\alpha, \mathcal{G}, \mathcal{D})$. $\qquad\square$

In the following, we apply Proposition 6.46 to obtain the rate function estimate. In general, from Figure 6.2, we know that b_0 can be obtained by solving

$$b_0 = (4c_1/\alpha)r_n(b_0).$$

For parametric models, we have the following result (see Section 5.2).

Example 6.47 In Example 6.45, assume that

$$\ln N_2(\epsilon, \mathcal{G}, n) \leq d \ln(n/\epsilon).$$

Then Theorem 6.25 implies that $r_n(b) = O(\sqrt{bd \ln n/n})$, and

$$\bar{r}_n^h(\alpha, \mathcal{G}, \mathcal{D}) = O\left(\frac{d \ln(n)}{n}\right).$$

For nonparametric models, we have the following result from Proposition 6.46.

Example 6.48   In Example 6.45, assume that

$$\ln N_2(\epsilon, \mathcal{G}, n) \leq c/\epsilon^p$$

for some $p < 2$. Then it can be shown from Theorem 6.25 that (we leave it to Exercise 6.9) $r_n(b) = O((\sqrt{b})^{1-0.5p}/\sqrt{n})$. This implies that

$$\bar{r}_n^h(\alpha, \mathcal{G}, \mathcal{D}) = O(n^{-1/(1+p/2)}).$$

In comparison, we may apply the uniform L_1 entropy analysis with

$$\ln N_1(\epsilon, \mathcal{G}, n) \leq c/\epsilon^p.$$

The multiplicative Chernoff bound in Corollary 4.13 has a suboptimal complexity of

$$\inf_{\epsilon > 0} \left[\epsilon + \frac{c}{\epsilon^p n} \right] = O(n^{-1/(1+p)}).$$

Example 6.49   Consider a function class $\mathcal{F}$ and the ERM method for least squares regression:

$$\hat{f} = \arg\min_{f \in \mathcal{F}} \frac{1}{n} \sum_{i=1}^{n} (f(X_i) - Y_i)^2,$$

where $Z_i = (X_i, Y_i)$ are iid samples from $\mathcal{D}$. Assume that $|f(X) - Y| \in [0, 1]$ for all X and Y. Example 3.18 implies that the loss function $\phi(f, Z) = [(f(X) - Y)^2 - (f_*(X) - Y)^2]$ satisfies the variance condition if the true regression function $f_* \in \mathcal{F}$.   Assume also that the empirical covering number of $\mathcal{F}$ satisfies

$$\ln N_2(\epsilon, \mathcal{F}, n) \leq \frac{c}{\epsilon^p} \tag{6.9}$$

for some constant $c > 0$ and $p > 0$. We consider the following two situations: $p \in (0, 2)$ and $p \geq 2$.
Let $h(f) = \phi(f, \mathcal{D})$ with $h_0(f) = 0$.

- $p \in (0, 2)$. The conditions of Corollary 6.44 hold with $c_0 = 0$. This implies the following bound (see Exercises 6.9) on the rate function with constant α:

$$\bar{r}^h(\alpha, \mathcal{F}, \mathcal{D}) = O\left(n^{-2/(2+p)}\right).$$

We thus have with probability at least $1 - \delta$,

$$\mathbb{E}_{\mathcal{D}} L(\hat{f}(X), Y) \leq \mathbb{E}_{\mathcal{D}} L(f_*(X), Y) + O\left(n^{-2/(2+p)} + \frac{\ln(1/\delta)}{n}\right).$$

- $p > 2$. The entropy integral of Theorem 6.25 implies that

$$R_n(\mathcal{F}^h(b), \mathcal{D}) \leq \frac{\tilde{c}_1}{n^{1/p}}$$

for some constant $\tilde{c}_1$. We thus obtain a rate of convergence of

$$\bar{r}^h(\alpha, \mathcal{F}, \mathcal{D}) = O\left(n^{-1/p}\right)$$

for local Rademacher complexity. It can be shown that this is the same rate as what we can obtain from the standard nonlocalized Rademacher complexity (see Exercise 6.7).

6.6 Historical and Bibliographical Remarks

The introduction of Rademacher complexity in machine learning was due to Koltchinskii (2001); Koltchinskii and Panchenko (2002); and Bartlett and Mendelson (2002). The treatment presented here mainly follows that of Bartlett and Mendelson (2002), and the proof of Lemma 6.29 was presented in Meir and Zhang (2003), which generalizes a result of Ledoux and Talagrand (2013) to handle offset functions. We also employs a generalized version of Rademacher complexity which we refer to as offset Rademacher complexity. The notation of offset Rademacher complexity was considered by Liang et al. (2015).

The concept of local Rademacher complexity was proposed in Bartlett et al. (2005). Our treatment follows their approach, which leads to the uniform convergence result presented in Corollary 6.34, and oracle inequality in Corollary 6.44. Similar results can be found in Bartlett et al. (2005), which also employed the notation of rate function, although the precise definition is different.

The idea of concentration inequality can be dated back to the Efron–Stein inequality in Efron and Stein (1981) and Steele (1986), which can be stated as follows.

Proposition 6.50 *Let $f(X_1, \ldots, X_n)$ be a function of n variables, and $\{X_i, X_i'\}$ $(1 \leq i \leq n)$ be $2n$ iid random variables, then*

$$\mathrm{Var}[f(X)] \leq \frac{1}{2}\mathbb{E}\sum_{i=1}^{n}(f(X) - f(X^{(i)}))^2, \tag{6.10}$$

where $X = [X_1, \ldots, X_n]$, and $X^{(i)} = [X_1, \ldots, X_{i-1}, X_i', X_{i+1}, \ldots, X_n]$.

This inequality may be regarded as a generalization of Chebyshev's inequality for the sum of iid random variables. Similarly, McDiarmid's inequality (McDiarmid, 1989) can be regarded as a generalization of the Chernoff bound. The generalization of Bernstein-style inequality for empirical processes, needed for establishing convergence rate faster than $O(1/\sqrt{n})$ and for the local Rademacher complexity analysis, is more complicated. Such an inequality was obtained first by Talagrand (1995, 1996b), and thus has been referred to as Talagrand's inequality. Its variations and improvements have been obtained by various researchers (Ledoux, 1997; Massart, 2000; Boucheron et al., 2000, 2003, 2013; Bousquet, 2002). Talagrand's inequality can also be used with matrix concentration techniques to obtain sharper tail bounds for the spectral norm of the sum of independent matrices (Tropp, 2015).

Exercises

6.1   Consider $\mathcal{G} = \{\phi(w, z) \colon w \in \Omega\}$ with $\phi(w, z) \in [0, 1]$. Given a dataset $\mathcal{S}_{n+m}$, we consider random partitions of $\mathcal{S}_{n+m}$ into disjoint subsets $\mathcal{S}_n \cup \mathcal{S}'_m$. Define

$$R(\mathcal{G}, \mathcal{S}_n, \mathcal{S}'_m) = \sup_{w \in \Omega} [\phi(w, \mathcal{S}_{n+m}) - \phi(w, \mathcal{S}_n)].$$

If $\mathcal{S}_{n+m} \sim \mathcal{D}^{n+m}$, then find constant $c_{n,m}$ so that $\epsilon_n(\mathcal{G}, \mathcal{D}) \leq c_{n,m} \mathbb{E}_{\mathcal{S}_n \cup \mathcal{S}'_m} R(\mathcal{G}, \mathcal{S}_n, \mathcal{S}'_m)$.

6.2   Given a dataset $\mathcal{S}_{n+m}$, we consider random partitions of $\mathcal{S}_{n+m}$ into disjoint subsets $\mathcal{S}_n \cup \mathcal{S}'_m$. Consider any function $f(Z) \in [a, b]$. Define

$$f(\mathcal{S}_n) = \frac{1}{n} \sum_{Z \in \mathcal{S}_n} f(Z), \quad f(\mathcal{S}_{n+m}) = \frac{1}{n+m} \sum_{Z \in \mathcal{S}_{n+m}} f(Z).$$

- Show that the sub-Gaussian inequality holds:

$$\frac{1}{\lambda} \ln \mathbb{E}_{\mathcal{S}_n \cup \mathcal{S}'_m} \exp\left(\lambda f(\mathcal{S}_n)\right) \leq f(\mathcal{S}_{n+m}) + \frac{\lambda(b-a)^2}{8n},$$

where the expectation is over random partitions. Hint: see Hoeffding (1963).
- Derive a Chernoff bound

$$\Pr(f(\mathcal{S}_n) - f(\mathcal{S}_{n+m}) \geq \epsilon),$$

where $\epsilon > 0$. Here the probability is with respect to all random partitions of $\mathcal{S}_{n+m}$.
- If $|\mathcal{G}| = N$ is finite, derive an upper bound of

$$\mathbb{E}_{\mathcal{S}_n \cup \mathcal{S}'_m} R(\mathcal{G}, \mathcal{S}_n, \mathcal{S}'_m)$$

by using the proof technique of Theorem 6.23, where the expectation is with respect to the random partition.

6.3   For general $\mathcal{G}$, with covering number $N(\epsilon, \mathcal{G}, L_\infty(\mathcal{S}_{n+m}))$, estimate

$$\mathbb{E}_{\mathcal{S}_n \cup \mathcal{S}'_m} R(\mathcal{G}, \mathcal{S}_n, \mathcal{S}'_m),$$

defined in the previous problem by using the chaining technique of Theorem 6.25. Here the expectation is with respect to the random partition.

6.4   In Theorem 6.25, assume that $0 \in \mathcal{G}$. If we replace covering number by packing number, then show that (6.7) can be improved to obtain

$$R(\mathcal{G}, \mathcal{S}_n) \leq \inf_{\epsilon \geq 0} \left[4\epsilon + 4 \int_\epsilon^\infty \sqrt{\frac{\ln M(\epsilon', \mathcal{G}, L_2(\mathcal{S}_n))}{n}} d\epsilon' \right].$$

6.5   Let $\mathcal{F} = \{f(w, x) : w \in \Omega\}$, where $x \in \mathcal{X}$, and each function $f(w, x)$ takes binary values in $\{\pm 1\}$. Consider $\mathcal{S}_n = \{(X_1, Y_1), \ldots, (X_n, Y_n)\}$, where $X_i \in \mathcal{X}$ and $Y_i \in \{\pm 1\}$. Let $\phi(w, X, Y) = \mathbb{1}(f(w, X) \neq Y)$, and $\mathcal{G} = \{\phi(w, X, Y) \colon w \in \Omega\}$. Let $R(\mathcal{F}, \mathcal{S}_n)$ be the Rademacher complexity of $\mathcal{F}$ on $\mathcal{S}_n$, and find $R(\mathcal{G}, \mathcal{S}_n)$.

6.6   Consider the least squares problem in Example 6.49. If $p = 2$, derive an oracle inequality using local Rademacher complexity.

6.7   Assume the empirical covering number of a function class $\mathcal{F}$ satisfies (6.9) with $p \geq 2$. Estimate the Rademacher complexity $R(\mathcal{F}, \mathcal{S}_n)$.

6.8 Assume that we have a VC subgraph class with finite VC dimension d. The variance condition (3.13) holds. Use Theorem 6.41 and Theorem 6.23 to derive a multiplicative-style uniform convergence result. Compare with Example 6.24.

6.9 In Example 6.48, prove the bound for $\bar{r}_n^h(\alpha, \mathcal{G}, \mathcal{D})$ when $p < 2$. Moreover assume that $p > 2$; find a bound for $\bar{r}_n^h(\alpha, \mathcal{G}, \mathcal{D})$.

6.10 Consider the variance condition (3.16) for some $\beta \in (0, 1)$. Use the result of Example 3.19 to write this condition in the form of (3.14) with β-dependent tuning parameters c_0 and c_1. Write an oracle inequality using Corollary 6.44. Consider the entropy number in Example 6.48, and compute the convergence rate in terms of β by optimizing the tuning parameters c_0 and c_1.

7

Algorithmic Stability Analysis

The theory of empirical processes has become an important tool to analyze the generalization ability of learning algorithms based on empirical risk minimization. However, in practical applications, we typically solve the empirical risk minimization problem using optimization methods such as stochastic gradient descent (SGD). Such an algorithm searches a model parameter along a path that does not cover the entire model space. Therefore the empirical process analysis may not be optimal to analyze the performance of specific computational procedures. In recent years, another theoretical tool, which we may refer to as *stability analysis*, has been proposed to analyze such computational procedures.

7.1 Algorithmic Stability

We consider an arbitrary randomized learning algorithm $\mathcal{A}$ that maps a training data $\mathcal{S}_n$ of n samples to a (random) weight vector $w \in \Omega$. An example of such randomized algorithm is SGD, which produces a random weight vector due to the randomness in selecting training examples during the training of SGD.

Similar to previous chapters, our goal is still to minimize the expected test loss

$$\phi(w, \mathcal{D}) = \mathbb{E}_{Z \sim \mathcal{D}} \phi(w, Z),$$

and we assume that $\mathcal{S}_n$ contains n iid samples, drawn from $\mathcal{D}$. Here the test loss $\phi(w, z)$ can be different from training loss as in regularized ERM method (6.1). But we consider a more general setting where the training algorithm may not necessarily correspond to an ERM method.

We are still interested in bounding the difference of training error and generalization of such an algorithm. We introduce the notation of algorithmic stability as follows.

Definition 7.1 An algorithm $\mathcal{A}$ is ϵ-uniformly stable if for all $\mathcal{S}_n$ and $\mathcal{S}'_n$ that differ by only one element:

$$\sup_{z \in \mathcal{Z}} [\mathbb{E}_{\mathcal{A}} \phi(\mathcal{A}(\mathcal{S}'_n), z) - \mathbb{E}_{\mathcal{A}} \phi(\mathcal{A}(\mathcal{S}_n), z)] \leq \epsilon,$$

where $\mathbb{E}_{\mathcal{A}}$ denotes the expectation over the internal randomization of the algorithm.

Stability can be used to derive an expected generalization bound for a learning algorithm. We have the following result, which shows that the expected generalization loss of a stable learning algorithm is bounded by the expected training loss.

Theorem 7.2 *If an algorithm $\mathcal{A}$ is ϵ-uniformly stable, then for $\mathcal{S}_n \sim \mathcal{D}^n$,*

$$\mathbb{E}_{\mathcal{S}_n} \mathbb{E}_{\mathcal{A}} \phi(\mathcal{A}(\mathcal{S}_n), \mathcal{D}) \leq \mathbb{E}_{\mathcal{S}_n} \mathbb{E}_{\mathcal{A}} \phi(\mathcal{A}(\mathcal{S}_n), \mathcal{S}_n) + \epsilon.$$

Proof Consider two independent samples of size n: $\mathcal{S}_n = \{Z_1, \ldots, Z_n\}$ and $\mathcal{S}'_n = \{Z'_1, \ldots, Z'_n\}$. Let $\mathcal{S}_n^{(i)} = \{Z_1, \ldots, Z_{i-1}, Z'_i, Z_{i+1}, \ldots, Z_n\}$. Let $p_t^{(i)}$ be the distribution obtained by $\mathcal{A}$ with $\mathcal{S}_n^{(i)}$. We have

$$\mathbb{E}_{\mathcal{S}_n} \mathbb{E}_{\mathcal{A}} \phi(\mathcal{A}(\mathcal{S}_n), \mathcal{D}) - \mathbb{E}_{\mathcal{S}_n} \mathbb{E}_{\mathcal{A}} \phi(\mathcal{A}(\mathcal{S}_n), \mathcal{S}_n)$$

$$= \frac{1}{n} \sum_{i=1}^{n} \mathbb{E}_{\mathcal{S}'_n} \mathbb{E}_{\mathcal{S}_n} \mathbb{E}_{\mathcal{A}} \phi(\mathcal{A}(\mathcal{S}_n^{(i)}), Z_i) - \frac{1}{n} \sum_{i=1}^{n} \mathbb{E}_{\mathcal{S}_n} \mathbb{E}_{\mathcal{A}} \phi(\mathcal{A}(\mathcal{S}_n), Z_i)$$

$$= \frac{1}{n} \sum_{i=1}^{n} \mathbb{E}_{\mathcal{S}'_n} \mathbb{E}_{\mathcal{S}_n} [\mathbb{E}_{\mathcal{A}} \phi(\mathcal{A}(\mathcal{S}_n^{(i)}), Z_i) - \mathbb{E}_{\mathcal{A}} \phi(\mathcal{A}(\mathcal{S}_n), Z_i)] \leq \epsilon.$$

The first equation used the fact that Z_i is independent of $\mathcal{S}_n^{(i)}$, and thus the distribution of $\phi(\mathcal{A}(\mathcal{S}_n^{(i)}), Z_i)$ is the same as that of $\phi(\mathcal{A}(\mathcal{S}_n), Z)$ with $Z \sim \mathcal{D}$. The inequality used the definition of uniform stability. $\square$

It is also possible to obtain a large probability statement for any uniformly stable algorithm. The proof relies on a concentration inequality for a leave-one-out estimate, which we leave to Section 7.6 (see Theorem 7.24). Using this result, we can obtain the following high-probability result that bounds the generalization loss in terms of training loss for uniformly stable algorithms.

Theorem 7.3 *Assume that $\mathcal{A}$ is ϵ uniformly stable. Let $\mathcal{S}_n = \{Z_1, \ldots, Z_n\} \sim \mathcal{D}^n$ and $\mathcal{S}'_n = \{Z'_1, \ldots, Z'_n\} \sim \mathcal{D}^n$ be independent training and validation sets of iid data from $\mathcal{D}$. Assume that there exists $\alpha \in (0, 1)$ such that for some $\delta \in (0, 1)$, we have the following inequality between the expected validation loss and the expected test loss. With probability at least $1 - \delta$,*

$$\alpha \mathbb{E}_{\mathcal{S}_n} \mathbb{E}_{\mathcal{A}} \phi(\mathcal{A}(\mathcal{S}_n), \mathcal{D}) \leq \frac{1}{n} \sum_{i=1}^{n} \mathbb{E}_{\mathcal{S}_n} \mathbb{E}_{\mathcal{A}} \phi(\mathcal{A}(\mathcal{S}_n), Z'_i) + \epsilon_n(\delta). \tag{7.1}$$

Then with probability at least $1 - \delta$,

$$\mathbb{E}_{\mathcal{A}} \phi(\mathcal{A}(\mathcal{S}_n), \mathcal{D}) \leq \mathbb{E}_{\mathcal{A}} \phi(\mathcal{A}(\mathcal{S}_n), \mathcal{S}_n) + (1 - \alpha) \mathbb{E}_{\mathcal{S}_n} \mathbb{E}_{\mathcal{A}} \phi(\mathcal{A}(\mathcal{S}_n), \mathcal{S}_n)$$
$$+ \epsilon_n(\delta/2) + (2 + 5\lceil \log_2 n \rceil) \epsilon \ln(2/\delta) + (3 - \alpha)\epsilon.$$

Proof We define

$$g(\mathcal{S}_n; z) = \mathbb{E}_{\mathcal{A}} \phi(\mathcal{A}(\mathcal{S}_n), \mathcal{D}) - \mathbb{E}_{\mathcal{A}} \phi(\mathcal{A}(\mathcal{S}_n), z).$$

Then $\mathbb{E}_Z g(\mathcal{S}_n; Z) = 0$ and $g(\mathcal{S}_n; z)$ is 2ϵ uniformly stable. Theorem 7.24 implies that with probability at least $1 - \delta/2$,

$$\bar{g}(\mathcal{S}_{n+1}) \leq 2\lceil \log_2 n \rceil \epsilon (1 + 2.5 \ln(2/\delta)), \tag{7.2}$$

where

$$\bar{g}(\mathcal{S}_{n+1}) = \frac{1}{n} \sum_{i=1}^{n} \Bigg[\Big(\mathbb{E}_\mathcal{A} \phi(\mathcal{A}(\mathcal{S}_{n+1}^{(i)}), \mathcal{D}) - \mathbb{E}_\mathcal{A} \phi(\mathcal{A}(\mathcal{S}_{n+1}^{(i)}), Z_i) \Big)$$

$$- \underbrace{\Big(\mathbb{E}_{\mathcal{S}_{n+1}^{(i)}} \mathbb{E}_\mathcal{A} \phi(\mathcal{A}(\mathcal{S}_{n+1}^{(i)}), \mathcal{D}) - \mathbb{E}_{\mathcal{S}_{n+1}^{(i)}} \mathbb{E}_\mathcal{A} \phi(\mathcal{A}(\mathcal{S}_{n+1}^{(i)}), Z_i) \Big)}_{\Delta_n} \Bigg].$$

Here $\mathcal{S}_{n+1} = \mathcal{S}_n \cup \{Z_{n+1}\}$ with $Z_{n+1} \sim \mathcal{D}$ independent of $\mathcal{S}_n$. Moreover, as in Theorem 7.24, we use the notation $\mathcal{S}_{n+1}^{(i)} = \{Z_1, \ldots, Z_{i-1}, Z_{n+1}, Z_{i+1}, \ldots, Z_n\}$.

In (7.1), we observe that $\mathbb{E}_{\mathcal{S}_n} \mathbb{E}_\mathcal{A} \phi(\mathcal{A}(\mathcal{S}_n), \mathcal{D})$ is a number that depends on $\mathcal{D}$, and $\mathbb{E}_{\mathcal{S}_n} \mathbb{E}_\mathcal{A} \phi(\mathcal{A}(\mathcal{S}_n), Z_i')$ depends only on Z_i'. Therefore by changing $\mathcal{S}_n$ to $\mathcal{S}_{n+1}^{(i)}$ and Z_i' to Z_i, we obtain the following equivalent form of (7.1). With probability at least $1 - \delta/2$,

$$\Delta_n = \frac{1}{n} \sum_{i=1}^{n} \Big[\mathbb{E}_{\mathcal{S}_{n+1}^{(i)}} \mathbb{E}_\mathcal{A} \phi(\mathcal{A}(\mathcal{S}_{n+1}^{(i)}), \mathcal{D}) - \mathbb{E}_{\mathcal{S}_{n+1}^{(i)}} \mathbb{E}_\mathcal{A} \phi(\mathcal{A}(\mathcal{S}_{n+1}^{(i)}), Z_i) \Big]$$

$$\leq (1 - \alpha) \mathbb{E}_{\mathcal{S}_n} \mathbb{E}_\mathcal{A} \phi(\mathcal{A}(\mathcal{S}_n), \mathcal{D}) + \epsilon_n(\delta/2)$$

$$\leq (1 - \alpha) \mathbb{E}_{\mathcal{S}_n} \mathbb{E}_\mathcal{A} \phi(\mathcal{A}(\mathcal{S}_n), \mathcal{S}_n) + \epsilon_n(\delta/2) + (1 - \alpha)\epsilon. \tag{7.3}$$

The first inequality is equivalent to (7.1). The second inequality used Theorem 7.2. It follows from the union bound that with probability $1 - \delta$, both (7.2) and (7.3) hold. This implies that

$$\mathbb{E}_\mathcal{A} \phi(\mathcal{A}(\mathcal{S}_n), \mathcal{D})$$

$$\leq \frac{1}{n} \sum_{i=1}^{n} [\mathbb{E}_\mathcal{A} \phi(\mathcal{A}(\mathcal{S}_{n+1}^{(i)}); \mathcal{D})] + \epsilon$$

$$= \frac{1}{n} \sum_{i=1}^{n} [\mathbb{E}_\mathcal{A} \phi(\mathcal{A}(\mathcal{S}_{n+1}^{(i)}); Z_i)] + \bar{g}(\mathcal{S}_{n+1}) + \Delta_n + \epsilon$$

$$\leq \frac{1}{n} \sum_{i=1}^{n} [\mathbb{E}_\mathcal{A} \phi(\mathcal{A}(\mathcal{S}_{n+1}^{(i)}); Z_i)] + 2\lceil \log_2 n \rceil \epsilon (1 + 2.5 \ln(2/\delta))$$

$$+ (1 - \alpha) \mathbb{E}_{\mathcal{S}_n} \mathbb{E}_\mathcal{A} \phi(\mathcal{A}(\mathcal{S}_n), \mathcal{S}_n) + \epsilon_n(\delta/2) + (2 - \alpha)\epsilon$$

$$\leq \frac{1}{n} \sum_{i=1}^{n} [\mathbb{E}_\mathcal{A} \phi(\mathcal{A}(\mathcal{S}_n); Z_i)] + 2\lceil \log_2 n \rceil \epsilon (1 + 2.5 \ln(2/\delta))$$

$$+ (1 - \alpha) \mathbb{E}_{\mathcal{S}_n} \mathbb{E}_\mathcal{A} \phi(\mathcal{A}(\mathcal{S}_n), \mathcal{S}_n) + \epsilon_n(\delta/2) + (3 - \alpha)\epsilon.$$

In the proof, the first inequality used uniform stability of $\mathcal{A}$. The second inequality used (7.2) and (7.3). The third inequality used the uniform stability of $\mathcal{A}$. $\qquad\square$

Example 7.4 For bounded loss $\phi(\cdot, \cdot) \in [0, 1]$, we can apply the additive Chernoff bound and let $\alpha = 1$ and

$$\epsilon_n(\delta) = \sqrt{\frac{\ln(1/\delta)}{2n}}$$

in (7.1). This leads to the following inequality. With probability at least $1 - \delta$,

$$\mathbb{E}_{\mathcal{A}}\phi(\mathcal{A}(\mathcal{S}_n), \mathcal{D}) \leq \mathbb{E}_{\mathcal{A}}\phi(\mathcal{A}(\mathcal{S}_n), \mathcal{S}_n) + (2 + 5\lceil \log_2 n \rceil)\epsilon \ln(2/\delta) + 2\epsilon + \sqrt{\frac{\ln(2/\delta)}{2n}}.$$

We note that in Example 7.4, if we employ a uniformly stable algorithm $\mathcal{A}(\mathcal{S}_n)$ that achieves approximate empirical risk minimization, then the same argument in the standard analyses of the ERM method (such as those in Chapter 3) can be used to derive an oracle inequality for $\mathcal{A}$ that holds in high probability. An important advantage of deriving such results using stability analysis instead of empirical process in Chapter 3 is that stability analysis does not have to rely on covering numbers (or related concept such as Rademacher complexity). As we will see later, stability analysis can be used with computational procedures such as SGD, for which the concept of covering numbers can be difficult to apply.

Example 7.5 For bounded loss $\phi(\cdot, \cdot) \in [0, 1]$, we can apply the multiplicative Chernoff bound (2.11) with $\alpha = 1 - \gamma$ for $\gamma \in (0, 1)$, and

$$\epsilon_n(\delta) = \frac{\ln(1/\delta)}{2\gamma n}$$

in (7.1). This leads to the following inequality. With probability at least $1 - \delta$,

$$\mathbb{E}_{\mathcal{A}}\phi(\mathcal{A}(\mathcal{S}_n), \mathcal{D}) \leq \mathbb{E}_{\mathcal{A}}\phi(\mathcal{A}(\mathcal{S}_n), \mathcal{S}_n) + \gamma \mathbb{E}_{\mathcal{S}_n}\mathbb{E}_{\mathcal{A}}\phi(\mathcal{A}(\mathcal{S}_n), \mathcal{S}_n)$$
$$+ (2 + 5\lceil \log_2 n \rceil)\epsilon \ln(2/\delta) + 3\epsilon + \frac{\ln(2/\delta)}{2\gamma n}.$$

The result implies that if one can design a stable learning algorithm that achieves near zero training loss, then the test loss is also near zero with large probability. One may also use Bernstein's inequality together with the variance condition to obtain a similar result. We leave it as an exercise.

In addition to uniform stability, we will also consider the following closely related concept of leave-one-out stability. It is easier to define training data dependent stability using leave-one-out stability, and to allow different training loss and test loss, as in (6.1).

Definition 7.6 Given datasets $\mathcal{S}_n = \{Z_1, \ldots, Z_n\} \subset \mathcal{S}_{n+1} = \{Z_1, \ldots, Z_n, Z_{n+1}\}$, let $\epsilon(\cdot, \cdot)$ be a function $\mathcal{Z} \times \mathcal{Z}^{n+1} \to \mathbb{R}$. The algorithm $\mathcal{A}(\mathcal{S}_n)$ is $\epsilon(\cdot, \cdot)$ leave-one-out stable if there exists $\bar{A}(\mathcal{S}_{n+1})$ such that for all $(Z_{n+1}, \mathcal{S}_{n+1})$,

$$\mathbb{E}_{\mathcal{A}}\phi(\mathcal{A}(\mathcal{S}_n), Z_{n+1}) - \mathbb{E}_{\bar{A}}\phi(\bar{A}(\mathcal{S}_{n+1}), Z_{n+1}) \leq \epsilon(Z_{n+1}, \mathcal{S}_{n+1}),$$

where $\mathbb{E}_{\mathcal{A}}$ denotes the expectation over the internal randomization of the algorithm.

The following result shows that the expected generalization loss of $\mathcal{A}$ on $\mathcal{S}_n$ can be bounded by the expected training loss of $\mathcal{A}$ on $\mathcal{S}_{n+1}$. The proof is left as an exercise.

Theorem 7.7 *If an algorithm $\mathcal{A}$ is $\epsilon(\cdot, \cdot)$-leave-one-out stable, then*

$$\mathbb{E}_{\mathcal{S}_n} \mathbb{E}_{\mathcal{A}} \phi(\mathcal{A}(\mathcal{S}_n), \mathcal{D}) \leq \mathbb{E}_{\mathcal{S}_{n+1}} \mathbb{E}_{\bar{\mathcal{A}}} \phi(\bar{\mathcal{A}}(\mathcal{S}_{n+1}), \mathcal{S}_{n+1})$$

$$+ \mathbb{E}_{\mathcal{S}_{n+1}} \frac{1}{n+1} \sum_{Z \in \mathcal{S}_{n+1}} \epsilon(Z, \mathcal{S}_{n+1}).$$

For certain problems, one can obtain more refined results using the data-dependent leave-one-out stability analysis of Theorem 7.7. We will mostly consider this approach in this chapter.

7.2 Regularized Empirical Risk Minimization

In this section, we consider empirical risk minimization with convex functions, and analyze its generalization using stability. Properties of convex functions that are useful for our purpose can be found in Appendix A. Additional background on convex analysis and convex optimization can be found in Rockafellar (2015) and Boyd and Vandenberghe (2004).

We can now analyze the empirical risk minimization method for convex objectives.

Theorem 7.8 *Assume that $\phi(w, z)$ is $G(z)$-Lipschitz in w on a closed convex set Ω. The training loss $\bar{\phi}(w, \mathcal{S}_n) = \phi(w, \mathcal{S}_n) + h(w)$ is λ strongly convex. Then the regularized empirical risk minimization method*

$$\mathcal{A}(\mathcal{S}_n) = \arg\min_{w \in \Omega} \bar{\phi}(w, \mathcal{S}_n)$$

is $\epsilon(Z_{n+1}, \mathcal{S}_{n+1}) = G(Z_{n+1})^2 / (\lambda(n+1))$ leave-one-out stable. If moreover we have $\sup_z G(z) \leq G$, then it is $\epsilon = 2G^2/(\lambda n)$ uniformly stable.

Assume $h(w) \geq 0$, then the following expected oracle inequality holds:

$$\mathbb{E}_{\mathcal{S}_n} \phi(\mathcal{A}(\mathcal{S}_n), \mathcal{D}) \leq \inf_{w \in \Omega} [\phi(w, \mathcal{D}) + h(w)] + \frac{\mathbb{E}_Z G(Z)^2}{\lambda(n+1)}.$$

Proof Consider $\mathcal{S}_n$ and $\mathcal{S}_{n+1} = \mathcal{S}_n \cup \{Z_{n+1}\}$. We define

$$\bar{\phi}(w, \mathcal{S}_{n+1}) = \phi(w, \mathcal{S}_{n+1}) + \frac{n}{n+1} h(w),$$

and let $\bar{\mathcal{A}}(\mathcal{S}_{n+1})$ be its minimizer on Ω. Using the optimality of $\mathcal{A}(\mathcal{S}_n)$ and Proposition A.8, we obtain

$$\nabla \bar{\phi}(\mathcal{A}(\mathcal{S}_n), \mathcal{S}_n)^\top (\bar{\mathcal{A}}(\mathcal{S}_{n+1}) - \mathcal{A}(\mathcal{S}_n)) \geq 0, \tag{7.4}$$

where $\nabla\bar{\phi}(w, \cdot)$ is the gradient with respect to w. Since

$$\bar{\phi}(\mathcal{A}(\mathcal{S}_n), \mathcal{S}_{n+1}) = \frac{n}{n+1}\bar{\phi}(\mathcal{A}(\mathcal{S}_n), \mathcal{S}_n) + \frac{1}{n+1}\phi(\mathcal{A}(\mathcal{S}_n), Z_{n+1}).$$

It follows that

$$\nabla\bar{\phi}(\mathcal{A}(\mathcal{S}_n), \mathcal{S}_{n+1})^\top(\bar{\mathcal{A}}(\mathcal{S}_{n+1}) - \mathcal{A}(\mathcal{S}_n))$$

$$= \left(\frac{n}{n+1}\nabla\bar{\phi}(\mathcal{A}(\mathcal{S}_n), \mathcal{S}_n) + \frac{1}{n+1}\nabla\phi(\mathcal{A}(\mathcal{S}_n), Z_{n+1})\right)^\top (\bar{\mathcal{A}}(\mathcal{S}_{n+1}) - \mathcal{A}(\mathcal{S}_n))$$

$$\geq \frac{1}{n+1}\nabla\phi(\mathcal{A}(\mathcal{S}_n), Z_{n+1})^\top(\bar{\mathcal{A}}(\mathcal{S}_{n+1}) - \mathcal{A}(\mathcal{S}_n))$$

$$\geq -\frac{G(Z_{n+1})}{n+1}\|\bar{\mathcal{A}}(\mathcal{S}_{n+1}) - \mathcal{A}(\mathcal{S}_n))\|_2.$$

The first inequality used (7.4). The second inequality used the Lipschitz property of ϕ. Since $\bar{\mathcal{A}}(\mathcal{S}_{n+1})$ is the minimizer of $\bar{\phi}(w, \mathcal{S}_{n+1})$ over $w \in \Omega$, we obtain from Proposition A.8 that

$$\|\mathcal{A}(\mathcal{S}_n) - \bar{\mathcal{A}}(\mathcal{S}_{n+1})\|_2 \leq \frac{G(Z_{n+1})}{\lambda(n+1)}.$$

It follows that

$$\phi(\mathcal{A}(\mathcal{S}_n), Z_{n+1}) - \phi(\bar{\mathcal{A}}(\mathcal{S}_{n+1}), Z_{n+1})$$

$$\leq G(Z_{n+1})\|\mathcal{A}(\mathcal{S}_n) - \bar{\mathcal{A}}(\mathcal{S}_{n+1})\|_2 \leq \frac{G(Z_{n+1})^2}{\lambda(n+1)}.$$

This proves the leave-one-out stability result. Similarly, we can prove the uniform stability result, which we leave as an exercise.

Now Theorem 7.7 implies that

$$\mathbb{E}_{\mathcal{S}_n}\phi(\mathcal{A}(\mathcal{S}_n), \mathcal{D}) \leq \mathbb{E}_{\mathcal{S}_{n+1}}\phi(\bar{\mathcal{A}}(\mathcal{S}_{n+1}), \mathcal{S}_{n+1}) + \mathbb{E}_{\mathcal{S}_{n+1}}\frac{1}{n+1}\sum_{Z \in \mathcal{S}_{n+1}}\frac{G(Z)^2}{\lambda(n+1)}$$

$$\leq \inf_w\left[\mathbb{E}_{\mathcal{S}_{n+1}}\phi(w, \mathcal{S}_{n+1}) + h(w)\right] + \mathbb{E}_{\mathcal{S}_{n+1}}\frac{1}{n+1}\sum_{Z \in \mathcal{S}_{n+1}}\frac{G(Z)^2}{\lambda(n+1)}$$

$$= \inf_w\left[\phi(w, \mathcal{D}) + h(w)\right] + \frac{\mathbb{E}_Z G(Z)^2}{\lambda(n+1)}.$$

In the derivation, the inequality used the fact that $\bar{\mathcal{A}}(\mathcal{S}_{n+1})$ is the minimizer of the regularized empirical risk, and $h(w) \geq 0$. $\qquad\square$

Example 7.9 We consider the binary linear support vector machine (SVM) formulation with $y \in \{\pm 1\}$, which employs the hinge loss

$$L(f(w, x), y) = \max(1 - f(w, x)y, 0), \quad g(w) = \frac{\lambda}{2}\|w\|_2^2,$$

with linear function class $\{f(w, x) = w^\top \psi(x) \colon w \in \mathbb{R}^d\}$, where $\psi(x) \in \mathbb{R}^d$ is a known feature vector. The loss $\phi(w, z) = L(f(w, x), y) + g(w)$ with $h(w) = 0$ is λ strongly convex. Moreover, the empirical minimizer $\mathcal{A}(\mathcal{S}_n)$ satisfies

$$\phi(\mathcal{A}(\mathcal{S}_n), \mathcal{S}_n) \leq \phi(0, \mathcal{S}_n) = 1.$$

Therefore $\|\mathcal{A}(\mathcal{S}_n)\|_2 \leq \sqrt{2/\lambda}$. This implies that we may consider the restriction of SVM to

$$\Omega = \left\{ w \colon \|w\|_2 \leq \sqrt{2/\lambda} \right\}$$

without changing the solution. It is clear that on Ω, $\phi(w, Z)$ with $Z = (X, Y)$ is $G(Z) = \|\psi(X)\|_2 + \sqrt{2\lambda}$ Lipschitz. From Theorem 7.8, we obtain the following expected generalization bound for SVM:

$$\mathbb{E}_{\mathcal{S}_n} \phi(\mathcal{A}(\mathcal{S}_n), \mathcal{D}) \leq \inf_{w \in \mathbb{R}^d} \phi(w, \mathcal{D}) + \frac{\mathbb{E}_X (\|\psi(X)\|_2 + \sqrt{2\lambda})^2}{\lambda(n+1)}.$$

Using Theorem 7.3, one can obtain an oracle inequality that holds with high probability. We leave it as an exercise.

Similar to the case of Lipschitz convex objective function, we have the following result for smooth convex functions.

Theorem 7.10   *Assume that $\phi(w, z)$ is λ-strongly convex and L-smooth in w on $\mathbb{R}^d$. Then the empirical risk minimization method*

$$\mathcal{A}(\mathcal{S}_n) = \arg \min_{w \in \mathbb{R}^d} \phi(w, \mathcal{S}_n)$$

is $\epsilon(Z_{n+1}, \mathcal{S}_{n+1}) = (1 + L/(2\lambda n)) \|\nabla \phi(\mathcal{A}(\mathcal{S}_{n+1}), Z_{n+1})\|_2^2 / (\lambda n)$ leave-one-out stable with respect to $\bar{\mathcal{A}}(\mathcal{S}_{n+1}) = \mathcal{A}(\mathcal{S}_{n+1})$.
  Moreover, if $L \leq 0.2\lambda n$, then the following expected oracle inequality holds:

$$\mathbb{E}_{\mathcal{S}_n} \phi(\mathcal{A}(\mathcal{S}_n), \mathcal{D}) \leq \inf_{w \in \mathbb{R}^d} \left[\phi(w, \mathcal{D}) + \frac{2.2}{\lambda n} \mathbb{E}_{Z \sim \mathcal{D}} \|\nabla \phi(w, Z)\|_2^2 \right].$$

Proof   Consider $\mathcal{S}_n$ and $\mathcal{S}_{n+1} = \mathcal{S}_n \cup \{Z_{n+1}\}$. Let

$$\mathcal{A}(\mathcal{S}_{n+1}) = \arg \min_{w \in \mathbb{R}^d} \phi(w, \mathcal{S}_{n+1}).$$

Using the optimality of $\mathcal{A}(\mathcal{S}_{n+1})$ and Proposition A.8, we obtain

$$\nabla \phi(\mathcal{A}(\mathcal{S}_{n+1}), \mathcal{S}_{n+1})^\top (\mathcal{A}(\mathcal{S}_n) - \mathcal{A}(\mathcal{S}_{n+1})) \geq 0. \tag{7.5}$$

Since

$$\phi(\mathcal{A}(\mathcal{S}_{n+1}), \mathcal{S}_n) = \frac{n+1}{n} \phi(\mathcal{A}(\mathcal{S}_{n+1}), \mathcal{S}_{n+1}) - \frac{1}{n} \phi(\mathcal{A}(\mathcal{S}_{n+1}), Z_{n+1}),$$

it follows that

$$\nabla\phi(\mathcal{A}(\mathcal{S}_{n+1}), \mathcal{S}_n)^\top (\mathcal{A}(\mathcal{S}_n) - \mathcal{A}(\mathcal{S}_{n+1}))$$

$$= \left(\frac{n+1}{n}\nabla\phi(\mathcal{A}(\mathcal{S}_{n+1}), \mathcal{S}_{n+1}) - \frac{1}{n}\nabla\phi(\mathcal{A}(\mathcal{S}_{n+1}), Z_{n+1}) \right)^\top (\mathcal{A}(\mathcal{S}_n) - \mathcal{A}(\mathcal{S}_{n+1}))$$

$$\geq -\frac{1}{n}\nabla\phi(\mathcal{A}(\mathcal{S}_{n+1}), Z_{n+1})^\top (\mathcal{A}(\mathcal{S}_n) - \mathcal{A}(\mathcal{S}_{n+1}))$$

$$\geq -\frac{\|\nabla\phi(\mathcal{A}(\mathcal{S}_{n+1}), Z_{n+1})\|_2}{n}\|\mathcal{A}(\mathcal{S}_{n+1}) - \mathcal{A}(\mathcal{S}_n))\|_2.$$

The first inequality used (7.5). Using the fact that $\mathcal{A}(\mathcal{S}_n)$ is the minimizer of $\phi(\cdot, \mathcal{S}_n)$, we obtain from Proposition A.8 that

$$\|\mathcal{A}(\mathcal{S}_n) - \mathcal{A}(\mathcal{S}_{n+1})\|_2 \leq \frac{\|\nabla\phi(\mathcal{A}(\mathcal{S}_{n+1}), Z_{n+1})\|_2}{\lambda n}. \tag{7.6}$$

We thus obtain

$$\phi(\mathcal{A}(\mathcal{S}_n), Z_{n+1}) - \phi(\mathcal{A}(\mathcal{S}_{n+1}), Z_{n+1})$$

$$\leq \nabla\phi(\mathcal{A}(\mathcal{S}_{n+1}), Z_{n+1})^\top (\mathcal{A}(\mathcal{S}_n) - \mathcal{A}(\mathcal{S}_{n+1})) + \frac{L}{2}\|\mathcal{A}(\mathcal{S}_n) - \mathcal{A}(\mathcal{S}_{n+1})\|_2^2$$

$$\leq \|\nabla\phi(\mathcal{A}(\mathcal{S}_{n+1}), Z_{n+1})\|_2\|\mathcal{A}(\mathcal{S}_n) - \mathcal{A}(\mathcal{S}_{n+1})\|_2 + \frac{L}{2}\|\mathcal{A}(\mathcal{S}_n) - \mathcal{A}(\mathcal{S}_{n+1})\|_2^2$$

$$\leq \left(\frac{1}{\lambda n} + \frac{L}{2\lambda^2 n^2} \right) \|\nabla\phi(\mathcal{A}(\mathcal{S}_{n+1}), Z_{n+1})\|_2^2.$$

The first inequality used the smoothness of ϕ. The second inequality used Cauchy–Schwarz. The third inequality used (7.6). This implies the stability result.

Next we want to apply Theorem 7.7, and need to bound the right-hand side. For this purpose, we consider an arbitrary $w \in \mathbb{R}^d$:

$$\frac{1}{n+1}\sum_{Z \in \mathcal{S}_{n+1}} \|\nabla\phi(\mathcal{A}(\mathcal{S}_{n+1}), Z)\|_2^2$$

$$\leq \frac{2}{n+1}\sum_{Z \in \mathcal{S}_{n+1}} \left[\|\nabla\phi(w, Z) - \nabla\phi(\mathcal{A}(\mathcal{S}_{n+1}), Z)\|_2^2 + \|\nabla\phi(w, Z)\|_2^2 \right]$$

$$\leq \frac{4L}{n+1}\sum_{Z \in \mathcal{S}_{n+1}} \left[\phi(w, Z) - \phi(\mathcal{A}(\mathcal{S}_{n+1}), Z) - \nabla\phi(\mathcal{A}(\mathcal{S}_{n+1}), Z)^\top (w - \mathcal{A}(\mathcal{S}_{n+1})) \right]$$

$$+ \frac{2}{n+1}\sum_{Z \in \mathcal{S}_{n+1}} \|\nabla\phi(w, Z)\|_2^2$$

$$= 4L[\phi(w, \mathcal{S}_{n+1}) - \phi(\mathcal{A}(\mathcal{S}_{n+1}), \mathcal{S}_{n+1}) - \nabla\phi(\mathcal{A}(\mathcal{S}_{n+1}), \mathcal{S}_{n+1})^\top (w - \mathcal{A}(\mathcal{S}_{n+1}))]$$

$$+ \frac{2}{n+1}\sum_{Z \in \mathcal{S}_{n+1}} \|\nabla\phi(w, Z)\|_2^2$$

$$= 4L[\phi(w, \mathcal{S}_{n+1}) - \phi(\mathcal{A}(\mathcal{S}_{n+1}), \mathcal{S}_{n+1})] + \frac{2}{n+1}\sum_{Z \in \mathcal{S}_{n+1}} \|\nabla\phi(w, Z)\|_2^2. \tag{7.7}$$

In this derivation, the first inequality used the algebraic calculation $\|a\|_2^2 \le 2\|b - a\|_2^2 + 2\|b\|_2^2$. The second inequality is due to Proposition A.7. The last equation used the fact that $\nabla\phi(\mathcal{A}(\mathcal{S}_{n+1}), \mathcal{S}_{n+1}) = 0$.

Now we obtain

$$
\begin{aligned}
\mathbb{E}_{\mathcal{S}_n}\phi(\mathcal{A}(\mathcal{S}_n), \mathcal{D}) \le {}& \mathbb{E}_{\mathcal{S}_{n+1}}\phi(\mathcal{A}(\mathcal{S}_{n+1}), \mathcal{S}_{n+1}) \\
& + \frac{(1 + L/(2\lambda n))}{\lambda n}\mathbb{E}_{\mathcal{S}_{n+1}}\frac{1}{n+1}\sum_{Z \in \mathcal{S}_{n+1}}\|\nabla\phi(\mathcal{A}(\mathcal{S}_{n+1}), Z)\|_2^2 \\
\le {}& \left(1 - \frac{4L(1 + L/(2\lambda n))}{\lambda n}\right)\mathbb{E}_{\mathcal{S}_{n+1}}\phi(\mathcal{A}(\mathcal{S}_{n+1}), \mathcal{S}_{n+1}) \\
& + \frac{4L(1 + L/(2\lambda n))}{\lambda n}\mathbb{E}_{\mathcal{S}_{n+1}}\phi(w, \mathcal{S}_{n+1}) \\
& + \frac{2(1 + L/(2\lambda n))}{\lambda n(n+1)}\mathbb{E}_{\mathcal{S}_{n+1}}\sum_{Z \in \mathcal{S}_{n+1}}\|\nabla\phi(w, Z)\|_2^2 \\
\le {}& \mathbb{E}_{\mathcal{S}_{n+1}}\phi(w, \mathcal{S}_{n+1}) + \frac{(2 + L/(\lambda n))}{\lambda n(n+1)}\mathbb{E}_{\mathcal{S}_{n+1}}\sum_{Z \in \mathcal{S}_{n+1}}\|\nabla\phi(w, Z)\|_2^2 \\
= {}& \phi(w, \mathcal{D}) + \frac{2(1 + L/(2\lambda n))}{\lambda n}\mathbb{E}_{Z \sim \mathcal{D}}\|\nabla\phi(w, Z)\|_2^2.
\end{aligned}
$$

In this derivation, the first inequality is an application of Theorem 7.7, with the leave-one-out stability result in the first part of the theorem. The second inequality used (7.7). The third inequality used the fact that $\phi(\mathcal{A}(\mathcal{S}_{n+1}), \mathcal{S}_{n+1}) \le \phi(w, \mathcal{S}_{n+1})$, and $1 - (4L(1 + L/(2\lambda n)))/(\lambda n) \ge 0$. We can now use $L/(\lambda n) \le 0.2$ to obtain the desired bound. $\qquad\square$

Example 7.11 We consider the linear ridge regression formulation with $y \in \mathbb{R}$, which employs the least squares loss

$$
L(f(w, x), y) = (f(w, x) - y)^2, \quad g(w) = \frac{\lambda}{2}\|w\|_2^2,
$$

with linear function class $\{f(w, x) = w^\top\psi(x): w \in \mathbb{R}^d\}$, where $\psi(x) \in \mathbb{R}^d$ is a known feature vector. The loss $\phi(w, z) = L(f(w, x), y) + g(w)$ is λ strongly convex. Moreover, $\phi(w, z)$ is

$$
L = 2\sup_X\|\psi(x)\|_2^2 + \lambda
$$

smooth for all $z = (x, y)$. If $L \le 0.2\lambda n$, we obtain from Theorem 7.10,

$$
\mathbb{E}_{\mathcal{S}_n}\phi(\mathcal{A}(\mathcal{S}_n), \mathcal{D}) \le \inf_{w \in \mathbb{R}^d}\left[\phi(w, \mathcal{D}) + \frac{8.8}{\lambda n}\mathbb{E}_X\|\psi(X)\|_2^2\mathbb{E}_{Y|X}(f(w, X) - Y)^2\right].
$$

In particular, if there exists w_* such that noise is uniformly bounded,

$$
\mathbb{E}_{Y|X}(f(w_*, X) - Y)^2 \le \sigma^2
$$

for all X, then

$$
\mathbb{E}_{\mathcal{S}_n}\phi(\mathcal{A}(\mathcal{S}_n), \mathcal{D}) \le \inf_{w \in \mathbb{R}^d}\left[\sigma^2 + \frac{\lambda}{2}\|w_*\|_2^2 + \frac{8.8\sigma^2}{\lambda n}\mathbb{E}_X\|\psi(X)\|_2^2\right].
$$

The result is superior to what can be obtained from Theorem 7.8 when σ^2 is small.

7.3 Stochastic Gradient Descent

Stochastic Gradient Descent (SGD) has been widely used in practical machine learning applications. Since it approximately implements the ERM method, one may use empirical process and uniform convergence to study its generalization behavior. However, one challenge is the lack of covering number bounds for general convex objective functions, although covering number results for special cases such as linear function classes exist. Another consideration is that in many applications, one may need to run SGD for finite iterations without achieving convergence to the minimum solution of ERM. In such a case, it is often much easier to obtain generalization analysis for SGD using the stability analysis, as demonstrated in Hardt et al. (2016).

Algorithm 7.1 Stochastic Gradient Descent Algorithm

Input: $\mathcal{S}_n$, $\bar{\phi}(w, z)$, w_0, learning rates $\{\eta_t\}$
Output: w_T
1 **for** $t = 1, 2, \ldots, T$ **do**
2 $\quad$ Randomly pick $Z \sim \mathcal{S}_n$
3 $\quad$ Let $w_t = \text{proj}_\Omega(w_{t-1} - \eta_t \nabla \bar{\phi}(w_{t-1}, Z))$
4 $\quad\quad$ where $\text{proj}_\Omega(v) = \arg\min_{u \in \Omega} \|u - v\|_2^2$
Return: w_T

A key lemma in Hardt et al. (2016) to analyze SGD for smooth convex function is the contraction property of SGD, as follows.

Lemma 7.12 (SGD Contraction) *Assume $\bar{\phi}(w)$ is an L-smooth and λ-strongly convex function of w on $\mathbb{R}^d$. Given any $w, w' \in \mathbb{R}^d$, we have for all $\eta \in [0, 1/L]$,*

$$\|\text{proj}_\Omega(w - \eta \nabla \bar{\phi}(w)) - \text{proj}_\Omega(w' - \eta \nabla \bar{\phi}(w'))\|_2 \leq (1 - \lambda\eta)\|w - w'\|_2.$$

Proof Let

$$\Delta_1 = \bar{\phi}(w) - \bar{\phi}(w') - \nabla\bar{\phi}(w')^\top (w - w'),$$
$$\Delta_2 = \bar{\phi}(w') - \bar{\phi}(w) - \nabla\bar{\phi}(w)^\top (w' - w).$$

We have

$$\|(w - \eta\nabla\bar{\phi}(w)) - (w' - \eta\nabla\bar{\phi}(w'))\|_2^2$$
$$= \|w - w'\|_2^2 - 2\eta(\nabla\bar{\phi}(w) - \nabla\bar{\phi}(w'))^\top (w - w') + \eta^2\|\nabla\bar{\phi}(w) - \nabla\bar{\phi}(w')\|_2^2$$
$$= \|w - w'\|_2^2 - 2\eta(\Delta_1 + \Delta_2) + \eta^2\|\nabla\bar{\phi}(w) - \nabla\bar{\phi}(w')\|_2^2$$
$$\leq \|w - w'\|_2^2 - 2\eta(\Delta_1 + \Delta_2) + \eta^2 L(\Delta_1 + \Delta_2)$$
$$\leq \|w - w'\|_2^2 - \eta(\Delta_1 + \Delta_2) \leq (1 - \eta\lambda)\|w - w'\|_2^2.$$

In the derivation, the first inequality used Proposition A.7. The second inequality used $\eta L \leq 1$. The third inequality used the strong convexity. We can now obtain the desired result by noticing that $\|\text{proj}_\Omega(u) - \text{proj}_\Omega(v)\|_2 \leq \|u - v\|_2$. $\quad\square$

We have the following uniform stability result for the SGD procedure. The proof is similar to that of Theorem 7.14, and we leave it as an exercise.

Theorem 7.13 *Assume that $\bar{\phi}(w, z) = \phi(w, z) + h(w)$ is λ-strongly convex and L-smooth in w on $\mathbb{R}^d$. Moreover, assume $\phi(w, z)$ is G Lipschitz on Ω. Define $b_0 = 0$, and for $t \geq 1$,*

$$b_t = (1 - \eta_t \lambda)b_{t-1} + \frac{2\eta_t}{n}G^2,$$

where $\eta_t \in [0, 1/L]$. Then after T steps, Algorithm 7.1 is $\epsilon = b_T$ uniformly stable with respect to $\phi(w, z)$. The result also holds for an arbitrary convex combination of the form $\sum_{t=0}^{T} \alpha_t w_t$ as the output of Algorithm 7.1, as long as the convex coefficient α_t (where $\alpha_t \geq 0$ and $\sum_{t=0}^{T} \alpha_t = 1$) are drawn from a known distribution.

We also have the following more refined result for SGD using the leave-one-out stability analysis.

Theorem 7.14 *Assume that $\bar{\phi}(w, z) = \phi(w, z) + h(w)$ is λ-strongly convex and L-smooth in w on $\mathbb{R}^d$. Moreover, assume $\phi(w, z)$ is $G(z)$ Lipschitz on Ω. Define $b_0 = 0$, and for $t \geq 1$,*

$$b_t = (1 - \eta_t \lambda)b_{t-1} + \frac{2\eta_t}{n+1}\mathbb{E}_{\mathcal{D}}G(Z)^2,$$

where $\eta_t \in [0, 1/L]$. We have the following result for Algorithm 7.1,

$$\mathbb{E}_{\mathcal{S}_n}\mathbb{E}_\mathcal{A}\phi(\mathcal{A}(\mathcal{S}_n), \mathcal{D}) \leq \mathbb{E}_{\mathcal{S}_{n+1}}\mathbb{E}_\mathcal{A}\phi(\mathcal{A}(\mathcal{S}_{n+1}), \mathcal{S}_{n+1}) + b_T,$$

where we use $\mathbb{E}_\mathcal{A}$ to denote the randomization in SGD. The result also holds for an arbitrary convex combination of the form $\sum_{t=0}^{T} \alpha_t w_t$ as the output of Algorithm 7.1, as long as the convex coefficient α_t (where $\alpha_t \geq 0$ and $\sum_{t=0}^{T} \alpha_t = 1$) is drawn from a known distribution.

Proof Let w_t be the intermediate steps of SGD on $\mathcal{S}_n$, and w_t' be the intermediate steps of SGD on $\mathcal{S}_{n+1} = \mathcal{S}_n \cup \{Z_{n+1}\}$. We consider a coupling of w_t and w_t', with the same randomization for w_t and w_t', except when we choose $Z = Z_{n+1}$ for update of w_t', we choose $Z = Z_i$ for updating of w_t with i drawn uniformly from $[n]$. It follows from Lemma 7.12 that with this coupling, at each time t, with probability $n/(n+1)$, we choose the same Z_i to update both w_t and w_t':

$$\|w_t - w_t'\|_2 \leq (1 - \lambda\eta_t)\|w_{t-1} - w_{t-1}'\|_2.$$

With probability $1/(n+1)$, we have

$$\|w_t - w'_t\|_2$$
$$\leq \|[w_{t-1} - \eta_t \nabla \bar{\phi}(w_{t-1}, Z_i)] - [w'_{t-1} - \eta_t \nabla \bar{\phi}(w'_{t-1}, Z_i)]\|_2$$
$$+ \eta_t \|\nabla \bar{\phi}(w'_{t-1}, Z_i) - \nabla \bar{\phi}(w'_{t-1}, Z_{n+1})\|_2$$
$$\leq (1 - \lambda \eta_t)\|w_{t-1} - w'_{t-1}\|_2 + \eta_t(\|\nabla \phi(w'_{t-1}, Z_{n+1})\|_2 + \|\nabla \phi(w'_{t-1}, Z_i)\|_2),$$

where i is uniformly from $[n]$. Note that the second inequality used Lemma 7.12 again. Therefore,

$$\mathbb{E}_{\mathcal{A}}\|w_t - w'_t\|_2 \leq (1 - \eta_t \lambda)\mathbb{E}_{\mathcal{A}}\|w_{t-1} - w'_{t-1}\|_2$$
$$+ \frac{\eta_t}{n(n+1)} \sum_{i=1}^{n}(G(Z_i) + G(Z_{n+1})).$$

We now define

$$s_t = \mathbb{E}_{\mathcal{S}_{n+1}}\mathbb{E}_{\mathcal{A}}\|w_t - w'_t\|_2 G(Z_{n+1}),$$

then we have

$$s_t \leq (1 - \eta_t \lambda)s_{t-1} + \mathbb{E}_{\mathcal{S}_{n+1}}\frac{\eta_t}{n(n+1)}\sum_{i=1}^{n}(G(Z_i) + G(Z_{n+1}))G(Z_{n+1})$$

$$= (1 - \eta_t \lambda)s_{t-1} + \frac{\eta_t}{n+1}[\mathbb{E}_{\mathcal{D}}G(Z)^2 + (\mathbb{E}_{\mathcal{D}}G(Z))^2]$$

$$\leq (1 - \eta_t \lambda)s_{t-1} + \frac{2\eta_t}{n+1}\mathbb{E}_{\mathcal{D}}G(Z)^2.$$

It follows from the definition of b_t that $s_t \leq b_t$. Therefore,

$$\mathbb{E}_{\mathcal{S}_{n+1}}\mathbb{E}_{\mathcal{A}}\|w_t - w'_t\|_2 G(Z_{n+1}) \leq b_t \leq b_T. \tag{7.8}$$

Assume that $\mathcal{A}(\mathcal{S}_n)$ returns an arbitrary convex combination $\sum_{t=0}^{T}\alpha_t w_t$, and $\mathcal{A}(\mathcal{S}_{n+1})$ returns $\sum_{t=0}^{T}\alpha_t w'_t$ with the same random coefficients α_t from the same known distribution. Let $\epsilon(Z_{n+1}, \mathcal{S}_{n+1}) = \mathbb{E}_{\mathcal{A}}\phi(\mathcal{A}(\mathcal{S}_n), Z_{n+1}) - \mathbb{E}_{\mathcal{A}}\phi(\mathcal{A}(\mathcal{S}_{n+1}), Z_{n+1})$, then from the Lipschitz condition of $\phi(w, Z_{n+1})$ and (7.8), we obtain

$$\mathbb{E}_{\mathcal{S}_{n+1}}\mathbb{E}_{\mathcal{A}}\epsilon(Z_{n+1}, \mathcal{S}_{n+1}) \leq \mathbb{E}_{\mathcal{S}_{n+1}}\mathbb{E}_{\mathcal{A}}\|\mathcal{A}(\mathcal{S}_n) - \mathcal{A}(\mathcal{S}_{n+1})\|_2 G(Z_{n+1}) \leq b_T.$$

We obtain from Theorem 7.7 that

$$\mathbb{E}_{\mathcal{S}_n}\mathbb{E}_{\mathcal{A}}\phi(\mathcal{A}(\mathcal{S}_n), \mathcal{D}) \leq \mathbb{E}_{\mathcal{S}_{n+1}}\mathbb{E}_{\mathcal{A}}\phi(\mathcal{A}(\mathcal{S}_{n+1}), \mathcal{S}_{n+1}) + b_T.$$

This proves the desired result. □

Example 7.15 We can obtain an oracle inequality from Theorem 7.14 by assuming further that after T SGD steps, Algorithm 7.1 approximately solves the empirical risk minimization problem as

$$\mathbb{E}_{\mathcal{A}}\phi(\mathcal{A}(\mathcal{S}_{n+1}), \mathcal{S}_{n+1}) \leq \inf_{w \in \Omega} \bar{\phi}(w, \mathcal{S}_{n+1}) + \epsilon_T(\mathcal{S}_{n+1})$$

for some $\epsilon_T(\cdot) \geq 0$. Here $\mathcal{A}$ may return a convex combination of w_t for $t \leq T$ (see Section 14.4 for examples of such convergence results). Using such a result, we obtain from Theorem 7.14 the following oracle inequality:

$$\mathbb{E}_{\mathcal{S}_n}\mathbb{E}_{\mathcal{A}}\phi(\mathcal{A}(\mathcal{S}_n), \mathcal{D}) \leq \inf_{w \in \Omega} \bar{\phi}(w, \mathcal{D}) + \mathbb{E}_{\mathcal{S}_{n+1}}\epsilon_T(\mathcal{S}_{n+1}) + b_T.$$

In particular, we consider $h(w) = 0$, a constant learning rate η for T steps, and a final estimator w_t from the algorithm with t drawn uniformly from 0 to $T - 1$. Then Theorem 14.5 implies that

$$\epsilon_T(\mathcal{S}_{n+1}) = \frac{\|w_0 - w\|_2^2}{2T\eta} + \frac{\eta}{2}G^2,$$

where we assume that $\|\nabla\phi(w, z)\|_2 \leq G$. In this case, $b_t = 2\eta t G^2/(n+1)$. This implies a bound

$$\mathbb{E}_{\mathcal{S}_n}\mathbb{E}_{\mathcal{A}}\phi(\mathcal{A}(\mathcal{S}_n), \mathcal{D}) \leq \inf_{w \in \Omega}\left[\phi(w, \mathcal{D}) + \frac{\|w_0 - w\|_2^2}{2T\eta}\right] + \frac{\eta}{2}G^2 + \frac{2\eta T G^2}{n+1}.$$

Note that this result allows $T > n$, which means we can run SGD repeatedly over the dataset $\mathcal{S}_n$. For example, we may take $T = n^2$, and $\eta = O(n^{-1.5})$ to obtain a convergence rate of $O(1/\sqrt{n})$.

In comparison, the online to batch conversion technique in Chapter 14 requires each data point Z in the algorithm to be drawn independently from $\mathcal{D}$. This means that the online to batch technique applies only when we run SGD over the dataset $\mathcal{S}_n$ once via sampling without replacement. It does not handle the situation that SGD is applied to the dataset repeatedly (as commonly done in practice).

Similar to Theorem 7.10, it is possible to remove the Lipschitz condition in Theorem 7.14, and obtain bounds in terms of smoothness only. However, the resulting bound will become more complex, and we will leave it as an exercise.

7.4 Gibbs Algorithm for Nonconvex Problems

Although it is possible to derive stability results for SGD for nonconvex problems under restrictive conditions, as shown in Hardt et al. (2016), the resulting bounds are rather weak. It is also difficult to establish stability results for the ERM solution of nonconvex optimization. However, in the following, we show that appropriate randomization can be used to achieve stability even in the nonconvex case. In particular, we consider a learning algorithm that randomly draws w from the following "posterior distribution," also referred to as the *Gibbs distribution*:

$$p(w|\mathcal{S}_n) \propto p_0(w) \exp\left(-\beta \sum_{Z \in \mathcal{S}_n} \phi(w, Z)\right), \tag{7.9}$$

where $\beta > 0$ is a tuning parameter, $p_0(w)$ is a prior on Ω. This randomized learning algorithm is often referred to as the *Gibbs algorithm*, and its test performance is measured by the expectation

$$\mathbb{E}_{\mathcal{A}}\phi(\mathcal{A}(\mathcal{S}_n), \mathcal{D}) = \mathbb{E}_{w \sim p(w|\mathcal{S}_n)}\phi(w, \mathcal{D}).$$

If $\beta \to \infty$, the method converges to ERM. We have the following characterization of Gibbs distribution, which means that it can be regarded as the entropy-regularized ERM over the probability distributions $\Delta(\Omega)$. Here $\mathrm{KL}(\cdot||\cdot)$ is the KL-divergence defined in Appendix B, which is always nonnegative.

Proposition 7.16 *Given any function $U(w)$, we have*

$$\min_{p \in \Delta(\Omega)} \left[\mathbb{E}_{w \sim p} U(w) + \mathrm{KL}(p||p_0) \right] = - \ln \mathbb{E}_{w \sim p_0} \exp(-U(w)),$$

and the solution is achieved by the Gibbs distribution $q(w) \propto p_0(w) \exp(-U(w))$. Here $\Delta(\Omega)$ denotes the set of probability distributions on Ω.

Proof Let $C = \mathbb{E}_{w \sim p_0} \exp(-U(w))$. Then we have

$$\mathbb{E}_{w \sim p} U(w) + \mathrm{KL}(p||p_0) = \mathbb{E}_{w \sim p} \ln \frac{p(w)}{p_0(w) \exp(-U(w))}$$

$$= \mathbb{E}_{w \sim p} \ln \frac{p(w)}{Cq(w)} \geq - \ln C.$$

The inequality used the fact that $\mathrm{KL}(p||q) \geq 0$, and the equality holds when $p(w) = q(w)$. $\qquad \square$

Proposition 7.16 implies that (7.9) satisfies

$$p(w|\mathcal{S}_n) = \arg \min_{p \in \Delta(\Omega)} \left[\mathbb{E}_{w \sim p} \phi(w, \mathcal{S}_n) + \frac{1}{\beta n} \mathrm{KL}(p||p_0) \right]. \qquad (7.10)$$

We can now state the uniform stability result for the Gibbs distribution.

Theorem 7.17 *Consider the Gibbs algorithm $\mathcal{A}$ described in (7.9). If for all z: $\sup_{w \in \Omega} \phi(w, z) - \inf_{w \in \Omega} \phi(w, z) \leq M$, then $\mathcal{A}$ is $\epsilon = 0.5(e^{2\beta M} - 1)M$ uniformly stable.*

Proof Consider $\mathcal{S}_n$ and $\mathcal{S}'_n$ that differ by one element. It follows that for any w,

$$\exp(-\beta M) \leq \frac{\exp(-\beta \phi(w, \mathcal{S}'_n))}{\exp(-\beta \phi(w, \mathcal{S}_n))} \leq \exp(\beta M).$$

This implies that

$$\exp(-\beta M) \leq \frac{\mathbb{E}_{w \sim p_0} \exp(-\beta \phi(w, \mathcal{S}'_n))}{\mathbb{E}_{w \sim p_0} \exp(-\beta \phi(w, \mathcal{S}_n))} \leq \exp(\beta M).$$

Therefore,

$$\frac{p(w|\mathcal{S}'_n)}{p(w|\mathcal{S}_n)} = \frac{\exp(-\beta \phi(w, \mathcal{S}'_n))}{\exp(-\beta \phi(w, \mathcal{S}_n))} \frac{\mathbb{E}_{w \sim p_0} \exp(-\beta \phi(w, \mathcal{S}_n))}{\mathbb{E}_{w \sim p_0} \exp(-\beta \phi(w, \mathcal{S}'_n))} \leq e^{2\beta M}.$$

This implies that

$$\left| \frac{p(w|\mathcal{S}'_n)}{p(w|\mathcal{S}_n)} - 1 \right| \leq \max \left(1 - e^{-2\beta M}, e^{2\beta M} - 1 \right) \leq e^{2\beta M} - 1.$$

Now let $\bar{\phi}(z) = \inf_w \phi(w, z) + 0.5M$. We know that $|\phi(w, z) - \bar{\phi}(z)| \le 0.5M$. Therefore

$$\mathbb{E}_{\mathcal{A}}\phi(\mathcal{A}(\mathcal{S}_n'), z) - \mathbb{E}_{\mathcal{A}}\phi(\mathcal{A}(\mathcal{S}_n), z)$$

$$= \mathbb{E}_{w \sim p(\cdot|\mathcal{S}_n)} \left(\frac{p(w|\mathcal{S}_n')}{p(w|\mathcal{S}_n)} - 1 \right) [\phi(w, z) - \bar{\phi}(z)]$$

$$\le \mathbb{E}_{w \sim p(\cdot|\mathcal{S}_n)} \left| \frac{p(w|\mathcal{S}_n')}{p(w|\mathcal{S}_n)} - 1 \right| |\phi(w, z) - \bar{\phi}(z)|$$

$$\le (e^{2\beta M} - 1) \cdot 0.5M.$$

This proves the desired result. $\qquad\square$

Example 7.18 Consider the Gibbs algorithm $\mathcal{A}$ described in (7.9) with bounded loss as in Theorem 7.17. We have the following expected oracle inequality:

$$\mathbb{E}_{\mathcal{S}_n} \mathbb{E}_{\mathcal{A}} \phi(\mathcal{A}(\mathcal{S}_n), \mathcal{D})$$

$$\le \mathbb{E}_{\mathcal{S}_n} \mathbb{E}_{\mathcal{A}} \phi(\mathcal{A}(\mathcal{S}_n), \mathcal{S}_n) + 0.5(e^{2\beta M} - 1)M$$

$$\le \mathbb{E}_{\mathcal{S}_n} \left[\mathbb{E}_{w \sim p(\cdot|\mathcal{S}_n)} \phi(w, \mathcal{S}_n) + \frac{1}{\beta n} \mathrm{KL}(p(\cdot|\mathcal{S}_n) \| p_0) \right] + 0.5(e^{2\beta M} - 1)M$$

$$\le \inf_{p \in \Delta(\Omega)} \left[\mathbb{E}_{w \sim p} \phi(w, \mathcal{D}) + \frac{1}{\beta n} \mathrm{KL}(p \| p_0) \right] + 0.5(e^{2\beta M} - 1)M.$$

The first inequality followed from Theorem 7.2 and Theorem 7.17. The second inequality used non negativity of KL-divergence. The last inequality used the fact that the Gibbs distribution minimizes (7.10).

We can also prove a more refined result using leave-one-out stability as follows.

Theorem 7.19 *Consider the Gibbs algorithm $\mathcal{A}$ described in (7.9). If for all z:* $\sup_{w \in \Omega} \phi(w, z) - \inf_{w \in \Omega} \phi(w, z) \le M$, *then $\mathcal{A}$ is*

$$\epsilon(Z_{n+1}, \mathcal{S}_{n+1}) = \beta e^{\beta M} \mathrm{Var}_{\mathcal{A}}[\phi(\mathcal{A}(\mathcal{S}_n), Z_{n+1})]$$

leave-one-out stable. If the loss function ϕ satisfies the variance condition (3.13), which we restate as

$$\mathrm{Var}_{Z \sim \mathcal{D}}[\phi(w, Z)] \le c_0^2 + c_1[\phi(w, \mathcal{D})],$$

then for $\beta > 0$ such that $c_2 = 1 - c_1 \beta e^{\beta M} > 0$, we have

$$c_2 \mathbb{E}_{\mathcal{S}_n} \mathbb{E}_{\mathcal{A}} \phi(\mathcal{A}(\mathcal{S}_n), \mathcal{D}) \le \inf_{p \in \Delta(\Omega)} \left[\mathbb{E}_{w \sim p} \phi(w, \mathcal{D}) + \frac{1}{\beta(n+1)} \mathrm{KL}(p \| p_0) \right] + \beta e^{\beta M} c_0^2$$

$$\le \inf_{w \in \Omega} \phi(w, \mathcal{D}) + \inf_{\epsilon > 0} \left[\epsilon - \frac{\ln p_0(\Omega(\epsilon))}{\beta(n+1)} \right] + \beta e^{\beta M} c_0^2,$$

where $\Omega(\epsilon) = \{w \in \Omega: \phi(w, \mathcal{D}) \le \inf_w \phi(w, \mathcal{D}) + \epsilon\}$.

Proof Let $\bar{\mathcal{A}}(\mathcal{S}_{n+1}, Z_{n+1})$ be the Gibbs algorithm with posterior $p(\cdot|\mathcal{S}_{n+1})$. Let $\tilde{\phi}(w, Z_{n+1}) = \phi(w, Z_{n+1}) - \mathbb{E}_{w' \sim p(\cdot|\mathcal{S}_n)} \phi(w', Z_{n+1})$. Then $|\tilde{\phi}(w, Z_{n+1})| \le M$. Note

$$\mathbb{E}_{w \sim p(\cdot|\mathcal{S}_{n+1})}\tilde{\phi}(w, Z_{n+1}) = \mathbb{E}_{w \sim p(\cdot|\mathcal{S}_n)} \frac{\exp(-\beta\tilde{\phi}(w, Z_{n+1}))\tilde{\phi}(w, Z_{n+1})}{\mathbb{E}_{w' \sim p(\cdot|\mathcal{S}_n)}\exp(-\beta\tilde{\phi}(w', Z_{n+1}))}, \tag{7.11}$$

$$\mathbb{E}_{w \sim p(\cdot|\mathcal{S}_n)}\tilde{\phi}(w, Z_{n+1}) = 0. \tag{7.12}$$

It follows that

$$\mathbb{E}_{w \sim p(\cdot|\mathcal{S}_n)}\phi(w, Z_{n+1}) - \mathbb{E}_{w \sim p(\cdot|\mathcal{S}_{n+1})}\phi(w, Z_{n+1})$$

$$= \mathbb{E}_{w \sim p(\cdot|\mathcal{S}_n)}\tilde{\phi}(w, Z_{n+1}) - \mathbb{E}_{w \sim p(\cdot|\mathcal{S}_{n+1})}\tilde{\phi}(w, Z_{n+1})$$

$$= \mathbb{E}_{w \sim p(\cdot|\mathcal{S}_n)}\left[1 - \frac{\exp(-\beta\tilde{\phi}(w, Z_{n+1}))}{\mathbb{E}_{w' \sim p(\cdot|\mathcal{S}_n)}\exp(-\beta\tilde{\phi}(w', Z_{n+1}))}\right]\tilde{\phi}(w, Z_{n+1})$$

$$= \frac{\mathbb{E}_{w \sim p(\cdot|\mathcal{S}_n)}\left[1 - \exp(-\beta\tilde{\phi}(w, Z_{n+1}))\right]\tilde{\phi}(w, Z_{n+1})}{\mathbb{E}_{w' \sim p(\cdot|\mathcal{S}_n)}\exp(-\beta\tilde{\phi}(w', Z_{n+1}))}$$

$$\leq \frac{\mathbb{E}_{w \sim p(\cdot|\mathcal{S}_n)}\left|\exp(-\beta\tilde{\phi}(w, Z_{n+1})) - 1\right||\tilde{\phi}(w, Z_{n+1})|}{\exp(-\mathbb{E}_{w' \sim p(\cdot|\mathcal{S}_n)}\beta\tilde{\phi}(w', Z_{n+1}))}$$

$$\leq \frac{\beta e^{\beta M}\mathbb{E}_{w \sim p(\cdot|\mathcal{S}_n)}|\tilde{\phi}(w, Z_{n+1})|^2}{\exp(-\mathbb{E}_{w' \sim p(\cdot|\mathcal{S}_n)}\beta\tilde{\phi}(w', Z_{n+1}))} = \beta e^{\beta M}\text{Var}_{w \sim p(\cdot|\mathcal{S}_n)}[\phi(w, Z_{n+1})].$$

In these derivations, the second equality used (7.11), and the third equality used (7.12). The first inequality used the Jensen inequality and the convexity of $\exp(\cdot)$; the second inequality used $|e^a - 1| \leq e^{|a|}|a|$. The last equation used (7.12). This proves the desired leave-one-out stability result. It follows that

$$\mathbb{E}_{\mathcal{S}_n}\mathbb{E}_{\mathcal{A}}\phi(\mathcal{A}(\mathcal{S}_n), \mathcal{D})$$

$$\leq \mathbb{E}_{\mathcal{S}_{n+1}}\mathbb{E}_{\mathcal{A}}\phi(\mathcal{A}(\mathcal{S}_{n+1}), \mathcal{S}_{n+1}) + \beta e^{\beta M}\mathbb{E}_{\mathcal{S}_n}\mathbb{E}_{Z \sim \mathcal{D}}\text{Var}_{\mathcal{A}}\phi(\mathcal{A}(\mathcal{S}_n), Z)$$

$$\leq \mathbb{E}_{\mathcal{S}_{n+1}}\left[\mathbb{E}_{w \sim p(\cdot|\mathcal{S}_{n+1})}\phi(w, \mathcal{S}_{n+1}) + \frac{1}{\beta(n+1)}\text{KL}(p(\cdot|\mathcal{S}_{n+1})||p_0)\right]$$

$$\quad + \beta e^{\beta M}\mathbb{E}_{\mathcal{S}_n}\mathbb{E}_{Z \sim \mathcal{D}}\text{Var}_{\mathcal{A}}\phi(\mathcal{A}(\mathcal{S}_n), Z)$$

$$\leq \inf_p\left[\mathbb{E}_{w \sim p}\phi(w, \mathcal{D}) + \frac{1}{\beta(n+1)}\text{KL}(p||p_0)\right] + \beta e^{\beta M}\mathbb{E}_{\mathcal{S}_n}\mathbb{E}_{Z \sim \mathcal{D}}\text{Var}_{\mathcal{A}}\phi(\mathcal{A}(\mathcal{S}_n), Z)$$

$$\leq \inf_p\left[\mathbb{E}_{w \sim p}\phi(w, \mathcal{D}) + \frac{1}{\beta(n+1)}\text{KL}(p||p_0)\right] + \beta e^{\beta M}[c_0^2 + c_1\mathbb{E}_{\mathcal{S}_n}\mathbb{E}_{\mathcal{A}}\phi(\mathcal{A}(\mathcal{S}_n), \mathcal{D})].$$

The first inequality follows from Theorem 7.7. The second inequality used the fact that KL-divergence is nonnegative. The third inequality used (7.10), and $\mathbb{E}_{\mathcal{S}_{n+1}}\phi(w, \mathcal{S}_{n+1}) = \phi(w, \mathcal{D})$. The last inequality used the variance condition. We can obtain the desired oracle inequality of the theorem by rearranging the terms.

The second part of the oracle inequality is achieved by taking

$$p(w) = \frac{p_0(w)\mathbb{1}(w \in \Omega(\epsilon))}{p_0(\Omega(\epsilon))},$$

so that $\text{KL}(p||p_0) = -\ln p_0(\Omega(\epsilon))$. $\qquad\square$

Example 7.20 Consider a parametric model, where $\Omega \subset \mathbb{R}^d$ is a compact set, and $w_* \in \arg\min_{w \in \Omega} \phi(w, \mathcal{D})$. Assume that $\phi(w, z) - \phi(w_*, z) \leq c_m \|w - w_*\|_2$, and $-\ln p_0(\{w \in \Omega : \|w - w_*\|_2 \leq \epsilon\}) \geq c_1' + c_2' d \ln(1/\epsilon)$. Then there exists $c_3' > 0$ such that for $\beta n \geq 1$,

$$\inf_{\epsilon > 0} \left[\epsilon - \frac{\ln p_0(\Omega(\epsilon))}{\beta(n+1)} \right] = \frac{c_2 c_3' d \ln(\beta n)}{\beta n}.$$

The oracle inequality in Theorem 7.19 becomes

$$c_2 \mathbb{E}_{\mathcal{S}_n} \mathbb{E}_{\mathcal{A}} \phi(\mathcal{A}(\mathcal{S}_n), \mathcal{D}) \leq \phi(w_*, \mathcal{D}) + \frac{c_3' d \ln(\beta n)}{\beta n} + \beta e^{\beta M} c_0^2.$$

Example 7.21 Consider the least squares problem of Example 3.18:

$$\phi(w, z) = (f(w, x) - y)^2 - (f(w_*, x) - y)^2, \quad (f(w, x) - y)^2 \in [0, 1],$$

and we assume that $f(w_*, x) = \mathbb{E}[y|x]$ with $w_* \in \Omega$. Then the variance condition is satisfied with $c_0 = 0$ and $c_1 = 2$. We can take β so that $4\beta e^\beta < 1$. In the parametric model case of Example 7.20, this leads to a fast rate

$$\mathbb{E}_{\mathcal{S}_n} \mathbb{E}_{w \sim \mathcal{A}} \mathbb{E}_{(X,Y)} (f(w, X) - Y)^2 \leq \mathbb{E}_{(X,Y)} (f(w_*, X) - Y)^2 + O\left(\frac{d \ln n}{n} \right).$$

7.5 Stochastic Gradient Langevin Dynamics

Similar to SGD, which solves ERM, the stochastic gradient Langevin dynamics (SGLD) algorithm can be used to sample from the Gibbs distribution. The resulting algorithm, described in Algorithm 7.2, is a slight modification of Algorithm 7.1 with the addition of Gaussian noise ϵ_t at each step.

Algorithm 7.2 Stochastic Gradient Langevin Dynamics Algorithm

Input: $\mathcal{S}_n$, $\bar{\phi}(w, z)$, p_0, learning rates $\{\eta_t\}$
Output: w_T
1 Draw $w_0 \sim p_0$
2 **for** $t = 1, 2, \ldots, T$ **do**
3 | Randomly pick $Z \sim \mathcal{S}_n$ uniformly at random
4 | Randomly generate $\epsilon_t \sim N(0, I)$
5 | Let $\tilde{w}_t = w_{t-1} - \eta_t \nabla \bar{\phi}(w_{t-1}, Z) + \sqrt{2\eta_t/\beta} \epsilon_t$
6 | Let $w_t = \text{proj}_\Omega(\tilde{w}_t)$, where $\text{proj}_\Omega(v) = \arg\min_{u \in \Omega} \|u - v\|_2^2$
Return: w_T

Since the addition of Gaussian noise is independent of the data, the stability analysis of SGD still holds. For strongly convex functions, we can thus obtain the following result. The proof is left as an exercise.

Theorem 7.22 *Assume that $\bar{\phi}(w, z) = \phi(w, z) + h(w)$ is λ-strongly convex and L-smooth in w on $\mathbb{R}^d$. Moreover, assume $\phi(w, z)$ is G Lipschitz on Ω. Define $b_0 = 0$, and for $t \geq 1$,*

$$b_t = (1 - \eta_t \lambda) b_{t-1} + \frac{2\eta_t}{n} G^2,$$

where $\eta_t \in [0, 1/L]$. Then after T steps, Algorithm 7.2 is $\epsilon = b_T$ uniformly stable. The result also holds for any random convex combinations of $\{w_t : t \leq T\}$ with combination coefficients from a known distribution.

It is also possible to derive stability result with nonconvex functions for SGLD. However, it is simpler to analyze the nonstochastic version (often referred to as unadjusted Langevin algorithm, or ULA), where line 5 of Algorithm 7.2 is replaced by the full gradient

$$\tilde{w}_t = w_{t-1} - \eta_t \nabla \bar{\phi}(w_{t-1}, \mathcal{S}_n) + \sqrt{2\eta_t/\beta} \epsilon_t. \tag{7.13}$$

Theorem 7.23 *Assume that for all z, z', $\bar{\phi}(w, z) - \bar{\phi}(w, z')$ is a G-Lipschitz function of w on $\Omega \subset \mathbb{R}^d$ (but $\bar{\phi}$ is not necessarily convex):*

$$\|\nabla \bar{\phi}(w, z) - \nabla \bar{\phi}(w, z')\|_2 \leq G.$$

Assume also that $\sup_{w,w' \in \Omega}[\phi(w, z) - \phi(w', z)] \leq M$ for all z. Then after T steps, ULA (with line 5 of Algorithm 7.2 replaced by (7.13)) is ϵ_T uniformly stable with

$$\epsilon_T = \frac{MG}{4n}\sqrt{2\beta \sum_{t=1}^{T} \eta_t}.$$

Proof Consider $\mathcal{S}_n \sim \mathcal{D}^n$ and $\mathcal{S}'_n = (\mathcal{S}_n \setminus \{Z_n\}) \cup \{Z'_n\}$, where $Z'_n \sim \mathcal{D}$ is a sample independent of $\mathcal{S}_n$. Let w_t and w'_t be the outputs of ULA with $\mathcal{S}_n$ and $\mathcal{S}'_n$ respectively. Moreover, let p_t be the distribution of w_t; let $p_{t,t-1}(w_t, w_{t-1})$ be the joint distribution of (w_t, w_{t-1}); let $\tilde{p}_{t,t-1}(\tilde{w}_t, w_{t-1})$ be the joint distribution of $(\tilde{w}_t, w_{t-1})$. Similarly, we define p'_t, $p'_{t,t-1}$ and $\tilde{p}'_{t,t-1}$.

We now let $\bar{w}_t(w) = w - \eta_t \nabla \bar{\phi}(w, \mathcal{S}_n)$ and $\bar{w}'_t(w) = w - \eta_t \nabla \bar{\phi}(w, \mathcal{S}'_n)$. Then

$$\tilde{p}_{t,t-1}(\cdot|w_{t-1} = w) = N(\bar{w}_t(w), (2\eta_t/\beta)I),$$
$$\tilde{p}'_{t,t-1}(\cdot|w'_{t-1} = w) = N(\bar{w}'_t(w), (2\eta_t/\beta)I).$$

We have

$$\mathrm{KL}(\tilde{p}_{t,t-1}(\cdot|w_{t-1} = w)\|\tilde{p}'_{t,t-1}(\cdot|w'_{t-1} = w))$$
$$= \mathrm{KL}\left(N(\bar{w}_t(w), (2\eta_t/\beta)I)\| N(\bar{w}'_t(w), (2\eta_t/\beta)I)\right)$$
$$= \frac{\beta\|\bar{w}_t(w) - \bar{w}'_t(w)\|_2^2}{4\eta_t} \leq \frac{\beta\eta_t G^2}{4n^2}. \tag{7.14}$$

The second equality used the formula for the KL-divergence of two Gaussian distributions. The last inequality used the Lipschitz condition of $\bar{\phi}$. We have

$$\mathrm{KL}(p_t\|p'_t) - \mathrm{KL}(p_{t-1}\|p'_{t-1})$$
$$= \mathrm{KL}(p_{t,t-1}\|p'_{t,t-1}) - \mathbb{E}_{w \sim p_t}\mathrm{KL}(p_{t,t-1}(\cdot|w_t = w)\|p'_{t,t-1}(\cdot|w'_t = w))$$
$$\quad - \mathrm{KL}(p_{t-1}\|p'_{t-1})$$
$$\leq \mathrm{KL}(p_{t,t-1}\|p'_{t,t-1}) - \mathrm{KL}(p_{t-1}\|p'_{t-1})$$
$$= \mathbb{E}_{w \sim p_{t-1}}\mathrm{KL}(p_{t,t-1}(\cdot|w_{t-1} = w)\|p'_{t,t-1}(\cdot|w'_{t-1} = w))$$
$$\leq \mathbb{E}_{w \sim p_{t-1}}\mathrm{KL}(\tilde{p}_{t,t-1}(\cdot|w_{t-1} = w)\|\tilde{p}'_{t,t-1}(\cdot|w'_{t-1} = w))$$
$$\leq \frac{\beta\eta_t G^2}{4n^2}.$$

The first inequality used the fact that KL-divergence is always nonnegative. The second inequality used the data processing inequality for KL-divergence (see Theorem B.4). The last inequality used (7.14).

By summing over $t = 1$ to $t = T$, and note that $p_0 = p_0'$, we obtain

$$\mathrm{KL}(p_T \| p_T') \le \frac{\beta G^2 \sum_{t=1}^{T} \eta_t}{4n^2}. \tag{7.15}$$

Therefore for any z, we have

$$\mathbb{E}_{\mathcal{A}} \phi(\mathcal{A}(\mathcal{S}_n'), z) - \mathbb{E}_{\mathcal{A}} \phi(\mathcal{A}(\mathcal{S}_n), z)$$

$$\le M \| p_T - p_T' \|_{\mathrm{TV}} \le M \sqrt{0.5 \mathrm{KL}(p_T \| p_T')} \le \frac{MG}{4n} \sqrt{2\beta \sum_{t=1}^{T} \eta_t}.$$

The first inequality used the definition of TV-norm in Proposition B.7. The second inequality used Pinsker's inequality of Theorem B.9. The last inequality used (7.15). This implies the desired result. □

The stability result in Theorem 7.23 can be applied to nonconvex functions. Moreover, the final bound depends on β. When $\beta \to 0$, we obtain a more and more stable algorithm. This is consistent with the analysis of the Gibbs algorithm. In comparison, the result of Theorem 7.22, which only applies to convex functions, does not depend on β.

7.6 Concentration of Uniformly Stable Leave-One-Out Estimate

This section proves a concentration inequality for an appropriately defined leave-one-out estimate of a uniformly stable algorithm, which is analogous to McDiarmid's inequality and Talagrand's inequality for empirical processes (see Chapter 6). Theorem 7.3 shows that this result can be used to obtain high-probability generalization bounds for uniformly stable algorithms.

Theorem 7.24 *Assume that $g(\mathcal{S}_n; z)$ is zero-mean with respect to z for all $\mathcal{S}_n$:*

$$\mathbb{E}_{Z \sim \mathcal{D}} g(\mathcal{S}_n; Z) = 0.$$

Assume also that $g(\mathcal{S}_n; z)$ is an ϵ uniformly stable function. That is, for all $z \in \mathcal{Z}$, and $\mathcal{S}_n'$ that differs from $\mathcal{S}_n$ by one element, we have

$$|g(\mathcal{S}_n; z) - g(\mathcal{S}_n'; z)| \le \epsilon.$$

Assume that $\mathcal{S}_{n+1} \sim \mathcal{D}^{n+1}$ contains $n + 1$ iid samples from $\mathcal{D}$. Let

$$\bar{g}(\mathcal{S}_{n+1}) = \frac{1}{n} \sum_{i=1}^{n} \left[g(\mathcal{S}_{n+1}^{(i)}; Z_i) - \mathbb{E}_{\mathcal{S}_{n+1}^{(i)}} g(\mathcal{S}_{n+1}^{(i)}; Z_i) \right],$$

where $\mathcal{S}_{n+1}^{(i)} = \{Z_1, \dots, Z_{i-1}, Z_{n+1}, Z_{i+1}, \dots, Z_n\}$. Then for all $\lambda \le 0.4/\epsilon$,

$$\ln \mathbb{E}_{\mathcal{S}_{n+1}} \exp \left((\lambda/L) \bar{g}(\mathcal{S}_{n+1}) \right) \le 1.5 \lambda^2 \epsilon^2,$$

where $L = \lceil \log_2 n \rceil$. This implies that with probability at least $1 - \delta$,

$$\bar{g}(\mathcal{S}_{n+1}) \leq L\epsilon + 2.5L\epsilon \ln(1/\delta).$$

The proof requires the following result from Boucheron et al. (2003).

Proposition 7.25 *Consider a functional $\tilde{g}(\mathcal{S})$, where $\mathcal{S} = [Z_1, \ldots, Z_m] \sim \mathcal{D}^m$ contains m iid samples from $\mathcal{D}$. Let $\mathcal{S}^{(i)} = [Z_1, \ldots, Z_{i-1}, Z_i', Z_{i+1}, \ldots, Z_m]$, where $\mathcal{S}' = \{Z_i'\} \sim \mathcal{D}^m$ are m iid samples from $\mathcal{D}$ that are independent of $\mathcal{S}$. Define*

$$V_+(\mathcal{S}) = \mathbb{E}_{\mathcal{S}'}\left[\sum_{i=1}^{m}(\tilde{g}(\mathcal{S}) - \tilde{g}(\mathcal{S}^{(i)})^2 \mathbf{1}(\tilde{g}(\mathcal{S}) > \tilde{g}(\mathcal{S}^{(i)})\Big|\mathcal{S}\right].$$

Assume that there exist positive constants a and b such that

$$V_+(\mathcal{S}) \leq a\tilde{g}(\mathcal{S}) + b,$$

then for $\lambda \in (0, 1/a)$,

$$\ln \mathbb{E}_{\mathcal{S}} \exp(\lambda \tilde{g}(\mathcal{S})) \leq \lambda \mathbb{E}_{\mathcal{S}}\tilde{g}(\mathcal{S}) + \frac{\lambda^2}{1 - a\lambda}(a\mathbb{E}_{\mathcal{S}}\tilde{g}(\mathcal{S}) + b).$$

Note that for the sake of simplicity, in the following proof our notation assumes that $g(\mathcal{S}_n, z)$ is invariant to the order of elements in $\mathcal{S}_n$. The analysis itself holds without this assumption, but directly working with the general version requires a more complex notation, which creates unnecessary difficulty for understanding the main argument. We will thus write the proof with this assumption so that the key idea of the proof is easier to follow. Consider a fixed $\mathcal{S}_{n+1} = \{Z_1, \ldots, Z_{n+1}\}$, we define for $i \leq m \leq n$,

$$\mathcal{S}_m^{(i)} = \{Z_1, \ldots, Z_{i-1}, Z_{n+1}, Z_{i+1}, \ldots, Z_m\},$$

and with this notation, we have $\mathcal{S}_{n+1}^{(i)} = \mathcal{S}_n^{(i)}$.

Now for all $1 \leq m' \leq m \leq n$, we define

$$\bar{g}_{m',m}(\mathcal{S}_{n+1}) = \frac{1}{m'}\sum_{i=1}^{m'}\left[g(\mathcal{S}_{n+1}^{(i)}; Z_i) - \mathbb{E}_{\mathcal{S}_m^{(i)}}g(\mathcal{S}_{n+1}^{(i)}; Z_i)\right].$$

It follows that $\bar{g}(\mathcal{S}_{n+1}) = \bar{g}_{n,n}(\mathcal{S}_{n+1})$.

Given $m' \leq m \leq n$, we denote by $\tilde{\mathcal{S}}_{m'}$ a uniformly selected subset of $\mathcal{S}_m$ of size m'. It is easy to see by symmetry that

$$\bar{g}_{m,m}(\mathcal{S}_{n+1}) = \frac{1}{m}\sum_{i=1}^{m}\left[g(\mathcal{S}_{n+1}^{(i)}; Z_i) - \mathbb{E}_{\mathcal{S}_m^{(i)}}g(\mathcal{S}_{n+1}^{(i)}; Z_i)\right]$$

$$= \mathbb{E}_{\tilde{\mathcal{S}}_{m'}}\frac{1}{m'}\sum_{Z_i \in \tilde{\mathcal{S}}_{m'}}\left[g(\mathcal{S}_{n+1}^{(i)}; Z_i) - \mathbb{E}_{\mathcal{S}_m^{(i)}}g(\mathcal{S}_{n+1}^{(i)}; Z_i)\right].$$

Therefore Jensen's inequality implies that

$$\ln \mathbb{E}_{\mathcal{S}_{n+1}} \exp(\lambda' \bar{g}_{m,m}(\mathcal{S}_{n+1}))$$

$$\leq \ln \mathbb{E}_{\mathcal{S}_{n+1}}\mathbb{E}_{\tilde{\mathcal{S}}_{m'}} \exp\left(\frac{\lambda'}{m'}\sum_{Z_i \in \tilde{\mathcal{S}}_{m'}}\left[g(\mathcal{S}_{n+1}^{(i)}; Z_i) - \mathbb{E}_{\mathcal{S}_m^{(i)}}g(\mathcal{S}_{n+1}^{(i)}; Z_i)\right]\right)$$

$$= \ln \mathbb{E}_{\mathcal{S}_{n+1}} \exp(\lambda' \bar{g}_{m',m}(\mathcal{S}_{n+1})). \tag{7.16}$$

The second inequality used the fact that all $\tilde{\mathcal{S}}_{m'}$ have identical distributions.

It is also easy to check the following equality by definition:

$$\bar{g}_{m',m}(\mathcal{S}_{n+1}) = \bar{g}_{m',m'}(\mathcal{S}_{n+1}) + \frac{1}{m'}\sum_{i=1}^{m'}\left[\mathbb{E}_{\mathcal{S}_{m'}^{(i)}}g(\mathcal{S}_{n+1}^{(i)};Z_i) - \mathbb{E}_{\mathcal{S}_m^{(i)}}g(\mathcal{S}_{n+1}^{(i)};Z_i)\right].$$

Now using this decomposition, and by applying Jensen's inequality to the convex function $\ln\mathbb{E}_{\mathcal{S}_{n+1}}\exp(g'(\mathcal{S}_{n+1}))$ with respect to $g'(\cdot)$, we obtain for all λ' and $\ell > 1$,

$$\ln\mathbb{E}_{\mathcal{S}_{n+1}}\exp\left(\lambda'\bar{g}_{m',m}(\mathcal{S}_{n+1})\right) \tag{7.17}$$

$$\leq \frac{\ell-1}{\ell}\ln\mathbb{E}_{\mathcal{S}_{n+1}}\exp\left(\frac{\ell\lambda'}{\ell-1}\bar{g}_{m',m'}(\mathcal{S}_{n+1})\right)$$

$$+ \frac{1}{\ell}\ln\mathbb{E}_{\mathcal{S}_{n+1}}\exp\left(\frac{\ell\lambda'}{m'}\sum_{i=1}^{m'}\left[\mathbb{E}_{\mathcal{S}_{m'}^{(i)}}g(\mathcal{S}_{n+1}^{(i)};Z_i) - \mathbb{E}_{\mathcal{S}_m^{(i)}}g(\mathcal{S}_{n+1}^{(i)};Z_i)\right]\right).$$

Now by fixing $\{Z_{m+1},\ldots,Z_n\}$, we may consider a function of $\mathcal{S}_{m'+1,\ldots,m} = \{Z_{m'+1},\ldots,Z_m\}$ defined as follows (we note that the function does not depend on Z_{n+1} due to the expectation with respect to Z_{n+1} over $\mathcal{S}_{m'}^{(i)}$ and $\mathcal{S}_m^{(i)}$):

$$g'(\mathcal{S}_{m'+1,m}) = \ln\mathbb{E}_{\mathcal{S}_{m'}}\exp\left(\frac{\lambda}{m'}\sum_{i=1}^{m'}[\mathbb{E}_{\mathcal{S}_{m'}^{(i)}}g(\mathcal{S}_{n+1}^{(i)};Z_i) - \mathbb{E}_{\mathcal{S}_m^{(i)}}g(\mathcal{S}_{n+1}^{(i)};Z_i)]\right).$$

We note that for $i \leq m'$, $[\mathbb{E}_{\mathcal{S}_{m'}^{(i)}}g(\mathcal{S}_{n+1}^{(i)};Z_i) - \mathbb{E}_{\mathcal{S}_m^{(i)}}g(\mathcal{S}_{n+1}^{(i)};Z_i)]$ as a function of $Z_i \sim \mathcal{D}$ has the same distribution as that of $[\mathbb{E}_{\mathcal{S}_{m'}}g(\mathcal{S}_n;Z) - \mathbb{E}_{\mathcal{S}_m}g(\mathcal{S}_n;Z)]$ (considered as a function of $Z \sim \mathcal{D}$). Since $\{Z_i\}$ are independent for $i \leq m'$, conditioned on $\mathcal{S}_{m'+1,m}$, it follows that

$$g'(\mathcal{S}_{m'+1,m}) = m'\ln\mathbb{E}_Z\exp\left(\frac{\lambda}{m'}[\mathbb{E}_{\mathcal{S}_{m'}}g(\mathcal{S}_n;Z) - \mathbb{E}_{\mathcal{S}_m}g(\mathcal{S}_n;Z)]\right). \tag{7.18}$$

We also have the following result, which is a direct consequence of uniform stability:

$$[\mathbb{E}_{\mathcal{S}_{m'}}g(\mathcal{S}_n;Z) - \mathbb{E}_{\mathcal{S}_m}g(\mathcal{S}_n;Z)] \leq (m-m')\epsilon. \tag{7.19}$$

In the following derivations, we further assume that $m \leq 2m'$. It implies that

$$(m-m')/m' \leq 1.$$

It follows that

$$g'(\mathcal{S}_{m'+1,m}) = m'\ln\mathbb{E}_Z\exp\left(\frac{\lambda}{m'}[\mathbb{E}_{\mathcal{S}_{m'}}g(\mathcal{S}_n;Z) - \mathbb{E}_{\mathcal{S}_m}g(\mathcal{S}_n;Z)]\right)$$

$$\leq m'\left[\mathbb{E}_Z\exp\left(\frac{\lambda}{m'}[\mathbb{E}_{\mathcal{S}_{m'}}g(\mathcal{S}_n;Z) - \mathbb{E}_{\mathcal{S}_m}g(\mathcal{S}_n;Z)]\right) - 1\right.$$

$$\left. - \frac{\lambda}{m'}\mathbb{E}_Z[\mathbb{E}_{\mathcal{S}_{m'}}g(\mathcal{S}_n;Z) - \mathbb{E}_{\mathcal{S}_m}g(\mathcal{S}_n;Z)]\right]$$

$$\leq \frac{(\lambda)^2}{m'}\phi(0.4)\underbrace{\mathbb{E}_Z(\mathbb{E}_{\mathcal{S}_{m'}}g(\mathcal{S}_n;Z) - \mathbb{E}_{\mathcal{S}_m}g(\mathcal{S}_n;Z))^2}_{g''(\mathcal{S}_{m'+1,m})}.$$

In derivation, the first equality used (7.18). The first inequality used $\log(z) \leq z-1$, and $\mathbb{E}_Z g(\cdot; Z) = 0$ (which is an assumption of the theorem). The second inequality used the fact that $\phi(z) = (e^z - z - 1)/z^2$ is increasing in z (this is the same derivation as that of Bennett's inequality), and $\frac{\lambda}{m'}[\mathbb{E}_{\mathcal{S}_{m'}} g(\mathcal{S}_n; Z) - \mathbb{E}_{\mathcal{S}_m} g(\mathcal{S}_n; Z)]] \leq 0.4$ (which follows from (7.19), and $\lambda(m - m')\epsilon/m' \leq \lambda\epsilon \leq 0.4$).

Using the Efron–Stein inequality (6.10) and the ϵ uniform stability of $g(\cdot, \cdot)$, we have

$$\mathbb{E}_{\mathcal{S}_{m'+1,m}} g''(\mathcal{S}_{m'+1,m}) \leq 0.5(m - m')\epsilon^2. \tag{7.20}$$

Note also that for $\mathcal{S}_{m'+1,m}$ and $\mathcal{S}'_{m'+1,m}$ that differ by one element, we have

$$(g''(\mathcal{S}_{m'+1,m}) - g''(\mathcal{S}'_{m'+1,m}))^2$$
$$\leq (2\epsilon \mathbb{E}_Z | [\mathbb{E}_{\mathcal{S}_{m'}} g(\mathcal{S}_n; Z) - \mathbb{E}_{\mathcal{S}_m} g(\mathcal{S}_n; Z)]| + \epsilon^2)^2$$
$$\leq 5\epsilon^2 g''(\mathcal{S}_{m'+1,m}) + 5\epsilon^4.$$

Therefore by summing over $\mathcal{S}'_{m'+1,m}$, which differs from $\mathcal{S}_{m'+1,m}$ at $j = m' + 1, \ldots, m$, we know that with g'', the condition of Proposition 7.25 holds with $a = 5(m - m')\epsilon^2$ and $b = 5(m - m')\epsilon^4$. Therefore,

$$\ln \mathbb{E}_{\mathcal{S}_{m'+1,m}} \exp(g'(\mathcal{S}_{m'+1,m}))$$
$$\leq \ln \mathbb{E}_{\mathcal{S}_{m'+1,m}} \exp\left(\frac{(\lambda)^2}{m'}\phi(0.4)g''(\mathcal{S}_{m'+1,m})\right)$$
$$\leq \frac{(\lambda)^2}{m'}\phi(0.4)\mathbb{E}_{\mathcal{S}_{m'+1,m}} g''(\mathcal{S}_{m'+1,m})$$
$$+ 2\frac{(\lambda)^4}{(m')^2}\phi(0.4)^2 \left(5(m - m')\epsilon^2 \mathbb{E}_{\mathcal{S}_{m'+1,m}} g''(\mathcal{S}_{m'+1,m}) + 5(m - m')\epsilon^4\right).$$

The second inequality used Proposition 7.25 for g'', with $a = 5(m-m')\epsilon^2$ and $b = 5(m-m')\epsilon^4$, and observe that $(1 - (\lambda^2/m')\phi(0.4)a)^{-1} \leq (1 - 5(0.4)^2\phi(0.4))^{-1} \leq 2$.

By combining the above inequality with (7.20), and using $\phi(0.4) \leq 0.58$ and $(m - m')/m' \leq 1$, we obtain

$$\ln \mathbb{E}_{\mathcal{S}_{n+1}} \exp\left(\frac{\lambda}{m'}\sum_{i=1}^{m'}[\mathbb{E}_{\mathcal{S}_{m'}^{(i)}} g(\mathcal{S}_{n+1}^{(i)}; Z_i) - \mathbb{E}_{\mathcal{S}_m^{(i)}} g(\mathcal{S}_{n+1}^{(i)}; Z_i)]\right)$$
$$\leq 0.3\lambda^2\epsilon^2 + 6\lambda^4\epsilon^4 \leq 1.5\lambda^2\epsilon^2. \tag{7.21}$$

The second inequality used $\lambda\epsilon \leq 0.4$.

Now consider an increasing sequence $1 = m_0 < m_1 < m_2 < \cdots < m_L = n$, where $m_\ell = \min(2^\ell, n)$. Let $\lambda_\ell = \lambda/\ell$ for $\ell > 0$ and $\lambda_0 = \lambda$. We have

$$\ell \ln \mathbb{E}_{\mathcal{S}_{n+1}} \exp\left(\lambda_\ell \bar{g}_{m_\ell, m_\ell}(\mathcal{S}_{n+1})\right)$$
$$\leq \ell \ln \mathbb{E}_{\mathcal{S}_{n+1}} \exp\left(\lambda_\ell \bar{g}_{m_{\ell-1}, m_\ell}(\mathcal{S}_{n+1})\right)$$
$$\leq (\ell - 1) \ln \mathbb{E}_{\mathcal{S}_{n+1}} \exp\left(\lambda_{\ell-1} \bar{g}_{m_{\ell-1}, m_{\ell-1}}(\mathcal{S}_{n+1})\right)$$
$$+ \ln \mathbb{E}_{\mathcal{S}_{n+1}} \exp\left(\frac{\lambda}{m_{\ell-1}}\sum_{i=1}^{m_{\ell-1}}[\mathbb{E}_{\mathcal{S}_{m_{\ell-1}}^{(i)}} g(\mathcal{S}_{n+1}^{(i)}; Z_i) - \mathbb{E}_{\mathcal{S}_{m_\ell}^{(i)}} g(\mathcal{S}_{n+1}^{(i)}; Z_i)]\right)$$
$$\leq (\ell - 1) \ln \mathbb{E}_{\mathcal{S}_{n+1}} \exp(\lambda_{\ell-1} \bar{g}_{m_{\ell-1}, m_{\ell-1}}(\mathcal{S}_{n+1})) + 1.5\lambda^2\epsilon^2.$$

The first inequality used (7.16). The second inequality used (7.17) for $\ell > 1$, and it becomes equality for $\ell = 1$. The third inequality used (7.21).

By summing ℓ from 1 to L, we obtain

$$L \cdot \ln \mathbb{E}_{\mathcal{S}_{n+1}} \exp \left(\lambda_L \bar{g}(\mathcal{S}_{n+1})\right) = L \cdot \ln \mathbb{E}_{\mathcal{S}_{n+1}} \exp \left(\lambda_L \bar{g}_{m_L, m_L}(\mathcal{S}_{n+1})\right) \leq 1.5 \lambda^2 \epsilon^2 L.$$

This implies the first desired bound.

The second inequality follows from the Markov's inequality as follows. Consider $\epsilon' = 2.5 \ln(1/\delta) > 0$ and take $\lambda = 0.4/\epsilon$. We have

$$\begin{aligned}
\ln \Pr[\bar{g}(\mathcal{S}_{n+1}) \geq L(1 + \epsilon')\epsilon] &\leq \ln \mathbb{E}_{\mathcal{S}_{n+1}} \exp \left(\lambda_L \bar{g}(\mathcal{S}_{n+1})\right) - \lambda_L L(1 + \epsilon')\epsilon \\
&\leq \left[1.5 \lambda^2 \epsilon^2 - (\lambda/L)L(1 + \epsilon')\epsilon\right] \leq -0.4\epsilon' = \ln \delta.
\end{aligned}$$

This implies the second bound.

7.7 Historical and Bibliographical Remarks

The idea of uniform stability for nonrandomized algorithms was introduced by Bousquet and Elisseeff (2002), where the authors also considered deriving concentration bounds using McDiarmid's inequality. However, concentration results obtained there were suboptimal. Better concentration bounds were obtained recently by Feldman and Vondrak (2019) and Bousquet et al. (2020). Theorem 7.24 is motivated by their analysis, and the result is comparable to that of Bousquet et al. (2020), but with a different proof. However, the concentration result holds only for uniform stability. The idea of using leave-one-out analysis to obtain expected oracle inequality was considered by Zhang (2003a). The leave-one-out stability analysis presented here generalizes the analysis of Zhang (2003a).

Randomized stability, discussed in this chapter, was introduced by Hardt et al. (2016) to analyze the generalization of stochastic gradient descent. It has become a popular theoretical tool for analyzing SGD-like procedures when it is necessary to run such algorithms multiple times over the data. For example, it is an essential technique in the generalization analysis of differentially private SGD (Bassily et al., 2020).

Gibbs distribution has its origin in physics (Gibbs, 1902). It has been studied in machine learning by McAllester (1999) in the supervised learning setting, and by Freund and Schapire (1997) in the online learning setting.

The SGLD algorithm was proposed by Welling and Teh (2011) for sampling from Bayesian posterior distributions (or Gibbs distributions). Its analysis has drawn significant interest, both for convergence and for generalization. The generalization analysis of SGLD for nonconvex functions in Theorem 7.23 is related to the information theoretical approach studied in some recent work (see Russo and Zou, 2016, 2019; Xu and Raginsky, 2017; Mou et al., 2018), which we will study further in Section 10.3.

The SGLD algorithm has also appeared in differential privacy, and in that setting it is referred to as the differentially private SGD (DP-SGD) algorithm (Abadi et al., 2016). Theorem 7.23 employs techniques simplified from the DP-SGD analysis (see Abadi et al., 2016). A more complex analysis that handles SGLD can be found in Li et al. (2020).

Exercises

7.1 Assume that the variance condition (3.13) holds. Use Bernstein's inequality to derive a bound for (7.1). Derive an oracle inequality using Theorem 7.3.

7.2 Prove Theorem 7.7.

7.3 In Example 7.9, assume that $\|\psi(X)\|_2 \le B$ for all X. Derive an oracle inequality for SVM that holds in high probability using Theorem 7.3.

7.4 Prove the uniform stability result in Theorem 7.8, under the assumption that $\sup_Z G(Z) \le G$.

7.5 Assume a learning algorithm $\mathcal{A}$ is deterministic and ϵ uniformly stable on training data of size n. Use McDiarmid's inequality to obtain a concentration bound. Apply it to the case of Exercise 7.4. Compare the result to that of Theorem 7.3.

7.6 Give an example to show that under the conditions of Theorem 7.10, ERM may not be uniformly stable.

7.7 Use Theorem 7.8 to derive an expected generalization bound for the ridge regression problem in Example 7.11.

7.8 Consider regularized binary linear logistic regression for $y \in \{\pm 1\}$:

$$L(f(w,x),y) = \ln(1 + \exp(-f(w,x)y)), \quad g(w) = \frac{\lambda}{2}\|w\|_2^2,$$

where $f(w,x) = w^\top \psi(x)$ for some known feature vector $\psi(x)$. Assume that there exists $B > 0$ such that $\sup_X \|\psi(X)\|_2 \le B$. Show that $\phi(w,z) = L(f(w,x),y) + g(w)$ is both Lipschitz (in a finite region) and smooth. Derive an expected oracle inequality using both Theorem 7.8 and Theorem 7.10. When does Theorem 7.10 give a better bound?

7.9 Prove Theorem 7.13.

7.10 Under the condition of previous problem with $\sup_X \|\psi(X)\|_2 \le B$. Assume we solve the regularized logistic regression problem using SGD. Assume that we choose a learning rate $\eta_t = 1/(L + \lambda t)$. Derive b_T and an oracle inequality using Theorem 7.14.

7.11 Assume that we remove the Lipschitz condition in Theorem 7.14. Derive a stability result and oracle inequality for SGD, similar in spirit to Theorem 7.10.

7.12 Consider binary linear classification with $L(f(w,x),y) = \mathbb{1}(f(w,x)y \le 0)$, where $y \in \{\pm 1\}$, $f(w,x) = w^\top \psi(x)$, with $\psi(x) \in \mathbb{R}^d$ and $\|\psi(x)\|_2 \le 1$. Let $p_0(w) = N(0, I)$, and assume that there exists $w_* \in \mathbb{R}^d$ so that $\mathbb{1}(f(w,x)y \le 0) = 0$ when $w \in \{w \colon \|w - w_*\|_2 \le \gamma\}$, where $\gamma > 0$. Use Theorem 7.19 to obtain an oracle inequality for the Gibbs algorithm.

7.13 Prove Theorem 7.22.

8

Model Selection

In previous chapters, we studied the generalization of supervised learning algorithms, when the model is given. That is, we assume that the loss function is $L(f(w, x), y)$, where the model class $\{f(w, x) \colon w \in \Omega\}$ is known. In practical applications, we often encounter the situation that many different model classes (such as SVM, neural networks, decision trees) are tried, and we want to select the best model to achieve the smallest test loss. A typical approach by practitioners is to select models via a validation set. One disadvantage is that model training and selection needs to be done separately. An alternative method allows model selection directly on the training data, using a data-dependent generalization bound as a regularization term. In this approach, we do not have to rely on a separate validation data, but employ a specially designed regularization term. We will discuss both approaches.

8.1 Model Selection Problem

Mathematically, we may regard a model, indexed by a hyperparameter $\theta \in \Theta$, as a learning algorithm $\mathcal{A}(\theta, \mathcal{S}_n)$ that maps the training data $\mathcal{S}_n$ to a prediction function $f \in \mathcal{F}$. In general, these algorithms may be completely different and the underlying model function classes not related to each other (e.g. one model may be decision tree, and another model may be support vector machine). However, in applications, one may also encounter the situation that the algorithms are related, and θ is a tuning parameter of the algorithm. For example, if we consider using stochastic gradient descent to train a classifier, the tuning parameter θ may be the learning rate schedule. If we consider using regularization methods, then θ may be the regularization parameter. If we consider training neural networks with different width, then the tuning parameter θ may be the width of the hidden layers. For such problems, each model $\mathcal{A}(\theta, \mathcal{S}_n) \in \mathcal{F}(\theta) = \{f(w, x) \colon w \in \Omega(\theta)\}$. The model functions $\mathcal{F} = \cup \mathcal{F}(\theta)$ have the same functional form. The goal of model selection is to find the best model hyperparameter θ so that the corresponding learning algorithm $\mathcal{A}(\theta, \cdot)$ achieves a small test error.

Definition 8.1 Consider a loss function $\phi(f, z) \colon \mathcal{F} \times \mathcal{Z} \to \mathbb{R}$, and a model family $\{\mathcal{A}(\theta, \mathcal{S}_n) \colon \Theta \times \mathcal{Z}^n \to \mathcal{F}, n \geq 0\}$. Consider $N \geq n \geq 0$, and iid dataset $\mathcal{S}_n \subset \mathcal{S}_N \sim \mathcal{D}^N$. A model selection algorithm $\bar{\mathcal{A}}$ maps $\mathcal{S}_N$ to $\hat{\theta} = \hat{\theta}(\mathcal{S}_N) \in \Theta$, and then trains a model $\hat{f} = \mathcal{A}(\hat{\theta}(\mathcal{S}_N), \mathcal{S}_n) = \bar{\mathcal{A}}(\mathcal{S}_N)$. It satisfies an $\epsilon_{n,N}(\cdot, \cdot)$ oracle inequality if there exists $\epsilon_{n,N}(\theta, \delta)$ such that for all $\delta \in (0, 1)$, with probability at least $1 - \delta$ over $\mathcal{S}_N$,

$$\phi(\mathcal{A}(\hat{\theta}(\mathcal{S}_N), \mathcal{S}_n), \mathcal{D}) \leq \inf_{\theta \in \Theta} \left[\mathbb{E}_{\mathcal{S}_n} \phi(\mathcal{A}(\theta, \mathcal{S}_n), \mathcal{D}) + \epsilon_{n,N}(\theta, \delta) \right].$$

More generally, a learning algorithm $\bar{\mathcal{A}} \colon \mathcal{S}_N \to \mathcal{F}$ is $\epsilon_{n,N}(\cdot, \cdot)$ adaptive to the model family $\{\mathcal{A}(\theta, \cdot) \colon \theta \in \Theta\}$ if there exists $\epsilon_{n,N}(\cdot, \cdot)$ such that for all $\delta \in (0, 1)$, with probability at least $1 - \delta$ over $\mathcal{S}_N$,

$$\phi(\bar{\mathcal{A}}(\mathcal{S}_N), \mathcal{D}) \leq \inf_{\theta \in \Theta} \left[\mathbb{E}_{\mathcal{S}_n} \phi(\mathcal{A}(\theta, \mathcal{S}_n), \mathcal{D}) + \epsilon_{n,N}(\theta, \delta) \right].$$

Note that we have used a slightly different notation $\phi(f, Z)$, instead of $\phi(w, Z)$ as in earlier chapters, to emphasize that in model selection, the prediction function $f(w, \cdot)$ from different models can be compared, but the parameter w of the functions may not be comparable when different models have different functional forms such as decision trees versus neural networks. Without causing confusion, one may consider f to be the function represented by w, so that $\phi(f, Z) = L(f(X), Y)$ and $\phi(w, Z) = L(f(w, X), Y)$. Similar to Definition 3.8, we use the simplified notation

$$\phi(f, \mathcal{D}) = \mathbb{E}_{Z \sim \mathcal{D}}\, \phi(f, Z), \quad \phi(f, \mathcal{S}_n) = \frac{1}{n} \sum_{Z \in \mathcal{S}_n} \phi(f, Z).$$

The concept adaptivity is more general than model selection, as the algorithm does not need to choose a specific model $\mathcal{A}(\theta, \cdot)$ indexed by θ. For example, a commonly used method to achieve adaptivity is model averaging, where we take the average of several different model outputs $\hat{f}_{\theta_j} = \mathcal{A}(\theta_j, \mathcal{S}_n)$ as

$$\hat{f}_{\mathrm{avg}}(x) = \frac{1}{k} \sum_{j=1}^{k} \hat{f}_{\theta_j}(x).$$

If different models have the same functional form, with a vector model parameter $w \in \mathbb{R}^d$: $\hat{f}_{\theta_j}(x) = f(\hat{w}_j, x)$. Then one may also average the model parameters as follows:

$$\hat{w}_{\mathrm{avg}} = \frac{1}{k} \sum_{j=1}^{k} \hat{w}_j.$$

In general, the training data $\mathcal{S}_n$ is a subset of $\mathcal{S}_N$, and we allow $n < N$ in order to analyze validation methods that are commonly used in practice. In addition to the large probability bounds in Definition 8.1, one may also derive bounds that hold for expectation over $\mathcal{S}_N$.

8.2 Model Selection on Validation Data

A frequently employed method for model hyperparameter tuning is to split a labeled data $\mathcal{S}_N$ into a training data $\mathcal{S}_n$ and a validation data $\bar{\mathcal{S}}_m$ with $N = m+n$. We can then train the models on the training data $\mathcal{S}_n$, and then evaluate on validation data $\bar{\mathcal{S}}_m$. We select the models according to their performance on the validation set.

In this section, we consider a countable sequence of models $\{\mathcal{A}(\theta, \cdot) : \theta = 1, 2, \ldots\}$ that can produce $\hat{f}_\theta = \mathcal{A}(\theta, \mathcal{S}_n) \in \mathcal{F}$ from the training data $\mathcal{S}_n$. Let $\{q(\theta) \geq 0\}$ be a sequence of nonnegative numbers that satisfies the inequality

$$\sum_{\theta=1}^{\infty} q(\theta) \leq 1. \tag{8.1}$$

Consider the following model selection algorithm, which trains a prediction function $\mathcal{A}(\theta, \mathcal{S}_n)$ on training data for any given a model θ, and then selects a model $\hat{\theta}$ to approximately minimize the following generic model selection criterion on the validation data:

$$Q(\hat{\theta}, \mathcal{A}(\hat{\theta}, \mathcal{S}_n), \bar{\mathcal{S}}_m) \leq \inf_\theta Q(\theta, \mathcal{A}(\theta, \mathcal{S}_n), \bar{\mathcal{S}}_m) + \tilde{\epsilon}, \tag{8.2}$$

where

$$Q(\theta, f, \bar{\mathcal{S}}_m) = \phi(f, \bar{\mathcal{S}}_m) + r_m(q(\theta)).$$

We have the following generic model selection result using the union bound of additive Chernoff bound. Similar results can be obtained for multiplicative Chernoff bounds, and Bernstein's inequalities.

Theorem 8.2 (Model Selection on Validation Data)   *Assume* $\sup_{Z,Z'}[\phi(f, Z) - \phi(f, Z')] \leq M$ *for all* f, *and the validation data* $\bar{\mathcal{S}}_m$ *contains* m *iid samples from* $\mathcal{D}$. *Given training data* $\mathcal{S}_n$, *consider* (8.2) *with*

$$r_m(q) = M\sqrt{\frac{\ln(1/q)}{2m}}.$$

Then with probability at least $1 - \delta$ *over the random selection of* $\mathcal{S}_m$,

$$\phi(\mathcal{A}(\hat{\theta}, \mathcal{S}_n), \mathcal{D}) \leq \inf_\theta Q(\theta, \mathcal{A}(\theta, \mathcal{S}_n), \bar{\mathcal{S}}_m) + \tilde{\epsilon} + M\sqrt{\frac{\ln(1/\delta)}{2m}}.$$

This implies the following oracle inequality. With probability at least $1 - \delta$ *over the random sampling of* $\bar{\mathcal{S}}_m$,

$$\phi(\mathcal{A}(\hat{\theta}, \mathcal{S}_n), \mathcal{D}) \leq \inf_\theta [\phi(\mathcal{A}(\theta, \mathcal{S}_n), \mathcal{D}) + r_m(q(\theta))] + \tilde{\epsilon} + M\sqrt{\frac{2\ln(2/\delta)}{m}},$$

where $q(\theta)$ *satisfies* (8.1).

Proof For each model θ, let $\hat{f}_\theta = \mathcal{A}(\theta, \mathcal{S}_n)$. We obtain from the additive Chernoff bound that with probability at least $1 - q(\theta)\delta$,

$$\mathbb{E}_{Z \sim \mathcal{D}} \phi(\hat{f}_\theta, Z) \leq \frac{1}{m} \sum_{Z \in \bar{\mathcal{S}}_m} \phi(\hat{f}_\theta, Z) + M\sqrt{\frac{\ln(1/(q(\theta)\delta))}{2m}}$$

$$\leq \frac{1}{m} \sum_{Z \in \bar{\mathcal{S}}_m} \phi(\hat{f}_\theta, Z) + M\sqrt{\frac{\ln(1/q(\theta))}{2m}} + M\sqrt{\frac{\ln(1/\delta)}{2m}}.$$

Taking the union bound over θ, we know that the claim holds for all $\theta \geq 1$ with probability at least $1 - \delta$. This result, combined with the definition of $\hat{\theta}$ in (8.2), leads to the first desired bound.

Now by applying the Chernoff bound for an arbitrary θ that does not depend on $\bar{\mathcal{S}}_m$, we obtain with probability at least $1 - \delta/2$,

$$Q(\theta, \hat{f}_\theta, \bar{\mathcal{S}}_m) \leq \mathbb{E}_{Z \sim \mathcal{D}} \phi(\hat{f}_\theta, Z) + r_m(q(\theta)) + M\sqrt{\frac{\ln(2/\delta)}{2m}}.$$

By combining this inequality with the first bound of the theorem, we obtain the second desired inequality. $\qquad\square$

A frequent choice of $q(\theta)$ is $q(\theta) = 1/(\theta(\theta + 1))$. In this case, r_m depends only logarithmically on θ, and the penalty $r_m(\theta)$ grows very slowly as θ increases. It means that for model selection with bounded loss functions, we can compare exponentially (in m) many models without paying a significant penalty.

Theorem 8.2 can be combined with uniform convergence results such as Corollary 6.21 to obtain a more precise statement for the ERM method, showing that a near optimal generalization bound can be obtained using the method of (8.2). This leads to an oracle inequality for model selection with ERM learners.

Corollary 8.3 *Consider a countable family of approximate ERM algorithms $\{\mathcal{A}(\theta, \cdot) \colon \theta = 1, 2, \ldots\}$, each of which is characterized by its model space $\mathcal{F}(\theta)$ and returns a function $\hat{f}_\theta \in \mathcal{F}(\theta)$ such that*

$$\phi(\hat{f}, \mathcal{S}_n) \leq \inf_{f \in \mathcal{F}(\theta)} \phi(f, \mathcal{S}_n) + \epsilon',$$

where we use the notation of Definition 8.1.

Assume further that $\sup_{Z,Z'}[\phi(f, Z) - \phi(f, Z')] \leq M$ for all f, and we use (8.2) to select the best model $\hat{\theta}$ on the validation data $\bar{\mathcal{S}}_m$, with the choice

$$r_m(q) = M\sqrt{\frac{\ln(1/q)}{2m}}.$$

Then the following result holds with probability at least $1 - \delta$ over random selection of $\mathcal{S}_n$ and $\bar{\mathcal{S}}_m$:

$$\phi(\mathcal{A}(\hat{\theta}, \mathcal{S}_n), \mathcal{D}) \leq \inf_\theta \left[\inf_{f \in \mathcal{F}(\theta)} \phi(f, \mathcal{D}) + 2R_n(\mathcal{G}(\theta), \mathcal{D}) + r_m(q(\theta)) \right]$$

$$+ \tilde{\epsilon} + \epsilon' + M\sqrt{\frac{2\ln(4/\delta)}{n}} + M\sqrt{\frac{2\ln(4/\delta)}{m}},$$

where $R_n(\mathcal{G}(\theta), \mathcal{D})$ is the Rademacher complexity of $\mathcal{G}(\theta) = \{\phi(f, \cdot) : f \in \mathcal{F}(\theta)\}$ and $q(\theta)$ satisfies (8.1).

Proof Consider any model θ. We have from Theorem 8.2 that with probability $1 - \delta/2$,

$$\phi(\mathcal{A}(\hat{\theta}, \mathcal{S}_n), \mathcal{D}) \leq [\phi(\mathcal{A}(\theta, \mathcal{S}_n), \mathcal{D}) + r_m(q(\theta))] + \tilde{\epsilon} + M\sqrt{\frac{2\ln(4/\delta)}{m}}.$$

Moreover, from Corollary 6.21 with $h(\cdot) = 0$, we know that with probability at least $1 - \delta/2$,

$$\phi(\mathcal{A}(\theta, \mathcal{S}_n), \mathcal{D}) \leq \inf_{f \in \mathcal{F}(\theta)} \phi(f, \mathcal{D}) + \epsilon' + 2R_n(\mathcal{G}(\theta), \mathcal{D}) + 2M\sqrt{\frac{\ln(4/\delta)}{2n}}.$$

Taking the union bound, both inequalities hold with probability at least $1 - \delta$, which leads to the desired bound. $\square$

In the application of Corollary 8.3, we often choose a nested function class $\mathcal{F}(\theta) \subset \mathcal{F}(\theta')$ when $\theta \leq \theta'$. This means we consider a sequence of model families that become more complex. A larger function class $\mathcal{F}(\theta)$ can achieve a smaller test loss $\inf_{f \in \mathcal{F}(\theta}\phi(f, \mathcal{D})$, but it also has a larger Rademacher complexity $R_n(\mathcal{G}(\theta), \mathcal{D})$. With the choice of $q(\theta) = 1/(\theta + 1)^2$, r_m depends only logarithmically on θ, and hence $R_n(\mathcal{G}(\theta), \mathcal{D})$ is the dominant penalty for overall generalization performance. It also implies that we should usually choose n to be larger than m in the training/validation split, as the dominant penalty $R_n(\mathcal{G}(\theta), \mathcal{D})$ decreases as n increases.

Example 8.4 Consider a $\{0, 1\}$–valued binary classification problem, with binary classifiers $\mathcal{F}(\theta) = \{f_\theta(w, x) \in \{0, 1\} : w \in \Omega(\theta)\}$ of VC-dimension $d(\theta)$. The Rademacher complexity of $\mathcal{G}(\theta)$ is no larger than $(16\sqrt{d(\theta)})/\sqrt{n}$ (see Example 6.26). Take $q(\theta) = 1/(\theta + 1)^2$. Then we have from Corollary 8.3 that

$$\mathbb{E}_{\mathcal{D}}\mathbb{1}(f_{\hat{\theta}}(\hat{w}, X) \neq Y) \leq \inf_{\theta, w \in \Omega(\theta)} \left[\mathbb{E}_{\mathcal{D}}\mathbb{1}(f_\theta(w, X) \neq Y) + \frac{32\sqrt{d(\theta)}}{\sqrt{n}} + \sqrt{\frac{\ln(\theta + 1)}{m}} \right]$$

$$+ \tilde{\epsilon} + \epsilon' + \sqrt{\frac{2\ln(4/\delta)}{n}} + \sqrt{\frac{2\ln(4/\delta)}{m}}.$$

This result shows that the model selection algorithm of (8.2) can automatically balance the model accuracy $\mathbb{E}_{\mathcal{D}}\mathbb{1}(f_\theta(w, X) \neq Y)$ and model dimension $d(\theta)$. it can adaptively choose the optimal model θ, up to a penalty of $O(\sqrt{\ln(\theta + 1)/n})$.

While we only considered the selection of discrete models with training data and validation data split, it is also possible to consider continuous models, if the learning algorithm is stable with respect to model hyperparameter θ. In such case, we may introduce a notion similar to covering numbers and then discrete the continuous model space accordingly.

8.3 Model Selection on Training Data Using Data Dependent Bounds

In the typical application of model selection, we can split a large labeled data into training and validation partitions, and employ the technique of Section 8.2 to do model selection on the validation data. However, the split effectively reduces training data size, and it is difficult to nest model selection procedures (i.e. to select model selection algorithms). To address this issue, an alternative approach is to do model selection directly on the training data ($\mathcal{S}_N = \mathcal{S}_n$) without any training and validation partition. This is possible if we have a sample-dependent generalization bound, as we will demonstrate in this section.

In the following, we still consider a countable sequence of models, parameterized by function families $\{\mathcal{F}(\theta) : \theta = 1, 2, \ldots\}$. Consider the following model selection algorithm, which simultaneously finds the model hyperparameter $\hat{\theta}$ and model function $\hat{f} \in \mathcal{F}(\hat{\theta})$ on the training data $\mathcal{S}_n$:

$$Q(\hat{\theta}, \hat{f}, \mathcal{S}_n) \leq \inf_{\theta, f \in \mathcal{F}(\theta)} Q(\theta, f, \mathcal{S}_n) + \tilde{\epsilon}, \tag{8.3}$$

where for $f \in \mathcal{F}(\theta)$,

$$Q(\theta, f, \mathcal{S}_n) = \phi(f, \mathcal{S}_n) + \tilde{R}(\theta, f, \mathcal{S}_n),$$

where $\tilde{R}$ is an appropriately chosen sample-dependent upper bound of the complexity for family $\mathcal{F}(\theta)$.

Sample-dependent uniform convergence bounds can be used to design $\tilde{R}$ in the model selection algorithm (8.3) on training data only, without splitting the training data into training versus validation partitions. The idea is similar to the model selection on validation data presented in Section 8.2, with data-dependent uniform convergence bound replacing the Chernoff bound. The following generic result shows that for this model selection method, we can obtain an oracle inequality from any sample-dependent uniform convergence bound.

Theorem 8.5 *Let $\{q(\theta) \geq 0\}$ be a sequence of numbers that satisfy (8.1). Assume that for each model θ, we have uniform convergence result as follows. With probability at least $1 - \delta$, for all $f \in \mathcal{F}(\theta)$,*

$$\alpha\phi(f, \mathcal{D}) \leq \phi(f, \mathcal{S}_n) + \hat{\epsilon}(\theta, f, \mathcal{S}_n) + \left(\frac{\ln(c_0/\delta)}{\lambda n}\right)^{\beta},$$

for some constants $\alpha, \lambda, \beta > 0$ and $c_0 \geq 1$. If we choose

$$\tilde{R}(\theta, f, \mathcal{S}_n) \geq \hat{\epsilon}(\theta, f, \mathcal{S}_n) + 2^{\max(0, \beta-1)} \left(\frac{\ln(c_0/q(\theta))}{\lambda n}\right)^{\beta},$$

then the following uniform convergence result holds. With probability at least $1 - \delta$, for all θ and $f \in \mathcal{F}(\theta)$,

$$\alpha\phi(f, \mathcal{D}) \leq \phi(f, \mathcal{S}_n) + \tilde{R}(\theta, f, \mathcal{S}_n) + 2^{\max(0, \beta-1)} \left(\frac{\ln(1/\delta)}{\lambda n}\right)^{\beta}.$$

If, moreover, we have for all θ and $f \in \mathcal{F}(\theta)$, the following concentration bound holds, with probability $1 - \delta$:

$$\phi(f, \mathcal{S}_n) + \tilde{R}(\theta, f, \mathcal{S}_n) \leq \mathbb{E}_{\mathcal{S}_n} \left[\alpha' \phi(f, \mathcal{S}_n) + \alpha'' \tilde{R}(\theta, f, \mathcal{S}_n) \right]$$
$$+ \epsilon'(\theta, f, \delta).$$

Then we have the following oracle inequality for (8.3). With probability at least $1 - \delta$,

$$\alpha \phi(\hat{f}, \mathcal{D}) \leq \inf_{\theta, f \in \mathcal{F}(\theta)} \left[\alpha' \phi(f, \mathcal{D}) + \alpha'' \mathbb{E}_{\mathcal{S}_n} \tilde{R}(\theta, f, \mathcal{S}_n) + \epsilon'(\theta, f, \delta/2) \right]$$
$$+ \tilde{\epsilon} + 2^{\max(0, \beta-1)} \left(\frac{\ln(2/\delta)}{\lambda n} \right)^{\beta}.$$

Proof Taking union bound over θ, each with probability $1 - 0.5q(\theta)\delta$, we obtain that with probability at least $1 - \delta/2$, for all θ and $f \in \mathcal{F}(\theta)$,

$$\alpha \phi(f, \mathcal{D}) \leq \phi(f, \mathcal{S}_n) + \hat{\epsilon}(\theta, f, \mathcal{S}_n) + \left(\frac{\ln(c_0/q(\theta))}{\lambda n} + \frac{\ln(2/\delta)}{\lambda n} \right)^{\beta}$$

$$\leq \phi(f, \mathcal{S}_n) + \hat{\epsilon}(\theta, f, \mathcal{S}_n) + 2^{\max(0, \beta-1)} \left(\frac{\ln(c_0/q(\theta))}{\lambda n} \right)^{\beta}$$

$$+ 2^{\max(0, \beta-1)} \left(\frac{\ln(2/\delta)}{\lambda n} \right)^{\beta}$$

$$\leq \phi(f, \mathcal{S}_n) + \tilde{R}(\theta, f, \mathcal{S}_n) + 2^{\max(0, \beta-1)} \left(\frac{\ln(2/\delta)}{\lambda n} \right)^{\beta}.$$

The first inequality used the union bound over all $\mathcal{F}(\theta)$. The second inequality used Jensen's inequality. The third inequality used the assumption of $\tilde{R}$. This proves the desired uniform convergence result.

Now since $\hat{f}$ is the solution of (8.3), it follows that for all θ and $f \in \mathcal{F}(\theta)$, with probability at least $1 - \delta/2$,

$$\alpha \phi(\hat{f}, \mathcal{D}) \leq \phi(\hat{f}, \mathcal{S}_n) + \tilde{R}(\hat{\theta}, \hat{f}, \mathcal{S}_n) + 2^{\max(0, \beta-1)} \left(\frac{\ln(2/\delta)}{\lambda n} \right)^{\beta}$$

$$\leq \phi(f, \mathcal{S}_n) + \tilde{R}(\theta, f, \mathcal{S}_n) + 2^{\max(0, \beta-1)} \left(\frac{\ln(2/\delta)}{\lambda n} \right)^{\beta} + \tilde{\epsilon}.$$

In addition, with probability at least $1 - \delta/2$,

$$\phi(f, \mathcal{S}_n) + \tilde{R}(\theta, f, \mathcal{S}_n) \leq \mathbb{E}_{\mathcal{S}_n} \left[\alpha' \phi(f, \mathcal{S}_n) + \alpha'' \tilde{R}(\theta, f, \mathcal{S}_n) \right] + \epsilon'(\theta, f, \delta/2).$$

Taking the union bound, and sum of the two inequalities, we obtain the desired oracle inequality. □

The result demonstrates that one can turn any sample-dependent uniform convergence bound into a model selection method. The algorithm itself does not depend on the concentration result involving ϵ'. In fact, an expected oracle inequality can be obtained even if we do not know ϵ', as shown in Exercises 8.2. The following example illustrates the roles of $\alpha, \alpha', \alpha'', \beta$, and λ.

Example 8.6 In Theorem 8.5, we consider the following absolute deviation loss

$$\phi(f, z) = |f(x) - y|,$$

and assume that $y \in [-1, 1]$. Assume also that we have function families $\{\mathcal{F}(\theta)\}$, each with $N(\theta)$ elements, and $|f(x)| \leq \theta$ for all $f(x) \in \mathcal{F}(\theta)$ ($\theta = 1, 2, \ldots$). We thus have $\phi(f, z) \in [0, \theta + 1]$. The multiplicative Chernoff bound in (2.11) implies that for any θ, with probability at least $1 - \delta$, for all $f \in \mathcal{F}(\theta)$,

$$(1 - \gamma)\phi(f, \mathcal{D}) \leq \phi(f, \mathcal{S}_n) + \frac{(\theta + 1)\ln(N(\theta)/\delta)}{2\gamma n}.$$

It implies the following result for $\gamma \in (0, 1)$:

$$(1 - \gamma)\phi(f, \mathcal{D}) \leq \phi(f, \mathcal{S}_n) + \frac{(\theta + 1)\ln(N(\theta))}{2\gamma n} + \frac{\lambda^2(\theta + 1)^2}{16\gamma^2} + \left(\frac{\ln(1/\delta)}{\lambda n}\right)^2.$$

In this derivation, we tried to decouple θ and δ so that the penalty term $\tilde{R}$ in the model selection method (8.3) does not depend on δ. Now we can take $\beta = 2$. It follows that we can take

$$\hat{\epsilon}(\theta, f, \mathcal{S}_n) = \frac{(\theta + 1)\ln(N(\theta))}{2\gamma n} + \frac{\lambda^2(\theta + 1)^2}{16\gamma^2},$$

$$\tilde{R}(\theta, f, \mathcal{S}_n) = \frac{(\theta + 1)\ln(N(\theta))}{2\gamma n} + \frac{\lambda^2(\theta + 1)^2}{16\gamma^2} + 2\left(\frac{\ln(1/q(\theta))}{\lambda n}\right)^2.$$

Both $\hat{\epsilon}$ and $\tilde{R}$ depend on the model index θ but not on the training data $\mathcal{S}_n$.

Now for all θ and $f \in \mathcal{F}(\theta)$, the multiplicative Chernoff bound (2.12) implies that for all θ and $f \in \mathcal{F}(\theta)$, with probability $1 - \delta$,

$$\phi(f, \mathcal{S}_n) \leq (1 + \gamma)\phi(f, \mathcal{D}) + \frac{(1 + \theta)(3 + 2\gamma)\ln(1/\delta)}{6\gamma n}.$$

Theorem 8.5 implies that the following oracle inequality holds:

$$(1 - \gamma)\phi(\hat{f}, \mathcal{D}) \leq \inf_{\theta, f \in \mathcal{F}(\theta)} [(1 + \gamma)\phi(f, \mathcal{D}) + \epsilon_n(\theta, \delta/2)] + \tilde{\epsilon} + \left(\frac{\ln(2/\delta)}{\lambda n}\right)^2,$$

where

$$\epsilon_n(\theta, \delta) = \frac{(\theta + 1)\ln N(\theta)}{2\gamma n} + \frac{\lambda^2(\theta + 1)^2}{16\gamma^2} + 2\left(\frac{\ln q(\theta)}{\lambda n}\right)^2 + \frac{(1 + \theta)(3 + 2\gamma)\ln\frac{1}{\delta}}{6\gamma n}.$$

If we take $\lambda = 1/\sqrt{n}$, then we have a complexity term of $\epsilon_n(\theta, \delta) = O(1/n)$.

Next we focus on bounded loss functions with Rademacher complexity analysis. In such case, we can simplify apply Theorem 8.5 with $\alpha = \alpha' = \alpha'' = 1$ and $\beta = 0.5$.

Theorem 8.7 *Consider the model selection algorithm in (8.3), with*

$$\tilde{R}(\theta, f, \mathcal{S}_n) = \tilde{R}(\theta) \geq 2R_n(\mathcal{F}(\theta), \mathcal{D}) + M(\theta)\sqrt{\frac{\ln(1/q(\theta))}{2n}},$$

where $M(\theta) = \sup_{f,z,z'} |\phi(f,z) - \phi(f,z')|$, *and* $q(\theta)$ *satisfies (8.1). Then with probability at least* $1 - \delta$, *for all* θ *and* $f \in \mathcal{F}(\theta)$,

$$\phi(f, \mathcal{D}) \leq \phi(f, \mathcal{S}_n) + \tilde{R}(\theta) + M(\theta)\sqrt{\frac{\ln(1/\delta)}{2n}}.$$

Moreover, we have the following oracle inequality. With probability of at least $1 - \delta$,

$$\phi(\hat{f}, \mathcal{D}) \leq \inf_{\theta, f \in \mathcal{F}(\theta)} \left[\phi(f, \mathcal{D}) + \tilde{R}(\theta) + 2M(\theta)\sqrt{\frac{\ln(2/\delta)}{2n}} \right] + \tilde{\epsilon}.$$

Proof Note that from Corollary 6.19, we obtain for any θ with $h = 0$, with probability $1 - \delta$, the following uniform convergence result holds for all $f \in \mathcal{F}(\theta)$:

$$\phi(f, \mathcal{D}) \leq \phi(f, \mathcal{S}_n) + 2R_n(\mathcal{F}(\theta), \mathcal{D}) + M(\theta)\sqrt{\frac{\ln(1/\delta)}{2n}}.$$

The choice of $\tilde{R}$ satisfies the condition of Theorem 8.5 with $c_0 = 1$ and $\beta = 0.5$. It implies the desired uniform convergence result.

Given fixed θ and $f \in \mathcal{F}(\theta)$, we know that

$$\left| [\phi(f, \mathcal{S}_n) + \tilde{R}(\theta)] - [\phi(f, \mathcal{S}'_n) + \tilde{R}(\theta)] \right| \leq M(\theta)$$

when $\mathcal{S}_n$ and $\mathcal{S}'_n$ differ by one element. From McDiarmid's inequality, we know that with probability at least $1 - \delta$,

$$\phi(f, \mathcal{S}_n) + \tilde{R}(\theta) \leq \phi(f, \mathcal{D}) + \tilde{R}(\theta) + M(\theta)\sqrt{\frac{\ln(1/\delta)}{2n}}.$$

It follows that we can take

$$\epsilon'(\theta, f, \delta) = M(\theta)\sqrt{\frac{\ln(1/\delta)}{2n}}$$

in Theorem 8.5, and obtain the desired oracle inequality. $\qquad\square$

Compared to Corollary 8.3, Theorem 8.7 achieves similar results using sample-dependent uniform convergence bounds. The resulting model selection algorithm (8.3) avoids partitioning data into training and validation parts, and can be used to design integrated algorithms that simultaneously estimate the model parameter and hyperparameter on the training data. However, the algorithm in (8.3) requires knowing the specific generalization bound for each model class, which may not be practical in some real applications.

Example 8.8 Consider the problem in Example 8.4. We can take $M(\theta) = 1$ and $h = 0$ in Theorem 8.7. It implies that the model selection method (8.3) with

$$\tilde{R}(\theta, f, \mathcal{S}_n) = \frac{32\sqrt{d(\theta)}}{\sqrt{n}} + \sqrt{\frac{\ln(\theta + 1)}{n}}$$

satisfies the following oracle inequality. With probability $1 - \delta$,

$$\mathbb{E}_{\mathcal{D}}\mathbb{1}(f_{\hat{\theta}}(\hat{\theta}, X) \neq Y) \leq \inf_{\theta, w \in \Omega_\theta}\left[\mathbb{E}_{\mathcal{D}}\mathbb{1}(f_\theta(w, X) \neq Y) + \frac{32\sqrt{d(\theta)}}{\sqrt{n}} + \sqrt{\frac{\ln(\theta + 1)}{n}}\right]$$
$$+ \sqrt{\frac{2\ln(2/\delta)}{n}}.$$

The result is comparable to that of Example 8.4.

It is also possible to develop a sample-dependent bound using the empirical Rademacher complexity. We note that an important property of Rademacher complexity is that for any function class $\mathcal{F}$, $R(\mathcal{F}, \mathcal{S}_n)$ is concentrated around $R_n(\mathcal{F}, \mathcal{D})$. This result follows directly from McDiarmid's inequality.

Theorem 8.9 (Concentration of Empirical Rademacher Complexity) *Consider h with decomposition 6.3 as $h(f, z) = h_0(f) + h_1(f, z)$. Assume that for some $M \geq 0$,*

$$\sup_{f \in \mathcal{F}}\sup_{z, z'}[|\phi(f, z) - \phi(f, z')| + |h_1(f, z) - h_1(f, z')|] \leq M.$$

We have with probability at least $1 - \delta$,

$$R_n^h(\mathcal{F}, \mathcal{D}) \leq R^h(\mathcal{F}, \mathcal{S}_n) + M\sqrt{\frac{\ln(1/\delta)}{2n}}.$$

Similarly, with probability at least $1 - \delta$, we have

$$R_n^h(\mathcal{F}, \mathcal{D}) \geq R^h(\mathcal{F}, \mathcal{S}_n) - M\sqrt{\frac{\ln(1/\delta)}{2n}}.$$

Proof Let $\mathcal{S}_n = \{Z_1, \ldots, Z_n\}$ and $\mathcal{S}'_n = \{Z'_1, \ldots, Z'_n\}$, where $Z_i = Z'_i$ except at a single index k. For any σ, we assume the sup of the following can be achieved at

$$\hat{f}(\sigma, \mathcal{S}_n) = \arg\max_{f \in \mathcal{F}}\left[\frac{1}{n}\sum_{i=1}^n \sigma_i[\phi(f, Z_i) + 0.5h_1(f, Z_i)] - 0.5h(f, \mathcal{S}_n)\right].$$

Let

$$\phi'(f, Z) = \phi(f, Z) + 0.5h_1(f, Z).$$

It follows that

$$\frac{1}{n}\sum_{i=1}^n \sigma_i\phi'(\hat{f}, Z'_i) - 0.5h(\hat{f}, \mathcal{S}'_n) \leq \frac{1}{n}\sum_{i=1}^n \sigma_i\phi(\hat{f}', Z'_i) - 0.5h(\hat{f}', \mathcal{S}'_n), \qquad (8.4)$$

where $\hat{f}$ is the short for $\hat{f}(\sigma, \mathcal{S}_n)$, and $\hat{f}'$ is the short for $\hat{f}(\sigma, \mathcal{S}'_n)$. Therefore,

$$R^h(\mathcal{F}, \mathcal{S}_n) - R^h(\mathcal{F}, \mathcal{S}'_n)$$

$$= \mathbb{E}_\sigma \left[\frac{1}{n} \sum_{i=1}^n \sigma_i \phi'(\hat{f}, Z_i) - \frac{1}{2} h(\hat{f}, \mathcal{S}_n) - \frac{1}{n} \sum_{i=1}^n \sigma_i \phi'(\hat{f}', Z'_i) + \frac{1}{2} h(\hat{f}', \mathcal{S}'_n) \right]$$

$$\leq \mathbb{E}_\sigma \left[\frac{1}{n} \sum_{i=1}^n \sigma_i \phi'(\hat{f}, Z_i) - \frac{1}{2} h(\hat{f}, \mathcal{S}_n) - \frac{1}{n} \sum_{i=1}^n \sigma_i \phi'(\hat{f}, Z'_i) + \frac{1}{2} h(\hat{f}, \mathcal{S}'_n) \right]$$

$$= \mathbb{E}_\sigma \left[\frac{1}{n} \sigma_k \phi'(\hat{f}, Z_k) - \frac{1}{n} \sigma_k \phi'(\hat{f}, Z'_k) + \frac{1}{2n} h_1(\hat{f}, Z'_k) - \frac{1}{2n} h_1(\hat{f}, Z_k) \right]$$

$$\leq M/n.$$

The first inequality used (8.4). Similarly, we have $R^h(\mathcal{F}, \mathcal{S}'_n) - R^h(\mathcal{F}, \mathcal{S}_n) \leq M/n$. This implies that $|R^h(\mathcal{F}, \mathcal{S}_n) - R^h(\mathcal{F}, \mathcal{S}'_n)| \leq M/n$. The desired bound is a direct consequence of McDiarmid's inequality. $\qquad\square$

This result, combined with Corollary 6.19, can be used to obtain the following sample-dependent uniform convergence result.

Corollary 8.10 *Consider h with decomposition (6.3) as $h(f, z) = h_0(f) + h_1(f, z)$. Assume that for some $M \geq 0$,*

$$\sup_{f \in \mathcal{F}} \sup_{z, z'} [|\phi(f, z) - \phi(f, z')| + |h_1(f, z) - h_1(f, z')|] \leq M.$$

Then with probability at least $1 - \delta$, for all $f \in \mathcal{F}$,

$$\phi(f, \mathcal{D}) \leq \phi(f, \mathcal{S}_n) + h(f, \mathcal{S}_n) + 2R^h(\mathcal{F}, \mathcal{S}_n) + 3M\sqrt{\frac{\ln(2/\delta)}{2n}}.$$

Proof With probability $1 - \delta/2$, Corollary 6.19 holds. With probability $1 - \delta/2$, Theorem 8.9 holds. The desired inequality follows by taking the union bound of the two events. $\qquad\square$

In order to apply the sample-dependent bound of Corollary 8.10, the right-hand side can be estimated using training data only. Although computationally the estimation of $R^h(\mathcal{F}, \mathcal{S}_n)$ can be quite challenging, it is statistically possible to do. One may also replace it by a sample-dependent upper bound, which are sometimes possible to derive. The following theorem is a direct consequence of Theorem 8.5. The proof is similar to that of Theorem 8.7.

Theorem 8.11 *Consider $h(\theta, f, \cdot)$ with decomposition (6.3) as $h(f, z) = h_0(f) + h_1(f, z)$. Assume that for some $M \geq 0$,*

$$\sup_{f \in \mathcal{F}(\theta)} \sup_{z, z'} [|\phi(f, z) - \phi(f, z')| + |h_1(\theta, f, z) - h_1(\theta, f, z')|] \leq M.$$

Let $\bar{R}(\theta, \mathcal{S}_n)$ be any upper bound of $R^{h(\theta, f, \cdot)}(\mathcal{F}(\theta), \mathcal{S}_n)$. Assume that

$$\tilde{R}(\theta, f, \mathcal{S}_n) \geq h(\theta, f, \mathcal{S}_n) + 2\bar{R}(\theta, \mathcal{S}_n) + 3M(\theta)\sqrt{\frac{\ln(2/q(\theta))}{2n}},$$

then the following uniform convergence result holds. With probability $1 - \delta$, for all θ and $f \in \mathcal{F}(\theta)$,

$$\phi(f, \mathcal{D}) \leq \phi(f, \mathcal{S}_n) + \tilde{R}(\theta, f, \mathcal{S}_n) + 3M(\theta)\sqrt{\frac{\ln(1/\delta)}{2n}}.$$

Consider the model selection algorithm in (8.3). We have the following oracle inequality. With probability of at least $1 - \delta$,

$$\phi(\hat{f}, \mathcal{D}) \leq \inf_{\theta, f \in \mathcal{F}(\theta)} \left[\phi(f, \mathcal{D}) + \mathbb{E}_{\mathcal{S}_n} \tilde{R}(\theta, f, \mathcal{S}_n) \right.$$

$$\left. + (4M(\theta) + 2\Delta_n(\bar{R}(\theta, \cdot)))\sqrt{\frac{\ln(2/\delta)}{2n}}\right] + \tilde{\epsilon},$$

where $\Delta_n(\cdot)$ is defined in Definition 6.17.

8.4 Bayesian Model Selection and Averaging

We have studied the Gibb's algorithm in Section 7.4. We showed that the algorithm is algorithmically stable, which can be used to show that it has good generalization performance in expectation. In this section, we further show that the Gibbs algorithm can be used for model selection.

We consider a family of Gibbs algorithms $\mathcal{A}(\theta, \mathcal{S}_n)$, and for each θ, the algorithm chooses a random $f \in \mathcal{F}(\theta)$ according to the probability

$$p(f|\theta, \mathcal{S}_n) = \frac{p_0(f|\theta) \exp\left(-\beta \sum_{Z \in \mathcal{S}_n} \phi(f, Z)\right)}{\exp(\Gamma(\theta|\mathcal{S}_n))}, \tag{8.5}$$

where $p_0(f|\theta)$ is a known prior on the model class $\mathcal{F}(\theta)$, and

$$\Gamma(\theta|\mathcal{S}_n) = \ln \mathbb{E}_{f \sim p_0(\cdot|\theta)} \exp\left(-\beta \sum_{Z \in \mathcal{S}_n} \phi(f, Z)\right).$$

Now, assume that we are further given a prior $p_0(\theta)$ on $\theta \in \Theta$, then the following algorithm is the Bayesian formula for Gibbs model selection, which randomly selects a model $\theta \in \Theta$ according to the posterior formula:

$$p(\theta|\mathcal{S}_n) \propto p_0(\theta) \exp\left(\Gamma(\theta|\mathcal{S}_n)\right). \tag{8.6}$$

After selecting θ, we then randomly select $f \in \mathcal{F}(\theta)$ according to (8.5).

Using the Bayesian formula, we obtain the joint posterior for both θ and f as:

$$p(\theta, f|\mathcal{S}_n) = p(\theta|\mathcal{S}_n)p(f|\theta, \mathcal{S}_n)$$

$$\propto p_0(\theta)p_0(f|\theta) \exp\left(-\beta \sum_{Z \in \mathcal{S}_n} \phi(f, Z)\right). \tag{8.7}$$

We simply randomly select a model from this distribution. This is still a Gibb's algorithm that defines a posterior distribution jointly on the hyperparameter θ

and the model function f. Theorem 7.19 can still be applied to obtain a generalization bound for this method.

Instead of selecting a model θ, and then obtaining the corresponding model parameter f using $\mathcal{A}(\theta, \mathcal{S}_n)$, it is observed in practice that model averaging, which simply averages different models, often leads to superior performance. To illustrate the idea, we consider the same setting as that of the Gibbs algorithm, which randomly picks a model from the posterior distribution (8.7). In model averaging, we simply use the averaged model output

$$\hat{f}(x) = \mathbb{E}_{(\theta, f) \sim p(\theta, f | \mathcal{S}_n)} f(x). \tag{8.8}$$

Since this particular model averaging method employs the posterior distribution, it is also referred to as Bayesian model averaging. The analysis of this method can be found in Chapter 15. If the loss function satisfies the α-exponential-concavity property defined in Definition 15.12, then one can obtain better results from model averaging, especially when the underlying model is misspecified. Such loss functions include log-loss, used in maximum-likelihood methods for conditional density estimation (e.g. logistic regression), and least squares regression with bounded target. For log-loss, model averaging is also the optimal estimation method under the Bayesian setting, where the underlying distribution is drawn according to a known prior (see Exercise 8.5). One may also come up with examples in which model averaging is superior to model selection, when model selection is unstable, as stated below. The construction is left to Exercise 8.6.

Proposition 8.12 *Consider the least squares regression problem*

$$\phi(f, z) = (f(x) - y)^2,$$

where $y \sim N(f_*(x), 1)$. We consider a model selection problem that contains only two models $\theta = 1, 2$, and each model contains only one (possibly misspecified) function $\mathcal{F}(\theta) = \{f_\theta(x)\}$, where $|f_\theta(x) - f_*(x)| \leq 1$ for all θ. Then there exists such a problem and an absolute constant $c_0 > 0$ so that given training data of size n, all model selection algorithms $\mathcal{A}_{sel}$ can only achieve an expected oracle inequality no better than

$$\mathbb{E}_{\mathcal{S}_n} \phi(\mathcal{A}_{sel}(\mathcal{S}_n), \mathcal{D}) \geq \inf_{\theta \in \{1,2\}} \phi(f_\theta, \mathcal{D}) + \frac{c_0}{\sqrt{n}}.$$

However, the Bayesian model averaging method $\mathcal{A}_{\mathrm{avg}}$ achieves an expected oracle inequality

$$\mathbb{E}_{\mathcal{S}_n} \phi(\mathcal{A}_{\mathrm{avg}}(\mathcal{S}_n), \mathcal{D}) \leq \inf_{\theta \in \{1,2\}} \phi(f_\theta, \mathcal{D}) + \frac{1}{c_0 n}.$$

8.5 Historical and Bibliographical Remarks

Model selection is an important topic in statistics. There are two classical asymptotic criteria for model selection, including the *Akaike information criterion* by Akaike (1974) (also referred to as AIC), and the *Bayesian information criterion* by Schwarz (1978) (also referred to as BIC). Both considered the parametric density estimation problem (negative-log likelihood loss) with $\phi(w, z) = -\ln p(y|w, x)$ in the asymptotic statistical setting, where $n \to \infty$. If the models are well specified, one can employ well-known classical asymptotic statistical techniques to derive these methods.

For AIC, one considers the ERM method (maximum-likelihood method) $\hat{f}_\theta$. If the model class $\mathcal{F}(\theta)$ is parametric, then one can show the following expected generalization bound

$$\phi(\hat{f}, \mathcal{D}) = \left[\phi(\hat{f}_\theta, \mathcal{S}_n) + \frac{d(\theta)}{n} + o_p\left(\frac{1}{n}\right) \right].$$

The leading excess risk term $\frac{d(\theta)}{n}$ on the right-hand side is AIC.

For BIC, one considers Bayesian model selection, and it can be shown using Laplace approximation that

$$-\Gamma(\theta|\mathcal{S}_n) = \phi(\hat{f}_\theta, \mathcal{S}_n) + \frac{d(\theta)\ln n}{2n} + O_p\left(\frac{1}{n}\right),$$

where $\hat{f}_\theta$ is the maximum likelihood estimate over $\mathcal{F}(\theta)$. The leading excess term $\frac{d(\theta)\ln n}{2n}$ on the right-hand side is BIC.

While simple, both AIC and BIC can only be applied in the asymptotic setting, and only for parametric models because both criteria depend linearly on the model parameter dimension $d(\theta)$. For nonparametric density estimation, one can employ a different criterion from information theory which may be regarded as a generalization of BIC, referred to as *minimum description length* (MDL) (see Rissanen, 1978; Barron et al., 1998; Grünwald, 2007). The MDL method, while not as easy to apply as BIC, is more consistent with the learning theory analysis which we investigated in this chapter. In fact, with our choice of $q(\theta)$ so that $\sum_\theta q(\theta) \leq 1$, the penalty $-\ln q(\theta)$ (which appears as model selection penalty) can be regarded as a coding length. Therefore the method considered in this chapter may be regarded as a generalized version of MDL.

Model selection has also been considered by Vapnik in his statistical learning approach, and was referred to as structural risk minimization (see Vapnik, 1999, 2013). The technique employs sample-dependent generalization bounds similar to those we considered in Section 8.3, with nested function classes.

Both Bayesian model selection and Bayesian model averaging have been used in practice (Raftery, 1995; Raftery et al., 1997; Wasserman, 2000; Robert, 2007).

The asymptotic analysis of Bayesian model selection for parametric models leads to BIC. For nonparametric models, as we have shown, the theoretical analysis of Bayesian model selection can be done either via the Gibbs algorithm or via MDL, and Bayesian model averaging can be analyzed using aggregation techniques studied in Chapter 15.

The concept of model selection is related to adaptive estimation in statistics (see Bickel, 1982; Birgé and Massart, 1997), which aims at optimal estimation across a family of models. This requires oracle inequalities similar to those of Section 8.3. Typically, the design of adaptive estimation methods also relies on data-dependent generalization analysis, similar to results developed in Section 8.3.

Exercises

8.1 In Theorem 8.2, we may consider model selection with

$$r_m(q) = \frac{\ln(1/q)}{2\gamma n}$$

for a fixed $\gamma > 0$. Use multiplicative Chernoff bound to obtain oracle inequalities similar to those of Theorem 8.2 and Corollary 8.3.

8.2 We can derive an expected oracle inequality under conditions of Theorem 8.5. Find a β dependent constant $C(\beta)$ such that the following expected oracle inequality holds:

$$\alpha \mathbb{E}_{\mathcal{S}_n} \phi(\hat{f}, \mathcal{D}) \leq \phi(f, \mathcal{D}) + \mathbb{E}_{\mathcal{S}_n} \tilde{R}(\theta, f, \mathcal{S}_n) + C(\beta) \left(\frac{1}{\lambda n} \right)^{\beta}.$$

Note that the inequality does not depend on ϵ'.

8.3 Consider a function family $\mathcal{F}$, and for each $f \in \mathcal{F}$, we have a complexity measure $c(f) \geq 0$. Let $\mathcal{F}(\theta) = \{f \in \mathcal{F}, c(f) \leq \theta\}$ for $\theta > 0$. Assume that we have a bound

$$\bar{R}(\theta) \geq R_n(\mathcal{F}(\theta), \mathcal{D})$$

for any $\theta > 0$. Assume that $\phi(f, z) \in [0, 1]$. Use Theorem 8.7 to obtain an oracle inequality for the following regularized ERM method:

$$\hat{f} = \arg\min_{f \in \mathcal{F}} \left[\frac{1}{n} \sum_{i=1}^{n} \phi(f, Z_i) + 2\bar{R}(2c(f))) + \sqrt{\ln(2 + \log_2(2c(f) + 1))/n} \right].$$

Hint: consider a sequence of function classes $\mathcal{F}(1), \mathcal{F}(2) \setminus \mathcal{F}(1), \mathcal{F}(4) \setminus \mathcal{F}(2), \ldots$.

8.4 Prove Theorem 8.11.

8.5 Consider the conditional density estimation problem

$$\phi(f, z) = -\ln p(y|f(x)).$$

Let $p_0(f)$ be a prior on $\mathcal{F}$, and assume that the true model is $p(y|f(x))$ is drawn according to the prior $p_0(f)$, and the corresponding data distribution $\mathcal{D} = \mathcal{D}_{f_*}$ has density $p_{f_*}(x, y) = p_*(x)p(y|f_*(x))$ for some unknown function $f_*(x)$. Show that for a given set of training data $\mathcal{S}_n$, the optimal Bayes estimator $\hat{f}_{\mathcal{S}_n}$ in terms of minimizing the expected loss

$$\mathbb{E}_{f_* \sim p_0} \mathbb{E}_{\mathcal{S}_n \sim \mathcal{D}_{f_*}^n} \mathbb{E}_{Z \sim \mathcal{D}_{f_*}} \phi(\hat{f}(Z))$$

is given by Bayesian model averaging over $p(y|f(x))$. Moreover, the Bayesian optimal model selection method is given by $\arg\max_\theta \Gamma(\theta|\mathcal{S}_n)$.

8.6 Show that the following example satisfies Proposition 8.12. Consider a one-dimensional problem with $x \sim \text{Uniform}(-1, 1)$. Assume that we choose $f_*(x)$ randomly from a two-function family $\{f_*^k(x) : k = 1, 2\}$, each with probability 0.5, where $f_*^1(x) = 1/\sqrt{n}$, and $f_*^2(x) = -1/\sqrt{n}$. Define two misspecified single-function model families $\{f_\theta(x)\}$ for $\theta = 1, 2$ as $f_\theta(x) = 0.5$ for $\theta = 1$ and $f_\theta(x) = -0.5$ for $\theta = 2$.

9

Analysis of Kernel Methods

A number of different kernel methods have appeared in the statistics literature. One such method, which employs the so-called reproducing kernel Hilbert space (RKHS), was popularized in machine learning through support vector machines (SVMs) in the 1990s (Cortes and Vapnik, 1995). This chapter presents an overview of RKHS kernel methods and their theoretical analysis. A more detailed treatment of RKHS kernel methods can be found in Schölkopf et al. (2018).

9.1 Introduction to Kernel Learning

In order to motivate kernel methods, we first consider the classical linear models, with the following real-valued function class $\mathcal{X} \to \mathbb{R}$ indexed by w:

$$\mathcal{F} = \{f(w, x) \colon f(w, x) = \langle w, \psi(x) \rangle\}, \tag{9.1}$$

where $\psi(x)$ is a predefined (possibly infinite-dimensional) feature vector for the input variable $x \in \mathcal{X}$, and $\langle \cdot, \cdot \rangle$ denotes an inner product in the feature vector space. In classical machine learning, the process of constructing the feature vector (or feature map) $\psi(x)$ is referred to as *feature engineering*, which is problem dependent. The feature vector is usually constructed by hand-crafted rules.

Given such a feature vector, we consider the following regularized ERM problem, with L_2 regularization:

$$\hat{w} = \arg\min_w \left[\frac{1}{n} \sum_{i=1}^n L(\langle w, \psi(X_i) \rangle, Y_i) + \frac{\lambda}{2} \|w\|^2 \right], \tag{9.2}$$

which employs the linear function class of (9.1).

If $\psi(x)$ is infinite dimensional (or its dimension is very large), then computationally it may not be feasible to work with $\psi(x)$ directly. The learning of the linear model class $\mathcal{F}$ can be achieved via an equivalent kernel formulation. We can define a kernel function $k(x, x')$ (also called reproducing kernel) as the inner product of their feature vectors:

$$k(x, x') = \langle \psi(x), \psi(x') \rangle. \tag{9.3}$$

One important observation, referred to as the *kernel trick*, can be described by the following result.

Proposition 9.1 *Assume that (9.3) holds. Consider a linear function $f(x) = \langle w, \psi(x) \rangle \in \mathcal{F}$ of (9.1). If w has a representation*

$$w = \sum_{i=1}^{n} \alpha_i \psi(x_i), \tag{9.4}$$

then

$$f(x) = \sum_{i=1}^{n} \alpha_i k(x_i, x) \tag{9.5}$$

and

$$\langle w, w \rangle = \sum_{i=1}^{n} \sum_{j=1}^{n} \alpha_i \alpha_j k(x_i, x_j). \tag{9.6}$$

The reverse is also true. That is, if $f(x)$ satisfies (9.5), then with w defined by (9.4), $f(x)$ can be equivalently expressed as $f(x) = \langle w, \psi(x) \rangle$, and (9.6) holds.

Proof Consider $f(x) = \langle w, \psi(x) \rangle$. If (9.4) holds, then

$$f(x) = \langle w, \psi(x) \rangle = \sum_{i=1}^{n} \alpha_i \langle \psi(x_i), \psi(x) \rangle = \sum_{i=1}^{n} \alpha_i k(x_i, x).$$

Moreover,

$$\langle w, w \rangle = \sum_{i=1}^{n} \sum_{j=1}^{n} \alpha_i \alpha_j \langle \psi(x_i), \psi(x_j) \rangle.$$

This implies (9.6). Similarly, the reverse direction holds. □

Proposition 9.1 implies if a linear machine learning algorithm produces a linear solution $f(x) = \langle w, \psi(x) \rangle$ with a weight vector w that satisfies (9.4), then the algorithm can be kernelized in that we can also use the kernel formulation (9.5) to represent the learned function.

In particular it can be shown that the solution $f(\hat{w}, x)$ of (9.2) satisfies (9.4), and thus can be kernelized. This result is often referred to as the representer theorem (Schölkopf et al., 2001).

Theorem 9.2 *For real-valued functions $f(x)$, the solution of (9.2) has the following kernel representation:*

$$\langle \hat{w}, \psi(x) \rangle = \bar{f}(\hat{\alpha}, x), \qquad \bar{f}(\hat{\alpha}, x) = \sum_{i=1}^{n} \hat{\alpha}_i k(X_i, x).$$

Therefore, the solution of (9.2) is equivalent to the solution of the following finite-dimensional kernel optimization problem:

$$\hat{\alpha} = \arg\min_{\alpha \in \mathbb{R}^n} \left[\frac{1}{n} \sum_{i=1}^{n} L\left(\bar{f}(\alpha, X_i), Y_i \right) + \frac{\lambda}{2} \alpha^\top K_{n \times n} \alpha \right], \tag{9.7}$$

with kernel Gram matrix

$$K_{n \times n} = \begin{bmatrix} k(X_1, X_1) & \cdots & k(X_1, X_n) \\ \cdots & \cdots & \cdots \\ k(X_n, X_1) & \cdots & k(X_n, X_n) \end{bmatrix}. \tag{9.8}$$

Proof Let

$$Q_1(w) = \frac{1}{n} \sum_{i=1}^{n} L(\langle w, \psi(X_i) \rangle, Y_i) + \frac{\lambda}{2} \|w\|^2$$

be the objective function of (9.2), and let

$$Q_2(\alpha) = \frac{1}{n} \sum_{i=1}^{n} L\left(\bar{f}(\alpha, X_i), Y_i\right) + \frac{\lambda}{2} \alpha^\top K_{n \times n} \alpha$$

be the objective function of (9.7).

The solution of (9.2) satisfies the following first-order optimality condition:

$$\frac{1}{n} \sum_{i=1}^{n} L_1'(\langle \hat{w}, \psi(X_i) \rangle, Y_i) \psi(X_i) + \lambda \hat{w} = 0.$$

Here, $L_1'(p, y)$ is the derivative of $L(p, y)$ with respect to p. We thus obtain the following representation as its solution:

$$\hat{w} = \sum_{i=1}^{n} \tilde{\alpha}_i \psi(X_i),$$

where

$$\tilde{\alpha}_i = -\frac{1}{\lambda n} L_1'(\langle \hat{w}, \psi(X_i) \rangle, Y_i) \qquad (i = 1, \ldots, n).$$

Using this notation, we obtain from Proposition 9.1 that

$$\langle \hat{w}, \psi(x) \rangle = \bar{f}(\tilde{\alpha}, x), \quad \langle \hat{w}, \hat{w} \rangle = \tilde{\alpha}^\top K_{n \times n} \tilde{\alpha}.$$

This implies that

$$Q_1(\hat{w}) = Q_2(\tilde{\alpha}) \geq Q_2(\hat{\alpha}) = Q_1(\tilde{w}),$$

where the last equality follows by setting $\tilde{w} = \sum_{i=1}^{n} \hat{\alpha}_i \psi(X_i)$. Proposition 9.1 implies that $Q_2(\hat{\alpha}) = Q_1(\tilde{w})$. It follows that $\tilde{w}$ is a solution of (9.2), which proves the desired result. □

We note that the kernel formulation does not depend on the feature $\psi(x)$, and thus can be computed even for an infinite-dimensional feature $\psi(x)$ as long as $k(x, x')$ is easy to compute.

Mathematically, the function space spanned by kernel functions of (9.5) with norm defined by (9.6) is referred to as a reproducing kernel Hilbert space (RKHS), which we can define formally in the following.

Definition 9.3 A symmetric function $k(x, x')$ is called a positive-definite kernel on $\mathcal{X} \times \mathcal{X}$ if for all $\alpha_1, \ldots, \alpha_m \in \mathbb{R}$ and $x_1, \ldots, x_m \in \mathcal{X}$, we have

$$\sum_{i=1}^{m} \sum_{j=1}^{m} \alpha_i \alpha_j k(x_i, x_j) \geq 0.$$

Definition 9.4 Given a symmetric positive-definite kernel, we define a function space $\mathcal{H}_0$ of the form

$$\mathcal{H}_0 = \left\{ f(x) : f(x) = \sum_{i=1}^{m} \alpha_i k(x_i, x) \right\},$$

with inner product defined as

$$\|f(x)\|_{\mathcal{H}}^2 = \sum_{i=1}^{m} \sum_{j=1}^{m} \alpha_i \alpha_j k(x_i, x_j).$$

The completion of $\mathcal{H}_0$ with respect to this inner product, defined as $\mathcal{H}$, is called the RKHS of kernel k.

We note that the RKHS norm of $f(x)$ in Definition 9.4 is well defined. That is, different representations lead to the same norm definition. The proof is left as an exercise.

Proposition 9.5 *Assume that for all $x \in \mathcal{X}$,*

$$\sum_{i=1}^{m} \alpha_i k(x_i, x) = \sum_{i=1}^{m'} \alpha_i' k(x_i', x),$$

then

$$\sum_{i=1}^{m} \sum_{j=1}^{m} \alpha_i \alpha_j k(x_i, x_j) = \sum_{i=1}^{m'} \sum_{j=1}^{m'} \alpha_i' \alpha_j' k(x_i', x_j').$$

We have derived kernel methods from linear models using the kernel trick. The following result shows that the reverse is also true. That is, there exists a feature representation of any RKHS. The result is a consequence of Mercer's theorem (Mercer, 1909).

Theorem 9.6 *A symmetric kernel function $k(x, x')$ is positive-definite if and only if there exists a feature map $\psi(x)$ so that it can be written in the form of (9.3). Moreover, let $\mathcal{H}$ be the RKHS of $k(\cdot, \cdot)$, then any function $f(x) \in \mathcal{H}$ can be written uniquely in the form of (9.1), with $\|f(x)\|_{\mathcal{H}}^2 = \langle w, w \rangle$.*

It is worth noting that although a decomposition (9.3) exists for a positive-definite kernel function, such decomposition may not be unique. Therefore it is possible to have different feature representations of an RKHS.

While the existence of decomposition stated in Theorem 9.6 is general, in practice, to construct a feature representation, one may use simple techniques such as Taylor expansion, as shown by the following example.

Example 9.7   If $x \in \mathbb{R}^d$, then a standard choice of kernel is the RBF (radial basis function) kernel:

$$k(x, x') = \exp \left[\frac{-\|x - x'\|_2^2}{2\sigma^2} \right].$$

It is easy to check that it can be written in the form of (9.3) using Taylor expansion:

$$k(x, x') = \exp \left[-\frac{\|x\|_2^2}{2\sigma^2} \right] \exp \left[-\frac{\|x'\|_2^2}{2\sigma^2} \right] \sum_{k=0}^{\infty} \frac{\sigma^{-2k}}{k!} (x^\top x')^k.$$

Given an RKHS $\mathcal{H}$, one may consider a norm constrained ERM problem in $\mathcal{H}$ as follows:

$$\hat{f}(\cdot) = \arg \min_{f(\cdot) \in \mathcal{H}} \frac{1}{n} \sum_{i=1}^{n} L(f(X_i), Y_i) \quad \text{subject to } \|f(\cdot)\|_{\mathcal{H}} \leq A. \tag{9.9}$$

The corresponding soft-regularized formulation with appropriate $\lambda > 0$ is

$$\hat{f}(\cdot) = \arg \min_{f(\cdot) \in \mathcal{H}} \left[\frac{1}{n} \sum_{i=1}^{n} L(f(X_i), Y_i) + \frac{\lambda}{2} \|f(\cdot)\|_{\mathcal{H}}^2 \right]. \tag{9.10}$$

The following result shows that if (9.3) holds, then $f(x) \in \mathcal{H}$ can be represented by a feature formulation (9.1). In this feature representation, we can write (9.10) equivalently as (9.2). The proof is left as an exercise.

Theorem 9.8   *Consider any kernel function $k(x, x')$ and feature map $\psi(x)$ that satisfies (9.3). Let $\mathcal{H}$ be the RKHS of $k(\cdot, \cdot)$. Then any $f(x) \in \mathcal{H}$ can be written in the form*

$$f(x) = \langle w, \psi(x) \rangle,$$

and

$$\|f(x)\|_{\mathcal{H}}^2 = \inf \{ \langle w, w \rangle : f(x) = \langle w, \psi(x) \rangle \}.$$

Consequently, the solution of (9.10) is equivalent to the solution of (9.2).

Note that Theorem 9.6 implies that there exists a feature representation of any RKHS, so that the RKHS norm is the same as the 2-norm of the linear weight. In this case, it is easy to see that (9.2) is equivalent to (9.10). Theorem 9.8 shows that the same conclusion holds for any decomposition (9.3) of the kernel function $k(x, x')$.

Example 9.9 In kernel ridge regression, we consider the least squares regression problem, which can be written as follows in the feature space representation:

$$\hat{w} = \arg\min_{w} \left[\frac{1}{n} \sum_{i=1}^{n} (\langle w, \psi(X_i) \rangle - Y_i)^2 + \frac{\lambda}{2} \langle w, w \rangle \right].$$

The primal kernel formulation is

$$\hat{\alpha} = \arg\min_{\alpha \in \mathbb{R}^n} \left[\frac{1}{n} \sum_{i=1}^{n} \left(\sum_{j=1}^{n} k(X_i, X_j)\alpha_j - Y_i \right)^2 + \frac{\lambda}{2} \alpha^\top K_{n \times n} \alpha \right].$$

There is also a dual formulation, which has the same solution:

$$\hat{\alpha} = \arg\max_{\alpha \in \mathbb{R}^n} \left[-\frac{\lambda}{2} \alpha^\top K_{n \times n} \alpha + \lambda \alpha^\top \mathbf{Y} - \frac{\lambda^2}{4} \alpha^\top \alpha \right],$$

where $\mathbf{Y}$ is the n-dimensional vector with Y_i as its component.

Example 9.10 Consider support vector machines for binary classification, where label $Y_i \in \{\pm 1\}$. Consider the following method in feature space:

$$\hat{w} = \arg\min_{w} \left[\frac{1}{n} \sum_{i=1}^{n} \max(0, 1 - \langle w, \psi(X_i) \rangle Y_i) + \frac{\lambda}{2} \langle w, w \rangle \right].$$

The primal kernel formulation is

$$\hat{w} = \arg\min_{\alpha} \left[\frac{1}{n} \sum_{i=1}^{n} \max \left(0, 1 - \sum_{j=1}^{n} \alpha_j k(X_i, X_j) Y_i \right) + \frac{\lambda}{2} \alpha^\top K_{n \times n} \alpha \right].$$

The equivalent dual kernel formulation is

$$\hat{\alpha} = \arg\max_{\alpha \in \mathbb{R}^n} \left[-\frac{\lambda}{2} \alpha^\top K_{n \times n} \alpha + \lambda \alpha^\top \mathbf{Y} \right], \quad \text{subject to } \alpha_i Y_i \in [0, 1/(\lambda n)].$$

A variation of the representer theorem can be obtained on functions defined on a finite set as follows.

Proposition 9.11 *Let $\mathcal{H}$ be the RKHS of a kernel $k(x, x')$ defined on a discrete set of n points $X_1, \ldots, X_n$. Let $K_{n \times n}$ be the Gram matrix defined on these points in (9.8), and K^+ be its pseudoinverse. Then for any function $f \in \mathcal{H}$, we have*

$$\|f\|_{\mathcal{H}}^2 = \mathbf{f}^\top K_{n \times n}^+ \mathbf{f}, \quad \text{where} \quad \mathbf{f} = \begin{bmatrix} f(X_1) \\ \vdots \\ f(X_n) \end{bmatrix}.$$

Proof We can express $f(x) = \sum_{i=1}^{n} \alpha_i k(x_i, x)$. Let $\alpha = [\alpha_1, \ldots, \alpha_n]^\top$, and we have $\mathbf{f} = \mathbf{K_{n \times n}} \alpha$. It follows that

$$\|f\|_{\mathcal{H}}^2 = \alpha^\top K_{n \times n} \alpha = \alpha^\top K_{n \times n} K_{n \times n}^+ K_{n \times n} \alpha = \mathbf{f}^\top K_{n \times n}^+ \mathbf{f}.$$

This proves the desired result. □

Proposition 9.11 establishes a link of kernel methods and Gaussian processes. In the Gaussian process view of kernel methods, the function values defined on a discrete set of n points $\{X_1, \ldots, X_n\}$ is a Gaussian $\mathbf{f} \sim N(\mathbf{m}, K_{n \times n})$, where $\mathbf{m} \in \mathbb{R}^n$ is the mean, and the kernel Gram matrix $K_{n \times n}$ is the covariance matrix. If the mean function is zero, then the density of the Gaussian is $\propto \exp(-0.5 \mathbf{f}^\top K_{n \times n}^+ \mathbf{f})$, which is closely related to Proposition 9.11. One can also extend Gaussian processes to infinitely many data points, with covariance of any two points given by the kernel function $k(x, x')$. For least squares regression, it can be shown that the posterior mean of the Gaussian process is equivalent to kernel ridge regression. For other loss functions, the inference may be different. Although Gaussian processes and kernel methods are closely related, one interesting fact is that samples from the Gaussian process corresponding to a kernel function $k(x, x')$ do not in general belong to the RKHS of the kernel function. Exercise 9.4 illustrates why this happens, and more discussions can be found in Neal (1998).

The RHKS representation in Proposition 9.11 can be directly used to obtain a semi-supervised formulation of kernel method, defined on both labeled and unlabeled data as follows.

Corollary 9.12 *Assume that we have labeled data $X_1, \ldots, X_n$, and unlabeled data $X_{n+1}, \ldots, X_{n+m}$. Let $K = K_{(n+m) \times (n+m)}$ be the kernel Gram matrix of a kernel k on these $m + n$ points, and let $\mathcal{H}$ be the corresponding RKHS. Then (9.10) defined on these data points is equivalent to*

$$\hat{f}(\cdot) = \arg \min_{\mathbf{f} \in \mathbb{R}^{n+m}} \left[\frac{1}{n} \sum_{i=1}^n L(f(X_i), Y_i) + \frac{\lambda}{2} \mathbf{f}^\top K^+ \mathbf{f} \right], \quad \mathbf{f} = \begin{bmatrix} f(X_1) \\ \vdots \\ f(X_{n+m}) \end{bmatrix}.$$

A drawback of kernel methods is that the computation requires the full kernel matrix $K_{n \times n}$, and thus it is at least quadratic in n. Moreover, the inference time is linear in n. Both are rather expensive if n is large.

9.2 Universal Approximation

An important question for learning methods is whether the underlying function class (model family) can approximate all measurable functions. A function class that can represent all functions is called a *universal approximator*. Since the set of continuous functions is dense in the set of measurable functions, we only require that all continuous functions can be approximated by the RKHS of a kernel function. The approximation can be measured using different metrics. For simplicity, we consider uniform approximation here.

Definition 9.13 A kernel $k(x, x')$ is called a universal kernel on $\mathcal{X} \subset \mathbb{R}^d$ (under the uniform convergence topology) if for any continuous function $f(x)$ on $\mathcal{X}$, and any $\epsilon > 0$, there exists $g(x) \in \mathcal{H}$ such that

$$\forall x \in \mathcal{X} : |f(x) - g(x)| \leq \epsilon,$$

where $\mathcal{H}$ is the RKHS of kernel $k(\cdot, \cdot)$.

For kernel methods, the universal approximation result was established in Park and Sandberg (1991). Following their approach, we present a more refined approximation bound for Lipschitz functions using translation invariant kernels on $\mathbb{R}^d$ include the RBF kernel as a special case. Since Lipschitz functions are dense in the set of continuous functions, this result implies universal approximation on any compact set $\mathcal{X} \subset \mathbb{R}^d$.

Theorem 9.14 *Consider a positive definite translation invariant kernel*

$$k(x, x') = h(\|x - x'\|/\sigma),$$

where $\| \cdot \|$ is a norm on $\mathbb{R}^d$. Assume that $h(\cdot) \in [0, 1]$, and

$$c_0 = \int h(\|x\|)dx \in (0, \infty), \qquad c_1 = \int \|x\| h(\|x\|)dx < \infty.$$

Assume that f is Lipschitz with respect to the norm $\| \cdot \|$: $\exists \gamma > 0$ such that $|f(x) - f(x')| \leq \gamma \|x - x'\|$ for all $x, x' \in \mathbb{R}^d$. If

$$\|f\|_1 = \int |f(x)|dx < \infty,$$

then for any $\epsilon > 0$ and $\sigma = \epsilon c_0/(\gamma c_1)$, there exists $\psi_\sigma(x) \in \mathcal{H}$, where $\mathcal{H}$ is the RKHS of $k(\cdot)$, so that $\|\psi_\sigma(x)\|_{\mathcal{H}} \leq (c_0 \sigma^d)^{-1} \|f\|_1$ and

$$\forall x: |f(x) - \psi_\sigma(x)| \leq \epsilon.$$

Proof We approximate f by the following function:

$$\psi_\sigma(x) = \int \alpha(z) h(\|x - z\|/\sigma)dz,$$

where $\alpha(z) = f(z)/(c_0 \sigma^d)$. Let

$$A = \int |\alpha(z)\alpha(x)| h(\|x - z\|/\sigma)dxdz,$$

then

$$A \leq \sqrt{\int \int |\alpha(z)\alpha(x)|dxdz} \sqrt{\int \int |\alpha(z)\alpha(x)| h(\|x - z\|/\sigma)^2 dxdz}$$

$$\leq \sqrt{\int \int |\alpha(z)|dz \int |\alpha(x)|dx} \cdot \sqrt{A}.$$

The first inequality used the Cauchy–Schwarz inequality. The second inequality used the fact that $h(\cdot) \in [0, 1]$. Therefore,

$$\sqrt{A} \leq \int |\alpha(x)|dx = (c_0 \sigma^d)^{-1} \|f\|_1.$$

The RKHS norm of $\psi_\sigma(x)$ is given by

$$\|\psi_\sigma(x)\|_{\mathcal{H}} = \sqrt{\int\int \alpha(z)\alpha(x)h(\|x - z\|/\sigma)dxdz} \leq \sqrt{A} \leq (c_0\sigma^d)^{-1}\|f\|_1.$$

In the following, we only need to show that $|f(x) - \psi_\sigma(x)| \leq \epsilon$ for all $x \in \mathbb{R}^d$. Using a change of variable for convolution, we also obtain the expression

$$\psi_\sigma(x) = c_0^{-1}\int f(x - \sigma z)h(\|z\|)dz.$$

Note that

$$f(x) = c_0^{-1}\int f(x)h(\|z\|)dz.$$

Since f is Lipschitz, we have

$$|f(x) - \psi_\sigma(x)| \leq c_0^{-1}\int |f(x) - f(x - \sigma z)|h(\|z\|)dz \leq \sigma\gamma c_0^{-1}c_1.$$

By setting $\epsilon = \sigma\gamma c_0^{-1}c_1$, we obtain the desired result. □

The parameter σ is often referred to as the bandwidth in the literature. Theorem 9.14 shows that it is useful to adjust the bandwidth in the kernel approximation because there is a trade-off between approximation error and RKHS norm. As we will see later, the RKHS norm affects generalization. While this result provides a specific approximation bound for Lipschitz functions, in the general situation, one can obtain a more qualitative universal approximate result without such a bound. One approach is to use the Stone–Weierstrass theorem, which states that a continuous function on a compact set in $\mathbb{R}^d$ can be uniformly approximated by polynomials. It implies the following result.

Theorem 9.15 *Consider a compact set $\mathcal{X}$ in $\mathbb{R}^d$. Assume that a kernel function $k(x, x')$ on $\mathcal{X} \times \mathcal{X}$ has a feature representation $k(x, x') = \sum_{i=1}^{\infty} c_i\psi_i(x)\psi_i(x')$, where each $\psi_i(x)$ is a real valued function, and $c_i > 0$. Assume the feature maps $\{\psi_i(x): i = 1, \ldots\}$ contain all monomials of the form $\{g(x) = \prod_{j=1}^{d} x_j^{\alpha_j} : x = [x_1, \ldots, x_d], \alpha_j \geq 0\}$. Then $k(x, x')$ is universal on $\mathcal{X}$.*

Proof Let $\mathcal{H}$ be the RKHS of $k(\cdot, \cdot)$. Note that according to Theorem 9.8, a function of the form $g(x) = \sum_{j=1}^{\infty} w_i\psi_i(x)$ has RKHS norm as $\|g\|_{\mathcal{H}}^2 \leq \sum_{i=1}^{\infty} w_i^2/c_i$. It follows from the assumption of the theorem that all monomials $p(x)$ have RKHS norm $\|p\|_{\mathcal{H}}^2 < \infty$. Therefore $\mathcal{H}$ contains all polynomials. The result of the theorem is now a direct consequence of the Stone–Weierstrass theorem. □

Example 9.16 Let $\alpha > 0$ be an arbitrary constant. Consider the kernel function

$$k(x, x') = \exp(\alpha x^\top x')$$

on a compact set of $\mathbb{R}^d$. Since

$$k(x, x') = \exp(-\alpha)\sum_{i=0}^{\infty} \frac{\alpha^i}{i!}(x^\top x' + 1)^i,$$

it is clear that the expansion of $(x^\top x' + 1)^i$ contains all monomials of order i. Therefore Theorem 9.15 implies that $k(x, x')$ is universal.

The following result is also useful when we consider compositions of kernels.

Theorem 9.17 *If $k(x, x')$ is a universal kernel on $\mathcal{X}$, and let $k'(x, x')$ be any other kernel function on $\mathcal{X} \times \mathcal{X}$. Then $k(x, x') + k'(x, x')$ is a universal kernel on $\mathcal{X}$. Moreover, let $u(x)$ be a real-valued continuous function on $\mathcal{X}$ so that*

$$\sup_{x \in \mathcal{X}} u(x) < \infty, \qquad \inf_{x \in \mathcal{X}} u(x) > 0.$$

Then $k'(x, x') = k(x, x')u(x)u(x')$ is a universal kernel on $\mathcal{X}$.

Proof Let $k(x, x') = \langle \psi(x), \psi(x') \rangle_{\mathcal{H}}$ with the corresponding RKHS denoted by $\mathcal{H}$, and let $k'(x, x') = \langle \psi'(x), \psi'(x') \rangle_{\mathcal{H}'}$ with RKHS $\mathcal{H}'$:

$$k(x, x') + k'(x, x') = \langle \psi(x), \psi(x') \rangle_{\mathcal{H}} + \langle \psi'(x), \psi'(x') \rangle_{\mathcal{H}'}.$$

Using feature representation, we can represent functions in the RKHS of $k(x, x') + k'(x, x')$ by $\langle w, \psi(x) \rangle_{\mathcal{H}} + \langle w', \psi'(x) \rangle_{\mathcal{H}'}$, and thus it contains $\mathcal{H} \oplus \mathcal{H}'$. This implies the first result.

For the second result, we know that $k'(x, x') = \langle \psi(x)u(x), \psi(x')u(x') \rangle_{\mathcal{H}}$, and thus its RHKS can be represented by $\langle w, \psi(x)u(x) \rangle_{\mathcal{H}}$. Since the universality of $k(x, x')$ implies that for any continuous $f(x)$, $f(x)/u(x)$ can be uniformly approximated by $\langle w, \psi(x) \rangle_{\mathcal{H}}$, we obtain the desired result. $\qquad \square$

Example 9.18 Consider the RBF kernel function

$$k(x, x') = \exp(-\alpha \|x - x'\|_2^2).$$

Since

$$k(x, x') = \exp(2\alpha x^\top x')u(x)u(x'),$$

where $u(x) = \exp(-\alpha \|x\|_2^2)$, Theorem 9.17 and Example 9.16 imply that $k(x, x')$ is universal on any compact set $\mathcal{X} \subset \mathbb{R}^d$.

One can also establish a relationship of universal kernel and the Gram matrix $K_{n \times n}$ in Theorem 9.2 as follows. It will be useful when we discuss neural tangent kernel in Chapter 11.

Theorem 9.19 *Let $k(x, x')$ be a universal kernel on $\mathcal{X}$. Consider n different data points $X_1, \ldots, X_n \in \mathcal{X}$, and let $K_{n \times n}$ be the Gram matrix defined in Theorem 9.2. Then $K_{n \times n}$ is full rank.*

Proof Consider a vector $Y = [Y_1, \ldots, Y_n] \in \mathbb{R}^n$. Given $\epsilon > 0$, there exists a continuous function $f(x)$ so that $|f(X_i) - Y_i| \leq \epsilon/\sqrt{n}$ for all i. Since $k(x, x')$ is universal, there exists $g(x) \in \mathcal{H}$ such that $|g(X_i) - f(X_i)| \leq \epsilon/\sqrt{n}$ for all i. Therefore $|g(X_i) - Y_i| \leq 2\epsilon/\sqrt{n}$ for all i.

Consider $\lambda = \epsilon^2/\|g\|_{\mathcal{H}}^2$, and let

$$\hat{g} = \arg\min_{g' \in \mathcal{H}} \left[\sum_{i=1}^{n} (g'(X_i) - Y_i)^2 + \lambda \|g'\|_{\mathcal{H}}^2 \right].$$

Then

$$\sum_{i=1}^{n} (\hat{g}(X_i) - Y_i)^2 \leq \sum_{i=1}^{n} (g(x) - Y_i)^2 + \lambda \|g\|_{\mathcal{H}}^2 \leq 5\epsilon^2.$$

Using Theorem 9.2, this implies that there exists $\alpha \in \mathbb{R}^n$ so that

$$\|K_{n \times n} \alpha - Y\|_2^2 \leq 5\epsilon^2.$$

Since ϵ is arbitrary, $K_{n \times n}$ has to be full rank. $\qquad\square$

9.3 Generalization Analysis

In this section, we study the generalization behavior of kernel methods using the Rademacher complexity analysis. In particular, we want to bound the Rademacher complexities of (9.9) and (9.10).

We will consider the feature representation (9.1), with the induced kernel (9.3). We know from Theorem 9.8 that if we define the function class

$$\mathcal{F}(A) = \{f(x) \in \mathcal{H} \colon \|f\|_{\mathcal{H}}^2 \leq A^2\},$$

then for any feature map that satisfies (9.3), $\mathcal{F}(A)$ can be equivalently written in the linear feature representation form as

$$\mathcal{F}(A) = \{f(x) = \langle w, \psi(x) \rangle \colon \langle w, w \rangle \leq A^2\}. \tag{9.11}$$

That is, kernel methods with RKHS regularization are equivalent to linear model with L_2 regularization. In the following, we will use the two representations interchangeably.

Theorem 9.20 *Consider $\mathcal{F}(A)$ defined in (9.11). We have the following bound for its Rademacher complexity:*

$$R(\mathcal{F}(A), \mathcal{S}_n) \leq A \sqrt{\frac{1}{n^2} \sum_{i=1}^{n} k(X_i, X_i)}.$$

Moreover let $\mathcal{F} = \mathcal{F}(+\infty)$, then

$$R^h(\mathcal{F}, \mathcal{S}_n) \leq \frac{1}{\lambda n^2} \sum_{i=1}^{n} k(X_i, X_i),$$

where in (6.3), we set

$$h(w, \mathcal{S}_n) = h_0(w) = \frac{\lambda}{2} \langle w, w \rangle. \tag{9.12}$$

Proof For convenience, let $\|w\| = \sqrt{\langle w, w \rangle}$. We have

$$
\begin{aligned}
R^h(\mathcal{F}, \mathcal{S}_n) &= \mathbb{E}_\sigma \sup_w \left[\frac{1}{n} \sum_{i=1}^n \sigma_i \langle w, \psi(X_i) \rangle - \frac{\lambda}{4} \langle w, w \rangle \right] \\
&= \mathbb{E}_\sigma \sup_w \left[\left\langle w, \frac{1}{n} \sum_{i=1}^n \sigma_i \psi(X_i) \right\rangle - \frac{\lambda}{4} \langle w, w \rangle \right] \\
&= \mathbb{E}_\sigma \frac{1}{\lambda} \left\| \frac{1}{n} \sum_{i=1}^n \sigma_i \psi(X_i) \right\|^2 \\
&= \frac{1}{\lambda n^2} \sum_{i=1}^n \|\psi(X_i)\|^2 = \frac{1}{\lambda n^2} \sum_{i=1}^n k(X_i, X_i).
\end{aligned}
$$

This proves the second bound. For the first bound, we note that

$$
R(\mathcal{F}(A), \mathcal{S}_n) \leq R^h(\mathcal{F}, \mathcal{S}_n) + \frac{\lambda A^2}{4} \leq \frac{1}{\lambda n^2} \sum_{i=1}^n k(X_i, X_i) + \frac{\lambda A^2}{4}.
$$

Optimize over $\lambda > 0$, and we obtain the desired result. $\square$

Corollary 9.21 *Let $\mathcal{G}(A) = \{L(f(x), y) : f(x) \in \mathcal{F}(A)\}$, where $\mathcal{F}(A)$ is defined in (9.11). If $L(p, y)$ is γ Lipschitz in p, then*

$$
R(\mathcal{G}(A), \mathcal{S}_n) \leq A\gamma \sqrt{\frac{1}{n^2} \sum_{i=1}^n k(X_i, X_i)},
$$

$$
R_n(\mathcal{G}(A), \mathcal{D}) \leq A\gamma \sqrt{\frac{\mathbb{E}_{X \sim \mathcal{D}} k(X, X)}{n}}.
$$

Moreover, let $\mathcal{G} = \mathcal{G}(+\infty)$, then

$$
R^h(\mathcal{G}, \mathcal{S}_n) \leq \frac{\gamma^2}{\lambda n^2} \sum_{i=1}^n k(X_i, X_i),
$$

$$
R_n^h(\mathcal{G}, \mathcal{D}) \leq \frac{\gamma^2 \mathbb{E}_{X \sim \mathcal{D}} k(X, X)}{\lambda n},
$$

where h is defined in (9.12).

Proof The first and the third inequalities follow from Theorem 9.20 and the Rademacher comparison theorem in Theorem 6.28. The second inequality follows from the derivation

$$R_n(\mathcal{G}(A), \mathcal{D}) = \mathbb{E}_{\mathcal{S}_n} R(\mathcal{G}, \mathcal{S}_n) \leq A\gamma \mathbb{E}_{\mathcal{S}_n} \sqrt{\frac{1}{n^2} \sum_{i=1}^{n} k(X_i, X_i)}$$

$$\overset{(a)}{\leq} A\gamma \sqrt{\frac{1}{n^2} \mathbb{E}_{\mathcal{S}_n} \sum_{i=1}^{n} k(X_i, X_i)}$$

$$= A\gamma \sqrt{\frac{1}{n} \mathbb{E}_{\mathcal{D}} k(X, X)}.$$

The derivation of (a) used Jensen's inequality and the concavity of $\sqrt{\cdot}$.

The fourth inequality of the corollary can be similarly derived. $\qquad \square$

Now using Theorem 6.31, we obtain the following result.

Corollary 9.22 *Assume that* $\sup_{p,y} L(p, y) - \inf_{p,y} L(p, y) \leq M$, *and* $L(p, y)$ *is* γ *Lipschitz with respect to* p. *Then with probability at least* $1 - \delta$, *for all* $f \in \mathcal{H}$ *with* $\|f\|_{\mathcal{H}} \leq A$,

$$\mathbb{E}_{\mathcal{D}} L(f(X), Y) \leq \frac{1}{n} \sum_{i=1}^{n} L(f(X_i), Y_i) + 2\gamma A \sqrt{\frac{\mathbb{E}_{\mathcal{D}} k(X, X)}{n}} + M \sqrt{\frac{\ln(1/\delta)}{2n}}.$$

Moreover, for (9.9), *if we solve it approximately up to suboptimality of* ϵ', *then we have with probability at least* $1 - \delta$,

$$\mathbb{E}_{\mathcal{D}} L(\hat{f}(X), Y) \leq \inf_{\|f\|_{\mathcal{H}} \leq A} \mathbb{E}_{\mathcal{D}} L(f(X), Y) + \epsilon' + 2\gamma A \sqrt{\frac{\mathbb{E}_{\mathcal{D}} k(X, X)}{n}}$$

$$+ M \sqrt{\frac{2 \ln(2/\delta)}{n}}.$$

Note that as $A \to \infty$, we have

$$\inf_{\|f\|_{\mathcal{H}} \leq A} \mathbb{E}_{\mathcal{D}} L(f(X), Y) \to \inf_{\|f\|_{\mathcal{H}} < \infty} \mathbb{E}_{\mathcal{D}} L(f(X), Y).$$

If $k(\cdot, \cdot)$ is a universal kernel, then

$$\lim_{A \to \infty} \inf_{\|f\|_{\mathcal{H}} \leq A} \mathbb{E}_{\mathcal{D}} L(f(X), Y) \to \inf_{\text{measurable } f} \mathbb{E}_{\mathcal{D}} L(f(X), Y).$$

Combine this with the generalization result of kernel method in Corollary 9.22, we know that as $n \to \infty$, and let $A \to \infty$, the following result is valid. With probability 1,

$$\mathbb{E}_{\mathcal{D}} L(\hat{f}(X), Y) \to \inf_{\text{measurable } f} \mathbb{E}_{\mathcal{D}} L(f(X), Y).$$

Such a result is referred to as *consistency*.

Example 9.23 For binary classification problem with $y \in \{\pm 1\}$, we may consider a classifier induced by a real-valued function $f(x)$ such that we predict $y = 1$ if $f(x) \geq 0$ and $y = -1$ otherwise. If $f(x)$ is taken from an RKHS, then we have the following margin bound. With probability $1 - \delta$, for all $f \in \mathcal{H}$ with $\|f\|_{\mathcal{H}} \leq A$,

$$\mathbb{E}_{\mathcal{D}} \mathbb{1}(f(X)Y \leq 0) \leq \frac{1}{n} \sum_{i=1}^{n} \mathbb{1}(f(X_i)Y_i \leq \gamma) + \frac{2A}{\gamma} \sqrt{\frac{\mathbb{E}_{\mathcal{D}} k(X, X)}{n}} + \sqrt{\frac{\ln(1/\delta)}{2n}}.$$

It says that if we can find a classifier with a small margin error, then we can achieve a good test classification error. Unlike the VC analysis in Chapter 4, the bound does not depend on the dimensionality of the feature vector $\psi(x)$, but rather on the classifier's RKHS norm A, and margin condition.

The bound can be obtained as a direct consequence of Corollary 9.22, using a loss function $L(p, y) = \min(1, \max(0, 1 - py/\gamma))$, which is γ^{-1} Lipschitz. In this case, $\mathbb{1}(f(x)y \leq 0) \leq L(f(x), y) \leq \mathbb{1}(f(x)y \leq \gamma)$.

We note that the Rademacher complexity analysis only leads to a convergence rate of $O(1/\sqrt{n})$. However, similar to the VC analysis, it is possible to obtain a margin bound of $O(\ln n/n)$ when the margin error is zero. This requires a different analysis stated in Theorem 4.21, together with the empirical L_∞ covering number of Theorem 5.20. We leave it to Exercise 9.5.

Example 9.24 For SVM loss, $\gamma = 1$. With hard regularization, we can take $M = (1 + AB)$, where we assume that $k(x, x) \leq B^2$. Consider $\hat{f}$ that solves (9.9) up to an accuracy of $\epsilon' > 0$. From Corollary 9.22, we obtain with probability at least $1 - \delta$,

$$\mathbb{E}_{\mathcal{D}} L(\hat{f}(X), Y) \leq \inf_{\|f\|_{\mathcal{H}} \leq A} \mathbb{E}_{\mathcal{D}} L(f(X), Y) + \epsilon' + \frac{2AB}{\sqrt{n}} + (1 + AB)\sqrt{\frac{2\ln(2/\delta)}{n}}.$$

Given an arbitrary competitor $f \in \mathcal{H}$, the optimal value of A would be $A = \|f\|_{\mathcal{H}}$. However, this requires us to know the value of $\|f\|_{\mathcal{H}}$, which is not feasible. In practice, it is more convenient to use the soft-regularized version (9.10), where the choice of λ is less sensitive than A, and it can be set independently of $\|f\|_{\mathcal{H}}$. The following result is a direct consequence of Corollary 9.21 and Theorem 6.14.

Corollary 9.25 *If $L(p, y)$ is γ-Lipschitz with respect to p, then we have the following expected oracle inequality for (9.10):*

$$\mathbb{E}_{\mathcal{S}_n} L(\hat{f}, \mathcal{D}) \leq \inf_{f \in \mathcal{H}} \left[L(f, \mathcal{D}) + \frac{\lambda}{2} \|f\|_{\mathcal{H}}^2 \right] + \frac{2\gamma^2 \mathbb{E}_{\mathcal{D}} k(X, X)}{\lambda n}.$$

Observe that in Corollary 9.25, the expected oracle inequality does not rely on the boundedness of $L(\cdot, \cdot)$. One may also obtain high probability inequalities by employing the technique of Chapter 8 and a union bound over a properly defined sequence of nested function classes.

Corollary 9.26 *Assume that $L(p, y) \geq 0$ is γ Lipschitz in p, and $\sup_y L(0, y) \leq M_0$. Let $B^2 = \sup_x k(x, x)$, then with probability at least $1 - \delta$, for all $f \in \mathcal{H}$,*

$$\left| \mathbb{E}_{\mathcal{D}} L(f(X), Y) - \frac{1}{n} \sum_{i=1}^{n} L(f(X_i), Y_i) \right| \leq \frac{1}{\sqrt{n}} (4M_0 + 4\gamma B \|f\|_{\mathcal{H}})$$

$$+ (3M_0 + 2\gamma B \|f\|_{\mathcal{H}}) \sqrt{\frac{\ln(2(2 + \log_2(1 + \gamma B \|f\|_{\mathcal{H}}/M_0))^2/\delta)}{2n}}.$$

Proof Let $A_\theta = 2^\theta A_0$ for $A_0 > 0$ to be determined later, with $q(\theta) = 1/(\theta + 1)^2$ for $\theta = 1, 2, \ldots$. Consider $\Omega_\theta = \{f \in \mathcal{H} : \|f\|_{\mathcal{H}} \leq A_\theta\}$. We know that $L(p, y) \leq L(0, y) + \gamma|p| \leq M_0 + \gamma A_\theta B$. Let $M_\theta = M_0 + \gamma A_\theta B$. Then Corollary 9.22 implies that with probability at least $1 - q(\theta)\delta$, for all $f \in \mathcal{H}$ with $\|f\|_{\mathcal{H}} \leq A_\theta$,

$$\left| \mathbb{E}_{\mathcal{D}} L(f(X), Y) - \frac{1}{n} \sum_{i=1}^{n} L(f(X_i), Y_i) \right| \leq \frac{2\gamma A_\theta B}{\sqrt{n}} + M_\theta \sqrt{\frac{\ln(2/(q(\theta)\delta))}{2n}}.$$

Taking the union bound, we have with probability $1 - \delta$, for all $f \in \mathcal{H}$ and all $\theta \geq 1$ such that $\|f\|_{\mathcal{H}} \leq A_\theta$,

$$\left| \mathbb{E}_{\mathcal{D}} L(f(X), Y) - \frac{1}{n} \sum_{i=1}^{n} L(f(X_i), Y_i) \right| \leq \frac{2\gamma A_\theta B}{\sqrt{n}} + M_\theta \sqrt{\frac{\ln(2/(q(\theta)\delta))}{2n}}.$$

We let $\theta(f) \geq 1$ be the smallest index such that $\|f\|_{\mathcal{H}} \leq A_\theta$. Then $A_{\theta(f)} \leq 2(A_0 + \|f\|_{\mathcal{H}})$, and thus $\theta(f) \leq \log_2(2 + 2\|f\|_{\mathcal{H}}/A_0)$. We can take $A_0 = M_0/(\gamma B)$. This implies the desired bound. $\qquad \square$

We can also obtain an oracle inequality as follows.

Corollary 9.27 *Assume that $L(p, y) \geq 0$ is γ-Lipschitz in p, $\sup_y L(0, y) \in [0, M_0]$, and $\sup_X k(X, X) \leq B^2$. Then with probability $1 - \delta$, we have the following oracle inequality for (9.10):*

$$L(\hat{f}, \mathcal{D}) \leq \inf_{f \in \mathcal{H}} \left[L(f, \mathcal{D}) + \frac{\lambda}{2} \|f\|_{\mathcal{H}}^2 + \epsilon_B \|f\|_{\mathcal{H}} \right] + 2\epsilon_M + \frac{\epsilon_B^2}{2\lambda},$$

where $\theta_0 = 1 + \log_2(1 + \gamma B \sqrt{2/(\lambda M_0)})$, and

$$\epsilon_M = \frac{4M_0}{\sqrt{n}} + 3M_0 \sqrt{\frac{\ln(2(1 + \theta_0)^2/\delta)}{2n}},$$

$$\epsilon_B = \frac{4\gamma B}{\sqrt{n}} + 2\gamma B \sqrt{\frac{\ln(2(1 + \theta_0)^2/\delta)}{2n}}.$$

Proof We note that $\|\hat{f}\|_{\mathcal{H}}^2 \leq 2M_0/\lambda$. Therefore Corollary 9.26 implies that with probability at least $1 - \delta$, for all $f \in \mathcal{H}$,

$$\left| \mathbb{E}_{\mathcal{D}} L(f(X), Y) - \frac{1}{n} \sum_{i=1}^{n} L(f(X_i), Y_i) \right| \leq \epsilon_M + \epsilon_B \|f\|_{\mathcal{H}}. \tag{9.13}$$

This implies that

$$L(\hat{f}, \mathcal{D}) \leq \frac{1}{n}\sum_{i=1}^{n} L(\hat{f}(X_i), Y_i) + \frac{\lambda}{2}\|\hat{f}\|_{\mathcal{H}}^2 \underbrace{- \frac{\lambda}{2}\|\hat{f}\|_{\mathcal{H}}^2 + \epsilon_M + \epsilon_B\|\hat{f}\|_{\mathcal{H}}}_{V}$$

$$\leq \frac{1}{n}\sum_{i=1}^{n} L(\hat{f}(X_i), Y_i) + \frac{\lambda}{2}\|\hat{f}\|_{\mathcal{H}}^2 + \epsilon_M + \frac{\epsilon_B^2}{2\lambda}$$

$$\leq \frac{1}{n}\sum_{i=1}^{n} L(f(X_i), Y_i) + \frac{\lambda}{2}\|f\|_{\mathcal{H}}^2 + \epsilon_M + \frac{\epsilon_B^2}{2\lambda}$$

$$\leq L(f, \mathcal{D}) + \frac{\lambda}{2}\|f\|_{\mathcal{H}}^2 + \epsilon_B\|f\|_{\mathcal{H}} + 2\epsilon_M + \frac{\epsilon_B^2}{2\lambda}.$$

The first inequality used (9.13). The second inequality can be obtained by maximizing V over $\|\hat{f}\|_{\mathcal{H}}$. The third inequality used the fact that $\hat{f}$ is the solution of (9.10). The last inequality used (9.13) again. □

Example 9.28 Consider the soft-regularized SVM in (9.10). We can let $\gamma = 1$ and $M_0 = 1/B$. It follows that if we take $\lambda = O(1/\sqrt{n})$, then we get an oracle inequality from Corollary 9.27 with a convergence rate of $O(\sqrt{\ln\ln n/n})$.

9.4 Vector-Valued Functions

We now consider vector-valued functions using kernels. In this case, we have $f(x): \mathcal{X} \to \mathbb{R}^q$ for some $q > 1$. Let $f(x) = [f_1(x), \ldots, f_q(x)]$. If we consider the feature space representation, then there are two possibilities. One is to treat these functions as sharing the same feature vector, but with different w:

$$f_\ell(x) = \langle w_\ell, \psi(x) \rangle \qquad (\ell = 1, \ldots, q).$$

Another view is to consider the same w, but with different features for different dimension:

$$f_\ell(x) = \langle w, \psi(x, \ell) \rangle. \tag{9.14}$$

The second view is more general because we may write the first view as follows. We concatenate the feature representation by letting $w = [w_1, \ldots, w_q]$ and $\psi(x, \ell) = [0, \ldots, 0, \psi(x), 0, \ldots, 0]$ with only the ℓth concatenating component to be $\psi(x)$, and the other components as zeros. With this representation, $\langle w, \psi(x, \ell) \rangle = \langle w_\ell, \psi(x) \rangle$. In the following discussions, we focus on (9.14).

Similar to (9.2), we have the following formulation in feature representation:

$$\hat{w} = \arg\min_{w \in \mathcal{H}} \left[\frac{1}{n}\sum_{i=1}^{n} L(\langle w, \psi(X_i, \cdot) \rangle, Y_i) + \frac{\lambda}{2}\|w\|^2 \right], \tag{9.15}$$

where $\langle w, \psi(X_i, \cdot) \rangle$ denotes the q-dimensional vector with $\langle w, \psi(X_i, \ell) \rangle$ as its ℓth component. Its solution has a kernel representation as follows. It may be regarded as a generalization of the representer theorem for scalar functions in Theorem 9.2.

Theorem 9.29 *Consider q-dimensional vector-valued function $f(x)$. Let $\hat{f}(x) = \langle \hat{w}, \psi(x, \cdot) \rangle$ with $\hat{w}$ being the solution of (9.15). Then*

$$\hat{f}(x) = \sum_{i=1}^{n} \mathbf{k}(x, X_i)\hat{\alpha}_i,$$

with

$$\langle \hat{w}, \hat{w} \rangle = \sum_{i=1}^{n} \sum_{j=1}^{n} \hat{\alpha}_i^{\top} \mathbf{k}(X_i, X_j)\hat{\alpha}_j,$$

where each $\hat{\alpha}_i \in \mathbb{R}^q$, and

$$\mathbf{k}(x, x') = \begin{bmatrix} k_{1,1}(x, x') & \cdots & k_{1,q}(x, x') \\ \vdots & & \vdots \\ k_{q,1}(x, x') & \cdots & k_{q,q}(x, x') \end{bmatrix},$$

and

$$k_{i,j}(x, x') = \langle \psi(x, i), \psi(x', j) \rangle \qquad (i, j = 1, \ldots, q).$$

Therefore the solution of (9.15) is equivalent to

$$\hat{\alpha} = \arg\min_{\alpha \in \mathbb{R}^{q \times n}} \left[\frac{1}{n} \sum_{i=1}^{n} L \left(\sum_{j=1}^{n} \mathbf{k}(X_i, X_j)\alpha_j, Y_i \right) \right.$$

$$\left. + \frac{\lambda}{2} \sum_{i=1}^{n} \sum_{j=1}^{n} \alpha_i^{\top} \mathbf{k}(X_i, X_j)\alpha_j \right]. \tag{9.16}$$

Proof The proof is similar to that of Theorem 9.2, and we define the objective in (9.15) as $Q_1(w)$. The objective in (9.16) is denoted by $Q_2(\alpha)$. The solution of (9.15) satisfies the following first-order optimality condition:

$$\frac{1}{n} \sum_{i=1}^{n} [\psi(X_i, 1), \ldots, \psi(X_i, q)] \nabla L_1(\hat{f}(X_i), Y_i) + \lambda \hat{w} = 0,$$

where $\nabla L_1(p, y)$ is the gradient of $L(p, y)$ with respect to p as a q-dimensional column vector. We thus obtain the following representation as its solution:

$$\hat{w} = \sum_{i=1}^{n} [\psi(X_i, 1), \ldots, \psi(X_i, q)] \tilde{\alpha}_i,$$

where

$$\tilde{\alpha}_i = -\frac{1}{\lambda n} \nabla L_1(\langle \hat{w}, \psi(X_i, \cdot) \rangle, Y_i) \quad (i = 1, \ldots, n).$$

Using this representation, we have

$$\hat{f}(x) = \begin{bmatrix} \langle \hat{w}, \psi(x,1) \rangle \\ \vdots \\ \langle \hat{w}, \psi(x,q) \rangle \end{bmatrix} = \sum_{i=1}^{n} \begin{bmatrix} \langle [\psi(X_i,1), \ldots, \psi(X_i,q)]\tilde{\alpha}_i, \psi(x,1) \rangle \\ \vdots \\ \langle [\psi(X_i,1), \ldots, \psi(X_i,q)]\tilde{\alpha}_i, \psi(x,q) \rangle \end{bmatrix}$$

$$= \sum_{i=1}^{n} \mathbf{k}(x, X_i)\tilde{\alpha}_i,$$

and

$$\langle \hat{w}, \hat{w} \rangle = \sum_{i=1}^{n} \left\langle [\psi(X_i,1), \cdots, \psi(X_i,q)]\tilde{\alpha}_i, \sum_{j=1}^{n} [\psi(X_j,1), \psi(X_j,q)]\tilde{\alpha}_j \right\rangle$$

$$= \sum_{i=1}^{n} \sum_{j=1}^{n} \tilde{\alpha}_i^\top \mathbf{k}(X_i, X_j)\tilde{\alpha}_j.$$

This implies that $Q_1(\hat{w}) = Q_2(\tilde{\alpha})$. Similarly, there exists $\tilde{w}$ such that $Q_1(\tilde{w}) = Q_2(\hat{\alpha})$. Therefore $Q_1(\hat{w}) = Q_2(\tilde{\alpha}) \geq Q_2(\hat{\alpha}) = Q_1(\tilde{w})$. This implies that $\tilde{w}$ is a solution of (9.15), which proves the result. $\qquad\square$

In order to obtain generalization analysis using Rademacher complexity for vector-valued functions, we can employ following generalization of Theorem 6.28. The proof is similar to that of Lemma 6.29.

Theorem 9.30 *Consider $L(p,y)$ that is γ_1-Lipschitz in p with respect to the L_1-norm:*

$$|L(p,y) - L(p',y)| \leq \gamma_1 \|p - p'\|_1.$$

Consider

$$\mathcal{G} \subset \{L([f_1(x), \cdots, f_q(x)], y) \colon f_j(x) \in \mathcal{F}_j \ (j = 1, \ldots, q)\},$$

then

$$R(\mathcal{G}, \mathcal{S}_n) \leq \gamma_1 \sum_{j=1}^{q} R(\mathcal{F}_j, \mathcal{S}_n).$$

For vector kernel method, we may consider the hard-constrained version using feature representation:

$$\hat{w} = \arg\min_{w \in \mathcal{H}} \frac{1}{n} \sum_{i=1}^{n} L(\langle w, \psi(X_i, \cdot) \rangle, Y_i) \quad \text{subject to } \langle w, w \rangle \leq A^2. \tag{9.17}$$

We have the following estimate of Rademacher complexity.

Lemma 9.31 *Let*

$$\mathcal{G} = \{L(\langle w, \psi(x, \cdot) \rangle, y) : \langle w, w \rangle \leq A^2\},$$

then with γ_1 defined in Theorem 9.30,

$$R(\mathcal{G}, \mathcal{S}_n) \leq \frac{\gamma_1 A}{n} \sum_{j=1}^{q} \sqrt{\sum_{i=1}^{n} k_{j,j}(X_i, X_i)}$$

and

$$R_n(\mathcal{G}, \mathcal{D}) \leq \gamma_1 A \sum_{j=1}^{q} \sqrt{\frac{1}{n} \mathbb{E}_{\mathcal{D}} k_{j,j}(X, X)}.$$

Proof We can set and let $\mathcal{F}_j = \{\langle w, \psi(x, j)\rangle \langle w, w\rangle \leq A^2\}$. From Theorem 9.20, we obtain

$$R(\mathcal{F}_j, \mathcal{S}_n) \leq \frac{A}{n} \sqrt{\sum_{i=1}^{n} k_{j,j}(X_i, X_i)},$$

and

$$R_n(\mathcal{F}_j, \mathcal{D}) \leq A \sqrt{\frac{1}{n} \mathbb{E}_{\mathcal{D}} k_{j,j}(X, X)}.$$

We can now apply Theorem 9.30 to obtain the desired bound.   □

If $k_{j,j}(x, x) \leq B^2$ for all j and x, then Corollary 9.31 implies a bound

$$R(\mathcal{G}, \mathcal{S}_n) \leq \frac{\gamma_1 q A B}{\sqrt{n}}.$$

One drawback of this bound is that the Rademacher complexity becomes linear in q, which is usually suboptimal when q is large. For such problems, one needs a more sophisticated estimation of Rademacher complexity.

Example 9.32 Consider the structured SVM loss function (Tsochantaridis et al., 2005) for q-class classification problem, with $y \in \{1, \ldots, q\}$, and for $f \in \mathbb{R}^q$,

$$L(f, y) = \max_{\ell}[\gamma(y, \ell) - (f_y - f_\ell)],$$

where $\gamma(y, y) = 0$ and $\gamma(y, \ell) \geq 0$. This loss tries to separate the true class y from alternative $\ell \neq y$ with margin $\gamma(y, \ell)$. It is Lipschitz with respect to $\|f\|_1$ with $\gamma_1 = 1$. Therefore for problems with $k_{\ell,\ell}(x, x) \leq B^2$ for all x and ℓ, we have from Corollary 9.31 that

$$R(\mathcal{G}, \mathcal{S}_n) \leq \frac{q A B}{\sqrt{n}}.$$

For the structured SVM loss, a better bound on Rademacher complexity, stated in Proposition 9.33, can be obtained from the covering number estimate of Theorem 5.20. The bound depends on q only logarithmically, and we leave its proof as an exercise.

Proposition 9.33 *Consider a loss function $L(f, y)$ that is γ_∞-Lipschitz in p with respect to the L_∞-norm:*

$$|L(p, y) - L(p', y)| \leq \gamma_\infty \|p - p'\|_\infty.$$

Let $\mathcal{F} = \{f(x) = [f_1(x), \ldots, f_q(x)] : f_\ell(x) = \langle w, \psi(x, \ell) \rangle, \langle w, w \rangle \leq A^2\}$. Assume that $\sup_{x, \ell} \langle \psi(x, \ell), \psi(x, \ell) \rangle \leq B^2$. Let $\mathcal{G} = \{L(f, y) : f \in \mathcal{F}\}$. Then there exists a constant $c_0 > 0$ such that

$$R(\mathcal{G}, \mathcal{S}_n) \leq \frac{c_0 \gamma_\infty A B \ln n \sqrt{\ln(nq)}}{\sqrt{n}}.$$

One may also consider the soft-regularized version of structured SVM

$$\hat{w} = \arg\min_w \left[\frac{1}{n} \sum_{i=1}^n L(\langle w, \psi(X_i, \cdot) \rangle, Y_i) + \frac{\lambda}{2} \langle w, w \rangle \right],$$

and analyze it using the stability analysis of Chapter 7. In fact, it can be easily checked that $L(\langle w, \psi(x, \cdot) \rangle, y)$ is B-Lipschitz in w when $\sup_{x, \ell} \|\psi(x, \ell)\|_2 \leq B$. Theorem 7.8 implies that for the structured SVM problem, we have an expected generalization bound of

$$\mathbb{E}_{\mathcal{S}_n} \mathbb{E}_{\mathcal{D}} L(\langle \hat{w}, \psi(X) \rangle, Y) \leq \inf_w \left[\mathbb{E}_{\mathcal{D}} L(\langle w, \psi(X) \rangle, Y) + \frac{\lambda}{2} \langle w, w \rangle \right] + \frac{B^2}{\lambda n}.$$

The structured SVM example shows that for some vector-valued estimation problems, stability analysis can be used to obtain results that may be more difficult to obtain using the theory of empirical processes.

9.5 Refined Analysis: Ridge Regression

Although the Rademacher complexity analysis leads to useful generalization results, they are not always tight. Moreover, to obtain a faster rate, we need to employ local Rademacher complexity analysis, as discussed in Section 6.5.

For the ridge regression problem,

$$\hat{w} = \arg\min_w \left[\frac{1}{n} \sum_{i=1}^n (w^\top \psi(X_i) - Y_i)^2 + \lambda w^\top w \right], \tag{9.18}$$

we show that it is possible to obtain faster rates more directly. Here we use the vector notation $u^\top v = \langle u, v \rangle$ for convenience.

For simplicity, we will consider the realizable case in that there exists w_* such that

$$Y = w_*^\top \psi(X) + \epsilon, \tag{9.19}$$

where ϵ is a zero-mean stochastic noise that may depend on X.

The following basic result is useful in the theoretical analysis of ridge regression.

Lemma 9.34 *Let $\{Y_i\}_1^n$ be independent samples conditioned on $\{X_i\}_1^n$ according to (9.19). Given any vector X that is independent of $\{Y_i\}_1^n$. If $\mathbb{E}[\epsilon_i|X_i] \leq \sigma^2$ for all i, then we have*

$$\mathbb{E}_{\{Y_i\}_1^n|\{X_i\}_1^n} \left[(\hat{w}^\top \psi(X) - w_*^\top \psi(X))^2 \right] \leq ((\sigma^2/n) + \lambda\|w_*\|_2^2) \, \|\psi(X)\|_{\hat{\Sigma}_\lambda^{-1}}^2 \,,$$

where

$$\hat{\Sigma}_\lambda = \frac{1}{n} \sum_{i=1}^n \psi(X_i)\psi(X_i)^\top + \lambda I.$$

Moreover if ϵ is sub-Gaussian,

$$\forall i: \quad \ln \mathbb{E}\exp[\mu\epsilon_i|X_i] \leq \frac{\mu^2\sigma^2}{2},$$

then the following inequalities hold for conditional probability of $\{Y_i\}_1^n|\{X_i\}_1^n$:

$$\Pr\left[\hat{w}^\top\psi(X) - w_*^\top\psi(X) \leq \left(\sqrt{\lambda}\|w_*\|_2 + \sigma\sqrt{\frac{2\ln(1/\delta)}{n}} \right) \|\psi(X)\|_{\hat{\Sigma}_\lambda^{-1}} \right] \leq \delta,$$

$$\Pr\left[w_*^\top\psi(X) - \hat{w}^\top\psi(X) \leq \left(\sqrt{\lambda}\|w_*\|_2 + \sigma\sqrt{\frac{2\ln(1/\delta)}{n}} \right) \|\psi(X)\|_{\hat{\Sigma}_\lambda^{-1}} \right] \leq \delta.$$

Proof We have

$$(\hat{w} - w_*) = \hat{\Sigma}_\lambda^{-1}\frac{1}{n}\sum_{i=1}^n \psi(X_i)Y_i - w_* = \hat{\Sigma}_\lambda^{-1}\frac{1}{n}\sum_{i=1}^n \psi(X_i)\epsilon_i - \lambda\hat{\Sigma}_\lambda^{-1}w_*.$$

Therefore

$$(\hat{w} - w_*)^\top\psi(X) = \frac{1}{n}\sum_{i=1}^n \underbrace{\psi(X)^\top\hat{\Sigma}_\lambda^{-1}\psi(X_i)}_{a_i}\,\epsilon_i - \lambda\psi(X)^\top\hat{\Sigma}_\lambda^{-1}w_*. \qquad (9.20)$$

We have

$$\frac{1}{n}\sum_{i=1}^n a_i^2 = \frac{1}{n}\sum_{i=1}^n \psi(X)^\top\hat{\Sigma}_\lambda^{-1}\psi(X_i)\psi(X_i)^\top\hat{\Sigma}_\lambda^{-1}\psi(X)$$

$$= \psi(X)^\top\hat{\Sigma}_\lambda^{-1}\hat{\Sigma}_0\hat{\Sigma}_\lambda^{-1}\psi(X)$$

$$\leq \|\psi(X)\|_{\hat{\Sigma}_\lambda^{-1}}^2. \qquad (9.21)$$

The inequality follows from the fact that $\hat{\Sigma}_0 \leq \hat{\Sigma}_\lambda$.

It follows that if $\mathrm{Var}[\epsilon_i|X_i] \le \sigma^2$, then

$$\mathbb{E}\left[(\hat{w}^\top\psi(X) - w_*^\top\psi(X))^2|\{X_i\}_1^n\right]$$

$$= \frac{1}{n^2}\sum_{i=1}^n \mathbb{E}\left[(a_i\epsilon_i)^2|X_i\right] + \lambda^2[\psi(X)^\top\hat{\Sigma}_\lambda^{-1}w_*]^2$$

$$\le \frac{1}{n^2}\sum_{i=1}^n a_i^2\sigma^2 + \lambda^2[\psi(X)^\top\hat{\Sigma}_\lambda^{-1}w_*]^2$$

$$\le \frac{\sigma^2}{n}\|\psi(X)\|_{\hat{\Sigma}_\lambda^{-1}}^2 + \lambda^2\|\psi(X)\|_{\hat{\Sigma}_\lambda^{-1}}^2\|w_*\|_{\hat{\Sigma}_\lambda^{-1}}^2$$

$$\le ((\sigma^2/n) + \lambda\|w_*\|_2^2)\,\|\psi(X)\|_{\hat{\Sigma}_\lambda^{-1}}^2\,.$$

The first equality used (9.20), and the fact that ϵ_i are independent and zero-mean random variables. The first inequality used $\mathbb{E}[\epsilon_i^2] \le \sigma^2$. The second inequality used (9.21) and the Cauchy–Schwarz inequality. The last inequality used $\|w_*\|_{\hat{\Sigma}_\lambda^{-1}}^2 \le \|w_*\|_2^2/\lambda$.

Moreover, if each ϵ_i is sub-Gaussian, then

$$\ln\mathbb{E}\left[e^{\mu(\hat{w}^\top\psi(X) - w_*^\top\psi(X))}|\{X_i\}_1^n\right]$$

$$= -\mu\lambda\psi(X)^\top\hat{\Sigma}_\lambda^{-1}w_* + \ln\mathbb{E}\left[e^{(\mu/n)\sum_{i=1}^n a_i\epsilon_i}|\{X_i\}_1^n\right]$$

$$\le -\mu\lambda\psi(X)^\top\hat{\Sigma}_\lambda^{-1}w_* + \frac{\mu^2\sigma^2}{2n^2}\sum_{i=1}^n a_i^2$$

$$\le \mu\lambda\|\psi(X)\|_{\hat{\Sigma}_\lambda^{-1}}\|w_*\|_{\hat{\Sigma}_\lambda^{-1}} + \frac{\mu^2\sigma^2}{2n}\|\psi(X)\|_{\hat{\Sigma}_\lambda}^2$$

$$\le \mu\sqrt{\lambda}\|\psi(X)\|_{\hat{\Sigma}_\lambda^{-1}}\|w_*\|_2 + \frac{\mu^2\sigma^2}{2n}\|\psi(X)\|_{\hat{\Sigma}_\lambda}^2.$$

The first equality used (9.20). The first inequality used the sub-Gaussian noise assumption. The second inequality used (9.21) and the Cauchy–Schwarz inequality. The last inequality used $\|w_*\|_{\hat{\Sigma}_\lambda^{-1}} \le \|w_*\|_2/\sqrt{\lambda}$. This implies that $\hat{w}^\top\psi(X) - w_*^\top\psi(X)$ is sub-Gaussian. The desired probability bounds follow from the standard sub-Gaussian tail inequalities in Theorem 2.12.   □

Lemma 9.34 implies that the model confidence at an arbitrary test data point X is proportional to $\|\psi(X)\|_{\hat{\Sigma}_\lambda^{-1}}$. This means that for ridge regression, one can obtain a *confidence interval* at any data point X. In particular, if we are interested in estimating $w_*^\top\psi(X_i)$ for all X_i in the training data, then by taking the union bound over $\{X_1, \ldots, X_n\}$, we obtain with probability $1 - \delta$,

$$\frac{1}{n}\sum_{i=1}^n(\hat{w}^\top\psi(X_i) - w_*^\top\psi(X_i))^2 = O\left(\left(\lambda\|w_*\|_2^2 + \frac{\sigma^2\ln(n/\delta)}{n}\right)\mathrm{trace}\left(\hat{\Sigma}_\lambda^{-1}\hat{\Sigma}_0\right)\right).$$

One can also use a generalization of the χ^2 tail probability bound to obtain a bound on the training prediction error more directly without paying a $\ln n$ penalty due to the union bound.

For the generalization performance of ridge regression on the test data, deriving large probability bounds requires concentration of $\hat{\Sigma}_\lambda^{-1}$ to $(\mathbb{E}\,\hat{\Sigma}_\lambda)^{-1}$. We will not consider such matrix concentration inequalities in this book. Nevertheless, one may also obtain an expected generalization bound without such a matrix concentration result when λ is at least $\Omega(1/n)$.

Theorem 9.35 *Assume that $\mathcal{S}_n = \{(X_i, Y_i)\}_1^n \sim \mathcal{D}^n$, and $\mathrm{Var}[\epsilon_i | X_i] \leq \sigma^2$ for all X_i. If we choose λ such that $\lambda n > B^2 \geq \sup_x \psi(x)^\top \psi(x)$, then (9.18) satisfies*

$$\mathbb{E}_{\mathcal{S}_n \sim \mathcal{D}^n} \mathbb{E}_{X \sim \mathcal{D}} (\hat{w}^\top \psi(X) - w_*^\top \psi(X))^2 \leq \frac{d_{1,\lambda'}}{n}(\sigma^2 + \lambda n \|w_*\|_2^2),$$

where

$$d_{1,\lambda'} = \mathrm{trace}\left((\Sigma_\mathcal{D} + \lambda' I)^{-1} \Sigma_\mathcal{D}\right), \quad \Sigma_\mathcal{D} = \mathbb{E}_\mathcal{D} \psi(X) \psi(X)^\top,$$

and $\lambda' = (\lambda n - B^2)/(n+1)$.

Proof Consider $\mathcal{S}_{n+1} = \{(X_1, Y_1), \ldots, (X_{n+1}, Y_{n+1})\}$. Let $\hat{w}$ be the solution with training data $\mathcal{S}_n$. Let

$$\hat{\Sigma}_{n+1} = \sum_{i=1}^{n+1} \psi(X_i)\psi(X_i)^\top,$$

$$\hat{\Sigma}_n = \sum_{i=1}^{n} \psi(X_i)\psi(X_i)^\top + \lambda n I,$$

then $\hat{\Sigma}_n \geq \hat{\Sigma}_{n+1} + (\lambda n - B^2)I$. It follows that

$$
\begin{aligned}
&\mathbb{E}\left[(\hat{w} - w_*)^\top \psi(X_{n+1})\right]^2 \\
&\leq (\sigma^2 + \lambda n \|w_*\|_2^2) \mathbb{E}\, \|\psi(X_{n+1})\|_{(\hat{\Sigma}_{n+1} + (\lambda n - B^2)I)^{-1}}^2 \\
&= \frac{\sigma^2 + \lambda n \|w_*\|_2^2}{n+1} \mathbb{E}\, \mathrm{trace}\left((\hat{\Sigma}_{n+1} + (\lambda n - B^2)I)^{-1} \hat{\Sigma}_{n+1}\right) \\
&\leq \frac{\sigma^2 + \lambda n \|w_*\|_2^2}{n+1} \mathrm{trace}\left((\mathbb{E}[\hat{\Sigma}_{n+1}] + (\lambda n - B^2)I)^{-1} [\mathbb{E}\hat{\Sigma}_{n+1}]\right) \\
&= \frac{\sigma^2 + \lambda n \|w_*\|_2^2}{n+1} d_{1,\lambda'}.
\end{aligned}
$$

In the above derivation, the first inequality used Lemma 9.34 and $\hat{\Sigma}_n^{-1} \leq (\hat{\Sigma}_{n+1} + (\lambda n - B^2)I)^{-1}$. The first equality used the symmetry of $X_1, \ldots, X_{n+1}$ conditioned on $\mathcal{S}_{n+1}$. The second inequality used Jensen's inequality and the concavity of the matrix function $\mathrm{trace}((A + \mu I)^{-1} A)$ for $\mu > 0$, where A is a symmetric positive semi-definite matrix (see Theorem A.18). $\qquad\square$

The quantity $d_{1,\lambda'}$ in Theorem 9.35 measures the effective dimension of ridge regression (see Hsu et al., 2012a). The following result gives an upper bound for $d_{1,\lambda'}$. The proof is left as an exercise.

Proposition 9.36 *Consider $\psi\colon \mathcal{X} \to \mathcal{H}$, and $\lambda > 0$. Let*

$$\dim(\lambda, \psi(\mathcal{X})) = \sup_{\mathcal{D}} \operatorname{trace}\left((\Sigma_{\mathcal{D}} + \lambda I)^{-1}\Sigma_{\mathcal{D}}\right),$$

where $\Sigma_{\mathcal{D}} = \mathbb{E}_{X\sim\mathcal{D}}\psi(X)\psi(X)^\top$. If $\dim(\mathcal{H}) < \infty$, then

$$\dim(\lambda, \psi(\mathcal{X})) \leq \dim(\mathcal{H}).$$

More generally, assume that $\mathcal{H}$ has a representation $\psi(x) = [\psi_j(x)]_{j=1}^\infty$ in 2-norm. Given any $\epsilon > 0$, define the ϵ-scale sensitive dimension as

$$d(\epsilon) = \min\left\{|S| : \sup_x \sum_{j\notin S}(\psi_j(x))^2 \leq \epsilon\right\},$$

then

$$\dim(\lambda, \psi(\mathcal{X})) \leq \inf_{\epsilon > 0}\left[d(\epsilon) + \frac{\epsilon}{\lambda}\right].$$

For finite-dimensional problems, where $\psi(x) \in \mathbb{R}^d$, the results of Theorem 9.35 and Proposition 9.36 imply that with $\lambda = B^2/n$, we have

$$\mathbb{E}_{\mathcal{S}_n\sim\mathcal{D}^n}\mathbb{E}_{X\sim\mathcal{D}}(\hat{w}^\top\psi(X) - w_*^\top\psi(X))^2 \leq \frac{d}{n}(\sigma^2 + B^2\|w_*\|_2^2).$$

This result is superior to the result from standard Rademacher complexity. Note that in Corollary 9.27, with $\lambda = \Omega(1/\sqrt{n})$, we can obtain a convergence of $O(1/(\lambda n))$. By choosing λ of order $1/\sqrt{n}$, we can obtain a rate of $O(1/\sqrt{n})$. In comparison, we can choose λ of order $O(1/n)$ in Theorem 9.35, and obtain a convergence rate of $O(d/n)$.

While the rate of $O(d/n)$ is optimal for the finite-dimensional case, the constant of $B^2\|w_*\|_2^2$ is suboptimal. To further improve this dependency, one needs to employ a more refined matrix concentration result, as in Hsu et al. (2012a).

For finite-dimensional problems, the result in Hsu et al. (2012a), in a simplified form, can be written as

$$\mathbb{E}_{\mathcal{S}_n\sim\mathcal{D}^n}\mathbb{E}_{X\sim\mathcal{D}}(\hat{w}^\top\psi(X) - w_*^\top\psi(X))^2 = O\left(\frac{\sigma^2 d}{n}\right) + \text{high-order terms}.$$

This implies $O(1/n)$ rate without the extra dependency on B^2 in the leading term. Additional results in the infinite-dimensional case, with nonzero approximation error term, can also be found in Hsu et al. (2012a).

Example 9.37 Consider kernel regression with a kernel that has a scale-sensitive dimension $d(\epsilon)$ in Proposition 9.36. We obtain from Theorem 9.35,

$$\mathbb{E}_{\mathcal{S}_n\sim\mathcal{D}^n}\mathbb{E}_{X\sim\mathcal{D}}(\hat{w}^\top\psi(X) - w_*^\top\psi(X))^2 \leq \left(\frac{d(\epsilon)}{n} + \frac{\epsilon(1 + 1/n)}{\lambda n - B^2}\right)(\sigma^2 + \lambda n\|w_*\|_2^2).$$

9.6 *G*-Optimal Design in RKHS

Lemma 9.34 shows that one can estimate the uncertainty (confidence interval) of the ridge regression prediction on an arbitrary data point X that is independent of the observed Y, and the uncertainty is measured by

$$\|\psi(X)\|_{\hat{\Sigma}_\lambda^{-1}} . \tag{9.22}$$

Assume that we are given a set of unlabeled data $\{\psi(X)\colon X \in \mathcal{X}\} \subset \mathcal{H}$, where $\mathcal{H}$ is an RKHS. Our goal is to select data $\mathcal{S}_n = \{X_1, \ldots, X_n\}$ from $\mathcal{X}$ to label, so that the ridge regression solution (9.18) has the smallest maximum uncertainty over $\mathcal{X}$. Using the uncertainty measure (9.22), we can find $\mathcal{S}_n$ by solving the following optimization problem:

$$\min_{\mathcal{S}_n} \sup_{X \in \mathcal{X}} \psi(X)^\top \Sigma_\lambda(\mathcal{S}_n)^{-1} \psi(X), \tag{9.23}$$

$$\Sigma_\lambda(\mathcal{S}_n) = \frac{1}{n} \sum_{X \in \mathcal{S}_n} \psi(X)\psi(X)^\top + \lambda I.$$

Note that in $\mathcal{S}_n$, we may select some $X \in \mathcal{X}$ multiple times.

This motivates the following closely related problem, which seeks the limiting distribution when $n \to \infty$.

Theorem 9.38 *Given a compact set $\psi(\mathcal{X}) \subset \mathcal{H}$, where $\mathcal{H}$ is an inner product space, let $\lambda > 0$; the λ-regularized G-optimal design is a probability distribution π over $\mathcal{X}$ that solves the problem*

$$\pi_G = \arg\min_{\pi \in \Delta(\mathcal{X})} \sup_{X \in \mathcal{X}} \psi(X)^\top \Sigma_\lambda(\pi)^{-1} \psi(X), \tag{9.24}$$

where $\Delta(\mathcal{X})$ denotes the probability distributions on $\mathcal{X}$, and

$$\Sigma_\lambda(\pi) = \mathbb{E}_{X \sim \pi} \psi(X)\psi(X)^\top + \lambda I.$$

Define the regularized D-optimal design as

$$\pi_D = \arg\min_{\pi \in \Delta(\mathcal{X})} -\ln\left|\Sigma_\lambda(\pi)\right|,$$

then the following inequality for π_D gives an upper bound for the G-optimal design:

$$\sup_{X \in \mathcal{X}} \psi(X)^\top \Sigma_\lambda(\pi_D)^{-1} \psi(X) \le \dim(\lambda, \psi(\mathcal{X})),$$

where $\dim(\lambda, \psi(\mathcal{X}))$ is defined in Proposition 9.36.

Proof Without loss of generality, we may assume that $\mathcal{X}$ is finite (we can take the limit of finite subset when $\mathcal{X}$ is infinite). We note that

$$\min_\pi -\ln\left|\Sigma_\lambda(\pi)\right|$$

is a convex optimization problem in π because $\ln|Z|$ is a concave function of Z (see Theorem A.18). The KKT (Karush–Kuhn–Tucker) condition of the optimal solution implies that there exists $\rho > 0$ such that for all $X \in \mathcal{X}$,

$$\begin{cases} \psi(X)^\top \Sigma_\lambda(\pi_D)^{-1}\psi(X) = \rho & \text{if } \pi_D(X) > 0, \\ \psi(X)^\top \Sigma_\lambda(\pi_D)^{-1}\psi(X) \leq \rho & \text{if } \pi_D(X) = 0. \end{cases}$$

Taking expectation over π_D, we obtain

$$\rho = \mathbb{E}_{X \sim \pi_D} \psi(X)^\top \Sigma_\lambda(\pi_D)^{-1}\psi(X) = \text{trace}(\Sigma_\lambda(\pi_D)^{-1}\Sigma(\pi_D)).$$

This implies the desired result. □

We note that neither π_G nor π_D is necessarily unique. Since π_D is the solution of a convex problem in π, one may use convex optimization techniques to find an approximation of π_D, which gives an approximate solution of the G-optimal design problem (9.24). In particular, the D-optimal design problem can be solved using a greedy algorithm which we state in Algorithm 9.1 (also see Algorithm 10.3 for a similar algorithm). The following convergence result shows that with $\eta \to 0$ and $n \to \infty$, we can achieve a bound of $\gamma_m \leq \dim(\lambda, \psi(\mathcal{X})) + o(1)$, which matches that of Theorem 9.38.

Theorem 9.39 *For Algorithm 9.1, we have*

$$\frac{\gamma_m}{1 + \eta(1-\eta)\gamma_m} \leq \frac{\dim(\lambda, \psi(\mathcal{X}))}{(1-\eta)^2} + \frac{\ln|\Sigma_\lambda(\pi_n)/\Sigma_\lambda(\pi_0)|}{\eta(1-\eta)n},$$

where $\gamma_m = \max_{X \in \mathcal{X}} \psi(X)^\top \Sigma_\lambda(\pi_{m-1})^{-1}\psi(X)$.

Proof Let

$$\tilde{\Sigma}_\lambda^{(i-1)} = \Sigma_\lambda(\pi_i) - \eta\psi(X_i)\psi(X_i)^\top. \tag{9.25}$$

We have for each $i \in [n]$,

$$\ln|\Sigma_\lambda(\pi_i)| - \ln|\Sigma_\lambda(\pi_{i-1})|$$
$$\geq \text{trace}((\Sigma_\lambda(\pi_i))^{-1}(\Sigma_\lambda(\pi_i) - \Sigma_\lambda(\pi_{i-1})))$$
$$= \eta\text{trace}((\Sigma_\lambda(\pi_i))^{-1}\psi(X_i)\psi(X_i)^\top) - \eta\text{trace}((\Sigma_\lambda(\pi_i))^{-1}\Sigma_0(\pi_{i-1}))$$
$$= \frac{\eta\psi(X_i)^\top(\tilde{\Sigma}_\lambda^{(i-1)})^{-1}\psi(X_i)}{1 + \eta\psi(X_i)^\top(\tilde{\Sigma}_\lambda^{(i-1)})^{-1}\psi(X_i)} - \eta\text{trace}((\Sigma_\lambda(\pi_i))^{-1}\Sigma_0(\pi_{i-1}))$$
$$\overset{(a)}{\geq} \frac{\eta\psi(X_i)^\top\Sigma_\lambda(\pi_{i-1})^{-1}\psi(X_i)}{1 + \eta\psi(X_i)^\top\Sigma_\lambda(\pi_{i-1})^{-1}\psi(X_i)} - \frac{\eta}{1-\eta}\text{trace}((\Sigma_\lambda(\pi_{i-1}))^{-1}\Sigma_0(\pi_{i-1}))$$
$$\geq \frac{\eta g_m(X_m)}{1 + \eta g_m(X_m)} - \frac{\eta}{1-\eta}\dim(\lambda, \psi(\cdot)).$$

The first inequality used Theorem A.18 with the matrix trace function $-\ln|\Sigma| = \text{trace}(-\ln\Sigma)$ which is convex in Σ. The first equality used the definition of π_i in terms of π_{i-1}. The second inequality used (9.25) and the Sherman–Morrison formula. Inequality (a) used $(\tilde{\Sigma}_\lambda^{(i-1)})^{-1} \geq \Sigma_\lambda(\pi_{i-1})^{-1}$ and $\eta z/(1+\eta z)$ is an increasing function of $z > 0$ to bound the first term, and used $\Sigma_\lambda(\pi_i) \geq (1-\eta)\Sigma_\lambda(\pi_{i-1})$ to bound the second term. The last inequality used the definition of m and $\dim(\cdot)$.

By summing over $i = 1$ to $i = n$, we obtain

$$n\frac{\eta g_m(X_m)}{1 + \eta g_m(X_m)} \leq n\frac{\eta}{1-\eta}\dim(\lambda, \psi(\cdot)) + \ln|\Sigma_\lambda(\pi_n)/\Sigma_\lambda(\pi_0)|.$$

The algorithm implies that $g_m(X_m) \geq (1-\eta)\gamma_m$. We can replace $g_m(X_m)$ by $(1-\eta)\gamma_m$ to obtain the desired result. $\qquad\square$

Algorithm 9.1 Greedy *G*-optimal Design

Input: $\mathcal{X}$, $\psi(\cdot)$, π_0, $\lambda > 0$, n, $\eta \in (0,1)$
Output: $\mathcal{S}_n$
1 **for** $i = 1, 2, \ldots, n$ **do**
2 $\quad$ Define $g_i(x) = \psi(x)^\top \Sigma_\lambda(\pi_{i-1})^{-1}\psi(x)$
3 $\quad$ Find X_i so that $g_i(X_i) \geq (1-\eta)\max_{X \in \mathcal{X}} g_i(X)$
4 $\quad$ Let $\pi_i = (1-\eta)\pi_{i-1} + \eta\mathbb{1}(X = X_i)$
5 Let $m = \arg\min_i g_i(X_i)$
6 **return** π_{m-1}

Example 9.40 If $\mathcal{H}$ is a (finite) d-dimensional space and $\|\psi(X)\|_\mathcal{H} \leq B$, then

$$\ln|\Sigma_\lambda(\pi_n)/\Sigma_\lambda(\pi_0)| \leq d\ln\operatorname{trace}(\Sigma_\lambda(\pi_n)/(d\Sigma_\lambda(\pi_0))) \leq d\ln(1 + B^2/(\lambda d)).$$

The first inequality used the inequality of arithmetic and geometric means (AM-GM). Since $\dim(\lambda, \psi(\cdot) \leq d$, we have

$$\frac{\gamma_m}{1 + \eta(1-\eta)\gamma_m} \leq \frac{d}{(1-\eta)^2} + \frac{d\ln(1 + B^2/(\lambda d))}{\eta(1-\eta)n}.$$

By taking $\eta = 0.25/d$ and $n = O(d\ln(1 + B^2/(\lambda d))$ in Theorem 9.39, we obtain obtain a bound of $\gamma_m = O(d)$, which matches Theorem 9.38 up to a constant.

Example 9.41 In general, we can define quantity $\operatorname{entro}(\lambda, \psi(\mathcal{X}))$ according to Proposition 15.8, so that

$$\ln|\Sigma_\lambda(\pi_n)/\Sigma_\lambda(\pi_0)| \leq \operatorname{entro}(\lambda, \psi(\mathcal{X})).$$

If we take $\eta = \min(0.1, 0.1/\dim(\lambda, \psi(\mathcal{X})))$ with an arbitrary $\pi_0 = \mathbb{1}(X = X_0)$ in Algorithm 9.1, then after $n = \lceil 8\operatorname{entro}(\lambda, \psi(\mathcal{X}))\rceil$ iterations, we have for $m \leq n$ in Theorem 9.39, thus we obtain

$$\frac{\gamma_m}{1 + 0.9 \cdot \frac{0.1}{\dim(\lambda, \psi(\mathcal{X}))}\gamma_m} \leq \frac{\dim(\lambda, \psi(\mathcal{X}))}{0.9^2} + \frac{\operatorname{entro}(\lambda, \psi(\mathcal{X}))}{\frac{0.1}{\dim(\lambda, \psi(\mathcal{X}))}0.9n}.$$

This implies that we can find $m \leq n$ so that

$$\gamma_m \leq 4\dim(\lambda, \psi(\mathcal{X})).$$

More generally, for any nonlinear function class $\mathcal{F}: \mathcal{X} \to \mathbb{R}$, we may define the corresponding nonlinear G-optimal design problem as follows.

Definition 9.42 Given any $\epsilon > 0$, the coverage coefficient of a distribution π on $\mathcal{X}$ with respect to a function class $\mathcal{F}: \mathcal{X} \to \mathbb{R}$ is defined as

$$\mathrm{CC}(\epsilon, \pi, \mathcal{F}) = \sup_{x \in \mathcal{X}} \sup_{f, f' \in \mathcal{F}} \frac{|f(x) - f'(x)|^2}{\epsilon + \mathbb{E}_{\tilde{x} \sim \pi}(f(\tilde{x}) - f'(\tilde{x}))^2}.$$

Given any $\epsilon > 0$, a G-optimal design π_G with respect to a function class $\mathcal{F}: \mathcal{X} \to \mathbb{R}$ is defined as the solution to

$$\pi_G(\epsilon, \mathcal{F}, \mathcal{X}) = \arg\min_{\pi \in \Delta(\mathcal{X})} \mathrm{CC}(\epsilon, \pi, \mathcal{F}),$$

where $\Delta(\mathcal{X})$ is the set of probability measures on $\mathcal{X}$.

The following result shows that nonlinear G-optimal design is a convex optimization problem.

Proposition 9.43 *The G-optimal design objective function* $\mathrm{CC}(\epsilon, \pi, \mathcal{F})$ *is convex in* π.

Proof Note that with fixed f, f', x, the following function of π

$$\frac{|f(x) - f'(x)|^2}{\epsilon + \mathbb{E}_{\tilde{x} \sim \pi}(f(\tilde{x}) - f'(\tilde{x}))^2}$$

is convex in π. Because sup of convex functions is still convex, we obtain the result. $\square$

The following result is a straightforward consequence of Theorem 9.38. Note that in the result, we do not assume that the feature representation $\psi(\cdot)$ is known.

Theorem 9.44 *Assume that* $\mathcal{F} \subset \mathcal{H}$, *where* $\mathcal{H}$ *is an RKHS. Assume that* $f(x)$ *has the feature representation* $f(x) = \langle w(f), \psi(x) \rangle$. *Let* $B = \sup_{f, f' \in \mathcal{F}} \|w(f) - w(f')\|_{\mathcal{H}}$ *be the diameter of* $\mathcal{F}$. *Then we have*

$$\mathrm{CC}(\epsilon, \pi_G(\epsilon, \mathcal{F}, \mathcal{X}), \mathcal{F}) \leq \dim(\epsilon/B^2, \psi(\mathcal{X})),$$

where $\dim(\cdot)$ *is defined in Proposition 9.36.*

Proof Let $\Sigma = \lambda I + \mathbb{E}_{x \sim \pi} \psi(x) \psi(x)^\top$, with $\lambda = \epsilon/B^2$. Then we have

$$\begin{aligned}
\mathrm{CC}(\epsilon, \pi, \mathcal{F}) &= \sup_{x \in \mathcal{X}} \sup_{f, f' \in \mathcal{F}} \frac{|f(x) - f'(x)|^2}{\epsilon + \mathbb{E}_{\tilde{x} \sim \pi}(f(\tilde{x}) - f'(\tilde{x}))^2} \\
&\leq \sup_{x \in \mathcal{X}} \sup_{f, f' \in \mathcal{F}} \frac{|f(x) - f'(x)|^2}{\lambda \|w(f) - w(f')\|_{\mathcal{H}}^2 + \mathbb{E}_{\tilde{x} \sim \pi}(f(\tilde{x}) - f'(\tilde{x}))^2} \\
&= \sup_{x \in \mathcal{X}} \sup_{f, f' \in \mathcal{F}} \frac{\langle w(f) - w(f'), \psi(x) \rangle^2}{(w(f) - w(f'))^\top \Sigma (w(f) - w(f'))} \\
&\leq \sup_{x \in \mathcal{X}} \psi(x)^\top \Sigma^{-1} \psi(x).
\end{aligned} \tag{9.26}$$

The first inequality used the assumption of this theorem which implies that $\lambda\|w(f) - w(f')\|_{\mathcal{H}}^2 \leq \epsilon$. The second inequality used the Cauchy–Schwarz inequality. The result is now a straightforward application of Theorem 9.38. □

Algorithm 9.2 Greedy Nonlinear G-optimal Design

Input: $\mathcal{F}$, $\mathcal{X}$, π_0, $\lambda > 0$, n, $\eta \in (0,1)$

Output: π_n

1 **for** $i = 1, 2, \ldots, n$ **do**

2   Define $\Delta\mathcal{F} = \{f(x) - f'(x) : f, f' \in \mathcal{F}\}$, and $\forall \Delta f \in \Delta\mathcal{F}, x \in \mathcal{X}$:

$$g_i(\Delta f, x) = \frac{|\Delta f(x)|^2}{\epsilon + \mathbb{E}_{x' \in \pi_{i-1}} \Delta f(x')^2}.$$

     Find $X_i \in \mathcal{X}, \Delta f_i \in \Delta\mathcal{F}$:

$$g_i(\Delta f_i, X_i) \geq (1 - \eta) \sup_{x \in \mathcal{X}} \sup_{\Delta f \in \Delta\mathcal{F}} g_i(\Delta f, x).$$

     Let $\pi_i = (1 - \eta)\pi_{i-1} + \eta \mathbb{1}(X = X_i)$

3 Let $m = \arg\min_i g_i(\Delta f_i, X_i)$

4 **return** π_{m-1}

Algorithm 9.2 is a direct generalization of Algorithm 9.1. It is easy to see from (9.26) that the following result holds with a proof nearly identical to that of Theorem 9.39. We leave the proof as an exercise.

Theorem 9.45 *Under the assumptions of Theorem 9.44, Algorithm 9.2 finds a solution that satisfies*

$$\frac{\gamma_m}{1 + \eta(1 - \eta)\gamma_m} \leq \frac{\dim(\lambda, \psi(\mathcal{X}))}{(1 - \eta)^2} + \frac{\ln|\Sigma_\lambda(\pi_n)/\Sigma_\lambda(\pi_0)|}{\eta(1 - \eta)n},$$

where $\lambda = \frac{\epsilon}{B^2}$, $\gamma_m = \sup_{x \in \mathcal{X}, \Delta f \in \Delta\mathcal{F}} g_m(\Delta f, x)$, $\Sigma_\lambda(\pi) = \lambda I + \mathbb{E}_{x \sim \pi} \psi(X)\psi(X)^\top$.

9.7 Historical and Bibliographical Remarks

In mathematics, reproducing kernel Hilbert space was introduced in the early 1900s by Stanislaw Zaremba and James Mercer (1909) in the studies of differential equations and integral equations. It was further developed by various researchers and most noticeably Aronszajn (1950) and Bergman (1970). The idea was brought to machine learning by Vapnik with collaborators, for his treatment of support vector machines (Boser et al., 1992; Cortes and Vapnik, 1995; Vapnik, 2013).

In statistics, kernel methods have been studied in the context of Kriging and Gaussian processes (Krige, 1951; Matheron, 1965). These methods are widely used in spatial statistics and computer experiments. Gaussian processes have been extensively used (see Rasmussen, 2003) both as kernel methods for prediction problems and as a method for hyperparameter tuning (see Bergstra et al., 2011).

Kernel methods have also been studied in statistics in the context of smoothing splines (see Craven and Wahba, 1978; Wahba, 1990), and their convergence rates have been investigated by Stone (1982, 1985).

As we have shown, kernel least squares regression is related to infinite-dimensional ridge regression. A more modern treatment of this subject can be found in Hsu et al. (2012a). The concept of kernel has also been frequently associated with kernel smoothing in statistics (Wand and Jones, 1994), which is a different way of using kernels than the RKHS of this chapter.

The representer theorem (Schölkopf et al., 2001) was observed by Wahba and Vapnik. Vapnik has also popularized the idea of the kernel trick, which can be used to kernelize machine learning algorithms that use linear features. This idea has been investigated further by various researchers to kernelize different machine learning algorithms. We refer the readers to Schölkopf et al. (2018) for a more thorough treatment of this subject.

The universal approximation of the kernel method has been shown by Park and Sandberg (1991), and studied further in Micchelli et al. (2006), which considered universal approximation from the view of kernel feature representations. It has also been investigated by Steinwart (2001) and Zhang (2004b) in the context of statistical consistency.

Vector-valued kernel functions have been studied by Micchelli and Pontil (2005) and Alvarez et al. (2012). Rademacher complexity for vector-valued functions has been investigated in Bartlett and Mendelson (2002), and the result is similar to Theorem 9.30. However, as we have pointed out in Section 9.4, the resulting bound is often suboptimal in the dependency of the vector dimension q. In comparison, stability analysis does not suffer from this problem.

The G-optimal design criterion has been widely used in experimental design (Fedorov, 2013). Theorem 9.38 can handle some infinite-dimensional problems, and is related to the well-known result in Kiefer and Wolfowitz (1960), where the equivalence of G-optimal design and D-optimal design (without regularization) was established. It is also known that the G-optimal design solution can be achieved with no more than $d(d+1)/2$ points. The convergence of Algorithm 9.1 and its variants can also be analyzed using techniques described in Section 10.4. While asymptotic formulations of nonlinear G-optimal design have been studied in statistics, the more general formulation presented in Definition 9.42 is new. Its applications in sequential estimation problems can be found in Section 17.5 and Section 18.4).

Exercises

9.1   Prove Proposition 9.5.

9.2   Prove Theorem 9.8.

9.3   In Example 9.9, assume that $K_{n \times n}$ is positive definite. Show that the primal and dual solutions are identical. Show that the minimum value of the primal objective function is the same as the maximum value of the dual objective function.

9.4   Assume that the Gram matrix $K_{n \times n}$ on $\{X_1, \ldots, X_n\}$ is positive definite. Consider a Gaussian process on these points with

$$\mathbf{f} \sim N(0, K_{n \times n}).$$

Compute $\mathbb{E}\|\mathbf{f}\|_{\mathcal{H}}^2$, and explain what happens when $n \to \infty$.

9.5   We consider linear models with L_2 regularization:

$$\mathcal{F}_A = \{f(w, x) = w^\top \psi(x) : \|w\|_2^2 \leq A\}.$$

Assume that $k(x, x) = \psi(x)^\top \psi(x) \leq B^2$ for all x. Using the covering number estimate of Theorem 5.20 and Theorem 4.21 to derive a multiplicative form of margin bound similar to the additive form margin bound of Example 9.23.

9.6   Show that the structured SVM problem in Example 9.32 satisfies Proposition 9.33.

- Use the empirical L_∞-covering number bound of Theorem 5.20 to derive an L_∞-covering number bound for the structured SVM loss $L(f, y)$ defined in the example, with a logarithmic dependence on q.
- Use chaining to obtain an estimate of the Rademacher complexity $R(\mathcal{G}, \mathcal{S}_n)$, and compare the result to that of Example 9.32.

9.7   Assume we want to solve the soft-regularized SVM of Example 9.23, with λ chosen based on the training data according to appropriate learning bounds. Assume we obtain the SVM solutions $\hat{w}_1, \ldots, \hat{w}_N$ at different choices $\lambda_1, \ldots, \lambda_N$. Assume that $k(X, X) \leq B^2$.

- Which bound do you use to select the best λ_j? Corollary 9.22, Corollary 9.26, or Corollary 9.27? And explain the procedure.
- Obtain an oracle inequality for your procedure.

9.8   Prove Proposition 9.33.

9.9   Prove Proposition 9.36.

9.10   In Proposition 9.36, consider $\psi(x) = [\psi_j(x)]_{j=1}^\infty$ so that $\psi_j(x)^2 \leq \frac{c_0}{j^q}$ for some $q > 0$.

- Find an upper bound for $d(\epsilon')$.
- Use the bound for $d(\epsilon')$ to find an upper bound for $d_{1,\lambda}$.
- Find the rate of convergence for ridge regression using Theorem 9.35.

9.11   In Example 9.41, for $n \geq 2m$, show how to generate n data with equal weighting so that

$$\sup_{x \in \mathcal{X}} \psi(x)^\top \left(\lambda n I + \sum_{i=1}^n \psi(X_i) \psi(X_i)^\top \right)^{-1} \psi(x) \leq \frac{\nu}{n - m} \dim(\lambda, \psi(\mathcal{X}))$$

with $\nu = 4$. More generally, show that for any $\nu > 1$, there exists $c_0 > 0$ and $m \leq \lceil c_0 \mathrm{entro}(\lambda, \psi(\mathcal{X})) \rceil$ such that when $n \geq 2m$, the result holds with ν.

9.12   Prove Theorem 9.45 by using the technique of (9.26) to adapt the proof of Theorem 9.39.

10

Additive and Sparse Models

In this chapter, we focus on *additive models* of the following form:

$$f([w, \theta], x) = \sum_{j=1}^{m} w_j \psi(\theta_j, x), \qquad (10.1)$$

where, for simplicity, we consider real-valued functions $\psi(\theta, \cdot) \colon \mathcal{X} \to \mathbb{R}$ first. In additive models, each $\psi(\theta, \cdot)$ may be regarded as a prediction function, which is parametrized by $\theta \in \Theta$. The goal of additive models is to find a combination of models $\psi(\theta, \cdot)$ so that the combined model $f([w, \theta], x)$ is more accurate than any single model $\psi(\theta, x)$.

10.1 Sparse Model Combination

In order to motivate sparse regularization, we will first consider the case that Θ is finite. Assume that Θ has m elements $\{\theta_1, \ldots, \theta_m\}$, then (10.1) can be regarded as a linear model with respect to the model parameter w, and we can simply denote it as

$$f(w, x) = \sum_{j=1}^{m} w_j \psi_j(x) = w^\top \psi(x),$$

with features $\psi_j(x) = \psi(\theta_j, x)$, and $\psi(x) = [\psi_1(x), \ldots, \psi_m(x)]$. We further assume that each feature $\psi_j(x)$ is a prediction function so that

$$\psi_j(x) \in [0, M].$$

If we do not consider regularization, then the model complexity is determined by the model dimensionality m. For example, the VC dimension of the linear decision function $\mathbb{1}(f(w, x) \geq 0)$ is m. If we consider regularization, such as kernel method or L_2 regularization, then we may consider the function class

$$\mathcal{F}' = \{f(w, x) = w^\top \psi(x) \colon \|w\|_2 \leq A\}. \qquad (10.2)$$

Using the Rademacher complexity analysis for kernel methods in Chapter 9, we know

$$R_n(\mathcal{F}', \mathcal{D}) \leq A\sqrt{\frac{m}{n} \mathbb{E}_{\mathcal{D}} k(x, x)},$$

with

$$k(x,x) = \frac{1}{m} \sum_{j=1}^{m} \psi_j(x)^2.$$

The normalization factor of $1/m$ is to make sure that $k(x,x)$ is bounded by M^2. This implies that

$$\mathbb{E}_{X \sim \mathcal{D}} k(X,X) \le \frac{1}{m} \sum_{j=1}^{m} \mathbb{E}_{X \sim \mathcal{D}} \psi_j(X)^2 \le M^2.$$

This gives a bound on the Rademacher complexity of $\mathcal{F}'$ as

$$R_n(\mathcal{F}', \mathcal{D}) \le \sqrt{\frac{m}{n}} AM,$$

which depends linearly on $\sqrt{m}$. This upper bound matches the worst-case lower bound below with $M = 1$.

Proposition 10.1 *Assume that the m feature functions $\{\psi_j(X)\}$ are orthonormal when $X \sim \mathcal{D}$. Then there exists an absolute constant $c > 0$ such that for sufficiently large n,*

$$R_n(\mathcal{F}', \mathcal{D}) \ge c \sqrt{\frac{m}{n}} A,$$

where $\mathcal{F}'$ is given by (10.2).

Proof When n is sufficiently large, the vectors $\{\psi_j\}$ are near orthonormal on the empirical distribution $\mathcal{S}_n$. Therefore with constant probability, $\mathcal{F}'$ is nearly an m-dimensional ball of radius A with respect to $L_2(\mathcal{S}_n)$. Therefore Theorem 5.3 implies that $M(\epsilon, \mathcal{F}, L_2(\mathcal{S}_n)) \ge 2^m$ at $\epsilon = c_0 A$ for some $c_0 > 0$. The Rademacher complexity lower bound is now a direct consequence of Sudakov minoration (see Theorem 12.4) with such ϵ. □

It follows from Proposition 10.1 that the factor $\sqrt{m}$ in $R_n(\mathcal{F}', \mathcal{D})$ cannot be removed in general with L_2 regularization (kernel methods) for additive models. To compensate the effect of m, a proper regularization term when m is large can be reformulated as

$$\mathcal{F}'' = \{f(w,x) \colon \|w\|_2^2 \le A^2/m\}.$$

This leads to a Rademacher complexity of

$$R_n(\mathcal{F}'', \mathcal{D}) \le \sqrt{\frac{1}{n}} AM.$$

Alternatively, one may consider other regularization conditions for model combination. One such regularization condition is sparse regularization or L_0 regularization, which is given as follows.

Definition 10.2 The sparsity pattern, or support of a weight vector $w \in \mathbb{R}^m$, is defined as

$$\text{supp}(w) = \{j \colon w_j \ne 0\},$$

and the L_0 norm of w is defined as

$$\|w\|_0 = |\mathrm{supp}(w)|.$$

The following example compares different regularization conditions with the RKHS functions.

Example 10.3 Consider RBFs of the form

$$\psi(\theta, x) = \exp(-\beta\|x - \theta\|_2^2)$$

for some $\beta > 0$. If we treat it as a kernel $k(\cdot, \cdot) = \psi(\cdot, \cdot)$ as in Chapter 9, then the corresponding RKHS is given by functions of the form

$$\tilde{f}(\alpha, x) = \sum_{j=1}^{m} \alpha_j \exp(-\beta\|x - \theta_j\|_2^2).$$

Let $\mathcal{H}$ be its RKHS, and the corresponding regularization is given by

$$\|\tilde{f}(\alpha, x)\|_{\mathcal{H}}^2 = \sum_{i=1}^{m}\sum_{j=1}^{m} \alpha_i \alpha_j \exp(-\beta\|\theta_i - \theta_j\|_2^2). \qquad (10.3)$$

If we use RBFs as basis functions in additive models, we have

$$f([w, \theta], x) = \sum_{j=1}^{m} w_j \exp(-\beta\|x - \theta_j\|_2^2).$$

In this case, the kernel associated with the additive model can be defined as

$$k(x, x') = \frac{1}{m}\sum_{i=1}^{m} \exp(-\beta\|x - \theta_j\|_2^2 - \beta\|x' - \theta_j\|_2^2).$$

The corresponding RKHS norm for additive model is different from (10.3), and can be defined instead as

$$\|f([w, \theta], x)\|^2 = m\sum_{j=1}^{m} w_j^2. \qquad (10.4)$$

However, even for simple one-dimensional functions such as

$$\sum_{j=1}^{m} \exp(-\|x - j\|_2^2)$$

with $\beta = 1$, the complexity measured by the RKHS norm in (10.4) can be rather large. Alternatively, one can also measure the complexity of $f([w, \theta], x)$ by the sparsity $\|w\|_0$.

For each sparsity pattern $F \subset \{1, \ldots, m\}$, we may define the $|F|$-dimensional sparse function class

$$\mathcal{G}_F = \{\phi(w, z) \colon \mathrm{supp}(w) \subset F\},$$

where $\phi(w, z) = L(f(w, x), y) = L(w^\top \psi(x), y)$. We can now consider the following sparse learning method:

$$\hat{w} = \arg\min_{w \in \mathbb{R}^d} \left[\frac{1}{n} \sum_{i=1}^{n} \phi(w, Z_i) + r(F) \right] \quad \text{subject to} \ \ \text{supp}(w) \subset F, \qquad (10.5)$$

with a properly defined regularizer $r(F)$ on the sparsity pattern F.

We note that the exact solution of (10.5) may be difficult to obtain because the sparsity constraint is nonconvex and discontinuous. In practice one often employs approximate solutions. Assume that we can find an approximate solution of (10.5), then we can obtain a generalization error bound that depends only logarithmically on m, and is linear with respect to the sparsity $|F|$. The following theorem is a direct consequence of Theorem 8.7, which employs an upper bound of the expected Rademacher complexity. Note that, similar to Theorem 8.11, one may also replace the expected (sample-independent) Rademacher complexity by the sample-dependent Rademacher complexity.

Theorem 10.4 *Assume* $\sup_{w,z,z'}[\phi(w,z) - \phi(w,z')] \leq M$. *Let* $\mathcal{S}_n$ *be* n *iid samples from* $\mathcal{D}$. *Then with probability at least* $1 - \delta$, *the following bound holds for all* $w \in \mathbb{R}^m$ *and sparsity pattern* F *such that* $\text{supp}(w) \subset F$:

$$\phi(w, \mathcal{D}) \leq \phi(w, \mathcal{S}_n) + r(F) + M\sqrt{\frac{\ln(1/\delta)}{2n}},$$

where

$$r(F) \geq 2R(\mathcal{G}_F, \mathcal{D}) + M\sqrt{\frac{|F|\ln(em/|F|) + \ln(|F|+1)^2}{2n}}$$

for all F. *Consider the sparse learning algorithm in (10.5). We have the following oracle inequality. With probability of at least* $1 - \delta$,

$$\phi(\hat{w}, \mathcal{D}) \leq \inf_{w \in \mathbb{R}^m, \text{supp}(w) \subset F} [\phi(w, \mathcal{D}) + r(F)] + 2M\sqrt{\frac{\ln(2/\delta)}{2n}}.$$

Proof We note that

$$\binom{m}{s} \leq \frac{m^s}{s!} \leq \frac{m^s}{s^s} \cdot \frac{s^s}{s!} \leq \frac{m^s}{s^s} \cdot e^s = (me/s)^s.$$

We can now consider each $\mathcal{G}_F$ as a model, with

$$q_F = \frac{(|F|+1)^{-2}}{(me/|F|)^{|F|}} \leq \frac{(|F|+1)^{-2}}{\binom{m}{|F|}}.$$

Therefore we have

$$\sum_{F: |F| \geq 1} q_F \leq \sum_{s \geq 1} \frac{1}{(s+1)^2} \sum_{F: |F|=s} \frac{1}{\binom{m}{|F|}} = \sum_{s \geq 1} \frac{1}{(s+1)^2} < 1.$$

For each index F, we may consider $\hat{w}$ as the ERM solution under the constraint $\text{supp}(w) \subset F$. We can thus apply Theorem 8.7 with models indexed by $F \subset \{1, \ldots, m\}$ to obtain the desired bounds. $\square$

Example 10.5   Consider the linear binary classification problem, with the loss function

$$L(f(w, x), y) = \mathbb{1}(w^\top \psi(x) y \leq 0).$$

In this problem, we know from the Rademacher complexity of VC class

$$R(\mathcal{G}_F, \mathcal{S}_n) \leq c_0 \sqrt{\frac{|F|}{n}}$$

for some constant $c_0 > 0$ (see Example 6.26). It follows that we may simply take

$$r(F) = c' \sqrt{\frac{|F| \ln m}{n}}$$

for a sufficiently large constant c', which leads to the following sparsity constrained optimization:

$$\hat{w} = \arg \min_{w \in \mathbb{R}^m} \left[\frac{1}{n} \sum_{i=1}^n L(w^\top \psi(X_i), Y_i) + \lambda \sqrt{\|w\|_0} \right],$$

with $\lambda = c' \sqrt{\frac{\ln m}{n}}$. We obtain the following oracle inequality. With probability at least $1 - \delta$,

$$\mathbb{E}_{\mathcal{D}} L(f(\hat{w}, X), Y) \leq \inf_{w \in \mathbb{R}^m} \left[\mathbb{E}_{\mathcal{D}} L(f(w, X), Y) + \lambda \sqrt{\|w\|_0} \right] + 2 \sqrt{\frac{\ln(2/\delta)}{2n}}.$$

The bound is linear in $\sqrt{\|w\|_0}$, and logarithmic in m.

The Rademacher complexity bound for sparse learning has a convergence rate of $O(\sqrt{1/n})$. For some specialized problems such as least squares regression, where the variance condition holds, we can obtain a better rate of $O(1/n)$ using local Rademacher complexity analysis. The resulting bound has a convergence rate of $O(\|w\|_0 \ln m/n)$, which is similar to the Bayesian information criterion (BIC) for parametric models in classical statistics (Schwarz, 1978).

10.2 L_1 Regularization

Sparse regularization can reduce the learning complexity. However, the optimization problem of (10.5) is in general NP-hard because the sparse L_0 regularization in Example 10.5 is nonconvex (Natarajan, 1995). To alleviate this computational problem, practitioners often solve a convex relaxation of L_0 regularization formulations, where the L_0 regularization $\|w\|_0$ is replaced by the L_1 regularization $\|w\|_1$. The resulting method is also referred to as *Lasso* (Tibshirani, 1996) or as *basis pursuit* (Chen et al., 2001).

In this section, we consider the general situation that Θ is infinite. For notation simplicity, we can define the function class

$$\Psi = \{\psi(\theta, x) \colon \theta \in \Theta\},$$

and its convex hull can be derived as (see Definition 5.12)

$$\text{CONV}(\Psi) = \left\{ \sum_{j=1}^{m} w_j \psi(\theta_j, x) \colon m > 0, \ \|w\|_1 = 1, \ w_j \geq 0, \ \theta_j \in \Theta \right\}.$$

The nonnegative L_1 regularized additive models are

$$\mathcal{F}^+_{A,L_1}(\Psi) = \{af(x) \colon a \in [0, A], \ f(x) \in \text{CONV}(\Psi)\}.$$

We may also consider the class of L_1 regularized additive models as

$$\mathcal{F}_{A,L_1}(\Psi) = \mathcal{F}^+_{A,L_1}(\Psi \cup -\Psi) = \left\{ \sum_{j=1}^{m} w_j \psi(\theta_j, x) \colon \|w\|_1 \leq A, \ \theta_j \in \Theta, \ m > 0 \right\}.$$

Note that in general, we have $\mathcal{F}^+_{A,L_1}(\Psi) \subset \mathcal{F}_{A,L_1}(\Psi)$. However, if $-f \in \Psi$ for all $f \in \Psi$, then $\mathcal{F}_{A,L_1}(\Psi) = \mathcal{F}^+_{A,L_1}(\Psi)$.

Definition 10.6 Let $\mathcal{F}_{L_1}(\Psi)$ be the point-wise closure of $\cup_{A>0}\mathcal{F}_{A,L_1}(\Psi)$, then for any $f \in \mathcal{F}_{L_1}(\Psi)$,

$$\|f\|_1 = \liminf_{\epsilon \to 0} \left\{ \|w\|_1 \colon \sup_x \left| f(x) - \sum_{j=1}^{m} w_j \psi(\theta_j, x) \right| \leq \epsilon \right\}.$$

For notational convenience, we write functions in $\mathcal{F}_{L_1}(\Psi)$ as

$$f(x) = w^\top \psi(x),$$

where $\psi(x)$ is the infinite-dimensional vector $[\psi(\theta, x)]_{\theta \in \Theta}$, and $\|f\|_1 = \|w\|_1$.

For smooth-loss functions (see Definition A.5), there is a strong relationship between L_1 regularization and L_0 regularization, in that functions with small L_1 norms can be sparsified. Such a sparsification result was first shown for the least squares loss, and referred to as Maurey's lemma in Pisier (1980–1).

Theorem 10.7 *Assume $L(p, y)$ is a γ-smooth function in p. Consider $f(x) = w^\top \psi(x) \in \mathcal{F}_{L_1}(\Psi)$. Let $\mathcal{D}$ be an arbitrary distribution over (x, y). Then there exists a sparse vector u so that $\|u\|_0 \leq N$, and*

$$\mathbb{E}_{\mathcal{D}} L(u^\top \psi(X), Y) \leq \mathbb{E}_{\mathcal{D}} L(w^\top \psi(X), Y)$$
$$+ \frac{\gamma[\|w\|_1^2 \sup_{\theta \in \Theta} \mathbb{E}_{\mathcal{D}} \psi(\theta, X)^2 - \mathbb{E}_{\mathcal{D}} f(X)^2]}{2N}.$$

Proof For simplicity, we only consider $f(x)$ such that for some $m > 0$,

$$f(x) = \sum_{j=1}^{m} w_j \psi(\theta_j, x),$$

and let $\psi_j(x) = \psi(\theta_j, x)$. Consider N iid random variable j_k $(k = 1, \ldots, N)$ that takes values in $\{1, \ldots, m\}$, so that $\Pr(j_k = j) = |w_j|/\|w\|_1$. Let

$$f_J(x) = \frac{1}{N} \sum_{k=1}^{N} u_{j_k} \psi_{j_k}(x), \qquad u_j = \text{sign}(w_j)\|w\|_1 \quad (j = 1, \ldots, N),$$

where $J = \{j_1, \ldots, j_N\}$. It is easy to check that for all x,

$$\mathbb{E}_J \, f_J(x) = f(x).$$

Note also from the smoothness assumption, we have

$$L(f_J(x), y) \leq L(f(x), y) + (f_J(x) - f(x))L_1'((f(x), y)) \\ + \frac{\gamma}{2}|f_J(x) - f(x)|^2,$$

where $L_1'(p, y)$ is the derivative of $L(p, y)$ with respect to p. Taking expectation with respect to J, we have

$$\mathbb{E}_J L(f_J(x), y) \leq L(f(x), y) + \frac{\gamma}{2}\mathbb{E}_J |f_J(x) - f(x)|^2$$

$$= L(f(x), y) + \frac{\gamma}{2N}\text{Var}_{j_1}[u_{j_1}\psi_{j_1}(x)]$$

$$= L(f(x), y) + \frac{\gamma}{2N}\mathbb{E}_{j_1}[\|w\|_1^2\psi_{j_1}(x)^2 - f(x)^2].$$

Therefore by taking expectation with respect to $\mathcal{D}$, we obtain

$$\mathbb{E}_J\mathbb{E}_\mathcal{D} L(f_J(X), Y) \leq \mathbb{E}_\mathcal{D} L(f(X), Y) + \frac{\gamma}{2N}\mathbb{E}_{j_1}\mathbb{E}_\mathcal{D}[\|w\|_1^2\psi_{j_1}(X)^2 - f(X)]$$

$$\leq \mathbb{E}_\mathcal{D} L(f(X), Y) + \frac{\gamma \sup_j[\|w\|_1^2\mathbb{E}_\mathcal{D}\psi_j(X)^2 - \mathbb{E}_\mathcal{D}f(X)^2]}{2N}.$$

Since each $f_J(X)$ can be expressed as a sparse combination of N functions, this implies the existence of u. □

Theorem 10.7 implies that L_1 regularization can be regarded as an approximation method to the L_0 regularized sparse learning problem. Conversely, if a target function is a sparse additive model, then it is easier to approximate it by L_1 regularization than L_2 regularization. In order to illustrate this, we will consider the L_1 regularization method for additive models, and investigate its generalization performance. The following result on Rademacher complexity for L_1 regularization is straightforward.

Theorem 10.8 *We have*

$$R(\text{CONV}(\Psi), \mathcal{S}_n) = R(\Psi, \mathcal{S}_n).$$

If either $\Psi = -\Psi$ *or* $0 \in \Psi$, *then the following equality holds:*

$$R(\mathcal{F}_{A,L_1}^+(\Psi), \mathcal{S}_n) = A \cdot R(\Psi, \mathcal{S}_n).$$

If $\Psi = -\Psi$, *then the following equality holds:*

$$R(\mathcal{F}_{A,L_1}(\Psi), \mathcal{S}_n) = A \cdot R(\Psi, \mathcal{S}_n).$$

Proof We will prove the second equality. Since $A \cdot \Psi \subset \mathcal{F}_{A,L_1}^+(\Psi, \mathcal{S}_n)$, we have

$$A \cdot R(\Psi, \mathcal{S}_n) \leq R(\mathcal{F}_{A,L_1}^+(\Psi), \mathcal{S}_n).$$

Moreover, consider any function

$$\sum_{j=1}^{m} w_j \psi(\theta_j, x) \colon \ \|w\|_1 \leq A, \ w_j \geq 0, \ \theta_j \in \Theta$$

and $\sigma_i \in \{\pm 1\}$, we know that under the conditions of the theorem,

$$\sum_{i=1}^{n} \sigma_i \sum_{j=1}^{m} w_j \psi(\theta_j, X_i) = \sum_{j=1}^{m} w_j \sum_{i=1}^{n} \sigma_i \psi(\theta_j, X_i)$$

$$\leq \sum_{j=1}^{m} w_j \sup_{j'} \sum_{i=1}^{n} \sigma_i \psi(\theta_{j'}, X_i)$$

$$= \|w\|_1 \sup_{j} \sum_{i=1}^{n} \sigma_i \psi(\theta_j, X_i)$$

$$\leq \|w\|_1 \sup_{\psi \in \Psi} \sum_{i=1}^{n} \sigma_i \psi(X_i)$$

$$\leq A \sup_{\psi \in \Psi} \sum_{i=1}^{n} \sigma_i \psi(X_i).$$

The first inequality used $w_j \geq 0$. The last inequality used the fact that $\|w\|_1 \leq A$ and $\sup_{\psi \in \Psi} \sum_{i=1}^{n} \sigma_i \psi(X_i) \geq 0$. This implies that

$$R(\mathcal{F}_{A,L_1}^{+}(\Psi), \mathcal{S}_n) \leq A \cdot R(\Psi, \mathcal{S}_n),$$

and thus we obtain the second desired equality of the theorem. The proof of the first equality of the theorem is similar. The third equality of the theorem holds because the condition implies that

$$R(\mathcal{F}_{A,L_1}(\Psi), \mathcal{S}_n) = R(\mathcal{F}_{A,L_1}^{+}(\Psi), \mathcal{S}_n).$$

This proves the desired result.   □

The following example shows that for a sparse target function, L_1 regularization is preferred over L_2 regularization due to smaller Rademacher complexity.

Example 10.9   Assume that $|\Psi| = N$, then $|\Psi \cup -\Psi| \leq 2N$. From Theorem 6.23, we have

$$R(\Psi \cup -\Psi, \mathcal{S}_n) \leq \|\psi\|_{L_2(\mathcal{S}_n)} \cdot \sqrt{\frac{2 \ln(2N)}{n}}.$$

Theorem 10.8 implies that

$$R(\mathcal{F}_{A,L_1}(\Psi), \mathcal{S}_n) \leq A \sup_{\psi \in \Psi} \|\psi\|_{L_2(\mathcal{S}_n)} \cdot \sqrt{\frac{2 \ln(2N)}{n}}.$$

If $|\psi(x)| \leq B$ for all $\psi \in \Psi$, then

$$R(\mathcal{F}_{A,L_1}(\Psi), \mathcal{S}_n) \leq AB \sqrt{\frac{2 \ln(2N)}{n}}.$$

We now consider the following sparse function class

$$\mathcal{F}_{m,L_0}(\Psi) = \left\{ f(x) = \sum_{j=1}^{m} w_j \psi_j(x) \colon |w_j| \leq 1, \psi_j(x) \in \Psi \right\}.$$

To represent this function class using L_1 regularization, we note that

$$\mathcal{F}_{m,L_0}(\Psi) \subset R(\mathcal{F}_{m,L_1}(\Psi)).$$

This implies a Rademacher complexity that depends logarithmically on N as

$$R(\mathcal{F}_{m,L_1}(\Psi), \mathcal{S}_n) \leq mB\sqrt{\frac{2\ln(2N)}{n}}. \tag{10.6}$$

If instead, we consider L_2 regularization, then we have to use the function class

$$\mathcal{F}_{m,L_0}(\Psi) \subset R(\mathcal{F}_{\sqrt{m},L_2}(\Psi)),$$

where

$$\mathcal{F}_{A,L_2}(\Psi) = \left\{ f(x) = \sum_{j=1}^{N} w_j \psi_j(x) \colon \sum_{j=1}^{N} w_j^2 \leq A^2, \psi_j(x) \in \Psi \right\}.$$

Since $\sum_j \|\psi_j(x)\|_2^2 \leq NB^2$, the corresponding Rademacher complexity is upper bounded as

$$R(\mathcal{F}_{\sqrt{m},L_2}(\Psi), \mathcal{S}_n) \leq B\sqrt{\frac{mN}{n}}. \tag{10.7}$$

If the vectors $[\psi(X) \colon X \in \mathcal{S}_n]$ are orthogonal for $\psi(X) \in \Psi$, then it is not difficult to check that a matching lower bound holds for $R(\mathcal{F}_{\sqrt{m},L_2}(\Psi), \mathcal{S}_n)$ (see Exercise 10.1). Since in sparse learning applications, we usually have $m \ll N$, the Rademacher complexity of L_1 approximation of sparse target in (10.6) is much smaller than the Rademacher complexity of L_2 approximation of sparse target in (10.7). The former depends logarithmically in N, while the latter depends polynomially in N.

The following result shows that the Rademacher complexity of L_1 combinations of functions with finite VC dimension can also be easily obtained.

Example 10.10 Assume that Ψ is a binary function class with VC dimension d, then we know that from Example 6.26,

$$R(\Psi, \mathcal{S}_n) \leq 16\sqrt{\frac{d}{n}}.$$

It follows that

$$R(\mathcal{F}_{A,L_1}(\Psi), \mathcal{S}_n) \leq AR(\Psi, S_n) + AR(-\Psi, \mathcal{S}_n) \leq 32A\sqrt{\frac{d}{n}}.$$

The following result shows that the Rademacher complexity of two-layer neural networks can be obtained easily using L_1 regularization.

Example 10.11 In two-layer neural networks, let Ψ be an L_2 regularized ReLU function class

$$\Psi = \left\{\psi(\theta, x) = \max(0, \theta^\top x) \colon \quad \|\theta\|_2 \leq \alpha, \|x\|_2 \leq \beta\right\},$$

and the corresponding L_1 regularized two-layer NN can be expressed as a function

$$f(x) = \sum_{j=1}^{m} w_j \psi(\theta_j, x) \colon \|w\|_1 \leq A, \|\theta\|_2 \leq \alpha, \|x\|_2 \leq \beta.$$

This function class belongs to $\mathcal{F}_{A,L_1}(\Psi)$. We thus obtain the following bound for L_1 regularized two-layer NN:

$$R(\mathcal{F}_{A,L_1}(\Psi), \mathcal{S}_n) \leq 2AR(\Psi, \mathcal{S}_n) \qquad \text{(Theorem 10.8)}$$
$$\leq 2A\alpha\beta/\sqrt{n}, \qquad \text{(Corollary 9.21)}$$

where we note that $\max(0, f)$ is 1-Lipschitz in f.

Next, we may consider the following hard-constrained L_1 regularized learning problem:

$$\hat{w} = \arg\min_{w} \frac{1}{n} \sum_{i=1}^{n} L(w^\top \psi(X_i), Y_i), \qquad \|w\|_1 \leq A. \tag{10.8}$$

Similarly, we may consider the soft-regularized version as

$$\hat{w} = \arg\min_{w} \frac{1}{n} \sum_{i=1}^{n} L(w^\top \psi(X_i), Y_i) + \lambda\|w\|_1. \tag{10.9}$$

Now by using Theorem 6.31, we obtain the following result.

Corollary 10.12 *Assume that $\sup_{p,p',y,y'}[L(p, y) - L(p', y')] \leq M$, and $L(p, y)$ is γ Lipschitz with respect to p. For fixed $A > 0$, with probability at least $1 - \delta$, for all $f(x) = w^\top \psi(x)$ such that $\|w\|_1 \leq A$,*

$$\mathbb{E}_{\mathcal{D}} L(w^\top \psi(X), Y) \leq \frac{1}{n} \sum_{i=1}^{n} L(w^\top \psi(X_i), Y_i) + 2\gamma AR_n(\Psi_\pm, \mathcal{D}) + M\sqrt{\frac{\ln(1/\delta)}{2n}},$$

where $\Psi_\pm = \{\psi(x) \colon \psi(x) \in \Psi \text{ or } -\psi(x) \in \Psi\}$. Moreover, for (10.8), if we solve it approximately up to sub-optimality of ϵ', then we have with probability at least $1 - \delta$,

$$\mathbb{E}_{\mathcal{D}} L(\hat{w}^\top \psi(X), Y) \leq \inf_{\|w\|_1 \leq A} \mathbb{E}_{\mathcal{D}} L(w^\top \psi(X), Y) + 2\gamma AR_n(\Psi_\pm, \mathcal{D}) + \epsilon'$$
$$+ M\sqrt{\frac{2\ln(2/\delta)}{n}}.$$

Example 10.13 If Ψ contains m functions $\{\psi_1(x), \ldots, \psi_m(x)\}$, each $|\psi_j(x)| \leq B$, then

$$R_n(\Psi_\pm, \mathcal{D}) \leq B\sqrt{\frac{2\ln(2m)}{n}}.$$

Therefore the bound of Corollary 10.12 implies the oracle inequality

$$\mathbb{E}_{\mathcal{D}}L(\hat{w}^\top\psi(X),Y) \le \inf_{\|w\|_1 \le A} \mathbb{E}_{\mathcal{D}}L(w^\top\psi(X),Y) + 2\gamma AB\sqrt{\frac{2\ln(2m)}{n}}$$

$$+ M\sqrt{\frac{2\ln(2/\delta)}{n}}.$$

This has a logarithmic dependency on m, similar to that of the sparsity constraint in Example 10.5.

Similar to the analysis of kernel method, we may analyze the soft L_1 regularization method by considering the sample-dependent bound below. The result is an application of Theorem 8.7, and similar to Corollary 9.26 for kernel methods.

Corollary 10.14 *Assume that $L(p,y) \ge 0$ is γ Lipschitz, $M_0 = \sup_y L(0,y)$, and $B = \sup_{x,\psi\in\Psi}|\psi(x)|$. Consider $A_0 > 0$, then with probability at least $1 - \delta$, the following inequality holds for all w:*

$$\mathbb{E}_{\mathcal{D}}L(w^\top\psi(X),Y) \le \frac{1}{n}\sum_{i=1}^n L(w^\top\psi(X_i),Y_i) + 4\gamma(A_0 + \|w\|_1)R_n(\Psi_\pm,\mathcal{D})$$

$$+ (M_0 + 2\gamma B(A_0 + \|w\|_1))\left[\sqrt{\frac{\ln(2 + \log_2(1 + \|w\|_1/A_0))}{n}} + \sqrt{\frac{\ln(1/\delta)}{2n}}\right].$$

Consider (10.9) *with*

$$\lambda \ge 4\gamma R_n(\Psi_\pm,\mathcal{D}) + 2\gamma B\sqrt{\frac{\ln(2 + \log_2(1 + M_0/(\lambda A_0)))}{n}}.$$

We have the following oracle inequality. With probability at least $1 - \delta$,

$$\mathbb{E}_{\mathcal{D}}L(\hat{w}^\top\psi(X),Y) \le \inf_w\left[\mathbb{E}_{\mathcal{D}}L(w^\top\psi(X),Y) + \left(\lambda + 4\gamma B\sqrt{\frac{\ln(2/\delta)}{2n}}\right)\|w\|_1\right]$$

$$+ \epsilon_n(\delta),$$

where

$$\epsilon_n(\delta) = 4\gamma A_0 R_n(\Psi_\pm,\mathcal{D}) + (M_0 + 2\gamma A_0 B)\sqrt{\frac{\ln((2 + \log_2(1 + M_0/(\lambda A_0))))}{n}}$$

$$+ (2M_0 + 4\gamma A_0 B)\sqrt{\frac{\ln(2/\delta)}{2n}}.$$

Proof Let $A_\theta = 2^\theta A_0$, with $q(\theta) = (1 + \theta)^{-2}$ for $\theta = 1, 2, \ldots$, and let $f(x) = w^\top\psi(x)$. Consider $\mathcal{F}(1) = \{w^\top\psi(x)\colon \|w\|_1 \le A_1\}$, and $\mathcal{F}(\theta) = \{w^\top\psi(x)\colon A_{\theta-1} \le \|w\|_1 \le A_\theta\}$ for $\theta > 1$. We have

$$R_n(\mathcal{F}(\theta),\mathcal{D}) \le \gamma A_\theta R_n(\Psi_\pm,\mathcal{D}).$$

Given any w, let θ be the smallest number such that $f(w,x) = w^\top\Psi(x) \in \mathcal{F}(\theta)$, then $A_\theta \le 2(A_0 + \|w\|_1)$. Therefore,

$$L(f(x), y) \leq L(0, y) + \gamma |f(x)| \leq M_0 + \gamma A_\theta B \leq M_0 + 2\gamma (A_0 + \|w\|_1) B.$$

We can take $h = 0$ in Theorem 8.7, $M(\theta) \leq M_0 + 2\gamma(A_0 + \|w\|_1)B$, and $1/q(\theta) \leq (2 + \log_2(1 + \|w\|_1/A_0))^2$. Let

$$\tilde{R}(\theta, f, \mathcal{S}_n) = 4\gamma(A_0 + \|w\|_1) R_n(\Psi_\pm, \mathcal{D})$$
$$+ (M_0 + 2\gamma B(A_0 + \|w\|_1)) \sqrt{\frac{\ln(2 + \log_2(1 + \|w\|_1/A_0))}{n}}. \quad (10.10)$$

This implies the desired uniform convergence result.

Now we would like to show the second desired oracle inequality. With the condition of λ, we have $\|\hat{w}\|_1 \leq M_0/\lambda$, and by considering $\|w\|_1 \leq M_0/\lambda$, we can redefine

$$\tilde{R}(\theta) = \tilde{R}(\theta, f, \mathcal{S}_n) = \lambda \|w\|_1 + 4\gamma A_0 R_n(\Psi_\pm, \mathcal{D})$$
$$+ (M_0 + 2\gamma A_0 B) \sqrt{\frac{\ln(2 + \log_2(1 + M_0/(\lambda A_0)))}{n}}.$$

This definition of $\tilde{R}(\theta)$ is an upper bound of (10.10). We can thus consider Theorem 8.7 again to obtain the desired oracle inequality, where we also use $2M_0 + 4\gamma A_0 B + 4\gamma B\|w\|_1$ as an upper bound for $2M(\theta)$. □

Example 10.15 Consider (10.9) with a function class Ψ of finite VC dimension (or pseudodimension) $\text{VC}(\Psi_\pm) = d$, which includes the two-layer neural network as a special case. Under the assumptions of Corollary 10.14, we have $R_n(\Psi_\pm, \mathcal{D}) = O(B\sqrt{d/n})$ (see Example 6.26). We can take $A_0 = M_0/(\gamma B)$ and set

$$\lambda = \tilde{O}\left(\gamma B \sqrt{\frac{d}{n}}\right)$$

to obtain

$$\mathbb{E}_\mathcal{D} L(\hat{w}^\top \psi(X), Y) \leq \inf_w \left[\mathbb{E}_\mathcal{D} L(w^\top \psi(X), Y) + \tilde{O}\left(\gamma B \sqrt{\frac{d + \ln(1/\delta)}{n}} \|w\|_1\right) \right]$$
$$+ \tilde{O}\left(M_0 \sqrt{\frac{d + \ln(1/\delta)}{n}}\right).$$

We use the notation $\tilde{O}(\cdot)$ to hide log-factors.

10.3 Information Theoretical Analysis with Entropy Regularization

We have analyzed the Gibbs algorithm in Section 7.4 using stability analysis. It is a randomized algorithm using the Gibbs distribution (or posterior distribution). From (7.10), we know that the Gibbs distribution can be regarded as the solution of an entropy-regularized empirical risk minimization problem. We will further investigate entropy-regularization as well as the closely related topic of information theoretical generalization analysis in this section.

Note that entropy regularization is closely related to L_1 regularization. Here we consider the case of convex hull, with weights $w \geq 0$, and $\sum_j w_j = 1$. For entropy regularization, we will consider a probability interpretation of w, which may now be regarded as a distribution over models, to be learned from the training data. Since we work with distributions in this section, in the following we will adopt a different notation, and replace the weight w by a general distribution $q(\theta)$ on Θ, where Θ may be either continuous or discrete.

Our goal is to find a distribution q on Θ, such that the additive model (10.1) is replaced by the average over $\psi(\theta, x) \in \Psi$ according to q:

$$f(q, x) = \int \psi(\theta, x) q(\theta) d\theta = \mathbb{E}_{\theta \sim q(\cdot)} \psi(\theta, x). \tag{10.11}$$

Since $q(\theta)$ is learned from the training data $\mathcal{S}_n$, we will call such a distribution $q(\theta)$ *posterior distribution*, using the Bayesian statistics analogy. Consider a *prior distribution* $q_0(\theta)$ on Θ (we use the term prior distribution to indicate that it does not depend on the training data $\mathcal{S}_n$), and we may consider the entropy regularization to regularize the posterior distribution q:

$$\mathrm{KL}(q\|q_0) = \int q(x) \ln \frac{q(\theta)}{q_0(\theta)} d\theta.$$

We have the following Rademacher complexity estimate for this entropy regularization.

Theorem 10.16   *Consider $h(q) = h_0(q) = \lambda \mathrm{KL}(q\|q_0)$, and $\mathcal{F} = \{f(q, x)\}$ in (10.11). The offset Rademacher complexity can be bounded as*

$$R^h(\mathcal{F}, \mathcal{S}_n) \leq \frac{\lambda}{2} \ln \mathbb{E}_{\theta \sim q_0} \exp \left[\frac{2}{\lambda^2 n^2} \sum_{i=1}^n \psi(\theta, X_i)^2 \right] \leq \frac{1}{\lambda n^2} \sup_\theta \sum_{i=1}^n \psi(\theta, X_i)^2.$$

Proof   We have

$$R^h(\mathcal{F}, \mathcal{S}_n) = \mathbb{E}_\sigma \sup_q \left[\frac{1}{n} \sum_{i=1}^n \sigma_i \mathbb{E}_{\theta \sim q} \psi(\theta, X_i) - \frac{\lambda}{2} \mathrm{KL}(q\|q_0) \right]$$

$$= \frac{\lambda}{2} \mathbb{E}_\sigma \ln \mathbb{E}_{\theta \sim q_0} \exp \left[\frac{2}{\lambda n} \sum_{i=1}^n \sigma_i \psi(\theta, X_i) \right]$$

$$\leq \frac{\lambda}{2} \ln \mathbb{E}_{\theta \sim q_0} \mathbb{E}_\sigma \exp \left[\frac{2}{\lambda n} \sum_{i=1}^n \sigma_i \psi(\theta, X_i) \right]$$

$$\leq \frac{\lambda}{2} \ln \mathbb{E}_{\theta \sim q_0} \exp \left[\frac{2}{\lambda^2 n^2} \sum_{i=1}^n \psi(\theta, X_i)^2 \right].$$

The first equation is the definition of Rademacher complexity (with offset). The second equation follows from Proposition 7.16. The first inequality used Jensen's inequality and the concavity of $\ln(\cdot)$. The second inequality follows from the sub-Gaussian exponential inequality. This implies the desired bound. $\square$

The above result for Rademacher complexity appeared in Meir and Zhang (2003), which immediately implies the following result.

Corollary 10.17   *Let $\mathcal{F}_A = \{f(q, x) \colon \mathrm{KL}(q\|q_0) \leq A^2\}$ be entropy regularized functions of (10.11). Then*

$$R(\mathcal{F}_A, \mathcal{S}_n) \leq \sqrt{\frac{2}{n}} A \sup_\theta \sqrt{\frac{1}{n} \sum_{i=1}^n \psi(\theta, X_i)^2} \; .$$

Proof   From Theorem 10.16, we have

$$R(\mathcal{F}_A, \mathcal{S}_n) \leq \frac{\lambda}{2} A^2 + \frac{1}{\lambda n^2} \sup_\theta \sum_{i=1}^n \psi(\theta, X_i)^2.$$

By optimizing over λ, we obtain the desired bound. $\square$

This bound holds for general function classes. In the case of finite family with $\Theta = \{\theta_1, \ldots, \theta_m\}$, and $q_0(\theta) = 1/m$ for all θ, we have

$$\mathrm{KL}(q\|q_0) \leq \ln m$$

for all q. Therefore entropy regularization implies a bound for L_1 regularization with nonnegative constraint $\sum_{j=1}^m w_j = 1$ and $w_j \geq 0$. Since this is exactly the convex hull of $\Psi = \{\psi(\theta, x)\}$, Corollary 10.17 implies that

$$R(\mathrm{CONV}(\Psi), \mathcal{S}_n) \leq \sqrt{\frac{2 \ln m}{n}} \sup_\theta \|\psi(\theta, \cdot)\|_{L_2(\mathcal{S}_n)},$$

which is identical to the Rademacher complexity of convex hull of finite function class obtained in Theorem 10.8 (by using Theorem 6.23).

Similar to Corollary 10.12 and Corollary 10.14, one can use the Rademacher complexity of entropy regularization and Theorem 6.31 to obtain uniform convergence and oracle inequalities for additive models with entropy regularization. In addition, a particularly interesting application of entropy regularization is the information theoretical approach to generalization analysis, which we describe in the following.

We now consider the notations introduced in Section 3.3, where we are interested in minimizing a loss function $\phi(w, z) \colon \Omega \times \mathcal{Z} \to \mathbb{R}$. We consider a general randomized algorithm $\mathcal{A} \colon \mathcal{Z}^n \to \Delta(\Omega)$, where $\Delta(\Omega)$ denotes probability measures on Ω. That is, given training data $\mathcal{S}_n$, $\mathcal{A}(\mathcal{S}_n)$ returns a posterior distribution $\hat{q}$ on Ω. It then randomly draws a model from $\hat{q}$ to make a prediction. The following uniform convergence result can be interpreted as a generalization bound for an arbitrary randomized learning algorithm.

Theorem 10.18   *Consider a randomized algorithm $\mathcal{A}$ that returns a distribution $\hat{q}(w|\mathcal{S}_n)$ on the parameter space Ω for each training data $\mathcal{S}_n \in \mathcal{Z}^n$. Let*

$$\Lambda(\lambda, w) = -\frac{1}{\lambda} \ln \mathbb{E}_{Z \sim \mathcal{D}} \exp(-\lambda \phi(w, Z)).$$

Then for any data independent distribution q_0 on Ω and $\lambda > 0$, we have

$$\mathbb{E}_{\mathcal{S}_n}\mathbb{E}_{w\sim\hat{q}(\cdot|\mathcal{S}_n)}\Lambda(1/(\lambda n), w) \leq \mathbb{E}_{\mathcal{S}_n}\mathbb{E}_{w\sim\hat{q}(\cdot|\mathcal{S}_n)}\frac{1}{n}\sum_{i=1}^{n}\phi(w, Z_i) + \lambda\mathbb{E}_{\mathcal{S}_n}\mathrm{KL}(\hat{q}||q_0).$$

Moreover, for any $\lambda > 0$, with probability at least $1 - \delta$ over $\mathcal{S}_n$,

$$\mathbb{E}_{w\sim\hat{q}(\cdot|\mathcal{S}_n)}\Lambda(1/(\lambda n), w) \leq \mathbb{E}_{w\sim\hat{q}(\cdot|\mathcal{S}_n)}\frac{1}{n}\sum_{i=1}^{n}\phi(w, Z_i) + [\lambda\mathrm{KL}(\hat{q}||q_0) + \lambda\ln(1/\delta)].$$

Proof Let

$$\Delta(\mathcal{S}_n) = \sup_{\hat{q}}\left[\mathbb{E}_{w\sim\hat{q}(\cdot|\mathcal{S}_n)}\left(\Lambda(1/(\lambda n), w) - \frac{1}{n}\sum_{i=1}^{n}\phi(w, Z_i)\right) - \lambda\mathrm{KL}(\hat{q}||q_0)\right].$$

We have

$$\ln\mathbb{E}_{\mathcal{S}_n\sim\mathcal{D}^n}\exp(\lambda^{-1}\Delta(\mathcal{S}_n))$$

$$= \ln\mathbb{E}_{\mathcal{S}_n\sim\mathcal{D}^n}\exp\left[\ln\mathbb{E}_{w\sim q_0}\exp\left(\lambda^{-1}\Lambda(1/(\lambda n), w) - \frac{\lambda^{-1}}{n}\sum_{i=1}^{n}\phi(w, Z_i)\right)\right]$$

$$= \ln\mathbb{E}_{w\sim q_0}\left[\exp\left(\lambda^{-1}\Lambda(1/(\lambda n), w)\right)\mathbb{E}_{\mathcal{S}_n\sim\mathcal{D}^n}\exp\left(-\frac{\lambda^{-1}}{n}\sum_{i=1}^{n}\phi(w, Z_i)\right)\right]$$

$$= \ln\mathbb{E}_{w\sim q_0}\left[\exp\left(\lambda^{-1}\Lambda(1/(\lambda n), w)\right)\left(\mathbb{E}_{Z\sim\mathcal{D}}\exp\left(-\frac{\lambda^{-1}}{n}\phi(w, Z)\right)\right)^n\right]$$

$$= \ln\mathbb{E}_{w\sim q_0}\left[\exp\left(\lambda^{-1}\Lambda(1/(\lambda n), w)\right)\left(\exp\left(-\frac{1}{\lambda n}\Lambda(1/(\lambda n), w)\right)\right)^n\right]$$

$$= 0.$$

The first equation used Proposition 7.16. The second equation used algebraic manipulation. The third equation used the independence of Z_i. The fourth equation used the definition of $\Lambda(\lambda, w)$. This implies that

$$\lambda^{-1}\mathbb{E}_{\mathcal{S}_n\sim\mathcal{D}^n}\Delta(\mathcal{S}_n) \leq \ln\mathbb{E}_{\mathcal{S}_n\sim\mathcal{D}^n}\exp(\lambda^{-1}\Delta(\mathcal{S}_n)) = 0.$$

This implies the first bound. For the second inequality, we know that

$$\Pr\left(\lambda^{-1}\Delta(\mathcal{S}_n) \geq \ln(1/\delta)\right) \leq \mathbb{E}_{\mathcal{S}_n}\exp\left(\lambda^{-1}\Delta(\mathcal{S}_n) - \ln(1/\delta)\right) = \delta.$$

This proves the second result. $\square$

The style of the generalization result stated in Theorem 10.18 is often referred to as *PAC-Bayes* analysis (McAllester, 1999), which can be applied to an arbitrary randomized learning algorithm $\mathcal{A}: \mathcal{Z}^n \to \Delta(\Omega)$. In the literature, it is often applied to bounded loss functions, for which we can estimate the logarithmic moment generating function $\Lambda(\lambda, w)$ easily. More generally, we may consider sub-Gaussian loss functions as in the following example.

Example 10.19 Assume that $\phi(w, Z)$ is uniformly sub-Gaussian: there exists $\sigma > 0$ so that

$$\forall w \in \Omega: \quad -\Lambda(\lambda, w) \leq -\phi(w, \mathcal{D}) + \frac{\lambda\sigma^2}{2}.$$

Then we obtain from Theorem 10.18 the following generalization bound. For any $\lambda > 0$, with probability at least $1 - \delta$,

$$\mathbb{E}_{w \sim \hat{q}(\cdot|\mathcal{S}_n)} \phi(w, \mathcal{D}) \leq \mathbb{E}_{w \sim \hat{q}(\cdot|\mathcal{S}_n)} \phi(w, \mathcal{S}_n) + \left[\lambda \mathrm{KL}(\hat{q}||q_0) + \frac{\sigma^2}{2\lambda n} + \lambda \ln(1/\delta) \right].$$

Assume that $\phi(w, Z)$ satisfies a uniform Bennett-style bound on the logarithmic moment generating function in Lemma 2.20, and the variance condition of (3.13), then we can obtain a fast rate result.

Corollary 10.20 *Under the assumptions of Theorem 10.18, and assume that there exists $b > 0$ so that*

$$-\Lambda(\lambda, w) \leq -\phi(w, \mathcal{D}) + \lambda\psi(\lambda b)\mathrm{Var}_{Z \sim \mathcal{D}}(\phi(w, Z)),$$

where $\psi(z) = (e^z - z - 1)/z^2$. Assume further that the variance condition of (3.13) holds. Then with probability at least $1 - \delta$,

$$\left(1 - \frac{c_1\psi(b/(\lambda n))}{\lambda n} \right) \mathbb{E}_{w \sim \hat{q}(\cdot|\mathcal{S}_n)} \phi(w, \mathcal{D})$$

$$\leq \mathbb{E}_{w \sim \hat{q}(\cdot|\mathcal{S}_n)} \phi(w, \mathcal{S}_n) + \left[\lambda \mathrm{KL}(\hat{q}||q_0) + \frac{c_0^2\psi(b/(\lambda n))}{\lambda n} + \lambda \ln(1/\delta) \right].$$

We also have the expected generalization error bound:

$$\left(1 - \frac{c_1\psi(b/(\lambda n))}{\lambda n} \right) \mathbb{E}_{\mathcal{S}_n} \mathbb{E}_{w \sim \hat{q}(\cdot|\mathcal{S}_n)} \phi(w, \mathcal{D})$$

$$\leq \mathbb{E}_{\mathcal{S}_n} \mathbb{E}_{w \sim \hat{q}(\cdot|\mathcal{S}_n)} \phi(w, \mathcal{S}_n) + \left[\lambda \mathbb{E}_{\mathcal{S}_n} \mathrm{KL}(\hat{q}||q_0) + \frac{c_0^2\psi(b/(\lambda n))}{\lambda n} \right].$$

Proof   We have

$$\Lambda(1/(\lambda n), w) \geq \phi(w, \mathcal{D}) - \frac{1}{\lambda n}\psi(b/(\lambda n))\mathrm{Var}_{Z \sim \mathcal{D}}(\phi(w, Z)) \quad \text{(assumption on } \Lambda)$$

$$\geq \phi(w, \mathcal{D}) - \frac{1}{\lambda n}\psi(b/(\lambda n))(c_0^2 + c_1\phi(w, \mathcal{D})) \quad \text{(variance condition)}$$

$$= \left(1 - \frac{c_1\psi(b/(\lambda n))}{\lambda n} \right) \phi(w, \mathcal{D}) - \frac{c_0^2\psi(b/(\lambda n))}{\lambda n}.$$

This estimate, together with Theorem 10.18, implies the desired bounds. $\square$

The result can be compared to the stability analysis of the Gibbs algorithm in Theorem 7.19, and to the local Rademacher complexity analysis in Theorem 6.41.

Example 10.21   Consider the least squares problem in Example 3.18 with either a convex or a nonconvex but realizable function class. Let

$$\phi(w, z) = (f(w, x) - y)^2 - (f_{\mathrm{opt}}(x) - y)^2.$$

We can take $b = M^2$, $c_0 = 0$, and $c_1 = 4M^2$. Let $\lambda = 4M^2/n$, and note that $\psi(b/(\lambda n)) = \psi(0.25) < 0.6$. We obtain the following bound from Corollary 10.20. With probability at least $1 - \delta$,

$$0.4\mathbb{E}_{w \sim \hat{q}(\cdot|S_n)}\phi(w, \mathcal{D}) \leq \mathbb{E}_{w \sim \hat{q}(\cdot|S_n)}\phi(w, S_n) + \frac{4M^2}{n}\left[\mathrm{KL}(\hat{q}||q_0) + \ln(1/\delta)\right].$$

For least squares regression with sub-Gaussian noise, one can also perform a more direct calculation of logarithmic moment generating function with a slightly improved result. See Proposition 12.21.

A more recent development of the information theoretical approach to generalization analysis is to rewrite the expected generalization result in Theorem 10.18 in terms of the mutual information between a learning algorithm $\mathcal{A}$ and the training data S_n. Using the notations of Theorem 10.18, we can define the mutual information of $\mathcal{A}$ and S_n as follows:

$$I(\mathcal{A}, S_n) = \mathbb{E}_{S_n}\mathbb{E}_{w \sim \hat{q}(\cdot|S_n)} \ln \frac{\hat{q}(w|S_n)}{\hat{q}(w)}, \qquad \hat{q}(w) = \mathbb{E}_{S_n}\hat{q}(w|S_n).$$

We note that the mutual information optimizes the expected KL-divergence in Theorem 10.18 over prior q_0:

$$I(\mathcal{A}, S_n) = \inf_{q_0} \mathbb{E}_{S_n}\mathrm{KL}(\hat{q}||q_0).$$

The following result is a direct consequence of Theorem 10.18 with $q_0(w) = \hat{q}(w)$.

Corollary 10.22   *Under the assumptions of Theorem 10.18, we have the following expected generalization bound for all $\lambda > 0$:*

$$\mathbb{E}_{S_n}\mathbb{E}_{\mathcal{A}}\Lambda(\lambda, \mathcal{D}) \leq \mathbb{E}_{S_n}\mathbb{E}_{\mathcal{A}}\frac{1}{n}\sum_{i=1}^{n}\phi(w, Z_i) + \lambda I(\mathcal{A}, S_n),$$

where $\mathbb{E}_{\mathcal{A}}$ denotes the expectation over the randomization of algorithm $\mathcal{A}$; that is, $w \sim \hat{q}(\cdot|S_n)$.

Similar to Example 10.19, we have the following result for sub-Gaussian loss functions. This is the result that is often stated in the literature.

Example 10.23   Assume that $\sup[\phi(w, z) - \phi(w, z')] \leq M$. Then we have the sub-Gaussian inequality

$$\Lambda(\lambda) \leq \frac{\lambda^2 M^2}{8}.$$

We obtain from Corollary 10.22,

$$\mathbb{E}_{S_n}\mathbb{E}_{\mathcal{A}}\phi(w, \mathcal{D}) \leq \mathbb{E}_{S_n}\mathbb{E}_{\mathcal{A}}\frac{1}{n}\sum_{i=1}^{n}\phi(w, Z_i) + \inf_{\lambda > 0}\left[\lambda I(\mathcal{A}, S_n) + \frac{M^2}{8\lambda n}\right]$$

$$= \mathbb{E}_{S_n}\mathbb{E}_{\mathcal{A}}\frac{1}{n}\sum_{i=1}^{n}\phi(w, Z_i) + M\sqrt{\frac{I(\mathcal{A}, S_n)}{2n}}.$$

We may also derive fast rate results for the mutual information generalization bound as follows.

Example 10.24   Under the conditions of Corollary 10.20, we obtain

$$\left(1 - \frac{c_1 \psi(b/(\lambda n))}{\lambda n}\right) \mathbb{E}_{\mathcal{S}_n} \mathbb{E}_{\mathcal{A}} \phi(w, \mathcal{D})$$

$$\leq \mathbb{E}_{\mathcal{S}_n} \mathbb{E}_{\mathcal{A}} \frac{1}{n} \sum_{i=1}^{n} \phi(w, Z_i) + \left[\lambda I(\mathcal{A}, \mathcal{S}_n) + \frac{c_0^2 \psi(b/(\lambda n))}{\lambda n}\right].$$

We now consider the Gibbs algorithm of (7.9), which we restate using notations of this section as follows:

$$\hat{q}(w|\mathcal{S}_n) \propto q_0(\theta) \exp\left(-\frac{1}{\lambda n} \sum_{i=1}^{n} \phi(w, Z_i)\right). \tag{10.12}$$

We have the following oracle inequality for the Gibbs algorithm.

Corollary 10.25   *The following expected oracle inequality holds for the Gibbs distribution (10.12):*

$$\mathbb{E}_{\mathcal{S}_n} \mathbb{E}_{w \sim \hat{q}} \Lambda(1/(\lambda n), w) \leq \inf_q \left[\mathbb{E}_{w \sim q} \phi(w, \mathcal{D}) + \lambda \mathrm{KL}(q\|q_0)\right],$$

where $\Lambda(\cdot)$ is defined in Theorem 10.18.

Proof   From Proposition 7.16, $\hat{q}$ is the solution of the following regularized empirical risk minimization problem:

$$\hat{q} = \arg\min_q \left[\mathbb{E}_{\theta \sim q} \frac{1}{n} \sum_{i=1}^{n} \phi(w, Z_i) + \lambda \mathrm{KL}(q\|q_0)\right]. \tag{10.13}$$

Therefore for any q, we obtain from Theorem 10.18,

$$\mathbb{E}_{\mathcal{S}_n} \mathbb{E}_{w \sim \hat{q}} \Lambda(1/(\lambda n), w) \leq \mathbb{E}_{\mathcal{S}_n}\left[\mathbb{E}_{w \sim \hat{q}} \frac{1}{n} \sum_{i=1}^{n} \phi(w, Z_i) + \lambda \mathrm{KL}(\hat{q}\|q_0)\right]$$

$$\leq \mathbb{E}_{\mathcal{S}_n}\left[\mathbb{E}_{w \sim q} \frac{1}{n} \sum_{i=1}^{n} \phi(w, Z_i) + \lambda \mathrm{KL}(q\|q_0)\right]$$

$$= \left[\mathbb{E}_{w \sim q} \phi(w, \mathcal{D}) + \lambda \mathrm{KL}(q\|q_0)\right].$$

The first inequality used Theorem 10.18. The second inequality used (10.13). The last equation used the fact that $Z_i \sim \mathcal{D}$. This implies the result. $\square$

We note that, similar to the analysis of least squares using Corollary 10.20 of Theorem 10.18, we may use Corollary 10.25 to obtain a simpler oracle inequality than that of the local Rademacher complexity. One interesting application, which we state in the following, is a simple analysis of conditional density estimation for Gibbs algorithms.

Corollary 10.26   *Consider the conditional density estimation problem with a density class $\{p(Y|w, X): w \in \Omega\}$. Let $\lambda = 1/(\alpha n)$ for some $\alpha \in (0, 1)$, and $\phi(w, Z) = -\ln p(Y|w, X)$ in (10.12). Then*

$$(1 - \alpha)\mathbb{E}_{\mathcal{S}_n \sim \mathcal{D}^n}\mathbb{E}_{w \sim \hat{q}}\mathbb{E}_{X \sim \mathcal{D}}D_\alpha(p(\cdot|w, X)||p_*(\cdot|X))$$

$$\leq \inf_q \left[\alpha\mathbb{E}_{w \sim q}\mathbb{E}_{X \sim \mathcal{D}}\mathrm{KL}(p_*(\cdot|X)||p(\cdot|w, X)) + \frac{\mathrm{KL}(q||q_0)}{n} \right],$$

where D_α is the α-divergence defined in (B.3), and $p_*(Y|X)$ is the true conditional density of $\mathcal{D}$.

Proof Consider $\phi'(w, Z) = \ln p_*(Y|X) - \ln p(Y|w, X)$. Then the Gibbs algorithm does not change if we replace $\phi(w, Z)$ with $\phi'(w, Z)$. By applying Corollary 10.25 with $\phi(w, Z)$ replaced by $\phi'(w, Z)$, we note that

$$\Lambda(1/(\lambda n), w) = -\frac{1}{\alpha} \ln \mathbb{E}_{(X,Y) \sim \mathcal{D}} \left(\frac{p(Y|w, X)}{p_*(Y|X)} \right)^\alpha$$

$$= -\frac{1}{\alpha} \ln \left[1 - (1 - \alpha)\mathbb{E}_{X \sim \mathcal{D}}D_\alpha(p(\cdot|w, X)||p_*(\cdot|X)) \right]$$

$$\geq \frac{1 - \alpha}{\alpha}\mathbb{E}_{X \sim \mathcal{D}}D_\alpha(p(\cdot|w, X)||p_*(\cdot|X)).$$

Moreover, $\mathbb{E}_\mathcal{D}\phi'(w, Z) = \mathbb{E}_X \mathrm{KL}(p_*(\cdot|X)||p(\cdot|w, X))$. The desired bound follows directly from Corollary 10.25. $\qquad \square$

Example 10.27 The squared Hellinger distance is α-divergence with $\alpha = 0.5$. Consider the following Gibbs algorithm with log-likelihood loss and $\lambda = 2/n$:

$$\hat{q}(w|\mathcal{S}_n) \propto q_0(\theta) \exp \left(0.5 \sum_{i=1}^n \ln p(Y_i|w, X_i) \right).$$

Corollary 10.26 implies that

$$\mathbb{E}_{\mathcal{S}_n \sim \mathcal{D}^n}\mathbb{E}_{w \sim \hat{q}}\mathbb{E}_{X \sim \mathcal{D}}H(p_*(\cdot|X)||p(\cdot|w, X))^2$$

$$\leq \inf_q \left[\mathbb{E}_{w \sim q}\mathbb{E}_{X \sim \mathcal{D}}\mathrm{KL}(p_*(\cdot|X)||p(\cdot|w, X)) + \frac{2\mathrm{KL}(q||q_0)}{n} \right].$$

One may also obtain high-probability oracle inequalities for the Gibbs algorithm. For example, we have the following result.

Theorem 10.28 *Assume that* $\sup_{w,z,z'}[\phi(w, z) - \phi(w, z')] \leq M$. *Let* q_0 *be a distribution on* Θ. *Let* $\hat{q}$ *be the Gibbs distribution of* (10.12). *Then with probability at least* $1 - \delta$,

$$\mathbb{E}_{w \sim \hat{q}}\phi(w, \mathcal{D}) \leq \inf_q [\mathbb{E}_{w \sim q}\phi(w, \mathcal{D}) + \lambda\mathrm{KL}(q||q_0)] + \frac{M^2}{8\lambda n} + 2M\sqrt{\frac{\ln(2/\delta)}{2n}}.$$

Proof Let $\Delta(\Omega)$ denote the set of posterior distributions $\hat{q}(\cdot|\mathcal{S}_n)$. We note that with $h(q) = \lambda\mathrm{KL}(q||q_0)$, Theorem 10.18 (with $\Delta_n(h) = 0$) implies that

$$\epsilon_n^h(\Delta(\Omega), \mathcal{D}) = \mathbb{E}_{\mathcal{S}_n \sim \mathcal{D}^n} \sup_{q \in \Delta(\Omega)} [\mathbb{E}_{w \sim q}\phi(w, \mathcal{S}_n) - \lambda\mathrm{KL}(q||q_0)] \leq \frac{M^2}{8\lambda n},$$

with a calculation similar to Example 10.19. We obtain the desired bound from Corollary 6.21. $\qquad \square$

10.4 Boosting and Greedy Algorithms

In (10.1), both w_j and θ_j need to be learned from the training data. A popular algorithm to do so is boosting, which assumes the existence of an ERM algorithm $\mathcal{A}$ that can learn $\hat{\theta} = \mathcal{A}(\widetilde{\mathcal{S}}_n)$ from any weighted version of data $\widetilde{\mathcal{S}}_n = \{(\rho_i, X_i, Y_i) \colon i = 1, \ldots, n\}$ as follows:

$$\sum_{i=1}^n \rho_i \widetilde{L}(\psi(\hat{\theta}, X_i), Y_i) \leq \inf_{\theta \in \Theta} \sum_{i=1}^n \rho_i \widetilde{L}(\psi(\theta, X_i), Y_i) + \widetilde{\epsilon}, \qquad (10.14)$$

where $\rho_i \geq 0$, and for simplicity, we normalize ρ_i so that $\sum_i \rho_i = 1$. The learner $\mathcal{A}$ is often referred to as a weak learner (or base learner) in the boosting literature.

In boosting, we repeatedly generate modified data $\widetilde{\mathcal{S}}_n^j$ ($j = 1, 2, \ldots$) from the training data $\mathcal{S}_n$ and apply $\mathcal{A}$ to obtain θ_j. We then find weight w_j to form the additive model in (10.1). There are two commonly used weaker learners. In AdaBoost, classification weak learner is employed, where $\psi(\theta, X_i) \in \{\pm 1\}$ and $Y_i \in \{\pm 1\}$ are both binary, and

$$\widetilde{L}(\psi(\theta, X), Y) = \mathbb{1}(\psi(\theta, X) \neq Y).$$

For AdaBoost, each dataset $\widetilde{\mathcal{S}}_n^j$ is formed by adjusting the weights $\{\rho_i\}$. In gradient boosting, $\mathcal{A}$ is assumed to be a regression learner, with

$$\widetilde{L}(\psi(\theta, X), Y) = (\psi(\theta, X) - Y)^2.$$

For gradient boosting, each dataset $\widetilde{\mathcal{S}}_n^j$ is formed by adjusting the response $\{Y_i\}$. Both AdaBoost and gradient boosting may be regarded as greedy algorithms, and their convergence will be analyzed in this section. In fact, the convergence analysis shows that greedy algorithms approximately solve the L_1 regularization problem. One may then use the Rademacher complexity analysis of L_1 regularization to analyze the generalization behavior of greedy algorithms.

Algorithm 10.1 AdaBoost

Input: $\mathcal{S}_n$, Ψ
Output: $f^{(T)}(x)$
1 Let $f^{(0)}(x) = 0$
2 Let $\rho_1 = \cdots = \rho_n = 1/n$
3 **for** $t = 1, 2, \ldots, T$ **do**
4 $\quad$ Find θ_t by approximately solving
5 $\quad$ $\theta_t \approx \arg\min_{\theta \in \Theta} \sum_{i=1}^n \rho_i \mathbb{1}(\psi(\theta, X_i) Y_i \leq 0)$
6 $\quad$ Let $r_t = \sum_{i=1}^n \rho_i \psi(\theta_t, X_i) Y_i$
7 $\quad$ Let $w_t = \frac{1}{2} \ln((1 + r_t)/(1 - r_t))$
8 $\quad$ Let $\rho_i = \rho_i \cdot \exp(-w_t \psi(\theta_t, X_i) Y_i)$ for $i = 1, \ldots, n$.
9 $\quad$ Normalize ρ_i so that $\sum_{i=1}^n \rho_i = 1$
10 $\quad$ Let $f^{(t)}(x) = f^{(t-1)}(x) + w_t \psi(\theta_t, x)$
Return: $f^{(T)}(x)$

Theorem 10.29 *Assume that $\Psi = \Psi_\pm$, $\psi(\theta, x) \in \{\pm 1\}$, and $y \in \{\pm 1\}$. Then AdaBoost implements the greedy algorithm to minimize the loss function*

$$L(f(x), y) = \exp(-f(x)y).$$

That is, at each time t, AdaBoost (with exact minimization in Line 5 of Algorithm 10.1) solves the following problem:

$$[w_t, \theta_t] = \arg\min_{w, \theta} \sum_{i=1}^{n} e^{-(f^{(t-1)}(X_i) + w\psi(\theta, X_i))Y_i}.$$

Moreover, the prediction function $f^{(T)}$ obtained by Algorithm 10.1 satisfies

$$\frac{1}{n}\sum_{i=1}^{n} e^{-f^{(T)}(X_i)Y_i} \leq \prod_{t=1}^{T} \sqrt{1 - r_t^2}.$$

Proof Let

$$[\tilde{w}_t, \tilde{\theta}_t] = \arg\min_{w, \theta} \sum_{i=1}^{n} e^{-(f^{(t-1)}(X_i) + w\psi(\theta, X_i))Y_i}.$$

By the definition of ρ_i, we know that

$$[\tilde{w}_t, \tilde{\theta}_t] = \arg\min_{w \in \mathbb{R}, \theta \in \Theta} \sum_{i=1}^{n} \rho_i e^{-w\psi(\theta, X_i)Y_i}. \tag{10.15}$$

It follows that $\tilde{w}_t$ is the solution of

$$\tilde{w}_t = \arg\min_{w} \sum_{i=1}^{n} \rho_i \left[e^{-w} \frac{\psi(\tilde{\theta}_t, X_i)Y_i + 1}{2} + e^{w} \frac{1 - \psi(\tilde{\theta}_t, X_i)Y_i}{2} \right].$$

Taking derivative with respect to w at $w = \tilde{w}_t$, we obtain

$$\sum_{i=1}^{n} \rho_i \left[-e^{-\tilde{w}_t} \frac{\psi(\tilde{\theta}_t, X_i)Y_i + 1}{2} + e^{\tilde{w}_t} \frac{1 - \psi(\tilde{\theta}_t, X_i)Y_i}{2} \right] = 0.$$

Therefore if we let $\tilde{r}_t = \sum_{i=1}^{n} \rho_i \psi(\tilde{\theta}_t, X_i)Y_i$, then

$$-e^{-\tilde{w}_t}(1 + \tilde{r}_t) + e^{\tilde{w}_t}(1 - \tilde{r}_t) = 0.$$

This implies that

$$\tilde{w}_t = \frac{1}{2} \ln \frac{1 + \tilde{r}_t}{1 - \tilde{r}_t},$$

and

$$\sum_{i=1}^{n} \rho_i e^{-\tilde{w}_t \psi(\tilde{\theta}_t, X_i)Y_i} = \sqrt{1 - \tilde{r}_t^2}. \tag{10.16}$$

Since $\Psi = \Psi_{\pm}$, the parameter $\tilde{\theta}_t$ that achieves the smallest classification error also achieves the smallest $1 - \tilde{r}_t^2$. This means that we can take $\tilde{\theta}_t = \theta_t$ and $\tilde{w}_t = w_t$ to achieve the minimum of (10.15). This proves the first desired result. Since $\rho_i \propto \exp(-f^{(t-1)}(X_i)Y_i)$ at each iteration t, we obtain from (10.16) that

$$\frac{\sum_{i=1}^{n} e^{-f^{(t)}(X_i)Y_i}}{\sum_{i=1}^{n} e^{-f^{(t-1)}(X_i)Y_i}} \leq \sqrt{1 - r_t^2}.$$

By using induction on t, we obtain the second desired bound. $\qquad\square$

In practice, one often observes that the test performance of AdaBoost improves even after AdaBoost achieves zero-training error. This phenomenon can be explained by the fact that AdaBoost tries to minimize the margin under L_1 constraints. This can be seen from the following simple corollary.

Corollary 10.30 *Under the assumptions of Theorem 10.29, and assume further that Ψ has VC-dimension d. Let*

$$\|f^{(T)}\|_1 = \sum_{t=1}^{T} w_t.$$

Assume that for $t = 1, \ldots, T$, we have $r_t \geq r_0 > 0$ in Algorithm 10.1. Then there exists an absolute constant C so that with probability at least $1 - \delta$,

$$\mathbb{E}_{(X,Y)\sim\mathcal{D}}\mathbb{1}(f^{(T)}(X)Y \leq 0) \leq \underbrace{\frac{1.5}{n}\sum_{i=1}^{n}\mathbb{1}(f^{(T)}(X_i)Y_i \leq 1)}_{\text{margin error}}$$

$$+ C\frac{(\|f^{(T)}\|_1 + 1)^2 d\ln n \ln(n + \|f^{(T)}\|_1) + \ln(1/\delta)}{n},$$

where margin error is upper bounded by

$$\exp\left(1 - 0.4\sum_{t=1}^{T}\min(1, w_t^2)\right) \leq \exp\left(1 - \frac{T}{10}\min\left(2, \ln\frac{1+r_0}{1-r_0}\right)^2\right).$$

Proof We note that $w_t \geq 0$. We have

$$r_t = \frac{e^{2w_t} - 1}{e^{2w_t} + 1},$$

which implies that

$$\sqrt{1 - r_t^2} = \frac{2e^{w_t}}{e^{2w_t} + 1} \leq \frac{1}{1 + 0.5w_t^2} \leq e^{-0.4\min(w_t^2, 1)},$$

where we used $(e^x + e^{-x})/2 \geq 1 + 0.5x^2$ and $1 + 0.5x \geq e^{0.4x}$ when $x \in [0, 1]$. Therefore, Theorem 10.29 implies that

$$\frac{1}{n}\sum_{i=1}^{n}\mathbb{1}(f^{(T)}(X_i)Y_i \leq 1) \leq \frac{1}{n}\sum_{i=1}^{n}e^{-f^{(T)}(X_i)Y_i+1} \leq e^{1-0.4\sum_{t=1}^{T}\min(1, w_t^2)}. \quad (10.17)$$

We also note that from Sauer's lemma and Theorem 5.21, we know that there exists a constant $C_0 > 0$ so that for any $A > 0$,

$$\ln N(\mathcal{F}_{A,L_1}(\Psi), \epsilon, L_\infty(\mathcal{S}_n)) \leq \frac{C_0 A^2 d\ln n \ln(n + A/\epsilon)}{\epsilon^2}.$$

The multiplicative bound in Theorem 4.21 with $\gamma = 0.1$ implies that with probability at least $1 - \delta$, for any $f \in \mathcal{F}_{A,L_1}(\Psi)$, we have

$$0.81\mathbb{E}_{(X,Y)\sim\mathcal{D}}\mathbb{1}(f(X)Y \le 0) \le \frac{1}{n}\sum_{i=1}^{n}\mathbb{1}(f^{(T)}(X_i)Y_i \le 0.1)$$

$$+ O\left(\frac{A^2 d \ln n \ln(n+A) + \ln(1/\delta)}{n}\right),$$

where $O(\cdot)$ hides an absolute constant. Taking union bound over $A = 1, 2, \ldots$, with probability $1 - \delta/(A(A+1))$, we obtain that for all $A \in \{1, 2, \ldots\}$ and $f \in \mathcal{F}_{A,L_1}$, we have

$$0.81\mathbb{E}_{(X,Y)\sim\mathcal{D}}\mathbb{1}(f(X)Y \le 0) \le \frac{1}{n}\sum_{i=1}^{n}\mathbb{1}(f^{(T)}(X_i)Y_i \le 0.1)$$

$$+ O\left(\frac{A^2 d \ln n \ln(n+A) + \ln(1/\delta)}{n}\right).$$

Now we apply this bound to $f^{(T)}$ with $A = \lceil \|f\|_1 \rceil$, and use (10.17), and obtain the desired bound. $\qquad\square$

For simplicity, we assume that each $r_t < 1 - \delta$ for some $\delta > 0$. Otherwise, the problem itself becomes easy. If each time AdaBoost achieves error $r_t \ge r_0 > 0$, then $\|f^{(T)}\|_1$ grow linearly but the margin error of Corollary 10.30 decreases exponentially. This shows that the generalization performance of AdaBoost can still reduce even when the training error goes to zero, because the margin error can still decrease.

While AdaBoost implements the greedy algorithm for the exponential loss and binary classification problem, gradient boosting can be applied to arbitrary loss functions using a least squares base learner. The resulting method, described in Algorithm 10.2, is referred to as gradient boosting. We use $L_1'(f, y)$ to denote the gradient of $L(f, y)$ with respect to f, which is also referred to as functional gradient in the boosting literature when evaluated on the training data.

Algorithm 10.2 Gradient Boosting

Input: $\mathcal{S}_n$, Ψ, $L(\cdot, \cdot)$
Output: $f^{(T)}(x)$
1 Let $f^{(0)}(x) = 0$
2 **for** $t = 1, 2, \ldots, T$ **do**
3   Let $g_i = L_1'(f^{(t-1)}(X_i), Y_i)$ $(i = 1, \ldots, n)$ be the functional gradients
4   Solve for $[w_t, \theta_t] = \arg\min_{w\in\mathbb{R}, \theta\in\Theta}\sum_{i=1}^{n}[w\psi(\theta, X_i) + g_i]^2$
5   Let $f^{(t)}(x) = f^{(t-1)}(x) + w_t\psi(\theta_t, x)$
Return: $f^{(T)}(x)$

Boosting is closely related to L_1 regularization. In Corollary 10.30, L_1 regularization bound is used to estimate the generalization of AdaBoost. Moreover, a slight modification of gradient boosting, described in Algorithm 10.3, can also be used to solve L_1 constrained optimization problems.

Algorithm 10.3 Gradient Boosting for L_1 Constrained Optimization

---

Input: $\mathcal{S}_n$, Ψ, $L(\cdot, \cdot)$, γ, $\{\eta_t > 0\}$

Output: $f^{(T)}(x)$

1 Let $f^{(0)}(x) = 0$
2 **for** $t = 1, 2, \ldots, T$ **do**
3   Let $g_i = L_1'(f^{(t-1)}(X_i), Y_i)$ $(i = 1, \ldots, n)$ be the functional gradients
4   Solve for $\theta_t = \arg\min_{\theta \in \Theta} \sum_{i=1}^n [\gamma \eta_t \psi(\theta, X_i) + g_i]^2$
5   Let $f^{(t)}(x) = (1 - \eta_t) f^{(t-1)}(x) + \eta_t \psi(\theta_t, x)$

Return: $f^{(T)}(x)$

The following result shows that Algorithm 10.3 converges to the solution of L_1 regularization problem.

Theorem 10.31 *Assume that* $\sup_\theta \|\psi(\theta, \cdot)\|_{L_2(\mathcal{S}_n)} \leq B$, *and* $L(f, y)$ *is a* γ-*smooth convex function with respect to* f. *If we take* $\eta_t = 2/(t + 1)$ *in Algorithm 10.3, then*

$$\frac{1}{n} \sum_{i=1}^n L(f^{(t)}(X_i), Y_i) \leq \inf_{f \in \mathrm{CONV}(\Psi)} \frac{1}{n} \sum_{i=1}^n L(f(X_i), Y_i) + \frac{10\gamma B^2}{T + 1}.$$

Proof Consider

$$f(x) = \sum_{j=1}^m u_j \psi(\tilde{\theta}_j, x),$$

where $u_j \geq 0$, and $\sum_{j=1}^m u_j = 1$. We obtain from the definition of η_t that for all $j = 1, \ldots, m$,

$$2\eta_t \sum_{i=1}^n g_i \psi(\theta_t, X_i) + \gamma \eta_t^2 \sum_{i=1}^n \psi(\theta_t, X_i)^2$$

$$\leq 2\eta_t \sum_{i=1}^n g_i \psi(\tilde{\theta}_j, X_i) + \gamma \eta_t^2 \sum_{i=1}^n \psi(\tilde{\theta}_j, X_i)^2.$$

Now multiplying the inequality by u_j and then summing over j, we obtain

$$2\eta_t \sum_{i=1}^n g_i \psi(\theta_t, X_i) + \gamma \eta_t^2 \sum_{i=1}^n \psi(\theta_t, X_i)^2$$

$$\leq 2\eta_t \sum_{i=1}^n g_i \sum_{j=1}^m u_j \psi(\tilde{\theta}_j, X_i) + \gamma \eta_t^2 \sum_{j=1}^m u_j \sum_{i=1}^n \psi(\tilde{\theta}_j, X_i)^2.$$

Therefore,

$$\eta_t \sum_{i=1}^n g_i \psi(\theta_t, X_i) \leq \eta_t \sum_{i=1}^n g_i f(X_i) + \frac{n\gamma}{2} \eta_t^2 B^2. \tag{10.18}$$

We have

$$\sum_{i=1}^{n} L(f^{(t)}(X_i), Y_i) = \sum_{i=1}^{n} L((1 - \eta_t)f^{(t-1)}(X_i) + \eta_t \psi(\theta_t, X_i), Y_i)$$

$$\leq \sum_{i=1}^{n} \left[L(f^{(t-1)}(X_i), Y_i) + \eta_t g_i(\psi(\theta_t, X_i) - f^{(t-1)}(X_i)) \right]$$

$$+ \frac{\eta_t^2 \gamma}{2} \sum_{i=1}^{n} ((\psi(\theta_t, X_i) - f^{(t-1)}(X_i))^2$$

$$\leq \sum_{i=1}^{n} \left[L(f^{(t-1)}(X_i), Y_i) + \eta_t g_i(f(X_i) - f^{(t-1)}(X_i)) \right] + \frac{n\eta_t^2 \gamma B^2}{2} + \frac{n\eta_t^2 \gamma}{2} 4B^2$$

$$\leq \sum_{i=1}^{n} L(f^{(t-1)}(X_i), Y_i) + \eta_t(L(f(X_i), Y_i) - L(f^{(t-1)}(X_i), Y_i)) + \frac{5n\gamma\eta_t^2 B^2}{2}.$$

The first inequality used γ-smoothness of $L(f, y)$ with respect to f, so that $L(f', y) \leq L(f, y) + L_1'(f, y)(f' - f) + 0.5\gamma(f' - f)^2$. The second inequality used (10.18). The third inequality used the convex of $L(f, y)$ with respect to f, so that $L(f, y) + L_1'(f, y)(f' - f) \leq L(f', y)$. Let

$$\beta_t = \frac{1}{n} \sum_{i=1}^{n} L(f^{(t)}(X_i), Y_i) - \frac{1}{n} \sum_{i=1}^{n} L(f(X_i), Y_i),$$

then we have shown with $\eta_t = 2/(t+1)$,

$$\beta_t \leq \frac{t-1}{t+1} \beta_{t-1} + \frac{10\gamma B^2}{(t+1)^2}.$$

Now multiply by $t(t+1)$, and we have

$$(t+1)t\beta_t \leq (t-1)t\beta_{t-1} + 10\gamma B^2.$$

By summing over $t = 1, 2, 3, \ldots, T$, we obtain the desired bound. $\qquad \square$

Algorithm 10.3 can be extended to solve hard-constrained L_1 regularization problem of the form $\|w\|_1 \leq A$. However this requires knowing A in advance. One may also use gradient boosting to solve the sparse approximation problem in the more general setting without specifying A. While results can be obtained for the original gradient boosting algorithm in Algorithm 10.2, a stronger convergence result can be obtained for a slight modification referred to as the fully corrective gradient boosting algorithm (see Shalev-Shwartz et al., 2010).

Theorem 10.32 (Shalev-Shwartz et al., 2010) *Assume that $L(p, y)$ is convex and γ smooth in p. Then at time T, the solution $f^{(T)}$ of Algorithm 10.4 satisfies*

$$\sum_{i=1}^{n} L(f^{(T)}(X_i), Y_i) \leq \inf_{f \in \mathcal{F}_{L_1}(\Psi)} \left[\sum_{i=1}^{n} L(f(X_i), Y_i) + \frac{2\gamma \|f\|_1^2 B^2}{T} \right],$$

where $B^2 = \sup_\theta \sum_{i=1}^{n} \psi(\theta, X_i)^2$.

Algorithm 10.4 Fully Corrective Gradient Boosting

Input: $\mathcal{S}_n$, Ψ, $L(\cdot, \cdot)$
Output: $f^{(T)}(x)$
1 Let $f^{(0)}(x) = 0$
2 **for** $t = 1, 2, \ldots, T$ **do**
3   Let $g_i = L_1'(f^{(t-1)}(X_i), Y_i)$ $(i = 1, \ldots, n)$ be functional gradients
4   Solve for $[\alpha_t, \theta_t] = \arg\min_{\alpha \in \mathbb{R}, \theta \in \Theta} Q_t(\alpha, \theta)$,
5   where $Q_t(\alpha, \theta) = \sum_{i=1}^n [\alpha\psi(\theta, X_i) + g_i]^2$
6   Let $w^{(t)} = \arg\min_{[w_s]} \sum_{i=1}^n L\left(\sum_{s=1}^t w_s \psi(\theta_s, X_i), Y_i\right)$
7   Let $f^{(t)}(x) = \sum_{s=1}^t w_s^{(t)} \psi(\theta_s, x)$
   Return: $f^{(T)}(x)$

One can use the relationship of greedy algorithm and L_1 regularization to analyze the generalization behavior of boosting. By combining a convergence analysis of greedy algorithm in terms of L_1 norm, with generalization analysis using L_1 regularization, one can show the consistency of boosting procedures (Zhang and Yu, 2005). It is also possible to investigate the generalization of boosting using margin with respect to the L_1 norm, similar to Corollary 10.30 (also see Schapire et al. 1998) for AdaBoost. In addition to the L_∞-covering number analysis, one may also use Rademacher complexity to derive such a data-dependent margin bound. This leads to a $O(1/\sqrt{n})$ convergence rate instead of a $O(1/n)$ convergence rate.

Corollary 10.33 *Assume that $Y \in \{\pm 1\}$, and $\psi(\theta, x) \in [-1, 1]$. Then $\forall \gamma > 0$, with probability $1 - \delta$: for all $f(x) = \sum_j w_j \psi(\theta_j, x)$, we have*

$$\mathbb{E}_{\mathcal{D}} \mathbf{1}(f(X)Y \leq 0) \leq \frac{1}{n} \sum_{i=1}^n \mathbf{1}(f(X_i)Y_i \leq \gamma) + 4(1 + \gamma^{-1}\|w\|_1)R_n(\Psi_\pm, \mathcal{D})$$

$$+ (3 + 2\gamma^{-1}\|w\|_1)\left[\sqrt{\frac{\ln(2 + \log_2(1 + \|w\|_1/\gamma))^2)}{2n}} + \sqrt{\frac{\ln(1/\delta)}{n}}\right].$$

Proof Let $L(p, y) = \min(1, \max(0, 1 - py/\gamma))$, which is γ^{-1} Lipschitz. Let $A_0 = \gamma$, $B = 1$, and $M_0 = 1$ by using the fact that

$$\mathbf{1}(f(X), Y) \leq L(f(X), Y) \leq \mathbf{1}(f(X)Y \leq \gamma).$$

The result is a direct consequence of Corollary 10.14 .   □

10.5 Sparse Recovery Analysis

We have shown that it is possible to approximate the L_1 regularized solution by sparse solutions using greedy boosting. On the other hand, L_1 regularization has frequently been used as an approximation technique to solve the nonconvex L_0 regularization problem. Under appropriate conditions, it can be shown that such a convex relaxation leads to exact or approximate solutions to the nonconvex problem.

We consider the same linear model (9.19), in the fixed design setting and with w_* replaced by the symbol $\bar{w}$ so that subscripts are less cluttered. We assume that $\bar{w}$ is sparse. For convenience, we replace the general feature map $\psi(x)$ by x. We also rescale the feature vector and target by $1/\sqrt{n}$, so that the factor $1/n$ (which denotes the average over the training data) is absorbed into x and y.

In the subsequent discussions, we will use the common convention in the high-dimensional statistics literature, so that symbols may carry meanings not consistent with other sections. Specifically, we will let X denote an $n \times p$ design matrix, and Y denote an n-dimensional observation vector. The model parameter w is p-dimensional. We assume the following sparse linear regression model:

$$Y = X\bar{w} + \epsilon, \tag{10.19}$$

where ϵ is an n-dimensional zero-mean noise vector with independent components. Note that due to the rescaling, we will assume that columns of X are bounded in 2-norms. The corresponding proper scaling of ϵ is to assume that each $\sqrt{n}\epsilon_i$ is σ sub-Gaussian.

We also assume that $\|\bar{w}\|_0 \ll p$. It is known that in this case, the complexity of learning $\bar{w}$ is $O(\|\bar{w}\|_0 \ln p)$ instead of $O(p)$ (see Example 10.5). We allow $p \gg n$, and in the statistics literature, this situation is referred to as *high dimensional*. Instead of solving the sparsity problem using L_0 regularization, one often employs the following L_1 regularization problem (Lasso) as a surrogate:

$$\hat{w} = \arg\min_w Q_{L_1}(w); \quad Q_{L_1}(w) = \frac{1}{2}\|Xw - Y\|_2^2 + \lambda\|w\|_1, \tag{10.20}$$

where $\lambda > 0$ is an appropriately chosen regularization parameter.

Under appropriate conditions, one can recover the true sparse parameter $\bar{w}$ using Lasso. This is referred to as the *sparse recovery* problem. In sparse recovery, theoretical questions we ask for Lasso is whether the solution $\hat{w}$ of Lasso with an appropriately chosen λ leads to a good estimate of $\bar{w}$ in the following sense:

- (Support Recovery) Does Lasso find the correct feature set: $\text{supp}(\hat{w}) = \text{supp}(\bar{w})$? Moreover, we say the Lasso solution is *sign consistent* if $\text{supp}(\hat{w}) = \text{supp}(\bar{w})$ and $\text{sign}(\hat{w}_j) = \text{sign}(\bar{w}_j)$ when $j \in \text{supp}(\bar{w})$.
- (Parameter Recovery) How good is the parameter estimation, or how small is $\|\hat{w} - \bar{w}\|_2$?

To answer these questions, we need to analyze the solution of the Lasso problem (10.20) using its KKT conditions at $\hat{w}$, which provide more precise characterizations of the solution than those from the empirical process analysis studied earlier. From the standard convex analysis (see Rockafellar, 2015), a solution of (10.20) satisfies the first-order optimality equation (KKT condition) in Proposition 10.34.

Proposition 10.34 *Let $\hat{F} = \text{supp}(\hat{w})$, then $\hat{w}$ is a solution of (10.20) if and only if*

$$X_{\hat{F}}^\top(X_{\hat{F}}\hat{w}_{\hat{F}} - Y) + \lambda\text{sign}(\hat{w})_{\hat{F}} = 0,$$
$$X_j^\top(X_{\hat{F}}\hat{w}_{\hat{F}} - Y) \in [-\lambda, \lambda] \qquad (j \notin \hat{F}),$$

where $X_{\hat{F}}$ contains columns of X with columns in $\hat{F}$, and X_j is the jth column of X.

Note that the first condition in the proposition implies that $\hat{w}$ is a solution with support restricted to $\hat{F}$:

$$Q_{L_1}(\hat{w}) = \min_w Q_{L_1}(w) \quad \text{subject to } \text{supp}(w) \subset \hat{F}.$$

In general, Lasso solutions may not be unique. For example, when $j \neq j' \in \hat{F}$ such that $X_j = X_{j'}$, then for any solution $\hat{w}$ such that $\hat{w}_j \neq 0$, we can construct $\tilde{w}$ so that $\tilde{w}_k = \hat{w}_k$ when $k \notin \{j, j'\}$, $\tilde{w}_j = 0$ and $\tilde{w}_{j'} = \hat{w}_j + \hat{w}_{j'}$. Then it is easy to show that $\tilde{w} \neq \hat{w}$ is also a Lasso solution. However, under suitable assumptions, we can also obtain the uniqueness of the Lasso solution.

Proposition 10.35 Let $\hat{F} = \text{supp}(\hat{w})$. If $X_{\hat{F}}^\top X_{\hat{F}}$ is positive definite, and

$$X_{\hat{F}}^\top(X_{\hat{F}}\hat{w}_{\hat{F}} - Y) + \lambda\text{sign}(\hat{w})_{\hat{F}} = 0,$$
$$X_j^\top(X_{\hat{F}}\hat{w}_{\hat{F}} - Y) \in (-\lambda, \lambda) \qquad (j \notin \hat{F}),$$

then $\hat{w}$ is the unique solution of (10.20).

Proof We only need to show that for any $\Delta w \neq 0$, $\hat{w} + \Delta w$ is not a solution. For $j \notin \hat{F}$, we define

$$\lambda_j' = |X_j^\top(X_{\hat{F}}\hat{w}_{\hat{F}} - Y)| < \lambda,$$

and let

$$Q_{L_1}'(w) = 0.5\|Xw - Y\|_2^2 + \lambda\sum_{j\in\hat{F}}|w_j| + \sum_{j\notin\hat{F}}\lambda_j'|w_j|.$$

Since there exists a subgradient $\nabla Q_{L_1}'(\hat{w}) = 0$, we know that $\hat{w}$ achieves the minimum of $Q_{L_1}'(w)$, and thus $Q_{L_1}'(\hat{w}+\Delta w) \geq Q_{L_1}'(\hat{w}) = Q_{L_1}(\hat{w})$. Now, if $\Delta w_j \neq 0$ for some $j \notin \hat{F}$, then $Q_{L_1}(\hat{w}+\Delta w) > Q_{L_1}'(\hat{w}+\Delta w) \geq Q_{L_1}(\hat{w})$, and thus $\hat{w}+\Delta w$ is not a solution of the original Lasso problem. If $\Delta w_j = 0$ for all $j \notin \hat{F}$, then $\text{supp}(\hat{w} + \Delta w) \subset \hat{F}$. However, the positive definiteness of $X_{\hat{F}}^\top X_{\hat{F}}$ means that $Q_{L_1}(w)$ is strictly convex when the support is restricted to $\hat{F}$, and hence the solution (with support restricted to $\hat{F}$) is unique. This implies that $\Delta w = 0$. $\square$

One important property of Lasso is that under suitable conditions, the method can find the set of nonzero elements $\text{supp}(\hat{w})$ that equals $\text{supp}(\bar{w})$. This property is referred to as *feature selection consistency* for the support recovery problem.

Proposition 10.36 Let $\bar{F} = \text{supp}(\bar{w})$. Let

$$\tilde{w}_{\bar{F}} = \bar{w}_{\bar{F}} + (X_{\bar{F}}^\top X_{\bar{F}})^{-1}(-\lambda\text{sign}(\bar{w})_{\bar{F}} + X_{\bar{F}}^\top\epsilon)$$

and $\tilde{w}_j = 0$ for $j \notin \bar{F}$. Assume that $X_{\bar{F}}^\top X_{\bar{F}}$ is positive definite, and

$$\text{sign}(\tilde{w}_{\bar{F}}) = \text{sign}(\bar{w}_{\bar{F}}),$$
$$|X_j^\top[-\lambda X_{\bar{F}}(X_{\bar{F}}^\top X_{\bar{F}})^{-1}\text{sign}(\bar{w})_{\bar{F}} + (X_{\bar{F}}(X_{\bar{F}}^\top X_{\bar{F}})^{-1}X_{\bar{F}}^\top - I)\epsilon]| < \lambda \quad (\forall j \notin \bar{F}).$$

Then $\hat{w} = \tilde{w}$ is the unique solution of (10.20) that is sign consistent.

Proof We note that for $j \notin \bar{F}$,

$$X_j^\top(X_{\bar{F}}\tilde{w}_{\bar{F}} - Y) = X_j^\top[-\lambda X_{\bar{F}}(X_{\bar{F}}^\top X_{\bar{F}})^{-1}\text{sign}(\bar{w})_{\bar{F}} + (X_{\bar{F}}(X_{\bar{F}}^\top X_{\bar{F}})^{-1}X_{\bar{F}}^\top - I)\epsilon].$$

By the assumption of the proposition, we have

$$|X_j^\top(X_{\bar{F}}\tilde{w}_{\bar{F}} - Y)| < \lambda \quad (\forall j \notin \bar{F}).$$

Moreover, we have

$$X_{\bar{F}}^\top(X_{\bar{F}}\tilde{w}_{\bar{F}} - Y) + \lambda\text{sign}(\tilde{w})_{\bar{F}} = X_{\bar{F}}^\top(X_{\bar{F}}\tilde{w}_{\bar{F}} - X_{\bar{F}}\bar{w}_{\bar{F}} - \epsilon) + \lambda\text{sign}(\bar{w})_{\bar{F}} = 0.$$

Therefore $\tilde{w}$ satisfies the KKT conditions of Proposition 10.34, and thus is a solution of the Lasso problem. Proposition 10.35 implies that $\tilde{w}$ is the unique solution of the Lasso problem. $\square$

Theorem 10.37 *Let* $\bar{F} = \text{supp}(\bar{w})$. *Assume that* $X_{\bar{F}}^\top X_{\bar{F}}$ *is positive definite, and*

$$\mu = \sup_{j \notin \bar{F}} |X_j^\top X_{\bar{F}}(X_{\bar{F}}^\top X_{\bar{F}})^{-1}\text{sign}(\bar{w})_{\bar{F}}| < 1.$$

Assume that we choose a sufficiently large λ *so that*

$$\lambda > (1 - \mu)^{-1}\sup_{j \notin \bar{F}}|X_j^\top(X_{\bar{F}}(X_{\bar{F}}^\top X_{\bar{F}})^{-1}X_{\bar{F}}^\top - I)\epsilon|.$$

If the weight $\bar{w}$ *is sufficiently large,*

$$\min_{j \in \bar{F}}|\bar{w}_j| > \|(X_{\bar{F}}^\top X_{\bar{F}})^{-1}\|_{\infty \to \infty}(\lambda + \|X_{\bar{F}}^\top\epsilon\|_\infty),$$

then the solution of (10.20) *is unique and sign consistent. Here* $\|M\|_{\infty \to \infty} = \sup_u[\|Mu\|_\infty/\|u\|_\infty]$ *is the maximum absolute row sum of* M.

Proof The proof is just a verification of Proposition 10.36. Since

$$\|(X_{\bar{F}}^\top X_{\bar{F}})^{-1}(-\lambda\text{sign}(\bar{w})_{\bar{F}} + X_{\bar{F}}^\top\epsilon)\|_\infty \leq \|(X_{\bar{F}}^\top X_{\bar{F}})^{-1}\|_{\infty \to \infty}(\lambda + \|X_{\bar{F}}^\top\epsilon\|_\infty),$$

we know that $\text{sign}(\tilde{w}_j) = \text{sign}(\bar{w}_j)$ for all $j \in \bar{F}$. This verifies the first condition. The second condition can be similarly verified as follows.

$$|X_j^\top[-\lambda X_{\bar{F}}(X_{\bar{F}}^\top X_{\bar{F}})^{-1}\text{sign}(\bar{w})_{\bar{F}} + (X_{\bar{F}}(X_{\bar{F}}^\top X_{\bar{F}})^{-1}X_{\bar{F}}^\top - I)\epsilon]|$$
$$\leq \mu\lambda + (1 - \mu)\lambda < \lambda,$$

where the inequality used the assumptions on μ and λ. This verifies the second condition. $\square$

If $\mu < 1$, then in order for the theorem to apply, we only need to choose a small λ when ϵ is small for the first condition to hold. When λ is small enough, then the second condition will also hold. Therefore the result means that given any $\bar{w}$, if $\mu < 1$, then as long as the noise ϵ is sufficiently small, we can obtain sign consistency using Lasso. The requirement of $\mu < 1$ is called the *irrepresentable condition* (Zhao and Yu, 2006), which is sufficient for the feature selection consistency of Lasso.

Example 10.38 It is known that if elements of $\sqrt{n}X$ have iid standard normal distributions, then for any fixed $\bar{w}$, such that $\|\bar{w}\|_0 = s$, the irrepresentable condition holds with high probability when $n = \Omega(s \ln p)$, where $\bar{w}$ is independent of X (see Exercise 10.7).

A stronger condition (*mutual incoherence condition*) guarantees support recovery for all $\bar{w}$ such that $\|\bar{w}\|_0 \leq s$. It assumes that $\sup_{i \neq j} |X_i^\top X_j| < 1/(2s - 1)$ when we normalize columns of X so that $\|X_i\|_2 = 1$ for all $i \in [p]$. Under this condition, the irrepresentable condition holds for all $\|\bar{w}\|_0 \in \mathbb{R}^p$ such that $\|\bar{w}\|_0 \leq s$. However, this stronger condition is only satisfied with $n = \Omega(s^2 \ln p)$ (see Exercise 10.8).

A slightly weaker condition $\mu \leq 1$ is necessary for the feature selection consistency of Lasso with sufficiently small noise ϵ. That is, when $\mu > 1$, we have the following inconsistency result of Lasso sated in Proposition 10.39.

Proposition 10.39 *Let $\bar{F} = \mathrm{supp}(\bar{w})$. Assume that $X_{\bar{F}}^\top X_{\bar{F}}$ is positive definite, and*

$$\mu = \sup_{j \notin \bar{F}} |X_j^\top (X_{\bar{F}}^\top X_{\bar{F}})^{-1} \mathrm{sign}(\bar{w})_{\bar{F}}| > 1.$$

Then for sufficiently small ϵ,

$$|X_j^\top [-\lambda X_{\bar{F}} (X_{\bar{F}}^\top X_{\bar{F}})^{-1} \mathrm{sign}(\bar{w})_{\bar{F}} + X_{\bar{F}} (X_{\bar{F}}^\top X_{\bar{F}})^{-1} X_{\bar{F}}^\top \epsilon]| > \lambda$$

for some $j \notin \bar{F}$. This implies that Lasso is not sign consistent.

Assume that $\mu < 1$. If the noise ϵ is non-stochastic, the conditions of Theorem 10.37 can be satisfied when ϵ is small. For stochastic zero-mean noise, the conditions can be satisfied when n is large, as shown in the Theorem 10.37.

Theorem 10.40 *Let $\bar{F} = \mathrm{supp}(\bar{w})$. Assume that the columns are normalized so that $\sup_j \|X_j\|_2^2 \leq B^2$ and (with the corresponding proper scaling) components of $\sqrt{n}\epsilon$ are independent zero-mean σ sub-Gaussian noise: $\ln \mathbb{E} e^{\lambda \epsilon_i} \leq \lambda^2 \sigma^2/(2n)$. Assume that $X_{\bar{F}}^\top X_{\bar{F}}$ is positive definite, and*

$$\mu = \sup_{j \notin \bar{F}} |X_j^\top X_{\bar{F}} (X_{\bar{F}}^\top X_{\bar{F}})^{-1} \mathrm{sign}(\bar{w})_{\bar{F}}| < 1.$$

Given $\delta \in (0,1)$, assume we choose a sufficiently large λ so that

$$\lambda > (1-\mu)^{-1}\sigma B\sqrt{\frac{2\ln(2p/\delta)}{n}},$$

$$\min_{j \in \bar{F}} |\bar{w}_j| > \|(X_{\bar{F}}^\top X_{\bar{F}})^{-1}\|_{\infty \to \infty}\left(\lambda + \sigma B\sqrt{\frac{2\ln(2p/\delta)}{n}}\right).$$

Then with probability at least $1 - \delta$, the solution of (10.20) is unique and sign consistent.

Proof Note that the sub-Gaussian probability tail inequality (Corollary 2.26) implies that for each fixed X_j, we have: if $j \in \bar{F}$, then

$$\Pr[|X_j^\top \epsilon| \geq \epsilon_0] \leq 2e^{-n\epsilon_0^2/(2B^2\sigma^2)},$$

and if $j \notin \bar{F}$,

$$\Pr[|X_j^\top(P_{\bar{F}} - I)\epsilon| \geq \epsilon_0] \leq 2e^{-n\epsilon_0^2/(2B^2\sigma^2)},$$

with $P_{\bar{F}} = X_{\bar{F}}(X_{\bar{F}}^\top X_{\bar{F}})^{-1}X_{\bar{F}}^\top$ denoting the projection matrix to the subspace spanned by X_j $(j \in \bar{F})$. Therefore by taking the union bound for $j = 1, \ldots, p$, we obtain the following inequalities. With probability at least $1 - \delta$,

$$\|X_j^\top \epsilon\|_\infty \leq \sigma B\sqrt{\frac{2\ln(2p/\delta)}{n}} \quad (j \in \bar{F}),$$

$$\|X_j^\top(P_{\bar{F}} - I)\epsilon\|_\infty \leq \sigma B\sqrt{\frac{2\ln(2p/\delta)}{n}} \quad (j \notin \bar{F}).$$

We can now verify that the conditions of Theorem 10.37 hold. This implies the desired result. $\qquad\square$

It is also possible to study the support recovery question without sign consistency, which leads to a slightly weaker condition. For parameter recovery, we often employ a condition that is weaker than the irrepresentable condition, referred to as the *restricted isometry property* (RIP) (Candes and Tao, 2005). The RIP requires the smallest eigenvalue of the matrix $X_F^\top X_F$ to be bounded away from zero for all subsets F such that $|F| \leq \text{const} \times \|\bar{w}\|_0$. A similar condition, referred to as the *restrictive eigenvalue condition* (RE), can be stated as follows.

Definition 10.41 (RE) An $n \times p$ matrix X satisfies the restricted eigenvalue condition $\text{RE}(F, c_0)$ for $F \subset [p]$ if the following quantity is nonzero:

$$\kappa_{\text{RE}}(F, c_0) = \min_{w \neq 0, \|w\|_1 \leq c_0\|w_F\|_1} \frac{\|Xw\|_2}{\|w\|_2}.$$

Under this condition, we have the following parameter estimation bound.

Theorem 10.42 *Let $\bar{F} = \text{supp}(\bar{w})$. Assume that the columns are normalized so that $\sup_j \|X_j\|_2 \leq B$ and (with the corresponding proper scaling) components of $\sqrt{n}\epsilon$ are independent zero-mean σ sub-Gaussian noise: $\ln \mathbb{E}e^{\lambda \epsilon_i} \leq \lambda^2\sigma^2/(2n)$.*

Assume that $\lambda \geq 2\sigma B\sqrt{\frac{2\ln(2p/\delta)}{n}}$. *Then with probability at least* $1-\delta$, *the solution of* (10.20) *satisfies*

$$\|\hat{w} - \bar{w}\|_2^2 \leq \frac{16\lambda^2\|\bar{w}\|_0}{\kappa_{\mathrm{RE}}(\bar{F}, 4)^2}.$$

Proof Let $\hat{w} = \bar{w} + \Delta\hat{w}$. From

$$\frac{1}{2}\|X\hat{w} - Y\|_2^2 + \lambda\|\hat{w}\|_1 \leq \frac{1}{2}\|X\bar{w} - Y\|_2^2 + \lambda\|\bar{w}\|_1,$$

we obtain

$$\frac{1}{2}\|X\Delta\hat{w}\|_2^2 - \epsilon^\top X\Delta\hat{w} + \lambda\|\hat{w}\|_1 - \lambda\|\bar{w}_{\bar{F}}\|_1 \leq 0. \tag{10.21}$$

From Corollary 2.26, and a union bound over $X_j^\top \epsilon$ for $j \in [p]$, we obtain the following sub-Gaussian tail probability inequality. With probability at least $1-\delta$,

$$\|\epsilon^\top X\|_\infty \leq \sigma B\sqrt{\frac{2\ln(2p/\delta)}{n}} \leq \lambda/2. \tag{10.22}$$

We obtain

$$\frac{1}{2}\|X\Delta\hat{w}\|_2^2 + \frac{\lambda}{2}\|\Delta\hat{w}\|_1$$
$$\leq \frac{1}{2}\|X\Delta\hat{w}\|_2^2 - \epsilon^\top X\Delta w + \lambda\|\Delta\hat{w}\|_1$$
$$\leq \frac{1}{2}\|X\Delta\hat{w}\|_2^2 - \epsilon^\top X\Delta w + \lambda\|\hat{w}\|_1 - \lambda\|\bar{w}_{\bar{F}}\|_1 + 2\lambda\|\Delta\hat{w}_{\bar{F}}\|_1$$
$$\leq 2\lambda\|\Delta\hat{w}_{\bar{F}}\|_1.$$

The first inequality used (10.22). The second inequality used the triangle inequality for $\|\cdot\|_1$ and $\hat{w}_{\bar{F}^c} = \Delta\hat{w}_{\bar{F}^c}$. The third inequality used (10.21). This implies the RE condition $\|\Delta\hat{w}\|_1 \leq 4\|\Delta\hat{w}_{\bar{F}}\|_1$. Therefore, we obtain

$$\frac{\kappa_{\mathrm{RE}}(\bar{F}, 4)}{2}\|\Delta\hat{w}\|_2^2 \leq 2\lambda\|\Delta\hat{w}_{\bar{F}}\|_1 \leq 2\lambda\sqrt{|\bar{F}|}\|\Delta\hat{w}\|_2.$$

This proves the desired bound. $\square$

It is also known that for random Gaussian matrices, RE (or RIP) is satisfied uniformly for all $\bar{F} = \mathrm{supp}(\bar{w})$ such that $\|\bar{w}\|_0 \leq s$ with large probability when $n = \Omega(s\ln p)$. This sample size requirement is weaker than that of the mutual incoherence condition in Example 10.38, which holds only when $n = \Omega(s^2\ln p)$. Moreover, the RE (or RIP) condition does not imply irrepresentable condition, and thus under RE (or RIP), Lasso may not necessarily select features consistently.

Sparse recovery results similar to those of Lasso can also be obtained using greedy algorithms, both for support recovery and for parameter recovery. For example, such results can be found in Tropp (2004) and Zhang (2009a, 2011).

10.6 Historical and Bibliographical Remarks

Additive models have been extensively studied in statistics (Friedman and Stuetzle, 1981; Huber, 1985; Buja et al., 1989), and more recently, sparse additive models were studied explicitly by Ravikumar et al. (2009). Two-layer neural networks can also be regarded as special cases of additive models. It is known that many additive model families are sufficiently large so that they are universal function approximators. For example, it is known that both boosted shallow decision trees and two-layer neural networks are universal function approximators.

The L_0 regularization method is a natural solution to the subset selection (variable selection) problem in classical statistics, where the goal is to choose a subset of the variables to fit the data. The subset selection problem can be regarded as a model selection problem, where each model corresponds to a subset of features. Model selection criteria such as AIC (Akaike, 1974) or BIC (Schwarz, 1978) can be applied. In the context of subset selection, AIC is closely related to the C_p criterion of Mallows (2000), which has also been used frequently in the statistics literature. The use of L_1 regularization as an alternative to L_0 regularization for variable selection has been popularized by the seminal work of Tibshirani (1996), where L_1 regularization is referred to as Lasso. This method is also referred to as basis pursuit (Chen et al., 2001) in the engineering literature.

In the machine learning literature, the Rademacher complexity of convex hull and L_1 regularization was first used by Koltchinskii and Panchenko (2002) to analyze model combination, and its simplicity helped the quick popularization of the Rademacher complexity as one of the main techniques for generalization analysis in supervised learning problems. The analysis presented in Section 10.2 follows this approach.

Entropy regularization can be regarded as a smoothed upper bound of convex hull regularization. Its use in machine learning appeared first in the online learning literature, and referred to as *multiplicative updates* (see Littlestone and Warmuth, 1994; Littlestone, 1988), which was used to combine a finite number of experts. It was shown that the polynomial dependency in the number of experts is needed with additive updates (corresponding to L_2 regularization), while logarithmic dependency in the number of experts can be achieved using multiplicative updates (corresponding to entropy regularization). The situation is analogous to Example 10.9. The connection of multiplicative update and entropy regularization was explicitly discussed in Zhang et al. (2002). The analysis of entropy regularization in the batch learning setting is often referred to as PAC-Bayes analysis (McAllester, 1999). The results stated in Theorem 10.18 can be found in Zhang (2006). In recent years, there has been renewed interest in entropy-regularization, due to the mutual information based generalization bound stated in Corollary 10.22. Although the bound is a direct consequence of previously known results, the analysis allows some additional applications (see Russo and Zou, 2016, 2019; Xu and Raginsky, 2017).

In the statistics literature, greedy algorithms have been used in projection pursuit and matching pursuit (Friedman and Stuetzle, 1981; Huber, 1985; Mallat and Zhang, 1993). The convergence analysis of greedy algorithm in the convex hull class (similar to Theorem 10.31) was obtained first by Jones (1992) for least squares regression, and later extended by Li and Barron (1999), Zhang (2003b), and Barron et al. (2008) for other loss functions. The method of greedy approximation in the convex hull of a function class is also referred to as Frank Wolfe's algorithm in the optimization literature (Frank and Wolfe, 1956; Clarkson, 2010).

The related boosting algorithms were pioneered by Freund and Schapire (1997) from the point of view of combining weak learners (see Theorem 10.29). Its connection to greedy algorithm was observed by Friedman et al. (2000), and this insight was further developed by Friedman (2001) into gradient boosting, which has been widely used in practical applications. The margin analysis of boosting in Corollary 10.30 was first developed by Schapire et al. (1998) and later by Koltchinskii and Panchenko (2002). The connection of boosting and L_1 regularization was explored by Zhang and Yu (2005) to prove the consistency of boosting procedure.

The sparse recovery problem was initially investigated for the compressed sensing problem (Donoho, 2006), where the goal is to reconstruct a sparse signal from its random projections. The problem can be regarded as solving a sparse regularized least squares regression problem, and both greedy algorithm and L_1 regularization can be used to recover the sparse signal. Since the signal dimension can be significantly larger than the number of examples, the theory is often referred to as high-dimensional statistical analysis (Wainwright, 2019). The support recovery of L_1 regularization in Theorem 10.37 under the *irrepresentable condition* was due to Zhao and Yu (2006), and a similar analysis was given by Tropp (2006) around the same time. The asymptotic properties of irrepresentable condition was investigated by Wainwright (2009).

For sparse least squares problem, it was shown in a seminal work (Candes and Tao, 2005) that a weaker condition, referred to as the RIP condition, can be used to obtain parameter estimation bounds in L_2-norm. This condition has been generalized to handle other sparse estimation problems. The RE condition introduced in Bickel et al. (2009) can be considered as a variant of RIP. Other variations, such as conditions suitable for obtaining estimation results in L_p-norms, can be found in Zhang (2009b).

Both support recovery and parameter recovery results can be established for greedy algorithms under conditions that are similar to irrepresentable condition (for support recovery) and RIP (for parameter estimation) (Tropp, 2004; Zhang, 2009a, 2011). In addition to L_1 regularization, which is convex, some nonconvex regularization methods have also been proposed in the literature (Fan and Li, 2001; Zhang, 2010). It was shown that by using appropriate numerical algorithms that can take advantage of the sparsity structure, one can solve nonconvex formulations, and obtain support recovery results under RIP-like conditions (Zhang, 2010; Zhang and Zhang, 2012).

Exercises

10.1 In Example 10.9, assume that the vectors $[\psi(X)\colon X \in \mathcal{S}_n]$ are orthogonal for $\psi(X) \in \Psi$. Derive a lower bound for the Rademacher complexity of $\mathcal{F}_{A,L_2}(\Psi)$ via direct calculation.

10.2 Let $w_* = e_1 \in \mathbb{R}^d$. Consider $\psi(x) = [\psi_1(x), \ldots, \psi_d(x)] \in \mathbb{R}^d$ such that for observations $\{(X_1, Y_1), \ldots, (X_n, Y_n)\}$, $n^{-1/2}[\psi_j(X_1), \ldots, \psi_j(X_n)]$ are d orthonormal vectors in $\mathbb{R}^n$ $(j = 1, \ldots, d)$, and $Y_i = w_*^\top \psi(X_i) + \epsilon_i$, where $\epsilon_i \sim N(0, \sigma^2)$ $(i = 1, \ldots, n)$ are zero-mean noises. Consider ridge regression:

$$\hat{w}(\lambda) = \arg\min_w \left[\frac{1}{n} \sum_{i=1}^n (w^\top \psi(X_i) - Y_i)^2 + \lambda \|w\|_2^2 \right].$$

Find the optimal λ so that

$$\mathbb{E}_\epsilon \|\hat{w}(\lambda) - w_*\|_2^2$$

is minimized. Compute the minimum value.

10.3 In the previous example. Consider the Lasso regression:

$$\hat{w}(\lambda) = \frac{1}{n} \sum_{i=1}^n (w^\top \psi(X_i) - Y_i)^2 + \lambda \|w\|_1.$$

For $\lambda > 0$, find an upper of

$$\mathbb{E}_\epsilon \|\hat{w}(\lambda) - w_*\|_2^2.$$

Find λ to approximately minimize the upper bound with logarithmic dependency on d, and compare to that of the ridge regression.

10.4 Consider the uniform convergence bound in Theorem 10.4. Let $\{1, \ldots, m\} = J_1 \cup \cdots \cup J_g$ be a nonoverlapping partition of $\{1, \ldots, m\}$ into g groups of size m/g each (we assume m/g is an integer). Let H contain the subsets of $\{1, \ldots, m\}$ that can be expressed as the union of one or more groups $\{J_\ell\}$. That is, if $J \in H$, then for all $\ell = 1, \ldots, g$, either $J_\ell \subset J$ or $J_\ell \cap J = \emptyset$.

In group sparsity, we consider only the sparse models indexed by $F \in H$.

- Derive a uniform convergence bound for group sparsity, where we consider a uniform bound that holds for all w and F with $\operatorname{supp}(w) \subset F$.
- Compare this bound to the sparse learning bound of Theorem 10.4, and derive an estimation method in (10.5) with $r(F)$ obtained using this bound. Explain when group sparsity performs better.

10.5 Use the Rademacher complexity of constrained entropy regularization in Corollary 10.17, and the same techniques in the proof of Corollary 10.14 for the following.

- Derive a data-dependent bound that holds uniformly for all $A > 0$.
- Use the bound to derive an oracle inequality for the soft regularization version of the Gibbs algorithm, and compare the result to Theorem 10.18.

10.6 Prove Proposition 10.39.

10.7 Consider Theorem 10.37. Assume that $\sqrt{n}X$ is an $n \times p$ random matrix, with iid standard Gaussian entries, and $\bar{F}$ is independent of X. Show that there exists an absolute constant $c_0 > 0$ so that if

$$n \geq c_0 |\bar{F}| \ln(p),$$

the irrepresentable condition $\mu < 1$ holds with probability at least 0.5.

10.8 Consider Theorem 10.37 with columns of X normalized: $\|X_i\|_2 = 1$ for all $i \in [p]$.

- Show that if the mutual incoherence condition $\sup_{i \neq j} |X_i^\top X_j| < 1/(2s-1)$ holds for some integer $s \geq 1$, then the irrepresentable condition holds for all $\bar{w}$ such that $\|\bar{w}\|_0 \leq s$.
- Show that if columns of X_i are normalized from X' where X' is an $n \times p$ random matrix with iid standard Gaussian entries, then the mutual incoherence condition holds with $n = \Omega(s^2 \ln p)$.

11

Analysis of Neural Networks

The idea of neural networks (NNs) can be dated back to the 1960s, and the key computational procedures for neural networks using stochastic gradient descent was developed in the 1980s. However, the training of neural networks was quite costly, and large-scale training of neural networks has only become practical with the advance of GPU computing in the 2010s.

A major difficulty to analyzing neural networks is its nonconvexity, and many of its empirically observed properties have not been fully explained by theory. This chapter presents some known theoretical results for neural networks, including some theoretical analysis that has been developed recently. While a general theory of neural networks is still under development, we will cover some existing results, including function approximation results and generalization analysis. In particular, we show that neural networks can be analyzed both using the kernel analysis of Chapter 9, and the L_1 regularization-based analysis of Chapter 10.

11.1 Introduction to Neural Networks

The simplest neural networks are two-layer neural networks that are closely related to additive models. With real-valued output, and d-dimensional input vector $x \in \mathbb{R}^d$, such two-layer neural networks can be written as follows as an additive model in (10.1):

$$f_m(w, x) = \sum_{j=1}^{m} u_j h(\theta_j^\top x + b_j), \qquad (11.1)$$

where $x \in \mathbb{R}^d$, $\theta_j \in \mathbb{R}^d$, $b_j \in \mathbb{R}$, $u_j \in \mathbb{R}$, and $w = \{[u_j, \theta_j, b_j] : j = 1, \ldots, m\}$. The function $h(\cdot)$ is referred to as an activation function, and some popular choices include rectified linear unit (ReLU) $h(z) = \max(0, z)$ and sigmoid $h(z) = 1/(1 + e^{-z})$ as shown in Figure 11.1.

In practice, the model parameters w are often trained using stochastic gradient descent (SGD). Since a two-layer neural network can be regarded as an additive model, we may apply the generalization analysis in Chapter 10 directly. Similar to kernel methods, it is known that two-layer neural networks are universal function approximators (see Section 11.2).

More generally, we may define a K-layer fully connected deep neural network with real-valued output as follows. Let $m^{(0)} = d$ and $m^{(K)} = 1$; we recursively define

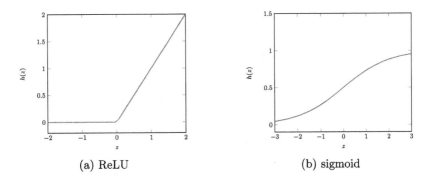

(a) ReLU   (b) sigmoid

Figure 11.1 Neural network activation functions

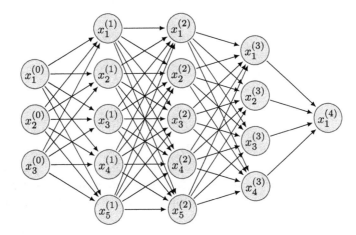

Figure 11.2 Four-layer fully connected neural network

$$x_j^{(0)} = x_j \quad (j = 1, \ldots, m^{(0)}),$$

$$x_j^{(k)} = h\left(\sum_{j'=1}^{m^{(k-1)}} \theta_{j,j'}^{(k)} x_{j'}^{(k-1)} + b_j^{(k)}\right) \quad (j = 1, \ldots, m^{(k)}), \qquad k = 1, 2, \ldots, K-1,$$

$$f(x) = x_1^{(K)} = \sum_{j=1}^{m^{(K-1)}} u_j x_j^{(K-1)},$$

where the model parameters can be represented by $w = \{[u_j, \theta_{j,j'}^{(k)}, b_j^{(k)}] : j, j', k\}$, with $m^{(k)}$ being the number of hidden units at layer k. Figure 11.2 illustrates a $K = 4$ layer neural network with $m^{(0)} = 3$, $m^{(1)} = m^{(2)} = 5$, $m^{(3)} = 4$, and $m^{(4)} = 1$.

11.2 Function Approximation

It is known that neural networks are universal function approximators. In fact, it is known that a two-layer neural network (11.1) is universal if $h(\cdot)$ is not a polynomial (Leshno et al., 1993).

Theorem 11.1 (Leshno et al., 1993)   *If h is a nonpolynomial continuous function, then the function class in (11.1) is dense in $C^0(K)$ for all compact subsets K of $\mathbb{R}^d$, where $C^0(K)$ denotes the set of continuous functions on K.*

A more refined result was obtained in Barron (1993), which considered functions with a certain smoothness property in Fourier representation.

Definition 11.2   Consider a real-valued function $f(x)\colon \mathbb{R}^d \to \mathbb{R}$. Assume that $f \in L_1(\mathbb{R}^d)$ has the following Fourier representation:

$$f(x) = \int_{\mathbb{R}^d} e^{i\omega^\top x} \tilde{f}(\omega)\, d\omega,$$

where $\tilde{f}(\omega)$ is the Fourier transform of $f(x)$ that may be a complex function. Define

$$C(f) = \int_{\mathbb{R}^d} \|\omega\|_2 |\tilde{f}(\omega)| d\omega.$$

Theorem 11.3 (Barron, 1993)   *If $h(z)$ is a bounded measurable function on the real line for which $\lim_{z\to-\infty} h(z) = 0$ and $\lim_{z\to\infty} h(z) = 1$. Consider $B_r = \{x \in \mathbb{R}^d\colon \|x\|_2 \le r\}$, and let f be a real-valued function defined on B_r such that $C(f) < \infty$. Then there exists a neural network (11.1) such that*

$$\int (f(x) - f(0) - f_m(w, x))^2\, d\mu(x) \le \frac{(2rC(f))^2}{m},$$

where μ is an arbitrary probability measure on B_r.

Proof   A key property of the complexity measure $C(f)$, shown in Barron (1993), is that $f(x) - f(0)$ belongs to the convex closure of functions

$$\{uh(\theta^\top x + b)\colon |u| \le 2rC(f)\},$$

where the closure is taken with respect to μ. This result, together with Theorem 10.7, implies Theorem 11.3.   □

Note that we can take any b so that $h(b) \ne 0$, and

$$f(0) = (f(0)/h(b))h(0^\top x + b).$$

It follows that if $f(x) - f(0)$ can be represented by a two-layer neural network (11.1) with m neurons, then $f(x)$ can be represented by a two-layer neural network (11.1) with $m+1$ neurons. Therefore Theorem 11.3 implies that any f with finite $C(f)$ can be approximated by a two-layer neural network. It can be shown that the function class $\{f\colon C(f) < \infty\}$ is dense on any compact set of $\mathbb{R}^d$. This implies the desired universal approximation result.

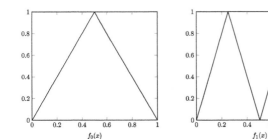
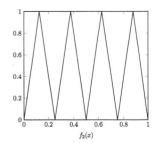

Figure 11.3 Plot of $f_k(x)$ with $k = 0, 1, 2$

Theorem 11.3 can also be applied to the ReLU activation function $h(z) = \max(0, z)$ via an intermediate function $h'(z) = h(z+1) - h(z)$, which satisfies the conditions of Theorem 11.3.

The universal approximation theory of Barron (1993) shows that a function can be efficiently represented by a two-layer neural network if $C(f)$ is small. However, for certain target functions with large $C(f)$, two-layer neural networks may require exponentially many nodes to represent. In some such cases, using deep representation can reduce the number of nodes needed to represent the functions. This phenomenon has been extensively investigated in the literature. A representative result along this line of research follows. It shows that a small deep neural network can efficiently represent a function that requires exponentially many nodes to represent with a shallow neural network. The construction appeared in Telgarsky (2016), which also includes functions defined on $\mathbb{R}^d$. Here we state a simplified result for $d = 1$.

Theorem 11.4 *Consider any integer $k \geq 3$. There exists $f(x) \colon [0, 1] \to [0, 1]$ computed by a $2k^2$-layer neural network with standard ReLU activation function, with no more than 2 neurons per layer so that*

$$\int_0^1 |f(x) - g(x)| dx \geq \frac{1}{16}, \tag{11.2}$$

where g is any function of a ReLU network with no more than k layers and $\leq 2^{k-2}$ nodes per layer.

Proof We will briefly explain the high-level intuition of Telgarsky (2016), which indicates what kind of functions are difficult to approximate with shallow neural networks. Consider the case of $d = 1$: a specific construction of a hard function $f(x)$ for shallow neural networks is via the function composition of the triangle function $f_0(x) = \max(0, \min(2x, 2(1 - x)))$ on $[0, 1]$. We may define $f_k(x) = f_0(f_{k-1}(x))$ with $k \geq 1$, as illustrated in Figure 11.3. Since $f_0(x)$ can be represented by a two-layer neural ReLU network with no more than two nodes per layer as $f_0(x) = 2\max(0, x) - 4\max(0, x - 0.5)$ in $[0, 1]$, $f_k(x)$ can be represented by a $2k$-layer neural network with no more than two nodes per layer.

It can be seen that $f_k(x)$ contains 2^k points that reach values of 1, and $2^k + 1$ points that reach values of 0. It follows that the number of solution segments of $f_k(x) = 0.5$, referred to as its crossing number, is 2^{k+1}.

It is easy to show that $f(x) - f_k(x)$ cannot be approximated well by a function $g(x)$ with crossing number $< 2^k$ in that the approximation error is lower bounded by (11.2).

Therefore in order to show that $f_k(x)$ cannot be approximated efficiently by shallow neural networks, we only need to show that the function of a shallow neural network cannot have many crossings unless it contains exponentially many nodes. Specifically, it can be shown (see Exercise 11.2) that an ℓ-layer ReLU network with no more than m ReLU nodes per layer has a crossing number of no larger than $2(2m)^\ell$. It follows that if a neural network can approximate $f_{k^2}(x)$ well, then $(2m) \geq 2^{(k^2-1)/\ell}$. Therefore the node number $m > 2^{k-2}$ if $\ell \leq k$. $\qquad \square$

At a high level, we note that function composition allows a deep neural network to reuse learned patterns (e.g. functions with high crossing numbers) to form more complex patterns. This corresponds to the intuition that shallow neural networks only learn basic lower-level features. To form high-level features, one needs to employ deeper neural networks that can combine basic features to form more complex features. Theorem 11.4 presents a mathematical model in which deep combinations of high-level features cannot be easily represented using shallow networks.

11.3 Random Feature Method

Assume that in two-layer neural networks, we do not train the parameters $[\theta, b]$, but randomly draw these parameters from a fixed distribution, then the resulting method becomes the random feature method. For notation simplicity, in this section, we do not include a bias term b. This does not affect generality because it is possible to change $x \in \mathbb{R}^d$ into $\tilde{x} = [x, 1] \in \mathbb{R}^{d+1}$, and change $\theta \in \mathbb{R}^d$ and $b \in \mathbb{R}$ into $\tilde{\theta} = [\theta, b] \in \mathbb{R}^{d+1}$, so that we have $\theta^\top x + b = \tilde{\theta}^\top \tilde{x}$.

With the simplified notation, we assume that $\{\theta_j : j = 1, \ldots, m\}$ are m independent samples drawn from a distribution μ on $\mathbb{R}^d$. A typical example is to take μ as a Gaussian distribution. The two-layer neural network in (11.1) can be written as

$$f_m(u, x) = \frac{1}{m} \sum_{j=1}^{m} u_j h(\theta_j^\top x). \tag{11.3}$$

It follows from Theorem 11.1 that (11.3) is universal with appropriate h. As $m \to \infty$, the law of large numbers implies that the limit can be written as

$$f_\infty(x) = \mathbb{E}_{\theta \sim \mu} u(\theta) h(\theta^\top x), \tag{11.4}$$

where $u(\theta)$ is a weight function. In this formulation, we may treat both $u(\theta)$ and $h(\theta^\top x)$ as infinite-dimensional vectors indexed by θ. In this setting, we may regard the limiting function class (11.4) as a linear system, in which we would like to learn the infinite-dimensional linear weight $u(\theta)$.

In order to learn this function class, it is necessary to impose a regularization condition on $u(\theta)$. Of particular interest, we may consider the L_2 regularization for random-feature method, where the function class is given by

$$\mathbb{E}_{\theta \sim \mu}|u(\theta)|^2 \leq A^2.$$

This function class induces a kernel class, and Theorem 9.8 implies the following result.

Proposition 11.5 *Consider any probability measure μ on $\mathbb{R}^d$. The function class (11.4) with L_2 regularization*

$$\|f\|_2 = \left(\mathbb{E}_{\theta \sim \mu}|u(\theta)|^2\right)^{1/2}$$

is equivalent to the RKHS function class defined in Definition 9.4 with kernel

$$k_\infty(x, x') = \mathbb{E}_{\theta \sim \mu} h(\theta, x) h(\theta, x').$$

Note that the equivalence also holds for the empirical measure on $\{\theta_1, \ldots, \theta_m\}$, which are independently drawn from μ. The kernel corresponding to (11.3) is

$$k_m(x, x') = \frac{1}{m} \sum_{j=1}^{m} h(\theta_j, x) h(\theta_j, x').$$

As $m \to \infty$, $k_m(x, x') \to k_\infty(x, x')$ in probability. This means that (11.3) with the L_2 regularizer

$$\frac{1}{m} \sum_{j=1}^{m} u_j^2 \leq A^2$$

converges to (11.4) with L_2 regularization. A particular class of random features are random Fourier features (aka random cosine features) on $\mathbb{R}^d$, considered in Rahimi and Recht (2007). This class of features can be written as

$$\psi(\theta, x) = \sqrt{2} \cos(\omega^\top x + b), \quad \theta = [\omega, b],$$

where ω is sampled from a distribution μ on $\mathbb{R}^d$, and b is sampled from the uniform distribution $U(0, 2\pi)$ on $[0, 2\pi]$. The following result (see Rudin, 2017), together with the convergence of (11.3) to (11.4), as used to justify the choice of Fourier random features in Rahimi and Recht (2007), with μ chosen as a probability measure.

Proposition 11.6 (Bochner's Theorem) *Any translation invariant kernel of the form $k(x, x') = k(x - x')$ can be written as*

$$k(x - x') = \mathbb{E}_{\omega \sim \mu, b \sim U[0, 2\pi]} 2 \cos(\omega^\top x + b) \cos(\omega^\top x' + b),$$

where μ is a nonnegative measure on $\mathbb{R}^d$ that may not be a probability measure (i.e. may not integrate to 1).

For the L_2-regularized random feature method, we immediately obtain the following Rademacher complexity result from Theorem 9.20.

Corollary 11.7 *Let*

$$\mathcal{F}_A^2 = \{\mathbb{E}_{\theta \sim \mu} u(\theta) h(\theta^\top x) \colon \mathbb{E}_{\theta \sim \mu} u(\theta)^2 \le A^2\},$$

then

$$R_n(\mathcal{F}_A^2, \mathcal{D}) \le A \sqrt{\frac{\mathbb{E}_{x \sim \mathcal{D}} \mathbb{E}_{\theta \sim \mu} h(\theta^\top x)^2}{n}}.$$

Similarly, we have the following result for (11.3).

Corollary 11.8 *Let*

$$\mathcal{F}_{A,m}^2 = \left\{ \frac{1}{m} \sum_{j=1}^m u_j h(\theta_j^\top x) \colon \|u\|_2 \le \sqrt{m} A \right\},$$

then

$$R_n(\mathcal{F}_{A,m}^2, \mathcal{D}) \le A \sqrt{\frac{\mathbb{E}_{x \sim \mathcal{D}} \sum_{j=1}^m h(\theta_j^\top x)^2}{mn}}.$$

We may compare the result of the kernel method to that of L_1 regularization, which requires an estimate of the Rademacher complexity of $h(\theta^\top x)$.

Proposition 11.9 *Let* $\mathcal{F} = \{h(\theta^\top x) \colon \theta \in \mathbb{R}^d\}$ *and* $\mathcal{F}_\pm = \mathcal{F} \cup -\mathcal{F}$. *Let*

$$\mathcal{F}_A^1 = \{\mathbb{E}_{\theta \sim \mu} u(\theta) h(\theta^\top x) \colon \mathbb{E}_{\theta \sim \mu} |u(\theta)| \le A\}.$$

Then for all monotone function $h(\cdot)$ *with* $h(\cdot) \in [-M, M]$,

$$R(\mathcal{F}_\pm, \mathcal{S}_n) \le M \frac{32\sqrt{d+1}}{\sqrt{n}},$$

$$R(\mathcal{F}_A^1, \mathcal{S}_n) \le AM \frac{32\sqrt{d+1}}{\sqrt{n}}.$$

Proof Since $h(\cdot)$ is monotone, we know that $\mathcal{F}$ is a VC-subgraph class with VC dimension $d + 1$. Therefore from Theorem 5.11 and the calculation in Example 6.26, we obtain

$$R(\mathcal{F}, \mathcal{S}_n) \le M \frac{16\sqrt{d+1}}{\sqrt{n}}.$$

This leads to the first bound. The second bound follows from Theorem 10.8. □

We note that $\mathbb{E}_{\theta \sim \mu} |u(\theta)| \le \sqrt{\mathbb{E}_{\theta \sim \mu} |u(\theta)|^2}$. Therefore the L_1 and L_2 regularized continuous random feature methods satisfy $\mathcal{F}_A^2 \subset \mathcal{F}_A^1$. Moreover, given any $A > 0$, there exists $f \in \mathcal{F}_A^1$ so that $\mathbb{E}_{\theta \sim \mu} |u(\theta)| \le A$ but $\mathbb{E}_{\theta \sim \mu} u(\theta)^2$ is arbitrarily large. For the finite random feature method (11.3), we have the following result.

Corollary 11.10 *Let*

$$\mathcal{F}^1_{A,m} = \left\{ \frac{1}{m} \sum_{j=1}^{m} u_j h(\theta_j^\top x) \colon \|u\|_1 \leq mA \right\}.$$

Assume that $h(\cdot) \in [-M, M]$ and $h(\cdot)$ is monotone. Then

$$R(\mathcal{F}^1_{A,m}, \mathcal{S}_n) \leq AM \frac{32\sqrt{d+1}}{\sqrt{n}}.$$

For the random kernel method with L_2 regularization, we require $\|u\|_2 \leq \sqrt{m}A$, which implies that $\|u\|_1 \leq mA$. However, the reverse is not true, as shown in the following example.

Example 11.11 Consider a target function that is represented by a single neuron

$$f_*(x) = u_1 h(\theta_1^\top x),$$

with $|u_1| \leq 1$ and $h(\cdot) \in [-1, 1]$. Then $f_* \in \mathcal{F}^1_{1,m}$ for all $m \geq 1$. Corollary 11.10 implies that the Rademacher complexity using L_1 regularization is $R_n(\mathcal{F}^1_{1,m}) = O(\sqrt{d/n})$, which is well behaved when $m \to \infty$.

However, if we employ L_2 regularization, then $f_* \in \mathcal{F}^2_{\sqrt{m},m}$. The corresponding Rademacher complexity bound becomes $R_n(\mathcal{F}^2_{\sqrt{m},m}) \leq \sqrt{m/n}$, which becomes infinity when $m \to \infty$.

More generally, when m is large, for sparse target that can be represented by $f_m(u, x)$ with a sparse u of small L_1 norm $\|u\|_1$, the random kernel method with L_2 regularization may be inferior to L_1 regularization when complexity is measured by Rademacher complexity.

11.4 Neural Tangent Kernel

In the random feature approach, the bottom-layer model parameter θ is fixed, and only the top-layer model parameter u is trained. However, in practical applications of neural networks, both the model parameter θ and parameter u are trained jointly. It is possible to generalize the kernel view to handle this case, which leads to the concept of neural tangent kernel (NTK) by Jacot et al. (2018).

To derive NTK, we start with a random initialization of the neural network (11.1) (again, for simplicity, we assume $b_j = 0$) at $[u, \theta] = [\tilde{u}, \tilde{\theta}]$, which we refer to as the NTK initialization. Here we independently draw m $d+1$-dimensional model parameters $[\tilde{u}_j, \tilde{\theta}_j] \in \mathbb{R}^{d+1}$ from a probability distribution μ on $\mathbb{R}^{d+1}$. The probability distribution is often chosen as an iid normal distribution. The resulting initial neural network is

$$\tilde{f}^{\text{NTK}}_m(x) = \frac{1}{\sqrt{m}} \sum_{j=1}^{m} \tilde{u}_j h(\tilde{\theta}_j^\top x), \tag{11.5}$$

which is similar to the random feature method (11.3), but $\tilde{u}_j$ is also drawn randomly. Note that in practice, we often choose μ to be a normal distribution with a diagonal covariance matrix. We do not make this assumption unless specified explicitly. However, to simplify the computation, throughout the section, we assume that μ is chosen so that

$$\mathbb{E}[\tilde{u}_j | \tilde{\theta}_j] = 0.$$

Given $x \in \mathbb{R}^d$, the variance of $\tilde{f}_m^{\mathrm{NTK}}(x)$ is

$$\mathrm{Var}_\mu(\tilde{f}_m^{\mathrm{NTK}}(x)) = \mathbb{E}_{[\tilde{u}_0, \tilde{\theta}_0] \sim \mu} \tilde{u}_0^2 h(\tilde{\theta}_0^\top x)^2.$$

This implies that the variance is finite when the right-hand side is finite. Moreover, the variance is independent of m as $m \to \infty$. This explains why we divide by $\sqrt{m}$ instead of dividing by m as in (11.3). Because of this normalization difference, we cannot obtain an explicit integration formulation similar to (11.4) for $\tilde{f}_m^{\mathrm{NTK}}(x)$ as $m \to \infty$. Nevertheless, we have the following limiting behavior of $\tilde{f}_m$ using the central limit theorem. This means that the $m \to \infty$ limit of the NTK initialization converges to a well-behaved random function as $m \to \infty$.

Proposition 11.12 *Assume that the central limit theorem holds for (11.5) (uniformly for all x) as $m \to \infty$. Then as $m \to \infty$, $\tilde{f}_m^{\mathrm{NTK}}(x)$ converges to a Gaussian process $\tilde{f}_\infty^{\mathrm{NTK}}(x)$ with zero-mean and covariance matrix,*

$$k(x, x') = \mathbb{E}_{[\tilde{u}_0, \tilde{\theta}_0] \sim \mu} \tilde{u}_0^2 h(\tilde{\theta}_0^\top x) h(\tilde{\theta}_0^\top x').$$

In general, neural networks are trained via SGD (see Algorithm 7.1), which employs gradients of the neural network. We have the following characterization of gradients at the NTK initialization.

Proposition 11.13 *Consider $\tilde{f}_m^{\mathrm{NTK}}(x)$ defined in (11.5). Let $h'(z)$ be the derivative of $h(\cdot)$. We have for all x and j,*

$$\mathbb{E}\|\nabla_{\tilde{u}_j} \tilde{f}_m^{\mathrm{NTK}}(x)\|_2^2 = \frac{1}{m} \mathbb{E}_{\tilde{\theta}_0 \sim \mu} h(\tilde{\theta}_0^\top x)^2,$$

$$\mathbb{E}\|\nabla_{\tilde{\theta}_j} \tilde{f}_m^{\mathrm{NTK}}(x)\|_2^2 = \frac{1}{m} \mathbb{E}_{[\tilde{u}_0, \tilde{\theta}_0] \sim \mu} \tilde{u}_0^2 h'(\tilde{\theta}_0^\top x)^2 \|x\|_2^2,$$

where the expectation is with respect to the random initialization. Moreover, for any x, as $m \to \infty$,

$$\|\nabla_{\tilde{u}} \tilde{f}_m^{\mathrm{NTK}}(x)\|_2^2 \xrightarrow{p} \mathbb{E}_{\tilde{\theta}_0 \sim \mu} h(\tilde{\theta}_0^\top x)^2,$$

$$\|\nabla_{\tilde{\theta}} \tilde{f}_m^{\mathrm{NTK}}(x)\|_2^2 \xrightarrow{p} \mathbb{E}_{[\tilde{u}_0, \tilde{\theta}_0] \sim \mu} \tilde{u}_0^2 h'(\tilde{\theta}_0^\top x)^2 \|x\|_2^2,$$

where the probability is with respect to the random initialization.

Proposition 11.13 shows that as $m \to \infty$, the gradient g of the NTK formulation has small L_∞-norm: $\|g\|_\infty \to 0$, although the L_2-norm is finite: $\|g\|_2 = O(1)$. We note that the progress of the SGD procedure is measured by the gradient 2-norm (e.g. see Theorem 14.9). Therefore in the NTK formulation, the convergence of

SGD is independent of m as $m \to \infty$, and the training process occurs in an infinitely small neighborhood of the initialization in terms of the L_∞-norm as $m \to \infty$. Assume for simplicity that $h(z)$ is a smooth function with derivative $h'(z)$, then we can perform a Taylor expansion in a small neighbor around $[\tilde{u}, \tilde{\theta}]$ to obtain a linear approximation around the initialization.

In the following discussion, we let $w = [u, \theta]$ and $\tilde{w} = [\tilde{u}, \tilde{\theta}]$. Let $B_\infty(\tilde{w}, r) = \{w \colon \|w - \tilde{w}\|_\infty \le r\}$. Let

$$f_{\mathrm{nn}}(w, x) = \frac{1}{\sqrt{m}} \sum_{j=1}^{m} u_j h(\theta_j^\top x),$$

and we can define its NTK approximation as

$$f_m^{\mathrm{NTK}}(w, x) = \tilde{f}_m^{\mathrm{NTK}}(x) + \frac{1}{\sqrt{m}} \sum_{j=1}^{m} \Big[(u_j - \tilde{u}_j) h(\tilde{\theta}_j^\top x)$$
$$+ \tilde{u}_j h'(\tilde{\theta}_j^\top x)(\theta_j - \tilde{\theta}_j)^\top x \Big]. \tag{11.6}$$

When $w \in B_\infty(\tilde{w}, r)$ for a sufficiently small r, we have $f_m^{\mathrm{NTK}}(w, x) \approx f_{\mathrm{nn}}(w, x)$ and $\nabla_w f_m^{\mathrm{NTK}}(w, x) \approx \nabla_w f_{\mathrm{nn}}(w, x)$. More formally, we may impose the following assumption for μ and h.

Assumption 11.14 For any x, $\delta \in (0, 1)$ and $\epsilon > 0$, there exist $A_0 > 0$, $r_0 > 0$, and $m_0 > 0$ such that when $m > m_0$, with probability at least $1 - \delta$ over random initialization, the following events hold uniformly for $w \in B_\infty(\tilde{w}, r_0)$:

- $|\tilde{f}_m^{\mathrm{NTK}}(x)| \le A_0$
- $\|\nabla_w f_m^{\mathrm{NTK}}(w, x)\|_2 + \|\nabla_w f_{\mathrm{nn}}(w, x)\|_2 \le A_0$
- $|f_m^{\mathrm{NTK}}(w, x) - f_{\mathrm{nn}}(w, x)| \le \epsilon$
- $\|\nabla_w f_m^{\mathrm{NTK}}(w, x) - \nabla_w f_{\mathrm{nn}}(w, x)\|_2 \le \epsilon$
- $\|\nabla_w f_m^{\mathrm{NTK}}(w, x)\|_\infty + \|\nabla_w f_{\mathrm{nn}}(w, x)\|_\infty \le m^{-1/4}$

The following result is not difficult to verify. We leave it as an exercise.

Proposition 11.15 *Assumption 11.14 holds for both ReLU and for sigmoid activation functions with Gaussian initialization $\tilde{w} \sim N(0, \sigma^2 I)$.*

Next, we will examine the property of $f_m^{\mathrm{NTK}}(w, x)$ when $m \to \infty$. Observe that the NTK approximation of the neural network is linear in the model parameter $w = [u, \theta]$, with random features $m^{-1/2} h(\tilde{\theta}_j^\top x)$ and $m^{-1/2} \tilde{u}_j h'(\tilde{\theta}_j^\top x) x$. This means that if we implicitly impose the L_2 regularization on the model parameter w, then we can obtain a kernel function class, which is well behaved as $m \to \infty$.

Proposition 11.16 *Consider the feature space NTK formulation (11.6). Then $f_m^{\mathrm{NTK}}(w, x) - \tilde{f}_m^{\mathrm{NTK}}(x)$ belongs to the RKHS function class defined in Definition 9.4 with kernel*

$$k_m^{\mathrm{NTK}}(x, x') = k_{m,1}^{\mathrm{NTK}}(x, x') + k_{m,2}^{\mathrm{NTK}}(x, x'),$$

where

$$k_{m,1}^{\text{NTK}}(x, x') = \frac{1}{m} \sum_{j=1}^{m} h(\tilde{\theta}_j^\top x) h(\tilde{\theta}_j^\top x'),$$

$$k_{m,2}^{\text{NTK}}(x, x') = \frac{1}{m} \sum_{j=1}^{m} \tilde{u}_j^2 h'(\tilde{\theta}_j^\top x) h'(\tilde{\theta}_j^\top x') x^\top x'.$$

Moreover, for any x, x', as $m \to \infty$, we have

$$k_{m,1}^{\text{NTK}}(x, x') \xrightarrow{p} k_{\infty,1}^{\text{NTK}}(x, x') = \mathbb{E}_{\tilde{\theta}_0 \sim \mu} h(\tilde{\theta}_0^\top x) h(\tilde{\theta}_0^\top x'),$$

$$k_{m,2}^{\text{NTK}}(x, x') \xrightarrow{p} k_{\infty,2}^{\text{NTK}}(x, x') = \mathbb{E}_{[\tilde{u}_0, \tilde{\theta}_0] \sim \mu} \tilde{u}_0^2 h'(\tilde{\theta}_0^\top x) h'(\tilde{\theta}_0^\top x') x^\top x',$$

where the probability is with respect to the random initialization.

In the NTK representation, the kernel $k_{\infty,1}^{\text{NTK}}$ is the same kernel as the random feature kernel in Proposition 11.5. The extra kernel $k_{\infty,2}^{\text{NTK}}$ in NTK corresponds to the fact that we allow θ to move away from the initialization $\tilde{\theta}$, while θ is fixed in the random feature kernel. It is not difficult to generalize NTK to deep neural networks by including kernels with respect to other layers.

Since for appropriate h, random feature kernel is universal, it follows that the NTK kernel $k_{\infty}^{\text{NTK}}(x, x') = k_{\infty,1}^{\text{NTK}}(x, x') + k_{\infty,2}^{\text{NTK}}(x, x')$ is also universal for such h. This implies that as $m \to \infty$, we can find a two-layer neural network within an infinitesimally small perturbation of the NTK initialization to approximate an arbitrary function $f(x)$.

Theorem 11.17 *Assume that the limiting NTK kernel $k_{\infty}^{\text{NTK}}(x, x')$ in Proposition 11.16 is universal. Consider an arbitrary function $f(x)$, and n distinct points $\{X_1, \ldots, X_n\}$. Consider a two-layer neural network with initialization (11.5). Given any $\epsilon > 0$ and $\delta \in (0,1)$, there exist $A > 0$ and m_0 such that when $m > m_0$, with probability at least $1 - \delta$, there exists $w \in B_\infty(\tilde{w}, r_m)$ that satisfy:*

- $r_m = A/m^{1/4}$ and $\|w - \tilde{w}\|_2 \leq A$.
- $|f_m^{\text{NTK}}(w, X_i) - f(X_i)| \leq \epsilon$ *for all* $i = 1, \ldots, n$.

Proof Since $k_{\infty}^{\text{NTK}}(x, x')$ is universal, its Gram matrix K_{∞}^{NTK} on $\{X_1, \ldots, X_n\}$ is invertible (see Theorem 9.19). There exists $\alpha \in \mathbb{R}^n$ so that $K_{\infty}^{\text{NTK}} \alpha = \Delta f$, where $\Delta f \in \mathbb{R}^n$ is the vector with $\Delta f_i = f(X_i) - \tilde{f}_m^{\text{NTK}}(X_i)$ as its components.

By Assumption 11.14, with probability at least $1 - \delta/3$, for sufficiently large m, $\Delta f_i = f(X_i) - \tilde{f}_m^{\text{NTK}}(X_i)$ is bounded $(i = 1, \ldots, n)$, and hence, α is bounded. It follows that there exists a constant $A > 1$ such that $A \geq 1 + \|\alpha\|_1 + \|\alpha\|_{K_{\infty}^{\text{NTK}}}$. Let $\mathcal{H}_m$ be the RKHS of k_m^{NTK}, and define

$$f_m(x) = \frac{A}{\max(A, \|f_m'\|_{\mathcal{H}_m})} f_m'(x), \quad f_m'(x) = \sum_{i=1}^{n} \alpha_i k_m^{\text{NTK}}(X_i, x)$$

in $\mathcal{H}_m$, then $\|f_m(x)\|_{\mathcal{H}_m} \le A$. Proposition 9.1 implies that there exists w such that $f_m^{\mathrm{NTK}}(w, x) = f_m(x)$ and $\|w - \tilde{w}\|_2 \le A$. Moreover, using (9.4), we can represent $w - \tilde{w}$ by

$$w - \tilde{w} = \frac{A}{\max(A, \|f_m'\|_{\mathcal{H}_m})} \sum_{i=1}^{n} \alpha_i \nabla_w f_m^{\mathrm{NTK}}(\tilde{w}, X_i).$$

Assumption 11.14 also implies that with probability at least $1 - \delta/3$,

$$\sup_{i=1,\ldots,n} \|\nabla_w f_m^{\mathrm{NTK}}(\tilde{w}, X_i)\|_\infty \le 1/m^{1/4}.$$

This implies that

$$\|w - \tilde{w}\|_\infty \le \|\alpha\|_1 \sup_{i=1,\ldots,n} \|\nabla_w f_m^{\mathrm{NTK}}(\tilde{w}, X_i)\|_\infty \le r_m = A/m^{1/4}.$$

Proposition 11.16 implies that as $m \to \infty$, $k_m^{\mathrm{NTK}}(\cdot) \to k_\infty^{\mathrm{NTK}}(\cdot)$, and thus $f_m^{\mathrm{NTK}}(w, X_i) - \tilde{f}_m^{\mathrm{NTK}}(X_i) \xrightarrow{p} \Delta f_i$ for all $i = 1, \ldots, n$. Therefore with probability at least $1 - \delta/3$, for sufficiently large m, $|f_m^{\mathrm{NTK}}(w, X_i) - f(X_i)| < \epsilon$ for $i = 1, \ldots, n$.

We obtain the desired result by taking the union bound of the three events with probability $1 - \delta/3$ each. $\qquad \square$

Theorem 11.17 implies that when $m \to \infty$, one can approximate an arbitrary function $f(x)$ using $f_m^{\mathrm{NTK}}(w, x)$ with $\|w - \tilde{w}\|_\infty \to 0$. In this regime, referred to as the *NTK regime*, Assumption 11.14 implies that the two-layer neural network can be approximated using the NTK approximation:

$$f(x) \approx f_m^{\mathrm{NTK}}(w, X_i) \approx f_{\mathrm{nn}}(w, x).$$

That is, the two-layer neural network is equivalent to a kernel method as $m \to \infty$. Moreover, Assumption 11.14 , together with an SGD convergence result such as Theorem 14.9, implies that as $m \to \infty$, SGD can find the minimizer of any loss function within the NTK regime.

Corollary 11.18 *Assume that the NTK kernel $k_\infty^{\mathrm{NTK}}(x, x')$ in Proposition 11.16 is universal. Let $f(x)$ be an arbitrary function, and $\{(X_1, Y_1), \ldots, (X_n, Y_n)\}$ be n distinct points. Consider a convex loss function $L(f(x), y)$ that is Lipschitz in $f(x)$. There exists $A > 0$ so that the following holds. For any $T > 0$, assume we run SGD from the NTK initialization* (11.5) *for T steps with constant learning rate $1/\sqrt{T}$, and return $f_{\mathrm{nn}}(w, x)$ with w chosen uniformly at random from the SGD iterates. Then as $m \to \infty$, $\|w - \tilde{w}\|_\infty \xrightarrow{p} 0$ and*

$$\mathbb{E}_w \frac{1}{n} \sum_{i=1}^{n} L(f_{\mathrm{nn}}(w, X_i), Y_i) \le \frac{1}{n} \sum_{i=1}^{n} L(f(X_i), Y_i) + \frac{A}{\sqrt{T}} + o_p(1),$$

where $\mathbb{E}_w$ indicates the randomness from the SGD iterates, and the convergence in probability is with respect to the randomness in the initialization.

Corollary 11.18 implies that as $m \to \infty$, the neural network training process using SGD is always inside the NTK regime. The property can be generalized to deep neural networks with more than two layers.

In the NTK regime, the generalization of neural network can be easily obtained using Rademacher complexity. Specifically, the following result can be obtained from Theorem 9.20.

Corollary 11.19 *Let*

$$\mathcal{F}_A^{\mathrm{NTK}}(\tilde{w}) = \{f_m^{\mathrm{NTK}}(w, x) \colon \|w - \tilde{w}\|_2^2 \leq A^2\},$$

then

$$R_n(\mathcal{F}_A^{\mathrm{NTK}}(\tilde{w}, \mathcal{D}) \leq A\sqrt{\frac{\mathbb{E}_{x \sim \mathcal{D}} k_m^{\mathrm{NTK}}(x, x)}{n}}.$$

11.5 Mean-Field Formulation

As pointed out in Section 11.4, the NTK approximation of neural networks (11.1) does not have a continuous integral formulation similar to that of the continuous random feature method (11.4), due to the $1/\sqrt{m}$ normalization in the NTK formula. The reason for this normalization is to ensure that (11.5) has a nonzero finite variance. In this section, we consider a different normalization of (11.1) (still ignoring b_j) as

$$f_m(x) = \frac{\alpha}{m} \sum_{j=1}^m u_j h(\theta_j^\top x), \tag{11.7}$$

with a scaling constant $\alpha > 0$. We assume that $\theta_j \in \mathbb{R}^d$ and $u_j \in \mathbb{R}$.

If we allow α to vary in m, and take $\alpha = \sqrt{m}$, then it leads to the NTK formulation (11.5) and (11.6). On the other hand, if we let $m \to \infty$ with α fixed, then we may treat $[u_j, \theta_j]$ as iid random samples from an underlying distribution q on $\mathbb{R}^{d+1}$. Similar to the continuous formulation of the random feature method, this leads to a continuous formulation of two-layer neural network as $m \to \infty$:

$$f_{\mathrm{mf}}(q, x) = \alpha \mathbb{E}_{[u,\theta] \sim q}\, uh(\theta^\top x). \tag{11.8}$$

This continuous formulation is referred to as the *mean-field* formulation in Mei et al. (2018). In this formulation, the distribution q on $\mathbb{R}^{d+1}$ characterizes the model, and can be trained using noisy gradient descent (see Mei et al., 2018). The finite two-layer neural network can be regarded as sampling from this distribution. In essence, this approach is a generalization of the random feature method but with the underlying random distribution trained to better fit the data, instead of using a fixed random distribution. The training of the underlying random distribution corresponds to feature learning in neural networks.

In the mean-field formulation, as $\alpha \to \infty$, the behavior of the resulting model becomes more and more similar to that of the NTK formulation. Therefore one may argue that the mean-field formulation is more general, while the NTK formulation is a limiting situation with $\alpha \to \infty$. One disadvantage of the mean-field formulation is that with standard random initialization of $[\tilde{u}, \tilde{\theta}]$, the initial function is always 0 in the continuous limit of $m \to \infty$. This is not desirable when we train a neural network in practice. On the other hand, the advantage of the mean-field formulation is that it allows $[u, \theta]$ to move outside a small neighbor of $[\tilde{u}, \tilde{\theta}]$, which is consistent with feature learning in practical neural network applications.

Convergence Analysis

It can be shown that in the continuous limit, neural network training converges to the optimal solution of the mean-field formulation (11.8), under suitable conditions (see Chizat and Bach, 2018; Mei et al., 2018). We will consider the entropy regularization model studied in Mei et al. (2018) for the mean-field formulation. It was shown in Mei et al. (2018) that for the mean-field formulation of two-layer neural networks, the Langevin algorithm converges to an entropy regularized ERM problem. In the following, we will prove this result for the continuous mean-field formulation, in which we seek a density function q on $\mathbb{R}^{d+1}$ to solve the following optimization problem:

$$\min_q \left[\frac{1}{n} \sum_{i=1}^n L(f_{\mathrm{mf}}(q, X_i), Y_i) + \mathbb{E}_{[u,\theta] \sim q} r(u, \theta) + \lambda \mathbb{E}_{[u,\theta] \sim q} \ln q([u, \theta]) \right],$$

where $f_{\mathrm{mf}}(q, x)$ is given by (11.8), and $r([u, \theta])$ is an appropriately chosen regularization term such as L_2 regularization.

In the convergence analysis, we employ a simplified notation with $w = [u, \theta] \in \mathbb{R}^{d+1}$, and take

$$p_0(w) \propto \exp(-r(w)/\lambda).$$

We thus obtain the following equivalent optimization problem:

$$q_* = \arg\min_q Q(q), \quad Q(q) = \left[\frac{1}{n} \sum_{i=1}^n L(f_{\mathrm{mf}}(q, X_i), Y_i) + \lambda \mathrm{KL}(q \| p_0) \right], \quad (11.9)$$

where

$$f_{\mathrm{mf}}(q, x) = \int \tilde{h}(w, x) q(w) dw, \qquad \tilde{h}(w, x) = \alpha u h(\theta^\top x).$$

The convergence theory of continuous two-layer neural networks to optimize (11.9) requires some knowledge on partial differential equations (PDEs). Since the required mathematical background is isolated from other parts of the book, we shall keep the discussion concise without concerning ourselves with issues such as the existence of PDE solutions. Readers who are not familiar with PDEs can skip the derivation.

In the convergence analysis, we will consider the continuous time noisy gradient descent, which can be described by a PDE. In this setting, the underlying mathematical model is to sample $m \to \infty$ neurons, each represented by an initial weight $w_0 \sim q_0$ at $t = 0$. When time t increases, we move each sampled neuron, represented by a weight w_t from the neuron distribution $q_t(w)$ at time t, using noisy gradient descent (Langevin algorithm). We assume that the moving neuron distribution of w_t at time t has density $q_t(w)$. Mathematically, the gradient descent method can be implemented as a stochastic partial differential equation (SDE):

$$dw_t = -\eta \tilde{g}(w_t, q_t)dt + \sqrt{2\lambda\eta}dB_t,$$

$$\tilde{g}(w, q) = \frac{1}{n} \sum_{i=1}^{N} L_1'(f_{\mathrm{mf}}(q, X_i), Y_i)\nabla_w \tilde{h}(w, X_i) + \nabla r(w),$$

where B_t is the standard Brownian motion and $L_1'(f, y)$ is the derivative of $L(f, y)$ with respect to f. The discretized version can be implemented using the SGLD algorithm (see Algorithm 7.2). It is well known that the dynamics of q_t satisfy the following Fokker–Planck equation (see Pavliotis, 2014, for example):

$$\frac{\partial q_t(w)}{\partial t} = \eta \nabla_w \cdot [q_t(w)\nabla_w g(w, q_t)], \tag{11.10}$$

where

$$g(w, q) = g_0(w, q) + \lambda \ln \frac{q(w)}{p_0(w)}, \quad g_0(w, q) = \frac{1}{n} \sum_{i=1}^{N} L_1'(f_{\mathrm{mf}}(q, X_i), Y_i)\tilde{h}(w, X_i).$$

We have the following general convergence result for (11.10).

Theorem 11.20 *Assume that $L(f, y)$ is convex in f. Moreover, for any density function q' on $\mathbb{R}^{d+1}$, the density*

$$q(w) \propto p_0(w) \exp\left(-\lambda^{-1} g_0(w, q')\right)$$

satisfies the logarithmic Soblev inequality (LSI) with parameter $\mu > 0$: for all density functions p on $\mathbb{R}^{d+1}$,

$$\mathrm{KL}(p\|q) \leq \frac{1}{2\mu} \mathbb{E}_{w \sim p}\left[\left\|\nabla \ln\left(\frac{p(w)}{q(w)}\right)\right\|_2^2\right]. \tag{11.11}$$

Then we have

$$Q(q_t) \leq Q(q_*) + e^{-2\eta\lambda\mu t}[Q(q_0) - Q(q_*)].$$

Proof We define a density function

$$q_t'(w) \propto p_0(w) \exp\left(-\lambda^{-1} g_0(w, q_t)\right),$$

then it is easy to verify that

$$q_t'(w) \propto q_t(w) \exp\left(-\lambda^{-1} g(w, q_t)\right). \tag{11.12}$$

We have

$$\frac{dQ(q_t)}{dt} = \int \frac{\delta Q(q_t)}{\delta q_t} \cdot \frac{\partial q_t(w)}{\partial t} dw$$

$$= \int g(w, q_t)\eta \nabla_w \cdot [q_t(w)\nabla_w g(w, q_t)]dw$$

$$= -\eta \int \|\nabla_w g(w, q_t)\|_2^2 q_t(w)dw$$

$$= -\eta\lambda^2 \int \left\|\nabla_w \ln \frac{q_t(w)}{q_t'(w)}\right\|_2^2 q_t(w)dw$$

$$\leq -\eta\lambda^2\mu \mathrm{KL}(q_t\|q_t'). \tag{11.13}$$

The first equation used calculus of variation. The second equation used (11.10), and the fact $g(w, q_t)$ may be considered as a functional gradient of Q with respect to q_t by treating q_t as an infinite-dimensional vector indexed by w. The third equation used integration by parts. The fourth equation used (11.12). The last inequality used (11.11), which is satisfied by q_t'. Moreover,

$$Q(q_*) - Q(q_t) \geq \int g(w, q_t)(q_*(w) - q_t(w))dw + \lambda\mathrm{KL}(q_*\|q_t)$$

$$\geq -\lambda \ln \mathbb{E}_{w\sim q_t} \exp\left(-\lambda^{-1}g(w, q_t)\right) - \mathbb{E}_{w\sim q_t}g(w, q_t)$$

$$= -\lambda\mathrm{KL}(q_t\|q_t'). \tag{11.14}$$

The first inequality used the fact that $Q(q) - \lambda\mathrm{KL}(q\|p_0)$ is convex in q, and $g_0(w, q_t)$ is the functional gradient of $Q(q_t) - \lambda\mathrm{KL}(q\|p_0)$ with respect to q as an infinite-dimensional vector indexed by w; it also used the fact that $\mathrm{KL}(q_*\|p_0) - \mathrm{KL}(q_t\|p_0) = \int \ln(q_t(w)/p_0(w))(q_*(w) - q_t(w))dw + \mathrm{KL}(q_*\|q_t)$. The second inequality used Proposition 7.16 (with $p = q_*$ and $p_0 = q_t$).

Now by combining (11.13) and (11.14), we obtain

$$\frac{d[Q(q_t) - Q(q_*)]}{dt} \leq -2\eta\lambda\mu[Q(q_t) - Q(q_*)].$$

By solving the differential equation, we obtain the result. □

Theorem 11.20 shows that the logarithmic Soblev inequality (11.11) implies that the two-layer neural network in the mean-field regime converges linearly. To obtain concrete examples for which (11.11) holds, we can employ the following well-known result.

Lemma 11.21 *Let $V(w)$ be a smooth and λ-strongly convex function on $\mathbb{R}^{d+1}$, and $U(w)$ be a smooth function so that $|U(w) - V(w)| \leq M < \infty$. Then the density*

$$q(w) = \frac{\exp(-U(w))}{\int \exp(-U(w))dw}$$

satisfies (11.11) with parameter $\mu = \lambda \exp(-2M)$.

Proof LSI holds for a strongly concave density function as a direct consequence of the Bakry–Emery criterion (Bakry and Émery, 1985). It is also known that LSI is stable under a bounded perturbation (see Holley and Stroock, 1987), which implies the result.   □

Example 11.22   Lemma 11.21 implies the following result. Assume that $g_0(w, q)$ is smooth in w: $\|\nabla_w^2 g_0(w,q)\|_2 \leq L$ for all w and q. If we take $r(w) = \lambda'\|w\|_2^\alpha$, then for any $\lambda' > 0$ and $\alpha > 2$, (11.11) is valid for some $\mu > 0$ (see Exercise 11.7). This implies that the convergence result in Theorem 11.20 holds.

Generalization Analysis

Because the parameter q of the mean-field model is a distribution, the two-layer NN in this continuous formulation can be regarded as a convex hull of the individual models $uh(\theta^\top x)$. We can thus apply the L_1-regularization result and the entropy-regularization result from Chapter 10 to compute the corresponding Rademacher complexity. The following result is identical to Proposition 11.9, except that we allow q to be learned for both parameters $[u, \theta]$.

Proposition 11.23   *Let*

$$\mathcal{F}_A^{\mathrm{mf}} = \{\mathbb{E}_{[u,\theta]\sim q}\, uh(\theta^\top x)\colon \mathbb{E}_{u\sim q}|u| \leq A\},$$

then

$$R(\mathcal{F}_A^{\mathrm{mf}}, \mathcal{S}_n) \leq AM\frac{32\sqrt{d+1}}{\sqrt{n}}.$$

Moreover, Theorem 11.20 shows that noisy gradient descent for the mean-field formulation leads to entropy regularization. We can analyze its generalization performance by using the Rademacher complexity analysis in Theorem 10.17, or by using Theorem 10.18 without assuming the boundedness of $uh(\cdot)$.

In addition to Theorem 11.20, it is also possible to prove convergence without entropy regularization under suitable conditions (see Chizat and Bach, 2018). One can study properties of the global solution of (11.8) as the limiting solution of the ERM method for two-layer neural networks. An interesting observation of the mean-field formulation (11.8) without entropy regularization is that any convex regularization in u leads to L_1 regularization, which implies that Proposition 11.23 can be directly applied for the solution of the mean-field formulation.

Proposition 11.24   *Consider an arbitrary distribution $\hat{\mathcal{D}}$ on $\mathcal{X} \times \mathcal{Y}$. Assume that $\sup\{|h(\theta^\top x)|\colon \theta \in \Omega\}$ is bounded. Let $\Delta(\mathbb{R} \times \Omega)$ be the set of probability measures on $(u, \theta) \in \mathbb{R} \times \Omega$. Consider the following optimization problem:*

$$\min_{q\in\Delta(\mathbb{R}\times\Omega)} \left[\mathbb{E}_{(X,Y)\sim\hat{\mathcal{D}}}L(\mathbb{E}_{[u,\theta]\sim q}\, uh(\theta^\top X), Y) + \mathbb{E}_{u\sim q}r(|u|)\right],$$

where $r(\cdot)$ is an increasing and strictly convex function on $\mathbb{R}_+$. Let $\hat{q}$ be an optimal solution. Then there exists $A > 0$ such that $|u| = A$ a.e. $u \sim \hat{q}(\cdot)$, and $\hat{q}$ is a solution to

$$\min_{q \in \Delta(\mathbb{R} \times \Omega)} \mathbb{E}_{(X,Y) \sim \hat{\mathcal{D}}} L(\mathbb{E}_{[u,\theta] \sim q} \, uh(\theta^\top X), Y) \qquad \mathbb{E}_{u \sim q} |u| \leq A.$$

Proof For notation simplicity, we consider discrete $\hat{q}$ (the continuous case is analogous except for more complex notations). Consider discrete values of $[u_1, \theta_1]$ with probability $\hat{q}_1 > 0$ and $[u_2, \theta_2]$ with probability $\hat{q}_2 > 0$. Without loss of generality, we may assume that $|u_1| \geq |u_2| \geq 0$.

We prove the first statement by contradiction. If $|u_1| > |u_2|$, then we can find $\delta > 0$, and let $\hat{q}_1' = \hat{q}_1 + \delta$, $\hat{q}_2' = \hat{q}_2 - \delta$, so that $|u_1'| = |u_2'|$ with $u_1' = u_1 \hat{q}_1 / \hat{q}_1'$ and $u_2' = u_2 \hat{q}_2 / \hat{q}_2'$. Let $\hat{q}'$ be the distribution on $[u, \theta]$ which equals $\hat{q}$ on all other points, except for a change of probability mass $\hat{q}_j$ on $[u_j, \theta_j]$ to a probability mass $\hat{q}_j'$ on $[u_j', \theta_j]$ $(j = 1, 2)$. The construction implies that $\mathbb{E}_{[u',\theta] \sim \hat{q}'} u'h(\theta^\top x) = \mathbb{E}_{[u,\theta] \sim \hat{q}} uh(\theta^\top x)$ and

$$\mathbb{E}_{u' \sim \hat{q}'} r(|u'|) - \mathbb{E}_{u \sim \hat{q}} r(|u|) = (\hat{q}_1 + \hat{q}_2) r\left(\frac{\hat{q}_1 |u_1| + \hat{q}_2 |u_2|}{\hat{q}_1 + \hat{q}_2}\right) - \sum_{j=1}^{2} \hat{q}_j r(|u_j|) < 0,$$

where we used $|u_1'| = |u_2'| = (\hat{q}_1 |u_1| + \hat{q}_2 |u_2|)/(\hat{q}_1 + \hat{q}_2)$. This is a contradiction to the optimality of $\hat{q}$. Therefore we must have $|u_1| = |u_2|$. This implies that $|u| = \text{const}$ when $u \sim \hat{q}(\cdot)$.

We prove the second statement by contradiction. If $\hat{q}$ is not a solution of the L_1 regularization formulation, then we can find $\hat{q}'$ with a smaller objective value so that $\mathbb{E}_{u' \sim \hat{q}'} |u'| \leq A$. From the previous analysis, we can also find a solution $\hat{q}'$ such that $|u'| = A'$ for some $A' \leq A$ with a smaller objective value. However, this is not possible because $\hat{q}'$ would lead to a smaller regularized loss than that of $\hat{q}$ with respect to the $r(\cdot)$ regularization formulation. □

Proposition 11.24 can be interpreted as follows. Even if we use L_2 regularization on u in a two-layer neural network, which seemingly is related to the kernel method, it effectively solves an L_1 regularization problem for the mean-field formulation, when we allow both u and θ to be optimized simultaneously. The optimization of θ modifies the L_2 regularization on u into the L_1 regularization with respect to the function class $\{h(\theta^\top x)\}$. This means Proposition 11.23 can be used to characterize the complexity of the mean-field formulation.

In the discrete mean-field formulation (11.7), $\{[u_j, \theta_j]\}$ may be regarded as m independent samples from q. In such a formulation, $[u_j, \theta_j]$ are trained simultaneously. The following result shows that with L_1 regularization, the Rademacher complexity is insensitive to m.

Corollary 11.25 *Let*

$$\mathcal{F}_{A,m}^{\text{mf}} = \left\{ \frac{1}{m} \sum_{j=1}^{m} u_j h(\theta_j^\top x) \colon \|u\|_1 \leq mA \right\}.$$

Assume that $h(\cdot) \in [-M, M]$ and $h(\cdot)$ is monotone. Then

$$R(\mathcal{F}^{\mathrm{mf}}_{A,m}, \mathcal{S}_n) \leq AM\frac{32\sqrt{d+1}}{\sqrt{n}}.$$

Note that unlike Corollary 11.10, where $\{\theta_j\}$ are random, Corollary 11.25 allows $\{\theta_j\}$ to be trained together with $\{u_j\}$. This means that it is more effective in learning the correct feature representation using a small m.

11.6 Analysis of Deep Neural Networks

It is possible to extend the NTK analysis to deep neural networks using an extension of the linear approximation (11.6) for two-layer neural networks without too much difficulty. We will not consider it here for simplicity. It has similar flaws as the kernel approaches for random features and for two-layer neural networks, in that the linearization requires model parameters to be restricted in a small region around the initialization.

An additional disadvantage of the NTK approximation is that it can be regarded as a shallow network approximation of a deep network using a linear model. According to Theorem 11.4, highly oscillating functions with large crossing numbers cannot be approximated efficiently with NTK, although they can be well approximated using deep neural networks. This is related to the fact that NTK cannot learn features efficiently. However, the efficient learning of feature representation is the key advantage of deep neural networks. Therefore in this section we will investigate the deep neural network method directly without considering the NTK approximation.

Here we consider a formulation of deep neural networks which may be considered as an extension of the mean-field formulation of two-layer neural networks, and then investigate its generalization. The deep function class is defined recursively as follows:

$$\mathcal{F}^{(1)} = \{\theta^\top x \colon \theta \in \Theta\},$$

and for $k = 2, \ldots, K$, using the notation of Section 10.2, we define

$$\mathcal{F}^{(k)} = \mathcal{F}_{A_k, L_1}(h \circ \mathcal{F}^{(k-1)}) \tag{11.15}$$

$$= \left\{ \sum_{j=1}^m w_j h(f_j(x)) \colon \|w\|_1 \leq A_k, \ f_j \in \mathcal{F}^{(k-1)}, m > 0 \right\}.$$

When $A_1, \ldots, A_k$ are sufficiently large, then it is clear that any function $f(x)$ that can be represented by a deep K-layer neural network that belongs to $\mathcal{F}^{(K)}$. The representation allows an arbitrary large m, and thus can handle continuous deep neural networks. This implies that it can be regarded as an extension of the two-layer mean-field formulation, which, as we have shown, also employs L_1-regularization implicitly.

For simplicity, we consider the case that $h \circ \mathcal{F}^{(1)}$ is bounded, and h is monotone and Lipschitz. The following result, first presented in Koltchinskii and Panchenko (2002), is a direct consequence of Theorem 10.8.

Theorem 11.26 *Consider K-layer neural networks defined by (11.15). Assume that $h(\theta^\top x) \in [-M, M]$ for all $\theta \in \Theta$ and $x \in \mathcal{X}$. Assume also that h is 1-Lipschitz and monotone. Then there exists a constant C, such that for all distribution D on $\mathcal{X}$, we have*

$$R(\mathcal{F}^{(k)}, \mathcal{S}_n) \leq A M \frac{32\sqrt{d+1}}{\sqrt{n}},$$

where $A = 2^{k-2} \prod_{\ell=2}^{k} A_\ell$.

Proof We prove the statement by induction. The case $k = 2$ follows from Corollary 11.10. Assume the statement holds at layer $k - 1$, then at layer k. We have

$$R(\mathcal{F}^{(k)}, \mathcal{S}_n) \leq A_k [R(h \circ \mathcal{F}^{(k-1)}, \mathcal{S}_n) + R(-h \circ \mathcal{F}^{(k-1)}, \mathcal{S}_n)]$$
$$\leq 2A_k R(\mathcal{F}^{(k-1)}, \mathcal{S}_n).$$

The first inequality used Theorem 10.8. The second inequality used Theorem 6.28 with $\gamma_i = 1$ and $h = 0$. Now by using induction, we obtain the desired bound. $\square$

The result implies that if we use L_1 regularization for every layer of a deep neural network, then the Rademacher complexity can be easily bounded using the multiplications of the layer-wise L_1-regularization parameters. For the ReLU function, the L_1 regularization can be moved to the last layer. It is also worth noticing that the learning complexity for the function composition example considered in Theorem 11.4 is still high if we measure it by L_1 regularization. This is not surprising because functions with exponentially many crossing numbers are complex, and L_1 regularization allows a large neural network with many neurons.

One benefit of the generalization bound in Theorem 11.26 is that the generalization performance does not depend on the number of neurons. Therefore the more neurons we use, the better. This is consistent with empirical observations that wide neural networks are easier to optimize. If we allow the number of neurons to approach infinity, then we obtain a continuous formulation of deep neural networks with the same learning bound measured by Rademacher complexity.

11.7 Double Descent and Benign Overfitting

Modern neural networks are usually overparameterized, in that the number of model parameters is significantly larger than the number of training data. This is consistent with both the NTK view and the mean-field view, where both consider the limit of $m \to \infty$. Without proper regularization, such a system will lead to overfitting based on classical statistics. However, with proper regularization such as RKHS regularization in the NTK view, and L_1 regularization in the mean-field view, such systems have bounded complexity when measured by quantities such

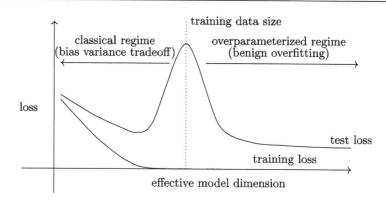

Figure 11.4 Double-descent curve

as the Rademacher complexity. In general, such a complexity measure implies a small effective model dimension as discussed in Section 9.5. In the classical setting, the effective dimension should be smaller than the number of training data, and one typically observes a U-shaped test loss as the model complexity increases. This is shown in Figure 1.1. However, some modern overparameterized models go beyond this regime, where it is observed that such models (including neural networks) exhibit the so-called *double-descent* phenomenon when the model size increases (see Belkin et al., 2019).

The double-descent phenomenon is illustrated in Figure 11.4. It can be seen that when the effective dimension is smaller than the number of training data, we are in the classical regime where the test loss has a U shape. In the overparameterized regime, the test loss is large when the effective model dimension is approximately the same as the number of training data, but it will decrease further when the effective dimension increases beyond the number of training data. In this regime, overfitting happens and the model generally starts interpolating the observed function value, which may potentially contain noise. Such overfitting is referred to as *benign overfitting* because even though the learned function overfits the noise, the test loss will decrease, and the minimum test loss that can be achieved is smaller than the minimum test loss that can be achieved in the classical regime.

A number of papers tried to explain the double-descent phenomenon, which occurs even for overparameterized linear regression models, noticeably with minimum L_2-norm estimator, where we try to fit a linear model with the smallest L_2-norm. This is equivalent to ridge regression with the regularization parameter approaching zero. Although double descent may look mysterious, it does not contradict classical learning theory. In classical learning theory, the more complex the model class, the lower the training loss required to obtain the optimal training loss, and the more overfitting one observes. In the extreme case that the model class is extremely complex, the optimal trade-off potentially requires the overfitting of the training data.

To explain what causes the double-descent phenomenon, we consider the following simple problem in the Bayesian setting with $(X, Y) \in \mathbb{R}^d \times \mathbb{R}$:

$$\begin{cases} Y &= w_*^\top X + \epsilon \\ X &\sim N(0, I_{d \times d}) \\ \epsilon &\sim N(0, \sigma^2) \\ w_* &\sim N\left(0, \frac{\tau^2}{d} I_{d \times d}\right). \end{cases} \tag{11.16}$$

We consider least squares regression in the overparameterized setting, where we observe $n \ll d$ training data $\{(X_i, Y_i) \colon i = 1, \ldots, n\}$. In this situation, the model belongs to a very complex function class because the target is a dense overparameterized family, with data generated by a dense target vector $w_* \in \Omega$. It is impossible to learn w_* accurately, but nevertheless, we will try to find $\hat{w}$ from the training data to achieve the smallest test loss:

$$\mathbb{E}_{(X,Y) \sim \mathcal{D}}(\hat{w}^\top X - Y)^2 = \|\hat{w} - w_*\|_2^2 + \sigma^2.$$

Note that we assume a generation process of w_* so that the optimal Bayes estimator, which is the best estimator among all possible learning algorithms, can be explicitly computed. We can then compare the results of other methods to this estimator. A simple calculation shows that the optimal Bayes estimator that minimizes the quantity is given by ridge regression:

$$\hat{w} = \arg\min_w \left[\sum_{i=1}^n (w^\top X_i - Y_i)^2 + \lambda d \|w\|_2^2 \right], \tag{11.17}$$

with $\lambda = \sigma^2 / \tau^2$. The following result compares the training loss and the test loss of ridge regression.

Theorem 11.27 *Consider* (11.16) *with fixed* τ, σ, n. *Let* $X = [X_1, \ldots, X_n]$ *be the* $d \times n$ *data matrix with response* $Y = [Y_1, \ldots, Y_n]^\top$. *Given any* $\delta \in (0, 1)$, *let*

$$c = \sqrt{\frac{\min(n, d)}{\max(n, d)}} + \sqrt{\frac{2 \ln(2/\delta)}{\max(n, d)}}.$$

Then with probability $1 - \delta$ *over the random choice of* X, *the following statements hold for the ridge regression estimator* (11.17). *There exists* $c', c'' \in [-\min(1, c), c]$ *such that the expected training loss and expected test loss satisfy the following equations. When* $d \leq n$,

$$\mathbb{E}\left[\frac{1}{n} \|X^\top \hat{w} - Y\|_2^2 \,\Big|\, X \right] = \left(1 - \frac{d}{n}\right) \sigma^2 + \frac{d^2}{n^2} \cdot \frac{\lambda^2(\tau^2(1 + c')^2 + (d/n)\sigma^2)}{((1 + c')^2 + \lambda d/n)^2},$$

$$\mathbb{E}\left[\|\hat{w} - w_*\|_2^2 + \sigma^2 \,\Big|\, X \right] = \sigma^2 + \frac{d}{n} \cdot \frac{(\lambda^2 \tau^2(d/n) + (1 + c'')^2 \sigma^2)}{((1 + c'')^2 + \lambda d/n)^2},$$

and when $d \geq n$,

$$\mathbb{E}\left[\frac{1}{n}\|X^\top \hat{w} - Y\|_2^2 \Big| X\right] = \frac{\lambda^2(\tau^2(1+c')^2 + \sigma^2)}{((1+c')^2 + \lambda)^2},$$

$$\mathbb{E}\left[\|\hat{w} - w_*\|_2^2 + \sigma^2 \Big| X\right] = \sigma^2 + \left(1 - \frac{n}{d}\right)\tau^2 + \frac{n}{d}\cdot\frac{(\lambda^2\tau^2 + (1+c'')^2\sigma^2)}{((1+c'')^2 + \lambda)^2}.$$

The conditional expectation is with respect to both w_* and $\{Y_i\}$.

Proof Let $Y = [Y_1, \ldots, Y_n]^\top$ and $\epsilon = Y - X^\top w_*$ be the noise vector. We can express

$$\hat{w} = X(X^\top X + \lambda dI_{n\times n})^{-1}X^\top w_* + X(X^\top X + \lambda dI_{n\times n})^{-1}\epsilon.$$

Let $K = \frac{1}{d}X^\top X$ be an $n \times n$ matrix. It is easy to verify that

$$\mathbb{E}\left[\frac{1}{n}\|X^\top \hat{w} - Y\|_2^2 \,|\, X\right] = \frac{\lambda^2}{n}\text{trace}((\tau^2 K + \sigma^2 I)(K + \lambda I)^{-2}), \qquad (11.18)$$

$$\mathbb{E}\left[\|\hat{w} - w_*\|_2^2 | X\right] = \left(1 - \frac{n}{d}\right)\tau^2 + \frac{1}{d}\text{trace}\left((\lambda^2\tau^2 I + \sigma^2 K)(K + \lambda I)^{-2}\right). \quad (11.19)$$

Since X is a $d \times n$ matrix with iid standard Gaussian entries, it is well known (see Rudelson and Vershynin, 2010, for example) that with probability at least $1 - \delta$, any singular value of X belongs to the interval

$$\left[\sqrt{\max(n,d)}(1 - c), \sqrt{\max(n,d)}(1 + c)\right].$$

If $d \leq n$, d eigenvalues of K belong to $[(n/d)(1 - \min(1,c))^2, (n/d)(1 + c)^2]$, and $n - d$ eigenvalues of K are zeros. We can now obtain the desired result by plugging this estimate into (11.18) and (11.19).

If $d \geq n$, then all n eigenvalues of K belong to $[(1 - \min(1,c))^2, (1 + c)^2]$. We can now obtain the desired result by plugging this estimate into (11.18) and (11.19). $\qquad\square$

The result of Theorem 11.27 focuses on the case $\min(n,d) \ll \max(n,d)$, which implies that $c', c'' \to 0$. It is also possible to derive more precise asymptotic results than that of Theorem 11.27 when $\sqrt{n/d} \to c \in (0,\infty)$ and $d, n \to \infty$. In such case, by using the Marchenko–Pastur law from the theory of random matrix (see Bai and Silverstein, 2010, Theorem 3.7 and Lemma 3.11), we can obtain the limiting eigenvalue distribution of K in the proof of Theorem 11.27, and use it to compute asymptotically precise characterizations of training and test losses. We leave the detailed calculations to Exercise 11.10. Specifically, when $\lambda = 0$, the following asymptotic expression is valid as $n \to \infty$ and $\sqrt{n/d} \to c < 1$:

$$\mathbb{E}\left[\frac{1}{n}\|X^\top \hat{w} - Y\|_2^2 \,|\, X\right] = \sigma^2 + \frac{n}{d-n}\sigma^2 + \left(1 - \frac{n}{d}\right)\tau^2 + o_p(1). \qquad (11.20)$$

To interpret Theorem 11.27, we first consider the classical regime, where $d/n \ll 1$ so that $c \approx 0$. With $\lambda = 0$, the training and test loss become

$$\text{training loss} \approx \left(1 - \frac{d}{n}\right)\sigma^2,$$

$$\text{test loss} \approx \left(1 + \frac{d}{n}\right)\sigma^2.$$

In this regime, we only overfit the training loss slightly by $(d/n)\sigma^2$, with a small generalization penalty $(d/n)\sigma^2$ for the test loss. The term $(d/n)\sigma^2$ corresponds to the estimation variance. The result is similar to that of the optimal $\lambda = \sigma^2/\tau^2$.

Next we consider the overparameterized regime, where $n/d \ll 1$ so that $c \approx 0$. The expected test loss is minimized with $\lambda = \sigma^2/\tau^2$, which corresponds to the choice of the optimal Bayes estimator. With $\lambda = \sigma^2/\tau^2$ and $c \approx 0$, we have

$$\text{training loss} \approx \frac{\sigma^4}{\tau^2 + \sigma^2},$$

$$\text{test loss} \approx \sigma^2 + \frac{n/d}{1 + \sigma^2/\tau^2}\sigma^2 + \left(1 - \frac{n}{d}\right)\tau^2.$$

If $\sigma \ll \tau$, then the training loss is approximately $\sigma^2(\sigma/\tau)^2$. It is significantly smaller than the test loss, which is approximately $(1 + n/d)\sigma^2 + (1 - n/d)\tau^2$. This shows that significant overfitting is necessary to achieve optimal performance in complex overparameterized models. We note the variance term becomes $(n/d)\sigma^2$ in the overparameterized case, and there is an extra bias term $(1 - n/d)\tau^2$.

We can also simply set $\lambda = 0$, corresponding to the minimum norm estimator, which is the focus in recent literature. In this case, we obtain that the training loss is zero, while test loss decreases as d increases:

$$\text{training loss} = 0,$$

$$\text{test loss} = \sigma^2 + \frac{n/d}{(1 + c'')^2}\sigma^2 + \left(1 - \frac{n}{d}\right)\tau^2.$$

When σ/τ is small, the test loss achieved at $\lambda = 0$ is close to the optimal test loss achieved at $\lambda = \sigma^2/\tau^2$, up to a difference of $O((n/d)\sigma^2)$.

More generally, when $\sqrt{d/n} \to c \in (0, 1)$, we can obtain (11.20) with $\lambda = 0$. This means even if we completely overfit the data, the resulting classifier still achieves near-optimal test performance since it nearly matches the result of the optimal Bayes estimator. The phenomenon that overfitting the noise is required to achieve near-optimal test performance is often referred to as *benign overfitting*.

The term $O((n/d)\sigma^2)$ in the overparameterized regime can be interpreted as estimation variance, which decreases as d increases. The reduction in variance, as d increases is what caused the double-descent phenomenon, which only happens in the overparameterized regime $d > n$. In contrast, when $d \ll n$, the variance term is $O((d/n)\sigma^2)$, which increases as d increases. Moreover, in our example, if we choose p out of d variables and perform regression with p parameters, then a similar calculation shows that in the overparameterized benign overfitting regime, the larger the chosen variable dimension p is, the smaller the variance term $O(\sigma^2 n/p)$ is, and the better the generalization error becomes. However, in the classical regime where the dimensionality p is smaller than n, the variance term is $O(\sigma^2 p/n)$, and we observe a classical U-shaped curve as in Figure 1.1 due to bias–variance trade-off. See Belkin et al. (2020) for a detailed analysis of this phenomenon for the minimum L_2-norm estimator.

One side effect of benign overfitting is that it is difficult to employ empirical process or stability techniques developed in earlier chapters in the overparameterized regime, because both methods work when the difference between the training loss and the test loss is small. However, such analysis may not be precise enough in the overparameterized regime when the difference between training loss and test loss becomes large. In fact, in the classical regime, we expect the generalization to behave as $O(\sigma^2 d/n)$, where d may also be replaced with the effective dimension as shown in Chapter 9. In the overparameterized regime with minimum regularization, we expect an additive variance-like term of $O(\sigma^2 n/d)$, in addition to a bias term of $(1 - n/d)\tau^2$. Even if τ is small, the variance term becomes smaller when d increases, and the bias term eventually dominates. However, classical learning theory has not developed effective technical tools to analyze the resulting bias terms in the general case.

The key insight that can be obtained from Theorem 11.27 is that if the true model belongs to a complex overparameterized model class, then to achieve near-optimal test performance, it is beneficial to overfit the training data. While it is often difficult to differentiate complex models from noise, the example in this section shows that overfitting is needed in overparameterized model learning, although the conclusion doesn't apply to observation noise in the classical regime where the effective dimension is smaller than n.

Intuitively, the reason that variance reduces when d increases is because overfitting to noise causes random perturbations in the estimated model parameter, and the perturbation belongs to the subspace spanned by the training data. Its effect on the test data becomes minor when d increases because the test data are nearly orthogonal to the training data. This means that test data are insensitive to a random perturbation of parameter in the subspace spanned by the training data. One can generalize this observation to the situation that test data are nearly orthogonal to the training data outside a low-dimensional space. This allows a more general covariance structure of the data matrix for which benign overfitting can happen. If the main function belongs to the low-dimensional space, then by using the classical statistical analysis inside the low-dimensional space, and orthogonality outside of the low-dimensional space, one can prove Bayes consistency of the minimum norm estimator even when such an estimator completely overfits the noise (Bartlett et al., 2020).

11.8 Historical and Bibliographical Remarks

Mathematical models of biological neurons appeared in the 1940s (McCulloch and Pitts, 1943). The idea was further developed into a computational model called perceptron by Rosenblatt (1962). However its limitation in representation power was soon recognized by Minsky and Papert (1969). To overcome the limitation, modern neural networks employ multilayer perceptrons with hidden layers, which can be trained using gradient descent (also referred to as back propagation) (Rumelhart et al., 1986). In fact, even two-layer neural networks are known to be universal (Leshno et al., 1993).

However, deep neural networks have additional benefits in representation power because high-level composite features can be more easily represented using deep networks with fewer neurons. There exist functions that can be represented by deep neural networks with a small number of nodes, but require an exponentially increasing number of nodes to represent using shallow neural networks (Telgarsky, 2016; Liang and Srikant, 2017). Related results show that deep neural networks can also represent any function with a fixed number of nodes per layer (Lu et al., 2017; Hanin, 2019). This implies that in order to represent a complex function, one can either increase a network's width or its depth. From representation point of view, depth is more important than width in that a wide shallow network can be represented by a fixed width deep neural network with a similar number of neurons (Vardi et al., 2022). Nevertheless, wide neural networks are generally easier to optimize, and it was observed in practice that with a fixed model size, the optimal trade-off between depth and width requires a balanced increase of both width and depth (Tan and Le, 2019).

The idea of using random features in machine learning was proposed by Huang et al. (2006). The resulting method is closely related to two-layer neural networks without optimizing the input layer (Rahimi and Recht, 2009). Its connection to kernel methods using random Fourier features was investigated in Rahimi and Recht (2007). One advantage of random Fourier features is that the computation may rely on fast Fourier transform (Le et al., 2013). Due to its simplicity and efficient computation, the method has been applied to various problems.

The formulation of infinitely wide neural networks as kernel methods or Gaussian processes had already been considered in the 1990s (Neal, 1995; Williams, 1997). However, the more rigorous development of neural tangent kernels has appeared more recently (Jacot et al., 2018). From the optimization perspective, it is known that with the NTK initialization in Section 11.4, if we let $m \to \infty$, then gradient descent finds a solution with zero training loss in an infinitely small neighborhood of the initialization (see Li and Liang, 2018; Zou et al., 2018; Allen-Zhu et al., 2019b,a; Du et al., 2019; Zou and Gu, 2019). These results are consistent with the existence of universal representation in a small neighborhood of the initialization in Theorem 11.17. This phenomenon is also referred to as the "lazy training" regime by Chizat et al. (2019). In the lazy training regime, the optimization problem is nearly linear, and the dynamics of gradient descent can be analyzed using a linear model approximation.

The mean-field view of neural networks was motivated by the mean-field analysis in statistical physics (Engel and Van den Broeck, 2001), where the interaction of a large number of neurons can be represented using the average effect according to their joint probability distribution. It was shown that using such a mean-field analysis, and techniques related to optimal transport, the continuous limit of two-layer neural networks converge globally by using either noisy gradient descent (Mei et al., 2018) or suitable activation functions such as ReLU (Chizat and Bach, 2018). The global convergence is possible because the mean-field formulation of two-layer neural networks is convex in the probability distribution of the model parameters, although the original discrete neural network is nonconvex in the model parameters. It was shown recently that the convexification of overparameterized neural networks can be extended to neural networks with more than two layers (Gu et al., 2020; Fang et al., 2022). However, the convergence analysis for deep neural networks is far more complex than the analysis of two-layer neural networks, and only specialized results can be established under limited conditions (Fang et al., 2021, 2022).

As we have shown in Section 11.5, the mean-field view employs a global L_1 regularization while the NTK formulation implicitly uses a local L_2 regularization. Therefore the two methods have different behaviors. In particular, L_1 regularization allows the mean-field formulation to learn feature representations, which is not possible in the NTK view. The solution behavior under the mean-field setting has also been investigated by Chizat and Bach (2020). Moreover, one can show that when the scaling parameter $\alpha \to \infty$, the convergence behavior of mean-field formulation approaches that of the NTK regime (see Mei et al., 2019; Chen et al., 2020).

It was observed by Zhang et al. (2017) that modern neural network training procedure can overfit a completely noisy target, and thus the model class of these neural networks is extremely complex. For such a complex model class, the classical learning theory does not fully explain its good generalization performance. The term benign overfitting is introduced to explain this mystery. The underlying assumption is that for certain computational procedures, such as the minimum norm estimator or estimator obtained from SGD, there is an implicit constraint of the search space (also referred to as *implicit bias*) so that among all models that achieve small training loss, the procedure can choose a model that performs well on the test set. Some recent mathematical analysis proved such claims more rigorously under appropriate conditions (Bartlett et al., 2020; Tsigler and Bartlett, 2020; Zou et al., 2021) under which test data are nearly orthogonal to the training data except for a small dimensionality $k < n$. Benign overfitting is closely related to the double-descent phenomenon observed in Belkin et al. (2019) and Nakkiran et al. (2021) for neural network training. This phenomenon has since drawn considerable theoretical interest (Hastie et al., 2022; Belkin et al., 2020; Mei and Montanari, 2022). The intuition of benign overfitting in Theorem 11.27 is analogous to the example given by Belkin et al. (2020) to illustrate double descent. The Bayesian argument in our analysis also implies that in order to achieve good test performance, it is necessary to overfit (also see Cheng et al., 2022). Both benign overfitting and double descent are still active research areas because the mathematical tools to handle the general situation have not been fully developed.

Exercises

11.1 Consider ReLU neural networks for approximating one-dimensional functions on $[0, 1]$. Prove that any piecewise linear function can be represented by a two-layer ReLU network.

11.2 For a k-layer ReLU neural network, with m nodes per layer, show that its output is a piecewise linear function. Estimate the maximum possible number of linear segments, hence the crossing number it may contain. How large should m be to achieve the same crossing number as that of the $f_{k^2}(x)$ function defined in the proof of Theorem 11.4?

11.3 Prove Proposition 11.12 and Proposition 11.13.

11.4 Prove Proposition 11.15.

11.5 Show if Assumption 11.14 holds, then starting from the NTK initialization, a finite number of gradient descent steps with finite step size remains in the NTK regime when m is sufficiently large.

11.6 Prove Proposition 11.16.

11.7 Consider Example 11.22. Let $r'(w) = 2(L/\lambda)\|w\|_2^2/(1 + \beta\|w\|_2^2)$.

- Show that $\|\nabla^2 r'(w)\|_2 \le c_0(L/\lambda)$ for some absolute constant c_0 independent of β.
- Show that if β is sufficiently small, then $V(w) = \lambda^{-1}[g_0(w, p) + r(w)] + r'(w)$ is strongly convex.
- Let $U(w) = \lambda^{-1}[g_0(w, p) + r(w)]$, then $|U(w) - V(w)| = |r'(w)|$ is bounded. Use Lemma 11.21 to show that (11.11) holds with some $\mu > 0$.

11.8 Consider (11.16), and assume that we randomly select p out of d variables and train a linear model using minimum L_2-norm estimator with the selected variables. Find the expected test loss for both $p < n$ and $p > n$.

11.9 Prove (11.18) and (11.19).

11.10 Consider Theorem 11.27 under the assumption that $\sqrt{n/d} \to c \in (0, 1)$ and $n \to \infty$. Consider the $n \times n$ matrix K in its proof. Lemma 3.11 of Bai and Silverstein (2010) implies that as $n \to \infty$,

$$g(\lambda) = \frac{1}{n}\text{trace}((K + \lambda I)^{-1}) = \frac{\sqrt{(1 + c^2 + \lambda)^2 - 4c^2} + c^2 - 1 - \lambda}{2c^2\lambda}.$$

Show that

$$\frac{1}{n}\text{trace}((\alpha K + \beta I)(K + \lambda I)^{-2}) = \alpha g(\lambda) + (\alpha\lambda - \beta)\frac{dg(\lambda)}{d\lambda}.$$

Use this formula to give closed-form expressions for (11.18) and (11.19).

12

Lower Bounds and Minimax Analysis

This chapter considers lower bounds for empirical processes and statistical estimation problems. We know that upper bounds for empirical processes and empirical risk minimization can be obtained from the covering number analysis. We show that under suitable conditions, lower bounds can also be obtained using covering numbers.

12.1 Lower Bounds for Empirical Processes

In previous chapters, such as Chapter 6, we showed that uniform convergence of empirical processes in terms of Rademacher complexity can be obtained using covering numbers and the chaining technique.

This section considers techniques to derive lower bounds. For simplicity, we will only consider empirical processes associated with a function family $\mathcal{F} = \{f(w, z) : w \in \Omega\}$, defined on the empirical measure $\mathcal{S}_n = \{Z_1, \ldots, Z_n\}$.

We shall first introduce the notation of Gaussian complexity, which is useful for obtaining lower bounds.

Definition 12.1 The empirical Gaussian complexity of $\mathcal{F}$ is defined as

$$G(\mathcal{F}, \mathcal{S}_n) = \mathbb{E}_g \sup_{f \in \mathcal{F}} \frac{1}{n} \sum_{i=1}^{n} g_i f(Z_i),$$

where $[g_1, \ldots, g_n]$ are independent standard normal random variables: $g_i \sim N(0, 1)$ for $i = 1, \ldots, n$.

The following result shows that Gaussian complexity and Rademacher complexity are equivalent up to a logarithmic factor in n.

Proposition 12.2 (Bartlett and Mendelson, 2002) *There exists an absolute constant $C > 0$ such that if $\mathcal{F} = -\mathcal{F}$, then*

$$C^{-1} R(\mathcal{F}, \mathcal{S}_n) \leq G(\mathcal{F}, \mathcal{S}_n) \leq C \ln n \, R(\mathcal{F}, \mathcal{S}_n).$$

Both Rademacher complexity and Gaussian complexity can be used to obtain expected uniform convergence for empirical processes. Upper bounds for both Rademacher complexity and Gaussian complexity can be obtained from covering numbers via Dudley's entropy integral, as shown in Theorem 6.25. However, the Gaussian complexity also has a lower bound using covering numbers, called

Sudakov minoration. Its proof relies on Slepian's lemma, which is a comparison lemma for Gaussian complexity, similar to the comparison lemma for Rademacher complexity in Lemma 6.29. The proof of this result can be found in Slepian (1962) and Joag-Dev et al. (1983).

Lemma 12.3 (Slepian's Lemma)   *Let $[X_1, \ldots, X_n]$ and $[Y_1, \ldots, Y_n]$ denote two zero-mean multivariate normal random vectors. Assume that*

$$\forall i \neq j, \qquad \mathbb{E}(X_i - X_j)^2 \geq \mathbb{E}(Y_i - Y_j)^2.$$

Then

$$\mathbb{E} \max_i X_i \geq \mathbb{E} \max_i Y_i.$$

Empirical process lower bounds rely on the packing number $M(\cdot)$, which is defined in Definition 5.1. Theorem 5.2 implies that it is equivalent to the covering number up to a scale of 2. The following result, referred to as *Sudakov minoration*, is a direct consequence of Slepian's lemma.

Theorem 12.4 (Sudakov Minoration)   *For any $\epsilon > 0$,*

$$\sqrt{\ln M(\epsilon, \mathcal{F}, L_2(\mathcal{S}_n))} \leq \frac{2\sqrt{n} G(\mathcal{F}, \mathcal{S}_n)}{\epsilon} + 1.$$

Proof   Let $\mathcal{F}_M = \{f_1, \ldots, f_M\} \subset \mathcal{F}$ be an ϵ packing subset of $\mathcal{F}$ under the $L_2(\mathcal{S}_n)$ metric. Consider independent standard Gaussian random variables $[g_1, \ldots, g_n]$:

$$\mathbb{E} \sup_{f \in \mathcal{F}} \frac{1}{n} \sum_{i=1}^{n} g_i f(Z_i) \geq \mathbb{E} \sup_{j \in [M]} \frac{1}{n} \sum_{i=1}^{n} g_i f_j(Z_i).$$

Let $g'_1, \ldots, g'_M$ be independent zero-mean normal random variables with variance $\epsilon^2/(2n)$ each. We then have for each $j \neq k$,

$$\mathbb{E} \left(\frac{1}{n} \sum_{i=1}^{n} g_i f_j(Z_i) - \frac{1}{n} \sum_{i=1}^{n} g_i f_k(Z_i) \right)^2$$

$$= \frac{1}{n^2} \sum_{i=1}^{n} (f_j(Z_i) - f_k(Z_i))^2$$

$$\geq \frac{1}{n} \epsilon^2 = \mathbb{E} \left(g'_j - g'_k \right)^2.$$

Using Slepian's lemma, we have

$$G(\mathcal{F}, L_2(\mathcal{S}_n)) \geq \mathbb{E} \sup_j g'_j.$$

We know from Theorem 2.1 that for all j and $z \geq 0$,

$$\Pr\left(g_j' \leq \frac{\epsilon z}{\sqrt{2n}}\right) \leq 1 - 0.5 e^{-(z+1)^2/2},$$

$$\Pr\left(g_j' \leq -\frac{\epsilon z}{\sqrt{2n}}\right) \leq 0.5 e^{-z^2/2},$$

and thus

$$\Pr\left(\sup_j g_j' \leq \frac{\epsilon z}{\sqrt{2n}}\right) \leq (1 - 0.5 e^{-(z+1)^2/2})^M,$$

$$\Pr\left(\sup_j g_j' \leq -\frac{\epsilon z}{\sqrt{2n}}\right) \leq 0.5^M e^{-Mz^2/2}.$$

We note that the desired inequality is trivial for $M \leq 2$. For $M \geq 3$,

$$\mathbb{E}\sup_j \frac{\sqrt{2n}g_j'}{\epsilon}$$

$$= -\int_{-\infty}^0 \Pr\left(\sup_j g_j' \leq \frac{\epsilon z}{\sqrt{2n}}\right) dz + \int_0^\infty \Pr\left(\sup_j g_j' \geq \frac{\epsilon z}{\sqrt{2n}}\right) dz$$

$$\geq \int_0^\infty \left(1 - (1 - 0.5 e^{-(z+1)^2/2})^M\right) dz - \int_{-\infty}^0 0.5^M e^{-Mz^2/2} dz$$

$$\geq \int_0^{\sqrt{2\ln M}-1} \left(1 - 0.5(1 - 0.5/M)^M\right) dz - \int_{-\infty}^0 0.5^M e^{-Mz^2/2} dz$$

$$\geq \int_0^{\sqrt{2\ln M}-1} \left(1 - 0.5/\sqrt{e}\right) dz - 0.5^{M+1} M^{-1/2} \int_{-\infty}^\infty e^{-z^2/2} dz$$

$$= (1 - 0.5/\sqrt{e})(\sqrt{2\ln M} - 1) - 0.5^{M+1}(3)^{-1/2}\sqrt{2\pi}$$

$$\geq 0.98\sqrt{\ln M} - 0.9.$$

This implies the desired bound. $\square$

A more precise characterization of Gaussian complexity, due to Talagrand (1996a), is to consider a generalization of covering numbers (*majorizing measures*), with a generalization of the chaining technique referred to as *generic chaining*. We consider any measure μ on $\mathcal{F}$, and let

$$\mu(f, \epsilon, L_2(\mathcal{S}_n)) = \mu\left(\{f' \in \mathcal{F} : \|f' - f\|_{L_2(\mathcal{S}_n)} \leq \epsilon\}\right).$$

Then $-\ln\mu(f, \epsilon, L_2(\mathcal{S}_n))$ may be regarded as a generalization of the entropy number of $\mathcal{F}$ localized around f. If we define

$$\gamma_2(\mathcal{F}, \mathcal{S}_n) = \inf_\mu \sup_{f \in \mathcal{F}} \int_0^\infty \sqrt{\frac{-\ln\mu(f, \epsilon, L_2(\mathcal{S}_n))}{n}} \, d\epsilon,$$

then the following result shows the equivalence of Gaussian complexity and the corresponding entropy integral in terms of majorizing measure (Talagrand, 1996a).

Theorem 12.5 (The Majorizing Measure Theorem)   *There exists an absolute constant $C > 0$ so that*

$$C^{-1}\gamma_2(\mathcal{F}, \mathcal{S}_n) \leq G(\mathcal{F}, \mathcal{S}_n) \leq C\gamma_2(\mathcal{F}, \mathcal{S}_n).$$

The result shows that the entropy integral bound for empirical processes is generally tight, although one may need to replace covering numbers by majorizing measures in certain situations. In other cases, the difference between covering number and majorizing measure is not significant.

12.2 Minimax Analysis for Statistical Estimation

We consider the general statistical estimation problem, where we want to estimate a certain quantity $\theta \in \Theta$ based on a sample Z from a distribution $\mathcal{D}$ on $\mathcal{Z}$. A learning algorithm (estimator) $\mathcal{A}$ is a (possibly random) map $\mathcal{Z} \to \Theta$. The quality of the estimated distribution dependent quantity $\theta \in \Theta$ can be measured by a general loss function

$$Q(\theta, \mathcal{D}),$$

and the goal is to find an estimator $\mathcal{A}$ that achieves the smallest loss $Q(\mathcal{A}(Z), \mathcal{D})$ when $Z \sim \mathcal{D}$.

Note that this definition can handle the general setting of supervised learning, where we observe n iid training examples $\mathcal{S}_n = \{Z_1, \ldots, Z_n\}$ from an unknown underlying distribution $\mathcal{D}$. In this case, we may simply take $Z = \mathcal{S}_n$ that is generated according to the product distribution $\mathcal{D}^n$. The model parameter space Θ can be regarded as the set of prediction functions, and we may denote θ by f, so that the learning algorithm $\mathcal{A}$ learns a function $\hat{f} = \mathcal{A}(\mathcal{S}_n)$.

Example 12.6   For a least squares problem, $f(x)$ is a real-valued regression function. Let $f_{\mathcal{D}}(x) = \mathbb{E}_{\mathcal{D}}[Y|X = x]$. We may define

$$Q(f, \mathcal{D}) = \mathbb{E}_{X \sim \mathcal{D}}(f(X) - f_{\mathcal{D}}(X))^2.$$

Example 12.7   For conditional density estimation with K classes $y \in \{1, \ldots, K\}$, we may consider Θ as the class of vector-valued density functions

$$f(x) = [p(y = 1|x), \ldots, p(y = K|x)].$$

For density estimation, the estimation quality can be measured by the KL-divergence

$$Q(f, \mathcal{D}) = \mathbb{E}_{X \sim \mathcal{D}} \mathbb{E}_{Y \sim p_{\mathcal{D}}(Y|X)} \ln \frac{p_{\mathcal{D}}(Y|X)}{p(Y|X)},$$

or by squared Hellinger distance:

$$Q(f, \mathcal{D}) = 2 - 2\mathbb{E}_{X \sim \mathcal{D}} \mathbb{E}_{Y \sim p_{\mathcal{D}}(Y|X)} \left(\frac{p(Y|X)}{p_{\mathcal{D}}(Y|X)} \right)^{1/2}.$$

Example 12.8 For K-class classification problems, if we are interested in classification accuracy, then we may use the excess classification error over the Bayes classification error as quality measure. Here,

$$f_{\mathcal{D}}(x) = \arg\max_{\ell} p_{\mathcal{D}}(Y = \ell | X = x)$$

is the optimal Bayes classifier. Let $f(x) \in \{1, \dots, K\}$ be any classifier, then we can define

$$Q(f, \mathcal{D}) = \mathbb{E}_{X \sim \mathcal{D}}[\Pr(Y = f_{\mathcal{D}}(X)|X) - \Pr(Y = f(X)|X)].$$

In statistical estimation, we do not know the true distribution $\mathcal{D}$, but can only observe a sample $\mathcal{S}_n$ from $\mathcal{D}^n$. In this case, we may consider a family of distributions $\mathcal{P}$ that contains $\mathcal{D}$. For each $\mathcal{D} \in \mathcal{P}$, a learning algorithm learns a quantity θ that depends on $\mathcal{D}$ from a sample $\mathcal{S}_n \sim \mathcal{D}^n$. We are interested in the worst-case expected risk of a learning algorithm $\mathcal{A}$ to measure the ability of the algorithm to learn the quantity θ with respect to a family of distributions $\mathcal{P}$.

Definition 12.9 Consider a distribution family $\mathcal{P}$ on sample space $\mathcal{Z}$, a parameter space Θ. A learning algorithm $\mathcal{A} \colon \mathcal{Z}^n \to \Theta$, a loss function $Q \colon \Theta \times \mathcal{P} \to \mathbb{R}$. Then the worst-case expected risk of a learning algorithm (i.e. a statistical estimator) $\mathcal{A}$ with respect to $\mathcal{P}$ is given by

$$r_n(\mathcal{A}, \mathcal{P}, Q) = \sup_{\mathcal{D} \in \mathcal{P}} \mathbb{E}_{\mathcal{S}_n \sim \mathcal{D}^n} \mathbb{E}_{\mathcal{A}} \, Q(\mathcal{A}(\mathcal{S}_n), \mathcal{D}),$$

where $\mathbb{E}_{\mathcal{A}}$ is the expectation over any internal randomization of $\mathcal{A}$. Moreover, the minimax risk is defined as

$$r_n(\mathcal{P}, Q) = \inf_{\mathcal{A}} r_n(\mathcal{A}, \mathcal{P}, Q).$$

The standard statistical framework for optimality is to find an algorithm with the smallest worse-case risk $r_n(\mathcal{A}, \mathcal{P}, Q)$. This type of analysis is referred to as *minimax analysis*. The minimax risk $r_n(\mathcal{P}, Q)$ depends only on sample size n, distribution family $\mathcal{P}$, and loss function Q. In nonparametric statistics, it is difficult to find the exact expression of minimax risk. Therefore we often consider rate optimal algorithms $\mathcal{A}$, which achieve the optimal minimax risk $r_n(\mathcal{P}, Q)$ up to a constant factor as $n \to \infty$.

In minimax analysis, we are interested in estimating the minimax risk (up to a constant factor). To establish an upper bound of $r_n(\mathcal{P}, Q)$, we consider specific learning algorithms and analyze their convergence rates. For example, if we consider the ERM method $\mathcal{A}_{\mathrm{erm}}$ for the least squares regression problem, then we may obtain an upper bound of

$$r_n(\mathcal{P}, Q) \leq r_n(\mathcal{A}_{\mathrm{erm}}, \mathcal{P}, Q) = O(n^{-r})$$

for some $r > 0$, based on the analysis of Example 6.49.

On the other hand, if we can show a lower bound $r_n(\mathcal{P}, Q) \geq cn^{-r}$ for some constant c that may depend on $\mathcal{P}$ but independent of n, then we know that the

ERM method achieves the optimal minimax lower bound. That is, no statistical estimator can perform much better than ERM up to a constant factor for this distribution family. If the lower bound is $O(n^{-r'})$ for $r' > r$, then ERM may not be optimal. As we will see, both situations can happen, depending on the entropy of the function class $\mathcal{F}$ to be estimated.

12.3 Lower Bounds Using Fano's Inequality

In this section, we will describe a general method to derive lower bounds for statistical estimation based on Fano's inequality, which is stated as follows.

Theorem 12.10 (Fano's Inequality) *Consider a finite family of distributions $\mathcal{P} = \{\mathcal{D}_1, \ldots, \mathcal{D}_N\}$. Assume that j is a random variable that is uniformly distributed in $\{1, \ldots, N\}$, and conditioned on j, $Z \sim \mathcal{D}_j$. Let $f(Z) \in \{1, \ldots, N\}$ be an estimate of the index j. Then*

$$\frac{1}{N} \sum_{j=1}^{N} \Pr_{Z \sim \mathcal{D}_j} (f(Z) \neq j) \geq 1 - \frac{I(j, Z) + \ln 2}{\ln(N)},$$

where

$$I(j, Z) = \mathbb{E}_{(j,Z) \sim p(j,Z)} \ln \frac{p(j, Z)}{p(j)p(Z)}$$

is the mutual information between random variables j and Z (see Appendix B).

In the following, we prove a generalization of the Fano's inequality, which is more convenient to apply for our purpose.

Theorem 12.11 *Consider a finite family of distributions $\mathcal{P} = \{\mathcal{D}_1, \ldots, \mathcal{D}_N\}$. Given a loss function Q on $\Theta \times \mathcal{P}$, let*

$$m = \sup_{\theta \in \Theta} \left| \{k : Q(\theta, \mathcal{D}_k) < \epsilon\} \right|.$$

Assume that j is a random variable that is uniformly distributed in $\{1, \ldots, N\}$, and conditioned on j, $Z \sim \mathcal{D}_j$. Given any (possibly random) estimator $\mathcal{A}(Z)$,

$$\frac{1}{N} \sum_{j=1}^{N} \Pr_{Z \sim \mathcal{D}_j} (Q(\mathcal{A}(Z), \mathcal{D}_j) < \epsilon) \leq \max \left(\frac{m}{N}, \frac{I(j, Z) + \ln 2}{\ln(N/m)} \right),$$

where $I(j, Z)$ is the mutual information of j and Z. The probability includes possible randomization in $\mathcal{A}$.

Proof Let p_j be the density function of Z for $\mathcal{D}_j$. Then the joint distribution of (j, Z) is given by

$$p(j, Z) = \frac{1}{N} p_j(Z).$$

We can introduce a random variable Z' with the same marginal distribution as Z, but independent of j:

$$p(Z') = \frac{1}{N} \sum_{j=1}^{N} p_j(Z').$$

Now, consider an arbitrary and possibly random estimator $\hat{\theta} = \mathcal{A}(Z)$. Let $\hat{\theta}' = \mathcal{A}(Z')$. By the data processing inequality for KL-divergence (see Theorem B.4), with input (j, Z) and binary output $h(j, Z) = \mathbb{1}(Q(\hat{\theta}, \mathcal{D}_j) < \epsilon)$, where $\mathbb{1}(\cdot)$ is the indicator function, we obtain

$$\mathrm{KL}(\mathbb{1}(Q(\hat{\theta}, \mathcal{D}_j) < \epsilon) \| \mathbb{1}(Q(\hat{\theta}', \mathcal{D}_j) < \epsilon)) \leq \mathrm{KL}((j, Z) \| (j, Z')) = I(j, Z).$$

Now let $q = \Pr(Q(\hat{\theta}, \mathcal{D}_j) < \epsilon)$ and $q' = \Pr(Q(\hat{\theta}', \mathcal{D}_j) < \epsilon)$, then our inequality can be rewritten as

$$\mathrm{KL}(q\|q') = q \ln \frac{q}{q'} + (1-q) \ln \frac{1-q}{1-q'} \leq I(j, Z).$$

Since $\hat{\theta}'$ is independent of j, and

$$|\{j \colon Q(\hat{\theta}', \mathcal{D}_j) < \epsilon\}| \leq m$$

for each $\hat{\theta}'$, we obtain

$$q' \leq m/N.$$

If $q \leq m/N$, we have proved the desired inequality. Otherwise, since $\mathrm{KL}(q\|q')$ as a function of q' is decreasing in $[0, q]$, we have

$$q \ln \frac{q}{m/N} + (1-q) \ln \frac{1-q}{1-m/N} \leq I(j, Z).$$

Since $q \ln q + (1-q) \ln(1-q) \geq -\ln 2$, we obtain

$$-\ln 2 + q \ln \frac{N}{m} + (1-q) \ln \frac{N}{N-m} \leq I(j, Z).$$

This implies that

$$q \leq \frac{I(j, Z) + \ln 2}{\ln(N/m)}.$$

We thus obtain the desired bound.   □

Example 12.12 In Theorem 12.11, if we take $\Theta = \{1, \ldots, N\}$, $Q(\theta, \mathcal{D}_j) = \mathbb{1}(\theta \neq j)$, and $\epsilon = 1$, then we have $m = 1$. Note that $1/N \leq \ln 2 / \ln(N)$, we obtain the following result

$$\frac{1}{N} \sum_{j=1}^{N} \Pr_{Z \sim \mathcal{D}_j} (\mathcal{A}(Z) = j) \leq \frac{I(j, Z) + \ln 2}{\ln N}.$$

This implies Fano's inequality of Theorem 12.10.

The following example gives an application of $m > 1$.

Example 12.13 In Theorem 12.11, if we take $\Theta = [1, N]$ for $N > 2$, $Q(\theta, \mathcal{D}_j) = |\theta - j|$, and $\epsilon = 1$, then we have $m = 2$. Note that $2/N \leq \ln 2/\ln(N/2)$, we obtain the following result:

$$\frac{1}{N} \sum_{j=1}^{N} \Pr_{Z \sim \mathcal{D}_j} (|\mathcal{A}(Z) - j| < 1) \leq \frac{I(j, Z) + \ln 2}{\ln(N/2)}.$$

The following result shows that if the distributions $\{\mathcal{D}_j\}$ are close to each other, then the mutual information $I(j, Z)$ in Theorem 12.11 is small.

Lemma 12.14 *The mutual information $I(j, Z)$ in Theorem 12.11 satisfies the inequality*

$$I(j, Z) \leq \frac{1}{N^2} \sum_{j=1}^{N} \sum_{k=1}^{N} \mathrm{KL}(\mathcal{D}_j \| \mathcal{D}_k) \leq \sup_{j,k} \mathrm{KL}(\mathcal{D}_j \| \mathcal{D}_k).$$

Proof We have

$$I(j, Z) = \frac{1}{N} \sum_{j=1}^{N} \mathbb{E}_{Z \sim \mathcal{D}_j} \ln \frac{p_{\mathcal{D}_j}(Z)}{\frac{1}{N} \sum_{k=1}^{N} p_{\mathcal{D}_k}(Z)}$$

$$\leq \frac{1}{N^2} \sum_{j=1}^{N} \sum_{k=1}^{N} \mathbb{E}_{Z \sim \mathcal{D}_j} \ln \frac{p_{\mathcal{D}_j}(Z)}{p_{\mathcal{D}_k}(Z)},$$

where the inequality used Jensen's inequality and the convexity of $-\ln z$. □

The following minimax risk lower bound is a direct application of generalized Fano's inequality to the product distribution of KL-divergence. We leave its proof as an exercise.

Theorem 12.15 *Consider a distributions family $\mathcal{P}$ that contains a finite subset of distributions $\{\mathcal{D}_1, \ldots, \mathcal{D}_N\}$. Let Q be a loss function on $\Theta \times \mathcal{P}$, and*

$$m = \sup_{\theta \in \Theta} \left| \{k : Q(\theta, \mathcal{D}_k) < \epsilon\} \right|.$$

Let $\mathcal{A}(\mathcal{S}_n)$ be an arbitrary (possibly random) estimator of $\mathcal{D}_j$ from iid data $\mathcal{S}_n = [Z_1, \ldots, Z_n] \sim \mathcal{D}_j^n$. If $m \leq N/2$ and

$$\ln(N/m) \geq \ln 4 + 2n \sup_{j,k} \mathrm{KL}(\mathcal{D}_j \| \mathcal{D}_k),$$

then

$$\frac{1}{N} \sum_{j=1}^{N} \Pr_{\mathcal{S}_n \sim \mathcal{D}_j^n} (Q(\mathcal{A}(\mathcal{S}_n), \mathcal{D}_j) < \epsilon) \leq 0.5,$$

where the probability also includes possible randomization in $\mathcal{A}$. If $Q(\cdot, \cdot)$ is non-negative, then this implies that $r_n(\mathcal{P}, Q) \geq 0.5\epsilon$.

The following example illustrates how to use the result.

Example 12.16 Consider the d-dimensional Gaussian mean estimation problem, where the goal is to estimate a Gaussian $N(\theta, I)$ with unknown mean $\theta \in \mathbb{R}^d$ such that $\|\theta\|_2 \leq 1$, based on observations $Z_1, \ldots, Z_n \sim \mathcal{D} = N(\theta, I)$. Let $\hat{\theta}$ be the estimated mean, and we define metric

$$Q(\hat{\theta}, \mathcal{D}) = Q(\hat{\theta}, \theta) = \|\hat{\theta} - \theta\|_2.$$

Then we are interested in the number of samples n needed to obtain an estimate as good as 0.5ϵ for some small $\epsilon > 0$.

In order to apply Theorem 12.15, we consider the ball $B(4\epsilon) = \{\theta \colon \|\theta\|_2 \leq 4\epsilon\}$. From Theorem 5.3, we know that there exists $N = ((4\epsilon)/(2\epsilon))^d = 2^d$ centers $\{\theta_j \colon j = 1, \ldots, N\}$ in $B(4\epsilon)$ such that $\|\theta_j - \theta_k\|_2 > 2\epsilon$ for $j \neq k$. Since $\|\hat{\theta} - \theta_j\|_2 + \|\hat{\theta} - \theta_k\|_2 \geq \|\theta_j - \theta_k\|_2 > 2\epsilon$, we obtain

$$|\{k \colon Q(\theta, \theta_k) < \epsilon\}| \leq 1.$$

Let $p_j = N(\theta_j, I)$. This implies that for all $\theta_j, \theta_k \in B(4\epsilon)$,

$$\mathrm{KL}(p_j \| p_k) = \frac{1}{2} \|\theta_j - \theta_k\|_2^2 \leq 32\epsilon^2.$$

The condition of Theorem 12.15 holds when

$$\ln(N) = \ln(2^d) \geq \ln 4 + 64n\epsilon^2 \geq \ln 4 + 2n \sup_{j,k} \mathrm{KL}(p_j \| p_k).$$

This implies that if

$$n \leq \frac{(d-2)\ln 2}{64\epsilon^2},$$

then for all mean estimator $\hat{\theta}$, there exists $\theta_j \in B(4\epsilon)$ so that for n iid samples from p_j,

$$\mathbb{E}\|\hat{\theta} - \theta_j\|_2 \geq 0.5\epsilon.$$

12.4 Minimax Analysis for Least Squares Regression

For the least squares regression problem in Example 12.6, we consider a function class $\mathcal{F}$ that contains the optimal prediction rule $f_{\mathcal{D}}(X) = \mathbb{E}[Y|X]$, and

$$Q_{\mathrm{LS}}(f, \mathcal{D}) = \mathbb{E}_{X \sim \mathcal{D}}(f(X) - f_{\mathcal{D}}(X))^2.$$

The following result is a direct consequence of Theorem 12.15.

Theorem 12.17 *Consider the regression model, where $X \sim \mathcal{D}_X$ with known $\mathcal{D}_X$, and*

$$Y = f_{\mathcal{D}}(X) + \epsilon,$$

where ϵ is zero-mean noise that may depend on $f_{\mathcal{D}}(\cdot) \in \mathcal{F}$. Assume there exists $\sigma > 0$ so that

$$\mathbb{E}_{X \sim \mathcal{D}_X}(f(X) - f'(X))^2 \geq 2\sigma^2 \mathrm{KL}(\mathcal{D}_f \| \mathcal{D}_{f'}),$$

where $\mathcal{D}_f$ is the distribution of (X, Y) when $f_\mathcal{D} = f$. If $\mathcal{F}$ contains N functions $f_1, \ldots, f_N$ such that

$$\ln N \geq \ln 4 + n\sigma^{-2} \sup_{j,k} \mathbb{E}_{X \sim \mathcal{D}}(f_j(X) - f_k(X))^2,$$

then

$$r_n(\mathcal{P}, \mathcal{Q}_{\mathrm{LS}}) \geq 0.125 \inf_{j \neq k} \mathbb{E}_{X \sim \mathcal{D}_X}(f_j(X) - f_k(X))^2.$$

Proof Define $Q(f, f') = \mathbb{E}_{X \sim \mathcal{D}}(f(X) - f'(X))^2$. Note that for each $f \in \mathcal{F}$, we associate a $\mathcal{D}_f \in \mathcal{P} = \{\mathcal{D}_f : f \in \mathcal{F}\}$. We also let $\epsilon = 0.25 \min_{j \neq k} Q(f_j, f_k)$, and it can be checked that for all $j \neq k$,

$$\max(Q(f, f_j), Q(f, f_k)) \geq (Q(f, f_j) + Q(f, f_k))/2 \geq Q(f_j, f_k)/4 \geq \epsilon.$$

This means that we can take $m = 1$, and obtain the theorem as a direct consequence of Theorem 12.15. $\qquad \square$

The following result implies that the condition of Theorem 12.17 holds for Gaussian noise.

Proposition 12.18 *Consider $\mathcal{D}_f(X, Y)$ so that $X \sim \mathcal{D}_X$ is identical for all $f \in \mathcal{F}$, and $Y \sim N(f(X), \sigma^2)$ for some constant $\sigma > 0$. Then*

$$\mathbb{E}_{X \sim \mathcal{D}_X}(f(X) - f'(X))^2 = 2\sigma^2 \mathrm{KL}(\mathcal{D}_f \| \mathcal{D}_{f'}).$$

Proof We consider a distribution $\mathcal{D}$ over $Z = (X, Y)$ associated with each $f \in \mathcal{F}$, with density defined as

$$p_\mathcal{D}(Z) = p_{\mathcal{D}_X}(X)\, p_{N(0,1)}((Y - f(X))/\sigma),$$

where $p_{\mathcal{D}_X}(X)$ is the density of $X \sim \mathcal{D}_X$ and $p_{N(0,1)}$ is the density of standard normal distribution. Using this notation, we have

$$\mathrm{KL}(\mathcal{D}_{\hat{f}} \| \mathcal{D}_f) = \frac{\mathbb{E}_X(\hat{f}(X) - f(X))^2}{2\sigma^2}.$$

This proves the desired result. $\qquad \square$

Similar results can also be obtained for other noise models such as Bernoulli noise, where $Y \in \{0, 1\}$.

Proposition 12.19 *Assume that $Y \in \{0, 1\}$ such that*

$$\mathbb{E}[Y|X] = f(X)$$

for some $f \in \mathcal{F}$, and let $\mathcal{D}_f(Z)$ be the distribution of $Z = (X, Y)$. If there exists $c \in (0, 0.5)$, and for all $f \in \mathcal{F}$ and X: $f(X) \in [c, 1 - c]$, then there exists $\sigma > 0$ such that for all $f, f' \in \mathcal{F}$,

$$\mathbb{E}_{X \sim \mathcal{D}_X}(f(X) - f'(X))^2 \geq 2\sigma^2 \mathrm{KL}(\mathcal{D}_f \| \mathcal{D}_{f'}).$$

Consider a distribution $\mathcal{D}_X$ over X, with the metric

$$\|f - f'\|_{L_2(\mathcal{D}_X)} = \left(\mathbb{E}_{X \sim \mathcal{D}_X}(f(X) - f'(X))^2\right)^{1/2}.$$

The following result shows that the corresponding metric entropy leads to a lower bound on the minimax risk.

Corollary 12.20 *If for some $C > 0$ and $\epsilon > 0$,*

$$C^{-1}\epsilon^{-q} \leq \ln M(\epsilon, \mathcal{F}, L_2(\mathcal{D}_X)) \leq C\epsilon^{-q}.$$

For a noise model that satisfies the condition of Theorem 12.17, we have

$$r_n(\mathcal{P}, Q_{\mathrm{LS}}) \geq C'n^{-2/(2+q)}$$

for some $C' > 0$.

Proof We consider an ϵ packing subset $\mathcal{F}'$ of $\mathcal{F}$ with size of at least $\exp(C^{-1}\epsilon^{-q})$. Since for some $C_0 > 0$,

$$\ln N(0.5C_0\epsilon, \mathcal{F}, L_2(\mathcal{D}_X)) \leq 0.5C^{-1}\epsilon^{-q},$$

it implies that there exists a ball of size $0.5C_0\epsilon$, which contains at least

$$\frac{\exp(C^{-1}\epsilon^{-q})}{\exp(0.5C^{-1}\epsilon^{-q})} = \exp(0.5C^{-1}\epsilon^{-q})$$

members of $\mathcal{F}'$.

This means we can find $N \geq \exp(0.5C^{-1}\epsilon^{-q})$ functions $\{f_1, \ldots, f_N\}$ such that

$$\sup_{j \neq k} Q(f_j, f_k) \leq C_0^2\epsilon^2,$$

$$\inf_{j \neq k} Q(f_j, f_k) \geq \epsilon^2,$$

where $Q(f, f') = \mathbb{E}_{X \sim \mathcal{D}_X}(f(X) - f'(X))^2$. Now let $n = \lceil (C'/\epsilon^2)^{(q+2)/2} \rceil$ for a sufficiently small constant C', then we have

$$\ln N \geq 0.5C^{-1}\epsilon^{-q} \geq \ln 4 + n\sigma^{-2}C_0^2\epsilon^2 \geq \ln 4 + n\sigma^{-2}\sup_{j \neq k} Q(f_j, f_k).$$

Theorem 12.17 implies that $r_n(\mathcal{P}, Q_{\mathrm{LS}}) \geq 0.125\epsilon^2$. Since $\epsilon^2 \geq C'n^{-2/(q+2)}$, we obtain the desired bound. $\qquad\square$

If the regression function class $\mathcal{F}$ is bounded, and has a uniform covering number of $O(\epsilon^{-q})$ for $q < 2$, then we know from the local Rademacher complexity analysis of Example 6.49 that for the empirical risk minimization method

$$\hat{f}_{\mathrm{erm}} = \arg\min_{f \in \mathcal{F}} \sum_{i=1}^{n}(f(X_i) - Y_i)^2,$$

the following risk bound holds:

$$\mathbb{E}_{\mathcal{S}_n \sim \mathcal{D}^n}\mathbb{E}_{X \sim \mathcal{D}_X}(\hat{f}_{\mathrm{erm}}(X) - f_{\mathcal{D}}(X))^2 = O(n^{-2/(q+2)}).$$

This matches the lower bound of Corollary 12.20.

For $q > 2$, the generalization bound for empirical risk minimization method is

$$\mathbb{E}_{\mathcal{S}_n \sim \mathcal{D}^n} \mathbb{E}_{X \sim \mathcal{D}_X} (\hat{f}_{\mathrm{erm}}(X) - f_{\mathcal{D}}(X))^2 = O(n^{-1/q}),$$

and since $1/q < 2/(q+2)$, the rate is inferior to the minimax rate. In general, this rate cannot be improved without additional assumptions (Birgé and Massart, 1993). Therefore when the nonparametric family has a large entropy, ERM can be suboptimal.

It is possible to achieve the optimal rate of $O(n^{-2/(q+2)})$ even when $q > 2$. One of the optimal methods is least squares on sieves, and a related method is the Gibbs algorithm with an appropriate prior. A third method is the exponential model aggregation method, studied in Section 15.3.

In the following, we consider the sieve method (Grenander, 1981; Geman and Hwang, 1982; Birgé and Massart, 1998), which, in our setting, is simply least squares regression on discrete ϵ-net.

Given a function class $\mathcal{F}$, instead of running least squares on $\mathcal{F}$ with

$$\hat{f} = \arg \min_{f \in \mathcal{F}} \sum_{i=1}^{n} (f(X_i) - Y_i)^2,$$

the sieve method considers a subset $\mathcal{F}_n \subset \mathcal{F}$, and then performs least squares regression restricted to this subset:

$$\hat{f}_{\mathcal{F}_n} = \arg \min_{f \in \mathcal{F}_n} \sum_{i=1}^{n} (f(X_i) - Y_i)^2.$$

The following result shows that with appropriate $\mathcal{F}_n$, we may achieve the minimax risk of Corollary 12.20.

Proposition 12.21 *Assume that the distribution of X is $\mathcal{D}_X$. Let $\mathcal{F}_n$ be an ϵ packing subset of $\mathcal{F}$ in the $L_2(\mathcal{D}_X)$ metric with $M(\epsilon, \mathcal{F}, L_2(\mathcal{D}_X))$ members. Assume there exists $b > 0$ such that $[f(X) - f'(X)] \leq 2b$ for all $f, f' \in \mathcal{F}$. Assume that $f_{\mathcal{D}} \in \mathcal{F}$ and Y is sub-Gaussian:*

$$\ln \mathbb{E}_{Y|X} \exp(\lambda(Y - f_{\mathcal{D}}(X))) \leq \frac{\lambda^2 b^2}{2}.$$

Then

$$\mathbb{E}_{\mathcal{S}_n \sim \mathcal{D}^n} \mathbb{E}_{X \sim \mathcal{D}_X} (\hat{f}_{\mathcal{F}_n}(X) - f_{\mathcal{D}}(X))^2 \leq \left[4\epsilon^2 + \frac{14b^2}{n} \ln M(\epsilon, \mathcal{F}, L_2(\mathcal{D}_X)) \right].$$

Proof Let $\phi(f, Z) = (f(X) - Y)^2 - (f_{\mathcal{D}}(X) - Y)^2$ with $Z = (X, Y)$. Let $\rho = b^{-2}/4$. Then we have

$$\Lambda(\rho, f) = -\frac{1}{\rho} \ln \mathbb{E}_Z e^{-\rho \phi(f, Z)} \qquad \text{(definition of } \Lambda \text{ in Theorem 10.18)}$$

$$= -\frac{1}{\rho} \ln \mathbb{E}_Z e^{-\rho(f(X) - f_{\mathcal{D}}(X))^2 + 2\rho(f(X) - f_{\mathcal{D}}(X))(Y - f_{\mathcal{D}}(X))} \qquad \text{(definition of } \phi)$$

$$\geq -\frac{1}{\rho} \ln \mathbb{E}_X e^{(-\rho + 2\rho^2 b^2)(f(X) - f_{\mathcal{D}}(X))^2} \qquad \text{(sub-Gaussian noise assumption)}$$

$$\geq \frac{1}{\rho} \left[1 - \mathbb{E}_X e^{-0.5\rho(f(X) - f_{\mathcal{D}}(X))^2} \right] \qquad (-\ln z \geq 1 - z)$$

$$\geq \frac{1}{\rho} \mathbb{E}_X e^{-2\rho b^2} 0.5\rho(f(X) - f_{\mathcal{D}}(X))^2 \qquad (1 - e^{-z} \geq e^{-a} z \text{ for } z \in [0, a])$$

$$\geq 0.3 \mathbb{E}_X (f(X) - f_{\mathcal{D}}(X))^2. \qquad (2\rho b^2 = 0.5)$$

It follows from Theorem 10.18 by setting $1/(\lambda n) = \rho = b^{-2}/4$ (which implies that $\lambda = 4b^2/n$) that for any random estimator $\hat{q}$ on $\mathcal{F}_n$,

$$0.3 \mathbb{E}_{\mathcal{S}_n} \mathbb{E}_{f \sim \hat{q}(\cdot | \mathcal{S}_n)} \mathbb{E}_X (f(X) - f_{\mathcal{D}}(X))^2$$

$$\leq \mathbb{E}_{\mathcal{S}_n} \mathbb{E}_{f \sim \hat{q}(\cdot | \mathcal{S}_n)} \frac{1}{n} \sum_{i=1}^n \phi(f, Z_i) + \frac{4b^2}{n} \mathbb{E}_{\mathcal{S}_n} \text{KL}(\hat{q} \| q_0). \qquad (12.1)$$

Let $\hat{q}$ correspond to the deterministic estimator $\hat{f}_{\mathcal{F}_n}$, and let q_0 be the uniform distribution on $\mathcal{F}_n$. Then $\text{KL}(\hat{q} \| q_0) \leq \ln |\mathcal{F}_n|$. Therefore we obtain

$$0.3 \mathbb{E}_{\mathcal{S}_n} Q_{\text{LS}}(\hat{f}_{\mathcal{F}_n}, \mathcal{D}) \leq \mathbb{E}_{\mathcal{S}_n} \frac{1}{n} \sum_{i=1}^n \phi(\hat{f}_{\mathcal{F}_n}, Z_i) + \frac{4b^2}{n} \ln |\mathcal{F}_n|$$

$$\leq \inf_{f \in \mathcal{F}_n} \mathbb{E}_{\mathcal{S}_n} \frac{1}{n} \sum_{i=1}^n \phi(f, Z_i) + \frac{4b^2}{n} \ln |\mathcal{F}_n|$$

$$\text{(} \hat{f}_{\mathcal{F}_n} \text{ is empirical risk minimizer on } \mathcal{F}_n)$$

$$\leq \inf_{f \in \mathcal{F}_n} Q_{\text{LS}}(f, \mathcal{D}) + \frac{4b^2}{n} \ln |\mathcal{F}_n| \leq \epsilon^2 + \frac{4b^2}{n} \ln |\mathcal{F}_n|.$$

The last inequality used the fact that $\mathcal{F}_n$ is an ϵ packing of $\mathcal{F}$ and $f_{\mathcal{D}} \in \mathcal{F}$. This implies the desired bound. $\qquad \square$

Example 12.22 Consider the covering number condition of Corollary 12.20. We note that

$$\inf_{\epsilon > 0} O\left(\epsilon^2 + \frac{1}{n} \ln M(\epsilon, \mathcal{F}, L_2(\mathcal{D}_X)) \right) = O(n^{-2/(2+q)}).$$

Therefore the upper bound of Proposition 12.21 matches the lower bound of Corollary 12.20.

The method of sieves can be regarded as a regularization method for ERM. The optimality of using a sieve versus ERM on the original function class implies that ERM can overfit if not used properly, which leads to suboptimality. It is suitable only for certain function classes but not others.

The following example gives a simple but intuitive illustration of such an overfitting phenomenon.

Example 12.23 Consider the function class

$$\mathcal{F} = \{f_0(x)\} \cup \{f_1(x) + \Delta f_1(x) : |\Delta f_1(x)| \le 1/\sqrt{n}\},$$

where $f_1(x) = f_0(x) + 0.5n^{-1/4}$.

If we consider ERM with sieve $\mathcal{F}_n = \{f_k(x): k = 0, 1\}$, then we have a convergence rate no worse than $O(1/n)$.

However, we have a overfitting problem with ERM on $\mathcal{F}$. To see this, we may consider the model

$$Y = f_0(X) + \epsilon, \quad \epsilon \sim N(0, 1),$$

and training data $(X_1, Y_1), \dots, (X_n, Y_n)$. Let $\delta_i = \Delta f_1(X_i)$ and $\epsilon_i = Y_i - f_0(X_i)$. Then we have

$$\sum_{i=1}^{n} \min_{|\delta_i| \le 1/\sqrt{n}} (f_1(X_i) + \delta_i - Y_i)^2 - \sum_{i=1}^{n} (f_0(X_i) - Y_i)^2$$

$$= \sum_{i=1}^{n} \min_{|\delta_i| \le 1/\sqrt{n}} (0.5n^{-1/4} + \delta_i - \epsilon_i)^2 - \sum_{i=1}^{n} \epsilon_i^2$$

$$\le \sqrt{n}(0.5 + n^{-1/4})^2 - n^{-1/4} \sum_{i=1}^{n} \epsilon_i - 2n^{-1/2} \sum_{i=1}^{n} |\epsilon_i|.$$

The inequality is achieved by setting $\delta_i = \text{sign}(\epsilon_i)/\sqrt{n}$. When n is large, this quantity is negative with large probability because the last term

$$-2n^{-1/2} \sum_{i=1}^{n} |\epsilon_i| = -2n^{1/2} \left[\mathbb{E}_{\epsilon \sim N(0,1)} |\epsilon| + O_p(1/\sqrt{n}) \right]$$

dominates with large probability. It implies that with large probability, ERM gives an estimator $\hat{f}(x) = f_1(x) + \Delta f_1(x)$ with $|\Delta f(x)| \le 1/\sqrt{n}$. This means that

$$\mathbb{E}_{\mathcal{S}_n} \mathbb{E}_X (\hat{f}(X) - f(X))^2 \ge c/\sqrt{n}$$

for some $c > 0$. Note that this is a suboptimal rate.

In addition to the ERM on sieve method, one may also employ the Gibbs algorithm (10.12) with $\lambda = 4b^2/n$ under the assumptions of Proposition 12.21. From (12.1) – and note that the Gibbs distribution $\hat{q}$ is the solution of the entropy regularized empirical risk minimization problem (see Proposition 7.16) – we obtain

$$0.3 \mathbb{E}_{\mathcal{S}_n} \mathbb{E}_{f \sim \hat{q}(\cdot | \mathcal{S}_n)} Q_{\text{LS}}(f, \mathcal{D}) \le \inf_q \left[Q_{\text{LS}}(f, \mathcal{D}) + +\frac{4b^2}{n} \mathbb{E}_{\mathcal{S}_n} \text{KL}(q \| q_0) \right].$$

If we choose prior q_0 to be uniform on a discrete net as in Proposition 12.21, we obtain the same rate. However, one may also choose an appropriate continuous prior q_0 to achieve a similar result without explicit discretization.

Another method that is closely related to the Gibbs algorithm is model aggregation, studied in Section 15.3. The generalization bound there implies that using model aggregation on a sieve $\mathcal{F}_n = \{f_1, \ldots, f_N\}$, with $N = M(\epsilon, \mathcal{F}, L_2(\mathcal{D}_X))$, we have

$$\mathbb{E}_{\mathcal{S}_n} Q_{\mathrm{LS}}(\hat{f}, \mathcal{D}) = O\left(\inf_j Q_{\mathrm{LS}}(f_j, \mathcal{D}) + n^{-1} \ln M(\epsilon, \mathcal{F}, L_2(\mathcal{D}_X))\right).$$

This achieves the same rate as that of Proposition 12.21. It follows that the exponential aggregation algorithm is also an optimal algorithm for least squares regression.

12.5 Minimax Analysis for Density Estimation

Assume that we are given a family of conditional distributions

$$\mathcal{F} = \{p(Y|X) \colon p \in \mathcal{F}\},$$

and the true conditional distribution $p_{\mathcal{D}} \in \mathcal{F}$. Similar to Section 12.4, we assume that all conditional densities share a marginal distribution $\mathcal{D}_X$ on X (which the learning algorithm does not need to know). The joint distribution is $\mathcal{P} = \{p(X, Y) = p_{\mathcal{D}_X}(X)p(Y|X) \colon p \in \mathcal{F}\}$.

Given any $p \in \mathcal{F}$, we are interested in minimizing its squared Hellinger distance to the true distribution

$$Q_H(p, \mathcal{D}) = H_{\mathcal{D}_X}(p \| p_{\mathcal{D}})^2 = \mathbb{E}_{X \sim \mathcal{D}_X} H(p(\cdot|X) \| p_{\mathcal{D}}(\cdot|X))^2.$$

Here $H_{\mathcal{D}_X}$ is the Hellinger distance between the joint probability $p_{\mathcal{D}_X}(X)p(Y|X) \in \mathcal{P}$. We focus on the case that there exists $c_{\mathcal{F}} > 0$ so that for all $p, p' \in \mathcal{F}$,

$$\mathbb{E}_{X \sim \mathcal{D}_X} \mathrm{KL}(p(\cdot|X) \| p'(\cdot|X)) \leq c_{\mathcal{F}} H_{\mathcal{D}_X} p \| p')^2. \tag{12.2}$$

For example, this condition holds if $\ln p(Y|X)$ is bounded.

The following result is a direct consequence of Theorem 12.15. The proof is similar to that of Theorem 12.17, and we leave it as an exercise.

Theorem 12.24 *Consider the conditional density estimation problem with $X \sim \mathcal{D}_X$, and assume that the true conditional probability is given by*

$$p_{\mathcal{D}}(Y|X) \in \mathcal{F}.$$

Assume that (12.2) holds. If $\mathcal{F}$ contains N conditional densities $p_1, \ldots, p_N$ such that

$$\ln N \geq \ln 4 + 2c_{\mathcal{F}} \sup_{j,k} H_{\mathcal{D}_X}(p_j \| p_k)^2,$$

then

$$r_n(\mathcal{P}, Q_H) \geq 0.125 \inf_{j \neq k} H_{\mathcal{D}_X}(p_j \| p_k)^2.$$

We have the following lower bound using metric entropy with respect to the Hellinger distance, which is analogous to Corollary 12.20.

Corollary 12.25 *If for some $C > 0$ and $\epsilon > 0$,*

$$C^{-1}\epsilon^{-q} \leq \ln M(\epsilon, \mathcal{F}, H_{\mathcal{D}_X}) \leq C\epsilon^{-q}.$$

Assume that (12.2) holds. Then we have

$$r_n(\mathcal{P}, \mathcal{Q}_H) \geq C' n^{-2/(2+q)}$$

for some $C' > 0$.

We also have the following upper bound using the Gibbs algorithm on sieves.

Proposition 12.26 *Assume that the distribution of X is $\mathcal{D}_X$. Let $\mathcal{F}_n$ be an ϵ packing subset of $\mathcal{F}$ under the $H_{\mathcal{D}_X}$ metric with $M(\epsilon, \mathcal{F}, H_{\mathcal{D}_X})$ members. Assume that $p_{\mathcal{D}} \in \mathcal{F}$ and (12.2) holds. Let $\hat{q}$ be a Gibbs distribution on $\mathcal{F}_n$ defined as*

$$\hat{q}(p|\mathcal{S}_n) \propto q_0(p) \exp\left(0.5 \sum_{i=1}^{n} \ln p(Y|X)\right),$$

where $q_0(p)$ is the uniform distribution on $\mathcal{F}_n$. Then

$$\mathbb{E}_{\mathcal{S}_n \sim \mathcal{D}^n} \mathbb{E}_{p \sim \hat{q}} \mathcal{Q}_H(p, \mathcal{D}) \leq c_{\mathcal{F}} \epsilon^2 + \frac{2 \ln M(\epsilon, \mathcal{F}, H_{\mathcal{D}_X})}{n}.$$

Proof Let $\Delta(\mathcal{F}_n)$ denote the set of probability distributions on $\mathcal{F}_n$. We obtain

$$\mathbb{E}_{\mathcal{S}_n \sim \mathcal{D}^n} \mathbb{E}_{p \sim \hat{q}} \mathcal{Q}_H(p||\mathcal{D}) \leq \inf_{q \in \Delta(\mathcal{F}_n)} \left[\mathbb{E}_{p \sim q} \mathbb{E}_{X \sim \mathcal{D}_X} \text{KL}(p_{\mathcal{D}}(\cdot|X)||p(\cdot|X)) + \frac{2\text{KL}(q||q_0)}{n} \right]$$

$$\leq \inf_{q \in \Delta(\mathcal{F}_n)} \left[c_{\mathcal{F}} \mathbb{E}_{p \sim q} H_{\mathcal{D}_X}(p_{\mathcal{D}}||p)^2 + \frac{2 \ln M(\epsilon, \mathcal{F}, H_{\mathcal{D}_X})}{n} \right].$$

The first inequality used Corollary 10.26 with $\alpha = 0.5$. The second inequality used (12.2) and $\text{KL}(q||q_0) \leq \ln M(\epsilon, \mathcal{F}, H_{\mathcal{D}_X})$. Since $\mathcal{F}_n$ is also an ϵ-cover of $\mathcal{F}_n$ in $H_{\mathcal{D}_X}$, we obtain the desired bound. $\square$

Under the condition of Corollary 12.25, we note that

$$\inf_{\epsilon > 0} O\left(\epsilon^2 + \frac{1}{n} \ln M(\epsilon, \mathcal{F}, H_{\mathcal{D}_X}) \right) = O(n^{-2/(2+q)}).$$

Therefore the upper bound of Proposition 12.26 matches the lower bound of Corollary 12.25.

12.6 Lower Bounds Using Assouad's Lemma

While the minimax risk analysis using Fano's inequality is applicable to a number of problems, the resulting bound employs KL-divergence, which can be infinity for certain distributions. In comparison, the analysis based on Assouad's lemma employs the TV-norm (see Appendix B) between distributions that is always finite. It is also easier to use this approach for some sequential estimation problems.

Lemma 12.27 (Generalized Assouad's Lemma) *Consider a finite family of distributions $\mathcal{P}$. Let $d \geq 1$ be an integer, and Q can be decomposed as*

$$Q(\theta, \mathcal{D}) = \sum_{j=1}^{d} Q_j(\theta, \mathcal{D}),$$

where $Q_j \geq 0$ are all nonnegative. Assume for all j, there exists a partition M_j of $\mathcal{P}$. We use notation $\mathcal{D}' \sim_j \mathcal{D}$ to indicate that $\mathcal{D}'$ and $\mathcal{D}$ belong to the same partition in M_j. Let $m_j(\mathcal{D})$ be the number of elements in the partition containing $\mathcal{D}$. Assume there exist $\epsilon, \beta \geq 0$ such that

$$\forall \mathcal{D}' \sim_j \mathcal{D}, \mathcal{D}' \neq \mathcal{D}: \quad \inf_{\theta} [Q_j(\theta, \mathcal{D}') + Q_j(\theta, \mathcal{D})] \geq \epsilon,$$

$$\forall \mathcal{D} \in \mathcal{P}: \quad \frac{1}{d(\mathcal{P})} \sum_{j=1}^{d} \sum_{\mathcal{D} \in \mathcal{P}_j} \frac{1}{m_j(\mathcal{D}) - 1} \sum_{\mathcal{D}' \sim_j \mathcal{D}} \|\mathcal{D}' - \mathcal{D}\|_{\mathrm{TV}} \leq \beta,$$

where $\mathcal{P}_j = \{\mathcal{D} \in \mathcal{P}: m_j(\mathcal{D}) > 1\}$ and $d(\mathcal{P}) = \sum_{j=1}^{d} |\mathcal{P}_j|$. Let $\mathcal{A}(Z)$ be any estimator, so we have

$$\frac{1}{|\mathcal{P}|} \sum_{\mathcal{D} \in \mathcal{P}} \mathbb{E}_{Z \sim \mathcal{D}} \mathbb{E}_{\mathcal{A}} Q(\mathcal{A}(Z), \mathcal{D}) \geq \frac{\epsilon d(\mathcal{P})}{2|\mathcal{P}|} [1 - \beta],$$

where $\mathbb{E}_{\mathcal{A}}$ is with respect to the internal randomization in $\mathcal{A}$.

Proof For notation convenience, assume there exists $d\mu(z)$ so that for all $\mathcal{D} \in \mathcal{P}$, $p_{\mathcal{D}}(z)d\mu(z)$ is the distribution of $\mathcal{D}$. Then

$$\frac{2}{|\mathcal{P}|} \sum_{j=1}^{d} \sum_{\mathcal{D} \in \mathcal{P}} \mathbb{E}_{Z \sim \mathcal{D}} Q_j(\mathcal{A}(Z), \mathcal{D}) \geq \frac{2}{|\mathcal{P}|} \sum_{j=1}^{d} \sum_{\mathcal{D} \in \mathcal{P}_j} \mathbb{E}_{Z \sim \mathcal{D}} Q_j(\mathcal{A}(Z), \mathcal{D})$$

$$= \frac{1}{|\mathcal{P}|} \sum_{j=1}^{d} \sum_{\substack{\mathcal{D} \in \mathcal{P}_j}} \frac{1}{m_j(\mathcal{D}) - 1} \sum_{\substack{\mathcal{D}' \sim_j \mathcal{D} \\ \mathcal{D}' \neq \mathcal{D}}} [\mathbb{E}_{Z \sim \mathcal{D}'} Q_j(\mathcal{A}(Z), \mathcal{D}') + \mathbb{E}_{Z \sim \mathcal{D}} Q_j(\mathcal{A}(Z), \mathcal{D})]$$

$$= \frac{1}{|\mathcal{P}|} \sum_{j=1}^{d} \sum_{\substack{\mathcal{D} \in \mathcal{P}_j}} \frac{1}{m_j(\mathcal{D}) - 1} \sum_{\substack{\mathcal{D}' \sim_j \mathcal{D} \\ \mathcal{D}' \neq \mathcal{D}}} \int [Q_j(\mathcal{A}(z), \mathcal{D}) p_{\mathcal{D}}(z) + Q_j(\mathcal{A}(z), \mathcal{D}') p_{\mathcal{D}'}(z)] d\mu(z)$$

$$\overset{(a)}{\geq} \frac{1}{|\mathcal{P}|} \sum_{j=1}^{d} \sum_{\substack{\mathcal{D} \in \mathcal{P}_j}} \frac{1}{m_j(\mathcal{D}) - 1} \sum_{\substack{\mathcal{D}' \sim_j \mathcal{D} \\ \mathcal{D}' \neq \mathcal{D}}} \int \epsilon \min(p_{\mathcal{D}}(z), p_{\mathcal{D}'}(z)) d\mu(z)$$

$$\overset{(b)}{=} \frac{1}{|\mathcal{P}|} \sum_{j=1}^{d} \sum_{\substack{\mathcal{D} \in \mathcal{P}_j}} \frac{1}{m_j(\mathcal{D}) - 1} \sum_{\substack{\mathcal{D}' \sim_j \mathcal{D} \\ \mathcal{D}' \neq \mathcal{D}}} \epsilon(1 - \|\mathcal{D} - \mathcal{D}'\|_{\mathrm{TV}}).$$

In this derivation, the first inequality used $Q_j(\cdot) \geq 0$; (a) used the assumption of the lemma, and (b) used the definition of TV-norm (see Appendix B). By rearranging the last term and using the definition of β, we obtain the desired bound. $\qquad\square$

The Assouad lemma stated here is a generalization of the typical Assouad lemma that appears in the literature. The latter is often stated with

$$\mathcal{P} = \{\mathcal{D}_\tau : \tau \in \{\pm 1\}^d\},$$

and M_j contains indices in $\{\pm 1\}^d$ that may differ from τ by only one coordinate j. The following result is a direct application of Assouad's lemma with this representation, and the TV-norm of product distributions is estimated by Theorem B.13.

Theorem 12.28 *Let $d \geq 1$ be an integer and $\mathcal{P}_d = \{\mathcal{D}_\tau : \tau \in \{-1, 1\}^d\}$ contain 2^d probability measures. Suppose that the loss function Q can be decomposed as*

$$Q(\theta, \mathcal{D}) = \sum_{j=1}^d Q_j(\theta, \mathcal{D}),$$

where $Q_j(\cdot, \cdot) \geq 0$. For any j and τ, let $\tau^{-[j]}$ be the index that differs with τ only by one coordinate j. Assume that there exists $\epsilon, \beta_j \geq 0$ such that

$$\forall \tau: \quad [Q_j(\theta, \mathcal{D}_\tau) + Q_j(\theta, \mathcal{D}_{\tau^{-[j]}})] \geq \epsilon, \quad H(\mathcal{D}_\tau \| \mathcal{D}_{\tau^{-[j]}}) \leq \beta_j.$$

Consider randomized $\mathcal{A}(\mathcal{S}_n)$ based on $\mathcal{S}_n \sim \mathcal{D}_\tau^n$ for some τ. We have

$$\frac{1}{2^d} \sum_\tau \mathbb{E}_{\mathcal{S}_n \sim \mathcal{D}_\tau^n} \mathbb{E}_{\mathcal{A}} Q(\mathcal{A}(\mathcal{S}_n), \mathcal{D}_\tau) \geq \frac{\epsilon d}{2} - \frac{\epsilon}{2} \sum_{j=1}^d \sqrt{2 - 2(1 - 0.5\beta_j^2)^n},$$

where $\mathbb{E}_{\mathcal{A}}$ is with respect to the internal randomization in $\mathcal{A}$. This implies that

$$r_n(\mathcal{P}_d, Q) \geq \frac{\epsilon d}{2} - \frac{\epsilon}{2} \sum_{j=1}^d \sqrt{2 - 2(1 - 0.5\beta_j^2)^n}.$$

In general, if we can choose $\beta_j = O(\epsilon)$, then Theorem 12.28 implies a bound of

$$r_n(\mathcal{P}_d, Q) \geq \Omega(d\epsilon)$$

when $n = O(1/\epsilon^2)$. The following example illustrates this with a specific application.

Example 12.29 Consider observations $Z_i \in \{0, 1\}^d$, where each Z_i has d components $Z_{i,j} \sim \text{Bernoulli}(\theta_j)$ for $j = 1, \ldots, d$. Let $\theta = [\theta_1, \ldots, \theta_d] \in (0, 1)^d$ be the model parameters to be estimated. For $\tau \in \{\pm 1\}^d$, we let $\theta_{\tau,j} = \epsilon^2(1 + \tau_j)/2$, where $\epsilon \in (0, 0.5)$. Let $\mathcal{D}_\tau$ be the corresponding Bernoulli distribution, and $\mathcal{P}_d = \{\mathcal{D}_\tau\}$. Define the metric

$$Q(\hat{\theta}, \theta) = \sum_{j=1}^d Q_j(\hat{\theta}, \theta), \quad Q_j(\hat{\theta}, \theta) = \left| \sqrt{\hat{\theta}_j} - \sqrt{\theta_j} \right|.$$

We cannot apply Theorem 12.15 directly on this subclass $\mathcal{P}_d$ because the KL-divergence of two distributions in $\mathcal{P}_d$ can be infinity. On the other hand, for all τ,

$$[Q_j(\theta, \mathcal{D}_\tau) + Q_j(\theta, \mathcal{D}_{\tau^{-[j]}})] \geq \epsilon$$

and

$$H(\mathcal{D}_\tau || \mathcal{D}_{\tau^{-[j]}}) \leq 2\epsilon.$$

We thus obtain from Theorem 12.28 that

$$r_n(\mathcal{P}_d, Q) \geq 0.5d\epsilon - 0.5d\epsilon\sqrt{2 - 2(1 - 2\epsilon^2)^n}.$$

For sufficiently small ϵ, with $n \leq 1/(6\epsilon^2)$, we obtain

$$r_n(\mathcal{P}_d, Q) \geq 0.1d\epsilon.$$

12.7 Historical and Bibliographical Remarks

While Rademacher complexity is more widely used in machine learning, Gaussian complexity has also been studied (Bartlett and Mendelson, 2002; Koltchinskii and Panchenko, 2002). Slepian's Lemma, which is the comparison lemma for Gaussian complexity, is more versatile than the corresponding Lemma 6.29 for Rademacher complexity. Among different applications, it directly implies Sudakov minoration as a lower bound for Gaussian complexity (Sudakov, 1969). It can also be used to obtain upper bounds on empirical L_2 covering numbers. Due to the convenience of Gaussian distributions, more sophisticated results such as generic chaining can be developed (Talagrand, 1996a).

The minimax criterion has become a widely adopted approach in statistical analysis. It has origins both from game theory and from statistical decision theory. The latter is closely related to Bayesian statistics, although the concept of minimax analysis has been studied mostly in the frequentist setting.

In parametric statistics, with suitable regularity conditions, the classical asymptotic lower bound for unbiased parameter estimation of a probability model is given by the Cramer–Rao inequality (Rao, 1992; Cramér, 2016). The matching upper bound can be achieved by the maximum likelihood method. This leads to the asymptotic optimality of the maximum likelihood method (under appropriate regularity conditions). In nonparametric statistics, one needs to consider other techniques originated from information theory to establish lower bounds for statistical convergence rates, usually up to a constant. Common techniques for lower bounds include Fano's inequality (Fano, 1961) and Assouad's lemma (Assouad, 1983). Assouad's method employs TV-norm and multiple hypothesis testing for a decomposable loss function. The idea of using TV-norm for hypothesis testing as a method to obtain lower bounds for statistical estimation was studied earlier by LeCam (1973). See (Yu, 1997) for a discussion of the relationship of these methods. These techniques have been employed in the minimax analysis of nonparametric statistical estimation problems (Birgé, 1986; Yang, 1999; Yang and

Barron, 1999). The condition used in the generalization of Fano's inequality in Theorem 12.11 is motivated by the analysis of Zhang (2006).

The method of sieves suggested in nonparametric statistics in the 1980s (Grenander, 1981; Geman and Hwang, 1982), although the suboptimality of ERM was only formally shown much later (Birgé and Massart, 1993). Both the sieve method and the exponential aggregation method are known to achieve the optimal convergence rate. The minimax analysis of the Gibbs algorithm can be found in Zhang (2006). Similar results hold for misspecified models for convex function classes when the variance condition holds (see Example 3.18). However, we can only achieve an inferior result with nonconvex function classes using ERM when competing to the optimal function in the function class (see Example 3.25 and Proposition 8.12). For general nonconvex function classes, it is known (see Example 15.21) that exponential model aggregation is superior to empirical risk minimization when model is misspecified (see Lecué, 2007; Audibert, 2007). The case of misspecified model does not affect the minimax analysis of this chapter, because we have only considered well-specified models in our analysis.

Exercises

12.1 Prove Proposition 12.2.

12.2 Consider the function class

$$\mathcal{F} = \{w^\top x : \|w\|_2 \le 1\}.$$

Consider empirical distribution $\mathcal{S}_n = \{X_1, \ldots, X_n\}$ so that $\|X_i\|_2 \le 1$ for all i.
Derive an upper bound for the Gaussian complexity $G(\mathcal{F}, \mathcal{S}_n)$, and obtain an upper bound for $N(\epsilon, \mathcal{F}, L_2(\mathcal{S}_n))$ using Sudakov minoration.

12.3 Prove Theorem 12.15 using Theorem 12.11, Lemma 12.14, and Theorem B.6.

12.4 Consider a function class defined on $[0, 1)$ as

$$\mathcal{F} = \{f_0(x)\} \cup \{f_0(x) + 0.1n^{-r/3} + n^{-r/2}\Delta f_u(x) : u \in \{\pm 1\}^n\},$$

with $r \in (0, 1]$.
Let $f_0(x) = 0$ and $\Delta f_u(x) = u_j \forall x \in [(j-1)/n, j/n)$ $(j = 1, \ldots, n)$, let

$$Y = f_*(x) + \epsilon, \quad \epsilon \sim N(0, 1),$$

for $f_* \in \mathcal{F}$, and let X be drawn uniformly from $[0, 1)$.
Consider the least squares problem

$$Q_{\mathrm{LS}}(f, \mathcal{D}) = \mathbb{E}_{X \sim \mathcal{D}}(f(X) - f_{\mathcal{D}}(X))^2,$$

and consider n samples $\mathcal{S}_n = \{(X_1, Y_1), \ldots, (X_n, Y_n)\}$.

- Find the minimax risk (up to a constant) for estimating f_* using these n samples.
- Show that there is a small enough constant c so that with probability at least 0.5, there are at least $0.1n$ buckets $[(j-1)/n, j/n)$ so that one and only one X_i belongs to $[(j-1)/n, j/n)$.
- Find a risk lower bound on the risk for the ERM method on $\mathcal{F}$ for sufficiently large n.

12.5 Prove Theorem 12.24 and Corollary 12.25.

12.6 Use Theorem 12.28 to derive a lower bound for Example 12.16.

12.7 Consider a distribution family $\mathcal{D}$ parametrized by $\theta_{\mathcal{D}} \in \mathbb{R}^d$, which we want to estimate from observations $Z_1, \ldots, Z_n \sim N(\theta_{\mathcal{D}}, I)$. Assume that $\theta_{\mathcal{D}}$ is sparse: $\|\theta_{\mathcal{D}}\|_0 = s$ for some $s \ll d$.

- Derive a lower bound for estimating θ with $Q(\theta, \mathcal{D}) = \|\theta - \theta_{\mathcal{D}}\|_2^2$.
- Derive a matching upper bound.

13

Probability Inequalities for Sequential Random Variables

In the sequential estimation problems investigated in the next few chapters, one observes a sequence of random variables $Z_t \in \mathcal{Z}$ for $t = 1, 2, \ldots$, where each Z_t may depend on the previous observations $\mathcal{S}_{t-1} = [Z_1, \ldots, Z_{t-1}] \in \mathcal{Z}^{t-1}$. The sigma algebra generated by $\{\mathcal{S}_t\}$ forms a natural filtration $\{\mathcal{F}_t\}$.

We say a sequence $\{\xi_t\}$ is adapted to the filtration $\{\mathcal{F}_t\}$ if each ξ_t is a function of $\mathcal{S}_t$. That is, each ξ_t at time t does not depend on future observations Z_s for $s > t$. Alternatively one may also say that ξ_t is measurable in $\mathcal{F}_t$. The sequence

$$\xi_t' = \xi_t - \mathbb{E}[\xi_t|\mathcal{F}_{t-1}], \text{ or equivalently } \xi_t'(\mathcal{S}_t) = \xi_t(\mathcal{S}_t) - \mathbb{E}_{Z_t|\mathcal{S}_{t-1}}\xi_t(\mathcal{S}_t),$$

is referred to as a *martingale difference sequence* with the property

$$\mathbb{E}[\xi_t'|\mathcal{F}_{t-1}] = \mathbb{E}_{Z_t|\mathcal{S}_{t-1}}\xi_t'(\mathcal{S}_t) = 0.$$

The sum of a martingale difference sequence

$$\sum_{s=1}^{t} \xi_s' = \sum_{s=1}^{t} \xi_s'(\mathcal{S}_s)$$

is referred to as a *martingale*, which satisfies the following equality for all t:

$$\mathbb{E}\left[\sum_{s=1}^{t} \xi_s'|\mathcal{F}_{t-1}\right] = \sum_{s=1}^{t-1} \xi_s', \text{ or } \mathbb{E}_{Z_t|\mathcal{S}_{t-1}} \sum_{s=1}^{t} \xi_s'(\mathcal{S}_s) = \sum_{s=1}^{t-1} \xi_s'(\mathcal{S}_s).$$

A martingale is a natural generalization of the sum of independent random variables (studied in Chapter 2) to the sequential estimation setting, where we allow each random variable to depend on previous random variables. This chapter studies probability inequalities and uniform convergence for martingales, which are essential in analyzing sequential statistical estimation problems.

In the following, we employ a slightly more refined notation, where each $\mathcal{Z} = \mathcal{Z}^{(x)} \times \mathcal{Z}^{(y)}$, and each $Z_t \in \mathcal{Z}$ can be written as $Z_t = (Z_t^{(x)}, Z_t^{(y)})$. We are interested in the conditional expectation with respect to $Z_t^{(y)}|Z_t^{(x)}, \mathcal{S}_{t-1}$, rather than with respect to $Z_t|\mathcal{S}_{t-1}$. This formulation is useful in many statistical estimation problems such as regression. Without causing confusion, throughout the chapter, we will adopt the following shortened notation for simplicity:

$$\mathbb{E}_{Z_t^{(y)}}[\cdot] = \mathbb{E}_{Z_t^{(y)}|Z_t^{(x)}, \mathcal{S}_{t-1}}[\cdot].$$

13.1 Martingale Exponential Inequalities

Using the technique of logarithmic moment generating functions, we can obtain martingale inequalities similar to those of Chapter 2.

Lemma 13.1 *Consider a sequence of real-valued random (measurable) functions $\xi_1(\mathcal{S}_1), \ldots, \xi_T(\mathcal{S}_T)$. Let $\tau \leq T$ be a stopping time so that $\mathbb{1}(t \leq \tau)$ is measurable in $\mathcal{S}_t$. We have*

$$\mathbb{E}_{\mathcal{S}_T} \exp\left(\sum_{i=1}^{\tau} \xi_i - \sum_{i=1}^{\tau} \ln \mathbb{E}_{Z_i^{(y)}} e^{\xi_i}\right) = 1.$$

Proof We prove the lemma by induction on T. When $T = 0$, the equality is trivial. Assume that the claim holds at $T - 1$ for some $T \geq 1$. Now we will prove the equation at time T using the induction hypothesis.

Note that $\tilde{\xi}_i = \xi_i \mathbb{1}(i \leq \tau)$ is measurable in $\mathcal{S}_i$. We have

$$\sum_{i=1}^{\tau} \xi_i - \sum_{i=1}^{\tau} \ln \mathbb{E}_{Z_i^{(y)}} e^{\xi_i} = \sum_{i=1}^{T} \tilde{\xi}_i - \sum_{i=1}^{T} \ln \mathbb{E}_{Z_i^{(y)}} e^{\tilde{\xi}_i}.$$

It follows that

$$\mathbb{E}_{Z_1, \ldots, Z_T} \exp\left(\sum_{i=1}^{\tau} \xi_i - \sum_{i=1}^{\tau} \ln \mathbb{E}_{Z_i^{(y)}} e^{\xi_i}\right)$$

$$= \mathbb{E}_{Z_1, \ldots, Z_T} \exp\left(\sum_{i=1}^{T} \tilde{\xi}_i - \sum_{i=1}^{T} \ln \mathbb{E}_{Z_i^{(y)}} e^{\tilde{\xi}_i}\right)$$

$$= \mathbb{E}_{Z_1, \ldots, Z_{n-1}, Z_T^{(x)}} \left[\exp\left(\sum_{i=1}^{T-1} \tilde{\xi}_i - \sum_{i=1}^{T-1} \ln \mathbb{E}_{Z_i^{(y)}} e^{\tilde{\xi}_i}\right) \underbrace{\mathbb{E}_{Z_T^{(y)}} \exp(\tilde{\xi}_T - \ln \mathbb{E}_{Z_T^{(y)}} e^{\tilde{\xi}_T})}_{=1}\right]$$

$$= \mathbb{E}_{Z_1, \ldots, Z_{T-1}} \exp\left(\sum_{i=1}^{T-1} \tilde{\xi}_i - \sum_{i=1}^{T-1} \ln \mathbb{E}_{Z_i^{(y)}} e^{\tilde{\xi}_i}\right)$$

$$= \mathbb{E}_{Z_1, \ldots, Z_{T-1}} \exp\left(\sum_{i=1}^{\min(\tau, T-1)} \xi_i - \sum_{i=1}^{\min(\tau, T-1)} \ln \mathbb{E}_{Z_i^{(y)}} e^{\xi_i}\right) = 1.$$

Note that the last equation follows from the induction hypothesis, and the fact that $\min(\tau, T - 1)$ is a stopping time $\leq T - 1$. $\qquad\square$

The following result is a direct consequence of Lemma 13.1, which generalizes Theorem 2.5 for sum of independent variables to martingales.

Theorem 13.2 *Consider a sequence of random functions $\xi_1(\mathcal{S}_1), \ldots, \xi_t(\mathcal{S}_t), \ldots,$ with filtration $\{\mathcal{F}_t\}$. We have for any $\delta \in (0, 1)$ and $\lambda > 0$,*

$$\Pr\left[\exists n > 0: \ -\sum_{i=1}^{n} \xi_i \geq \frac{\ln(1/\delta)}{\lambda} + \frac{1}{\lambda} \sum_{i=1}^{n} \ln \mathbb{E}_{Z_i^{(y)}} e^{-\lambda \xi_i}\right] \leq \delta.$$

Moreover, consider a sequence of $\{z_t \in \mathbb{R}\}$ adapted to $\{\mathcal{F}_t\}$, and events A_t on $\mathcal{F}_t$:

$$\ln \Pr\left[\exists n > 0: \sum_{i=1}^{n} \xi_i \leq z_n \ \& \ \mathcal{S}_n \in A_n\right] \leq \inf_{\lambda > 0} \sup_{n > 0} \sup_{\mathcal{S}_n \in A_n}\left[\lambda z_n + \sum_{i=1}^{n} \ln \mathbb{E}_{Z_i^{(y)}} e^{-\lambda \xi_i}\right].$$

Proof We will prove the result for a finite time sequence $\xi_1(\mathcal{S}_1), \ldots, \xi_T(\mathcal{S}_T)$. It implies the desired result by letting $T \to \infty$. Let

$$\xi_\tau(\lambda) = -\sum_{i=1}^{\tau} \ln \mathbb{E}_{Z_i^{(y)}} e^{-\lambda \xi_i} - \lambda \sum_{i=1}^{\tau} \xi_i,$$

where τ is a stopping time, then we have from Lemma 13.1: $\mathbb{E} e^{\xi_\tau(\lambda)} = 1$. Now for any given sequence of $\tilde{z}_n(\mathcal{S}_n)$ and A_n, define the stopping time τ as either T, or the first time step n, so that

$$\xi_n(\lambda) \geq -\tilde{z}_n(\mathcal{S}_n) \ \& \ \mathcal{S}_n \in A_n$$

for each sequence $\mathcal{S}_T$. It follows that

$$\Pr\left(\exists n: \xi_n(\lambda) \geq -\tilde{z}_n(\mathcal{S}_n) \ \& \ \mathcal{S}_n \in A_n\right) \inf_{n>0, \mathcal{S}_n \in A_n} e^{-\tilde{z}_n(\mathcal{S}_n)}$$

$$\leq \mathbb{E}\left[e^{\xi_\tau(\lambda) + \tilde{z}_\tau(\mathcal{S}_\tau)} \mathbb{1}(\mathcal{S}_\tau \in A_\tau)\right] \inf_{n>0, \mathcal{S}_n \in A_n} e^{-\tilde{z}_n(\mathcal{S}_n)}$$

$$\leq \mathbb{E}\left[e^{\xi_\tau(\lambda) + \tilde{z}_\tau(\mathcal{S}_\tau)} \mathbb{1}(\mathcal{S}_\tau \in A_\tau) e^{-\tilde{z}_\tau(\mathcal{S}_\tau)}\right]$$

$$\leq \mathbb{E} e^{\xi_\tau(\lambda)} = 1.$$

Therefore we obtain

$$\ln \Pr\left[\exists n > 0: -\lambda \sum_{i=1}^{n} \xi_i \geq -\tilde{z}_n(\mathcal{S}_n) + \sum_{i=1}^{n} \ln \mathbb{E}_{Z_i^{(y)}} e^{-\lambda \xi_i} \ \& \ \mathcal{S}_n \in A_n\right]$$

$$\leq \sup_{n>0: \ \mathcal{S}_n \in A_n} \tilde{z}_n(\mathcal{S}_n).$$

Let $\tilde{z}(\mathcal{S}_n) = \ln \delta$, and we obtain the first inequality. Let

$$\tilde{z}_n(\mathcal{S}_n) = \lambda z_n + \sum_{i=1}^{n} \ln \mathbb{E}_{Z_i^{(y)}} e^{-\lambda \xi_i},$$

and we obtain the second inequality. $\qquad\square$

One difference between Theorem 13.2 and Theorem 2.5 is that in the latter case, one may optimize over λ to obtain an inequality in terms of the rate function $I_X(z)$. However, for sequential problems, we cannot directly optimize λ in the first inequality of Theorem 13.2 without paying a penalty associated with uniform convergence over λ (which typically leads to an additional $\ln n$ term) This is because for sequential problems, the conditional expectation may still depend on the observation $\mathcal{S}_n$, and thus optimizing over λ leads to sample dependent λ. The second inequality in Theorem 13.2 resolves this issue by restricting the optimization over λ in a restricted event A_n.

Now by using the logarithmic moment generating functions of Chapter 2, we obtain the following results.

Theorem 13.3 (Martingale Sub-Gaussian Inequality)   *Consider a sequence of random functions* $\xi_1(S_1), \ldots, \xi_t(S_t), \ldots$ *. Assume each ξ_i is sub-Gaussian with respect to $Z_i^{(y)}$:*

$$\ln \mathbb{E}_{Z_i^{(y)}} e^{\lambda \xi_i} \leq \lambda \mathbb{E}_{Z_i^{(y)}} \xi_i + \frac{\lambda^2 \sigma_i^2}{2}$$

for some σ_i that may depend on S_{i-1} and $Z_i^{(x)}$. Then for all $\sigma > 0$, with probability at least $1 - \delta$,

$$\forall n > 0: \sum_{i=1}^{n} \mathbb{E}_{Z_i^{(y)}} \xi_i < \sum_{i=1}^{n} \xi_i + \left(\sigma + \frac{\sum_{i=1}^{n} \sigma_i^2}{\sigma} \right) \sqrt{\frac{\ln(1/\delta)}{2}}.$$

Proof   We can let $\lambda = \sqrt{2 \ln(1/\delta)}/\sigma$, and then apply the first inequality of Theorem 13.2.   □

Since we allow σ_i to be data dependent in Theorem 13.3, we cannot in general choose $\sigma^2 = \sum_{i=1}^{n} \sigma_i^2$. However, if σ_i does not depend on data, then we can further optimize σ for specific time horizon n. In particular, a direct consequence of the sub-Gaussian inequality is the additive Chernoff bound, which can be stated below. It is often referred to as Azuma's inequality (Azuma, 1967).

Theorem 13.4 (Azuma's Inequality)   *Consider a sequence of random functions $\xi_1(S_1), \ldots, \xi_n(S_n)$ with a fixed number $n > 0$. If for each i, $\sup \xi_i - \inf \xi_i \leq M_i$ for some constant M_i, then with probability at least $1 - \delta$,*

$$\frac{1}{n} \sum_{i=1}^{n} \mathbb{E}_{Z_i^{(y)}} \xi_i < \frac{1}{n} \sum_{i=1}^{n} \xi_i + \sqrt{\frac{\sum_{i=1}^{n} M_i^2 \ln(1/\delta)}{2n^2}}.$$

Proof   Using the sub-Gaussian moment bound (see Example 2.14), we can obtain the desired bound by taking $\sigma_i = M_i/2$, and $4\sigma^2 = \sum_{i=1}^{n} M_i^2$ in Theorem 13.3.   □

For the analogy of multiplicative Chernoff bound, we can obtain a weaker version than Corollary 2.18.

Theorem 13.5   *Consider a sequence of random functions $\xi_1(S_1), \ldots, \xi_t(S_t), \ldots$ such that $\xi_i \in [0, 1]$ for all i. We have for $\lambda > 0$, with probability at least $1 - \delta$,*

$$\forall n > 0: \frac{1}{n} \sum_{i=1}^{n} \mathbb{E}_{Z_i^{(y)}} \xi_i < \frac{\lambda}{1 - e^{-\lambda}} \frac{1}{n} \sum_{i=1}^{n} \xi_i + \frac{\ln(1/\delta)}{(1 - e^{-\lambda}) n}.$$

Similarly, for $\lambda > 0$, with probability at least $1 - \delta$,

$$\forall n > 0: \frac{1}{n} \sum_{i=1}^{n} \mathbb{E}_{Z_i^{(y)}} \xi_i > \frac{\lambda}{e^{\lambda} - 1} \frac{1}{n} \sum_{i=1}^{n} \xi_i - \frac{\ln(1/\delta)}{(e^{\lambda} - 1) n}.$$

Proof We obtain from Lemma 2.15 and Theorem 13.2 that with probability at least $1 - \delta$,

$$-\sum_{i=1}^{n} \xi_i < \frac{\ln(1/\delta)}{\lambda} + \frac{1}{\lambda} \sum_{i=1}^{n} \ln(1 + (e^{-\lambda} - 1)\mathbb{E}_{Z_i^{(y)}} \xi_i)$$

$$\leq \frac{\ln(1/\delta)}{\lambda} + \frac{1}{\lambda} \sum_{i=1}^{n} (e^{-\lambda} - 1)\mathbb{E}_{Z_i^{(y)}} \xi_i.$$

This implies the first bound. Moreover, with probability at least $1 - \delta$,

$$-\sum_{i=1}^{n} [1 - \xi_i] < \frac{\ln(1/\delta)}{\lambda} + \frac{1}{\lambda} \sum_{i=1}^{n} \ln(1 + (e^{-\lambda} - 1)\mathbb{E}_{Z_i^{(y)}} [1 - \xi_i])$$

implies that

$$\sum_{i=1}^{n} \xi_i < \frac{\ln(1/\delta)}{\lambda} + \frac{1}{\lambda} \sum_{i=1}^{n} \ln(1 + (e^{\lambda} - 1)\mathbb{E}_{Z_i^{(y)}} \xi_i)$$

$$\leq \frac{\ln(1/\delta)}{\lambda} + \frac{1}{\lambda} \sum_{i=1}^{n} (e^{\lambda} - 1)\mathbb{E}_{Z_i^{(y)}} \xi_i.$$

This implies the second bound. $\qquad \square$

We can also obtain the following Bennett/Bernstein-style inequality, which is often referred to as the Freedman's inequality (Freedman, 1975).

Theorem 13.6 (Freedman's Inequality) *Consider a sequence of random functions $\xi_1(\mathcal{S}_1), \ldots, \xi_n(\mathcal{S}_n)$. Assume that $\xi_i \geq \mathbb{E}_{Z_i^{(y)}} \xi_i - b$ for some constant $b > 0$. Then for any $\lambda \in (0, 3/b)$, with probability at least $1 - \delta$,*

$$\forall n > 0: \sum_{i=1}^{n} \mathbb{E}_{Z_i^{(y)}} \xi_i < \sum_{i=1}^{n} \xi_i + \frac{\lambda \sum_{i=1}^{n} \mathrm{Var}_{Z_i^{(y)}}(\xi_i)}{2(1 - \lambda b/3)} + \frac{\ln(1/\delta)}{\lambda}.$$

This implies that for all $\sigma > 0$, with probability at least $1 - \delta$:

$$\forall n > 0: \sum_{i=1}^{n} \mathbb{E}_{Z_i^{(y)}} \xi_i < \sum_{i=1}^{n} \xi_i + \sigma\sqrt{2\ln(1/\delta)} + \frac{b\ln(1/\delta)}{3} \ \text{ or } \ \sum_{i=1}^{n} \mathrm{Var}_{Z_i^{(y)}}(\xi_i) > \sigma^2.$$

Proof Using the logarithmic moment generating function (2.13), we obtain the first inequality directly from the first inequality of Theorem 13.2.

Moreover, we can obtain from the second inequality of Theorem 13.2 with $A_n = \{\mathcal{S}_n: \sum_{i=1}^{n} \mathrm{Var}_{Z_i^{(y)}}(\xi_i) \leq \sigma^2\}$, $z_n = \sum_{i=1}^{n} \mathbb{E}_{Z_i^{(y)}} \xi_i - \epsilon - \epsilon^2 b/(6\sigma^2)$, and the rate function estimate corresponding to the third inequality of Lemma 2.9:

$$\Pr\left[\exists n > 0: \sum_{i=1}^{n} \xi_i \leq z_n \text{ and } \mathcal{S}_n \in A_n\right] \leq \exp\left(-\frac{\epsilon^2}{2\sigma^2}\right).$$

This implies the second desired inequality with $\epsilon = \sigma\sqrt{2\ln(1/\delta)}$. $\qquad \square$

Under the conditions of Theorem 13.6, we may also obtain (see Exercise 13.1) for $V_0 > 0$, with probability at least $1 - \delta$:

$$\forall n > 0 : \sum_{i=1}^{n} \mathbb{E}_{Z_i^{(y)}} \xi_i < \sum_{i=1}^{n} \xi_i + \sqrt{4 \left(V_0 + \sum_{i=1}^{n} \mathrm{Var}_{Z_i^{(y)}}(\xi_i) \right) \ln((\hat{\ell}+1)^2/\delta)} \quad (13.1)$$

$$+ \frac{b \ln((\hat{\ell}+1)^2/\delta)}{3}, \qquad \text{where } \hat{\ell} = \left\lfloor 1 + \log_2 \left(1 + \sum_{i=1}^{n} \mathrm{Var}_{Z_i^{(y)}}(\xi_i)/V_0 \right) \right\rfloor.$$

13.2 Self-Normalizing Vector Martingale Inequalities

The following result is useful in the analysis of contextual bandits. The proof technique is similar to that of Theorem 2.29.

Theorem 13.7 *Let $\{(X_t, \epsilon_t)\}$ be a sequence in $\mathbb{R}^d \times \mathbb{R}$ with respect to a filtration $\{\mathcal{F}_t\}$ so that ϵ_t is conditional zero-mean sub-Gaussian noise: for all $\lambda \in \mathbb{R}$,*

$$\ln \mathbb{E}[e^{\lambda \epsilon_t} | X_t, \mathcal{F}_{t-1}] \leq \frac{\lambda^2}{2} \sigma^2.$$

Let Λ_0 be a positive definite matrix, and

$$\Lambda_t = \Lambda_0 + \sum_{s=1}^{t} X_s X_s^\top.$$

Then for any $\delta > 0$, with probability at least $1 - \delta$, for all $t \geq 0$,

$$\left\| \sum_{s=1}^{t} \epsilon_s X_s \right\|_{\Lambda_t^{-1}}^2 < \sigma^2 \ln \frac{|\Lambda_0^{-1} \Lambda_t|}{\delta^2}.$$

Proof Let $\xi \sim N(0, \Lambda_0^{-1})$ be a normal random variable. We have for all $0 \leq \lambda \leq \sigma^{-2}/2$,

$$\exp \left(\lambda \left\| \sum_{s=1}^{t} \epsilon_s X_s \right\|_{\Lambda_t^{-1}}^2 \right)$$

$$= \mathbb{E}_{\tilde{\xi} \sim N(0, \Lambda_t^{-1})} \exp \left(\sqrt{2\lambda} \sum_{s=1}^{t} \epsilon_s \tilde{\xi}^\top X_s \right)$$

$$= |\Lambda_0^{-1} \Lambda_t|^{1/2} \mathbb{E}_{\xi \sim N(0, \Lambda_0^{-1})} \exp \left(\sqrt{2\lambda} \sum_{s=1}^{t} \epsilon_s \xi^\top X_s - \sum_{s=1}^{t} \frac{1}{2} (\xi^\top X_s)^2 \right)$$

$$\leq |\Lambda_0^{-1} \Lambda_t|^{1/2} \mathbb{E}_\xi \exp \left(\sqrt{2\lambda} \sum_{s=1}^{t} \epsilon_s \xi^\top X_s - \sum_{s=1}^{t} \frac{2\lambda \sigma^2}{2} (\xi^\top X_s)^2 \right)$$

$$\leq |\Lambda_0^{-1} \Lambda_t|^{1/2} \mathbb{E}_\xi \exp \left(\sum_{s=1}^{t} \sqrt{2\lambda} \epsilon_s \xi^\top X_s - \sum_{s=1}^{t} \ln \mathbb{E}_{\epsilon_s | X_s, \mathcal{F}_{s-1}} \exp \left(\sqrt{2\lambda} \epsilon_s \xi^\top X_s \right) \right).$$

The first equality used Gaussian integration. The second equality used the density of Gaussian distribution and $\Lambda_t = \Lambda_0 + \sum_{s=1}^{t} X_s X_s^\top$. The first inequality used $2\lambda \sigma^2 \leq 1$. The second inequality used the sub-Gaussian assumption. Now by taking expectation with respect to $\{(\epsilon_s, X_s)\}_{s=1}^{t}$, and applying Lemma 13.1, we obtain

$$\mathbb{E}\exp\left(\lambda\left\|\sum_{s=1}^{t}\epsilon_s X_s\right\|_{\Lambda_t^{-1}}^2\right) \leq |\Lambda_0^{-1}\Lambda_t|^{1/2}.$$

Using Markov inequality, we obtain

$$\Pr\left(\left\|\sum_{s=1}^{t}\epsilon_s X_s\right\|_{\Lambda_t^{-1}}^2 \geq z\right)\exp(\lambda z) \leq |\Lambda_0^{-1}\Lambda_t|^{1/2}.$$

Now we can take $\lambda = \sigma^{-2}/2$ and $\exp(\lambda z) = |\Lambda_0^{-1}\Lambda_t|^{1/2}/\delta$ to obtain the desired bound. $\qquad\square$

The main application of self-normalizing vector martingale inequality is to bound the confidence interval for linear sequential prediction problems, shown by the following example. Such a result can be used to analyze the regret of linear contextual bandits (see Section 17.2).

Example 13.8 Consider a sequence of observations $\{(X_1, Y_1), \ldots, (X_t, Y_t), \ldots\}$, and at each time t, X_t may depend on $\mathcal{S}_{t-1} = \{(X_1, Y_1), \ldots, (X_{t-1}, Y_{t-1})\}$. Assume that $Y_t|X_t$ is independent of $\mathcal{S}_{t-1}$, and generated according to a model

$$Y_t = f_*(X_t) + \epsilon_t, \quad f_*(X_t) = w_*^\top X_t,$$

where ϵ_t is a zero-mean sub-Gaussian noise as in Theorem 13.7. Assume that at each time t, we solve

$$\hat{w}_t = \arg\min_w \left[\sum_{s=1}^{t}(X_t^\top w - Y_t)^2 + \lambda I\right].$$

We can take $\Lambda_0 = \lambda I$ in Theorem 13.7, $\hat{f}_t(x) = \hat{w}_t^\top x$, and obtain the following bound of prediction confidence interval (see the proof of Theorem 17.8):

$$|\hat{f}_t(X) - f_*(X)| \leq \left[\sqrt{\lambda}\|w_*\| + \left\|\sum_{s=1}^{t}\epsilon_s X_s\right\|_{\Lambda_t^{-1}}\right]\|X\|_{\Lambda_t^{-1}}.$$

The result is analogous to the result of Lemma 9.34. We note that due to the dependency of X_s and $\mathcal{S}_{s-1}$, Lemma 9.34 can not be applied. Self-bounding martingale inequality can be used to obtain a confidence interval estimation. However, for independent data, the bound from Theorem 13.7 is worse than that of Lemma 9.34 by an extra factor $\sqrt{\ln|\Lambda_t/\lambda|}$. We know from Proposition 15.8 that this log-determinant term is $\tilde{O}(\sqrt{d})$ for d-dimensional problems.

One may also obtain a Bennett-style self-normalizing vector martingale inequality. We first introduce a lemma.

Lemma 13.9 *Let Σ_0 be a $d\times d$ symmetric positive definite matrix, and $\{\psi(X_t)\}$ be a sequence of vectors in $\mathbb{R}^d$. Let $\Sigma_t = \Sigma_0 + \sum_{s=1}^{t}\psi(X_s)\psi(X_s)^\top$, then*

$$\sum_{s=1}^{t}\frac{\psi(X_s)^\top\Sigma_{s-1}^{-1}\psi(X_s)}{1+\psi(X_s)^\top\Sigma_{s-1}^{-1}\psi(X_s)} \leq \ln|\Sigma_0^{-1}\Sigma_t|.$$

Proof We have

$$\frac{\psi(X_s)^\top \Sigma_{s-1}^{-1} \psi(X_s)}{1 + \psi(X_s)^\top \Sigma_{s-1}^{-1} \psi(X_s)} = \psi(X_s)^\top \Sigma_s^{-1} \psi(X_s)$$

$$= \text{trace}(\Sigma_s^{-1}(\Sigma_s - \Sigma_{s-1}))$$
$$= \text{trace}(\nabla \ln |\Sigma_s|(\Sigma_s - \Sigma_{s-1}))$$
$$\leq \ln |\Sigma_s| - \ln |\Sigma_{s-1}|.$$

The first equality is due to the Sherman–Morrison formula. The last inequality used the fact that $\ln |Z|$ is a concave function of Z (see Theorem A.18). Now by summing over $s = 1$ to $s = t$, we obtain the desired bound. $\quad\square$

Theorem 13.10 *Let $\{(X_t, \epsilon_t)\}$ be a sequence in $\mathbb{R}^d \times \mathbb{R}$ with respect to a filtration $\{\mathcal{F}_t\}$ so that*

$$\mathbb{E}[\epsilon_t | X_t, \mathcal{F}_{t-1}] = 0, \qquad \text{Var}[\epsilon_t | X_t, \mathcal{F}_{t-1}] \leq \sigma^2.$$

Let Λ_0 be a positive definite matrix, and

$$\Lambda_t = \Lambda_0 + \sum_{s=1}^t X_s X_s^\top.$$

If there exists $\alpha > 0$ such that $|\epsilon_t| \leq \alpha$, then for any $\delta > 0$, with probability at least $1 - \delta$, for all $t \geq 0$,

$$\left\| \sum_{s=1}^t \epsilon_s X_s \right\|_{\Lambda_t^{-1}}^2 \leq 1.3\sigma^2 \ln |\Lambda_0^{-1}\Lambda_t| + 4\alpha^2 \ln(2/\delta).$$

Proof For $t \geq 1$, let $\hat{w}_t = \Lambda_t^{-1} \sum_{s=1}^t \epsilon_s X_s$ $f_t = \hat{w}_{t-1}^\top X_t$, and $b_t = 1 + X_t^\top \Lambda_{t-1}^{-1} X_t$. Then we have the following decomposition (proof is left as Exercise 13.6)

$$\left\| \sum_{s=1}^t \epsilon_s X_s \right\|_{\Lambda_t^{-1}}^2 = \sum_{s=1}^t \frac{(b_s - 1)\epsilon_s^2 + 2\epsilon_s f_s - f_s^2}{b_s}. \qquad (13.2)$$

The right-hand side can be bounded using martingale concentration techniques because b_s and f_s are all measurable in $[X_s, \mathcal{F}_{s-1}]$.

The assumption of the theorem implies that

$$|2\epsilon_s f_s / b_s| \leq 2\alpha f_s / \sqrt{b_s}.$$

By using the sub-Gaussian exponential inequality of bounded random variable in Lemma 2.15, we obtain from Theorem 13.2 that, with probability at least $1 - \delta/2$,

$$\sum_{s=1}^t \frac{2\epsilon_s f_s - f_s^2}{b_s} \leq \sum_{s=1}^t \frac{2\lambda\alpha^2 f_s^2 - f_s^2}{b_s} + \frac{\ln(2/\delta)}{\lambda}.$$

By setting $\lambda = 0.5\alpha^{-2}$, we obtain

$$\sum_{s=1}^{t} \frac{2\epsilon_s f_s - f_s^2}{b_s} \leq 2\alpha^2 \ln(2/\delta). \tag{13.3}$$

Moreover, since

$$(1 - b_s^{-1})\epsilon_s^2 \leq \alpha^2,$$

we obtain with probability at least $1 - \delta/2$,

$$\sum_{s=1}^{t}(1 - b_s^{-1})\epsilon_s^2 \leq \frac{1}{\lambda\alpha^2}\sum_{s=1}^{t}(e^{\lambda\alpha^2} - 1)(1 - b_s^{-1})\mathbb{E}_{\epsilon_s}\epsilon_s^2 + \frac{\ln(2/\delta)}{\lambda}.$$

The inequality used the second inequality of Theorem 13.5. We now set $\lambda = 0.5\alpha^{-2}$, and obtain

$$\sum_{s=1}^{t}(1 - b_s^{-1})\epsilon_s^2 \leq 1.3\sigma^2\sum_{s=1}^{t}(1 - b_s^{-1}) + 2\alpha^2\ln(2/\delta)$$

$$\leq 1.3\sigma^2 \ln|\Lambda_0^{-1}\Lambda_t| + 2\alpha^2 \ln(2/\delta). \tag{13.4}$$

The second equality used Lemma 13.9.

The result of the theorem follows by taking the union bound of the two events corresponding to (13.3) and (13.4) with probability $1 - \delta/2$ each, and (13.2). $\square$

A similar proof can be used to obtain a more refined result, with an even weaker dependence on the range of ϵ_t. Such a result is useful for the analysis of variance-weighted linear regression. We leave it as Exercise 13.7.

13.3 Uniform Convergence

Similar to iid problems, it is possible to derive martingale uniform convergence results. Such results are useful for analyzing statistical estimation in the sequential decision setting, such as estimation problems in online learning, bandits, and reinforcement learning.

Consider a real-valued function class $\mathcal{F}$ on $\mathcal{Z}$, and a sequence of observations $Z_1, \ldots, Z_n \in \mathcal{Z}$, and let $\mathcal{S}_n = [Z_1, \ldots, Z_n]$. We assume that each Z_t may depend on $\mathcal{S}_{t-1}$. In uniform convergence, we are generally interested in estimating the following quantity:

$$\sup_{f \in \mathcal{F}}\left[\frac{1}{n}\sum_{i=1}^{n}[-f(Z_i) + \mathbb{E}_{Z_i^{(y)}}f(Z_i)]\right].$$

However, by using logarithmic moment generating function directly, one can get a more general and simplified result as a direct consequence of Theorem 13.2. In the following theorem, $M(\epsilon, \mathcal{F}, \|\cdot\|_\infty)$ is the ϵ L_∞ packing number of $\mathcal{F}$ defined in Chapter 5, with the metric $\|f\|_\infty = \sup_Z |f(Z)|$.

Theorem 13.11   *We have for any $\lambda > 0$, with probability at least $1 - \delta$, for all $n \geq 1$ and $f \in \mathcal{F}$,*

$$\left[-\sum_{i=1}^{n} f(Z_i) - \frac{1}{\lambda} \sum_{i=1}^{n} \ln \mathbb{E}_{Z_i^{(y)}} e^{-\lambda f(Z_i)} \right] \leq \inf_{\epsilon > 0} \left[2n\epsilon + \frac{\ln(M(\epsilon, \mathcal{F}, \| \cdot \|_\infty))/\delta)}{\lambda} \right].$$

Moreover, for all $n \geq 1$,

$$\mathbb{E} \sup_{f \in \mathcal{F}} \left[-\sum_{i=1}^{n} f(Z_i) - \frac{1}{\lambda} \sum_{i=1}^{n} \ln \mathbb{E}_{Z_i^{(y)}} e^{-\lambda f(Z_i)} \right] \leq \inf_{\epsilon > 0} \left[2n\epsilon + \frac{\ln(M(\epsilon, \mathcal{F}, \| \cdot \|_\infty)))}{\lambda} \right].$$

Proof   Let $\mathcal{F}_\epsilon \subset \mathcal{F}$ be an ϵ maximal packing of $\mathcal{F}$, with $|\mathcal{F}_\epsilon| \leq M(\epsilon, \mathcal{F}, \| \cdot \|_\infty)$. We obtain from Theorem 13.2, and the uniform bound over $\mathcal{F}_\epsilon$, that with probability at least $1 - \delta$,

$$\sup_{f \in \mathcal{F}_\epsilon} \left[-\sum_{i=1}^{n} f(Z_i) - \frac{1}{\lambda} \sum_{i=1}^{n} \ln \mathbb{E}_{Z_i^{(y)}} e^{-\lambda f(Z_i)} \right] \leq \frac{\ln(M(\epsilon, \mathcal{F}, \| \cdot \|_\infty))/\delta)}{\lambda}.$$

Since $\mathcal{F}_\epsilon$ is also an ϵ L_∞ cover of $\mathcal{F}$ (see Theorem 5.2), we obtain

$$\sup_{f \in \mathcal{F}} \left[-\sum_{i=1}^{n} f(Z_i) - \frac{1}{\lambda} \sum_{i=1}^{n} \ln \mathbb{E}_{Z_i^{(y)}} e^{-\lambda f(Z_i)} \right]$$

$$\leq 2n\epsilon + \sup_{f \in \mathcal{F}_\epsilon} \left[-\sum_{i=1}^{n} f(Z_i) - \frac{1}{\lambda} \sum_{i=1}^{n} \ln \mathbb{E}_{Z_i^{(y)}} e^{-\lambda f(Z_i)} \right].$$

This implies the first inequality. The second inequality is left as an exercise.   □

If the loss function satisfies the variance condition, then we can obtain the following uniform convergence result.

Corollary 13.12   *Assume that for all $f \in \mathcal{F}$ and Z_t: $-f(Z_t) + \mathbb{E}_{Z_t^{(y)}} f(Z_t) \leq b$, and the following variance condition holds for all $f \in \mathcal{F}$ and S_t:*

$$\text{Var}_{Z_t^{(y)}}[f(Z_t)] \leq c_0^2 + c_1 \mathbb{E}_{Z_t^{(y)}}[f(Z_t)],$$

then with probability at least $1 - \delta$, for all $f \in \mathcal{F}$,

$$(1 - \lambda c_1 \phi(\lambda b)) \sum_{t=1}^{n} \mathbb{E}_{Z_t^{(y)}}[f(Z_t)] \leq \sum_{t=1}^{n} f(Z_t) + \lambda n c_0^2 \phi(\lambda b)$$

$$+ \inf_{\epsilon > 0} \left[2n\epsilon + \frac{\ln(M(\epsilon, \mathcal{F}, \| \cdot \|_\infty))/\delta)}{\lambda} \right],$$

where $\phi(z) = (e^z - z - 1)/z^2$.

Proof Note that by employing the moment estimation of Bennett's inequality in Lemma 2.20, we obtain

$$\frac{1}{\lambda} \ln \mathbb{E}_{Z_t^{(y)}} e^{-\lambda f(Z_t)}$$

$$\leq -\mathbb{E}_{Z_t^{(y)}}[f(Z_t)] + \lambda\phi(\lambda b) \operatorname{Var}_{Z_t^{(y)}}[f(Z_t)]$$

$$\leq -\mathbb{E}_{Z_t^{(y)}}[f(Z_t)] + \lambda\phi(\lambda b)[c_0^2 + c_1 \mathbb{E}_{Z_t^{(y)}}[f(Z_t)]].$$

We can now obtain the desired bound from Theorem 13.11. □

Example 13.13 We consider least squares regression of Example 3.18, with $(x, y) = (Z^{(x)}, Z^{(y)})$. In the realizable case, the variance condition is satisfied with $c_0 = 0$, $c_1 = 2M^2$, and $b = 2M^2$. If we choose $\lambda = 0.2M^{-2}$, then $\lambda c_1 \phi(\lambda b) < 0.5$. Corollary 13.12 implies that with probability $1 - \delta$, for all $\phi \in \mathcal{G}$,

$$\sum_{i=1}^{n} \mathbb{E}_{Z_t^{(y)}}[\phi(Z_t)] \leq 2 \sum_{i=1}^{n} \phi(Z_t) + \inf_{\epsilon > 0} \left[4n\epsilon + 10M^2 \ln(M(\epsilon, \mathcal{G}, \|\cdot\|_\infty)/\delta)\right].$$

Since $(f(x) - y)^2$ is a $2M$ Lipschitz in $f(x)$, we obtain

$$\sum_{i=1}^{n} \mathbb{E}_{Z_t^{(y)}}[\phi(Z_t)] \leq 2 \sum_{i=1}^{n} \phi(Z_t) + \inf_{\epsilon > 0} \left[8nM\epsilon + 10M^2 \ln(M(\epsilon, \mathcal{F}, \|\cdot\|_\infty)/\delta)\right].$$

Note that the result of Theorem 13.11 can be improved using chaining with L_∞ cover. Similar to Proposition 4.20, we have the following result (see Exercise 13.4).

Proposition 13.14 *Consider a bounded function class $\mathcal{F}$ such that $|f(Z)| \leq b$ for all $f \in \mathcal{F}$. Then with probability $1 - \delta$, for all $f \in \mathcal{F}$, we have*

$$\frac{1}{n} \sum_{i=1}^{n} \mathbb{E}_{Z_i^{(y)}}[f(Z_i)] \leq \frac{1}{n} \sum_{i=1}^{n} f(Z_i)$$

$$+ C \inf_{\epsilon_0 > 0} \left[\epsilon_0 + \int_0^\infty \sqrt{\frac{\ln(M(\epsilon, \mathcal{F}, \|\cdot\|_\infty))}{n}} + b\sqrt{\frac{\ln(1/\delta)}{n}}\right],$$

where C is an absolute constant.

In addition to chaining, it is also possible to work with empirical covering numbers, which is needed for VC class. We will not discuss it here, but leave it as Exercise 13.5.

For realizable least squares problem with sub-Gaussian noise, one may also obtain a simpler estimate more directly. The result is useful both for contextual bandits and for some reinforcement learning problems.

Theorem 13.15 *Let $\{(X_t, \epsilon_t)\}$ be a filtered sequence in $\mathcal{X} \times \mathbb{R}$ so that ϵ_t is conditional zero-mean sub-Gaussian noise: for all $\lambda \in \mathbb{R}$,*

$$\ln \mathbb{E}[e^{\lambda\epsilon_t}|X_t, \mathcal{S}_{t-1}] \leq \frac{\lambda^2}{2}\sigma^2,$$

where $\mathcal{S}_{t-1}$ denotes the history data. Assume that $Y_t = f_*(X_t) + \epsilon_t$, with $f_*(x) \in \mathcal{F} : \mathcal{X} \to \mathbb{R}$. Let $\hat{f}_t$ be an approximate ERM solution for some $\epsilon' > 0$:

$$\left(\sum_{s=1}^{t} (\hat{f}_t(X_s) - Y_s)^2 \right)^{1/2} \leq \min_{f \in \mathcal{F}} \left(\sum_{s=1}^{t} (f(X_s) - Y_s)^2 \right)^{1/2} + \sqrt{t}\epsilon'.$$

Then with probability at least $1 - \delta$, for all $t \geq 0$,

$$\sum_{s=1}^{t} (\hat{f}_t(X_t) - f_*(X_t))^2 \leq \inf_{\epsilon > 0} \left[8t(\epsilon + \epsilon')(\sigma + 2\epsilon + 2\epsilon') + 12\sigma^2 \ln \frac{2N(\epsilon, \mathcal{F}, \|\cdot\|_\infty)}{\delta} \right].$$

Proof Let $\eta = \sigma^{-2}/4$, and for $f \in \mathcal{F}$, let

$$\phi(f, Z_t) = [(f(X_t) - Y_t)^2 - (f_*(X_t) - Y_t)^2].$$

Let $\mathcal{F}_\epsilon$ be an $\epsilon \|\cdot\|_\infty$ cover of $\mathcal{F}$ with $N = N(\epsilon, \mathcal{F}, \|\cdot\|_\infty)$ members. Given any $f \in \mathcal{F}_\epsilon$,

$$\begin{aligned}
\ln & \mathbb{E}_{Y_t | X_t, \mathcal{S}_{t-1}} \exp(-\eta\phi(f, Z_t)) \\
&= -\eta(f(X_t) - f_*(X_t))^2 \\
&\quad + \ln \mathbb{E}_{Y_t | X_t, \mathcal{S}_{t-1}} \exp(-2\eta(f(X_t) - f_*(X_t))(f_*(X_t) - Y_t)) \\
&\leq -\eta(f(X_t) - f_*(X_t))^2 + \frac{4\eta^2\sigma^2}{2}(f(X_t) - f_*(X_t))^2 \\
&= -\frac{(f(X_t) - f_*(X_t))^2}{8\sigma^2}.
\end{aligned}$$

The inequality used the sub-Gaussian noise assumption. It follows from Theorem 13.11 that with probability at least $1 - \delta/2$, for all $f \in \mathcal{F}_\epsilon$ and $t \geq 0$,

$$\sum_{i=1}^{t} -\eta\phi(f, Z_i) \leq -\sum_{i=1}^{t} \frac{(f(X_i) - f_*(X_i))^2}{8\sigma^2} + \ln(2N/\delta). \tag{13.5}$$

Using Exercise 13.3, we have with probability at least $1 - \delta/2$, for all $t \geq 0$,

$$\underbrace{\sum_{i=1}^{t} (f_*(X_i) - Y_i)^2}_{A} \leq 2t\sigma^2 + 3\sigma^2 \ln(2/\delta). \tag{13.6}$$

It follows that with probability at least $1 - \delta$, for all $t \geq 0$ and $f \in \mathcal{F}_\epsilon$, both (13.5) and (13.6) hold. Now, let $f \in \mathcal{F}_\epsilon$ so that $\|\hat{f}_t - f\|_\infty \leq \epsilon$. This implies that

$$\sum_{i=1}^{t}[(f(X_i) - Y_i)^2 - (f_*(X_i) - Y_i)^2] \leq \left(\sqrt{\sum_{i=1}^{t}(\hat{f}_t(X_i) - Y_i)^2} + \sqrt{t}\epsilon\right)^2 - A$$

$$\leq \left(\sqrt{A} + \sqrt{t}(\epsilon + \epsilon')\right)^2 - A$$

$$\overset{(a)}{\leq} (\epsilon' + \epsilon)^2 t + 2\sqrt{t}(\epsilon' + \epsilon)\sigma\sqrt{2t + 3\ln(2/\delta)}$$

$$\leq 4(\epsilon' + \epsilon)^2 t + 3\sigma t(\epsilon' + \epsilon) + \sigma^2 \ln(2/\delta). \tag{13.7}$$

In the derivations, the first inequality used $|f(X_i) - Y_i| \leq |\hat{f}_t(X_i) - Y_i| + \epsilon$ for all i. The second inequality used the fact that $\hat{f}_t$ is approximate ERM. (a) follows from (13.6). The last inequality used $2a\sigma\sqrt{2b + 3c} \leq 3a\sigma\sqrt{b} + 3a^2 + \sigma^2 c$. We thus obtain

$$\left(\sum_{i=1}^{t}(\hat{f}(X_i) - f_*(X_i))^2\right)^{1/2}$$

$$\leq \sqrt{\epsilon t} + \left(\sum_{i=1}^{t}(f(X_i) - f_*(X_i))^2\right)^{1/2} \qquad \text{(triangle inequality)}$$

$$\leq \sqrt{\epsilon^2 t} + \left(8\sigma^2 \ln(2N/\delta) + 8\sigma^2 \sum_{i=1}^{t}\eta\phi(f, Z_i)\right)^{1/2} \qquad \text{(from (13.5))}$$

$$= \sqrt{\epsilon^2 t} + \left(8\sigma^2 \ln(2N/\delta) + 2\sum_{i=1}^{t}[(f(X_i) - Y_i)^2 - (f_*(X_i) - Y_i)^2]\right)^{1/2}$$

$$\leq \sqrt{\epsilon^2 t} + \left(10\sigma^2 \ln(2N/\delta) + 8t(\epsilon' + \epsilon)^2 + 6\sigma t(\epsilon' + \epsilon)\right)^{1/2} \qquad \text{(from (13.7))}$$

$$\leq \left(12\sigma^2 \ln(2N/\delta) + 16t(\epsilon + \epsilon')^2 + 8\sigma t(\epsilon + \epsilon')\right)^{1/2},$$

where the last inequality used $\sqrt{a} + \sqrt{b} \leq \sqrt{6a + 1.2b}$. This implies the bound. $\square$

13.4 Minimax Analysis for Sequential Statistical Estimation

We may consider a generalization of the statistical estimation problem in Section 12.2 for supervised learning to the sequential decision setting.

Consider a general sequential estimation problem, where we observe data $Z_t \in \mathcal{Z}$ from the environment by interacting with the environment using a sequence of learned policies $\pi_t \in \Pi$. At each time t, the observation history is $\mathcal{S}_{t-1} = [(Z_1, \pi_1), \ldots, (Z_{t-1}, \pi_{t-1})]$. Based on the history, the player (or learning algorithm), denoted by $\hat{q}$, determines the next *policy* $\pi_t \in \Pi$ that can interact with the environment. Based on the policy π_t, environment generates the next observation $Z_t \in \mathcal{Z}$ according to an unknown distribution $q(Z_t | \pi_t, \mathcal{S}_{t-1})$.

In the sequential decision literature, the symbol $\mathcal{A}$ is often used to denote the action space of the learning algorithm. We will follow this convention, and thus will use the symbol $\hat{q}$ to denote a learning algorithm. The following definition summarizes the sequential statistical estimation problem in the realizable case.

Definition 13.16 (Sequential Statistical Estimation) Consider a family of environment distributions $\mathcal{P}_{\mathcal{Z}}$, where each $q \in \mathcal{P}_{\mathcal{Z}}$ determines the probability for generating Z_t based on policy π_t as $q(Z_t|\pi_t, \mathcal{S}_{t-1})$. Consider also a family of learning algorithms, represented by $\mathcal{P}_{\mathcal{A}}$. Each learning algorithm $\hat{q} \in \mathcal{P}_{\mathcal{A}}$ maps the history $\mathcal{S}_{t-1}$ deterministically to the next policy $\pi_t \in \Pi$ as $\pi_t = \hat{q}(\mathcal{S}_{t-1})$. Given $q \in \mathcal{P}_{\mathcal{Z}}$, and $\hat{q} \in \mathcal{P}_{\mathcal{A}}$, the data generation probability is fully determined as

$$p(\mathcal{S}_n|\hat{q}, q) = \prod_{t=1}^{n} q(Z_t|\hat{q}(\mathcal{S}_{t-1}), \mathcal{S}_{t-1}).$$

After observing $\mathcal{S}_n$ for some n, the learning algorithm $\hat{q}$ determines a distribution $\hat{q}(\theta|\mathcal{S}_n)$, and draw estimator $\theta \in \Theta$ according to $\hat{q}(\theta|\mathcal{S}_n)$. The learning algorithm suffers a loss (also referred to as regret) $Q(\theta, q)$. The overall probability of θ and $\mathcal{S}_n$ is

$$p(\theta, \mathcal{S}_n|\hat{q}, q) = \hat{q}(\theta|\mathcal{S}_n) \prod_{t=1}^{n} q(Z_t|\hat{q}(\mathcal{S}_{t-1}), \mathcal{S}_{t-1}). \tag{13.8}$$

Note that although the notation in Definition 13.16 assumes that π_t is a deterministic function of $\mathcal{S}_{t-1}$, it can also incorporate randomized algorithms. In such case, a policy is simply a distribution over the random choices. Since a random choice can always be characterized by a distribution (over the random choices) that is a deterministic function of $\mathcal{S}_{t-1}$, when we consider *random policies* in subsequent chapters, it should be understood that such policies can be handled by Definition 13.16. An example follows.

Example 13.17 (Online Learning (Non-adversarial)) We consider a parameter space Ω, and at each time t, the learning algorithm chooses a parameter $w_t \in \Omega$ according to a probability distribution $\pi_t(\cdot)$ on Ω. This probability distribution is the policy. Given $w_t \sim \pi_t$, we then observe a $Z_t \sim q_t$ from an unknown distribution q_t. We assume that the loss function ℓ is known. After n rounds, let $\theta(\mathcal{S}_n) = [\pi_1, \ldots, \pi_n]$, and we suffer a loss

$$Q(\theta, q) = \sum_{t=1}^{n} \mathbb{E}_{w_t \sim \pi_t} \mathbb{E}_{Z_t \sim q_t} \ell(w_t, Z_t) - \inf_{w \in \Omega} \sum_{t=1}^{n} \mathbb{E}_{Z \sim q_t} \ell(w, Z_t).$$

In non-adversarial online learning, the policy π_t only affects the final loss, but does not affect the observation Z_t. However, for some problems, the policy taken by the learning algorithm may affect the next observation. Such problems are usually more complex to analyze.

Example 13.18 (MAB) We consider the multiarmed bandit problem, where we have K arms from $\mathcal{A} = \{1, \ldots, K\}$. For each arm $a \in \mathcal{A}$, we have a probability distribution q_a on $[0, 1]$. If we pull an arm $a \in \mathcal{A}$, we observe a random reward

$r \in [0, 1]$ from a distribution q_a that depends on the arm a. Our goal is to find the best arm $\theta \in \Theta = \mathcal{A}$ with the largest expected reward $\mathbb{E}_{r \sim q_a}[r]$, and the loss $Q(\theta, q) = \sup_a \mathbb{E}_{r \sim q_a}[r] - \mathbb{E}_{r \sim q_\theta}[r]$. In this case, a policy π_t is a probability distribution over $\mathcal{A}$. The learning algorithm defines a probability distribution $\hat{q}(\mathcal{S}_{t-1})$ over $\mathcal{A}$ at each time, and draw $a_t \sim \hat{q}(\mathcal{S}_{t-1})$. The observation Z_t is the reward r_t which is drawn from q_{a_t}.

In this example, the learned policy affects the observation, but it does not need to interact with the environment. In contextual bandits and reinforcement learning, the policy interacts with the environment.

Example 13.19 (Contextual Bandits)   In contextual bandits, we consider a context space $\mathcal{X}$ and action space $\mathcal{A}$. Given a context $x \in \mathcal{X}$, we can take an action $a \in \mathcal{A}$, and observe a reward $r \sim q_{x,a}$. A policy π is a map $\mathcal{X} \to \Delta(\mathcal{A})$, where $\Delta(\mathcal{A})$ denotes the set of probability distributions over $\mathcal{A}$ (with an appropriately defined sigma algebra). The policy π_t interacts with the environment to generate the next observation as the environment generates x_t, the player takes an action $a_t \sim \pi_t(x_t)$, and then the environment generates the reward $r_t \sim q_{x_t, a_t}$.

For sequential estimation problems, we may define the minimax risk similar to Definition 12.9 as follows.

Definition 13.20   Consider an environment distribution family $\mathcal{P}_{\mathcal{Z}}$, learning algorithm distribution family $\mathcal{P}_{\mathcal{A}}$. Then the worst-case expected risk of a learning algorithm $\hat{q} \in \mathcal{P}_{\mathcal{A}}$ with respect to $\mathcal{P}_{\mathcal{Z}}$ is given by

$$r_n(\hat{q}, \mathcal{P}_{\mathcal{Z}}, Q) = \sup_{q \in \mathcal{P}_{\mathcal{Z}}} \mathbb{E}_{\theta, \mathcal{S}_n \sim p(\cdot|\hat{q}, q)} Q(\theta, q),$$

where $p(\cdot|\hat{q}, q)$ is defined in (13.8). Moreover, the minimax risk is defined as

$$r_n(\mathcal{P}_{\mathcal{A}}, \mathcal{P}_{\mathcal{Z}}, Q) = \inf_{\hat{q} \in \mathcal{P}_{\mathcal{A}}} r_n(\hat{q}, \mathcal{P}_{\mathcal{Z}}, Q).$$

We note that in the sequential decision setting, the following result for KL-divergence is a straightforward extension of Theorem B.6 by using the chain-rule of KL-divergence.

Lemma 13.21   *Let $\mathcal{P}' \subset \mathcal{P}_{\mathcal{Z}}$ be a finite subset. For any $q_0 \in \mathcal{P}_{\mathcal{Z}}$ and $\hat{q} \in \mathcal{P}_{\mathcal{A}}$. Assume that for any step t, history $\mathcal{S}_{t-1}$:*

$$\frac{1}{|\mathcal{P}'|} \sum_{q' \in \mathcal{P}'} \mathrm{KL}(q_0(\cdot|\hat{q}(\mathcal{S}_{t-1}), \mathcal{S}_{t-1}) || q'(\cdot|\hat{q}(\mathcal{S}_{t-1}), \mathcal{S}_{t-1}))) \leq \beta_t^2.$$

Then for any learning algorithm $\hat{q} \in \mathcal{P}_{\mathcal{A}}$, and sequence of size n, we have

$$\frac{1}{|\mathcal{P}'|} \sum_{q' \in \mathcal{P}'} \mathrm{KL}(p(\cdot|\hat{q}, q_0) || p(\cdot|\hat{q}, q'))) \leq \sum_{t=1}^{n} \beta_t^2.$$

Proof We have

$$\frac{1}{|\mathcal{P}'|} \sum_{q'\in\mathcal{P}'} \mathrm{KL}(p(\cdot|\hat{q},q_0) \,||\, p(\cdot|\hat{q},q'))) = \frac{1}{|\mathcal{P}'|} \sum_{q'\in\mathcal{P}'} \mathbb{E}_{\mathcal{S}_n\sim p(\cdot|\hat{q},q_0)} \ln\left(\frac{p(\mathcal{S}_n,|\hat{q},q_0)}{p(\mathcal{S}_n|\hat{q},q')}\right)$$

$$= \frac{1}{|\mathcal{P}'|} \sum_{q'\in\mathcal{P}'} \mathbb{E}_{\mathcal{S}_n\sim p(\cdot|\hat{q},q_0)} \left[\ln\left(\frac{p(\mathcal{S}_{n-1}|\hat{q},q_0)}{p(\mathcal{S}_{n-1}|\hat{q},q')}\right) + \ln\frac{q_0(Z_n|\hat{q}(\mathcal{S}_{n-1}),\mathcal{S}_{n-1})}{q'(Z_n|\hat{q}(\mathcal{S}_{n-1}),\mathcal{S}_{n-1})}\right]$$

$$= \frac{1}{|\mathcal{P}'|} \sum_{q'\in\mathcal{P}'} \mathbb{E}_{\mathcal{S}_n\sim p(\cdot|\hat{q},q_0)} \left[\ln\left(\frac{p(\mathcal{S}_{n-1}|\hat{q},q_0)}{p(\mathcal{S}_{n-1}|\hat{q},q')}\right) + \mathrm{KL}\left(q_0(\cdot|\hat{q},\mathcal{S}_{n-1}) \,||\, q'(\cdot|\hat{q},\mathcal{S}_{n-1})\right)\right]$$

$$\leq \frac{1}{|\mathcal{P}'|} \sum_{q'\in\mathcal{P}'} \mathbb{E}_{\mathcal{S}_{n-1}\sim p(\cdot|\hat{q},q_0)} \ln\left(\frac{p(\mathcal{S}_{n-1}|\hat{q},q_0)}{p(\mathcal{S}_{n-1}|\hat{q},q')}\right) + \beta_n^2$$

$$\leq \cdots \leq \sum_{t=1}^{n} \beta_t^2.$$

This implies the bound. $\qquad\qquad\square$

By using Lemma 13.21 to replace Theorem B.6 with $\alpha = 1$, we obtain the following straightforward generalization of Theorem 12.15 from Fano's inequality.

Theorem 13.22 *Consider a finite distribution family $\mathcal{P}_{\mathcal{Z}} = \{q^1,\ldots,q^N\}$. Assume for some $\hat{q} \in \mathcal{P}_{\mathcal{A}}$, if for all time step t, and history $\mathcal{S}_{t-1}$,*

$$\frac{1}{N^2} \sum_{q\in\mathcal{P}_{\mathcal{Z}}} \sum_{q'\in\mathcal{P}_{\mathcal{Z}}} \mathrm{KL}(q(\cdot|\hat{q}(\mathcal{S}_{t-1}),\mathcal{S}_{t-1})||q'(\cdot|\hat{q}(\mathcal{S}_{t-1}),\mathcal{S}_{t-1}))) \leq \beta_t^2.$$

Let Q be a loss function on $\Theta \times \mathcal{P}_{\mathcal{Z}}$, and

$$m = \sup_{\theta\in\Theta} \left| \{k : Q(\theta,q^k) < \epsilon\} \right|.$$

If $m \leq N/2$ and

$$\ln(N/m) \geq \ln 4 + 2\sum_{t=1}^{n} \beta_t^2,$$

then

$$\frac{1}{N} \sum_{j=1}^{N} \Pr_{\theta,\mathcal{S}_n\sim p(\cdot|\hat{q},q^j)} \left(Q(\theta,q^j) < \epsilon\right) \leq 0.5,$$

where the probability also includes possible randomization in $\mathcal{A}$. If $Q(\cdot,\cdot)$ is nonnegative, then this implies that $r_n(\hat{q},\mathcal{P}_{\mathcal{Z}},Q) \geq 0.5\epsilon$.

We can also obtain the following result from Fano's inequality in Theorem 13.22, which is stated in a style that is similar to Theorem 12.28, but with Hellinger distance replaced by KL-divergence.

Corollary 13.23 *Let $d \geq 32$ be an integer and let $\mathcal{P}_d = \{q^\tau : \tau \in \{-1,1\}^d\}$ contain 2^d probability measures. Suppose that the loss function Q can be decomposed as*

$$Q(\theta, q) = \sum_{j=1}^{d} Q_j(\theta, q),$$

where $Q_j \geq 0$ are all nonnegative. For any j and τ, let $\tau^{-[j]}$ be the index that differs with τ only by one coordinate j. Assume there exists $\epsilon, \beta \geq 0$ such that

$$\forall \tau: \quad [Q_j(\theta, q^\tau) + Q_j(\theta, q^{\tau^{-[j]}})] \geq \epsilon.$$

Assume for some $\hat{q} \in \mathcal{P}_\mathcal{A}$,

$$\sup_{q,q' \in \mathcal{P}_\mathcal{Z}} \sup_{\mathcal{S}_{t-1}} \mathrm{KL}(q(\cdot|\hat{q}(\mathcal{S}_{t-1}), \mathcal{S}_{t-1})\|q'(\cdot|\hat{q}(\mathcal{S}_{t-1}), \mathcal{S}_{t-1}))) \leq \beta_t^2.$$

If $\sum_{t=1}^{n} \beta_t^2 \leq (d/32 - 1)$, then $r_n(\hat{q}, \mathcal{P}_d, Q) \geq d\epsilon/16$.

Proof Consider drawing $\tau_i \in \{\pm 1\}^d$ from uniform distribution $i = 1, \ldots, N$, where $N = \lfloor \exp(d/16) \rfloor$. For any fixed $1 \leq i < j \leq N$, using the Chernoff bound with $|\tau_i - \tau_j| \in [0, 2]^d$ and $\mathbb{E}\|\tau_i - \tau_j\|_1 = d$, we obtain

$$\Pr(\|\tau_i - \tau_j\|_1 \leq d/2) \leq \exp(-d/8).$$

Therefore

$$\Pr(\exists i \neq j: \|\tau_i - \tau_j\|_1 \leq d/2) \leq N(N-1)\exp(-d/8) < 1.$$

It follows there exists a subset of T of $\{\pm 1\}^d$ with N members so that for $\tau_i \neq \tau_j \in T$,

$$\frac{1}{2}\|\tau_i - \tau_j\|_1 \geq d/4.$$

This implies that

$$Q(\theta, q^{\tau_i}) + Q(\theta, q^{\tau_j}) \geq d\epsilon/4.$$

It follows that

$$m = \sup_{\theta \in \Theta} \left| \{k: Q(\theta, q^{\tau_k}) < d\epsilon/8\} \right| = 1.$$

Since the condition of the corollary implies that

$$\ln(N) \geq \ln 4 + 2\sum_{t=1}^{n} \beta_t^2,$$

the desired result is a direct consequence of Theorem 13.22. □

While Theorem 13.22 and Corollary 13.23 can be applied to online learning problems, it is not convenient to use for bandit problems. For bandit problems, we will employ the following result which directly follows from Assouad's lemma.

Theorem 13.24 *Let $d \geq 1$ and $m \geq 2$ be integers, and let $\mathcal{P}_{\mathcal{Z}} = \{q^\tau : \tau \in \{1, \ldots, m\}^d\}$ contain m^d probability measures. Suppose that the loss function Q can be decomposed as*

$$Q(\theta, q) = \sum_{j=1}^{d} Q_j(\theta, q),$$

where $Q_j \geq 0$ are all nonnegative. For each j, $\tau \sim_j \tau'$ if $\tau = \tau'$ or if τ and τ' differs by only one component j. Assume that there exists $\epsilon, \beta \geq 0$ such that

$$\forall \tau' \sim_j \tau, \tau' \neq \tau: \quad [Q_j(\theta, q^\tau) + Q_j(\theta, q^{\tau'})] \geq \epsilon,$$

and there exists q_j^τ such that all $\tau' \sim_j \tau$ map to the same value: $q_j^{\tau'} = q_j^\tau$. Given any learning algorithm $\hat{q}$, if for all τ, $j \in [d]$, time step t, and $\mathcal{S}_{t-1}$,

$$\frac{1}{m} \sum_{\tau' \sim_j \tau} \mathrm{KL}(q_j^\tau(\cdot | \hat{q}(\mathcal{S}_{t-1}), \mathcal{S}_{t-1}) \| q^{\tau'}(\cdot | \hat{q}(\mathcal{S}_{t-1}), \mathcal{S}_{t-1}))) \leq \beta_{j,t}^2,$$

then

$$\frac{1}{m^d} \sum_{\tau} \mathbb{E}_{\theta, \mathcal{S}_n \sim p(\cdot | \hat{q}, q^\tau)} Q(\theta, q^\tau) \geq 0.5 d\epsilon \left(1 - \sqrt{\frac{2}{d} \sum_{j=1}^{d} \sum_{t=1}^{n} \beta_{j,t}^2} \right).$$

Proof We have

$$\frac{1}{dm^d} \sum_{\tau} \sum_{j=1}^{d} \frac{1}{m-1} \sum_{\tau' \sim_j \tau} \| p(\cdot | \hat{q}, q^\tau) - p(\cdot | \hat{q}, q^{\tau'}) \|_{\mathrm{TV}}$$

$$\leq \frac{1}{dm^d} \sum_{\tau} \sum_{j=1}^{d} \frac{1}{m-1} \sum_{\tau' \sim_j \tau, \tau' \neq \tau} \left[\| p(\cdot | \hat{q}, q_j^\tau) - p(\cdot | \hat{q}, q^{\tau'}) \|_{\mathrm{TV}} \right.$$

$$\left. + \| p(\cdot | \hat{q}, q_j^\tau) - p(\cdot | \hat{q}, q^\tau) \|_{\mathrm{TV}} \right]$$

$$= \frac{2}{dm^d} \sum_{\tau} \sum_{j=1}^{d} \frac{1}{m} \sum_{\tau' \sim_j \tau} \| p(\cdot | \hat{q}, q_j^\tau) - p(\cdot | \hat{q}, q^{\tau'}) \|_{\mathrm{TV}}$$

$$\leq \frac{2}{m^d} \sum_{\tau} \sqrt{ \frac{1}{dm} \sum_{j=1}^{d} \sum_{\tau' \sim_j \tau} \| p(\cdot | \hat{q}, q_j^\tau) - p(\cdot | \hat{q}, q^{\tau'}) \|_{\mathrm{TV}}^2 }$$

$$\leq \frac{2}{m^d} \sum_{\tau} \sqrt{ \frac{1}{2dm} \sum_{j=1}^{d} \sum_{\tau' \sim_j \tau} \mathrm{KL}(p(\cdot | \hat{q}, q_j^\tau) \| p(\cdot | \hat{q}, q^{\tau'})) }$$

$$\leq \sqrt{ \frac{2}{d} \sum_{j=1}^{d} \sum_{t=1}^{n} \beta_t^2 }.$$

The first inequality is triangle inequality for TV-norm. The first equality used $\hat{q}_j^\tau = \hat{q}_j^{\tau'}$ when $\tau \sim_j \tau'$. The second inequality used Jensen's inequality and the concavity of $\sqrt{\cdot}$. The third inequality used Theorem B.9. The last inequality used Lemma 13.21. Now in Lemma 12.27, we let $M_j(q^\tau) = \{q^{\tau'} : \tau' \sim_j \tau\}$ be the partitions. The result is a simple application of Lemma 12.27 with $m_j(q^\tau) = m$, $|\mathcal{P}| = m^d$, and $d(\mathcal{P}) = dm^d$. $\qquad\square$

Example 13.25 Consider estimating the mean of a d-dimensional Gaussian random variable $Z \sim N(\theta, I_{d \times d})$. Each time, the player draws an action $a_t \in \{1, \dots, d\}$, and the environment draws $\tilde{Z}_t \sim N(\theta, I_{d \times d})$, and reveals only the a_t-th component $Z_t = \tilde{Z}_{t,a_t}$. After T rounds, we would like to estimate the mean as $\hat{\theta}$, and measure the quality with $Q(\hat{\theta}, \theta) = \|\hat{\theta} - \theta\|_2^2$. In this case, a policy π_t can be regarded as a distribution over $\{1, \dots, d\}$, and we draw $a_t \sim \pi_t$.

To obtain an upper bound of the loss, we can simply randomly pick a_t, and use the following unbiased estimator:

$$\hat{\theta}_j = \frac{d}{n} \sum_{t=1}^n Z_{t,a_t} \mathbb{1}(a_t = j).$$

This implies that

$$\mathbb{E} \|\hat{\theta} - \theta\|_2^2 = \frac{d^2}{n}.$$

To obtain a lower bound of the loss, we consider Corollary 13.23, with $\theta^\tau = \epsilon\tau/(\sqrt{d})$ and $\mathcal{P}_{\mathcal{Z}} = \{N(\theta^\tau, I_{d \times d}) : \tau \in \{\pm 1\}^d$. Consider the decomposition

$$Q(\theta, q^\tau) = \sum_{j=1}^d Q_j(\theta, q^\tau), \quad Q_j(\theta, q^\tau) = (\theta_j - \theta_j^\tau)^2.$$

This implies that

$$\forall \tau: \quad [Q_j(\theta, q^\tau) + Q_j(\theta, q^{\tau^{-[j]}})] \geq \epsilon^2/d.$$

Let Z_t and Z'_t be the observations under $q, q' \in \mathcal{P}_{\mathcal{Z}}$, then for any a_t, $\mathrm{KL}(Z_t, Z'_t) \leq \beta_t^2 = 2\epsilon^2/d$. When

$$2n\epsilon^2 \leq d^2/32 - d,$$

we have

$$r_n(\mathcal{P}_{\mathcal{A}}, \mathcal{P}_{\mathcal{Z}}, Q) \geq \epsilon^2/16.$$

This matches the upper bound up to a constant.

13.5 Historical and Bibliographical Remarks

Sequential estimation problems have many applications that involve random observations over time. The formal mathematical tool to study such random variables is stochastic process (Doob, 1953). Martingale and Martingale difference sequences are natural mathematical concepts in stochastic processes that can be regarded as a generalization of the sum of independent random variables. The martingale difference sequence is also a mathematical formalization of a fair game, where the expected outcome at each play is zero. Martingale concentration means that the cumulative mean of such a game should be close to zero. Azuma's inequality (Azuma, 1967) may be regarded as a generalization of Hoeffding's inequality with a similar proof. It can be used to prove McDiarmid's inequality in Chapter 6. Freedman's inequality (Freedman, 1975) can be regarded as a generalization of Bernstein's inequality for independent random variables. It has been widely used in sequential decision problems with refined variance control. The treatment given in this chapter using Lemma 13.1 follows Zhang (2005). Theorem 13.7 was obtained in Abbasi-Yadkori et al. (2011) to analyze linear contextual bandits. Theorem 13.10 was used by Zhou et al. (2021) to analyze variance-weighted regression for model-based reinforcement learning for linear mixture MDP. However, better analysis of variance weighted regression can be obtained using a more refined result in Exercise 13.7 (also see Zhou and Gu (2022)).

Exercises

13.1 In Freedman's inequality, we want to remove the condition

$$\text{or } \sum_{i=1}^{n} \text{Var}_{Z_i^{(y)}}(\xi_i) > \sigma^2$$

by deriving a data-dependent probability bound that depends on the empirical conditional standard deviation (instead of a predefined σ) as

$$\hat{\sigma} = \sqrt{\frac{1}{n} \sum_{i=1}^{n} \text{Var}_{Z_i^{(y)}}(\xi_i)}.$$

- Show how to derive such an inequality using uniform convergence over a sequence of σ^2 of $V_0, 2V_0, 4V_0, \ldots$.
- Apply the result to $\xi_i \in [0, b]$ that satisfies the variance condition

$$\text{Var}_{Z_i^{(y)}}(\xi_i) \leq c_1 \mathbb{E}_{Z_i^{(y)}} \xi_i.$$

  Obtain a probability inequality to upper bound $\sum_{i=1}^{n} \mathbb{E}_{Z_i^{(y)}} \xi_i$ in terms of $\sum_{i=1}^{n} \xi_i$, with probability at least $1 - \delta$.

13.2 Use Lemma 13.1 to prove the second inequality of Theorem 13.11.

13.3 Let $\{\xi_i\}$ be a sequence of dependent zero-mean sub-Gaussian random variables:

$$\ln \mathbb{E}_{\xi_i} \exp(\lambda \xi_i) \leq 0.5 \lambda^2 \sigma^2.$$

Use the logarithmic moment generating function estimate in Theorem 2.29 to show that with probability $1 - \delta$, for all $t \geq 0$,

$$\sum_{i=1}^{t} \xi_i^2 \leq 2t\sigma^2 + 3\sigma^2 \ln(1/\delta).$$

13.4 Consider a bounded function class $\mathcal{F}$ such that $|f(Z)| \leq b$ for all $f \in \mathcal{F}$.

- If $|\mathcal{F}| \leq N$ is finite, show that with probability $1 - \delta$, for all $f \in \mathcal{F}$,

$$\frac{1}{n}\sum_{i=1}^{n}\mathbb{E}_{Z_i^{(y)}}[f(Z_i)] \leq \frac{1}{n}\sum_{i=1}^{n}f(Z_i) + b\sqrt{\frac{2\ln(N/\delta)}{n}}.$$

- Show that every $f \in \mathcal{F}$ can be expressed as the summation of

$$f(Z) = \sum_{\ell=0}^{\infty}f_\ell(Z),$$

where $|f_\ell(Z)| \leq 3 \cdot 2^\ell b$, using a decomposition similar to that in the proof of Theorem 6.25. Use this decomposition to prove Proposition 13.14.

13.5 Consider a bounded function class $\mathcal{F}$ such that $f(Z) \in [0,1]$ for all $f \in \mathcal{F}$. Let $N_\infty(\epsilon, \mathcal{F}, 2n)$ be L_∞ uniform covering number of $\mathcal{F}$ in Definition 4.4. Consider a sequence of samples $\{Z_t, Z_t'\}$ such that Z_t' has the same distribution of Z_t conditioned on $\mathcal{S}_{t-1} = [Z_1, \ldots, Z_{t-1}]$.

- Find

$$\Pr\left[\sup_{f \in \mathcal{F}}\frac{1}{n}\sum_{i=1}^{n}[f(Z_i') - f(Z_i)] \geq \epsilon\right]$$

using $N_\infty(\epsilon, \mathcal{F}, 2n)$.

- Let $\hat{f}$ be an arbitrary estimator that depends on $\mathcal{S}_n$, and find

$$\Pr\left[\frac{1}{n}\sum_{i=1}^{n}\mathbb{E}_{Z_i^{(y)}}[\hat{f}(Z_i)] - \hat{f}(Z_i') \geq \epsilon\right].$$

- Use the previous two results to find

$$\Pr\left[\sup_{f \in \mathcal{F}}\frac{1}{n}\sum_{i=1}^{n}\mathbb{E}_{Z_i^{(y)}}[f(Z_i)] - f(Z_i) \geq \epsilon\right].$$

13.6 Prove (13.2) by using Theorem 15.6 with $Y_t = \epsilon_t$ (and set $\sigma = 0$ in the theorem).

13.7 Assume that in Theorem 13.10, we replace the condition $|\epsilon_t| \leq \alpha$ by

$$\forall t \geq 1: \ |\epsilon_t|\min\left(1, \alpha'\|X_t\|_{\Lambda_{t-1}^{-1}}\right) \leq \alpha,$$

where $\alpha' > 0$. Let

$$\beta_t(\alpha, \delta) = \sqrt{1.3\sigma^2\ln|\Lambda_0^{-1}\Lambda_t| + 4(\alpha^2 + \sigma^2)\ln(2/\delta)}.$$

If we can choose α' so that inequality $\alpha' \geq \alpha\beta_T(\alpha, \delta)/(1.5\sigma^2)$ always holds for some $T > 0$, then with probability at least $1 - 1.5\delta$, for all $0 \leq t \leq T$, we have

$$\left\|\sum_{s=1}^{t}\epsilon_sX_s\right\|_{\Lambda_t^{-1}} \leq \beta_t(\alpha, \delta).$$

The proof of this statement is similar to that of Theorem 13.10.

- Show that we have decomposition $\epsilon_t = \epsilon_t^{(1)} + \epsilon_t^{(2)}$, where

$$\epsilon_t^{(1)} = \epsilon_t\mathbb{1}(|\epsilon_t| \leq \alpha) - \mathbb{E}[\epsilon_t\mathbb{1}(|\epsilon_t| \leq \alpha)|X_s, \mathcal{F}_{s-1}]),$$
$$\epsilon_t^{(2)} = \epsilon_t\mathbb{1}(|\epsilon_t| > \alpha) - \mathbb{E}[\epsilon_t\mathbb{1}(|\epsilon_t| > \alpha)|X_s, \mathcal{F}_{s-1}]).$$

- Show that (13.4) still holds for probability at least $1 - \delta/2$.
- (13.3) holds with ϵ_t replaced by $\epsilon_t^{(1)}$ with probability at least $1 - \delta/2$.
- Define events

$$E_t = \left\{ \mathcal{S}_t \colon \left\| \sum_{s=1}^t \epsilon_s X_s \right\|_{\Lambda_t^{-1}} \leq \beta_t(\alpha, \delta) \right\},$$

$$E' = \left\{ \forall t \colon (13.3) \text{ holds for } \epsilon_t^{(1)}, \text{ and } (13.4) \text{ holds} \right\}.$$

Show that under $\cap_{s<t} E_s$, $|\epsilon_s f_s| \leq \beta_{s-1} |\epsilon_s| \|X_s\|_{\Lambda_{t-1}^{-1}} \leq M/2$ $(s = 1, \ldots, t)$, and thus for $s = 1, \ldots, t$, $\epsilon_s^{(2)} f_s \in [-M, M]$ (with respect to the conditional distribution over $\epsilon_s^{(2)}$), where $M = 2(\alpha/\alpha')\beta_T$.

- Show that under $E_t^c \cap E' \cap_{s<t} E_s$, the following event holds:

$$\sum_{s=1}^t \frac{2\epsilon_s^{(2)} f_s - f_s^2}{b_s} \geq 4\sigma^2 \ln(2/\delta). \tag{13.9}$$

Let $A_t = E' \cap_{s<t} E_s$. Use the second inequality of Theorem 13.2 and (2.13) to show that

$$\Pr\left(\exists t \in [T] \colon A_t \,\&\, (13.9) \text{ holds}\right) \leq 0.5\delta.$$

- Show that $\Pr\left(\cap_{t \in [T]} E_t \cap E'\right) \geq 1 - 1.5\delta$, and this implies the desired result.

13.8 Derive a lower bound on Example 13.25 using Theorem 13.24, and compare to the result obtained in the example from Corollary 13.23.

14

Basic Concepts of Online Learning

In online learning, we consider a learning model that is different from that of supervised learning, in that we make predictions sequentially and obtain feedback after predictions are made. In this chapter, we introduce this learning model as well as some first-order online learning algorithms.

14.1 Online Learning Model

We will use the notations that are consistent with earlier chapters on supervised learning. In online learning, we consider observing $Z_t = (X_t, Y_t)$ one by one in a time sequence from $t = 1, 2, \ldots$. At each time step, we try to predict the next datum in the sequence, and then obtain a feedback of the prediction.

More formally, the online learning model can be considered as a repeated game. For $t = 1, 2, \ldots$:

- An adversary picks (X_t, Y_t), and reveals X_t only.
- An online learning algorithm $\mathcal{A}$ predicts $\hat{f}_{t-1}(X_t)$.
- The value of Y_t is revealed and a loss $L(\hat{f}_{t-1}(X_t), Y_t)$ is computed.

The goal of online learning is to minimize the aggregated loss

$$\sum_{t=1}^{T} L(\hat{f}_{t-1}(X_t), Y_t).$$

In general, an online algorithm $\mathcal{A}$ picks a prediction model $f(x)$ from $\mathcal{F} = \{f(w, x) \colon w \in \Omega\}$ by learning a model parameter $w_{t-1} \in \Omega$ at time t based on previously observed data $\mathcal{S}_{t-1} = \{Z_1, \ldots, Z_{t-1}\}$. That is, we take $\hat{f}_{t-1}(X_t) = f(w_{t-1}, X_t)$ with $w_{t-1} = \mathcal{A}(\mathcal{S}_{t-1})$. We are interested in the following inequality, referred to as *regret bound*, where the aggregated loss of an online algorithm is compared to the optimal aggregated loss:

$$\sum_{t=1}^{T} L(f(w_{t-1}, X_t), Y_t) - \inf_{w \in \Omega} \sum_{t=1}^{T} L(f(w, X_t), Y_t) \leq \epsilon_T. \tag{14.1}$$

In many situations, online regret bounds hold for all sequences $\{Z_t\}$, although the definition can also be modified to hold in expectation. In the online learning literature, the choice of prediction functions in the form $f(w_{t-1}, x)$ is referred to as *proper learning*, since it matches the function form of

$\{f(w, X): w \in \Omega\}$, with which it competes. More generally, one may also consider *improper online learning*, where $\hat{f}_{t-1}(x)$ may not belong to the function class $\{f(w, x): w \in \Omega\}$. We do not differentiate the two situations in our discussion.

To differentiate from online learning, the standard supervised learning setting is often referred to as *batch learning* in the machine learning literature. Regret bound analysis can be considered as a generalization of the oracle inequality in batch learning. We will show later that a regret bound directly implies an oracle inequality using a simple technique called *online to batch conversion*.

14.2 Perceptron Algorithms

In this section, we will study a simple online learning algorithm called the perceptron algorithm, which is a precursor to modern neural networks.

Consider the binary classification problem with $Y \in \{\pm 1\}$, and linear functions

$$f(w, X) = w^\top X,$$

with prediction rule

$$\begin{cases} 1 & f(w, X) \geq 0, \\ -1 & \text{otherwise.} \end{cases}$$

The loss function is a binary classification error: $\mathbb{1}(f(w, X)Y \leq 0)$. The perceptron algorithm (Rosenblatt, 1957, 1962) is an online learning algorithm that takes data sequentially, as in Algorithm 14.1. It is mistake-driven, which means it only updates the model weight vector when the prediction makes a mistake. The algorithm belongs to the family of linear classifiers. In many applications, one needs to design the linear features by hand.

Algorithm 14.1 Perceptron Algorithm
___
Input: Sequence $(X_1, Y_1), \ldots, (X_T, Y_T)$
Output: w_s
1 Let $w_0 = 0$
2 **for** $t = 1, 2, \ldots, T$ **do**
3 Observe X_t and predict label $\text{sign}(w_{t-1}^\top X_t)$
4 Observe Y_t and compute mistake $\mathbb{1}(w_{t-1}^\top X_t Y_t \leq 0)$
5 **if** $w_{t-1}^\top X_t Y_t > 0$ **then**
6   // No mistake
7   Let $w_t = w_{t-1}$
8 **else**
9   // A mistake is observed
10   Let $w_t = w_{t-1} + X_t Y_t$
11 Randomly pick s from 0 to $T - 1$
Return: w_s

Note that the random choice of the returned predictor in the perceptron algorithm is for the purpose of online to batch conversion, which we will discuss later. In the following, we first state the mistake bound of perceptron as follows.

Theorem 14.1 *Consider the perceptron algorithm in algorithm 14.1. Consider $\gamma > 0$ and weight vector w_* such that for all t*

$$w_*^\top X_t Y_t \geq \gamma.$$

Then we have the following mistake bound:

$$\sum_{t=1}^{T} \mathbb{1}(w_{t-1}^\top X_t Y_t \leq 0) \leq \frac{\|w_*\|_2^2 \sup\{\|X_t\|_2^2\}}{\gamma^2}.$$

Proof Let $M = \sup_t \|X_t\|_2$, and let $\eta = \gamma/M^2$. Assume that we have a mistake at time step t, then we have

$$(\eta w_{t-1} - w_*)^\top X_t Y_t \leq 0 - w_*^\top X_t Y_t \leq -\gamma.$$

This implies that

$$\begin{aligned}
\|\eta w_t - w_*\|_2^2 &= \|\eta w_{t-1} + \eta X_t Y_t - w_*\|_2^2 \\
&= \|\eta w_{t-1} - w_*\|_2^2 + 2\eta(\eta w_{t-1} - w_*)^\top X_t Y_t + \eta^2 \|X_t\|_2^2 \\
&\leq \|\eta w_{t-1} - w_*\|_2^2 - 2\eta\gamma + \eta^2 M^2 \\
&\leq \|\eta w_{t-1} - w_*\|_2^2 - \frac{\gamma^2}{M^2}.
\end{aligned}$$

Note also that $\|\eta w_t - w_*\|_2^2 = \|\eta w_{t-1} - w_*\|_2^2$ if there is no mistake at time step t. Therefore by summing over $t = 1$ to $t = t$, we obtain

$$0 \leq \|\eta w_t - w_*\|_2^2 \leq \|\eta w_0 - w_*\|_2^2 - \frac{\gamma^2}{M^2} k,$$

where k is the number of mistakes. This implies the bound. $\qquad\square$

The perceptron mistake bound can be regarded as an online version of the margin bound discussed in Chapter 9, where empirical process was used to obtain similar margin bounds for the ERM method. The technique required for analyzing the ERM method is much more complicated.

Using essentially the same proof, we can also obtain a mistake bound for multiclass classification problems (Collins, 2002). In comparison, the analysis of the ERM method for multiclass classification is more complex, as discussed in Section 9.4.

For multiclass prediction with q classes $y \in \{1, \ldots, q\}$, we may use the notations of Section 9.4, and consider a vector prediction function $f(x) \in \mathbb{R}^q$, with linear prediction model for class ℓ in (9.14) defined as

$$f_\ell(x) = w^\top \psi(x, \ell).$$

The predicted class for each x is

$$\hat{y}(w, x) \in \arg\max_{\ell} [w^\top \psi(x, \ell)],$$

and the error (or mistake) for an instance x with true label y is

$$\mathbb{1}(\hat{y}(w, x) \neq y).$$

Algorithm 14.2 Multiclass Perceptron Algorithm

Input: Sequence $(X_1, Y_1), \ldots, (X_T, Y_T)$
Output: w_s
1   Let $w_0 = 0$
2   **for** $t = 1, 2, \ldots, T$ **do**
3   Observe X_t and predict label $\hat{Y}_t \in \arg\max_\ell \{w_{t-1}^\top \psi(X_t, \ell)\}$
4   Observe Y_t and compute mistake $\mathbb{1}(\hat{Y}_t \neq Y_t)$
5   **if** $\hat{Y}_t == Y_t$ **then**
6   // No mistake
7   Let $w_t = w_{t-1}$
8   **else**
9   // A mistake is observed
10   Let $w_t = w_{t-1} + [\psi(X_t, Y_t) - \psi(X_t, \hat{Y}_t)]$
11   Randomly pick s from 0 to $T - 1$
Return: w_s

Theorem 14.2 *Consider Algorithm 14.2. We have the following mistake bound:*

$$\sum_{t=1}^T \mathbb{1}(\hat{Y}_t \neq Y_t) \leq \inf_{\gamma > 0, w} \left[\sum_{t=1}^T 2\max\left(0, 1 - \gamma^{-1} \min_{\ell \neq Y_t} w^\top [\psi(X_t, Y_t) - \psi(X_t, \ell)]\right) \right.$$
$$\left. + \frac{\|w\|_2^2 \sup\{\|\psi(X_t, Y_t) - \psi(X_t, Y_\ell)\|_2^2\}}{\gamma^2} \right].$$

Proof The proof is basically the same as that of the binary case. Given any $\gamma > 0$ and w, we let $\psi_t = \psi(X_t, Y_t) - \psi(X_t, \hat{Y}_t)$, $M = \sup\{\|\psi_t\|_2\}$, and $\eta = \gamma/M^2$. Assume that we have a mistake at time step t, then we have $\hat{Y}_t \neq Y_t$, and $w_{t-1}^\top \psi_t \leq 0$. This implies that

$$(\eta w_{t-1} - w_*)^\top \psi_t \leq 0 - w_*^\top \psi_t \leq \max(0, \gamma - w_*^\top \psi_t) - \gamma.$$

Therefore by taking

$$\|\eta w_t - w_*\|_2^2 = \|\eta w_{t-1} + \eta \psi_t - w_*\|_2^2$$
$$= \|\eta w_{t-1} - w_*\|_2^2 + 2\eta(\eta w_{t-1} - w_*)^\top \psi_t + \eta^2 \|\psi_t\|_2^2$$
$$\leq \|\eta w_{t-1} - w_*\|_2^2 + 2\eta \max(0, \gamma - w_*^\top \psi_t) - 2\eta\gamma + \eta^2 M^2$$
$$\leq \|\eta w_{t-1} - w_*\|_2^2 + 2\eta \max(0, \gamma - w_*^\top \psi_t) - \frac{\gamma^2}{M^2}.$$

Note also that $\|\eta w_t - w_*\|_2^2 = \|\eta w_{t-1} - w_*\|_2^2$ if there is no mistake at time step t. Therefore by summing over $t = 1$ to $t = T$, we obtain

$$0 \le \|\eta w_T - w_*\|_2^2 \le 2\eta \sum_{t=1}^{T} \max(0, \gamma - w_*^\top \psi_t) + \|\eta w_0 - w_*\|_2^2 - \frac{\gamma^2}{M^2} k,$$

where k is the number of mistakes. This implies the bound. $\qquad\square$

Unlike Theorem 14.1, Theorem 14.2 does not require that there exists $\gamma > 0$ so that $w_*^\top \psi(X, Y) \ge w_*^\top \psi(X, \ell) + \gamma$ for all $\ell \ne Y$. The bound is thus a soft-margin bound, with a margin-based hinge loss as penalty. In the special case of hard-margin condition, where $w_*^\top \psi(X, Y) \ge w_*^\top \psi(X, \ell) + \gamma$ for all $\ell \ne Y$, we obtain the simpler mistake bound:

$$\sum_{t=1}^{T} \mathbf{1}(\hat{Y}_t \ne Y_t) \le \frac{\|w\|_2^2 \sup\{\|\psi(X_t, Y_t) - \psi(X_t, Y_\ell)\|_2^2\}}{\gamma^2}.$$

This is analogous to the binary class perceptron mistake bound of Theorem 14.1.

14.3 Online to Batch Conversion

In online learning, each time, we train a model using historic data, and then test on the next datum. This naturally corresponds to the generalization performance. If we assume that in online learning, the observed data are random, with $Z_t = (X_t, Y_t) \sim \mathcal{D}$, then by taking expectation, we can obtain an expected oracle inequality.

Specially, we may consider an online algorithm $\mathcal{A}$ such that it returns a weight vector $w_t = \mathcal{A}(\mathcal{S}_t)$ with $\mathcal{S}_t = \{Z_1, \ldots, Z_t\}$. Assume that we have a regret bound of the general form

$$\sum_{t=1}^{T} \phi(w_{t-1}, Z_t) \le \epsilon(\mathcal{S}_T). \tag{14.2}$$

By taking expectations, we obtain an expected generalization bound of

$$\mathbb{E}_{\mathcal{S}_T} \sum_{t=1}^{T} \mathbb{E}_Z \phi(w_{t-1}, Z) \le \mathbb{E}_{\mathcal{S}_T} \epsilon(\mathcal{S}_T).$$

This implies that if we select s uniformly from 0 to $T - 1$, then

$$\mathbb{E}_{\mathcal{S}_T} \mathbb{E}_s \mathbb{E}_Z \phi(w_s, Z) \le \mathbb{E}_{\mathcal{S}_T} \epsilon(\mathcal{S}_T)/T.$$

For example, for the perceptron algorithm, we may let

$$\phi(w, Z) = \mathbf{1}(\hat{y}(w, X) \ne Y) - 2 \max\left(0, 1 - \gamma^{-1} \min_{\ell \ne Y} w^\top [\psi(X, Y) - \psi(X, \ell)]\right),$$

then the following expected generalization bound can be obtained from the perceptron mistake bound of Theorem 14.2.

Proposition 14.3 *Consider Algorithm 14.2, with s chosen uniformly at random from 0 to $T-1$. If $Z_t = (X_t, Y_t) \sim \mathcal{D}$ are iid observations, then we have*

$$\mathbb{E}_{\mathcal{S}_{T-1}} \mathbb{E}_s \mathbb{E}_{Z \sim \mathcal{D}} \mathbf{1}(\hat{y}(w_s, X) \neq Y)$$

$$\leq \inf_{\gamma > 0, w} \left[2\mathbb{E}_{Z \sim \mathcal{D}} \max\left(0, 1 - \gamma^{-1} \min_{\ell \neq Y_t} w^\top [\psi(X, Y) - \psi(X, \ell)]\right) \right.$$

$$\left. + \frac{\|w\|_2^2 \sup\{\|\psi(X, Y) - \psi(X, Y')\|_2^2\}}{\gamma^2 \, T} \right],$$

where the prediction rule $\hat{y}(w, x) \in \arg\max_\ell w^\top \psi(x, \ell)$ is consistent with Algorithm 14.2.

Proof We simply note that

$$\mathbb{E}_{\mathcal{S}_{T-1}} \sum_{t=1}^T \mathbb{E}_{Z \sim \mathcal{D}} \mathbf{1}(\hat{y}(w_{t-1}, X) \neq Y) = \mathbb{E}_{\mathcal{S}_T} \sum_{t=1}^T \mathbf{1}(\hat{y}(w_{t-1}, X_t) \neq Y_t),$$

and

$$\sum_{t=1}^T 2\mathbb{E}_{Z \sim \mathcal{D}} \max\left(0, 1 - \gamma^{-1} \min_{\ell \neq Y_t} w^\top [\psi(X, Y) - \psi(X, \ell)]\right)$$

$$= \mathbb{E}_{\mathcal{S}_T} \sum_{t=1}^T 2\max\left(0, 1 - \gamma^{-1} \min_{\ell \neq Y_t} w^\top [\psi(X_t, Y_t) - \psi(X_t, \ell)]\right).$$

Now, a straightforward application of Theorem 14.2 implies that

$$\mathbb{E}_{\mathcal{S}_{T-1}} \sum_{t=1}^T \mathbb{E}_{Z \sim \mathcal{D}} \mathbf{1}(\hat{y}(w_{t-1}, X) \neq Y)$$

$$\leq \inf_{\gamma > 0, w} \left[2T\mathbb{E}_{Z \sim \mathcal{D}} \max\left(0, 1 - \gamma^{-1} \min_{\ell \neq Y_t} w^\top [\psi(X, Y) - \psi(X, \ell)]\right) \right.$$

$$\left. + \frac{\|w\|_2^2 \sup\{\|\psi(X, Y) - \psi(X, Y')\|_2^2\}}{\gamma^2} \right].$$

This implies the desired result. $\square$

From Chapter 13, we know that one can further employ martingale tail probability bounds to obtain a high-probability result of the following form: with probability at least $1 - \delta$ over $\mathcal{S}_T$,

$$\sum_{t=1}^T \mathbb{E}_{Z \sim \mathcal{D}} \phi(w_{t-1}, Z) \leq \sum_{t=1}^T \phi(w_{t-1}, Z_t) + \epsilon(\delta). \tag{14.3}$$

We may combine this bound with (14.2), and obtain the following probability bound for the randomized estimator s, uniformly chosen from 0 to $T-1$. With probability at least $1 - \delta$ over $\mathcal{S}_T$,

$$\mathbb{E}_s \mathbb{E}_{Z \sim \mathcal{D}} \phi(w_s, Z) \leq \frac{\epsilon(\delta) + \epsilon(\mathcal{S}_T)}{T}.$$

The following result is a concrete example on how to use martingale inequalities and online mistake bound to derive high-probability generalization error bound.

Proposition 14.4 *Consider Algorithm 14.1, with s uniformly drawn from 0 to $T - 1$. Assume $w_*^\top XY \geq \gamma > 0$ for all $Z = (X, Y)$. If $Z_t = (X_t, Y_t) \sim \mathcal{D}$, then with probability at least $1 - \delta$,*

$$\mathbb{E}_s \mathbb{E}_{Z \in \mathcal{D}} \mathbb{1}(\hat{y}(w_s, X) \neq Y)$$
$$\leq \inf_{\lambda > 0} \left[\frac{\lambda}{1 - e^{-\lambda}} \frac{\|w_*\|_2^2 \sup_X \|X\|_2^2}{\gamma^2 T} + \frac{\ln(1/\delta)}{(1 - e^{-\lambda}) T} \right].$$

Proof Let

$$\{\xi_i = \mathbb{1}(w_{i-1}^\top X_i Y_i \leq 0) : i = 1, 2, \ldots, n\}$$

be a sequence of random variables. Theorem 13.5 implies that for any $\lambda > 0$, with probability at least $1 - \delta$,

$$\frac{1}{T} \sum_{i=1}^{T} \mathbb{E}_{(X_i, Y_i) \sim \mathcal{D}} \xi_i \leq \frac{\lambda}{1 - e^{-\lambda}} \frac{1}{T} \sum_{i=1}^{T} \xi_i + \frac{\ln(1/\delta)}{(1 - e^{-\lambda}) T}.$$

Also note that the mistake bound in Theorem 14.1 implies that

$$\sum_{i=1}^{T} \xi_i \leq \frac{\|w_*\|_2^2 \sup\{\|X\|_2^2\}}{\gamma^2}.$$

Since $\mathbb{E}_{(X,Y) \sim \mathcal{D}} \mathbb{1}(w_{i-1}^\top XY \leq 0) = \mathbb{E}_{(X_i, Y_i) \sim \mathcal{D}} \xi_i$, we obtain the desired result. $\square$

14.4 Online Convex Optimization

One can extend the analysis of perceptron algorithms to general convex loss functions, leading to the so-called online convex optimization, introduced into machine learning by Zinkevich (2003). A general first-order algorithm for online convex optimization, which we refer to as online gradient descent, can be found in Algorithm 14.3. Its analysis is given in Theorem 14.5.

Algorithm 14.3 Online Gradient Descent

Input: Sequence of loss functions $\ell_1, \ldots, \ell_T$ defined on Ω
Output: $\hat{w}$
1 Let $w_0 = 0$
2 **for** $t = 1, 2, \ldots, T$ **do**
3   Observe loss $\ell_t(w_{t-1})$
4   Let $\tilde{w}_t = w_{t-1} - \eta_t \nabla \ell_t(w_{t-1})$
5   Let $w_t = \arg\min_{w \in \Omega} \|w - \tilde{w}_t\|_2^2$
6 Let $\hat{w} = T^{-1} \sum_{t=1}^{T} w_{t-1}$ or $\hat{w} = w_s$ for a random s from 0 to $T - 1$
Return: $\hat{w}$

Theorem 14.5   *Let* $\{\ell_t(w) : w \in \Omega\}$ *be a sequence of real-valued convex loss functions defined on a convex set* Ω. *Assume that all* $\ell_t(w)$ *are G-Lipschitz (i.e.* $\|\nabla \ell_t(w)\|_2 \leq G$). *If we let* $\eta_t = \eta > 0$ *be a constant in Algorithm 14.3. Then for all* $w \in \Omega$, *we have*

$$\sum_{t=1}^{T} \ell_t(w_{t-1}) \leq \sum_{t=1}^{T} \ell_t(w) + \frac{\|w_0 - w\|_2^2}{2\eta} + \frac{\eta T}{2} G^2.$$

Proof   We have the following inequality:

$$
\begin{aligned}
\|\tilde{w}_t - w\|_2^2 &= \|w_{t-1} - w - \eta \nabla \ell_t(w_{t-1})\|_2^2 \\
&= \|w_{t-1} - w\|_2^2 - 2\eta \nabla \ell_t(w_{t-1})^\top (w_{t-1} - w) + \eta^2 \|\nabla \ell_t(w_{t-1})\|_2^2 \\
&\leq \|w_{t-1} - w\|_2^2 - 2\eta \nabla \ell_t(w_{t-1})^\top (w_{t-1} - w) + G^2 \eta^2 \\
&\leq \|w_{t-1} - w\|_2^2 - 2\eta [\ell_t(w_{t-1}) - \ell_t(w)] + G^2 \eta^2,
\end{aligned}
$$

where the first inequality used the Lipschitz condition, and the second inequality used the convexity condition.

Since $w_t \in \Omega$ is the projection of $\tilde{w}_t$ onto Ω and $w \in \Omega$, we also have

$$\|w_t - w\|_2^2 \leq \|\tilde{w}_t - w\|_2^2.$$

Therefore, we have

$$\|w_t - w\|_2^2 \leq \|w_{t-1} - w\|_2^2 - 2\eta [\ell_t(w_{t-1}) - \ell_t(w)] + G^2 \eta^2.$$

Now we may sum over $t = 1$ to $t = T$, and obtain

$$\|w_T - w\|_2^2 \leq \|w_0 - w\|_2^2 - 2\eta \sum_{t=1}^{T} [\ell_t(w_{t-1}) - \ell_t(w)] + T G^2 \eta^2.$$

Rearrange the terms and we obtain the desired bound. $\square$

The analysis technique of Theorem 14.5 is quite similar to that of the perceptron mistake bound. In fact, we may state the following more general result which includes both online convex optimization and perceptron mistake analysis as special cases. We leave its proof as an exercise.

Theorem 14.6   *Consider Algorithm 14.5 with the update rule replaced by the following method:*

$$\tilde{w}_t = w_{t-1} - \eta_t g_t.$$

If we can choose g_t *so that*

$$g_t^\top (w - w_{t-1}) \leq \tilde{\ell}_t(w) - \ell_t(w_{t-1}),$$

then

$$\sum_{t=1}^{T} \ell_t(w_{t-1}) \leq \sum_{t=1}^{T} \tilde{\ell}_t(w) + \frac{\|w_0 - w\|_2^2}{2\eta} + \frac{\eta T}{2} G^2.$$

Note that in Theorem 14.6, $\ell_t(w_{t-1})$ may not necessarily be a convex function of w_{t-1}.

Example 14.7   Theorem 14.5 is a special case of Theorem 14.6 by taking $\tilde{\ell}_t(w) = \ell_t(w)$ and $g_t = \nabla \ell_t(w_{t-1})$.

Example 14.8   When $w_{t-1}^\top X_t Y_t \leq 0$, we have

$$-(w - w_{t-1})^\top X_t Y_t \leq \gamma - w^\top X_t Y_t - \gamma$$
$$\leq \max(0, \gamma - w^\top X_t Y_t) - \gamma \mathbb{1}(w_{t-1}^\top X_t Y_t \leq 0).$$

When $w_{t-1}^\top X_t Y_t > 0$, we have

$$0 \leq \max(0, \gamma - w^\top X_t Y_t) - \gamma \mathbb{1}(w_{t-1}^\top X_t Y_t \leq 0).$$

Therefore let $g_t = -\mathbb{1}(w_{t-1}^\top X_t Y_t \leq 0) X_t Y_t$, then

$$(w - w_{t-1})^\top g_t \leq \max(0, \gamma - w^\top X_t Y_t) - \gamma \mathbb{1}(w_{t-1}^\top X_t Y_t \leq 0).$$

This implies that Theorem 14.1 is a special case of Theorem 14.6 by taking $\tilde{\ell}_t(w) = \max(0, \gamma - w^\top X_t Y_t)$ and $\ell_t(w_{t-1}) = \gamma \mathbb{1}(w_{t-1}^\top X_t Y_t \leq 0)$.

We may also obtain an oracle inequality for Algorithm 14.3 as follows.

Theorem 14.9   *Consider loss function $\phi(w, Z) \in [0, M]$ with $Z \sim \mathcal{D}$, and $w \in \Omega$, where Ω is a convex set. Assume that $\phi(w, Z)$ is convex and G-Lipschitz with respect to w. Let $[Z_1, \ldots, Z_T] \sim \mathcal{D}^T$ be independent samples, and consider $\hat{w}$ obtained from Algorithm 14.3, with $\ell_i(w) = \phi(w, Z_i)$ and $\eta_t = \eta > 0$. Then with probability at least $1 - \delta$,*

$$\mathbb{E}_{Z \sim \mathcal{D}} \phi(\hat{w}, Z) \leq \inf_{w \in \Omega} \left[\mathbb{E}_{Z \sim \mathcal{D}} \phi(w, Z) + \frac{1}{2\eta T} \|w - w_0\|_2^2 \right] + \frac{\eta}{2} G + M \sqrt{\frac{2\ln(2/\delta)}{T}}.$$

Proof   Note that the convexity and Jensen's inequality imply

$$\mathbb{E}_{Z \sim \mathcal{D}} \phi(\hat{w}, Z) \leq \frac{1}{T} \sum_{t=1}^T \mathbb{E}_{Z_t} \phi(w_{t-1}, Z_t). \tag{14.4}$$

Moreover, using Azuma's inequality, we have with probability at least $1 - \delta/2$,

$$\frac{1}{T} \sum_{t=1}^T \mathbb{E}_{Z_t} \phi(w_{t-1}, Z_t) \leq \frac{1}{T} \sum_{t=1}^T \phi(w_{t-1}, Z_t) + M \sqrt{\frac{\ln(2/\delta)}{2T}}. \tag{14.5}$$

Using Theorem 14.5, we obtain

$$\frac{1}{T} \sum_{t=1}^T \phi(w_{t-1}, Z_t) \leq \frac{1}{T} \sum_{t=1}^T \phi(w, Z_t) + \frac{\|w_0 - w\|_2^2}{2\eta T} + \frac{\eta}{2} G^2. \tag{14.6}$$

Using the Chernoff bound, we have with probability at least $1 - \delta/2$,

$$\frac{1}{T} \sum_{t=1}^T \phi(w, Z_t) \leq \mathbb{E}_{Z \sim \mathcal{D}} \phi(w, Z) + M \sqrt{\frac{\ln(2/\delta)}{2T}}. \tag{14.7}$$

By taking the union bound, and combining the four inequalities, we obtain the following. With probability at least $1 - \delta$,

$$\mathbb{E}_{Z \sim \mathcal{D}} \phi(\hat{w}, Z) \le \frac{1}{T} \sum_{t=1}^{T} \mathbb{E}_{Z_t} \phi(w_{t-1}, Z_t)$$

$$\le \frac{1}{T} \sum_{t=1}^{T} \phi(w_{t-1}, Z_t) + M \sqrt{\frac{\ln(2/\delta)}{2T}}$$

$$\le \frac{1}{T} \sum_{t=1}^{T} \phi(w, Z_t) + \frac{\|w_0 - w\|_2^2}{2\eta T} + \frac{\eta}{2} G^2 + M \sqrt{\frac{\ln(2/\delta)}{2T}}$$

$$\le \mathbb{E}_{Z \sim \mathcal{D}} \phi(w, Z) + \frac{\|w_0 - w\|_2^2}{2\eta T} + \frac{\eta}{2} G^2 + M \sqrt{\frac{2 \ln(2/\delta)}{T}}.$$

The first inequality used (14.4). The second inequality used (14.5). The third inequality used (14.6). The last inequality used (14.7). □

If we take $\eta = O(1/\sqrt{T})$, then we obtain a convergence result of $O(1/\sqrt{T})$ in Theorem 14.9. This result can be compared to that of Corollary 9.27, which has a similar convergence rate if we set $\lambda = 1/(\eta T)$.

In Corollary 9.27, the loss function does not have to be convex, and the theorem applies to ERM, which implies the following bound for the ERM estimator:

$$\mathbb{E}_{\mathcal{D}} \phi(\hat{w}, Z) \le \mathbb{E}_{\mathcal{D}} \phi(w, Z) + \lambda \|w\|_2^2$$
$$+ O\left(\sqrt{\frac{\ln((\lambda + B^2)/(\delta \lambda))}{n}} \right) + O\left(\frac{B^2 \ln((\lambda + B^2)/(\delta \lambda))}{\lambda n} \right).$$

This result is similar to that of Theorem 14.9 with $\eta = 1/(\lambda T)$.

However, the result in Theorem 14.9 does not apply to ERM, but rather the specific online learning procedure for convex functions described in Algorithm 14.3. We note that the definitions of Lipschitz constants are different, with $G \le \gamma B$, where γ is the Lipschitz of the loss function, and $B = \sup\{\|X\|_2\}$. In addition, one may regard the regret bound in the online learning analysis as an analogy of the Rademacher complexity bound for ERM estimator. Azuma's inequality is the counterpart of McDiarmid's inequality to obtain the concentration results.

The techniques used in online learning analysis are closely related to the stability analysis of Chapter 7. In fact, these two techniques often lead to similar results. Stability analysis has the advantage of allowing the computational procedure (SGD) to go through the data more than once, while the online to batch conversion technique only allows the computational procedure (online algorithm) to go through the training data once.

For vector-valued functions, the Rademacher complexity analysis is trickier unless one works with covering numbers. This is due to the fact that the corresponding comparison lemma based on the Lipschitz loss assumption may depend on the dimensionality of the vector function, as discussed in Section 9.4. However, the Lipschitz parameter of $\phi(w, \cdot)$ in Theorem 14.9 is with respect to the model parameter, and thus the difficulty of Rademacher complexity analysis does not exist. In particular, we may directly analyze the structured-SVM loss of Example 9.32 without much difficulty using online learning (or stability analysis).

Example 14.10 Consider the structured-SVM loss of Example 9.32, where

$$\phi(w, z) = \max_\ell [\gamma(y, \ell) - w^\top (\psi(x, y) - \psi(x, \ell))].$$

If $\|\psi(x, y) - \psi(, \ell)\|_2 \leq B$, then we can take $G = B$. Using Theorem 14.5, we obtain

$$\frac{1}{T} \sum_{t=1}^{T} \phi(w_{t-1}, Z_t) \leq \frac{1}{T} \sum_{t=1}^{T} \phi(w, Z_t) + \frac{\|w_0 - w\|_2^2}{2\eta T} + \frac{\eta}{2} B^2.$$

By taking expectation, and using Jensen's inequality with $\lambda = 1/(\eta T)$, we obtain

$$\mathbb{E}_{\mathcal{S}_T} \mathbb{E}_{Z \sim \mathcal{D}} \phi(\hat{w}, Z) \leq \mathbb{E}_{Z \sim \mathcal{D}} \phi(w, Z) + \frac{\lambda}{2} \|w_0 - w\|_2^2 + \frac{1}{2\lambda T} B^2.$$

For L_2 regularization (or kernel methods), one can obtain a better bound using strong convexity. Observe that for regularized loss, we take

$$\ell_t(w) = \phi(w, Z_t) + \frac{\lambda}{2} \|w - w_0\|_2^2. \tag{14.8}$$

If $\phi(w, z)$ is convex in w, then $\ell_t(w)$ is λ strongly convex.

The following result holds for strongly convex loss functions, and the specific learning rate schedule was proposed by Shalev-Shwartz et al. (2011) to solve SVMs.

Theorem 14.11 *Consider convex loss functions $\ell_t(w) \colon \Omega \to \mathbb{R}$, which are G-Lipschitz (i.e. $\|\nabla \ell_t(w)\|_2 \leq G$) and λ strongly convex. If we let $\eta_t = 1/(\lambda t) > 0$ in Algorithm 14.3, then for all $w \in \Omega$, we have*

$$\sum_{t=1}^{T} \ell_t(w_{t-1}) \leq \sum_{t=1}^{T} \ell_t(w) + \frac{1 + \ln T}{2\lambda} G^2.$$

Proof Similar to the proof of Theorem 14.5, we have

$$\begin{aligned}
\|w_t - w\|_2^2 &\leq \|\tilde{w}_t - w\|_2^2 \\
&= \|w_{t-1} - w - \eta_t \nabla \ell_t(w_{t-1})\|_2^2 \\
&= \|w_{t-1} - w\|_2^2 - 2\eta_t \nabla \ell_t(w_{t-1})^\top (w_{t-1} - w) + \eta_t^2 \|\nabla \ell_t(w_{t-1})\|_2^2 \\
&\leq \|w_{t-1} - w\|_2^2 + 2\eta_t [\ell_t(w) - \ell_t(w_{t-1})] - \eta_t \lambda \|w_{t-1} - w\|_2^2 + G^2 \eta_t^2 \\
&= (1 - \lambda \eta_t) \|w_{t-1} - w\|_2^2 + 2\eta_t [\ell_t(w) - \ell_t(w_{t-1})] + G^2 \eta_t^2,
\end{aligned}$$

where strong convexity is used to derive the second inequality. Note that $1 - \eta_t \lambda = \eta_t/\eta_{t-1}$ and for notation convenience we take $1/\eta_0 = 0$. This implies that

$$\eta_t^{-1} \|w_t - w\|_2^2 \leq \eta_{t-1}^{-1} \|w_{t-1} - w\|_2^2 + 2[\ell_t(w) - \ell_t(w_{t-1})] + G^2 \eta_t.$$

By summing over $t = 1$ to $t = T$, we obtain

$$\eta_T^{-1}\|w_T - w\|_2^2 \le \eta_0^{-1}\|w_0 - w\|_2^2 + 2\sum_{t=1}^{T}[\ell_t(w) - \ell_t(w_{t-1})] + G^2\sum_{t=1}^{T}\frac{1}{\lambda t}.$$

Using $\sum_{t=1}^{T}(1/t) \le 1 + \ln T$, we obtain the desired bound. $\qquad\square$

It is possible to remove the $\ln T$ factor if we use weighted regret, as shown in the following theorem.

Theorem 14.12 *Consider convex loss functions $\ell_t(w) \colon \Omega \to \mathbb{R}$, which are G-Lipschitz (i.e. $\|\nabla \ell_t(w)\|_2 \le G$) and λ strongly convex. If we let $\eta_t = 2/(\lambda(t+1)) > 0$ in Algorithm 14.3, then all $w \in \Omega$, we have*

$$\sum_{t=1}^{T}\frac{2(t+1)}{T(T+3)}\ell_t(w_{t-1}) \le \sum_{t=1}^{T}\frac{2(t+1)}{T(T+3)}\ell_t(w) + \frac{2G^2}{\lambda(T+3)}.$$

Proof As in the proof of Theorem 14.11, we have

$$\|w_t - w\|_2^2 \le (1 - \eta_t\lambda)\|w_{t-1} - w\|_2^2 + 2\eta_t[\ell_t(w) - \ell_t(w_{t-1})] + G^2\eta_t^2.$$

This implies that $\eta_t^{-2}(1 - \eta_t\lambda) \le \eta_{t-1}^{-2}$, where we set $\eta_0^{-2} = 0$:

$$\eta_t^{-2}\|w_t - w\|_2^2 \le \eta_{t-1}^{-2}\|w_{t-1} - w\|_2^2 + 2\eta_t^{-1}[\ell_t(w) - \ell_t(w_{t-1})] + G^2.$$

By summing over $t = 1$ to $t = T$, we obtain

$$\eta_T^{-2}\|w_T - w\|_2^2 \le \eta_0^{-2}\|w_0 - w\|_2^2 + 2\sum_{t=1}^{T}\eta_t^{-1}[\ell_t(w) - \ell_t(w_{t-1})] + G^2 T.$$

This leads to the bound. $\qquad\square$

Using batch to online conversion, we can obtain the following expected oracle inequality as a straightforward result of Theorem 14.11 and Theorem 14.12.

Corollary 14.13 *Consider the regularized loss function (14.8) with $w_0 = 0$, where $\phi(w, z)$ is convex in w, and G-Lipschitz in w. Moreover assume that $d(\Omega) = \sup\{\|w\|_2 \colon w \in \Omega\}$. If $Z_1, \ldots, Z_T \sim \mathcal{D}$ are independent samples, then we can obtain the following expected oracle inequality for Algorithm 14.3 if we take the learning rate in Theorem 14.11:*

$$\mathbb{E}_{\mathcal{S}_T}\mathbb{E}_{\mathcal{D}}\phi(\hat{w}, Z) + \frac{\lambda}{2}\|\hat{w}\|_2^2 \le \inf_{w\in\Omega}\left[\mathbb{E}_{\mathcal{D}}\phi(w, Z) + \frac{\lambda}{2}\|w\|_2^2\right] + \frac{\ln(eT)}{2\lambda T}[G + \lambda d(\Omega)]^2.$$

We can also obtain the following expected oracle inequality for Algorithm 14.3 if we take the learning rate in Theorem 14.12 with

$$\hat{w}' = \sum_{t=1}^{T} \frac{2(t+1)}{T^2 + 3T} w_{t-1},$$

then

$$\mathbb{E}_{\mathcal{S}_T} \mathbb{E}_{\mathcal{D}} \phi(\hat{w}', Z) + \frac{\lambda}{2} \|\hat{w}'\|_2^2 \leq \inf_{w \in \Omega} \left[\mathbb{E}_{\mathcal{D}} \phi(w, Z) + \frac{\lambda}{2} \|w\|_2^2 \right] + \frac{2[G + \lambda d(\Omega)]^2}{\lambda(T+3)}.$$

Proof Note that $\ell_t(w)$ is λ-strongly convex in w. Moreover, it is $G + \lambda d(\Omega)$ Lipschitz. We simply take expectation and apply Jensen's inequality to obtain the desired bounds. $\qquad\square$

In the stochastic setting, the online gradient algorithm is often referred to as the *stochastic gradient descent* algorithm (SGD). The results in Corollary 14.13 directly imply both a generalization bound and a convergence bound for SGD. In order to obtain concentration bounds, or obtain an oracle inequality without the assumption of $d(\Omega)$, one can apply the technique of sample dependent bounds similar to the analysis of kernel methods as in Corollary 9.26 and Corollary 9.27. If we restrict $\mathcal{D}$ to the uniform distribution of training data, then Corollary 14.13 implies a convergence of SGD to a minimizer of the training loss. However, once we go through the data more than once, Corollary 14.13 cannot be used to obtain a generalization bound for SGD. In this case, we have to combine the convergence analysis of Corollary 14.13 and the stability analysis of Theorem 7.14 to obtain a generalization bound if we run SGD multiple times over the data. We leave the resulting bound as an exercise. Moreover, some recent work studied the generalization of SGD (and the related SGLD method) using the mutual information-based generalization bound of Corollary 10.22.

14.5 Online Nonconvex Optimization

Consider the online optimization problem with a nonconvex but bounded loss function $\ell_t(w)$. In this case, in order to obtain a meaningful online regret bound, it is necessary to consider randomized algorithms. We have the following negative result for any deterministic algorithm.

Proposition 14.14 *Consider $\Omega = \{w_0, w_1, \ldots, w_T\}$ that contains T members. Given any deterministic online learning algorithm $\mathcal{A}$ that returns a model parameter w_{t-1} based on $\{\ell_s : s = 1, \ldots, t-1\}$, there exists a loss sequence $\ell_t(w) \in \{0, 1\}$ so that*

$$\inf_w \sum_{t=1}^{T} \ell_t(w) = 0, \qquad \sum_{t=1}^{T} \ell_t(w_{t-1}) = T.$$

Proof We simply pick the loss at each time t so that

$$\ell_t(w) = \mathbb{1}(w = w_{t-1}).$$

In this case, after time T, there exists one $w \in \Omega$ that differs from $w_1, \ldots, w_T$. It follows that $\sum_{t=1}^{T} \ell_t(w) = 0$. □

In general, Proposition 14.14 implies that for a deterministic online learning algorithm, the worst-case regret for nonconvex loss cannot be logarithmic in the size of the model family Ω. To resolve this difficulty, one needs to employ randomized algorithms. In fact, it is known that the Gibbs algorithm considered in Section 7.4 for nonconvex supervised learning problems can also be used for nonconvex online learning. In the online learning context, this algorithm is often referred to as Hedge. In the setting of general online (nonconvex) optimization, the Gibbs distribution of (7.9) can be defined after time t as follows:

$$p_t(w) \propto p_0(w) \exp\left(-\eta \sum_{s=1}^{t} \ell_s(w)\right), \qquad (14.9)$$

where $p_0(w)$ is a prior on Ω.

Algorithm 14.4 Hedge Algorithm

Input: T, prior $p_0(w)$ on Ω, learning rate $\eta > 0$
1 Randomly draw $w_0 \sim p_0(w)$
2 **for** $t = 1, 2, \ldots, T$ **do**
3 $\quad$ Observe loss $\ell_t(w_{t-1})$
4 $\quad$ Randomly draw $w_t \sim p_t(w)$ according to (14.9)

We have the following result for the Hedge algorithm, using conditions similar to those of Theorem 7.17.

Theorem 14.15 *Assume that for all t,*

$$\sup_{w \in \Omega} \ell_t(w) - \inf_{w \in \Omega} \ell_t(w) \leq M,$$

then Algorithm 14.4 has regret

$$\sum_{t=1}^{T} \mathbb{E}_{w_{t-1} \sim p_{t-1}(\cdot)} \ell_t(w_{t-1}) \leq \inf_{p \in \Delta(\Omega)} \left[\mathbb{E}_{w \sim p} \sum_{t=1}^{T} \ell_t(w) + \frac{1}{\eta} \mathrm{KL}(p \| p_0)\right] + \frac{\eta T M^2}{8},$$

where $\Delta(\Omega)$ denotes the set of probability distributions on Ω.

Proof Let

$$Z_t = -\ln \mathbb{E}_{w \sim p_0} \exp\left(-\eta \sum_{s=1}^{t} \ell_s(w)\right)$$

be the log-partition function for observations up to time t. We have

$$Z_{t-1} - Z_t = \ln \mathbb{E}_{w \sim p_{t-1}} \exp\left(-\eta \ell_t(w)\right)$$

$$\leq -\eta \mathbb{E}_{w \sim p_{t-1}} \ell_t(w) + \frac{\eta^2 M^2}{8},$$

where the first equation is simple algebra, and the inequality follows from the estimate of logarithmic moment generation function in Lemma 2.15. By summing over $t = 1$ to T, and noticing that $Z_0 = 0$, we obtain

$$\sum_{t=1}^{T} \mathbb{E}_{w_{t-1} \sim p_{t-1}(\cdot)} \ell_t(w_{t-1}) \leq \frac{1}{\eta} Z_T + \frac{\eta T M^2}{8}.$$

The desired bound follows by applying Proposition 7.16 to reformulate the log-partition function Z_T. $\qquad\square$

If Ω contains a discrete number of functions, and consider p to be a measure concentrated on a single $w \in \Omega$, then $\mathrm{KL}(p\|p_0) = \ln(1/p_0(w))$. We thus obtain from Theorem 14.15

$$\sum_{t=1}^{T} \mathbb{E}_{w_{t-1} \sim p_{t-1}(\cdot)} \ell_t(w_{t-1}) \leq \inf_{w \in \Omega} \left[\sum_{t=1}^{T} \ell_t(w) + \frac{1}{\eta} \ln \frac{1}{p_0(w)} \right] + \frac{\eta T M^2}{8}.$$

If $|\Omega| = N$ with $p_0(w) = 1/N$, then by setting $\eta = \sqrt{8 \ln N/(T M^2)}$, we obtain

$$\sum_{t=1}^{T} \mathbb{E}_{w_{t-1} \sim p_{t-1}(\cdot)} \ell_t(w_{t-1}) \leq \inf_{w \in \Omega} \sum_{t=1}^{T} \ell_t(w) + M \sqrt{\frac{T \ln N}{2}}.$$

This matches the generalization result using empirical process in Chapter 3. Large probability bounds can be obtained by using online to batch conversion with Azuma's inequality. Theorem 14.15 is also comparable to the stability analysis of Gibbs algorithm in Example 7.18.

We note that the proof of Theorem 14.15 relied on the logarithmic moment generating function in the proof of Chernoff bound, which leads to a regret of $O(\sqrt{T})$. In Theorem 14.11, it is shown that for strongly convex problems, one can obtain an online regret bound of $O(\ln T)$. The following result shows that if the variance condition holds, then similar results can be obtained for nonconvex problems as well by using Bennett's inequality. The resulting bound is similar to that of the stability analysis in Theorem 7.19.

Theorem 14.16 *Assume that at each step t, we draw $\ell_t \sim \mathcal{D}_t$, where $\mathcal{D}_t$ is an arbitrary sequence of distributions, and the variance condition holds:*

$$\mathrm{Var}_{\ell_t \sim \mathcal{D}_t}[\ell_t(w)] \leq c_1 \mathbb{E}_{\ell_t \sim \mathcal{D}_t}[\ell_t(w)].$$

Assume that $-\inf_{t,w}[\ell_t(w)] \leq M$, and we choose a small enough $\eta > 0$ so that $\eta c_1 \phi(-\eta M) < 1$, where $\phi(z) = (e^z - 1 - z)/z^2$. Then Algorithm 14.4 has regret

$$\mathbb{E} \sum_{t=1}^{T} \ell_t(w_{t-1}) \leq \frac{1}{1 - \eta c_1 \phi(-\eta M)} \inf_{p \in \Delta(\Omega)} \left[\mathbb{E}_{w \sim p} \sum_{t=1}^{T} \mathbb{E}_{\ell_t \sim \mathcal{D}_t} \ell_t(w) + \frac{1}{\eta} \mathrm{KL}(p\|p_0) \right],$$

where $\Delta(\Omega)$ denotes the set of probability measures on Ω.

Proof Let

$$Z_t = -\mathbb{E} \ln \mathbb{E}_{w \sim p_0} \exp\left(-\eta \sum_{s=1}^{t} \ell_s(w)\right)$$

be the log-partition function for observations up to time t. We have

$$\mathbb{E}\, Z_{t-1} - \mathbb{E}\, Z_t$$
$$= \mathbb{E} \ln \mathbb{E}_{w \sim p_{t-1}} \exp\left(-\eta \ell_t(w)\right)$$
$$\leq \mathbb{E}\left[\mathbb{E}_{w \sim p_{t-1}} \exp\left(-\eta \ell_t(w)\right) - 1\right]$$
$$\leq -\eta \mathbb{E}\, \mathbb{E}_{w \sim p_{t-1}} \ell_t(w) + \eta^2 \mathbb{E}\, \mathbb{E}_{w \sim p_{t-1}} \phi(-\eta M) \mathrm{Var}_{\ell_t \sim \mathcal{D}_t}[\ell_t(w)]$$
$$\leq -\eta \mathbb{E}\, \mathbb{E}_{w \sim p_{t-1}} \ell_t(w) + \eta^2 \mathbb{E}\, \mathbb{E}_{w \sim p_{t-1}} \phi(-\eta M) \mathrm{Var}_{\ell_t \sim \mathcal{D}_t}[\ell_t(w)]$$
$$\leq -\eta(1 - \eta c_1 \phi(-\eta M)) \mathbb{E}\, \mathbb{E}_{w \sim p_{t-1}} \mathbb{E}_{\ell_t \sim \mathcal{D}_t} \ell_t(w).$$

The first inequality used $\ln z \leq z - 1$. The second inequality used the fact that $\phi(z)$ is an increasing function of z, which was used to estimate the moment generating function in Bennett's inequality. The last inequality used the variance condition. By summing over $t = 1$ to T, and notice that $Z_0 = 0$, we obtain

$$\mathbb{E} \sum_{t=1}^{T} \mathbb{E}_{w_{t-1} \sim p_{t-1}(\cdot)} \ell_t(w_{t-1}) \leq \frac{1}{\eta(1 - \eta c_1 \phi(-\eta M))} Z_T.$$

The desired bound follows by applying Proposition 7.16 to reformulate the log-partition function Z_T. □

Since for the Gibbs distribution, if we replace $\ell_t(w)$ by $\ell_t(w) - \ell_t(w_*)$ for any $w_* \in \Omega$, the posterior is unchanged. Therefore if $\ell_t(w) - \ell_t(w_*)$ satisfies the variance condition, and $|\Omega| = N$ is finite, then we obtain from Theorem 14.16

$$\mathbb{E} \sum_{t=1}^{T} \ell_t(w_{t-1}) \leq \sum_{t=1}^{T} \mathbb{E}_{\ell_t \sim \mathcal{D}_t} \ell_t(w_*) + \frac{\ln N}{\eta(1 - \eta c_1 \phi(-\eta M))},$$

which does not grow when T increases. This matches the result of empirical process analysis in Chapter 3 using the variance condition and Bernstein's inequality. The result is also comparable with that of Theorem 7.19.

14.6 Historical and Bibliographical Remarks

The perceptron algorithm for binary classification was studied in Rosenblatt (1957, 1962) and Novikoff (1963), and is the precursor of neural networks. It is also closely related to support vector machines (SVMs), because the perceptron mistake bound depends on the concept of margin, which motivated the design of SVM loss. The idea of online learning was motivated by the analysis of the perceptron algorithm, and a number of different online learning algorithms were developed in the 1990s by the computational learning community. The multiclass perceptron algorithm was used by Collins (2002) for natural language processing and achieved great success for a number of problems using hand-tuned features.

Although the standard analysis of perceptron algorithms assumes that the data is linear separable, the result in Theorem 14.2 allows the data to be nonseparable.

The idea of online to batch conversion has been frequently used to obtain algorithms with performance guarantees in the supervised learning setting using online learning techniques. The high-probability results can be obtained as direct consequences of martingale exponential tail inequalities.

One can extend the mistake analysis of the perceptron algorithms to general convex loss functions, leading to the analysis of online convex optimization. The problem was introduced into machine learning by Zinkevich (2003), and the stochastic optimization setting was studied by Zhang (2004a). The resulting proof technique is also very similar to that of the first-order gradient descent methods in the optimization literature (Nesterov, 2014). If we assume that each online sample is drawn from an iid distribution, then the online learning technique can be used to analyze both the convergence behavior and the generalization performance of the underlying stochastic optimization problem. The analysis of nonsmooth strongly convex function was studied by Shalev-Shwartz et al. (2011), with a convergence rate of $O(\ln T/T)$ using the standard online to batch conversion. The $O(\ln T/T)$ can be improved to $O(1/T)$ using weighted averaging as shown in Rakhlin et al. (2012) and Shamir and Zhang (2013). The results for convex and strongly convex problems match the lower bounds of Agarwal et al. (2009).

The Hedge algorithm is the online counterpart of the Gibbs algorithm, which was named in Freund and Schapire (1997). It is related to the weighted majority algorithm and the Winnow algorithm studied by Littlestone and Warmuth (1994); Littlestone (1988). The analysis is analogous to the stability analysis of the Gibbs algorithm in Section 7.4. In fact, online learning heavily relies on a similar stability argument, which can be seen clearly in the analysis of online convex optimization.

Exercises

14.1 Prove Theorem 14.6.

14.2 Consider Corollary 14.13. Show that even if $d(\Omega) = \infty$, we can still derive an oracle inequality for $\hat{w}$ of the form

$$\mathbb{E}_{\mathcal{S}_T}\mathbb{E}_{\mathcal{D}}\phi(\hat{w}, Z) \leq \inf_{w \in \Omega}\left[\mathbb{E}_{\mathcal{D}}g_w(Z) + \frac{\lambda}{2}\|w\|_2^2\right] + \epsilon_T. \tag{14.10}$$

Derive such a bound.

14.3 For the previous problem, obtain a large probability statement of an oracle inequality which is of the form (14.10).

Hint: First derive a sample-dependent version of the sub-Gaussian inequality with boundedness condition $|g_{\hat{w}_{t-1}}(z) - g_0(z)| \leq G\|\hat{w}_{t-1}\|_2$, where the concentration term depends on the sample dependent quantity

$$O\left(G\sqrt{\sum_{t=1}^{T}\|w_{t-1}\|_2^2}\right).$$

Then obtain the desired oracle inequality.

14.4 Assume that we run SGD for a strongly convex problem more than once over the data
      with a learning rate schedule $\eta_t = 1/(\lambda t)$. Use Theorem 14.11 and Theorem 7.14 to obtain
      an oracle inequality.

14.5 Use Theorem 14.16 to obtain an upper bound for the least squares problem in Section 12.4,
      and compare the result to that of Proposition 12.21 and Corollary 12.20.

15

Online Aggregation and Second-Order Algorithms

In Chapter 14, we introduced the basic definitions of online learning, and analyzed a number of first-order algorithms. In this chapter, we consider more advanced online learning algorithms that inherently exploit second-order information.

15.1 Bayesian Posterior Averaging

Consider conditional probability density estimation with log-loss (negative-log-likelihood), where the loss function is

$$\phi(w, Z) = -\ln p(Y|w, X).$$

Although we consider conditional probability models for online learning, in the regret bound analysis, we do not have to assume that the true conditional model of $p_*(Y|X)$ is given by $p(Y|w, X)$ for any w.

Example 15.1 For discrete $y \in \{1, \ldots, K\}$, we have

$$p(y|w, x) = \frac{\exp(f_y(w, x))}{\sum_{k=1}^{K} \exp(f_k(w, x))},$$

and (let $Z = (x, y)$):

$$\phi(w, Z) = -f_y(w, x) + \ln \sum_{k=1}^{K} \exp(f_k(w, x)).$$

Example 15.2 For least squares regression with noise variance σ^2, we may have

$$p(y|w, x) = \frac{1}{\sqrt{2\pi}\sigma} \exp\left(-\frac{(y - f(w, x))^2}{2\sigma^2}\right),$$

and (let $Z = (x, y)$):

$$\phi(w, Z) = \frac{(y - f(w, x))^2}{2\sigma^2} + \ln(\sqrt{2\pi}\sigma).$$

We may also consider the noise as part of the model parameter, and let

$$p(y|[w,\sigma],x) = \frac{1}{\sqrt{2\pi}\sigma}\exp\left(-\frac{(y-f(w,x))^2}{2\sigma^2}\right),$$

$$\phi([w,\sigma],Z) = \frac{(y-f(w,x))^2}{2\sigma^2} + \ln(\sqrt{2\pi}\sigma).$$

In the Bayesian setting, the optimal statistical estimation of posterior density for log-loss is the Bayesian posterior averaging estimator. Here we consider a prior $p_0(w)$ on Ω. Given the training data $\mathcal{S}_n = \{Z_1, \ldots, Z_n\}$, the posterior distribution is

$$p(w|\mathcal{S}_n) = \frac{\prod_{i=1}^n p(Y_i|w,X_i)p_0(w)}{\int_\Omega \prod_{i=1}^n p(Y_i|w',X_i)p_0(w')\,dw'}. \tag{15.1}$$

Unlike ERM, the Bayesian posterior averaging method does not use $p(y|\hat{w},x)$ for a specific $\hat{w} \in \Omega$ that is estimated from the training data, but instead uses the averaged probability estimate over the posterior as follows:

$$\hat{p}(y|x,\mathcal{S}_n) = \int_\Omega p(y|w,x)p(w|\mathcal{S}_n)\,dw. \tag{15.2}$$

As pointed out in Section 14.1, such a method is referred to as improper online learning.

In the online setting, we have the following result, which may be regarded as a generic regret bound for the Bayesian posterior model averaging method.

Theorem 15.3 *We have*

$$-\sum_{t=1}^T \ln\hat{p}(Y_t,|X_t,\mathcal{S}_{t-1}) = -\ln \mathbb{E}_{w\sim p_0}\prod_{t=1}^T p(Y_t|w,X_t)$$

$$= \inf_{q\in\Delta(\Omega)}\left[-\mathbb{E}_{w\sim q}\sum_{t=1}^T \ln p(Y_t|w,X_t) + \mathbb{E}_{w\sim q}\ln\frac{q(w)}{p_0(w)}\right],$$

where $\Delta(\Omega)$ is the set of probability distributions over Ω.

Proof We have

$$\ln\hat{p}(Y_t,|X_t,\mathcal{S}_{t-1}) = \ln\int_\Omega p(Y_t|w,X_t)p(w|\mathcal{S}_{t-1})\,dw$$

$$= \ln\frac{\int_\Omega \prod_{i=1}^t p(Y_i|w,X_i)p_0(w)dw}{\int_\Omega \prod_{i=1}^{t-1} p(Y_i|w',X_i)p_0(w')dw'}$$

$$= \ln\mathbb{E}_{w\in p_0}\prod_{i=1}^t p(Y_i|w,X_i) - \ln\mathbb{E}_{w\in p_0}\prod_{i=1}^{t-1} p(Y_i|w,X_i).$$

By summing over $t = 1$ to $t = T$, we obtain

$$\sum_{t=1}^{T} \ln \hat{p}(Y_t, |x_t, \mathcal{S}_{t-1}) = \ln \mathbb{E}_{w \in p_0} \prod_{t=1}^{T} p(Y_t|w, X_t)$$

$$= \sup_{q} \left[\mathbb{E}_{w \sim q} \ln \prod_{t=1}^{T} p(Y_t|w, X_t) - \mathbb{E}_{w \sim q} \ln \frac{q(w)}{p_0(w)} \right],$$

where the second equality used Proposition 7.16. This implies the desired result.
$\square$

The following result is a direct consequence of Theorem 15.3.

Corollary 15.4 *If $\Omega = \{w_1, \ldots\}$ is discrete, then*

$$-\sum_{t=1}^{T} \ln \hat{p}(Y_t, |X_t, \mathcal{S}_{t-1}) \leq \inf_{w \in \Omega} \left[-\sum_{t=1}^{T} \ln p(Y_t|w, X_t) - \ln p_0(w) \right].$$

Proof Given any $w' \in \Omega$, if we choose $q(w) = 1$ when $w = w'$, and $q(w) = 0$ when $w \neq w'$, then

$$-\mathbb{E}_{w \sim q} \sum_{t=1}^{T} \ln p(Y_t|w, X_t) + \mathbb{E}_{w \sim q} \ln \frac{q(w)}{p_0(w)} = -\sum_{t=1}^{T} \ln p(Y_t|w', X_t) - \ln p_0(w').$$

This implies the result.
$\square$

If $|\Omega| = N$ is finite, and $p_0(w) = 1/N$ is the uniform distribution on Ω, then we have

$$-\sum_{t=1}^{T} \ln \hat{p}(Y_t, |X_t, \mathcal{S}_{t-1}) \leq \inf_{w \in \Omega} \left[-\sum_{t=1}^{T} \ln p(Y_t|w, X_t) + \ln N \right].$$

This means that we have a constant regret which is independent of T.

If we use online to batch conversion, then by taking expectation, we have

$$-\frac{1}{T} \mathbb{E}_{\mathcal{S}_T} \sum_{t=1}^{T} \mathbb{E}_{Z \sim \mathcal{D}} \ln \hat{p}(Y|X, \mathcal{S}_{t-1}) \leq \inf_{w \in \Omega} \left[-\mathbb{E}_{Z \sim \mathcal{D}} \ln p(Y|w, X) + \frac{\ln N}{T} \right].$$

Therefore the statistical convergence rate of the Bayesian posterior averaging algorithm for density estimation problems is naturally $\ln N/T$. This rate is generally superior to that of ERM, which is suboptimal when the entropy number grows quickly in ϵ (see Section 12.4 and Section 12.5). In comparison, under similar conditions, the Bayesian posterior averaging algorithm can achieve the optimal minimax convergence rate of Theorem 12.24 under a suitable prior. We may also compare the Bayesian posterior average algorithm to the Gibbs algorithm studied in Proposition 12.26. In particular, the Gibbs algorithm, which is a proper learning algorithm that samples a model from a generalized posterior distribution, can bound the Hellinger distance between the estimated conditional density and the true conditional density. On the other hand, the Bayesian posterior averaging method, which is an improper learning algorithm that employs the posterior mean, can bound the KL-divergence between the estimated conditional density and the true conditional density. The result for posterior averaging is stronger because a small KL-divergence implies a small Hellinger distance (see Proposition B.12) but not vice versa.

It is worth mentioning that the Bayesian posterior averaging result of this section is valid even when the true conditional density does not belong to the model class, and thus can directly handle model misspecification with $\ln N/T$ regret. However, the Gibbs algorithm will not achieve a $\ln T/T$ regret under misspecification.

15.2 Ridge Regression as Bayesian Posterior Averaging

The general regret bound for Bayesian posterior averaging can be used to analyze the ridge regression method. Consider the following linear prediction problem with least squares loss:

$$f(w, x) = w^\top \psi(x),$$

with loss function

$$(y - f(w, x))^2.$$

Consider the ridge regression estimator

$$\hat{w}(\mathcal{S}_n) = \arg \min_w \left[\sum_{i=1}^n (Y_i - w^\top \psi(X_i))^2 + \|w\|_{\Lambda_0}^2 \right], \tag{15.3}$$

where Λ_0 is a symmetric positive definite matrix, which is often chosen as λI for some $\lambda > 0$ in applications. We have the following Bayesian interpretation of ridge regression.

Proposition 15.5 *Consider the probability model*

$$p(y|w, x) = N(w^\top \psi(x), \sigma^2),$$

with prior

$$p_0(w) = N(0, \sigma^2 \Lambda_0^{-1}).$$

Then given $\mathcal{S}_n = \{(X_1, Y_1), \ldots, (X_n, Y_n)\}$, *we have*

$$p(w|\mathcal{S}_n) = N(\hat{w}(\mathcal{S}_n), \sigma^2 \hat{\Lambda}(\mathcal{S}_n)^{-1}),$$

where $\hat{w}(\mathcal{S}_n)$ *is given by* (15.3) *and*

$$\hat{\Lambda}(\mathcal{S}_n) = \sum_{i=1}^n \psi(X_i)\psi(X_i)^\top + \Lambda_0.$$

Given x, *the posterior distribution of* y *is*

$$\hat{p}(y|x, \mathcal{S}_n) = N\left(\hat{w}(\mathcal{S}_n)^\top \psi(x), \sigma^2 + \sigma^2 \psi(x)^\top \hat{\Lambda}(\mathcal{S}_n)^{-1} \psi(x) \right).$$

Proof It is clear that

$$p(w|S_n) \propto \exp\left(-\sum_{i=1}^{n}\frac{(w^\top\psi(X_i)-Y_i)^2}{2\sigma^2} - \frac{\|w\|_{\Lambda_0}^2}{2\sigma^2}\right).$$

Note that (15.3) implies that

$$\sum_{i=1}^{n}\frac{(w^\top\psi(X_i)-Y_i)^2}{2\sigma^2} + \frac{\|w\|_{\Lambda_0}^2}{2\sigma^2}$$

$$= \sum_{i=1}^{n}\frac{(\hat{w}^\top\psi(X_i)-Y_i)^2}{2\sigma^2} + \frac{\|\hat{w}\|_{\Lambda_0}^2}{2\sigma^2} + \frac{1}{2\sigma^2}(w-\hat{w})^\top\hat{\Lambda}(S_n)(w-\hat{w}). \qquad (15.4)$$

This implies the first desired result. Moreover, given x, and letting the random variable $u = w^\top\psi(x)$ with $w \sim p(w|S_n)$, we have

$$u|x, S_n \sim N(\hat{w}^\top\psi(x), \sigma^2\psi(x)^\top\hat{\Lambda}(S_n)^{-1}\psi(x)).$$

Since in posterior distribution the observation $y|u \sim u + \epsilon$ with $\epsilon \sim N(0, \sigma^2)$, we know that

$$y|x, S_n \sim N(\hat{w}^\top\psi(x), \sigma^2\psi(x)^\top\hat{\Lambda}^{-1}\psi(x) + \sigma^2).$$

This implies the desired result. $\qquad\square$

We note that the probability calculation in Theorem 15.3 is only for the purpose of calculating the posterior distribution. In particular, the calculation does not assume that the underlying model is correct. That is, the observed Y_t may not satisfy the underlying probability model. The result of Theorem 15.3 implies the following predictive loss bound for ridge regression for all sequences S_T.

Theorem 15.6 *Consider the ridge regression method of (15.3). We have the following result for any $\sigma \geq 0$ and for all observed sequence S_T:*

$$\sum_{t=1}^{T}\left[\frac{(Y_t - \hat{w}(S_{t-1})^\top\psi(X_t))^2}{b_t} + \sigma^2\ln b_t\right]$$

$$= \inf_w\left[\sum_{t=1}^{T}(Y_t - w^\top\psi(X_t))^2 + \|w\|_{\Lambda_0}^2\right] + \sigma^2\ln\left|\Lambda_0^{-1}\Lambda_T\right|,$$

where

$$\Lambda_t = \Lambda_0 + \sum_{s=1}^{t}\psi(X_s)\psi(X_s)^\top$$

and $b_t = 1 + \psi(X_t)^\top\Lambda_{t-1}^{-1}\psi(X_t)$.

Proof   Assume $w \in \mathbb{R}^d$. We note from Gaussian integration that

$$\mathbb{E}_{w \sim p_0} \prod_{i=1}^{T} p(Y_i | w, X_i)$$

$$= \int \frac{|\Lambda_0^{-1}|^{-1/2}}{(2\pi)^{(T+d)/2} \sigma^T \sigma^d} \exp\left(-\frac{1}{2\sigma^2} \sum_{i=1}^{T} (Y_i - w^\top \psi(X_i))^2 - \frac{\|w\|_{\Lambda_0}^2}{2\sigma^2}\right) dw$$

$$= \frac{|\Lambda_0^{-1} \Lambda_T|^{-1/2}}{(2\pi)^{T/2} \sigma^T} \exp\left(-\frac{1}{2\sigma^2} \sum_{i=1}^{T} (Y_i - \hat{w}(\mathcal{S}_T)^\top \psi(X_i))^2 - \frac{\|\hat{w}(\mathcal{S}_T)\|_{\Lambda_0}^2}{2\sigma^2}\right),$$

where the last equation used Gaussian integration with decomposition (15.4).
That is,

$$- \ln \mathbb{E}_{w \sim p_0} \prod_{i=1}^{T} p(Y_i | w, X_i) = T \ln(\sqrt{2\pi} \sigma) + \frac{1}{2} \ln |\Lambda_0^{-1} \Lambda_T|$$

$$+ \frac{1}{2\sigma^2} \sum_{i=1}^{T} (Y_i - \hat{w}(\mathcal{S}_T)^\top \psi(X_i))^2 + \frac{\|\hat{w}(\mathcal{S}_T)\|_{\Lambda_0}^2}{2\sigma^2}.$$

Moreover, from Proposition 15.5, we have

$$\sum_{i=1}^{T} - \ln p(Y_t | \hat{w}(\mathcal{S}_{t-1}), X_t)$$

$$= \sum_{t=1}^{T} \left[\frac{(Y_t - \hat{w}(\mathcal{S}_{t-1})^\top \psi(X_t))^2}{2\sigma^2 b_t} + \frac{1}{2} \ln(b_t) + \ln(\sqrt{2\pi} \sigma)\right].$$

The desired result now follows from Theorem 15.3.   □

Theorem 15.6 does not require Y_t to be generated according to the probability model $N(w^\top \psi(x), \sigma^2)$. Therefore the formula holds for all σ. In particular, by matching σ dependent terms, we have

$$\sum_{t=1}^{T} \sigma^2 \ln b_t = \sigma^2 \ln |\Lambda_0^{-1} \Lambda_T|.$$

By choosing specific σ in Theorem 15.6, we can obtain the following result.

Corollary 15.7   *Assume that $Y_t \in [0, M]$ for $t \geq 1$. Consider the ridge regression method of (15.3), and let*

$$\hat{Y}_t = \max(0, \min(M, \hat{w}(\mathcal{S}_{t-1})^\top \psi(X_t))).$$

We have

$$\sum_{t=1}^{T} (Y_t - \hat{Y}_t)^2 \leq \inf_w \left[\sum_{t=1}^{T} (Y_t - w^\top \psi(X_t))^2 + \|w\|_{\Lambda_0}^2\right] + M^2 \ln |\Lambda_0^{-1} \Lambda_T|,$$

where

$$\Lambda_T = \Lambda_0 + \sum_{s=1}^{T} \psi(X_s)\psi(X_s)^\top.$$

Proof We can apply Theorem 15.6 by taking $\sigma^2 = M^2$. By using the following inequality

$$0 \le \frac{1 - b_t}{b_t} + \ln b_t,$$

we obtain

$$\sum_{t=1}^{T}(Y_t - \hat{Y}_t)^2 \le \sum_{t=1}^{T}\left[(Y_t - \hat{Y}_t)^2 + M^2\frac{1 - b_t}{b_t} + M^2\ln b_t\right]$$

$$\le \sum_{t=1}^{T}\left[(Y_t - \hat{Y}_t)^2 + (Y_t - \hat{Y}_t)^2\frac{1 - b_t}{b_t} + M^2\ln b_t\right] \qquad (15.5)$$

$$\le \sum_{t=1}^{T}\left[\frac{(Y_t - \hat{w}(\mathcal{S}_{t-1})^\top\psi(X_i))^2}{b_t} + M^2\ln b_t\right],$$

where b_t is defined in Theorem 15.6. Note that (15.5) used $1 - b_t \le 0$ and $(Y_t - \hat{Y}_t)^2 \le M^2$. The desired result is now a direct application of Theorem 15.6. $\square$

In order to interpret the regret bound in Corollary 15.7, we need to find an interpretable upper bound of $\Lambda_0^{-1}\Lambda_T$. For $\Lambda_0 = \lambda I$, we have the following result.

Proposition 15.8 *Given any $\mathcal{X}$ and $\psi\colon \mathcal{X} \to \mathcal{H}$, where $\mathcal{H}$ is an inner product space. Then for each $\lambda > 0$ and integer T, the embedding entropy of $\psi(\cdot)$ can be defined as*

$$\mathrm{entro}(\lambda, \psi(\mathcal{X})) = \sup_{\mathcal{D}} \ln\left|I + \frac{1}{\lambda}\mathbb{E}_{X\sim\mathcal{D}}\psi(X)\psi(X)^\top\right|.$$

If $\sup_{X\in\mathcal{X}}\|\psi(X)\|_{\mathcal{H}} \le B$ and $\dim(\mathcal{H}) < \infty$, then

$$\mathrm{entro}(\lambda, \psi(\mathcal{X})) \le \dim(\mathcal{H})\ln\left(1 + \frac{B^2}{\dim(\mathcal{H})\lambda}\right).$$

Moreover, generally, assume that $\mathcal{H}$ has representation $\psi(x) = [\psi_j(x)]_{j=1}^{\infty}$ with 2-norm, and given any $\epsilon > 0$,

$$d(\epsilon) = \min\left\{|S| : \sup_x \sum_{j\notin S}(\psi_j(x))^2 \le \epsilon\right\}.$$

Then

$$\mathrm{entro}(\lambda, \psi(\mathcal{X})) \le \inf_{\epsilon>0}\left[d(\epsilon)\ln\left(1 + \frac{B^2}{\lambda d(\epsilon)}\right) + \frac{\epsilon}{\lambda}\right].$$

Proof Let $A = I + (\lambda)^{-1}\mathbb{E}_{X\sim\mathcal{D}}\psi(X)\psi(X)^\top$ and $d = \dim(\mathcal{H})$, then

$$\mathrm{trace}(A) \le d + (\lambda)^{-1}\mathbb{E}_{X\sim\mathcal{D}}\mathrm{trace}(\psi(X)\psi(X)^\top) \le d + B^2/\lambda.$$

Using the AM-GM inequality, we have

$$|A| \le [\mathrm{trace}(A)/d]^d \le (1 + B^2/(d\lambda))^d.$$

This implies the first desired bound. The proof of the second bound is left as an exercise. $\square$

Example 15.9 Consider Corollary 15.7 with $\Lambda_0 = \lambda I$. We can use Proposition 15.8 to obtain

$$\sum_{t=1}^{T}(Y_t - \hat{Y}_t)^2 \le \inf_w \left[\sum_{t=1}^{T}(Y_t - w^\top\psi(X_t))^2 + \|w\|_{\Lambda_0}^2\right] + M^2 d\ln\left(1 + \frac{TB^2}{d\lambda}\right),$$

where we assume that $\|\psi(x)\|_2 \le B$, and d is the dimension of $\psi(x)$.

We note that we can also obtain regret bounds for infinite-dimensional feature maps using Proposition 15.8. The resulting bound is similar to that of the effective dimension bound in Proposition 9.36. The latter is slightly better by a logarithmic factor. Using Proposition 15.8, we can obtain regret bounds for nonparametric models such as kernel methods.

Example 15.10 Consider the RKHS induced by the RBF kernel

$$k(x, x') = \exp\left[\frac{-\|x - x'\|_2^2}{2}\right],$$

on $\{x \in \mathbb{R}^d: \|x\|_2 \le 1\}$ with

$$k(x, x') = \exp\left(-\frac{\|x\|_2^2}{2}\right)\exp\left(-\frac{\|x'\|_2^2}{2}\right)\sum_{j=0}^{\infty}\frac{1}{j!}(x^\top x')^j.$$

The feature can be expressed as $\psi = [\psi_{j,k}]$, where k corresponds to the Taylor expansion terms of $(x^\top x')^j$. Given $j_0 \ge 2$, the total number of terms in $\{\psi_{j,k}: j \le j_0\}$) is

$$\binom{j_0 + d}{d} \le (j_0 + d)^d.$$

Moreover, when $j_0 \ge 4$,

$$\sum_{j>j_0}\sum_{k}\psi_{j,k}(x)^2 = e^{-\|x\|_2^2}\sum_{j>j_0}\frac{(x^\top x)^j}{j!} \le \frac{1}{(j_0+1)!}\sum_{j>j_0}\frac{(j_0+1)!}{j!} < \frac{1}{e^{j_0+1}}e^1 = e^{-j_0}.$$

This implies that for $\epsilon \le e^{-4}$, we can set $j_0 = \lceil\ln(1/\epsilon)\rceil \ge 4$ to obtain

$$d(\epsilon) \le (\ln(1/\epsilon) + d + 1)^d.$$

Proposition 15.8 implies that if $d \geq 4$, we can take $B = 1$ and $\epsilon = \exp(-d)$:

$$\text{entro}(\lambda, \psi(\mathcal{X})) \leq (2d+1)^d \ln\left(1 + \frac{1}{\lambda}\right) + \frac{e^{-d}}{\lambda}.$$

Similarly, from Proposition 9.36, we also obtain the following bound for the effective dimension:

$$\dim(\lambda, \psi(\mathcal{X})) \leq (2d+1)^d + \frac{e^{-d}}{\lambda}.$$

If we consider the case of online to batch conversion, where $Z_t = (X_t, Y_t)$ comes from an underlying distribution, then we can replace $Y_t \in [0, M]$ by $\mathbb{E}_{\mathcal{D}}[Y|X] \in [0, M]$ and $\text{Var}_{\mathcal{D}}[Y|X] \leq \sigma^2$. This naturally leads to the following result.

Corollary 15.11 *Consider an arbitrary sequence $\{(X_t, Y_t)\}$, where $Y_t|X_t$ is generated from a distribution $\mathcal{D}$. Assume that $f_*(X_t) = \mathbb{E}[Y_t|X_t] \in [0, M]$ and $\text{Var}[Y_t|X_t] \leq \sigma^2$. Consider the ridge regression method of (15.3), and let*

$$\hat{f}(w, x) = \max(0, \min(M, w^\top \psi(X))).$$

We have

$$\mathbb{E}_{\mathcal{S}_T} \sum_{t=1}^{T} (f_*(X_t) - \hat{f}(\hat{w}(\mathcal{S}_{t-1}), X_t))^2$$

$$\leq \mathbb{E}_{\mathcal{S}_T} \inf_w \sum_{t=1}^{T} \left[(f_*(X_t) - w^\top \psi(X_t))^2 + \|w\|_{\Lambda_0}^2\right] + (M^2 + \sigma^2)\mathbb{E}_{\mathcal{S}_T} \ln\left|\Lambda_0^{-1}\Lambda_T\right|,$$

where $\Lambda_T = \Lambda_0 + \sum_{s=1}^{T} \psi(X_s)\psi(X_s)^\top$.

Proof We have the following derivation, which is similar to that of Corollary 15.7:

$$\mathbb{E}_{\mathcal{S}_T} \sum_{t=1}^{T} \left[\sigma^2 + (f_*(X_t) - \hat{f}(\hat{w}_{t-1}(\mathcal{S}_{t-1}), X_t))^2\right]$$

$$\leq \mathbb{E}_{\mathcal{S}_T} \sum_{t=1}^{T} \Big[[\sigma^2 + (f_*(X_t) - \hat{f}(\hat{w}_{t-1}(\mathcal{S}_{t-1}), X_t))^2]$$

$$+ [\sigma^2 + (f_*(X_t) - \hat{f}(\hat{w}_{t-1}(\mathcal{S}_{t-1}), X_t))^2]\frac{1 - b_t}{b_t} + [M^2 + \sigma^2]\ln b_t\Big]$$

$$\leq \mathbb{E}_{\mathcal{S}_T} \sum_{t=1}^{T} \left[\frac{(Y_t - \hat{w}_{t-1}(\mathcal{S}_{t-1})^\top \psi(X_t))^2}{b_t} + [M^2 + \sigma^2]\ln b_t\right].$$

In this derivation, the proof of the first inequality is the same as that of (15.5). The last inequality used (by noticing the truncation definition of $\hat{f}(w, x)$) is

$$(f_*(X_t) - \hat{f}(\hat{w}_{t-1}(\mathcal{S}_{t-1}), X_t))^2 \leq (f_*(X_t) - \hat{w}_{t-1}(\mathcal{S}_{t-1})^\top \psi(X_t))^2.$$

Now using Theorem 15.6, we obtain

$$\mathbb{E}_{\mathcal{S}_T} \sum_{t=1}^{T} \left[\sigma^2 + (f_*(X_t) - \hat{f}(\hat{w}(\mathcal{S}_{t-1}), X_t))^2 \right]$$

$$\leq \inf_w \left[\mathbb{E}_{\mathcal{S}_T} \sum_{t=1}^{T} (Y_t - w^\top \psi(X_t))^2 + \|w\|_{\Lambda_0}^2 \right] + [M^2 + \sigma^2] \mathbb{E}_{\mathcal{S}_T} \ln |\Lambda_0^{-1} \Lambda_T|$$

$$= \inf_w \left[\mathbb{E}_{\mathcal{S}_T} \sum_{t=1}^{T} [\sigma^2 + (f_*(X_t) - w^\top \psi(X_t))^2] + \|w\|_{\Lambda_0}^2 \right] + [M^2 + \sigma^2] \mathbb{E}_{\mathcal{S}_T} \ln |\Lambda_0^{-1} \Lambda_T|.$$

This implies the result. $\qquad\qquad\square$

If we assume that $(X_t, Y_t) \sim \mathcal{D}$ are iid examples, then by taking expectation with respect to $\mathcal{D}$, and by using Jensen's inequality for the concave log-determinant function, we obtain from Corollary 15.11 that with $\Lambda_0 = \lambda I$, we have

$$\mathbb{E}_{\mathcal{S}_T} \frac{1}{T} \sum_{t=1}^{T} \mathbb{E}_{X \sim \mathcal{D}} (f_*(X) - \hat{f}(\hat{w}(\mathcal{S}_{t-1}), X))^2$$

$$\leq \inf_w \mathbb{E}_{X \sim \mathcal{D}} \left[(f_*(X) - w^\top \psi(X))^2 + \lambda \|w\|_2^2 \right]$$

$$+ \frac{M^2 + \sigma^2}{T} \ln \left| I + \frac{T}{\lambda} \mathbb{E}_{X \sim \mathcal{D}} \psi(X) \psi(X)^\top \right|.$$

Note that this bound is superior to the Rademacher complexity bound, and the best convergence rate that can be achieved is $O(\ln T / T)$. The result can be compared to Theorem 9.35, where log-determinant is replaced by trace.

15.3 Exponential Model Aggregation

Exponential model aggregation is a generalization of Bayesian model averaging by using the average prediction over the Gibbs distribution (which may be regarded as a generalization of the Bayesian posterior distribution). Consider a general loss function with $Z = (X, Y)$:

$$\phi(w, Z) = L(f(w, X), Y),$$

where $L(f, y)$ is convex with respect to f. Consider a prior $p_0(w)$ on Ω, and the following form of Gibbs distribution (which we will also refer to as posterior):

$$p(w|\mathcal{S}_n) \propto \exp \left[-\eta \sum_{i=1}^{n} \phi(w, Z_i) \right] p_0(w), \qquad (15.6)$$

where $\eta > 0$ is a learning rate parameter. The exponential model aggregation algorithm computes

$$\hat{f}(x|\mathcal{S}_n) = \int_\Omega f(w, x) p(w|\mathcal{S}_n) \, dw, \qquad (15.7)$$

where $p(w|\mathcal{S}_n)$ is given by (15.6).

Algorithm 15.1 Online Exponential Model Aggregation

Input: $\eta > 0$, $\{f(w, x) \colon w \in \Omega\}$, prior $p_0(w)$
Output: $\hat{f}(\cdot | \mathcal{S}_T)$
1 **for** $t = 1, 2, \ldots, T$ **do**
2   Observe X_t
3   Let $\hat{f}_t = \hat{f}(X_t | \mathcal{S}_{t-1})$ according to (15.7)
4   Observe Y_t
5   Compute $L(\hat{f}_t, Y_t)$
Return: $\hat{f}(\cdot | \mathcal{S}_T)$

In order to analyze Algorithm 15.1, we need to employ the concept of α-exponential concavity introduced in the following.

Definition 15.12 A convex function $g(u)$ is α-exponentially concave for some $\alpha > 0$ if

$$e^{-\alpha g(u)}$$

is concave in u.

The following property is convenient to show exponential concavity.

Proposition 15.13 *A convex function $\phi(u)$ is α-exponentially concave if*

$$\alpha \nabla \phi(u) \nabla \phi(u)^\top \leq \nabla^2 \phi(u).$$

Proof We have

$$\nabla^2 e^{-\alpha \phi(u)} = e^{-\alpha \phi(u)} \left[-\alpha \nabla^2 \phi(u) + \alpha^2 \nabla \phi(u) \nabla \phi(u)^\top \right] \leq 0.$$

This implies the concavity of $\exp(-\alpha \phi(u))$. $\qquad\square$

Proposition 15.14 *If a convex function $\phi(u)$ is α-exponentially concave for some $\alpha > 0$, then it is also β-exponentially concave for $\beta \in (0, \alpha]$.*

Proof Let $h(u) = \exp(-\alpha \phi(u))$. We note that $\exp(-\beta \phi(u)) = g(h(u))$, where $g(z) = z^{\beta/\alpha}$ is an increasing and concave function. Since $h(u)$ is concave, $g(h(u))$ is also concave. $\qquad\square$

Example 15.15 We note that if $\phi(u)$ is both Lipschitz $\|\nabla \phi(u)\|_2 \leq G$, and λ-strongly convex, then

$$(\lambda/G^2) \nabla \phi(u) \nabla \phi(u)^\top \leq \lambda I \leq \nabla^2 \phi(u).$$

Proposition 15.13 implies that $\phi(u)$ is λ/G^2-exponentially concave.

The following proposition says that the property of exponential concavity holds under a linear transformation of the model parameter. Therefore in general, the exponential concavity criterion is easier to satisfy than strong convexity.

Proposition 15.16 *Assume $\phi(u)$ is α-exponentially concave in u. Let $\tilde{\phi}(w) = \phi(w^\top X)$, then $\tilde{\phi}$ is also α-exponentially concave in w.*

Proof Since $e^{-\alpha\phi(u)}$ is concave, we know $e^{-\alpha\tilde{\phi}(w)} = e^{-\alpha\phi(w^\top X)}$ is also concave. □

Example 15.17 Consider the loss function $L(u, y) = (u - y)^2$. If $|u - y| \leq M$, then $L(u, y)$ is α-exponentially concave in u with $\alpha \leq 1/(2M^2)$.

Example 15.18 Consider a function $f(\cdot)$, and let $L(f(\cdot), y) = -\ln f(y)$, then $L(f(\cdot), y)$ is α-exponentially concave in $f(\cdot)$ for $\alpha \leq 1$. This loss function is applicable to conditional probability estimate $\ln f(y|x)$.

For exponentially concave loss functions, we have the following result for the exponential model aggregation algorithm.

Theorem 15.19 *Assume that $L(f, y)$ is η-exponentially concave. Then (15.7) satisfies the following regret bound:*

$$\sum_{t=1}^{T} L(\hat{f}(X_t|\mathcal{S}_{t-1}), Y_t) \leq \inf_q \left[\mathbb{E}_{w \sim q} \sum_{t=1}^{T} L(f(w, X_t), Y_t) + \frac{1}{\eta} \mathbb{E}_{w \sim q} \ln \frac{q(w)}{p_0(w)} \right].$$

Proof Since $e^{-\eta L(f,y)}$ is concave in f, we obtain from Jensen's inequality

$$\ln \int e^{-\eta L(f(w,x),y)} p(w|\mathcal{S}_{t-1}) dw \leq \ln e^{-\eta L(\hat{f}(x|\mathcal{S}_{t-1}),y)}.$$

With $(x, y) = (X_t, Y_t)$, this can be equivalently rewritten as

$$L(\hat{f}(X_t|\mathcal{S}_{t-1}), Y_t) \leq \frac{-1}{\eta} \ln \frac{\int_\Omega \exp(-\eta \sum_{i=1}^{t} L(f(w, X_i), Y_i)) p_0(w) dw}{\int_\Omega \exp(-\eta \sum_{i=1}^{t-1} L(f(w, X_i), Y_i)) p_0(w) dw}.$$

By summing over $t = 1$ to $t = T$, we obtain

$$\sum_{t=1}^{T} L(\hat{f}(X_t|\mathcal{S}_{t-1}), Y_t) \leq \frac{-1}{\eta} \ln \int_\Omega \exp\left(-\eta \sum_{i=1}^{T} L(f(w, X_i), Y_i) \right) p_0(w) dw.$$

Using Proposition 7.16, we obtain the desired result. □

Example 15.20 Theorem 15.3 is a special case of Theorem 15.19, with $\eta = 1$, $L(f(\cdot|w, x), y) = -\ln P(y|w, x)$ and $f(\cdot|w, x) = P(\cdot|w, x)$. In this case,

$$\exp(-L(f(\cdot|\cdot), y)) = f(y|\cdot)$$

is a component of $f(\cdot|\cdot)$ indexed by y, and thus concave in $f(\cdot|\cdot)$.

The following result holds for nonlinear least squares regression, which generalizes the ridge regression result.

Example 15.21 Assume that $L(f, y) = (f - y)^2$, and $\sup |f(w, x) - y| \leq M$. Then for $\eta \leq 1/(2M^2)$, $L(f, y)$ is η-exponentially concave. Therefore we have

$$\sum_{t=1}^{T}(\hat{f}(X_t|\mathcal{S}_{t-1}) - Y_t)^2 \le \inf_{q} \left[\mathbb{E}_{w\sim q} \sum_{t=1}^{T}(f(w, X_t) - Y_t)^2 + \frac{1}{\eta}\mathbb{E}_{w\sim q}\ln\frac{q(w)}{p_0(w)} \right].$$

In particular, if Ω is countable, then

$$\sum_{t=1}^{T}(\hat{f}(X_t|\mathcal{S}_{t-1}) - Y_t)^2 \le \inf_{w\in\Omega} \left[\sum_{t=1}^{T}(f(w, X_t) - Y_t)^2 + \frac{1}{\eta}\ln\frac{1}{p_0(w)} \right].$$

We may also compare this result for model aggregation to that of the Gibbs algorithm in Theorem 14.16 that randomly samples a model from the Gibbs distribution (also see Corollary 10.25). We note that model aggregation is superior for misspecified models, because the regret with respect to the best function in the function class is still $O(1/n)$. In comparison, using ERM or the Gibbs algorithm, one can only achieve a worst-case regret of $O(1/\sqrt{n})$ when competing with the best function in a nonconvex function class (see lower bounds in Example 3.25 and Proposition 8.12).

Example 15.22 In Example 15.21, if we assume further that $f(w, x) = w^\top \psi(x)$ is linear, $\sigma^2 = 1/(2\eta)$ and $p_0(w) \sim N(0, \sigma^2/\lambda)$. Let $q = N(\hat{w}(\mathcal{S}_{t-1}), \hat{\Sigma})$ be the posterior distribution of ridge regression. This implies that the model aggregation estimator is given by the posterior mean $\hat{f}(x|\mathcal{S}_{t-1}) = \hat{w}(\mathcal{S}_{t-1})^\top x$, where $\hat{w}(\mathcal{S}_{t-1})$ is the ridge regression solution. One can thus obtain a bound similar to Corollary 15.7 from Theorem 15.19. We leave it as an exercise.

15.4 Second-Order Online Convex Optimization

We note that ridge regression may be regarded as a second-order method. This section shows that a similar analysis can be extended to more general second-order methods for α-exponentially concave loss functions.

In general, we consider online learning with loss functions $\ell_1(w), \ldots, \ell_T(w)$, where we assume that each $\ell_t(w)$ is α-exponentially concave. Algorithm 15.2, referred to as the *online Newton step* (ONS) in Hazan et al. (2007), may be regarded as a generalization of the online ridge regression algorithm.

Algorithm 15.2 Online Newton Step

Input: $\eta > 0$, w_0, A_0, and a sequence of loss functions $\ell_t(w)$
Output: w_T
1 **for** $t = 1, 2, \ldots, T$ **do**
2   Observe loss $\ell_t(w_{t-1})$
3   Let $g_t = \nabla\ell_t(w_{t-1})$
4   Let $A_t = A_{t-1} + g_t g_t^\top$
5   Let $\tilde{w}_t = w_{t-1} - \eta A_t^{-1} g_t$
6   Let $w_t = \arg\min_{w\in\Omega}(w - \tilde{w}_t)^\top A_t(w - \tilde{w}_t)$
Return: w_T

The following result shows that ONS can achieve a logarithmic regret under exponential concavity. The result is analogous to that of the first-order gradient descent for strongly convex loss functions. However, it employs the condition of α-exponential concavity, which is strictly weaker than strong convexity according to Example 15.15 and Proposition 15.16.

Theorem 15.23 *Assume that for all t, the loss function $\ell_t \colon \Omega \to \mathbb{R}$ is α-exponentially concave and Lipschitz: $\|\nabla \ell_t\|_2 \leq G$. Let $\eta^{-1} = \beta < 0.5 \min (\alpha, 1/(G\Delta_2))$. Then ONS has the regret bound*

$$\sum_{t=1}^{T} \ell_t(w_{t-1}) \leq \inf_{w \in \Omega} \left[\sum_{t=1}^{T} \ell_t(w) + \frac{1}{2\eta}(w - w_0)^\top A_0(w - w_0) \right] + \frac{\eta}{2} \ln \frac{|A_T|}{|A_0|},$$

where $\Delta_2 = \sup\{\|w' - w\|_2 \colon w, w' \in \Omega\}$ is the diameter of Ω.

We will first prove the following lemma.

Lemma 15.24 *For a function $\ell_t \colon \Omega \to \mathbb{R}$ that satisfies the conditions of Theorem 15.23, we have*

$$\ell_t(w') \geq \ell_t(w) + \nabla \ell_t(w)^\top (w' - w) + \frac{\beta}{2}(w' - w)^\top \nabla \ell_t(w) \nabla \ell_t(w)^\top (w' - w)$$

for all $w, w' \in \Omega$.

Proof Since $\exp(-\alpha \ell_t(w))$ is concave and $2\beta \leq \alpha$, we know that the function $h(x) = \exp(-2\beta \ell_t(w))$ is concave, which implies that

$$h(w') \leq h(w) + \nabla h(w)^\top (w' - w).$$

That is,

$$\exp(-2\beta \ell_t(w')) \leq \exp(-2\beta \ell_t(w))[1 - 2\beta \nabla \ell_t(w)^\top (w' - w)].$$

By taking logarithm on each side, we obtain

$$\begin{aligned}
-2\beta \ell_t(w') &\leq -2\beta \ell_t(w) + \ln[1 - 2\beta \nabla \ell_t(w)^\top (w' - w)] \\
&\leq -2\beta \ell_t(w) - 2\beta \nabla \ell_t(w)^\top (w' - w) - \frac{1}{4}(2\beta \nabla \ell_t(w)^\top (w' - w))^2,
\end{aligned}$$

where the second inequality is because $\ln(1 - z) \leq -z - z^2/4$ when $|z| < 1$, and $|2\beta \nabla \ell_t(w)^\top (w' - w)| \leq 2\beta G \Delta_2 < 1$. $\qquad \square$

Proof of Theorem 15.23 Consider $w \in \Omega$, then from Lemma 15.24, we obtain

$$-(w_{t-1} - w)^\top g_t \leq \ell_t(w) - \ell_t(w_{t-1}) - \frac{1}{2\eta}[(w - w_{t-1})^\top g_t]^2. \tag{15.8}$$

Using this inequality, we obtain:

$$
\begin{aligned}
(\tilde{w}_t &- w)^\top A_t (\tilde{w}_t - w) \\
&= (w_{t-1} - \eta A_t^{-1} g_t - w)^\top A_t (w_{t-1} - \eta A_t^{-1} g_t - w) \\
&= (w_{t-1} - w)^\top A_t (w_{t-1} - w) - 2\eta (w_{t-1} - w)^\top g_t + \eta^2 g_t^\top A_t^{-1} g_t \\
&\leq (w_{t-1} - w)^\top A_t (w_{t-1} - w) + 2\eta [\ell_t(w) - \ell_t(w_{t-1})] - [(w - w_{t-1})^\top g_t]^2 \\
&\quad + \eta^2 g_t^\top A_t^{-1} g_t \\
&\overset{(a)}{=} (w_{t-1} - w)^\top A_{t-1} (w_{t-1} - w) + 2\eta [\ell_t(w) - \ell_t(w_{t-1})] \\
&\quad + \eta^2 \mathrm{trace}(A_t^{-1}(A_t - A_{t-1})) \\
&\overset{(b)}{\leq} (w_{t-1} - w)^\top A_{t-1} (w_{t-1} - w) + 2\eta [\ell_t(w) - \ell_t(w_{t-1})] \\
&\quad + \eta^2 [\ln |A_t| - \ln |A_{t-1}|].
\end{aligned}
$$

The first inequality used (15.8). We used $g_t g_t^\top = A_t - A_{t-1}$ twice for the last two terms in (a). In (b), we used the concavity of the log-determinant function $\ln |A| = \mathrm{trace}(\ln(A))$ and Theorem A.18.

Now, by using the fact that $(w_t - w)^\top A_t (w_t - w) \leq (\tilde{w}_t - w)^\top A_t (\tilde{w}_t - w)$, we obtain

$$
\begin{aligned}
(w_t - w)^\top A_t (w_t - w) &\leq (w_{t-1} - w)^\top A_{t-1} (w_{t-1} - w) \\
&\quad + 2\eta [\ell_t(w) - \ell_t(w_{t-1})] + \eta^2 [\ln |A_t| - \ln |A_{t-1}|].
\end{aligned}
$$

We can now sum over $t = 1$ to $t = T$:

$$
\begin{aligned}
(w_T - w)^\top A_T (w_T - w) &\leq (w_0 - w)^\top A_0 (w_0 - w) \\
&\quad + 2\eta \sum_{t=1}^{T} [\ell_t(w) - \ell_t(w_{t-1})] + \eta^2 [\ln |A_T| - \ln |A_0|].
\end{aligned}
$$

This implies the desired bound. $\qquad\square$

Using Proposition 15.8, we obtain a regret bound that is logarithmic in T for ONS. If we let $A_0 = \lambda I$, then

$$
\sum_{t=1}^{T} \ell_t(w_{t-1}) \leq \inf_{w \in \Omega} \left[\sum_{t=1}^{T} \ell_t(w) + \frac{\lambda}{2\eta} \|w - w_0\|_2^2 \right] + \frac{\eta d}{2} \ln \left(1 + \frac{TG^2}{d\lambda} \right).
$$

If $\ell_t(w) = L(f(w, X_t), Y_t)$ with $(X_t, Y_t) \sim \mathcal{D}$, then this implies the following online to batch conversion bound for s randomly chosen from 0 to $T - 1$:

$$
\begin{aligned}
\mathbb{E}_{\mathcal{S}_T} \mathbb{E}_s \mathbb{E}_{\mathcal{D}} L(f(w_s, X), Y) &\leq \inf_{w \in \Omega} \left[\mathbb{E}_{\mathcal{D}} L(f(w, X), Y) + \frac{\lambda}{2\eta T} \|w - w_0\|_2^2 \right] \\
&\quad + \frac{\eta d}{2T} \left(1 + \frac{TG^2}{d\lambda} \right).
\end{aligned}
$$

15.5 Adaptive Gradient Method

In many applications, such as neural networks or learning with sparse features, the gradient $\nabla \ell_t(w)$ may have highly varying scales for different components of the model parameter w. In practice, a popular method called AdaGrad (adaptive subgradient method), which tries to normalize different components, is effective for such problems.

Algorithm 15.3 describes AdaGrad with diagonal matrix inversion. The corresponding full matrix version employs $G_t = A_t^{1-p}$ instead of $G_t = \operatorname{diag}(A_t)^{1-p}$. The standard implementation of AdaGrad in the literature employs $p = 0.5$. The version presented in Algorithm 15.3 is a generalization, which includes both AdaGrad ($p = 0.5$) and the standard SGD ($p = 1$) as special cases.

Algorithm 15.3 Adaptive Subgradient Method (AdaGrad)

Input: $\eta > 0$, w_0, A_0, $p \in [0.5, 1]$, and a sequence of loss functions $\ell_t(w)$
Output: w_T
1 **for** $t = 1, 2, \ldots, T$ **do**
2 $\quad$ Observe loss $\ell_t(w_{t-1})$
3 $\quad$ Let $g_t = \nabla \ell_t(w_{t-1})$
4 $\quad$ Let $A_t = A_{t-1} + g_t g_t^\top$
5 $\quad$ Let $G_t = \operatorname{diag}(A_t)^{1-p}$ $\quad$ (full matrix version : $G_t = A_t^{1-p}$)
6 $\quad$ Let $\tilde{w}_t = w_{t-1} - \eta G_t^{-1} g_t$
7 $\quad$ Let $w_t = \arg\min_{w \in \Omega} (w - \tilde{w}_t)^\top G_t (w - \tilde{w}_t)$
Return: w_T

The commonly used diagonal matrix inversion version of AdaGrad has the same computational complexity as the first-order gradient method, and thus can be regarded as a modification of SGD. However, its analysis is closely related to second-order online methods studied in this chapter. In fact, we can obtain a regret bound for AdaGrad by using the techniques of analyzing ONS (but without assuming exponential concavity). The result shows that, under suitable conditions, it is beneficial to use AdaGrad rather than SGD when gradients have different scales.

Theorem 15.25 *Assume that for all t, the loss function $\ell_t \colon \Omega \to \mathbb{R}$ is convex. Then AdaGrad method (diagonal version) with $p \in [0.5, 1)$ has the following regret bound:*

$$\sum_{t=1}^{T} \ell_t(w_{t-1}) \leq \inf_{w \in \Omega} \sum_{t=1}^{T} \ell_t(w) + \frac{\eta}{2p} \operatorname{trace}(\operatorname{diag}(A_T)^p) + \frac{\Delta_q^2}{2\eta} \operatorname{trace}(\operatorname{diag}(A_T)^p)^{(1-p)/p},$$

where $q = 2p/(2p-1)$ and $\Delta_q = \sup\{\|w' - w\|_q \colon w, w' \in \Omega\}$ is the L_q-diameter of Ω.

Proof Consider $w \in \Omega$. The convexity of ℓ_t implies that

$$-2\eta(w_{t-1} - w)^\top g_t \leq 2\eta[\ell_t(w) - \ell_t(w_{t-1})].$$

Let $G_t = \text{diag}(A_t)^{1-p}$. We obtain the following result:

$$(\tilde{w}_t - w)^\top G_t(\tilde{w}_t - w)$$
$$= (w_{t-1} - \eta G_t^{-1} g_t - w)^\top G_t(w_{t-1} - \eta G_t^{-1} g_t - w)$$
$$= (w_{t-1} - w)^\top G_t(w_{t-1} - w) - 2\eta(w_{t-1} - w)^\top g_t + \eta^2 g_t^\top G_t^{-1} g_t$$
$$\leq (w_{t-1} - w)^\top G_t(w_{t-1} - w) + 2\eta[\ell_t(w) - \ell_t(w_{t-1})] + \eta^2 g_t^\top G_t^{-1} g_t$$
$$\stackrel{(a)}{=} (w_{t-1} - w)^\top G_{t-1}(w_{t-1} - w) + (w_{t-1} - w)^\top (G_t - G_{t-1})(w_{t-1} - w)$$
$$\quad + 2\eta[\ell_t(w) - \ell_t(w_{t-1})] + \eta^2 \text{trace}((G_t^{1/(1-p)})^{p-1}(G_t^{1/(1-p)} - G_{t-1}^{1/(1-p)}))$$
$$\stackrel{(b)}{\leq} (w_{t-1} - w)^\top G_{t-1}(w_{t-1} - w) + (w_{t-1} - w)^\top (G_t - G_{t-1})(w_{t-1} - w)$$
$$\quad + 2\eta[\ell_t(w) - \ell_t(w_{t-1})] + \eta^2 p^{-1}[\text{trace}(G_t^{p/(1-p)}) - \text{trace}(G_{t-1}^{p/(1-p)})].$$

The first inequality used the convexity of ℓ_t. In (a), we used the fact that $g_t^\top G_t^{-1} g_t = \text{trace}((G_t^{1/(1-p)})^{p-1}(G_t^{1/(1-p)} - G_{t-1}^{1/(1-p)}))$. In (b), we used the fact that $h(B) = p^{-1}\text{trace}(B^p)$ is concave in B, and with $B = G_t^{1/(1-p)}$ and $B' = G_{t-1}^{1/(1-p)}$, Theorem A.18 implies that $\text{trace}(B^{p-1}(B - B')) \leq p^{-1}[\text{trace}(B^p) - \text{trace}((B')^p)]$.

Now let $p' = p/(1 - p)$. We can use the fact that $(w_t - w)^\top G_t(w_t - w) \leq (\tilde{w}_t - w)^\top G_t(\tilde{w}_t - w)$, and then sum over $t = 1$ to $t = T$. This implies that

$$\sum_{t=1}^T \ell_t(w_{t-1}) \leq \sum_{t=1}^T \ell_t(w) + \frac{R_T}{2\eta} + \frac{\eta}{2p}\left[\text{trace}(G_T^{p'}) - \text{trace}(G_0^{p'})\right],$$

where

$$R_T = (w_0 - w)^\top G_0(w_0 - w) + \sum_{t=1}^T (w_{t-1} - w)^\top (G_t - G_{t-1})(w_{t-1} - w)$$
$$\leq \Delta_q^2 \text{trace}(G_0^{p'})^{1/p'} + \sum_{t=1}^T \Delta_q^2 \text{trace}(|G_t - G_{t-1}|^{p'})^{1/p'}$$
$$\leq \Delta_q^2 \text{trace}(G_T^{p'})^{1/p'}.$$

In the derivation, we note that $\text{trace}(|G|^{p'})^{1/p'}$ is the vector p'-norm of the diagonal of G. The first inequality used Hölder's inequality and $2/q + 1/p' = 1$. The second inequality used the triangle inequality of p'-norm. This implies the bound. $\square$

Since

$$\text{trace}(\text{diag}(A_T)^p) = O(T^p),$$

if we take optimal $\eta = O(\Delta_q \text{trace}(\text{diag}(A_T)^p)^{-1/q})$ in Theorem 15.25, then the regret bound becomes

$$O(\Delta_q \text{trace}(\text{diag}(A_T)^p)^{1/(2p)}) = O(\Delta_q\sqrt{T}),$$

similar to that of Theorem 14.5 for $p \in [0.5, 1]$. In fact, the SGD bound of Theorem 14.5 is a counterpart of $p = 1$ in Theorem 15.25.

However, for $p < 1$, the bound of Theorem 15.25 uses the L_q-diameter with $q > 2$, and in this case Δ_q of AdaGrad can be significantly smaller than Δ_2 for SGD. This situation becomes important when the gradient has different scales, and dimensions with smaller gradients can benefit from larger model parameters corresponding to such dimensions. If the gradient is sufficiently sparse, then $\text{trace}(\text{diag}(A_T)^p)^{1/(2p)}$ with $p < 1$ can be similar to $\text{trace}(\text{diag}(A_T))^{1/2}$, but $\Delta_q \ll \Delta_2$. The bound of Theorem 15.25 for $p < 1$ will be superior. In the specific case of $p = 0.5$ (i.e. $q = \infty$), we know Δ_2 can be as large as $\Omega(\sqrt{d}\Delta_\infty)$, where d is the dimension of the model parameter.

15.6 Historical and Bibliographical Remarks

In classical statistics, Bayesian posterior averaging is known to be the optimal method for density estimation if the underlying Bayesian model assumption is correct. Its online learning analysis, without assuming the correctness of the underlying model, has been explored in Vovk (1990), who considered more general aggregation strategies. The same idea has also been used by Yang and Barron (1999) to derive optimal statistical estimators in statistical minimax analysis. Vovk later used the same technique to study ridge regression, and obtained Corollary 15.7 in Vovk (2001).

The aggregation method is known to be optimal for many statistical estimation problems, and has been investigated by many researchers both in the online setting, and in the supervised learning setting. For additional details on this topic, we refer the readers to the literature (Tsybakov, 2003; Audibert, 2007, 2009; Dalalyan and Tsybakov, 2007; Lecué, 2007; Rigollet and Tsybakov, 2007; Dai et al., 2012; Lecué and Rigollet, 2014). The idea of exponential concavity was introduced by Kivinen and Warmuth (1999) to analyze aggregation methods for a general class of convex optimization problems with conditions weaker than strong convexity. The idea was later adopted by Hazan et al. (2007) to analyze the second-order online Newton step method.

AdaGrad was proposed in Duchi et al. (2011), and the original motivation was to improve the effectiveness of SGD for training with sparse features. The proof technique is closely related to that of online Newton step. The method itself has been widely adopted in the training of neural networks, with multiple variations. In particular, the idea of AdaGrad became an important component in the popular Adam optimizer for deep learning (Kingma and Ba, 2015). We note that the original version of AdaGrad in Duchi et al. (2011) was only with $p = 0.5$, where a version of AdaGrad with full matrix $G_t = A^{1/2}$ was also considered. We also note that the resulting bound stated in Duchi et al. (2011) relied on the L_2 diameter of Ω. Theorem 15.25 modified the statement so that its advantage over Theorem 14.5 is more explicit.

Exercises

15.1 Consider the conditional density estimation problem, with function class $\mathcal{F} = \{p(y|w, x) : w \in \Omega\}$ and log-loss. Consider the upper bound of Corollary 15.4 for Bayesian posterior averaging. Under which conditions can you derive a matching lower bound using Theorem 12.15? Compare the results to Corollary 12.25 and Proposition 12.26.

15.2 Prove the second inequality of Proposition 15.8.

15.3 In Proposition 15.8, consider $\psi(x) = [\psi_j(x)]_{j=1}^{\infty}$ so that $\psi_j(x)^2 \leq c_0 \mu^j$ for $\mu \in (0,1)$.

- Find an upper bound for $d(\epsilon)$.
- Use the bound for $d(\epsilon)$ to find an upper bound for the log-determinant function

$$\ln \left| I + \frac{1}{\lambda} \mathbb{E}_{X \sim \mathcal{D}} \psi(X)\psi(X)^{\top} \right|.$$

- Derive a generalization bound for ridge regression using Corollary 15.11.
- Compare to Theorem 9.35, with $\lambda_{1,\lambda}$ estimated from Proposition 9.36.

15.4 In Example 15.21, we assume that $f_*(X_t) = \mathbb{E}[Y_t|X_t]$ but f_* may not belong to the function class $\{f(w, x)\}$. Derive a regret bound for the Hedge algorithm using Theorem 14.16 and compare to that of the result for exponential model aggregation.

15.5 In Example 15.22, obtain a regret bound from Theorem 15.19, and compare to that of Corollary 15.7.

15.6 In Algorithm 15.3. Let $G_t = \text{trace}(\text{diag}(A_t))^{1/2}I$. Derive a regret bound by mimicking the proof of Theorem 15.25.

16

Multiarmed Bandits

In supervised learning and online learning, we assume that the outcome y of an observation is fully observed. For example, for online image classification, we first predict the label $\hat{y}$ of an image x, and then the true label y is revealed.

In comparison, for bandit problems, we consider the so-called *partial informa-tion* setting, where only the outcome of the action taken is observed. For the online classification example, we may assume that an image is multiply classified, and we only predict one label, which is correct if the image contains the label and incorrect otherwise. Assume the feedback we receive only says whether the pre-dicted label $\hat{y}$ is correct or not, but not what the true labels are, then it becomes a bandit problem. In this chapter, we will investigate some bandit algorithms that are commonly used.

16.1 Multiarmed Bandit Problem

The multi-armed bandit problem can be regarded as a repeated game, similar to online learning.

Definition 16.1 In the multi-armed bandit (or MAB) problem, we consider K arms. The environment generates a sequence of reward vectors for time steps $t \geq 1$ as $r_t = [r_t(1), \ldots, r_t(K)]$. Each $r_t(a)$ is associated with an *arm* $a \in \{1, \ldots, K\}$. In the literature, an arm a is also referred to as an *action*. At each time step $t = 1, 2, \ldots, T$:

- The player pulls one of the arms $a_t \in \{1, \ldots, K\}$.
- The environment returns the reward $r_t(a_t)$, but does not reveal information on any other arm $a \neq a_t$.

At each time t, a (randomized) bandit algorithm takes the historic observations observed so far, and maps it to a distribution $\hat{\pi}_{t-1}$ over actions $a \in \{1, \ldots, K\}$. We then draw a random action a_t (arm) from $\hat{\pi}_{t-1}$. Here $\hat{\pi}_{t-1}$ is referred to as policy.

In the adversarial bandit problem, we are given an arbitrary reward sequence $\{[r_1(1), \ldots, r_t(K)]: t \geq 1\}$ beforehand. The adversary in this setting, called *ob-livious*, decides the rewards of all the rounds before the game starts (but may take advantage of the bandit algorithm's weakness). For this reward sequence, the expected cumulative reward of a randomized bandit algorithm is

$$\mathbb{E} \sum_{t=1}^{T} r_t(a_t),$$

where the randomization is over the internal randomization of the bandit algorithm. The expected regret is defined as

$$\text{REG}_T = \max_a \sum_{t=1}^{T} r_t(a) - \mathbb{E} \sum_{t=1}^{T} r_t(a_t). \tag{16.1}$$

If the bandit algorithm is deterministic (i.e. pulling a single arm a_t only at any time step), then the regret is

$$\text{REG}_T = \max_a \sum_{t=1}^{T} r_t(a) - \sum_{t=1}^{T} r_t(a_t).$$

In the adversarial bandit problem, our goal is to minimize the expected regret REG_T (and the expectation is with respect to the internal randomization of the algorithm instead of the data).

Another form of bandit problem, called the *stochastic bandit*, assumes that the reward $r_t(a)$ is drawn independently from a distribution $\mathcal{D}_a$, with mean $\mu(a) = \mathbb{E}_{r_t(a) \sim \mathcal{D}_a}[r_t(a)]$. In this setting, the goal of the bandit is to find a that maximizes the expected reward $\mu(a)$. We are interested in the expected regret defined as

$$\text{REG}_T = T \max_a \mu(a) - \mathbb{E} \sum_{t=1}^{T} \mu(a_t). \tag{16.2}$$

Again, this regret is defined for each realization of the stochastic rewards, and the expectation is with respect to the randomness of the algorithm. If algorithm is deterministic and outputs a_t at each time t, then

$$\text{REG}_T = T \max_a \mu(a) - \sum_{t=1}^{T} \mu(a_t).$$

We can further include randomization over data into the regret of stochastic bandit, by considering expected regret as follows:

$$\mathbb{E}\,\text{REG}_T = T \max_a \mu(a) - \mathbb{E} \sum_{t=1}^{T} \mu(a_t),$$

where the expectation is with respect to both the data and the internal randomization of the learning algorithm.

16.2 Upper Confidence Bound for Stochastic MAB

An important algorithm for stochastic bandits is the *Upper Confidence Bound* (UCB), which is a deterministic algorithm presented in Algorithm 16.1. In this method, we define for each $a = 1, \ldots, K$,

$$\hat{n}_t(a) = \sum_{s=1}^{t} \mathbb{1}(a_s = a), \quad \hat{\mu}_t(a) = \frac{1}{\hat{n}_t(a)} \sum_{s=1}^{t} r_s(a_s)\mathbb{1}(a_s = a), \tag{16.3}$$

and a properly defined $c_t(a)$, so that the following upper confidence bound holds for an optimal arm $a_* \in \arg\max_a \mu(a)$ with high probability:

$$\mu(a_*) \leq \hat{\mu}_{t-1}(a_*) + \hat{c}_{t-1}(a_*).$$

Algorithm 16.1 UCB Algorithm

Input: K and $T \geq K$

1 **for** $a = 1, \ldots, K$ **do**
2   Let $\hat{n}_0(a) = 0$
3   Let $\hat{\mu}_0(a) = 0$

4 **for** $t = 1, 2, \ldots, T$ **do**
5   **if** $t \leq K$ **then**
6   Let $a_t = t$

7   **else**
8   Let $a_t \in \arg\max_a[\hat{\mu}_{t-1}(a) + \hat{c}_{t-1}(a)]$ according to (16.3)

9   Pull arm a_t and observe reward $r_t(a_t)$

We first establish a regret bound for UCB that holds in high probability. The corresponding analysis is more intuitive. A generic result can be obtained as follows. We note that while the algorithm only uses UCB, the analysis requires both upper and lower confidence bounds.

Lemma 16.2 *Let $a_* \in \arg\max_a \mu(a)$. Let*

$$\delta_1 = \Pr\left[\exists t > K : \mu(a_*) > \hat{\mu}_{t-1}(a_*) + \hat{c}_{t-1}(a_*)\right]$$

be the probability that the upper confident bound fails on a_*. Let

$$\delta_2 = \Pr\left[\exists t > K \,\&\, a \in \{1, \ldots, K\} \setminus \{a_*\} : \mu(a) < \hat{\mu}_{t-1}(a) - \hat{c}'_{t-1}(a)\right]$$

be the probability that the lower confident bound fails on $a \neq a_*$. Then for Algorithm 16.1, we have with probability at least $1 - \delta_1 - \delta_2$,

$$\mathrm{REG}_T \leq \sum_{a=1}^{K}[\mu(a_*) - \mu(a)] + \sum_{t=K+1}^{T}[\hat{c}_{t-1}(a_t) + \hat{c}'_{t-1}(a_t)]\mathbb{1}(a_t \neq a_*).$$

Proof We have with probability $1 - \delta_1 - \delta_2$, the following hold for all $t > K$:

$$\mu(a_*) \leq \hat{\mu}_{t-1}(a_*) + \hat{c}_{t-1}(a_*), \qquad \text{(upper confidence bound)}$$
$$\hat{\mu}_{t-1}(a_t)\mathbb{1}(a_t \neq a_*) \leq [\mu(a_t) + \hat{c}'_{t-1}(a_t)]\mathbb{1}(a_t \neq a_*). \quad \text{(lower confidence bound)}$$

It follows that for all $t > K$,

$$\mu(a_*)\mathbb{1}(a_t \neq a_*)$$
$$\leq [\hat{\mu}_{t-1}(a_*) + \hat{c}_{t-1}(a_*)]\mathbb{1}(a_t \neq a_*) \qquad \text{(upper confidence bound)}$$
$$\leq [\hat{\mu}_{t-1}(a_t) + \hat{c}_{t-1}(a_t)]\mathbb{1}(a_t \neq a_*) \qquad \text{(UCB algorithm)}$$
$$\leq [\mu(a_t) + \hat{c}'_{t-1}(a_t) + \hat{c}_{t-1}(a_t)]\mathbb{1}(a_t \neq a_*). \qquad \text{(lower confidence bound)}$$

For $t \leq K$, we have

$$\mu(a_*) = \mu(a_t) + [\mu(a_*) - \mu(a_t = t)].$$

We obtain the bound by summing over $t = 1$ to $t = T$.   □

The analysis of the bandit problem in Lemma 16.2 is similar to the empirical process analysis of ERM. This technique can be used in other bandit problems such as linear bandits. We note that although the algorithm uses an upper confidence bound, it only requires the bound to hold for the optimal arm a_*. The regret analysis, however, relies on both upper confidence and lower confidence bounds. The lower confidence bound needs to hold for all arms a, which implies that it holds for a_t. The estimation of lower confidence requires uniform convergence. However, the upper confidence bound does not have to satisfy for all a_t, and thus its estimation does not require uniform convergence. Given upper and lower confidence bounds, the regret bound for MAB becomes an estimation of the summation of the confidence bounds, which requires showing that the confidence bounds shrink to zero as the time step goes to infinity. A careful analysis of the confidence interval size using Martingale exponential inequality leads to the following result for MAB.

Theorem 16.3 *Assume that rewards $r_t(a) \in [0,1]$. Let $a_* \in \arg\max_a \mu(a)$. With a choice of*

$$\hat{c}_t(a) = \sqrt{\frac{\ln(2(\hat{n}_t(a)+1)^2/\delta)}{2\hat{n}_t(a)}},$$

we have with probability at least $1 - \delta$,

$$\mathrm{REG}_T \leq (K-1) + \sqrt{8\ln(2KT^2/\delta)(T-K)K}.$$

Proof Given any integer $m \geq 1$ and $a \in \{1, \ldots, K\}$, we know that the sequence $r(a_t)\mathbb{1}(a_t = a)$ satisfies the sub-Gaussian bound in Theorem 13.3 with $\sigma_i = 0.51(a_i = a)$. This means that $\sum_{i=1}^t \sigma_i^2 = 0.25\hat{n}_t(a)$. By letting $\sigma = 0.5\sqrt{m}$ for a constant m, and considering the event $\hat{n}_t(a) = m$, we obtain with probability at most $0.5\delta/(m+1)^2$,

$$\exists t \geq 1 \colon \mu(a) > \hat{\mu}_t(a) + \hat{c}_t(a) \quad \& \quad \hat{n}_t(a) = m.$$

Similarly, with probability at most $(0.5/K)\delta/(m+1)^2$,

$$\exists t \geq 1 \colon \mu(a) < \hat{\mu}_t(a) - \hat{c}'_t(a) \quad \& \quad \hat{n}_t(a) = m,$$

where the lower confidence interval size is defined as

$$\hat{c}'_t(a) = \sqrt{\frac{\ln(2K(\hat{n}_t(a)+1)^2/\delta)}{2\hat{n}_t(a)}}.$$

It follows that the failure probability of the upper confidence bound is given by

$$\Pr\left[\exists t > K : \mu(a_*) > \hat{\mu}_t(a_*) + \hat{c}_t(a_*)\right]$$

$$\leq \sum_{m=1}^{\infty} \Pr\left[\exists t > K : \hat{n}_t(a_*) = m \ \& \ \mu(a_*) > \hat{\mu}_t(a_*) + \hat{c}_t(a_*)\right]$$

$$\leq \sum_{m=1}^{\infty} 0.5\delta/(m+1)^2 \leq 0.5\delta.$$

Moreover, the failure probability of the lower confidence bound is given by

$$\Pr\left[\exists t > K \ \& \ a \in \{1,\dots,K\} : \mu(a) < \hat{\mu}_t(a) - \hat{c}'_t(a)\right]$$

$$\leq \sum_{a=1}^{K} \Pr\left[\exists t > K : \mu(a) < \hat{\mu}_t(a) - \hat{c}'_t(a)\right]$$

$$\leq \sum_{a=1}^{K} \sum_{m=1}^{\infty} \Pr\left[\exists t > K : \hat{n}_t(a) = m \ \& \ \mu(a) < \hat{\mu}_t(a) - \hat{c}'_t(a)\right]$$

$$\leq \sum_{a=1}^{K} \sum_{m=1}^{\infty} \frac{\delta}{2K(m+1)^2} \leq \delta/2.$$

The following bound follows from Lemma 16.2. With probability at least $1 - \delta$,

$$\sum_{t=1}^{T}[\mu(a_*) - \mu(a_t)] - \sum_{a=1}^{K}[\mu(a_*) - \mu(a)] \leq \sum_{t=K+1}^{T}[\hat{c}_{t-1}(a_t) + \hat{c}'_{t-1}(a_t)]$$

$$\leq 2\sum_{t=K+1}^{T} \sqrt{\frac{\ln(2K(\hat{n}_{t-1}(a_t)+1)^2/\delta)}{2\hat{n}_{t-1}(a_t)}}$$

$$= 2\sum_{a=1}^{K}\sum_{t=K+1}^{T} \sqrt{\frac{\ln(2K(\hat{n}_{t-1}(a_t)+1)^2/\delta)}{2\hat{n}_{t-1}(a_t)}}\mathbb{1}(a_t = a)$$

$$\overset{(a)}{=} 2\sum_{a=1}^{K}\sum_{m=1}^{\hat{n}_T(a)-1} \sqrt{\frac{\ln(2K(m+1)^2/\delta)}{2m}}$$

$$\leq 2\sum_{a=1}^{K}\int_{0}^{\hat{n}_T(a)-1} \sqrt{\frac{\ln(2K\hat{n}_T(a)^2/\delta)}{2t}}dt$$

$$= 4\sum_{a=1}^{K} \sqrt{\frac{\ln(2K\hat{n}_T(a)^2/\delta)(\hat{n}_T(a)-1)}{2}}$$

$$\leq 4\sqrt{\frac{\ln(2KT^2/\delta)(T-K)K}{2}}.$$

Equation (a) used the fact that for each arm a, with $a_t = a$, $\hat{n}_{t-1}(a_t)$ takes values from $m = 1$ to $m = \hat{n}_T(a) - 1$, once for each value. In the derivation of the last inequality, we used Jensen's inequality and the concavity of $\sqrt{z}$, which implies that

$$\sum_{a=1}^{K} \sqrt{\hat{n}_T(a) - 1} \leq \sqrt{K \sum_{a=1}^{K} (\hat{n}_T(a) - 1)} = \sqrt{K(T - K)}.$$

This implies the desired bound. $\qquad\square$

Example 16.4 Assume in Theorem 16.3, $\mu(a_*) \approx 0$. In such case, we can use the following multiplicative Chernoff bound in Theorem 13.5 to obtain an upper confidence bound. We know that with probability at most $1 - \delta$,

$$\mu(a) \leq \frac{e}{e-1}\hat{\mu}_t(a) + \frac{e \ln(1/\delta)}{(e-1)\hat{n}_t(a)} \quad \& \quad \hat{n}_t(a) = m.$$

This implies that we may use an upper confidence bound

$$\hat{c}_t(a) = \frac{1}{e-1}\hat{\mu}_t(a) + \frac{e \ln(2(\hat{n}_t(a) + 1)^2/\delta)}{(e-1)\hat{n}_t(a)}$$

in Algorithm 16.1. In order to obtain a better regret bound than that of Theorem 16.3, we also need to use the multiplicative Chernoff bound for the lower confidence interval, and than repeat the analysis of Theorem 16.3 with such a multiplicative lower confidence interval bound. We leave it as an exercise.

Example 16.5 Assume for each arm a, the reward $r_t(a)$ is a sub-Gaussian random variable, but different arms have different reward distributions:

$$\ln \mathbb{E} \exp(\lambda r_t(a)) \leq \lambda \mathbb{E} r_t(a) + \frac{\lambda^2}{2} M(a)^2,$$

where $M(a)$ is known. Then one can obtain a bound similar to Theorem 16.3, with an arm-dependent UCB estimate involving $M(a)$.

One can also obtain a refined version of Lemma 16.2 that replies on the gap between a_* and any other a.

Lemma 16.6 *Let $a_* \in \arg\max_a \mu(a)$. Let*

$$\delta_1 = \Pr\left[\exists t > K : \mu(a_*) > \hat{\mu}_{t-1}(a_*) + \hat{c}_{t-1}(a_*)\right],$$

$$\delta_2 = \Pr\left[\exists t > K, a \in \{1, \dots, K\} \setminus \{a_*\} : \mu(a) < \hat{\mu}_{t-1}(a) - \hat{c}'_{t-1}(a)\right].$$

Define $\Delta(a) = \mu(a_*) - \mu(a)$, and

$$T(a) = \max\left\{m \colon \Delta(a) \leq \hat{c}_{t-1}(a) + \hat{c}'_{t-1}(a), \hat{n}_{t-1}(a) = m, K < t \leq T\right\} \cup \{0\}.$$

Then for Algorithm 16.1, we have with probability at least $1 - \delta_1 - \delta_2$,

$$\mathrm{REG}_T \leq \inf_{\Delta_0 > 0}\left[\sum_{a=1}^{K} T(a)\Delta(a)\mathbb{1}(\Delta(a) > \Delta_0) + (T - K)\Delta_0\right] + \sum_{a=1}^{K} \Delta(a).$$

Proof The proof of Lemma 16.2 shows that with probability at least $1 - \delta$, for all $t \geq K + 1$,

$$\mu(a_*) \leq \mu(a_t) + [\hat{c}'_{t-1}(a_t) + \hat{c}_{t-1}(a_t)]\mathbb{1}(a_t \neq a_*),$$

which implies that

$$\Delta(a_t) \leq [\hat{c}'_{t-1}(a_t) + \hat{c}_{t-1}(a_t)]\mathbb{1}(a_t \neq a_*).$$

Using the assumption of the lemma, we obtain for all $a \neq a_*$ and $1 \leq t \leq T$, $\hat{n}_{t-1}(a)\mathbb{1}(a_t = a) \leq T(a)$.

It follows that for all $a \neq a_*$, let t be the last time such that $a_t = a$, then $t \leq T$ and $\hat{n}_T(a) = \hat{n}_{t-1}(a_t) + 1 \leq T(a) + 1$. We thus obtain the following regret bound for any $\Delta_0 \geq 0$:

$$\sum_{t=1}^{T}[\mu(a_*) - \mu(a_t)] = \sum_{a=1}^{K} \hat{n}_T(a)\Delta(a)$$

$$\leq \sum_{a=1}^{K}\Delta(a) + \sum_{a=1}^{K}(\hat{n}_T(a) - 1)\Delta_0 + \sum_{a=1}^{K}(\hat{n}_T(a) - 1)\Delta(a)\mathbb{1}(\Delta(a) > \Delta_0)$$

$$\leq \sum_{a=1}^{K}\Delta(a) + (T - K)\Delta_0 + \sum_{a=1}^{K}T(a)\Delta(a)\mathbb{1}(\Delta(a) > \Delta_0).$$

The second inequality used $\sum_{a=1}^{K} \hat{n}_T(a) = T - K$ and $\hat{n}_T(a) - 1 \leq T(a)$. This implies the bound. $\qquad\square$

We note that in Lemma 16.6, δ_1 is still the failure probability for the upper confidence bound, and δ_2 is the failure probability for the lower confidence bound. The intuition of the quantity $T(a)$ is that after we have pulled arm a for more than $T(a)$ times, the confidence interval for a becomes smaller than the gap $\Delta(a)$, which means that we will not choose arm a in the future. That is, $T(a)$ is the maximum number of times that one will pull a particular arm a. This means that the regret caused by choosing a is upper bounded by $T(a)\Delta(a)$.

Using Lemma 16.6, we can now obtain a gap-dependent bound in Theorem 16.7.

Theorem 16.7 *Assume that the reward $r_t(a) \in [0, 1]$. Let $a_* \in \arg\max_a \mu(a)$. With a choice of*

$$\hat{c}_t(a) = \sqrt{\frac{\ln(2(\hat{n}_t(a) + 1)^2/\delta)}{2\hat{n}_t(a)}},$$

we have

$$\text{REG}_T \leq \inf_{\Delta_0 > 0}\left[(T - K)\Delta_0 + \sum_{a=1}^{K}\frac{2\ln(2KT^2/\delta)}{\Delta(a)}\mathbb{1}(\Delta(a) > \Delta_0)\right] + \sum_{a=1}^{K}\Delta(a).$$

Proof From the proof of Theorem 16.3, we know that with the choice of

$$\hat{c}_t'(a) = \sqrt{\frac{\ln(2K(\hat{n}_t(a)+1)^2/\delta)}{2\hat{n}_t(a)}},$$

the inequality $\Delta(a) \le \hat{c}_{t-1}(a) + \hat{c}_{t-1}'(a)$ in the definition of $T(a)$ implies that

$$\Delta(a) \le \sqrt{\frac{2\ln(2KT^2/\delta)}{\hat{n}_{t-1}(a)}}.$$

This implies that

$$\hat{n}_{t-1}(a) \le \frac{2\ln(2KT^2/\delta)}{\Delta(a)^2}.$$

Therefore

$$T(a) \le \frac{2\ln(2KT^2/\delta)}{\Delta(a)^2}.$$

This implies the desired result from Lemma 16.6. □

Example 16.8 We may take $\Delta_0 = 0$ in the gap-dependent regret bound of Theorem 16.7, and obtain

$$\text{REG}_T \le \sum_{a=1}^{K} \frac{2\ln(2KT^2/\delta)}{\Delta(a)} + K.$$

Example 16.9 The gap-dependent regret bound of Theorem 16.7 implies the gap-independent regret bound of Theorem 16.3. In fact, if we take

$$\Delta_0 = \sqrt{\frac{K\ln(KT/\delta)}{T}},$$

then we obtain a regret of

$$\text{REG}_T = O\left(\sqrt{KT\ln(KT/\delta)}\right)$$

from Theorem 16.7.

Results we have obtained so far require the construction of UCB knowing the confidence level δ. This might be inconvenient for some applications. In the following, we show that using a similar analysis, it is possible to obtain a regret analysis with a construction of UCB that does not depend on either T or δ. In the analysis, we will first introduce a lemma to replace Lemma 16.6 without the need to consider events that hold uniformly for all t. Lemma 16.10 is a variant of Lemma 16.6 that considers each specific time step t separately. It leads to a similar result that holds in expectation.

Lemma 16.10 *Let $a_* \in \arg\max_a \mu(a)$. For $t > K$, define*

$$\delta_1(t) = \Pr\left[\mu(a_*) > \hat{\mu}_{t-1}(a_*) + \hat{c}_{t-1}(a_*)\right],$$
$$\delta_2(t) = \Pr\left[\exists a \in \{1,\ldots,K\}\setminus\{a_*\} : \mu(a) < \hat{\mu}_{t-1}(a) - \hat{c}_{t-1}'(a)\right],$$

and let

$$\delta = \sum_{t>K} [\delta_1(t) + \delta_2(t)].$$

Define $\Delta(a) = \mu(a_*) - \mu(a)$, $M = \sup_a \Delta(a)$, *and*

$$T(a) = \max \{m : \Delta(a) \le \hat{c}_{t-1}(a) + \hat{c}'_{t-1}(a), \hat{n}_{t-1}(a) = m, K < t \le T\} \cup \{0\}.$$

Then for Algorithm 16.1, we have

$$\mathbb{E} \, \mathrm{REG}_T \le \inf_{\Delta_0 > 0} \left[\sum_{a=1}^{K} T(a)\Delta(a)\mathbb{1}(\Delta(a) > \Delta_0) + (T-K)\Delta_0 \right] + (K+\delta)M.$$

Proof We obtain for any fixed $t > K$ that with probability $1 - \delta_1(t)$,

$$\mu(a_*) \le \hat{\mu}_{t-1}(a_t) + \hat{c}_{t-1}(a_t).$$

Moreover, with probability $1 - \delta_2(t)$,

$$\hat{\mu}_{t-1}(a_t) \le \mu(a_t) + \hat{c}'_{t-1}(a_t).$$

It follows from the same derivation of Lemma 16.2 that with probability $1 - \delta_1(t) - \delta_2(t)$,

$$\Delta(a_t) = \mu(a_*) - \hat{\mu}_{t-1}(a_t) \le \hat{c}_{t-1}(a_t) + \hat{c}_{t-1}(a_t).$$

This implies that $\hat{n}_{t-1}(a_t) \le T(a_t)$. It follows that for all $t > K$,

$$\Pr(\hat{n}_{t-1}(a_t) > T(a_t)) \le \delta_1(t) + \delta_2(t). \tag{16.4}$$

Now let

$$\delta(a) = \sum_{t=K+1}^{T} \mathbb{E} \, \mathbb{1}(a_t = a, \hat{n}_{t-1}(a) > T(a)),$$

then

$$\sum_{a=1}^{K} \delta(a) = \sum_{a=1}^{K} \sum_{t=K+1}^{T} \Pr(a_t = a, \hat{n}_{t-1}(a) > T(a))$$

$$= \sum_{t=K+1}^{T} \Pr(\hat{n}_{t-1}(a_t) > T(a_t)) \le \delta.$$

The last inequality used (16.4) and the definition of δ.

Now we have for any fixed a,

$$\mathbb{E} \, \hat{n}_T(a) = 1 + \mathbb{E} \sum_{t=K+1}^{T} \mathbb{1}(a_t = a)$$

$$= 1 + \sum_{t=K+1}^{T} \mathbb{E} \, \mathbb{1}(a_t = a, \hat{n}_{t-1}(a) \le T(a)) + \sum_{t=K+1}^{T} \mathbb{E} \, \mathbb{1}(a_t = a, \hat{n}_{t-1}(a) > T(a))$$

$$\le 1 + T(a) + \delta(a). \tag{16.5}$$

The last inequality used the definition of $\delta(a)$.

We can now bound the expected regret as follows:

$$\mathbb{E} \sum_{t=1}^{T} [\mu(a_*) - \mu(a_t)] = \sum_{a=1}^{K} \Delta(a) \mathbb{E} \, \hat{n}_T(a)$$

$$\leq \sum_{a=1}^{K} \Delta(a) \mathbb{E} \, (\hat{n}_T(a) - 1) \mathbb{1}(\Delta(a) > \Delta_0)$$

$$+ \sum_{a=1}^{K} \Delta(a) \mathbb{E} \, (\hat{n}_T(a) - 1) \mathbb{1}(\Delta(a) \leq \Delta_0) + KM$$

$$\leq \sum_{a=1}^{K} [T(a) \Delta(a) \mathbb{1}(\Delta(a) > \Delta_0) + \delta(a) M] + \Delta_0 \mathbb{E} \sum_{a=1}^{K} (\hat{n}_T(a) - 1) + KM$$

$$\leq \sum_{a=1}^{K} \Delta(a) T(a) \mathbb{1}(\Delta(a) > \Delta_0) + (T - K) \Delta_0 + (\delta + K) \cdot M.$$

The first inequality used $\Delta(a) \leq M$. The second inequality used $\Delta(a) \leq M$ and (16.5). The last inequality used $\sum_a \delta(a) \leq \delta$ and $\sum_a [\hat{n}_T(a) - 1] = T - K$. This implies the desired bound. $\qquad \square$

Theorem 16.11 *Assume that the reward $r_t(a) \in [0, 1]$. Let $a_* \in \arg\max_a \mu(a)$. With a choice of*

$$\hat{c}_t(a) = \sqrt{\frac{\alpha \ln t}{2 \hat{n}_t(a)}}$$

for $\alpha > 1$, we have

$$\mathbb{E} \, \mathrm{REG}_T \leq \inf_{\Delta_0 > 0} \left[\sum_{a=1}^{K} \frac{2\alpha \ln(T)}{\Delta(a)} \mathbb{1}(\Delta(a) > \Delta_0) + T \Delta_0 \right] + \frac{\alpha + 1}{\alpha - 1}(K + 1).$$

Proof Using the same analysis of Theorem 16.3, we know that for any fixed $t = K + 1, \ldots, T$, with probability at least $1 - (t - 1)^{-\alpha}$,

$$\mu(a_*) \leq \hat{\mu}_{t-1}(a_*) + \hat{c}_{t-1}(a_*).$$

Moreover, with probability at least $1 - K(t - 1)^{-\alpha}$, for all a,

$$\hat{\mu}_{t-1}(a) \leq \mu(a) + \hat{c}'_{t-1}(a) \qquad c'_{t-1}(a) = \sqrt{\frac{\alpha \ln(t-1)}{2 \hat{n}_{t-1}(a)}}.$$

Therefore we can choose $\delta_1(t) = (t - 1)^{-\alpha}$ and $\delta_2(t) = K(t - 1)^{-\alpha}$. We have

$$\delta = \sum_{t=K+1}^{\infty} [\delta_1(t) + \delta_2(t)] \leq (K + 1) \sum_{t=K}^{\infty} t^{-\alpha}$$

$$\leq (K + 1) K^{-\alpha} + (K + 1) \int_{K}^{\infty} t^{-\alpha} dt \leq \frac{2}{\alpha - 1}(K + 1).$$

The inequality $\Delta(a) \leq \hat{c}_{t-1}(a) + \hat{c}'_{t-1}(a)$ in the definition of $T(a)$ implies that

$$\hat{n}_{t-1}(a) \leq \frac{2\alpha \ln(T)}{\Delta(a)^2}.$$

It follows that

$$T(a) \leq \frac{2\alpha \ln(T)}{\Delta(a)^2}.$$

We can now apply Lemma 16.10 to obtain the desired bound. $\square$

16.3 Lower Bounds for Stochastic MAB

The following result gives a lower bound on any consistent algorithm for MAB.

Theorem 16.12 (Lai and Robbins, 1985) *Assume $r_t(a) \in \{0, 1\}$. Consider an algorithm such that $\forall \beta \in (0, 1)$, $\lim_{T \to \infty}(\mathrm{REG}_T/T^\beta) = 0$, then*

$$\liminf_{T \to \infty} \frac{\mathbb{E}\left[\sum_{t=1}^T \mathbb{1}(a_t = a)\right]}{\ln T} \geq \frac{1}{\mathrm{KL}(\mu(a), \mu_*)}$$

for all a, where $\mu_* = \max_a \mu(a)$.

The result implies that

$$\liminf_{T \to \infty} \frac{\mathbb{E}\,\mathrm{REG}_T}{\ln T} \geq \sum_{a=1}^K \frac{\Delta(a)}{\mathrm{KL}(\mu(a), \mu_*)} \mathbb{1}(\mu(a) < \mu_*).$$

Since $\mathrm{KL}(\mu(a), \mu_*)^{-1} = \Omega(\Delta(a)^{-2})$, it follows that the UCB bound in Theorem 16.11 has the worst-case optimal dependency on the gap $\Delta(a)$ up to a constant. One may also obtain more refined dependency on $\Delta(a)$ using the KL-divergence version of the Hoeffding's inequality in Theorem 2.17. This leads to KL-UCB as in Garivier and Cappé (2011); Maillard et al. (2011), with a gap-dependence that matches the lower bound of Theorem 16.12.

By taking $\Delta_0 = O(\sqrt{K \ln(T)/T})$ in Theorem 16.11, we can obtain a gap-independent expected regret bound similar to Theorem 16.3:

$$\mathbb{E}\,\mathrm{REG}_T = O\left(\sqrt{KT \ln(T)}\right).$$

The lower bound, stated in Theorem 16.13, is $\Omega(\sqrt{KT})$. It only matches the regret bound for UCB in Theorem 16.11 up to a $\log(T)$ factor. It is known that there exists an algorithm that can remove this $\log T$ factor, and achieve the lower bound up to a constant (Audibert and Bubeck, 2009).

Theorem 16.13 *Given $K \geq 2$ and $T \geq 1$, there exists a distribution over the assignment of rewards $r_t(a) \in [0, 1]$ such that the expected regret of any algorithm (where the expectation is taken with respect to both the randomization over rewards and the algorithm's internal randomization) is at least*

$$\min(0.02T, 0.06\sqrt{KT}).$$

Proof We apply Theorem 13.24 with $d = 1$ and $m = K$. We consider a family of K distributions $\mathcal{P}_{\mathcal{Z}} = \{q^\tau, \tau = 1, \ldots, K\}$, and for each arm a, the distribution $q^\tau(a)$ is a Bernoulli distribution $r \in \{0, 1\}$ with mean $\mathbb{E}[r] = 0.5 + \epsilon \mathbb{1}(a = \tau)$ with $\epsilon \in (0, 0.1]$ to be determined later. We also define $q_0(a)$ as a Bernoulli distribution $r \in \{0, 1\}$ with mean $\mathbb{E}[r] = 0.5$. By construction $q^\tau \sim_1 q^{\tau'}$ for all $\tau, \tau' \in [K]$, we can map them all to $q_1^\tau = q_0$.

If we pull an arm θ, we have

$$Q(\theta, q^\tau) = \epsilon \mathbb{1}(\theta \neq \tau).$$

It is clear that $[Q(\theta, q^\tau) + Q(\theta, q^{\tau'})] \geq \epsilon$ for $\tau \neq \tau'$. Consider $n \leq T$ samples generated sequentially by an arbitrary bandit algorithm and $q^\tau(a)$, and let the resulting distribution generate $\mathcal{S}_n$ as $p^\tau(\mathcal{S}_n)$, where $\mathcal{S}_n = \{a_1, r_1, \ldots, a_n, r_n\}$.

Let $\epsilon = \min(0.1, 0.24\sqrt{K/T})$. We have for all a_t,

$$\frac{1}{K} \sum_{\tau=1}^K \mathrm{KL}(q_0(a_t) \| q^\tau(a_t)) = \frac{1}{K} \sum_{\tau=1}^K \mathrm{KL}(q_0(a_t) \| q^\tau(a_t)) \mathbb{1}(a_t = \tau)$$

$$= \frac{1}{K} \mathrm{KL}(0.5 \| 0.5 + \epsilon) \leq \frac{0.5\epsilon^2}{K(0.5 + \epsilon)(0.5 - \epsilon)} \leq \frac{2.1}{K} \epsilon^2.$$

The first inequality is left as Exercise 16.4. The second inequality used $\epsilon \leq 0.1$. Theorem 13.24 (with $d = 1$, $m = K$, and $\beta_{1,t}^2 = \frac{2.1}{K}\epsilon^2$) implies that at the end of the nth iteration, $\hat{\theta}$ of any learning algorithm satisfies

$$\frac{1}{K} \sum_{\tau=1}^K \mathbb{E}_{q^\tau} \mathbb{E}_{\hat{\theta}} \, Q(\hat{\theta}, q^\tau) \geq 0.5\epsilon \left(1 - \sqrt{2 \times 2.1(n/K)\epsilon^2}\right)$$

$$\geq 0.25\epsilon = 0.25 \min\left(0.1, 0.24\sqrt{K/T}\right).$$

The second inequality used $(n/K)\epsilon^2 \leq 0.24^2$. Since this holds for all steps $n \leq T$, we obtain the desired bound. $\qquad\square$

It is worth noting that due to the special structure of MAB, Theorem 13.22 is not suitable because $\hat{q}(\mathcal{S}_{t-1})$ may pick an arm $a_t = \tau$ for any q^τ, and in such case, $\mathrm{KL}(q^\tau \| q^{\tau'}) = \mathrm{KL}(0.5 + \epsilon \| 0.5)$ for all $\tau' \neq \tau$. Therefore a direct application of Theorem 13.22 can only lead to a loose lower bound of $\Omega(\sqrt{T})$. We leave the detailed calculation to an exercise.

16.4 Arm Elimination Algorithm for Stochastic Linear Bandits

In the standard MAB problem, the regret bound scales with the number of arms K. This might not be desirable for problems that contain many arms. In order to deal with such problems, we need to impose additional structures that model correlations among arms. A popular model for such problems is stochastic linear bandits, which allow large action (arm) space. In this section, we assume that the set of arms (or actions) is $\mathcal{A}$, which is finite: $|\mathcal{A}| = K$. Each time, we pull one arm $a \in \mathcal{A}$. We also know a feature vector $\phi(a) \in \mathcal{H}$ (where $\mathcal{H}$ is an inner product space) so that the expected reward is a linear function:

$$\mu(a) = \theta_*^\top \psi(a),$$

with an unknown parameter $\theta_* \in \mathcal{H}$ to be estimated. In this section, we present an arm-elimination method for stochastic linear bandits in Algorithm 16.2 with regret depending linearly on $\dim(\lambda, \psi(\mathcal{A}), T)$ and logarithmically on K. Here $\dim(\lambda, \psi(\mathcal{A}), T)$ is defined in Proposition 9.36). The lower-order term also depends on the quantity $\mathrm{entro}(\lambda, \psi(\mathcal{A}), T)$ in Proposition 15.8.

Algorithm 16.2 Arm Elimination for Stochastic Linear Bandit

Input: $\mathcal{A}, \{\psi(a) : a \in \mathcal{A}\}$

1 Let $\mathcal{A}_0 = \mathcal{A}$
2 **for** $\ell = 1, 2, \ldots, L$ **do**
3 $\quad$ Set parameters $\lambda_\ell, T_\ell, \beta_\ell, n_\ell, \eta_\ell$
4 $\quad$ Use Algorithm 9.1 (with $\lambda = \lambda_\ell, n = n_\ell, \eta = \eta_\ell$) to obtain a policy
$\quad$ $\sum_{i=1}^{m_\ell} \pi_{\ell,i} \mathbb{1}(a = a_{\ell,i})$ with $m_\ell \leq n_\ell$ examples $\{a_{\ell,s} \in \mathcal{A}_{\ell-1}\}$
5 $\quad$ For each $i = 1, \ldots, T_\ell$, pull $a_{\ell,i}$ for $J_\ell = \lceil T_\ell \pi_{\ell,i} \rceil$ times, and observe
$\quad$ rewards $r_{\ell,i,j} \in [0,1]$ ($j = 1, \ldots, J_\ell$)
6 $\quad$ Let $\theta_\ell = \arg\min_\theta \sum_{i=1}^{m_\ell} \sum_{j=1}^{J_\ell} \left[(\theta^\top \psi(a_{\ell,i}) - r_{\ell,i,j})^2 + \lambda_\ell \|\theta\|_2^2 \right]$
7 $\quad$ Let $a_\ell = \arg\max_{a \in \mathcal{A}_{\ell-1}} \theta_\ell^\top \psi(a)$
8 $\quad$ Let $\mathcal{A}_\ell = \{a \in \mathcal{A}_{\ell-1} : \theta_\ell^\top \psi(a) \geq \theta_\ell^\top \psi(a_\ell) - \beta_\ell\}$

Theorem 16.14 *Assume that we know* $\|\theta_*\|_2 \leq B$. *Let* $a_* \in \arg\max_{a \in \mathcal{A}} \mu(a)$. *Given* $\eta > 0$, *for each* $\ell \geq 1$, *we set*

$$\lambda_\ell = \alpha^2/(B^2 T_\ell), \qquad T_\ell = 2^{\ell-1},$$
$$n_\ell = \lceil 8\,\mathrm{entro}(\lambda_\ell, \psi(\mathcal{A})) \rceil, \quad \eta_\ell = \min(0.1, 0.1/\dim(\lambda_\ell, \psi(\mathcal{A}))),$$
$$\beta_\ell = 2 \left(\alpha + \sqrt{\frac{\ln(2K(\ell+1)^2/\delta)}{2}} \right) \sqrt{\frac{4\dim(\lambda_\ell, \psi(\mathcal{A}))}{T_\ell}}$$

in Algorithm 16.2. We also define $\beta_0 = 0.5$. *It follows that* $\forall \ell \geq 0$, $a_* \in \mathcal{A}_\ell$ *and*

$$\sup\{\mu(a_*) - \mu(a) : a \in \mathcal{A}_\ell\} \leq 2\beta_\ell.$$

This implies that after iteration L, *and we have pulled total number of* $T \leq (2^L - 1) + \sum_{\ell=1}^L n_\ell$ *arms, with probability at least* $1 - \delta$:

$$\mathrm{REG}_T \leq 2 \sum_{\ell=1}^L (n_\ell + T_\ell)\beta_{\ell-1}.$$

Proof The claim holds for $\ell = 0$. Assume the claim holds for $\ell - 1$, and consider stage ℓ. Let $\Sigma_\ell = \sum_{i=1}^{m_\ell} J_\ell[\psi(a_{\ell,i})\psi(a_{\ell,i})^\top + \lambda_\ell I]$ and $\tilde{\Sigma}_\ell = \sum_{i=1}^{m_\ell} \pi_{\ell,i}[\psi(a_{\ell,i})\psi(a_{\ell,i})^\top + \lambda_\ell I]$. From Example 9.41, we have for all $a \in \mathcal{A}_{\ell-1}$,

$$\|\psi(a)\|_{\Sigma_\ell^{-1}}^2 \leq \frac{\|\psi(a)\|_{\tilde{\Sigma}_\ell^{-1}}^2}{T_\ell} \leq \frac{4\dim(\lambda_\ell, \psi(\mathcal{A}))}{T_\ell}.$$

It follows from Lemma 9.34 (with $\sigma = 0.5$ since $r_{\ell,s} \in [0,1]$) and a union bound over $a \in \mathcal{A}_{\ell-1}$ that with probability at least $1 - \delta/(\ell+1)^2$, for all $a \in \mathcal{A}_{\ell-1}$,

$$\theta_\ell^\top \psi(a) - 0.5\beta_\ell \leq \theta_*^\top \psi(a) \leq \theta_\ell^\top \psi(a) + 0.5\beta_\ell. \tag{16.6}$$

Therefore,

$$\theta_\ell^\top \psi(a_*) \geq \theta_*^\top \psi(a_*) - 0.5\beta_\ell \geq \theta_*^\top \psi(a_\ell) - 0.5\beta_\ell \geq \theta_\ell^\top \psi(a_\ell) - \beta_\ell.$$

The first and the third inequalities used (16.6). The second inequality used the definition of a_* as the optimal arm. Because $a_* \in \mathcal{A}_{\ell-1}$ by the induction hypothesis, we know that $a_* \in \mathcal{A}_\ell$.

Moreover, if $a \in \mathcal{A}_\ell$, then

$$\theta_*^\top \psi(a) \geq \theta_\ell^\top \psi(a) - 0.5\beta_\ell \geq \theta_\ell^\top \psi(a_\ell) - 1.5\beta_\ell \geq \theta_\ell^\top \psi(a_*) - 1.5\beta_\ell$$
$$\geq \theta_*^\top \psi(a_*) - 2\beta_\ell.$$

The second inequality used the definition of $\mathcal{A}_\ell$. The third inequality used the definition of a_ℓ. The first and the last inequalities used (16.6). By taking the union bound over ℓ, we complete the proof. □

Example 16.15 For finite-dimensional linear bandits, we can take $\dim(\mathcal{H}) = d$ and $\alpha = 1$ in Theorem 16.14. Proposition 15.8 implies that

$$\dim(\lambda_\ell, \psi(\mathcal{A})) \leq d, \quad \text{entro}(\lambda_\ell, \psi(\mathcal{A})) \leq d\ln(1 + (BB')^2/(\lambda_\ell d)) = O(d\ell),$$

where we assume that $B' = \sup_a \|\psi(a)\|_2$. We thus have $n_\ell = O(d\ln T)$. One can obtain a regret of

$$O\left(\sqrt{Td\ln(KT)}\right).$$

If we ignore the log-factors, this generalizes the result of MAB. In fact, we note that MAB can be regarded as a linear bandit with $\psi(a) = e_a \in \mathbb{R}^K$, where e_a is the vector with value 1 at component a, and value 0 elsewhere. Therefore with $d = K$, we recover MAB results up to logarithmic factors.

Example 16.16 We may also consider nonparametric problems with infinite-dimensional embedding. We assume that

$$\dim(\lambda_\ell, \psi(\mathcal{A})) = \lambda_\ell^{-q}$$

for some $q \in (0,1)$. In Theorem 16.14, with $\alpha = \sqrt{\ln(8KT/\delta)}$, we can upper bound $T_0(\alpha)$ by a constant, and obtain a regret of

$$O\left(\sqrt{(\ln(KT))^{1-q}T^{q+1}}\right).$$

16.5 Thompson Sampling for Stochastic MAB

As a popular algorithm for bandit problems, Thompson sampling has a rather long history (Thompson, 1933). The basic idea is to consider a prior distribution on the mean of the reward distribution of every arm. At any time step, sample a mean from the posterior for each arm, and then pick the arm with the highest sampled mean.

In practice, it will be convenient to use a model so that the posterior is simple. This can be achieved with conjugate priors. For example, we can assume a Gaussian prior and reward likelihood:

$$\mu(a) \sim N(0,1), \quad r_t(a) \sim N(\mu(a), 1).$$

Then the posterior for arm a after time step $t-1$ is given by the normal distribution $N(\hat{\mu}_{t-1}(a), \hat{V}_{t-1}(a))$, where

$$\hat{\mu}_{t-1}(a) = \frac{\sum_{s=1}^{t-1} \mathbb{1}(a_s = a)r_s(a_s)}{1 + \sum_{s=1}^{t-1} \mathbb{1}(a_s = a)}, \quad \hat{V}_{t-1}(a) = \frac{1}{1 + \sum_{s=1}^{t-1} \mathbb{1}(a_s = a)}. \tag{16.7}$$

This leads to Algorithm 16.3.

Algorithm 16.3 Thompson Sampling (Gaussian)

Input: K and T
1 **for** $t = 1, 2, \ldots, T$ **do**
2   **for** $a = 1, \ldots, K$ **do**
3   Sample $\tilde{\mu}_t(a) \sim N(\hat{\mu}_{t-1}(a), \hat{V}_{t-1}(a))$ according to (16.7)
4   Let $a_t = \arg\max_a \tilde{\mu}_t(a)$
5   Pull arm a_t and observe reward $r_t(a_t)$

Alternatively, for binary rewards $r_t(a) \in \{0, 1\}$, we can use Beta prior with Bernoulli likelihood:

$$\mu(a) \sim \text{Beta}(1,1), \quad r_t(a) \sim \text{Bernoulli}(\mu(a)).$$

The posterior for arm a after time step $t-1$ is given by the Beta distribution

$$\text{Beta}(1 + \hat{n}_{t-1}^1(a), 1 + \hat{n}_{t-1}^0(a)),$$

where for $y \in \{0, 1\}$,

$$\hat{n}_{t-1}^y(a) = \sum_{s=1}^{t-1} \mathbb{1}(a_s = a)\mathbb{1}(r_s(a_s) = y). \tag{16.8}$$

This leads to Algorithm 16.4.

It is known (Agrawal and Goyal, 2013a) that for Thompson sampling, we can obtain a regret bound of $O(\sqrt{TK \ln K})$ for Gaussian Thompson sampling, and a bound of $O(\sqrt{TK \ln T})$ for Beta Thompson sampling. Moreover, near-optimal

---

Algorithm 16.4 Thompson Sampling (Beta)

Input: K and T

1 **for** $t = 1, 2, \ldots, T$ **do**
2 $\quad$ **for** $a = 1, \ldots, K$ **do**
3 $\quad\quad$ Sample $\tilde{\mu}_t(a) \sim \text{Beta}(1 + \hat{n}^1_{t-1}(a), 1 + \hat{n}^0_{t-1}(a))$ according to (16.8)
4 $\quad$ Let $a_t = \arg\max_a \tilde{\mu}_t(a)$
5 $\quad$ Pull arm a_t and observe reward $r_t(a_t) \in \{0, 1\}$

---

gap-dependent bounds can also be obtained. In general, one may analyze Thompson sampling using techniques similar to the analysis of UCB, by upper bounding the number of times each suboptimal arm can be pulled based on confidence interval calculations. The analysis requires an anti-concentration argument, as illustrated in Exercise 16.7.

16.6 EXP3 for Adversarial MAB

The UCB algorithm can only be applied to stochastic bandit problems. For adversarial bandits, one can use an exponential weighting method motivated from the Hedge algorithm for online learning. The algorithm, referred to as EXP3 (Auer et al., 2002b), is given in Algorithm 16.5.

Algorithm 16.5 EXP3

Input: K, T, $\gamma \in (0, 1]$

1 **for** $a = 1, \ldots, K$ **do**
2 $\quad$ Let $w_0(a) = 1$
3 **for** $t = 1, 2, \ldots, T$ **do**
4 $\quad$ Let $w_{t-1} = \sum_{a=1}^K w_{t-1}(a)$
5 $\quad$ **for** $a = 1, \ldots, K$ **do**
6 $\quad\quad$ Let $\hat{\pi}_t(a) = (1 - \gamma)w_{t-1}(a)/w_{t-1} + \gamma/K$
7 $\quad$ Sample a_t according to $\hat{\pi}_t(\cdot)$
8 $\quad$ Pull arm a_t and observe reward $r_t(a_t) \in [0, 1]$
9 $\quad$ **for** $a = 1, \ldots, K$ **do**
10 $\quad\quad$ Let $\hat{r}_t(a, a_t) = r_t(a_t)\mathbb{1}(a = a_t)/\hat{\pi}_t(a_t)$
11 $\quad\quad$ Let $w_t(a) = w_{t-1}(a)\exp(\gamma \hat{r}_t(a, a_t)/K)$

Conditioned on the observations made before time step t, the reward estimator $\hat{r}_t(a, a_t)$ is a random estimator with respect to the random selection of the next arm $a_t \sim \hat{\pi}_t(\cdot)$. It converts a partial information problem (where we only observe the reward $r_t(a_t)$ at a_t) into a full information problem, where the reward $\hat{r}_t(a, a_t)$ as a function of a is defined for all arms $a \in \{1, \ldots, K\}$. With the choice of

$\hat{r}_t(a, a_t)$, $\hat{r}_t(a, a_t)$ is an unbiased estimator of the full information reward vector $[r_t(a) : a \in \{1, \ldots, K\}]$:

$$r_t(a) = \mathbb{E}_{a_t \sim \hat{\pi}_t(\cdot)} \hat{r}_t(a, a_t).$$

The following regret bound holds for the EXP3 algorithm.

Theorem 16.17 *Consider Algorithm 16.5. Let $G_* = \max_a \sum_{i=1}^{T} r_t(a)$. We have the following bound for the adversarial regret (16.1):*

$$\mathrm{REG}_T \leq (e-1)\gamma G_* + \frac{K \ln K}{\gamma}.$$

Proof We have

$$\sum_{a=1}^{K} \hat{\pi}_t(a) \hat{r}_t(a, a_t) = r_t(a_t), \tag{16.9}$$

$$\sum_{a=1}^{K} \hat{\pi}_t(a) \hat{r}_t(a, a_t)^2 = \hat{r}_t(a_t, a_t) r_t(a_t) \leq \hat{r}_t(a_t, a_t). \tag{16.10}$$

It follows that for all $t \geq 1$,

$$\frac{w_t}{w_{t-1}} = \sum_{a=1}^{K} \frac{w_t(a)}{w_{t-1}} = \sum_{a=1}^{K} \frac{w_{t-1}(a)}{w_{t-1}} \exp(\gamma \hat{r}_t(a, a_t)/K)$$

$$= \sum_{a=1}^{K} \frac{\hat{\pi}_t(a) - \gamma/K}{1 - \gamma} \exp(\gamma \hat{r}_t(a, a_t)/K) \qquad \text{(definition of } \hat{\pi}_t(a))$$

$$\stackrel{(a)}{\leq} \sum_{a=1}^{K} \frac{\hat{\pi}_t(a) - \gamma/K}{1 - \gamma} \left[1 + \gamma \hat{r}_t(a, a_t)/K + (e-2)(\gamma \hat{r}_t(a, a_t)/K)^2\right]$$

$$\leq 1 + \frac{1}{1 - \gamma} \left[\sum_{a=1}^{K} \hat{\pi}_t(a) \gamma \hat{r}_t(a, a_t)/K + \sum_{a=1}^{K} \hat{\pi}_t(a)(e-2)(\gamma \hat{r}_t(a, a_t)/K)^2\right]$$

$$\stackrel{(b)}{\leq} 1 + \frac{\gamma/K}{1 - \gamma} r_t(a_t) + \frac{(e-2)(\gamma/K)^2}{1 - \gamma} \hat{r}_t(a_t, a_t).$$

In (a), we used $\exp(z) \leq 1 + z + (e-2)z^2$ when $z \leq 1$, and $\gamma \hat{r}_t(a, a_t)/K \leq 1$. In (b), we used (16.9) and (16.10).

Therefore,

$$\ln \frac{w_t}{w_{t-1}} \leq \ln\left(1 + \frac{\gamma/K}{1 - \gamma} r_t(a_t) + \frac{(e-2)(\gamma/K)^2}{1 - \gamma} \hat{r}_t(a_t, a_t)\right)$$

$$\leq \frac{\gamma/K}{1 - \gamma} r_t(a_t) + \frac{(e-2)(\gamma/K)^2}{1 - \gamma} \hat{r}_t(a_t, a_t).$$

The second inequality follows from $\ln(1 + z) \leq z$.

Now, by summing over t, and letting

$$G_T = \sum_{t=1}^{T} r_t(a_t),$$

we obtain

$$'\ln\frac{w_T}{w_0} \le \frac{\gamma/K}{1-\gamma}G_T + \frac{(e-2)(\gamma/K)^2}{1-\gamma}\sum_{t=1}^{T}\sum_{a=1}^{K}\hat{r}_t(a,a_t),$$

where we used $\hat{r}_t(a_t,a_t) = \sum_{a=1}^{K}\hat{r}_t(a,a_t)$. Note that for all a',

$$\ln\frac{w_T}{w_0} \ge \ln\frac{w_T(a')}{w_0} = \frac{\gamma}{K}\sum_{t=1}^{T}\hat{r}_t(a',a_t) - \ln K.$$

It follows that

$$\frac{\gamma}{K}\sum_{t=1}^{T}\hat{r}_t(a',a_t) \le \frac{\gamma/K}{1-\gamma}G_T + \frac{(e-2)(\gamma/K)^2}{1-\gamma}\sum_{t=1}^{T}\sum_{a=1}^{K}\hat{r}_t(a,a_t) + \ln K.$$

Observe that, conditioned on the history,

$$\mathbb{E}_{a_t\sim\hat{\pi}_t}\hat{r}_t(a,a_t) = r_t(a).$$

We obtain the following bound by taking expectation:

$$\mathbb{E}\frac{\gamma}{K}\sum_{t=1}^{T}r_t(a') \le \frac{\gamma/K}{1-\gamma}\mathbb{E}G_T + \frac{(e-2)(\gamma/K)^2}{1-\gamma}\mathbb{E}\sum_{t=1}^{T}\sum_{a=1}^{K}r_t(a) + \ln K$$

$$\le \frac{\gamma/K}{1-\gamma}\mathbb{E}G_T + \frac{(e-2)(\gamma/K)^2}{1-\gamma}KG_* + \ln K.$$

Let a' be the optimal arm, and rearrange, so we obtain

$$G_* \le \frac{1}{1-\gamma}\mathbb{E}G_T + \frac{(e-2)\gamma}{(1-\gamma)}G_* + \frac{K}{\gamma}\ln K.$$

This implies the desired result. □

If we take

$$\gamma = \sqrt{\frac{K\ln K}{(e-1)g}}$$

for some $g \ge \max(G_*, K\ln K)$ in Theorem 16.17, then we obtain a bound

$$\mathrm{REG}_T \le 2\sqrt{e-1}\sqrt{gK\ln K}.$$

In particular, with $g = T$, we have

$$\mathrm{REG}_T \le 2\sqrt{e-1}\sqrt{TK\ln K}.$$

16.7 Historical and Bibliographical Remarks

The multiarmed bandit problem has a long history (Robbins, 1952), with many practical applications. An important theoretical development on this topic was given in Lai and Robbins (1985), where the authors studied asymptotic properties of the MAB problem. It was shown by Agrawal (1995) and Auer et al. (2002a) that a simple algorithm using upper confidence bounds provides a satisfactory solution to this problem.

The asymptotic lower bound for MAB was obtained by Lai and Robbins (1985). The matching upper bound can be found in Garivier and Cappé (2011) and Maillard et al. (2011). Finite sample lower bound can be found in Auer et al. (2002b), and the result is similar to that of Theorem 16.13. The matching upper bound was obtained by Audibert and Bubeck (2009).

The linear bandit problem was first studied by Auer (2002), which was later adopted in many other follow-up works. The model can be regarded as a direct generalization of MAB, but it can also directly handle large action space (number of arms). A different generalization of MAB to large action space is to consider continuous actions, such as actions in a metric space (Kleinberg et al., 2008). However, without additional structures comparable to linear bandits, the optimal regret can become near linear in T.

While Thompson sampling has a long history, its theoretical analysis has only been established very recently (see Agrawal and Goyal, 2012, 2013a; Kaufmann et al., 2012). We will analyze a variant of Thompson sampling in Chapter 17.

The techniques to analyze MAB can be extended to handle contextual bandit problems, which we will investigate in Chapter 17. We also refer the readers to Lattimore and Szepesvári (2020) for further studies on bandit problems.

Exercises

16.1 Finish Example 16.4 by analyzing the corresponding UCB algorithm and obtain its regret bound in the style of Theorem 16.3.

16.2 Finish Example 16.5 by deriving the corresponding UCB algorithm and its regret bound in the style of Theorem 16.3.

16.3 Consider MAB with K arms and rewards in $[0, 1]$. We want to obtain a gap-dependent regret bound using the KL Chernoff bound in Theorem 2.17. For each a and t, estimate $T(a)$ in Lemma 16.10 with $\delta_1(t) = \delta_2(t) = O((t-1)^{-\alpha})$, and obtain a regret bound with $\Delta_0 = 0$. Let $T \to \infty$, and compare the result to the lower bound in Theorem 16.12.

16.4 Let $\mathrm{KL}(q_1 \| q_2) = q_1 \ln(q_1/q_2) + (1 - q_1) \ln((1 - q_1)/(1 - q_2))$ for $q_1, q_2 \in (0, 1)$. Show that $\mathrm{KL}(q_1 \| q_2) \leq 0.5(q_1 - q_2)^2 / \min(q_1(1 - q_1), q_2(1 - q_2))$.

16.5 Construct a lower bound for the MAB problem using Theorem 13.22, and compare it to the result of Theorem 16.13.

16.6 In Algorithm 16.2, if an arm $a \neq a_*$ has a gap $\Delta(a) = \mu(a_*) - \mu(a) > 0$. In what stage ℓ will the arm get eliminated? Use this to derive a gap-dependent bound for the algorithm.

16.7 In Algorithm 16.3, assume that the reward is Gaussian for all a: $r_t(a) \sim N(\mu(a), \sigma^2)$. Let a_* be the best arm. At each time t, for each arm a and $\epsilon > 0$,

- estimate an upper bound of the probability of $|\mu(a) - \tilde{\mu}_t(a)| \leq \epsilon$
- estimate a lower bound of the probability of $\tilde{\mu}_t(a_*) \geq \mu(a_*) + \epsilon$ (which is referred to as anti-concentration)
- use these results to show that the confidence interval of $\tilde{\mu}_t(a_*) - \mu(a_*)$ shrinks
- use an UCB-style analysis to derive a regret bound for Algorithm 16.3.

17

Contextual Bandits

In the standard multiarmed bandit problem, one observes a fixed number of arms. To achieve optimal regret bounds, one estimates confidence intervals of the arms by counting. In the contextual bandit problem, one observes side information for each arm, which can be used as features for more accurate confidence interval estimation.

Definition 17.1 (Contextual Bandit Problem) In contextual bandits, we consider a context space $\mathcal{X}$ and an action space $\mathcal{A}$. Given context $x \in \mathcal{X}$, we take an action $a \in \mathcal{A}$, and observe a reward $r \in \mathbb{R}$ that can depend on (x, a). The contextual bandit problem is a repeated game: at each time step t:

- The player observes a sample $x_t \in \mathcal{X}$.
- The player chooses precisely one action (or arm) $a_t \in \mathcal{A}$.
- The reward r_t is revealed.

Note that in this chapter, we will follow the convention in the bandit literature of using $\mathcal{A}$ to denote the action space instead of the learning algorithm. We may also introduce the notation of *policy* for contextual bandits. Using the notation of Section 13.4, a bandit learning algorithm returns a policy $\hat{q}(\mathcal{S}_{t-1})$ based on the history $\mathcal{S}_{t-1}$.

Definition 17.2 A policy π for a contextual bandit is a map $\mathcal{X} \to \Delta(\mathcal{A})$, where $\Delta(\mathcal{A})$ denotes probability measures over $\mathcal{A}$ with an appropriately defined σ-algebra. One may also write it as a conditional distribution $\pi(a|x)$, and the policy draws $a \sim \pi(\cdot|x)$ when it observes context x. A contextual bandit algorithm $\hat{q}$ maps historic observations

$$\mathcal{S}_{t-1} = \{(x_1, a_1, r_1), \dots, (x_{t-1}, a_{t-1}, r_{t-1})\}$$

to a policy $\pi_t = \hat{q}(\cdot|\mathcal{S}_{t-1})$ at each time step t, and pulls an arm $a_t \sim \pi_t(\cdot|x_t)$ based on the observation x_t. In this chapter, we will also write the history-dependent policy as $a_t \sim \hat{q}(a_t|x_t, \mathcal{S}_{t-1})$.

The contextual bandit problem includes the multiarmed bandit problem as a special case if we take $x = x_0$ to be a fixed context for all time steps.

Similar to the case of multiarmed bandit problem, we may also consider the adversarial setting with an oblivious adversary as follows. At each time step t, we have the information of all rewards $[r_t(a) : a \in \mathcal{A}]$, but only the value of $r_t(a_t)$ for the chosen arm a_t is revealed. The goal is to maximize the expected cumulative reward

$$\sum_{t=1}^{T} \mathbb{E}_{a_t \sim \pi_t}[r_t(a_t)].$$

If we are given a policy class Π, then regret of a contextual bandit algorithm with respect to Π can be written as

$$\text{REG}_T = \sup_{\pi \in \Pi} \sum_{t=1}^{T} \mathbb{E}_{a_t \sim \pi}[r_t(a_t)] - \sum_{t=1}^{T} \mathbb{E}_{a_t \sim \pi_t}[r_t(a_t)]. \tag{17.1}$$

If we consider the stochastic contextual bandit setting with unknown *value functions*

$$f_*(x, a) = \mathbb{E}[r|x, a], \qquad f_*(x) = \max_{a \in \mathcal{A}} f(x, a)$$

that do not change over time, then the goal becomes to maximize the expected reward:

$$\sum_{t=1}^{T} \mathbb{E}_{a_t \sim \pi_t}[f_*(x_t, a_t)].$$

The regret of the algorithm that produces policy sequence $\{\pi_t\}$ is

$$\text{REG}_T = \sum_{t=1}^{T} \mathbb{E}_{a_t \sim \pi_t}[f_*(x_t) - f_*(x_t, a_t)]. \tag{17.2}$$

17.1 EXP4 for Adversarial Contextual Bandits

The EXP4 algorithm is a generalization of the EXP3 algorithm for the adversarial multiarmed bandit problem (Auer et al., 2002b). It can be regarded as a policy-based method for adversarial contextual bandits. EXP4 can be applied to the case that the action space $\mathcal{A} = \{1, \ldots, K\}$ is finite, and it works in the setting of "experts." An expert in EXP4 can be regarded as a policy.

Assume that we have an expert class indexed by w:

$$\mathcal{G} = \{[\hat{q}_t(\cdot|w, x_t)]_{t=1,2,\ldots} : w \in \Omega\}.$$

Given any context $x_t \in \mathcal{X}$, an expert w returns a probability distribution $\hat{q}_t(\cdot|w, x_t)$ on $a_t \in \{1, \ldots, K\}$.

Let $p_0(w)$ be a prior on Ω, then the EXP4 algorithm, presented in Algorithm 17.1, has a regret bound that is logarithmic in $|\mathcal{G}|$ for finite $\mathcal{G}$, if the regret is to compete with the best expert in $\mathcal{G}$. EXP4 can also be regarded as a generalization of EXP3, which has K experts, and each expert pulls one arm $a \in \{1, \ldots, K\}$ constantly.

Example 17.3 Any stationary policy can be regarded as an expert. As an example, we may consider experts of logistic policies (parametrized by w) defined as

$$\hat{q}_t(a|w,x) = \hat{q}(a|w,x) = \frac{\exp(w^\top \psi(x,a))}{\sum_{\ell=1}^{K} \exp(w^\top \psi(x,\ell))},$$

with Gaussian prior $p_0(w)$:

$$w \sim N(0,\sigma^2).$$

Algorithm 17.1 EXP4

Input: K, T, $\mathcal{G}$, $p_0(\cdot)$, $\gamma \in (0,1]$, $\eta > 0$, $b \geq 0$

1 Let $u_0(w) = 1$
2 **for** $t = 1, 2, \ldots, T$ **do**
3   Observe x_t
4   **for** $a = 1, \ldots, K$ **do**
5   Let $\hat{\pi}_t(a) = (1-\gamma)\mathbb{E}_{w \sim p_{t-1}(w)}\hat{q}_t(a|w,x_t) + \gamma/K$
6   Sample a_t according to $\hat{\pi}_t(\cdot)$
7   Pull arm a_t and observe reward $r_t(a_t) \in [0,1]$
8   Let $\hat{r}_t(w,x_t,a_t) = \hat{q}_t(a_t|w,x_t)(r_t(a_t) - b)/\hat{\pi}_t(a_t)$
9   Let $u_t(w) = u_{t-1}(w)\exp(\eta\hat{r}_t(w,x_t,a_t))$
10   Let $p_t(w) = p_0(w)u_t(w)/\mathbb{E}_{w \sim p_0(w)}u_t(w)$

Note that conditioned on the history, the estimator $\hat{r}_t(w,x_t,a_t)$ is a random estimator that depends on the partial reward $r_t(a_t)$ received for $a_t \sim \hat{\pi}_t(a)$. Moreover, it is an unbiased estimator of the following shifted reward of w, according to policy $\hat{q}_t(\cdot|w,x_t)$:

$$\mathbb{E}_{a_t \sim \hat{\pi}_t}\hat{r}_t(w,x_t,a_t) = \mathbb{E}_{a \sim \hat{q}_t(a|w,x_t)}(r_t(a) - b), \tag{17.3}$$

which relies on the full reward vector $[r_t(a)]$ at time step t over all arms a.

Both parameter γ and b control exploration. The original EXP4 set $b = 0$, and in such case we need to set $\gamma > 0$. The larger γ is, the more uniform $\hat{q}_t(a)$ becomes, and thus we explore more.

Similarly, the larger b is, the more penalty we put on arms that have been observed, and this favors arms that are not observed in the future. In the full information case, where all $r_t(a)$ are observed at every time step, the parameter b doesn't affect the algorithm. However, in the partial information case, if we set $b = 0$, we need $\gamma > 0$ to perform exploration. On the other hand, if we choose $b = 1$, then we can set $\gamma = 0$.

Theorem 17.4 *For any K, $T \geq 0$, and any $\gamma \in (0,1]$, $\eta > 0$ and $b \geq 0$. Consider any expert class $\mathcal{G} = \{[\hat{q}_t(\cdot|w,x)]_{t=1,2,\ldots} : w \in \Omega\}$ with prior $p_0(w)$. Let*

$$R_T(w) = \mathbb{E}\sum_{t=1}^{T}\mathbb{E}_{a \sim \hat{q}_t(\cdot|w,x_t)}r_t(a)$$

be the reward of expert w. Then the expected reward of Algorithm 17.1 satisfies

$$\mathbb{E} \sum_{t=1}^{T} r_t(a_t) \geq (1 - \gamma) \max_q \left[\mathbb{E}_{w \sim q} R_T(w) - \frac{1}{\eta} \mathrm{KL}(q \| p_0), \right]$$

$$- c(\eta, b) \eta \sum_{t=1}^{T} \sum_{a=1}^{K} |r_t(a) - b|,$$

where the expectation is with respect to the randomization of the algorithm,

$$c(\eta, b) = \phi(z_0) \max(b, 1 - b), \quad z_0 = \max(0, \eta(1 - b)K/\gamma),$$

and $\phi(z) = (e^z - 1 - z)/z^2$.

Proof The proof is similar to that of Theorem 16.17. By the definition of $\hat{\pi}_t(a_t)$, we have

$$\tilde{\rho}_t(a_t) = \mathbb{E}_{w \sim p_{t-1}(w)} \hat{q}_t(a_t | w, x_t) / \hat{\pi}_t(a_t) \leq 1/(1 - \gamma). \tag{17.4}$$

Therefore,

$$\mathbb{E}_{w \sim p_{t-1}(w)} \hat{r}_t(w, x_t, a_t) = \mathbb{E}_{w \sim p_{t-1}(w)} \hat{q}_t(a_t | w, x_t) [r_t(a_t) - b] / \hat{\pi}_t(a_t)$$

$$\leq \frac{1}{1 - \gamma} r_t(a_t) - \tilde{\rho}_t(a_t) b. \tag{17.5}$$

The first equation used the definition of $\hat{r}$. The inequality used (17.4). Moreover,

$$\mathbb{E}_{w \sim p_{t-1}(w)} \hat{r}_t(w, x_t, a_t)^2$$
$$= \mathbb{E}_{w \sim p_{t-1}(w)} \hat{q}_t(a_t | w, x_t)^2 ((r_t(a_t) - b) / \hat{\pi}_t(a_t))^2$$
$$\leq \max(b, 1 - b) \mathbb{E}_{w \sim p_{t-1}(w)} \hat{q}_t(a_t | w, x_t) (|r_t(a_t) - b| / \hat{\pi}_t(a_t)^2)$$
$$\leq \frac{\max(b, 1 - b)}{1 - \gamma} (|r_t(a_t) - b| / \hat{\pi}_t(a_t)). \tag{17.6}$$

The first equation used the definition of $\hat{r}$. The first inequality used $|r_t(a_t) - b| \leq \max(b, 1 - b)$. The second inequality used (17.4).

If we let

$$W_t = \mathbb{E}_{w \sim p_0(w)} u_t(w),$$

then

$$\ln \frac{W_t}{W_{t-1}} = \ln \mathbb{E}_{w \sim p_0(w)} \frac{u_t(w)}{W_{t-1}}$$
$$= \ln \mathbb{E}_{w \sim p_{t-1}(w)} \exp(\eta \hat{r}_t(w, x_t, a_t))$$
$$\leq \ln \mathbb{E}_{w \sim p_{t-1}(w)} \left[1 + (\eta \hat{r}_t(w, x_t, a_t)) + \phi(z_0)(\eta \hat{r}_t(w, x_t, a_t))^2 \right]$$
$$\leq \mathbb{E}_{w \sim p_{t-1}(w)} (\eta \hat{r}_t(w, x_t, a_t)) + \phi(z_0) \mathbb{E}_{w \sim p_{t-1}(w)} (\eta \hat{r}_t(w, x_t, a_t))^2$$
$$\leq \frac{\eta}{1 - \gamma} r_t(a_t) - \eta \tilde{\rho}_t(a_t) b + \frac{c(\eta, b) \eta^2}{(1 - \gamma)} \frac{|r_t(a_t) - b|}{\hat{\pi}_t(a_t)}.$$

The second equality used the definition of u_t. The first inequality used $\exp(z) \leq 1 + z + \phi(z_0) z^2$ when $z = \eta \hat{r}_t(w, x_t, a_t) \leq z_0$; the second inequality used $\ln(1 + z) \leq z$; and the third inequality used (17.5) and (17.6).

Now we can sum over $t = 1$ to $t = T$, and obtain

$$\ln \frac{W_T}{W_0} \leq \frac{\eta}{1 - \gamma} \sum_{t=1}^{T} r_t(a_t) - \eta b \sum_{t=1}^{T} \tilde{\rho}_t(a_t) + \frac{c(\eta, b)\eta^2}{(1 - \gamma)} \sum_{t=1}^{T} \frac{|r_t(a_t) - b|}{\hat{\pi}_t(a_t)}.$$

Note that $W_0 = 1$. We can take expectation with respect to the randomization of the algorithm, and obtain

$$\mathbb{E} \ln \mathbb{E}_{w \sim p_0(w)} \exp\left(\eta \sum_{t=1}^{T} \hat{r}_t(w, x_t, a_t) \right)$$

$$\leq \frac{\eta}{1 - \gamma} \mathbb{E} \sum_{t=1}^{T} r_t(a_t) - \eta T b + \frac{c(\eta, b)\eta^2}{(1 - \gamma)} \mathbb{E} \sum_{t=1}^{T} \sum_{a=1}^{K} |r_t(a) - b|. \qquad (17.7)$$

The derivation also used $\mathbb{E}\, \tilde{\rho}_t(a_t) = \mathbb{E}\, \mathbb{E}_{a_t \sim \hat{\pi}_t} \tilde{\rho}_t(a_t) = 1$ and

$$\mathbb{E} \frac{|r_t(a_t) - b|}{\hat{\pi}_t(a_t)} = \mathbb{E}\, \mathbb{E}_{a_t \sim \hat{\pi}_t} \frac{|r_t(a_t) - b|}{\hat{\pi}_t(a_t)} = \mathbb{E} \sum_{a=1}^{K} |r_t(a) - b|.$$

We can lower bound the left-hand side of (17.7) as:

$$\mathbb{E} \ln \mathbb{E}_{w \sim p_0(w)} \exp\left(\eta \sum_{t=1}^{T} \hat{r}_t(w, x_t, a_t) \right)$$

$$= \mathbb{E} \max_q \left[\mathbb{E}_{w \sim q} \eta \sum_{t=1}^{T} \hat{r}_t(w, x_t, a_t) - \mathrm{KL}(q \| p_0) \right]$$

$$\geq \max_q \left[\mathbb{E}_{w \sim q} \eta \mathbb{E} \sum_{t=1}^{T} \hat{r}_t(w, x_t, a_t) - \mathrm{KL}(q \| p_0) \right]$$

$$= \max_q \left[\mathbb{E}_{w \sim q} \eta [R_T(w) - bT] - \mathrm{KL}(q \| p_0) \right].$$

The first equality used Proposition 7.16. The last equation used (17.3) and the definition of R_T. By plugging this estimate into the left-hand side of (17.7), we obtain the desired result. $\qquad \square$

The following result is a direct consequence of Theorem 17.4. It can be regarded as a direct generalization of Theorem 16.17.

Corollary 17.5 *Let $\eta = \gamma/K$ and $b = 0$. Assume that the uniform random policy belongs to Ω and $|\Omega| = N < \infty$. Let $p_0(w)$ be the uniform prior over Ω, then*

$$G_* - \mathbb{E} \sum_{t=1}^{T} r_t(a_t) \leq (e - 1)\gamma G_* + \frac{K \ln N}{\gamma},$$

where the expectation is with respect to the randomization of the algorithm, and

$$G_* = \arg\max_w \sum_{t=1}^{T} \mathbb{E}\, \mathbb{E}_{a \sim \hat{q}_t(\cdot | w, x_t)}[r_t(a)].$$

Proof We have $\eta \hat{r}_t(w, x_t, a_t) \leq 1$, and thus $c(\eta, b) = e - 2$. Note that the uniform random policy belonging to Ω implies that

$$\frac{1}{K} \sum_{t=1}^{T} \sum_{a=1}^{K} r_t(a) \leq G_*.$$

We consider Theorem 17.4, with q defined as $q(w) = \mathbb{1}(w = w_*)$, where w_* achieves the maximum of G_*. This implies

$$\mathbb{E} \sum_{t=1}^{T} r_t(a_t) \geq (1 - \gamma) \left[G_* - \frac{K}{\gamma} \ln N \right] - (e - 2) \gamma G_*.$$

This implies the bound.   □

Example 17.6 We can take $\gamma = 0$ and $b = 1$ in Algorithm 17.1. By noting that $\phi(z)$ is an increasing function of z and $\eta(1 - b) \leq 0$, we may take

$$c(\eta, b) = 0.5.$$

Theorem 17.4 implies that

$$\mathbb{E} \sum_{t=1}^{T} r_t(a_t) \geq \max_q \left[R_T(w) - \frac{1}{\eta} \mathrm{KL}(q \| p_0) \right] - 0.5 \eta K T.$$

In the finite policy case $|\Omega| = N$ with uniform prior,

$$G_* - \mathbb{E} \sum_{t=1}^{T} r_t(a_t) \leq \frac{\ln N}{\eta} + 0.5 \eta K T.$$

By choosing $\eta = \sqrt{\ln N / (KT)}$, we obtain

$$G_* - \mathbb{E} \sum_{t=1}^{T} r_t(a_t) \leq 2\sqrt{KT \ln N}.$$

We can compare EXP4 to its full information counterpart Hedge in Algorithm 14.4. We note that in the online setting of the Hedge algorithm, we observe the information for all arms $a \in \{1, \ldots, K\}$ even if a is not pulled. In this case, it is possible to replace $\hat{r}_t(w, x_t, a_t)$ by $r_t(w, x_t) = -\ell_t(w_{t-1})$, and we do not have to explore in order to obtain rewards for different arms. This removes the K dependency in the resulting online regret bound. Using the same notation of Theorem 17.4, we obtain the following Hedge online regret bound (in the full information case) from Theorem 14.15:

$$\mathbb{E} \sum_{t=1}^{T} r_t(a_t) \geq \max_q \left[R_T(w) - \frac{1}{\eta} \mathrm{KL}(q \| p_0) \right] - \eta T / 8.$$

Assume that $|\Omega| = N < \infty$. Let $p_0(w)$ be the uniform prior over Ω, then we obtain the following online regret bound for Hedge (in the full information case):

$$G_* - \mathbb{E} \sum_{t=1}^{T} r_t(a_t) \leq \frac{\ln N}{\eta} + \frac{\eta T}{8}.$$

With $\eta = \sqrt{\ln N / T}$, we obtain the full information regret bound of

$$G_* - \mathbb{E} \sum_{t=1}^{T} r_t(a_t) \leq 2\sqrt{T \ln N},$$

which does not contain the factor K.

17.2 Linear UCB for Stochastic Contextual Bandits

The EXP4 algorithm tries to find the best policy in a policy class. We can also design an algorithm that finds the best value function from a value function class. In particular, if $f_*(x, a)$ is a linear function, then we can directly generalize the UCB algorithm to find a near-optimal value function, and use its induced greedy policy to select an arm to pull. We first introduce the following definition, which generalizes stochastic linear bandit models in Section 16.4 to the contextual bandit setting.

Definition 17.7 The stochastic linear contextual bandit (or stochastic contextual bandit with linear payoff) is a contextual bandit problem, where the reward at each time step t is given by

$$r_t(a) = r_t(x_t, a) = w_*^\top \psi(x_t, a) + \epsilon_t(x_t, a), \tag{17.8}$$

where $\epsilon_t(x, a)$ is a zero-mean random variable. We assume that $\mathcal{H}$ is a known inner product space, $w_* \in \mathcal{H}$ is the unknown model parameter, and the feature vector $\psi(x, a) \in \mathcal{H}$ is known.

In the stochastic linear bandit model, the number of arms can be either infinite or finite, and an UCB-style algorithm is presented in Algorithm 17.2. Note that the algorithm selects an arm that has the largest confidence bound adjusted reward. This methodology is referred to as *optimism in the face of uncertainty*, and is a direct generalization of upper confidence bound (UCB) for MAB. Therefore we call Algorithm 17.2 linear UCB, although it is also referred to as OFUL (optimism in the face of uncertainty linear) bandit in the literature (Abbasi-Yadkori et al., 2011).

Algorithm 17.2 Linear UCB Algorithm

Input: λ, T, $\{\beta_t\}$
1   Let $A_0 = \lambda I$
2   Let $w_0 = 0$
3   Let $b_0 = 0$
4   **for** $t = 1, 2, \ldots, T$ **do**
5   Observe x_t
6   Let $a_t \in \arg\max_a \left[w_{t-1}^\top \psi(x_t, a) + \beta_{t-1} \sqrt{\psi(x_t, a)^\top A_{t-1}^{-1} \psi(x_t, a)} \right]$
7   Pull arm a_t and observe reward $r_t(x_t, a_t)$
8   Let $b_t = b_{t-1} + r_t(x_t, a_t)\psi(x_t, a_t)$
9   Let $A_t = A_{t-1} + \psi(x_t, a_t)\psi(x_t, a_t)^\top$
10   Let $w_t = A_t^{-1} b_t$

In order to analyze Algorithm 17.2, we need to obtain a uniform confidence interval for the linear bandit problem using either Theorem 13.7 or Theorem 13.10. The bound stated below holds uniformly for all arms (possibly infinitely many) and both for lower and upper confidence bounds.

Lemma 17.8 *Assume that in the stochastic linear bandit model, $\|w_*\|_{\mathcal{H}} \leq B$ for some constant B, and in Algorithm 17.2, assume that $\{\beta_t\}$ is any sequence so that*

$$\Pr\left[\forall 0 \leq t \leq T: \beta_t \geq \sqrt{\lambda}B + \left\|\sum_{s=1}^{t} \epsilon_s(x_s, a_s)\psi(x_s, a_s)\right\|_{A_t^{-1}}\right] \geq 1 - \delta. \quad (17.9)$$

Then with probability at least $1 - \delta$, for all $t = 0, \ldots, T$ and $u \in \mathcal{H}$,

$$|u^\top(w_t - w_*)| \leq \beta_t\sqrt{u^\top A_t^{-1}u}.$$

Proof We have

$$u^\top(w_t - w_*) = u^\top A_t^{-1}\sum_{s=1}^{t} r_s(x_s, a_s)\psi(x_s, a_s) - u^\top w_*$$

$$= u^\top A_t^{-1}\sum_{s=1}^{t} \epsilon_s(x_s, a_s)\psi(x_s, a_s) - \lambda u^\top A_t^{-1}w_*$$

$$\leq \|u\|_{A_t^{-1}}\left\|\sum_{s=1}^{t} \epsilon_s(x_s, a_s)\psi(x_s, a_s)\right\|_{A_t^{-1}} + \lambda\|u\|_{A_t^{-1}}\|w_*\|_{A_t^{-1}}$$

$$\leq \|u\|_{A_t^{-1}}\left[\left\|\sum_{s=1}^{t} \epsilon_s(x_s, a_s)\psi(x_s, a_s)\right\|_{A_t^{-1}} + \sqrt{\lambda}B\right] \leq \beta_t\|u\|_{A_t^{-1}}.$$

The second equality used (17.8). The first inequality used the Cauchy–Schwarz inequality. The last inequality used the definition of β_t. This implies the desired bound. $\qquad\square$

Example 17.9 Assume that noise in (17.8) satisfies the sub-Gaussian conditions of Theorem 13.7, and assume that $d = \dim(\mathcal{H})$ is finite dimensional, with $B' = \sup_{x,a}\|\psi(x, a)\|_{\mathcal{H}}$. Then in Lemma 17.8 we can set

$$\beta_t = \sqrt{\lambda}B + \sigma\sqrt{2\ln(1/\delta) + d\ln(1 + T(B')^2/d\lambda)}$$

so that (17.9) holds. Note that Proposition 15.8 is used to obtain a bound on the log-determinant function.

Example 17.10 Assume that noise in (17.8) satisfies the conditions of Theorem 13.10. Then in Lemma 17.8 we can set

$$\beta_t = \sqrt{\lambda}B + 2\alpha\sqrt{\ln(2/\delta)} + 1.2\sigma\sqrt{\mathrm{entro}(\lambda/T, \psi(\mathcal{X} \times \mathcal{A}))}$$

so that (17.9) holds. Note that $\mathrm{entro}(\cdot)$ is defined in Proposition 15.8.

The confidence interval estimate in Lemma 17.8 can be used to obtain a regret bound for the UCB method in Algorithm 17.2, and the proof is similar to that of Theorem 16.3.

Theorem 17.11   *Assume that in the stochastic linear bandit model, $r_t(x_t, a_t) \in [0, 1]$ and $\|w_*\|_2 \leq B$ for some constant B. Let $\mu_t(x, a) = \mathbb{E}_{\epsilon_t(x,a)} r_t(x, a) = w_*^\top \psi(x, a)$. Let $a_*(x) \in \arg\max_a \mu_t(x, a)$ be the optimal arm for each context x. Then in Algorithm 17.2, with probability at least $1 - \delta$,*

$$\mathbb{E}\sum_{t=1}^{T}[\mu_t(x_t, a_*(x_t)) - \mu_t(x_t, a_t)] \leq 3\sqrt{\ln|A_T/\lambda| \sum_{t=1}^{T}\beta_{t-1}^2} + 2\ln|A_T/\lambda|,$$

where $\{\beta_t\}$ is any sequence that satisfies (17.9).

Proof   We have for $t \geq 1$,

$$w_*^\top\psi(x_t, a_*(x_t))$$

$$\leq w_{t-1}^\top\psi(x_t, a_*(x_t)) + \beta_{t-1}\sqrt{\psi(x_t, a_*(x_t))^\top A_{t-1}^{-1}\psi(x_t, a_*(x_t))}$$

$$\leq w_{t-1}^\top\psi(x_t, a_t) + \beta_{t-1}\sqrt{\psi(x_t, a_t)^\top A_{t-1}^{-1}\psi(x_t, a_t)}$$

$$\leq w_*^\top\psi(x_t, a_t) + 2\beta_{t-1}\sqrt{\psi(x_t, a_t)^\top A_{t-1}^{-1}\psi(x_t, a_t)},$$

where the first and the third inequalities used Lemma 17.8 . The second inequality is due to the UCB choice of a_t in Algorithm 17.2.

Let E_t be the event of $\|\psi(x_t, a_t)\|_{A_{t-1}} \leq 1$. Since $w_*^\top\psi(x_t, a) \in [0, 1]$, we have

$$w_*^\top\psi(x_t, a_*(x_t)) - w_*^\top\psi(x_t, a_t) \leq 2\beta_{t-1}\|\psi(x_t, a_t)\|_{A_{t-1}^{-1}}\mathbb{1}(E_t) + \mathbb{1}(E_t^c).$$

By summing over $t = 1$ to $t = T$, we obtain

$$\sum_{t=1}^{T}[\mu_t(x_t, a_*(x_t)) - \mu_t(x_t, a_t)]$$

$$\leq 2\sum_{t=1}^{T}\beta_{t-1}\|\psi(x_t, a_t)\|_{A_{t-1}^{-1}}\mathbb{1}(E_t) + \sum_{t=1}^{T}\mathbb{1}(E_t^c)$$

$$\leq 2\sum_{t=1}^{T}\beta_{t-1}\sqrt{\frac{2\|\psi(x_t, a_t)\|_{A_{t-1}^{-1}}^2}{1 + \|\psi(x_t, a_t)\|_{A_{t-1}^{-1}}^2}} + 2\sum_{t=1}^{T}\frac{\psi(x_t, a_t)^\top A_{t-1}^{-1}\psi(x_t, a_t)}{1 + \psi(x_t, a_t)^\top A_{t-1}^{-1}\psi(x_t, a_t)}$$

$$\leq 3\sqrt{\sum_{t=1}^{T}\beta_{t-1}^2}\sqrt{\sum_{t=1}^{T}\frac{\psi(x_t, a_t)^\top A_{t-1}^{-1}\psi(x_t, a_t)}{1 + \psi(x_t, a_t)^\top A_{t-1}^{-1}\psi(x_t, a_t)}} + 2\ln|A_T/\lambda|.$$

The second inequality used simple algebraic inequalities under E_t and E_t^c. The third inequality used the Cauchy–Schwarz inequality and Lemma 13.9. We can now apply Lemma 13.9 again to obtain the desired bound. $\square$

Example 17.12 In order to interpret the results of Theorem 17.11, we may consider the noise assumption and the choice of β_t in Example 17.9 with $\sigma = 0.5$. It implies a bound:

$$\mathbb{E}\sum_{t=1}^{T}[\mu_t(x_t, a_*(x_t)) - \mu_t(x_t, a_t)] = \tilde{O}\left(\sqrt{\lambda dT}B + d\sqrt{T}\right),$$

where $\tilde{O}$ hides logarithmic factors. By setting λ to be sufficiently small, we obtain

$$\mathbb{E}\sum_{t=1}^{T}[\mu_t(x_t, a_*(x_t)) - \mu_t(x_t, a_t)] = \tilde{O}(d\sqrt{T}).$$

Similarly, under the conditions of Example 17.10 with $\alpha = 1$, we obtain

$$\mathbb{E}\sum_{t=1}^{T}[\mu_t(x_t, a_*(x_t)) - \mu_t(x_t, a_t)] = \tilde{O}\left(\sigma\tilde{d}\sqrt{T} + \sqrt{\tilde{d}T}\right),$$

where $\tilde{d} = \text{entro}(\lambda/T, \psi(\mathcal{X} \times \mathcal{A}))$ with $\lambda = O(1)$.

For a stochastic linear bandit with possibly infinitely many arms, the bound in Example 17.12 is optimal up to a logarithmic factor, as shown by the following result.

Theorem 17.13 *Given any integer $d \geq 1$ and $T \geq 1$, there exists a (noncontextual) stochastic linear bandit problem with 2^d arms corresponding to feature vectors $\{\pm 1\}^d$, and reward $r \in [-0.5, 0.5]$, so that regret of any bandit algorithm is at least*

$$\min\left(0.05T, 0.12d\sqrt{T}\right).$$

Proof Consider 2^d arms, represented by feature vectors $\psi(a) = a \in \{-1, 1\}^d$. The reward r of pulling arm a (without context) is in $\{-0.5, 0.5\}$, and

$$\mathbb{E}[r|a] = w^\top a$$

for some $w \in \{-\epsilon, \epsilon\}^d$, where $\epsilon \in (0, 0.5/d]$ will be specified later. Using notations of Theorem 13.24 with τ changed to w and $m = 2$, $\mathcal{P}_{\mathcal{Z}} = \{q_w(r|a)\}$, where each $q_w(r|a)$ is a $\{-0.5, 0.5\}$-valued binary random variable Bernoulli$(0.5 + w^\top a) - 0.5$. A policy π is a probability distribution on $\mathcal{A}$, and we can define $q_w(r|\pi) = \mathbb{E}_{a \sim \pi} q_w(r|a)$.

Let θ indicate an arbitrary arm returned by a learning algorithm, represented by its feature vector $\theta \in \{\pm 1\}^d$. It follows that the regret of pulling arm θ is

$$Q(\theta, w) = \sum_{j=1}^{d} Q_j(\theta, w), \quad Q_j(\theta, w) = \epsilon - w_j\theta_j.$$

This means that for $w \sim_j w'$ and $w \neq w'$ ($w' \sim_j w$ means that w' and w are identical except at the jth component),

$$Q_j(\theta, q_w) + Q_j(\theta, q_{w'}) \geq 2\epsilon.$$

Let $w^{(j)} = w - w_j e_j$ be the vector with value zero at the jth component but the same value as that of w elsewhere.

Now we can let $\epsilon = \min\left(0.1/d, 0.24\sqrt{1/T}\right)$. Given any learning algorithm $\hat{q}$, for all w, time step t, and a_t represented by feature representation in $\{-1, 1\}^d$,

$$\frac{1}{2} \sum_{w' \sim_j w} \mathrm{KL}(q_{w^{(j)}}(\cdot|\hat{q}(\mathcal{S}_{t-1}), \mathcal{S}_{t-1}) \| q_{w'}(\cdot|\hat{q}(\mathcal{S}_{t-1}), \mathcal{S}_{t-1}))$$

$$\leq \frac{1}{2} \sup_{a_t} \sum_{w' \sim_j w} \mathrm{KL}(0.5 + (w^{(j)})^\top a_t \| 0.5 + (w')^\top a_t)$$

$$\leq 2.1\epsilon^2,$$

where the last inequality follows from Exercise (16.4)

$$\mathrm{KL}(q_1 \| q_2) = q_1 \ln \frac{q_1}{q_2} + (1 - q_2) \ln \frac{1 - q_1}{1 - q_2} \leq \frac{(q_1 - q_2)^2}{2 \min(q_1(1 - q_1), q_2(1 - q_2))}.$$

Here we set $q_1 = 0.5 + (w^{(j)})^\top a$ and $q_2 = 0.5 + (w')^\top a$. This implies that $q_1, q_2 \in [0.4, 0.6]$ and $|q_1 - q_2| \leq \epsilon$.

We can now take $\beta_{j,t}^2 = 2.1\epsilon^2$ and apply Theorem 13.24. For $n \leq T$,

$$\frac{1}{2^d} \sum_w \mathbb{E}_{\theta, \mathcal{S}_n \sim p(\cdot|\hat{q}, q_w)} Q(\theta, q_w) \geq d\epsilon \left(1 - \sqrt{2 \times 2.1 n \epsilon^2}\right)$$

$$\geq 0.5 d\epsilon = 0.5 d \min\left(0.1/d, 0.24\sqrt{1/T}\right).$$

Since this holds for all $n \leq T$, we obtain the bound. $\qquad\square$

We note that the lower bound in Theorem 17.13 requires 2^d number of arms. However, for K arms with small K, this bound is suboptimal.

Example 17.14 The stochastic multiarmed bandit with K arms and rewards in $[0, 1]$ can be considered as a stochastic linear bandit, where we take $w_* = [\mu(1), \dots, \mu(K)]$, and $\psi(a, x) = e_a$ for $a \in \{1, \dots, K\}$. Therefore we may choose $B = \sqrt{K}$, so that $\|w_*\|_2 \leq B$. We can also choose $\lambda = 1$ and $M = 1$. Theorem 17.11 implies a suboptimal bound (ignoring log factors):

$$\mathbb{E} \sum_{t=1}^T [\mu_t(x_t, a_*(x_t)) - \mu_t(x_t, a_t)] = \tilde{O}(K\sqrt{T}).$$

The extra $\sqrt{K}$ factor is due to the analysis not taking advantage of the fact that only a finite number of arms are available. In comparison, Algorithm 16.2 for the noncontextual stochastic linear bandit achieves a regret of $\tilde{O}(\sqrt{KT})$ according to Theorem 16.14 and Example 16.15.

The extra dependency on d (and K) is due to the uniform confidence interval over all $u \in \mathbb{R}^d$ in Lemma 17.8. To obtain better dependence on K, one needs to obtain a confidence interval for a fixed u as in Lemma 9.34, instead of uniform over all $u \in \mathbb{R}^d$. One difficulty for obtaining nonuniform result for in Algorithm 17.2 is that A_t depends on $\epsilon_s(a_s, t_s)$ for $s \leq t$, which breaks the independence argument in Lemma 9.34.

A more complex scheme, presented in Auer (2002) and Chu et al. (2011), can be used to derive such a nonuniform convergence result, which leads to an improved bound for stochastic linear bandits with finitely many arms. The resulting bound is similar to that of Theorem 16.14.

It is also relatively easy to apply Thompson sampling to the stochastic linear bandit model. Consider the prior and likelihood functions defined as

$$w \sim p_0(w) = N(0, (\sigma^2/\lambda)I),$$
$$r_t(x, a) \sim N(w^\top \psi(x, a), \sigma^2).$$

At the beginning of any time step t, after we have observed data up to time $t - 1$, the posterior is

$$w \sim N(w_{t-1}, \Sigma_{t-1}), \quad \sigma^2 \Sigma_{t-1}^{-1} = \lambda I + \sum_{s<t} \psi(x_s, a_s)\psi(x_s, a_s)^\top.$$

The Thompson sampling method samples $\tilde{w}$ from the posterior and plays an arm that is optimal with respect to $\tilde{w}$. The algorithm is presented in Algorithm 17.3.

Algorithm 17.3 Thompson Sampling for Linear Contextual Bandits

---

Input: λ, σ, T

1   Let $A_0 = \lambda I$
2   Let $w_0 = 0$
3   Let $b_0 = 0$
4   **for** $t = 1, 2, \ldots, T$ **do**
5   Sample $\tilde{w}_{t-1} \sim N(w_{t-1}, \sigma^2 A_{t-1}^{-1})$
6   Observe x_t
7   Let $a_t \in \arg\max_a \left[\tilde{w}_{t-1}^\top \psi(x_t, a) \right]$
8   Pull arm a_t and observe reward $r_t(x_t, a_t)$
9   Let $b_t = b_{t-1} + r_t(x_t, a_t)\psi(x_t, a_t)$
10   Let $A_t = A_{t-1} + \psi(x_t, a_t)\psi(x_t, a_t)^\top$
11   Let $w_t = A_t^{-1} b_t$

In Section 17.4, we will analyze a variant of Thompson sampling with optimistic prior for the more general nonlinear contextual bandit problem. However, the theoretical result for the standard Thompson sampling without such an optimistic prior is inferior to that of linear UCB, although Thompson sampling can be an effective practical algorithm in many applications (see Chapelle and Li, 2011).

17.3 Nonlinear UCB with Eluder Coefficient

One may generalize stochastic linear contextual bandits using nonlinear function approximation as follows.

Definition 17.15 The stochastic nonlinear contextual bandit is a contextual bandit problem, where the reward at each time step t is given by

$$r_t(a) = r_t(x_t, a) = f_*(x_t, a) + \epsilon_t(x_t, a),$$

where $\epsilon_t(x, a)$ is a zero-mean random variable, where we assume that $f_*(x, a) \in \mathcal{F}$ for a known function class $\mathcal{F} \colon \mathcal{X} \times \mathcal{A} \to \mathbb{R}$. Given any $f(x, a) \in \mathcal{F}$, we also define

$$f(x) = \max_{a \in \mathcal{A}} f(x, a),$$

and the greedy policy of f as: $\pi_f(x) \in \arg\max_{a \in \mathcal{A}} f(x, a)$.

For the stochastic nonlinear bandit model, we may generalize Algorithm 17.2 as in Algorithm 17.4. In general, we say $\mathcal{F}_t$ is a version space if $f_* \in \mathcal{F}_t$ with high probability. Choosing the optimal f_t in a properly defined version space is a natural generalization of upper confidence bound. The algorithm directly implements the optimism in the face of the uncertainty principle.

Algorithm 17.4 Version Space UCB Algorithm

Input: λ, T, $f_0 \in \mathcal{F}$
1 Let $\mathcal{F}_0 = \{f_0\}$
2 **for** $t = 1, 2, \ldots, T$ **do**
3   Observe x_t
4   Let $f_t \in \arg\max_{f \in \mathcal{F}_{t-1}} f(x_t)$
5   Let $a_t \in \arg\max_a f_t(x_t, a)$
6   Pull arm a_t and observe reward $r_t(x_t, a_t) \in [0, 1]$
7   Let $\mathcal{F}_t$ be an appropriate version space based on $\mathcal{S}_t = \{(x_s, a_s)\}_{s=1}^t$.

The following result shows that with an appropriately defined version space, Algorithm 17.4 is a generalization of Algorithm 17.2. We leave its proof to an exercise.

Proposition 17.16 *Assume that $\mathcal{F} = \{f(w, x, a) = w^\top \psi(x, a) : w \in \mathbb{R}^d\}$. Let*

$$\mathcal{F}_t = \left\{ f(w, \cdot) \colon \phi_t(w) \leq \phi_t(w_t) + \beta_t^2 \right\},$$

where $w_t = \arg\min_w \phi_t(w)$, and

$$\phi_t(w) = \sum_{s=1}^t (w^\top \psi(x_s, a_s) - r_s(x_s, a_s))^2 + \lambda \|w\|_2^2.$$

Then Algorithm 17.4 is equivalent to Algorithm 17.2. In particular, we have

$$\mathcal{F}_{t-1} = \{ f(w, x, a) \colon \|w - w_{t-1}\|_{A_{t-1}} \leq \beta_{t-1} \},$$

and

$$\max_{f \in \mathcal{F}_{t-1}} f(x_t, a) = w_{t-1}^\top \psi(x_t, a) + \beta_{t-1} \|\psi(x_t, a)\|_{A_{t-1}^{-1}}.$$

In general, the version space $\mathcal{F}_t$ in Algorithm 17.4 contains functions that fit well on historic data $\mathcal{S}_t$. In order to analyze such a version space algorithm, we need to introduce the concept of eluder coefficient.

Definition 17.17 Given a function class $\mathcal{F}$, its eluder coefficient $\mathrm{EC}(\epsilon, \mathcal{F}, T)$ is defined as the smallest number d so that for any sequence $\{(x_t, a_t)\}_{t=1}^T$ and $\{f_t\}_{t=1}^T \in \mathcal{F}$:

$$\sum_{t=2}^T [f_t(x_t, a_t) - f_*(x_t, a_t)] \leq \sqrt{d \sum_{t=2}^T \left(\epsilon + \sum_{s=1}^{t-1} |f_t(x_s, a_s) - f_*(x_s, a_s)|^2 \right)}.$$

The intuition behind the eluder coefficient is that, on average, if functions in the version space have small in-sample prediction error

$$\sum_{s=1}^{t-1} |f_t(x_s, a_s) - f_*(x_s, a_s)|^2$$

on the training data at each time step t, then the confidence interval $|f_t(x_t, a_t) - f_*(x_t, a_t)|$ on the next data point is also small (on average). This allows us to obtain the following generic theorem for version space–based upper confidence bound algorithm.

Lemma 17.18 *In Algorithm 17.4, assume that $f_* \in \mathcal{F}_{t-1}$ for all $t \leq T$, and there exists $\hat{f}_t$ and $\beta_t > 0$ such that*

$$\sup_{f \in \mathcal{F}_t} \sum_{s=2}^t |f(x_s, a_s) - \hat{f}_t(x_s, a_s)|^2 \leq \beta_t^2.$$

Then we have the following regret bound:

$$\sum_{t=2}^T [f_*(x_t) - f_*(x_t, a_t)] \leq \sqrt{\mathrm{EC}(\epsilon, \mathcal{F}, T) \left(\epsilon T + 4 \sum_{t=2}^T \beta_{t-1}^2 \right)}.$$

Proof We have

$$\begin{aligned} f_*(x_t) &- f_*(x_t, a_t) \\ &= f_*(x_t) - f_t(x_t) + f_t(x_t, a_t) - f_*(x_t, a_t) \\ &\leq f_t(x_t, a_t) - f_*(x_t, a_t). \end{aligned}$$

The first equality used $f_t(x_t, a_t) = f_t(x_t)$. The inequality used the fact that $f_* \in \mathcal{F}_{t-1}$ and thus $f_t(x_t) = \max_{f \in \mathcal{F}_{t-1}} f(x_t) \geq f_*(x_t)$.

We can now obtain

$$\sum_{t=2}^T [f_*(x_t) - f_*(x_t, a_t)]$$

$$\leq \sum_{t=2}^T [f_t(x_t, a_t) - f_*(x_t, a_t)]$$

$$\leq \sqrt{\mathrm{EC}(\epsilon, \mathcal{F}, T) \sum_{t=2}^T \left(\epsilon + \sum_{s=1}^{t-1} |f_t(x_s, a_s) - f_*(x_s, a_s)|^2 \right)}$$

$$\leq \sqrt{\mathrm{EC}(\epsilon, \mathcal{F}, T) \left(\epsilon T + 4 \sum_{t=2}^T \beta_{t-1}^2 \right)}.$$

The second inequality used the definition of $\mathrm{EC}(\epsilon, \mathcal{F}, T)$, and the third inequality used

$$\sum_{s=1}^{t-1} |f_t(x_s, a_s) - f_*(x_s, a_s)|^2$$

$$\leq 4 \sum_{s=1}^{t-1} [|f_t(x_s, a_s) - \hat{f}_{t-1}(x_s, a_s)|^2 + |f_*(x_s, a_s) - \hat{f}_{t-1}(x_s, a_s)|^2] \leq 4\beta_{t-1}^2.$$

This proves the desired bound. $\qquad\square$

Lemma 17.18 is a generic regret analysis for version space upper confidence bound algorithm, and the proof idea is similar to the upper confidence bound analysis in multi-armed bandits. It reduces the bandit regret analysis to in-sample prediction error estimation. The latter can be bounded using Theorem 13.15. This implies the following result.

Theorem 17.19 *Assume that*

$$r_t = f_*(x_t, a_t) + \epsilon_t,$$

where ϵ_t is conditional zero-mean sub-Gaussian noise: for all $\lambda \in \mathbb{R}$,

$$\ln \mathbb{E}[e^{\lambda \epsilon_t} | X_t, \mathcal{F}_{t-1}] \leq \frac{\lambda^2}{2}\sigma^2.$$

In Algorithm 17.4, we define

$$\hat{f}_t = \arg\min_{f \in \mathcal{F}} \sum_{s=1}^{t} (f(x_s, a_s) - r_s)^2,$$

and

$$\mathcal{F}_t = \left\{ f \in \mathcal{F}: \sum_{s=1}^{t} (f(x_s, a_s) - \hat{f}_t(x_s, a_s))^2 \leq \beta_t^2 \right\},$$

where

$$\beta_t^2 \geq \inf_{\epsilon>0} \left[8\epsilon t(\sigma + 2\epsilon) + 12\sigma^2 \ln(2N(\epsilon, \mathcal{F}, \|\cdot\|_\infty)/\delta) \right].$$

Then with probability at least $1 - \delta$,

$$\sum_{t=2}^{T} [f_*(x_t) - f_*(x_t, a_t)] \leq \sqrt{\mathrm{EC}(\epsilon, \mathcal{F}, T)\left(\epsilon T + 4\sum_{t=2}^{T} \beta_{t-1}^2\right)}.$$

Proof We note that Theorem 13.15 (with $\epsilon' = 0$) implies that $f_* \in \mathcal{F}_{t-1}$ for all $t \geq 2$. The result is a direct consequence of Lemma 17.18. $\qquad\square$

The following result shows that if a function class can be embedded into a RKHS (which does not need to be known to the algorithm), then its eluder coefficient is bounded.

Proposition 17.20 *Assume that $\mathcal{F} \subset \mathcal{H}$, where $\mathcal{H}$ is a RKHS that does not need to be known to the learning algorithm. For all $f \in \mathcal{H}$, we have the feature representation $f(x,a) = \langle w(f), \psi(x,a) \rangle$. Assume $\|w(f) - w(f_*)\|_{\mathcal{H}} \leq B$ for all $f \in \mathcal{F}$ and $f - f_* \in [-1,1]$ for all $f \in \mathcal{F}$. Then*

$$\mathrm{EC}(1, \mathcal{F}, T) \leq 2\mathrm{entro}(1/(B^2 T), \psi(\mathcal{X} \times \mathcal{A})), \tag{17.10}$$

where $\mathrm{entro}(\cdot)$ *is defined in Proposition 15.8. More generally, we have*

$$\mathrm{EC}(\epsilon, \mathcal{F}, T) \leq 4\mathrm{entro}(\lambda, \psi(\mathcal{X} \times \mathcal{A}))$$

with $\epsilon = \lambda B^2 T + \frac{2}{T}\mathrm{entro}(\lambda, \psi(\mathcal{X} \times \mathcal{A}))$.

Proof Let $A_0 = (\lambda T)I$ and $A_t = A_0 + \sum_{s=1}^{T} \psi(x_s, a_s)\psi(x_s, a_s)^\top$. Let $f_*(x,a) = \langle w_*, \psi(x,a) \rangle$ and $f_t(x,a) = \langle w_t, \psi(x,a) \rangle$. By using the Cauchy–Schwarz inequality, we obtain

$$|f_t(x_t, a_t) - f_*(x_t, a_t)| \leq \|w_t - w_*\|_{A_{t-1}} \|\psi(x_t, a_t)\|_{A_{t-1}^{-1}}. \tag{17.11}$$

We also have the following derivations:

$$\sum_{t=1}^{T} |f_t(x_t, a_t) - f_*(x_t, a_t)|$$

$$\leq \sum_{t=1}^{T} \|w_t - w_*\|_{A_{t-1}} \cdot \underbrace{\|\psi(x_t, a_t)\|_{A_{t-1}^{-1}} \cdot \mathbb{1}(\|\psi(x_t, a_t)\|_{A_{t-1}^{-1}} \leq 1)}_{b_t} \quad \text{(from (17.11))}$$

$$+ \sum_{t=1}^{T} \mathbb{1}(\|\psi(x_t, a_t)\|_{A_{t-1}^{-1}} \geq 1) \qquad\qquad (|f_t - f_*| \leq 1)$$

$$\leq \sqrt{\sum_{t=1}^{T} \|w_t - w_*\|_{A_{t-1}}^2} \sqrt{\sum_{t=1}^{T} b_t^2 + 2\sum_{t=1}^{T} \frac{\|\psi(x_t, a_t)\|_{A_{t-1}^{-1}}^2}{1 + \|\psi(x_t, a_t)\|_{A_{t-1}^{-1}}^2}}$$

$$\leq \sqrt{\sum_{t=1}^{T} \|w_t - w_*\|_{A_{t-1}}^2} \sqrt{2\ln|A_0^{-1} A_T| + 2\ln|A_0^{-1} A_T|}.$$

The second inequality used the Cauchy–Schwarz inequality to bound the first summation term, and algebra to bound the second summation term. The last inequality used Proposition 15.8 to bound the second summation term, and the following derivation to simplify the first term:

$$\sum_{t=1}^{T} b_t^2 \leq 2\sum_{t=1}^{T} \frac{\|\psi(x_t, a_t)\|_{A_{t-1}^{-1}}^2}{1 + \|\psi(x_t, a_t)\|_{A_{t-1}^{-1}}^2} \qquad\qquad \text{(algebra)}$$

$$\leq 2\ln|A_0^{-1} A_T|. \qquad\qquad \text{(Lemma 13.9)}$$

Let $d = \ln|A_0^{-1}A_T|$. We obtain

$$\sum_{t=1}^{T} |f_t(x_t, a_t) - f_*(x_t, a_t)|$$

$$\leq \sqrt{\sum_{t=1}^{T} \|w_t - w_*\|_{A_{t-1}}^2} \sqrt{2\ln|A_0^{-1}A_T|} + 2\ln|A_0^{-1}A_T|$$

$$\leq \sqrt{4d \sum_{t=1}^{T} \|w_t - w_*\|_{A_{t-1}}^2 + 8d^2}$$

$$= \sqrt{4d \sum_{t=1}^{T} \left[(\lambda T \|w_t - w_*\|_{\mathcal{H}}^2 + 2d/T) + \sum_{s=1}^{t-1} |f_t(x_s, a_s) - f_*(x_s, a_s)|^2 \right]}.$$

This implies the second desired bound. The proof of the first bound is left as an exercise. □

Example 17.21 If $\mathcal{F} \subset \mathcal{H} = \{w^\top \psi(x, a) \colon w \in \mathbb{R}^d\}$ can be embedded into a d-dimensional linear function class for a finite d, then we have the following bound from Proposition 17.20 and Proposition 15.8:

$$\mathrm{EC}(1, \mathcal{F}, T) \leq 2d \ln(1 + T(BB')^2/d).$$

Since Theorem 5.3 implies that the covering number of $\mathcal{F}$ is also $\tilde{O}(d)$, we can obtain the following regret bound from Theorem 17.19:

$$\sum_{t=2}^{T} [f_*(x_t) - f_*(x_t, a_t)] = \tilde{O}(d\sqrt{T}),$$

which is consistent with that of Theorem 17.11. One may also use Proposition 15.8 to obtain bounds for nonparametric models such as RKHS induced by RBF kernels (also see Example 15.10).

We note that unlike Algorithm 17.2, Algorithm 17.4 does not use the feature representation $\psi(x, a)$ explicitly. That is, Algorithm 17.4 allows a nonlinear function class that may be embedded in an RKHS with unknown feature $\psi(x, a)$. Therefore the algorithm is more flexible. Moreover, if we consider a function class $\mathcal{F}$ that can be represented as a function in RKHS $\mathcal{H}$, it may be a small subset of $\mathcal{H}$, which has a small covering number. This can also reduce the overall complexity.

In the literature, one often employs a slightly different concept called *eluder dimension*, which is defined in (17.22). We note that Definition 17.17 is more general because it can be shown that a small eluder dimension implies a small eluder coefficient (also see Dann et al., 2021). We leave it as an exercise.

Definition 17.22 (Eluder Dimension)   Given $\epsilon > 0$, the eluder dimension $\mathrm{Edim}(\mathcal{F}, \epsilon)$ of a function class $\mathcal{F}$ is the length of the longest possible sequence of elements $\{(x_t, a_t)\}$ so that for some $\epsilon' \geq \epsilon$ and $f' \in \mathcal{F}$, $\forall t \geq 2$,

$$\exists f_t \in \mathcal{F}: \quad \sum_{s=1}^{t-1} |f_t(x_s, a_s) - f'(x_s, a_s)| \leq (\epsilon')^2, \quad |f_t(x_t, a_t) - f'(x_t, a_t)| > \epsilon'.$$

17.4 Nonlinear Contextual Bandits with Decoupling Coefficient

The optimism-based contextual bandit algorithm described in Algorithm 17.4 requires an assumption on eluder coefficients, which may not behave well for general nonlinear function classes. In general, eluder coefficients allow mild nonlinearity, but the underlying structural assumption is analogous to linear function classes. On the other hand, it is known that if the number of arms K is finite, then it is possible to design a contextual bandit algorithm with sublinear regret. In this section, we present a variation of Thompson sampling called *Feel-Good Thompson sampling*, which can solve general nonlinear contextual bandits with a finite number of arms, as well as certain nonlinear contextual bandits with an infinite number of arms.

Definition 17.23   Given any value function $f \in \mathcal{F}$, let $\pi_f(x) \in \arg\min_a f(x, a)$ be the greedy policy induced by f. Given $\epsilon > 0$, the decoupling coefficient $\mathrm{DC}(\epsilon, \mathcal{F})$ of a function class $\mathcal{F}$ is defined as the smallest $d > 0$, so that for all distribution p on $\mathcal{F}$,

$$\mathbb{E}_{f \sim p}[f(x, \pi_f(x)) - f_*(x, \pi_f(x))]$$
$$\leq \sqrt{d\left(\epsilon + \mathbb{E}_{f' \sim p}\mathbb{E}_{f \sim p}[f'(x, \pi_f(x)) - f_*(x, \pi_f(x))]^2\right)}.$$

The following result indicates that the decoupling coefficient allows linear embedding of the function class with linear weight that can depend on the context x. This allows it to deal with much more general nonlinear function classes that cannot be handled by an eluder coefficient, such as general nonlinear function classes with a finite number of arms.

Definition 17.24 (Linearly Embeddable Condition)   Let $\mathcal{H}$ be a vector space with inner product $\langle \cdot, \cdot \rangle$. We say a function class $\mathcal{F}$ is linearly embeddable in $\mathcal{H}$ if there exists $\psi: \mathcal{X} \times \mathcal{A} \to \mathcal{H}$, and $w: \mathcal{F} \times \mathcal{X} \to \mathcal{H}$, so that for all $f \in \mathcal{F}$ and $(x, a) \in \mathcal{X} \times \mathcal{A}$, we have

$$f(x, a) = \langle w(f, x), \psi(x, a) \rangle.$$

The following result shows that decoupling coefficients can be estimated for linear embeddable function classes.

Proposition 17.25   *Assume that $\mathcal{F}$ satisfies Definition 17.24, and $\|w(f, x) - w(f_*, x)\|_{\mathcal{H}} \leq B$. Then*

$$DC(\lambda B^2, \mathcal{F}) \leq \dim(\lambda, \psi(\mathcal{X} \times \mathcal{A})),$$

where $\dim(\cdot)$ *is defined in Proposition 9.36.*

Proof Let $A(p) = \mathbb{E}_{f \sim p} \psi(x, \pi_f(x)) \psi(x, \pi_f(x))^\top$. We have

$$\mathbb{E}_{f \sim p}[f(x, \pi_f(x)) - f_*(x, \pi_f(x))]$$
$$= \mathbb{E}_{f \sim p} \langle w(f, x) - w(f_*, x), \psi(x, \pi_f(x)) \rangle$$
$$\leq \sqrt{\mathbb{E}_{f \sim p} \|w(f, x) - w(f_*, x)\|^2_{A(p)+\lambda I} \; \mathbb{E}_{f \sim p} \|\psi(x, \pi_f(x))\|^2_{(A(p)+\lambda I)^{-1}}}$$
$$= \sqrt{[\mathbb{E}_{f \sim p} \mathbb{E}_{f' \sim p}(f'(x, \pi_f(x)) - f_*(x, \pi_f(x)))^2 + \lambda \|w(f, x) - w(f_*, x)\|^2_{\mathcal{H}}]}$$
$$\times \sqrt{\mathrm{trace}((A(p) + \lambda I)^{-1} A(p))}.$$

The first inequality is Cauchy–Schwarz. We can now use $\lambda \|w(f, x) - w(f_*, x)\|^2_2 \leq \lambda B^2$ to obtain the desired bound. $\qquad \square$

Example 17.26 If there are only K arms: $a \in \{1, \ldots, K\}$, then $DC(\epsilon, \mathcal{F}) \leq K$ for all $\epsilon > 0$. This can be achieved by embedding all $f(x, a)$ to a weight vector $w(x)$ such that $w(x) = [f(1, x), \ldots, f(K, x)]$, and $\psi(x, a) = e_a$. The decoupling coefficient is bounded by $DC(0, \mathcal{F}) \leq K$.

This example shows that the decoupling coefficient in Definition 17.23 for finite arm nonlinear contextual bandits is always finite, which is a property that does not hold for eluder coefficient in Definition 17.17.

Example 17.27 Assume $\mathcal{F} \subset \mathcal{H}$ is linearly embeddable in an inner product space $\mathcal{H}$ with ψ. If $\mathcal{H}$ is finite dimensional, then $DC(0, \mathcal{F}) \leq \dim(\mathcal{H})$. An estimate for infinite-dimensional embeddings can be found in Proposition 9.36.

We now present an algorithm, referred to as *Feel-Good Thompson sampling*, which adds an optimistic prior to Thompson sampling. The resulting algorithm solves nonlinear contextual bandits under small decoupling coefficients. Given history $S_{t-1} = \{(x_1, a_1, r_1), \ldots, (x_{t-1}, a_{t-1}, r_{t-1})\}$, let $p_0(f)$ be an arbitrary prior distribution on $\mathcal{F}$. We define

$$p(f|S_{t-1}) \propto p_0(f) \exp \left(-\sum_{s=1}^{t-1} L(f, x_s, a_s, r_s) \right), \qquad (17.12)$$

where $L(f, x, a, r) = -\lambda f(x) + \eta(f(x, a) - r)^2$. The term $\lambda f(x)$ (referred to as the Feel-Good term) favors an optimistic value function $f(x)$, which plays a similar role to the upper confidence bound.

Algorithm 17.5 Feel-Good Thompson Sampling for Contextual Bandits

---

Input: p_0, T

1 **for** $t = 1, 2, \ldots, T$ **do**
2 $\quad$ Observe $x_t \in \mathcal{X}$
3 $\quad$ Draw $f_t \sim p(f|S_{t-1})$ according to (17.12)
4 $\quad$ Pull arm $a_t = \pi_{f_t}(x_t)$
5 $\quad$ Observe reward $r_t \in [0, 1]$

To analyze Algorithm 17.5, we need the following lemma, which can be used to reduce regret for contextual bandit problems into online regret analysis for random Gibbs algorithms.

Lemma 17.28 *Given any distribution p on f, we have for all $\mu > 0$,*

$$\underbrace{\mathbb{E}_{f \sim p}\left[f_*(x) - f_*(x, \pi_f(x))\right]}_{\text{bandit regret}} \leq \frac{DC(\epsilon, \mathcal{F})}{4\mu} + \sqrt{DC(\epsilon, \mathcal{F})\epsilon}$$

$$+ \mathbb{E}_{f' \sim p}\left[\underbrace{[f_*(x) - f'(x)]}_{\text{Feel-Good term}} + \mu \mathbb{E}_{f \sim p}\underbrace{[(f'(x, \pi_f(x)) - f_*(x, \pi_f(x)))^2]}_{\text{least squares loss}}\right].$$

Proof We note that $f(x) = f(x, \pi_f(x)))$. Therefore

$$\mathbb{E}_{f \sim p}[f_*(x) - f_*(x, \pi_f(x))] = \mathbb{E}_{f \sim p}[f_*(x) - f(x)]$$
$$+ \mathbb{E}_{f \sim p}[f(x, \pi_f(x)) - f_*(x, \pi_f(x))].$$

Using Definition 17.23, we have

$$\mathbb{E}_{f \sim p}[f(x, \pi_f(x)) - f_*(x, \pi_f(x))]$$
$$\leq \sqrt{DC(\epsilon, \mathcal{F})\left(\epsilon + \mathbb{E}_{f' \sim p}\mathbb{E}_{f \sim p}[(f'(x, \pi_f(x)) - f_*(x, \pi_f(x)))^2]\right)}$$
$$\leq \sqrt{DC(\epsilon, \mathcal{F})\epsilon} + \frac{DC(\epsilon, \mathcal{F})}{4\mu} + \mu \mathbb{E}_{f' \sim p}\mathbb{E}_{f \sim p}[(f'(x, \pi_f(x)) - f_*(x, \pi_f(x)))^2].$$

By combining the two inequalities, we obtain the desired bound. □

The lemma implies that bandit regret can be upper bounded with the Feel-Good term plus least squares loss. Next we show that both can be bounded using online learning analysis similar to that of Theorem 14.15 and Theorem 14.16.

Lemma 17.29 *Assume that $f \in [0,1]$ for all $f \in \mathcal{F}$. If $\eta \leq 0.5$, then the following bound holds for Algorithm 17.5:*

$$\mathbb{E}\sum_{t=1}^{T}\mathbb{E}_{f \sim p(\cdot|\mathcal{S}_{t-1})}\left[(0.5/\sqrt{e})\eta(f(x_t, a_t) - f_*(x_t, a_t))^2 + \lambda(f_*(x_t) - f(x_t))\right]$$

$$\leq \inf_{p}\left[\mathbb{E}_{f \sim p}\sum_{t=1}^{T}\Delta L(f, x_t, a_t, r_t) + KL(p\|p_0)\right] + \lambda^2 T/4,$$

where $\Delta L(f, x, a, r) = L(f, x, a, r) - L(f_*, x, a, r)$.

Proof Let

$$Z_t = -\ln \mathbb{E}_{f \sim p_0}\exp\left(-\sum_{t=1}^{t}\Delta L(f, x_t, a_t, r_t)\right)$$

be the log-partition function for observations up to time t. Let $p_{t-1}(f) = p(f|\mathcal{S}_{t-1})$.

We have

$$\mathbb{E}[Z_{t-1} - Z_t] = \mathbb{E} \ln \mathbb{E}_{f \sim p_{t-1}} \exp \left(-\Delta L(f, x_t, a_t, r_t) \right)$$

$$\leq \frac{1}{2} \mathbb{E} \ln \mathbb{E}_{f \sim p_{t-1}} \exp \left(2\lambda (f(x_t) - f_*(x_t)) \right)$$

$$+ \frac{1}{2} \mathbb{E} \ln \mathbb{E}_{f \sim p_{t-1}} \underbrace{\exp \left(-2\eta ((f(x_t, a_t,) - r_t)^2 - (f_*(x_t, a_t) - r_t)^2) \right)}_{A_t}$$

$$\leq \lambda \mathbb{E}_{f \sim p_{t-1}} (f(x_t) - f_*(x_t)) + \frac{\lambda^2}{4} + A_t. \tag{17.13}$$

The first inequality follows from Jensen's inequality and the convexity of the function $\ln \mathbb{E}_Z \exp(Z)$ in Z. The second inequality used the estimate of logarithmic moment generation function in Lemma 2.15 with $f - f_* \in [-1, 1]$.

Next, we introduce the simplified notation

$$\Delta f(x, a) = f(x, a) - f_*(x, a)$$

and bound A_t as follows:

$$A_t = \frac{1}{2} \mathbb{E} \ln \mathbb{E}_{f \sim p_{t-1}} \exp \left(-2\eta (\Delta f(x_t, a_t)^2 + 4\eta (\Delta f(x_t, a_t) \epsilon(x_t, a_t)) \right)$$

$$\leq \frac{1}{2} \mathbb{E} \ln \mathbb{E}_{f \sim p_{t-1}} \mathbb{E}_{r_t | x_t, a_t} \exp \left(-2\eta (\Delta f(x_t, a_t)^2 + 4\eta \Delta f(x_t, a_t)(r_t - f_*(x_t, a_t)) \right)$$

$$\leq \frac{1}{2} \mathbb{E} \ln \mathbb{E}_{f \sim p_{t-1}} \exp \left(-2\eta (1 - \eta) \Delta f(x_t, a_t,)^2 \right)$$

$$\leq -\eta (1 - \eta) e^{-2\eta(1-\eta)} \mathbb{E} \, \mathbb{E}_{f \sim p_{t-1}} \Delta f(x_t, a_t)^2. \tag{17.14}$$

The first inequality used Jensen's inequality to move $\mathbb{E}_{r_t | x_t, a_t}$ into the concave function $\ln(\cdot)$. The second inequality used Lemma 2.15 and $\mathbb{E}\left[r_t | x_t, a_t\right] = f_*(x_t, a_t)$. The third inequality used $\ln \mathbb{E} \exp(Z) \leq \exp(c) \mathbb{E}[Z]$ when $c \leq Z \leq 0$.

By combining the previous inequalities, and summing over t, we obtain

$$\mathbb{E} \sum_{t=1}^{T} \left[0.5\eta e^{-0.5} \mathbb{E}_{f \sim p_{t-1}} \Delta f(x_t, a_t,)^2 + \lambda \mathbb{E}_{f \sim p_{t-1}} (f_*(x_t) - f(x_t)) \right]$$

$$\leq \mathbb{E} \sum_{t=1}^{T} \left[\eta (1 - \eta) e^{-2\eta(1-\eta)} \mathbb{E}_{f \sim p_{t-1}} \Delta f(x_t, a_t,)^2 + \lambda \mathbb{E}_{f \sim p_{t-1}} (f_*(x_t) - f(x_t)) \right]$$

$$\leq \mathbb{E} \sum_{t=1}^{T} \left[-A_t + \lambda \mathbb{E}_{f \sim p_{t-1}} (f_*(x_t) - f(x_t)) \right]$$

$$\leq \sum_{t=1}^{T} [\ln Z_t - \ln Z_{t-1} + \lambda^2 / 4]$$

$$= Z_T + \lambda^2 T / 4.$$

The first inequality used $\eta \leq 0.5$. The second inequality used (17.14). The third inequality used (17.13). We can now use Proposition 7.16 to reformulate the log-partition function Z_T, and obtain the desired bound. $\square$

Theorem 17.30 *Assume that $f \in [0,1]$ for all $f \in \mathcal{F}$. If $\eta \leq 0.5$, then the following bound holds for Algorithm 17.5:*

$$\mathbb{E} \, \mathrm{REG}_T \leq \frac{1}{\lambda} \mathbb{E} \inf_p \left[\mathbb{E}_{f \sim p} \sum_{t=1}^T \Delta L(f, x_t, a_t, r_t) + \mathrm{KL}(p \| p_0) \right]$$
$$+ \frac{\lambda T}{4} + \sqrt{\mathrm{DC}(\epsilon, \mathcal{F}) \epsilon} \, T + \frac{\lambda \mathrm{DC}(\epsilon, \mathcal{F})}{\eta} T,$$

where $\Delta L(f, x, a, r) = L(f, x, a, r) - L(f_*, x, a, r)$.

Proof With $\lambda \mu = 0.5 \eta / \sqrt{e}$, we obtain

$\mathbb{E} \, \mathrm{REG}_T$

$$\leq \sum_{t=1}^T \frac{\mathrm{DC}(\epsilon, \mathcal{F})}{4\mu} + \sqrt{\mathrm{DC}(\epsilon, \mathcal{F}) \epsilon} \, T$$

$$+ \frac{1}{\lambda} \mathbb{E} \sum_{t=1}^T \mathbb{E}_{f' \sim p(\cdot | \mathcal{S}_{t-1})} \left[\lambda [f_*(x_t) - f'(x_t)] + \lambda \mu (f'(x_t, a_t) - f_*(x_t, a_t))^2 \right]$$

(Lemma 17.28)

$$\leq \sum_{t=1}^T \frac{\mathrm{DC}(\epsilon, \mathcal{F})}{4\mu} + \sqrt{\mathrm{DC}(\epsilon, \mathcal{F}) \epsilon} \, T$$

$$+ \frac{1}{\lambda} \mathbb{E} \inf_p \left[\mathbb{E}_{f \sim p} \sum_{t=1}^T \Delta L(f, x_t, a_t, r_t) + \mathrm{KL}(p \| p_0) \right] + \lambda T / 4, \quad \text{(Lemma 17.29)}$$

which implies the result by noting that $\mu^{-1} \leq 4\lambda / \eta$. □

Example 17.31 Consider the special case that both the number of arms and the function class $\mathcal{F}$ are finite in Theorem 17.30. We have

$$\inf_p \left[\mathbb{E}_{f \sim p} \sum_{t=1}^T \Delta L(f, x_t, a_t, r_t) + \mathrm{KL}(p \| p_0) \right] \leq \ln |\mathcal{F}|.$$

Since $\mathrm{DC}(0, \mathcal{F}) \leq |\mathcal{A}|$, we obtain the following bound for nonlinear contextual bandit problems with $\epsilon = 0$, $\eta = 0.5$ and $\lambda = \sqrt{\ln |\mathcal{F}| / (|\mathcal{A}| T)}$:

$$\mathbb{E} \, \mathrm{REG}_T = O\left(\sqrt{|\mathcal{A}| T \ln |\mathcal{F}|} \right).$$

Example 17.32 For infinite $\mathcal{F}$, the term

$$\kappa = \inf_p \left[\mathbb{E}_{f \sim p} \sum_{t=1}^T \Delta L(f, x_t, a_t, r_t) + \mathrm{KL}(p \| p_0) \right]$$

can be regarded as the analogy of ERM sample complex caused by covering numbers. If we define the following ball in L_∞ metric:

$$\mathcal{F}(\epsilon) = \left\{ f \in \mathcal{F} : \sup_{x,a,r} |\Delta L(f,x,a,r)| \leq \epsilon \right\},$$

then we may take $p(f) = p_0(f) \mathbb{1}(f \in \mathcal{F}(\epsilon))/p_0(\mathcal{F}(\epsilon))$ to obtain $\kappa \leq \epsilon - \ln p_0(\mathcal{F}(\epsilon))$. We thus obtain

$$\kappa \leq \inf_{\epsilon > 0} [\epsilon - \ln p_0(\mathcal{F}(\epsilon))].$$

Next, we show that the result obtained in Example 17.31 matches the following lower bound up to logarithmic factors.

Theorem 17.33   *Consider $K \geq 2$ and $d \geq 1$. There exists a bandit problem with $\{0,1\}$-valued rewards, such that the realizable condition holds with $|\mathcal{A}| = K$, $|\mathcal{F}| = K^d$, so that the expected regret of any bandit algorithm $\hat{q}$ is at least*

$$\min\left(0.02T, 0.06\sqrt{KdT} \right).$$

Proof   We would like to apply Theorem 13.24 with $m = K$. We consider finite $\mathcal{X} = \{1, \ldots, d\}$ with d different contexts. Consider the class of all possible deterministic policies $\mathcal{G} = \{\tau \colon \mathcal{X} \to [K]\}$, which contains $|\mathcal{G}| = K^d$ policies. For each policy τ, we define its value function

$$f^\tau(x,a) = \begin{cases} 0.5 + \epsilon & \text{if } a = \tau(x), \\ 0.5 & \text{otherwise,} \end{cases}$$

where $\epsilon \in (0, 0.1]$ will be specified later. For each j, we assume also that

$$f_j^\tau(x,a) = \begin{cases} 0.5 & \text{if } x = j, \\ f^\tau(x,a) & \text{otherwise.} \end{cases}$$

We now consider the $\{0,1\}$-valued reward distribution

$$q^\tau(r|x,a) = \text{Bernoulli}(f^\tau(x,a)), \qquad q_j^\tau(r|x,a) = \text{Bernoulli}(f_j^\tau(x,a)).$$

Given a (random) policy π that returns a distribution $\pi(a|x)$ for all $x \in \mathcal{X}$, we can define

$$q^\tau(r|\pi,x) = \mathbb{E}_{a \sim \pi(\cdot|x)} q^\tau(r|x,a),$$

and similarly for $q_j^\tau(r|\pi,x)$. Let $\tau \sim_j \tau'$ if $\tau(x)$ and $\tau'(x)$ differs at most at $x = j$. Assume that we choose context in $\mathcal{X}$ uniformly at random. Let $\theta = \theta(\cdot|x)$ be a policy learned from a bandit algorithm. We can decompose the regret of θ as

$$Q(\theta, q^\tau) = \frac{1}{d} \sum_{j=1}^{d} \epsilon \, \mathbb{E}_{a \sim \theta(\cdot|x=j)} \mathbb{1}\left(a \neq \tau(j) \right) = \sum_{j=1}^{d} Q_j(\theta, q^\tau),$$

where

$$Q_j(\theta, q^\tau) = \frac{\epsilon}{d} \, \mathbb{E}_{a \sim \theta(\cdot|j)} \mathbb{1}(a \neq \tau(j)).$$

This implies that when $\tau \sim_j \tau'$ and $\tau \neq \tau'$,

$$Q_j(\theta, q^\tau) + Q_j(\theta, q^{\tau'}) \geq \frac{\epsilon}{d}.$$

We can now set $\epsilon = \min(0.1, 0.24\sqrt{Kd/T})$, and apply Theorem 13.24 with $m = K$. Given any bandit algorithm $\hat{q}$, and time step t, we have

$$\frac{1}{K} \sum_{\tau' \sim_j \tau} \mathrm{KL}(q_j^\tau(\cdot|\hat{q}(\mathcal{S}_{t-1}), \mathcal{S}_{t-1})||q^{\tau'}(\cdot|\hat{q}(\mathcal{S}_{t-1}), \mathcal{S}_{t-1})))$$

$$\leq \frac{1}{dK} \sup_{a_t} \sum_{\tau' \sim_j \tau} \mathrm{KL}(q_j^\tau(\cdot|a_t, x_t = j)||q^{\tau'}(\cdot|a_t, x_t = j))$$

$$= \frac{1}{dK}\mathrm{KL}(0.5||0.5 + \epsilon) \leq \frac{2.1}{dK}\epsilon^2.$$

The first inequality used the fact that $\mathrm{KL}(\cdot||\cdot) = 0$ when $x_t \neq j$, and the probability of $x_t = j$ is $1/d$. The last inequality used $\epsilon \leq 0.1$ and Exercise 16.4. We can thus take $\beta_{j,t}^2 = \frac{2.1}{dK}\epsilon^2$ in Theorem 13.24, and obtain at the end of the $n \leq T$ iteration that $\hat{\theta}$ returned by $\hat{q}$ satisfies

$$\frac{1}{K^d} \sum_\tau \mathbb{E}_{q^\tau} \mathbb{E}_{\hat{\theta}} \, Q(\hat{\theta}, q^\tau) \geq 0.5d\frac{\epsilon}{d}\left(1 - \sqrt{2 \times \frac{2.1n}{dK}\epsilon^2}\right)$$

$$\geq 0.25\epsilon = 0.25\min\left(0.1, 0.24\sqrt{Kd/T}\right).$$

The second inequality used $n\epsilon^2/(dK) \leq 0.24^2$. Since this bound holds for all $n \leq T$, we obtain the desired result. $\qquad\square$

17.5 Nonlinear Bandits with Coverage Coefficient

In this section, we consider the pure exploration setting for nonlinear contextual bandits.

Definition 17.34 Consider a stochastic contextual bandit problem, in which the context comes from a fixed distribution: $x \sim \mathcal{D}$. Let π_E be a bandit policy, (referred to as an *exploration policy*). Given any integer T, the goal of the pure exploration problem in contextual bandits is to design an exploration policy π_E, and draw T samples $x_t \sim \mathcal{D}$ and $a_t \sim \pi_E(\cdot|x_t)$ ($t = 1, \ldots, T$), so that one can learn a bandit policy $\hat{\pi}$ from the samples with small regret:

$$\mathrm{REG}(\hat{\pi}) = \mathbb{E}_{x \sim \mathcal{D}}\mathbb{E}_{a \sim \hat{\pi}(\cdot|x)}[f_*(x) - f_*(x, a)],$$

where f_* is the true value function.

In the following, we show that it is possible to design a pure exploration strategy to solve the stochastic nonlinear bandit problem if the problem is realizable and linearly embeddable. This is comparable to the problems that we can solve with Feel-Good Thompson sampling from Section 17.4. However, instead of the decoupling coefficient, we will introduce the following concept of the coverage coefficient.

Definition 17.35 The contextual coverage coefficient of a contextual bandit policy π is defined as

$$\mathrm{CC}_{\mathcal{X}}(\epsilon, \pi, \mathcal{F}) = \sup_{x \in \mathcal{X}} \mathrm{CC}(\epsilon, \pi(\cdot|x), \mathcal{F}),$$

where

$$\mathrm{CC}(\epsilon, \pi(\cdot|x), \mathcal{F}) = \sup_{a \in \mathcal{A}} \sup_{f, f' \in \mathcal{F}} \frac{|f(x, a) - f'(x, a)|^2}{\epsilon + \mathbb{E}_{\tilde{a} \sim \pi(\cdot|x)}(f(x, \tilde{a}) - f'(x, \tilde{a}))^2}$$

is defined for any distribution over $\mathcal{A}$ according to Definition 9.42.

The coverage coefficient in Definition 17.35 is the conditional version of the coverage coefficient in Definition 9.42. Theorem 9.44 implies that the coverage coefficient is small for linearly embeddable function classes.

Proposition 17.36 *Let $\mathcal{F}$ be a function class that is linearly embeddable in $\mathcal{H}$ according to Definition 17.24. Let π_G be a pure exploration policy so that for each $x \in \mathcal{X}$, $\pi_G(\cdot|x)$ is the solution of the G-optimal design problem (over $\mathcal{A}$, conditioned on x) in Definition 9.42:*

$$\pi_G(\cdot|x) = \min_{\pi \in \Delta(\mathcal{A})} \mathrm{CC}\left(\epsilon, \pi, \mathcal{F}_x\right), \quad \mathcal{F}_x = \{f(x, \cdot) : f \in \mathcal{F}\},$$

then with $\|w(f, x) - w(f', x)\|_{\mathcal{H}} \leq B$ for all $f, f' \in \mathcal{F}$,

$$\mathrm{CC}_{\mathcal{X}}(\epsilon, \pi_G, \mathcal{F}) \leq \dim(\epsilon/B^2, \psi(\mathcal{X} \times \mathcal{A})).$$

The following proposition shows that one can reduce the contextual bandit problem in the pure exploration setting to a supervised least squares regression problem. It plays a similar role to Lemma 17.28, which employs the decoupling coefficient.

Proposition 17.37 *Assume that $f_* \in \mathcal{F}$, and the context x is drawn from a fixed distribution $\mathcal{D}$ on $\mathcal{X}$. For any exploration policy π_E, and $f \in \mathcal{F}$, we have*

$$\mathrm{REG}(\pi_f) \leq 2\sqrt{d\epsilon} + 2\sqrt{d\mathbb{E}_{x \sim \mathcal{D}}\mathbb{E}_{a \sim \pi_E(\cdot|x)}(f(x, a) - f_*(x, a))^2},$$

where $d = \mathrm{CC}_{\mathcal{X}}(\epsilon, \pi_E, \mathcal{F})$ and π_f is the greedy policy of f.

Proof We note that

$$\mathbb{E}_{x \sim \mathcal{D}}\left[f_*(x) - f_*(x, \pi_f(x))\right]$$
$$\leq \mathbb{E}_{x \sim \mathcal{D}}\left[f_*(x, \pi_{f_*}(x)) - f(x, \pi_{f_*}(x)) + f(x, \pi_f(x)) - f_*(x, \pi_f(x))\right]$$
$$\leq 2\mathbb{E}_{x \sim \mathcal{D}} \sup_{a \in \mathcal{A}} |f(x, a) - f_*(x, a)|$$
$$\leq 2\sqrt{\mathbb{E}_{x \sim \mathcal{D}} \sup_{a \in \mathcal{A}} (f(x, a) - f_*(x, a))^2}$$
$$\leq 2\sqrt{d\epsilon + d\mathbb{E}_{x \sim \mathcal{D}}\mathbb{E}_{a \sim \pi_E(\cdot|x)} (f(x, a) - f_*(x, a))^2}.$$

The first inequality used the fact that $0 \leq -f(x, \pi_{f_*}(x)) + f(x, \pi_f(x))$, which follows from the definition of greedy policy π_f. The third inequality used Jensen's inequality and the concavity of $\sqrt{\cdot}$. The last inequality used the definition of coverage coefficient. This implies the desired bound. $\qquad\square$

Proposition 17.37 reduces a bandit problem in the pure exploration setting to a supervised learning problem. We can simply draw T samples $x_1, \ldots, x_T$ from $\mathcal{D}$, and draw $a_t \sim \pi(\cdot|x_t)$. This means that the generalization error

$$\mathbb{E}_{x \sim \mathcal{D}} \mathbb{E}_{a \sim \pi_E(\cdot|x)} (f(x, a) - f_*(x, a))^2$$

can be established for the ERM method or the Gibbs algorithm as in Section 12.4.

Example 17.38   Assume that both $\mathcal{F}$ and $\mathcal{A}$ are finite. Let π_E be the uniform distribution over $\mathcal{A}$ and let $\epsilon = 0$. We have $\text{CC}_{\mathcal{X}}(0, \pi_E, \mathcal{F}) \leq K$. Given T samples with the pure exploration policy π_E, let

$$f_T = \arg\min_{f \in \mathcal{F}} \sum_{t=1}^{T} (f(x_t, a_t) - r_t)^2.$$

Then it follows from Section 12.4 that with probability $1 - \delta$,

$$\mathbb{E}_{x \sim \mathcal{D}} \left(f_T(x, \pi(x)) - f_*(x, \pi(x))\right)^2 = O\left(\frac{\ln(|\mathcal{F}|/\delta))}{T}\right).$$

This implies that

$$\text{REG}(\pi_{f_T}) = O\left(\sqrt{\frac{|\mathcal{A}| \ln(|\mathcal{F}|/\delta)}{T}}\right).$$

In the pure exploration setting, the performance of the greedy policy of f_T is comparable to that of Thompson sampling in Example 17.31 by using online to batch conversion.

17.6 Historical and Bibliographical Remarks

The EXP4 algorithm was studied in Auer et al. (2002b) as an extension of EXP3. It handles general policy classes that can change over time, and thus the result can be directly applied to a contextual bandit in the adversarial setting. The problem of contextual bandit (or bandit with side information) was formulated more explicitly by Langford and Zhang (2007). It was argued in Langford and Zhang (2007) that EXP4 is not an efficient algorithm for contextual bandit because the computation of

$$\mathbb{E}_{w \sim p_{t-1}(w)} \hat{q}_t(a|w, x_t)$$

is difficult to implement efficiently. An empirical risk-minimization oracle-based method called *epoch greedy* was investigated in Langford and Zhang (2007).

However, epoch greedy has a suboptimal regret of $O(T^{2/3})$ instead of the regret of $O(\sqrt{T})$ for EXP4. The gap was closed in subsequent works (Dudik et al., 2011; Agarwal et al., 2014) using more complicated algorithms with empirical minimization oracles. However, these algorithms are policy based, and the empirical minimization problems require solutions of classification problems. More recently, significant interest has been given to value function-based approaches that use regression instead of classification (see Agarwal et al., 2012).

The first model for a value function-based approach to the contextual bandit problem is the stochastic linear bandit model, where the number of arms can be infinite. The UCB-style algorithms for this model have been analyzed in the literature (Auer, 2002; Dani et al., 2008; Abbasi-Yadkori et al., 2011; Chu et al., 2011). One version of the resulting UCB algorithm is described in Algorithm 17.2, and was analyzed in Dani et al. (2008) and Abbasi-Yadkori et al. (2011). A matching lower bound similar to Theorem 17.13 was also obtained by Dani et al. (2008). It is relatively easy to apply Thompson sampling to linear contextual bandits (see Agrawal and Goyal, 2013b; Russo and Van Roy, 2016). However, the regret bound obtained in Agrawal and Goyal (2013b) is superlinear in d, and hence inferior to that of the ridge regression with UCB. The suboptimality can be addressed by using Feel-Good Thompson sampling (Zhang, 2022).

The idea of eluder dimension was introduced by Russo and Van Roy (2013), and adopted recently by various researchers as a technique to generalize UCB-[based] based linear bandit and reinforcement learning models to nonlinear models. The resulting technique can be considered as a nonlinear generalization of UCB. Section 17.3 employs a different treatment via eluder coefficient instead of eluder dimension. The concept of eluder coefficient was introduced by Dann et al. (2021), and it was shown that a small eluder dimension implies a small eluder coefficient. We note that eluder coefficient was referred to as decoupling coefficient in Dann et al. (2021). However, due to the close relationship of eluder coefficient and eluder dimension, and the distinctive difference between eluder coefficient and decoupling coefficient, we adopt the more appropriate term eluder coefficient in this book.

The value function-based approach to nonlinear contextual bandit problems was considered in Agarwal et al. (2012). A general solution to this problem using online regression oracle was obtained by Foster and Rakhlin (2020). It was shown by Simchi-Levi and Xu (2021) that this method can be regarded as an approximate solution of Dudik et al. (2011). More recently, it was shown by Zhang (2022) that general nonlinear contextual bandits can also be solved using a modification of Thompson sampling, referred as Feel-Good Thompson sampling, which incorporates an optimistic exploration term. It was shown in Zhang (2022) that this optimistic term is necessary, and without this term, the standard Thompson sampling algorithm will not be able to solve the nonlinear contextual bandit problem.

Exercises

17.1 In Algorithm 17.2 for stochastic linear contextual bandits, we consider a pure exploration scheme where we choose the arm in line 6 according to confidence as

$$a_t \in \arg\max_a \psi(x_t, a)^\top A_{t-1}^{-1} \psi(x_t, a).$$

Similar to Lemma 17.8, we would like to derive an upper confidence bound after step T, but instead of a uniform bound for all $u \in \mathbb{R}^d$, we consider a bound for any fixed vector $u \in \mathbb{R}^d$. Given any fixed $u \in \mathbb{R}^d$, show that with probability at least $1 - \delta$,

$$|u^\top(w_* - w_T)| \leq \tilde{\beta}_T \sqrt{u^\top A_T^{-1} u}$$

for some $\tilde{\beta}_T$ that is independent of d.

- Show that for appropriately defined γ_t,

$$u^\top(w_* - w_T) = \lambda u^\top A_T^{-1} w_* + \sum_{t=1}^{T} \gamma_t \epsilon_t(x_t, a_t),$$

where $\{\gamma_t\}$ and $\{\epsilon_t(x_t, a_t)\}$ are independent.

- Use Azuma's inequality to obtain a concentration bound so that

$$\Pr\left[|u^\top(w_* - w_T)| > \tilde{\beta}_T \sqrt{u^\top A_T^{-1} u}\right] \leq \delta,$$

with appropriately chosen $\tilde{\beta}_T$ independent of d. As in Lemma 17.8, we assume that $\|w_*\|_2 \leq B$ with known B, and for all t, $r_t(x_t, a_t) \in [0, M]$.

- Assume we have K arms. Define $\tilde{\beta}_T$ so that with probability at least $1 - \delta$, the following inequality holds uniformly for all $a \in \{1, \ldots, K\}$:

$$|\psi(x_{T+1}, a)^\top(w_* - w_T)| \leq \tilde{\beta}_T \sqrt{\psi(x_{T+1}, a)^\top A_T^{-1} \psi(x_{T+1}, a)}.$$

Compare this bound to that of Lemma 17.8. Why can we not use this better $\tilde{\beta}_T$ for β_T in the original Algorithm 17.2?

17.2 Consider stochastic linear bandit with $K = 2^s$ arms and feature dimension d with $s \leq d$. Construct an example, so that the regret of any bandit algorithm is at least

$$\Omega(\sqrt{sdT}).$$

17.3 Prove Proposition 17.16.

17.4 Prove (17.10) by using the following inequality with $A_{t-1} = B^{-2} I + A_{t-1}$:

$$|f_t(x_t, a_t) - f_*(x_t, a_t)|^2 \leq \left(\|w_t - w_*\|_{A_{t-1}}^2 + 1\right) \min\left(1, \|\psi(x_t, a_t)\|_{A_{t-1}^{-1}}^2\right).$$

17.5 Compute the eluder coefficient of a function class under the conditions of Example 9.10.

17.6 Use Theorem 13.22 to derive a lower bound for the construction in Theorem 17.33, and compare the result to that of Theorem 17.33.

17.7 Show that the eluder coefficient $\mathrm{EC}(\epsilon, \mathcal{F}, T) = \tilde{O}(\mathrm{Edim}(\mathcal{F}, \epsilon))$, where $\tilde{O}$ hides a logarithmic factor.

17.8 Assume that $\mathcal{F}$ is linearly embeddable with $\dim(\epsilon, \psi(\mathcal{X})) \leq c_0/\epsilon^p$ for some $p, c_0 > 0$, and assume that $\mathcal{F}$ has $L_\infty(\mathcal{D})$ covering number $N(\epsilon, \mathcal{F}, L_\infty(\mathcal{D})) \leq c_1/\epsilon^q$ for some $c_1, q > 0$. Derive a regret bound for an appropriately designed bandit algorithm in the pure exploration setting.

18

Reinforcement Learning

This chapter describes some theoretical results of reinforcement learning, and the analysis may be regarded as a natural generalization of technique introduced for contextual bandit problems. In the literature, there are two formulations of reinforcement learning, episodic reinforcement learning, and reinforcement learning with discounted rewards. We focus on episodic reinforcement learning in this chapter, due to its close relationship with contextual bandits. Generally speaking, results for episodic reinforcement learning can be converted into results for discounted reinforcement learning. An episodic MDP, illustrated in Figure 18.1, can be formally defined.

Definition 18.1 An episodic Markov decision process (MDP) of length H, denoted by $M = \text{MDP}(\mathcal{X}, \mathcal{A}, P)$, contains a state space $\mathcal{X}$, an action space $\mathcal{A}$, and probability measures $\{P^h(r^h, x^{h+1}|x^h, a^h)\}_{h=1}^H$. At each step $h \in [H] = \{1, \dots, H\}$, we observe a state $x^h \in \mathcal{X}$ and take action $a^h \in \mathcal{A}$. We then get a reward r^h and go to the next state x^{h+1} with probability $P^h(r^h, x^{h+1}|x^h, a^h)$. We assume that x^1 is drawn from an unknown but fixed distribution.

A random policy π is a set of conditional probability $\pi^h(a^h|x^h)$ that determines the probability of taking action a^h on state x^h at step h. If a policy π is deterministic, then we also write the action a^h it takes at x^h as $\pi^h(x^h) \in \mathcal{A}$.

The policy π interacts with the MDP in an episode as follows: for step $h = 1, \dots, H$, the player observes x^h, and draws $a^h \sim \pi(a^h|x^h)$; the MDP returns (r^h, x^{h+1}). The reward of the episode is

$$\sum_{h=1}^H [r^h].$$

The observation $(x, a, r) = \{(x^h, a^h, r^h)\}_{h=1}^H$ is called a trajectory, and each policy π, when interacting with the MDP, defines a distribution over trajectories, which we denote as $(x, a, r) \sim \pi$. The value of a policy π is defined as its expected reward:

$$V_\pi = \mathbb{E}_{(x,a,r)\sim\pi} \sum_{h=1}^H [r^h].$$

We note that the state x^{H+1} has no significance as the episode ends after taking action a^h at x^h and observe the reward r^h.

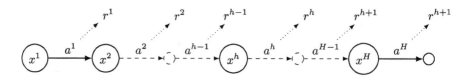

Figure 18.1 Episodic Markov decision process

With this definition of episodic MDP, we can now introduce the episodic reinforcement learning problem as follows.

Definition 18.2 In episodic reinforcement learning (RL), we consider an episodic MDP. The player interacts with the MDP via a repeated game: at each time (episode) t:

- The player chooses a policy π_t based on historic observations.
- The policy interacts with the MDP, and generates a trajectory $(x_t, a_t, r_t) = \{(x_t^h, a_t^h, r_t^h)\}_{h=1}^H \sim \pi_t$.

The regret of episodic reinforcement learning is

$$\sum_{t=1}^T [V_* - V_{\pi_t}],$$

where $V_* = \sup_\pi V_\pi$ is the optimal value function.

One may also define the optimal value function within a policy class, and define the regret with respect to the optimal policy in this class. Note that in the case of contextual bandits, EXP4 can be used to solve such a problem. However, it is nontrivial to generalize an EXP4-style algorithm to handle episodic RL without suffering an exponential dependency in H. Therefore we will focus on value function-based algorithms by extending value function-based contextual bandit analysis. Under the realizability assumption, the resulting regret bound can compete with the optimal value function achieved with the best policy over the class of all possible policies.

Example 18.3 (Contextual Bandits) Consider the episodic MDP with $H = 1$. We observe $x^1 \in \mathcal{X}$, take action $a^1 \in \mathcal{A}$, and observe reward $r^1 \in \mathbb{R}$. This case is the same as contextual bandits.

Example 18.4 (Tabular MDP) In a Tabular MDP, both $\mathcal{X}$ and $\mathcal{A}$ are finite: $|\mathcal{X}| = S$ and $|\mathcal{A}| = A$. It follows that the transition probability at each step h

$$\{P^h(x^{h+1}|x^h, a^h) : h = 1, \ldots, H\}$$

can be expressed using HS^2A numbers. The expected reward $\mathbb{E}[r^h|x^h, a^h]$ can be expressed using HSA numbers.

Example 18.5 (LQR) A linear quadratic regulator (LQR) has state space $\mathcal{X} = \mathbb{R}^d$ and $\mathcal{A} = \mathbb{R}^k$. The transition probability is given by

$$x^{h+1} = A^h x^h + B^h a^h + \epsilon^h,$$

where $\epsilon^h \sim N(0, \sigma^2 I)$ is Gaussian noise. The reward is

$$r^h = -[(x^h)^\top Q^h x^h + (a^h)^\top R^h a^h],$$

where Q^h and R^h are positive semi-definite matrices.

18.1 Value Functions of Episodic MDP

In a value function-based approach to RL, we consider value functions as follows.

Definition 18.6 Given any policy π, we can define its value function (also referred to as the Q-function in the literature) starting at a state–action pair (x^h, a^h) at step h as

$$Q_\pi^h(x^h, a^h) = \sum_{h'=h}^{H} \mathbb{E}_{r^{h'} \sim \pi|(x^h, a^h)}[r^{h'}],$$

where $r^{h'} \sim \pi|(x^h, a^h)$ is the reward distribution at step h' conditioned on starting from state–action pair (x^h, a^h) at step h. Similarly, we also define

$$V_\pi^h(x^h) = \sum_{h'=h}^{H} \mathbb{E}_{r^{h'} \sim \pi|x^h}[r^{h'}].$$

By convention, we set $V_\pi^{H+1}(x^{H+1}) \equiv 0$.

We note that the value of a policy π can be expressed as

$$V_\pi = \mathbb{E}_{x^1} V_\pi^1(x^1),$$

where the distribution of x^1 is independent of π.

The following result is a straightforward application of the definition of value function. We leave it as an exercise.

Proposition 18.7 *We have*

$$Q_\pi^h(x^h, a^h) = \mathbb{E}_{r^h, x^{h+1}|x^h, a^h}[r^h + V_\pi^{h+1}(x^{h+1})],$$
$$V_\pi^h(x^h) = \mathbb{E}_{a^h \sim \pi^h(\cdot|x^h)} Q_\pi^h(x^h, a^h).$$

We may also define the optimal value functions that are the best possible value function achieved by any policy, starting from an arbitrary state x^h or state–action pair (x^h, a^h) at step h.

Definition 18.8 The optimal value functions starting at step h are given by

$$Q_*^h(x^h, a^h) = \sup_\pi Q_\pi^h(x^h, a^h), \qquad V_*^h(x^h) = \sup_\pi V_\pi^h(x^h).$$

We also define the optimal value as $V_* = \mathbb{E}_{x^1} V_*^1(x^1)$.

In the following, for notation simplicity, we assume that the solution to

$$\arg\max_{a \in \mathcal{A}} Q_*^h(x^h, a)$$

can be achieved by some $a \in \mathcal{A}$ so that the greedy policy in Theorem 18.9 can be properly defined. The following theorem describes key properties of optimal value functions and optimal policy for reinforcement learning. The proof is straightforward, and we leave it as an exercise.

Theorem 18.9 *The optimal Q-function Q_* satisfies the Bellman equation:*

$$Q_*^h(x^h, a^h) = \mathbb{E}_{r^h, x^{h+1} | x^h, a^h} \left[r^h + V_*^{h+1}(x^{h+1}) \right].$$

The optimal value function satisfies

$$V_*^h(x^h) = \max_{a \in \mathcal{A}} Q_*^h(x^h, a),$$

and the optimal value function can be achieved using a deterministic greedy policy π_*:

$$\pi_*^h(x^h) \in \arg \max_{a \in \mathcal{A}} Q_*^h(x^h, a).$$

Theorem 18.9 motivates the following definition of Bellman error for reinforcement learning.

Definition 18.10 We say f is a candidate Q-function if $f = \{f^h(x^h, a^h): \mathcal{X} \times \mathcal{A} \to \mathbb{R}: h \in [H+1]\}$, with $f^{H+1}(\cdot) = 0$. Define

$$f^h(x^h) = \arg \max_{a \in \mathcal{A}} f^h(x^h, a),$$

and define its greedy policy π_f as a deterministic policy that satisfies

$$\pi_f^h(x^h) \in \arg \max_{a \in \mathcal{A}} f^h(x^h, a).$$

Given an MDP M, we also define the Bellman operator of f as

$$(\mathcal{T}^h f)(x^h, a^h) = \mathbb{E}_{r^h, x^{h+1} | x^h, a^h} [r^h + f^{h+1}(x^{h+1})],$$

and its Bellman error as

$$\mathcal{E}^h(f, x^h, a^h) = f^h(x^h, a^h) - (\mathcal{T}^h f)(x^h, a^h),$$

where the conditional expectation is with respect to the MDP M.

Theorem 18.9 implies that

$$\mathcal{E}^h(Q_*, x^h, a^h) = 0, \quad \forall h \in [H].$$

The following theorem shows that the difference of the true value of policy π_f and the candidate value function $f^1(x^1)$ are close if (and only if) the average Bellman error is small along the path generated by π_f. Since Bellman error can be evaluated on real data, we can use this decomposition to design reinforcement algorithms and obtain their regret bounds.

Theorem 18.11 *Consider any candidate value function $f = \{f^h(x^h, a^h): \mathcal{X} \times \mathcal{A} \to \mathbb{R}\}$, with $f^{H+1}(\cdot) = 0$. Let π_f be its greedy policy. Then*

$$[f^1(x^1) - V_{\pi_f}^1(x^1)] = \mathbb{E}_{(x,a,r) \sim \pi_f | x^1} \sum_{h=1}^{H} \mathcal{E}^h(f, x^h, a^h).$$

Proof We prove the following statement by induction from $h = H$ to $h = 1$.

$$[f^h(x^h) - V_{\pi_f}^h(x^h)] = \mathbb{E}_{\{(x^{h'},a^{h'},r^{h'})\}_{h'=h}^{H} \sim \pi_f | x^h} \sum_{h'=h}^{H} \mathcal{E}^{h'}(f, x^{h'}, a^{h'}). \tag{18.1}$$

When $h = H$, we have $a^H = \pi_f^H(x^H)$ and

$$\mathcal{E}^H(f, x^H, a^H) = f^H(x^H, a^H) - \mathbb{E}_{r^H | x^H, a^H}[r^H] = f^H(x^H) - V_\pi^H(x^H).$$

Therefore (18.1) holds. Assume that the equation holds at $h + 1$ for some $1 \leq h \leq H - 1$. Then at h, we have

$$\mathbb{E}_{\{(x^{h'},a^{h'},r^{h'})\}_{h'=h}^{H} \sim \pi_f | x^h} \sum_{h'=h}^{H} \mathcal{E}^{h'}(f, x^{h'}, a^{h'})$$

$$= \mathbb{E}_{x^{h+1},r^h,a^h \sim \pi_f | x^h}[\mathcal{E}^h(f, x^h, a^h) + f^{h+1}(x^{h+1}) - V_{\pi_f}^{h+1}(x^{h+1})]$$

$$= \mathbb{E}_{x^{h+1},r^h,a^h \sim \pi_f | x^h}[f^h(x^h, a^h) - r^h - V_{\pi_f}^{h+1}(x^{h+1})]$$

$$= \mathbb{E}_{a^h \sim \pi_f | x^h}[f^h(x^h, a^h) - V_{\pi_f}^h(x^h)]$$

$$= [f^h(x^h) - V_{\pi_f}^h(x^h)].$$

The first equation used the induction hypothesis. The second equation used the definition of Bellman error. The third equation used Proposition 18.7. The last equation used $a^h = \pi_f(x^h)$ and thus, by definition, $f^h(x^h, a^h) = f^h(x^h)$. □

In value function-based methods, we consider the following assumptions.

Assumption 18.12 Given a candidate value function class $\mathcal{F}$ of functions $f = \{f^h(x^h, a^h) : \mathcal{X} \times \mathcal{A} \to \mathbb{R}\}$, with $f^{H+1}(\cdot) = 0$, we assume that (realizable assumption)

$$Q_* = f_* \in \mathcal{F}.$$

Moreover, we assume that $f^1(x^1) \in [0, 1]$ and $r^h + f^{h+1}(x^{h+1}) \in [0, 1]$ $(h \geq 1)$.

Bellman error plays an important role in the analysis of reinforcement learning algorithms. For a value function-based approach to reinforcement learning, we would like to approximate Bellman error by minimizing least squares loss

$$(f^h(x^h, a^h) - r^h - f^{h+1}(x^{h+1}))^2. \tag{18.2}$$

By taking conditional expectation with respect to (x^h, a^h), we obtain

$$\mathbb{E}_{r^h, x^{h+1} | x^h, a^h}(f^h(x^h, a^h) - r^h - f^{h+1}(x^{h+1}))^2$$

$$= \mathcal{E}^h(f, x^h, a^h)^2 + \mathbb{E}_{r^h, x^{h+1} | x^h, a^h}\underbrace{\left(r^h + f^{h+1}(x^{h+1}) - (\mathcal{T}^h f)(x^h, a^h)\right)^2}_{f\text{-dependent zero-mean noise}}.$$

Since noise variance depends on f, if we use (18.2) to estimate f, we will favor f with smaller noise variance, which may not have zero Bellman error. To overcome this issue, one can estimate the noise variance term, and then subtract it from

(18.2) to obtain the term $\mathcal{E}^h(f, x^h, a^h)^2$. This requires an additional assumption referred to as *Bellman completeness* (or simply *completeness*).

Definition 18.13 (Bellman Completeness)   A candidate value function class $\mathcal{F}$ is complete with respect to another candidate value function class $\mathcal{G}$ if for any $h \in [H]$, $f \in \mathcal{F}$, there exists $g \in \mathcal{G}$ so that for all $h \in [H]$,

$$g^h(x^h, a^h) = (T^h f)(x^h, a^h) = \mathbb{E}_{r^h, x^{h+1}|x^h, a^h}\left[r^h + f^{h+1}(x^{h+1})\right].$$

We say $\mathcal{F}$ is complete if $\mathcal{F}$ is complete with respect to itself.

Note that if $\mathcal{F}$ is complete with respect to $\mathcal{G}$, then we may use the solution of

$$\min_{g^h \in \mathcal{G}^h} \sum_{s=1}^{t}(g^h(x_s^h, a_s^h) - r_s^h - f^{h+1}(x_s^{h+1}))^2$$

to estimate $(T^h f)(x^h, a^h)$, which can be used to cancel the variance term in (18.2). This motivates the following loss function

$$L^h(f, g, x^h, a^h, r^h, x^{h+1}) = [(f^h(x^h, a^h) - r^h - f^{h+1}(x^{h+1}))^2$$
$$-(g^h(x^h, a^h) - r^h - f^{h+1}(x^{h+1}))^2]. \qquad (18.3)$$

The following result is a counterpart of Theorem 13.15.

Theorem 18.14   *Assume that assumption 18.12 holds, $\mathcal{F}$ is complete with respect to $\mathcal{G}$, and $g^h(\cdot) \in [0, 1]$ for all $g \in \mathcal{G}$. Consider (18.3), and let*

$$\mathcal{F}_t = \left\{ f \in \mathcal{F}: \sup_{g \in \mathcal{G}} \sum_{h=1}^{H} \sum_{s=1}^{t} L^h(f, g, x_s^h, a_s^h, r_s^h, x_s^{h+1}) \leq \beta_t^2 \right\},$$

where

$$\beta_t^2 \geq 4\epsilon t(4 + \epsilon)H + 2\ln\left(16M(\epsilon, \mathcal{F}, \|\cdot\|_\infty)^2 M(\epsilon, \mathcal{G}, \|\cdot\|_\infty)/\delta^2\right),$$

with $M(\cdot)$ denotes the $\|\cdot\|_\infty$ packing number, and $\|f\|_\infty = \sup_{h,x,a}|f^h(x, a)|$. Then with probability at least $1 - \delta$, for all $t \leq n$, $Q_* \in \mathcal{F}_t$ and for all $f \in \mathcal{F}_t$,

$$\sum_{s=1}^{t} \sum_{h=1}^{H} \mathcal{E}^h(f, x_s^h, a_s^h)^2 \leq 4\beta_t^2.$$

Proof   Let $\mathcal{F}_\epsilon$ be an $\epsilon \|\cdot\|_\infty$ packing subset of $\mathcal{F}$ of size M_1, and let $\mathcal{G}_\epsilon$ be an $\epsilon \|\cdot\|_\infty$ packing subset of $\mathcal{G}$ of size M_2.

For all $f \in \mathcal{F}$ and $g \in \mathcal{G}$ (or $g \in \mathcal{F}$), we introduce the simplified notations

$$\epsilon_s^h(f) = r_s^h + f_s^{h+1}(x_s^{h+1}) - (T^h f)(x_s^h, a_s^h),$$
$$\Delta_s^h(f, g) = ((T^h f)(x_s^h, a_s^h) - g^h(x_s^h, a_s^h)).$$

We have the following sub-Gaussian inequality (see Lemma 2.15) for any fixed $f_\epsilon \in \mathcal{F}_\epsilon$, $h \in [H]$, and $\rho \in \mathbb{R}$:

$$\ln \mathbb{E}_{r_s^h, x_s^{h+1}|x_s^h, a_s^h} \exp(\rho \epsilon_s^h(f_\epsilon)) \leq \frac{\rho^2}{8}.$$

Using this logarithmic moment generating function, we can now obtain the following statement from Theorem 13.11, by taking a uniform bound over $\mathcal{G}_\epsilon \times \mathcal{F}_\epsilon$, and consider both under- and overestimation (for the absolute value on the left-hand side). With probability at least $1 - \delta/2$, for all $f_\epsilon \in \mathcal{F}_\epsilon$, $g_\epsilon \in \mathcal{G}_\epsilon$ and $t \geq 0$,

$$\underbrace{\left| \sum_{s=1}^{t} \sum_{h=1}^{H} \Delta_s^h(f_\epsilon, g_\epsilon) \epsilon_s^h(f_\epsilon) \right|}_{A} \leq \sum_{s=1}^{t} \sum_{h=1}^{H} \frac{\Delta_s^h(f_\epsilon, g_\epsilon)^2}{8} + \ln(4M_1 M_2/\delta). \qquad (18.4)$$

In the following, for each $f \in \mathcal{F}$, we choose $f_\epsilon \in \mathcal{F}_\epsilon$ so that $\|f - f_\epsilon\|_\infty \leq \epsilon$. Similarly, for each $g \in \mathcal{G}$, we choose $g_\epsilon \in \mathcal{G}_\epsilon$ so that $\|g - g_\epsilon\|_\infty \leq \epsilon$. Then

$$\left| \sum_{s=1}^{t} \sum_{h=1}^{H} \Delta_s^h(f, g) \epsilon_s^h(f) \right|$$

$$\leq \left| \sum_{s=1}^{t} \sum_{h=1}^{H} \Delta_s^h(f, g) \epsilon_s^h(f_\epsilon) \right| + 2\epsilon \sum_{s=1}^{t} \sum_{h=1}^{H} |\Delta_s^h(f, g)|$$

$$\geq \underbrace{\left| \sum_{s=1}^{t} \sum_{h=1}^{H} \Delta_s^h(f_\epsilon, g_\epsilon) \epsilon_s^h(f_\epsilon) \right|}_{A} + 4H\epsilon t.$$

The first inequality used $|\epsilon_s^h(f) - \epsilon_s^h(f_\epsilon)| \leq 2\epsilon$. The second inequality used the ϵ-covering property $|\Delta_s^h(f, g) - \Delta_s^h(f_\epsilon, g_\epsilon)| \leq 2\epsilon$, $|\epsilon_s^h(f_\epsilon)| \leq 1$, and $|\Delta_s^h(f, g)| \leq 1$. We also have

$$A \leq \frac{1}{8} \sum_{s=1}^{t} \sum_{h=1}^{H} \Delta_s^h(f_\epsilon, g_\epsilon)^2 + \ln(4M_1 M_2/\delta)$$

$$\leq \frac{1}{8} \sum_{s=1}^{t} \sum_{h=1}^{H} (\Delta_s^h(f, g) + 2\epsilon)^2 + \ln(4M_1 M_2/\delta)$$

$$\leq \frac{1}{4} \sum_{s=1}^{t} \sum_{h=1}^{H} (\Delta_s^h(f, g))^2 + \epsilon^2 Ht + \ln(4M_1 M_2/\delta).$$

The first inequality used (18.4). The second inequality used the ϵ-covering property $|\Delta_s^h(f, g) - \Delta_s^h(f_\epsilon, g_\epsilon)| \leq 2\epsilon$. The last inequality used standard algebra inequalities $|a + 2\epsilon|^2/8 \leq (a^2/4) + \epsilon^2$ to simplify the terms.

That is, we have shown that with probability at least $1 - \delta/2$, for all $f \in \mathcal{F}$ and $g \in \mathcal{G}$ and $t \geq 0$,

$$\left| \sum_{s=1}^{t} \sum_{h=1}^{H} \Delta_s^h(f, g) \epsilon_s^h(f) \right| \leq \frac{1}{4} \sum_{s=1}^{t} \sum_{h=1}^{H} \Delta_s^h(f, g)^2$$

$$+ \epsilon t H(4 + \epsilon) + \ln(4M_1 M_2/\delta). \qquad (18.5)$$

Similarly, with probability at least $1 - \delta/2$, for all $f \in \mathcal{F}$ and $t \geq 0$,

$$\left| \sum_{s=1}^{t} \sum_{h=1}^{H} \Delta_s^h(f,f) \epsilon_s^h(f) \right| \leq \frac{1}{4} \sum_{s=1}^{t} \sum_{h=1}^{H} \Delta_s^h(f,f)^2$$
$$+ \epsilon t H(4+\epsilon) + \ln(4M_1/\delta). \qquad (18.6)$$

We have with probability at least $1 - \delta$, both (18.5) and (18.6) hold. We obtain with probability at least $1 - \delta$, for all $t \geq 0$, $f \in \mathcal{F}$, $g \in \mathcal{G}$,

$$\left| \sum_{h=1}^{H} \sum_{s=1}^{t} [\Delta_s^h(f,f) - \Delta_s^h(f,g)] \, \epsilon_s^h(f) \right|$$
$$\leq \frac{1}{4} \sum_{h=1}^{H} \sum_{s=1}^{t} [\Delta_s^h(f,f)^2 + \Delta_s^h(f,g)^2] + 0.5\beta_t^2. \qquad (18.7)$$

Therefore

$$\sum_{s=1}^{t} \sum_{h=1}^{H} L^h(f,g,x_s^h,a_s^h,r_s^h,x_s^{h+1})$$
$$= \sum_{s=1}^{t} \sum_{h=1}^{H} \left[\Delta_s^h(f,f)^2 - \Delta_s^h(f,g)^2 + 2[\Delta_s^h(f,f) - \Delta_s^h(f,g)]\epsilon_s^h(f) \right]$$
$$\geq \sum_{s=1}^{t} \sum_{h=1}^{H} \left[0.5\Delta_s^h(f,f)^2 - 1.5\Delta_s^h(f,g)^2 \right] - \beta_t^2, \qquad \text{(by (18.7))}$$

and

$$\sum_{s=1}^{t} \sum_{h=1}^{H} L^h(Q_*,g,x_s^h,a_s^h,r_s^h,x_s^{h+1})$$
$$= \sum_{s=1}^{t} \sum_{h=1}^{H} \left[\Delta_s^h(Q_*,Q_*)^2 - \Delta_s^h(Q_*,g)^2 + 2[\Delta_s^h(Q_*,Q_*) - \Delta_s^h(Q_*,g)]\epsilon_s^h(f) \right]$$
$$\leq \sum_{s=1}^{t} \sum_{h=1}^{H} \left[1.5\Delta_s^h(Q_*,Q_*)^2 - 0.5\Delta_s^h(Q_*,g)^2 \right] + \beta_t^2. \qquad \text{(by (18.7))}$$

Taking sup over $g \in \mathcal{G}$, and note that $\Delta_s^h(Q_*,Q_*) = 0$, and that $\mathcal{F}$ is complete with respect to $\mathcal{G}$, we obtain

$$\sup_{g \in \mathcal{G}} \sum_{s=1}^{t} \sum_{h=1}^{H} L^h(Q_*,g,x_s^h,a_s^h,r_s^h,x_s^{h+1}) \leq \beta_t^2,$$

$$\sup_{g \in \mathcal{G}} \sum_{s=1}^{t} \sum_{h=1}^{H} L^h(f,g,x_s^h,a_s^h,r_s^h,x_s^{h+1}) \geq 0.5 \sum_{s=1}^{t} \sum_{h=1}^{H} \underbrace{\Delta_s^h(f,f)^2}_{\mathcal{E}^h(f,x_s^h,a_s^h)^2} - \beta_t^2.$$

In the two displayed inequalities, the first implies that $Q_* \in \mathcal{F}_t$. The second implies that if $f \in \mathcal{F}_t$, then

$$\beta_t^2 \geq 0.5 \sum_{s=1}^{t} \sum_{h=1}^{H} \mathcal{E}^h(f,x_s^h,a_s^h)^2 - \beta_t^2,$$

which implies the second result of the theorem. $\qquad\qquad\square$

18.2 *Q*-type Model-Free Linear MDP

Linear MDP is a special MDP can be defined as follows.

Definition 18.15 (Linear MDP) Let $\mathcal{H} = \{\mathcal{H}^h\}$ be a sequence of vector spaces with inner products $\langle \cdot, \cdot \rangle$. An MDP $M = \text{MDP}(\mathcal{X}, \mathcal{A}, P)$ is a linear MDP with feature maps $\phi = \{\phi^h(x^h, a^h) \colon \mathcal{X} \times \mathcal{A} \to \mathcal{H}^h\}_{h=1}^H$ if for all $h \in [H]$, there exists a map $\nu^h(x^{h+1}) \colon \mathcal{X} \to \mathcal{H}^h$ and $\theta^h \in \mathcal{H}^h$ such that

$$dP^h(x^{h+1}|x^h, a^h) = \langle \nu^h(x^{h+1}), \phi^h(x^h, a^h) \rangle d\mu^{h+1}(x^{h+1}),$$

$$\mathbb{E}[r^h|x^h, a^h] = \langle \theta^h, \phi^h(x^h, a^h) \rangle.$$

Here $\langle \cdot, \cdot \rangle$ denotes the inner product in $\mathcal{H}^h$ for different h, and the conditional probability measure $dP^h(\cdot|x^h, a^h)$ is absolute continuous with respect to a measure $d\mu^{h+1}(\cdot)$ with density $\langle \nu^h(x^{h+1}), \phi^h(x^h, a^h) \rangle$. In general, we assume that $\nu^h(\cdot)$ and θ^h are unknown. We may assume $\phi(\cdot)$ to be either known or unknown.

Example 18.16 (Tabular MDP) In a tabular MDP, we assume that $|\mathcal{A}| = A$ and $|\mathcal{X}| = S$. Let $d = AS$, and we can encode the space of $\mathcal{X} \times \mathcal{A}$ into a d-dimensional vector with components indexed by (x, a). Let $\phi^h(x, a) = e_{(x,a)}$ and let $\nu^h(x^{h+1})$ be a d-dimensional vector so that its (x, a) component is $P^h(x^{h+1}|x^h = x, a^h = a)$. Similarly, we can take θ^h as a d-dimensional vector so that its (x, a) component is $\mathbb{E}[r^h|x^h = x, a^h = a]$. Therefore tabular MDP is a linear MDP with $d = AS$.

Example 18.17 (Low-Rank MDP) For a low-rank MDP, we assume that the transition probability matrix can be decomposed as

$$P^h(x^{h+1}|x^h, a^h) = \sum_{j=1}^d P^h(x^{h+1}|z = j)P^h(z = j|x^h, a^h).$$

In this case, we can set $\phi^h(x^h, a^h) = [P^h(z = j|x^h, a^h)]_{j=1}^d$, and $\nu^h(x^{h+1}) = [P^h(x^{h+1}|z = j)]_{j=1}^d$. Therefore a low-rank MDP is a linear MDP with rank as dimension.

We have the following structural result for linear MDP, which is useful in our analysis.

Proposition 18.18 *In a linear MDP with feature map $\phi^h(x^h, a^h)$ on vector spaces $\mathcal{H}^h$ ($h \in [H]$). Consider the linear candidate Q function class*

$$\mathcal{F} = \left\{ \langle w^h, \phi^h(x^h, a^h) \rangle : w^h \in \mathcal{H}^h, h \in [H] \right\}.$$

Any function $g^{h+1}(x^{h+1})$ on $\mathcal{X}$ satisfies

$$(\mathcal{T}^h g^{h+1})(x^h, a^h) \in \mathcal{F}.$$

It implies that $\mathcal{F}$ is complete, and $Q_* \in \mathcal{F}$. Moreover, $\forall f \in \mathcal{F}$,

$$\mathcal{E}^h(f, x^h, a^h) \in \mathcal{F}.$$

Proof Let

$$u_g^h = \int g^{h+1}(x^{h+1})\nu^h(x^{h+1})d\mu^{h+1}(x^{h+1}).$$

We have

$$\mathbb{E}_{x^{h+1}|x^h,a^h} g^{h+1}(x^{h+1}) = \int g^{h+1}(x^{h+1})\langle \nu^h(x^{h+1}), \phi^h(x^h,a^h)\rangle d\mu^{h+1}(x^{h+1})$$
$$= \langle u_g^h, \phi^h(x^h,a^h)\rangle.$$

This implies that

$$(\mathcal{T}^h g)(x^h,a^h) = \langle \theta^h + u_g^h, \phi^h(x^h,a^h)\rangle \in \mathcal{F}.$$

Since $Q_*^h(x^h,a^h) = (\mathcal{T}^h Q_*)(x^h,a^h)$, we know $Q_*^h(x^h,a^h) \in \mathcal{F}$.

Similarly, since $(\mathcal{T}^h f)(x^h,a^h) \in \mathcal{F}$, we know that $f \in \mathcal{F}$ implies

$$\mathcal{E}^h(f,x^h,a^h) = f^h(x^h,a^h) - (\mathcal{T}^h f)(x^h,a^h) \in \mathcal{F}.$$

This proves the desired result. $\qquad\square$

Proposition 18.18 implies that if the feature map ϕ is known, then a linear MDP with linear function class is both realizable and complete.

Algorithm 18.1 Bellman Error UCB Algorithm

Input: $\lambda, T, \mathcal{F}, \mathcal{G}$
1 Let $\mathcal{F}_0 = \{f_0\}$
2 Let $\beta_0 = 0$
3 **for** $t = 1, 2, \ldots, T$ **do**
4 $\quad$ Observe x_t^1
5 $\quad$ Let $f_t \in \arg\max_{f \in \mathcal{F}_{t-1}} f(x_t^1)$.
6 $\quad$ Let $\pi_t = \pi_{f_t}$
7 $\quad$ Play policy π_t and observe trajectory (x_t, a_t, r_t)
8 $\quad$ Let

$$\mathcal{F}_t = \left\{ f \in \mathcal{F} : \sup_{g \in \mathcal{G}} \sum_{h=1}^{H}\sum_{s=1}^{t} L^h(f,g,x_s^h,a_s^h,r_s^h,x_s^{h+1}) \leq \beta_t^2 \right\}$$

$\quad$ with appropriately chosen β_t, where $L^h(\cdot)$ is defined in (18.3).
9 **return** randomly chosen π_t from $t = 1$ to $t = T$

We can generalize the UCB algorithm for contextual bandit to the UCB algorithm for reinforcement learning in Algorithm 18.1. It is again an implementation of the optimism in the face of uncertainty principle. Its analysis is similar to that of Algorithm 17.4. We may define an extension of the eluder coefficient as follows, which is similar to Definition 17.17. For convenience, we define it in terms of expectation, which is more general than the definition without expectation in Definition 17.17.

Definition 18.19 (Q-type Bellman eluder coefficient)   Given a candidate Q function class $\mathcal{F}$, its Q-type Bellman eluder coefficient $\mathrm{EC}_Q(\epsilon, \mathcal{F}, T)$ is the smallest number d so that for any filtered sequence $\{f_t, (x_t, r_t, a_t) \sim \pi_{f_t}\}_{t=1}^T$,

$$\mathbb{E} \sum_{t=2}^{T} \sum_{h=1}^{H} \mathcal{E}^h(f_t, x_t^h, a_t^h) \leq \sqrt{d\, \mathbb{E} \sum_{h=1}^{H} \sum_{t=2}^{T} \left(\epsilon + \sum_{s=1}^{t-1} \mathcal{E}^h(f_t, x_s^h, a_s^h)^2 \right)}.$$

One may also replace the sum $\sum_{s=1}^{t-1} \mathcal{E}^h(f_t, x_s^h, a_s^h)^2$ on the right-hand side of Definition 18.19 by

$$\sum_{s=1}^{t-1} \mathbb{E}_{(\tilde{x}_s, \tilde{a}_s) \sim \pi_{f_s}} \mathcal{E}^h(f_t, \tilde{x}_s^h, \tilde{a}_s^h)^2.$$

We will not consider this variant for the Q-type problem, but will employ this variant for the V-type problem in Definition 18.27.

For linear MDP, one can employ Proposition 17.20 and Proposition 15.8 to obtain an estimate of the eluder coefficient.

Proposition 18.20   *Assume that a linear MDP has (possibly unknown) feature maps $\phi^h(x^h, a^h)$ in inner product spaces $\{\mathcal{H}^h\}$, each with inner product $\langle \cdot, \cdot \rangle = \langle \cdot, \cdot \rangle_{\mathcal{H}^h}$. Assume also that the candidate Q-function class $\mathcal{F}$ can be embedded into the linear function space $\mathcal{F} \subset \{\langle w^h, \phi^h(x^h, a^h) \rangle : w^h \in \mathcal{H}^h\}$, and there exists $B > 0$ such that $\|\mathcal{E}^h(f, \cdot, \cdot)\|_{\mathcal{H}^h} \leq B$. Assume that $|\mathcal{E}^h(f, x^h, a^h)| \in [0, 1]$, then*

$$\mathrm{EC}_Q(1, \mathcal{F}, T) \leq 2 \sum_{h=1}^{H} \mathrm{entro}(1/(B^2 T), \phi^h(\cdot)),$$

where $\mathrm{entro}(\cdot)$ is defined in Proposition 15.8. In particular, if $\{\mathcal{H}^h\}$ are finite dimensional, then we have

$$\mathrm{EC}_Q(1, \mathcal{F}, T) \leq 2 \sum_{h=1}^{H} \dim(\mathcal{H}^h) \ln(1 + T(BB')^2),$$

where $B' = \sup_h \sup_{x^h, a^h} \|\phi^h(x^h, a^h)\|_{\mathcal{H}^h}$.

We note that $\mathcal{F}$ may be nonlinear by itself, although it can be embedded into a linear function space. One may also choose a sufficiently large RKHS to realize such an embedding assumption. We can now prove a direct extension of Theorem 17.19 as follows. Similar to Theorem 17.19, the structural assumption of the MDP is characterized by Definition 18.19, which may include examples other than linear MDP. For simplicity, we state the result in expectation, and leave the high-probability bound as an exercise.

Theorem 18.21   *Assume that Assumption 18.12 holds, $\mathcal{F}$ is complete with respect to $\mathcal{G}$, and $g^h(\cdot) \in [0, 1]$ for all $g \in \mathcal{G}$. Assume also that β_t is chosen in Algorithm 18.1 according to*

$$\beta_t^2 \geq \inf_{\epsilon > 0} \left[4\epsilon t(4 + \epsilon)H + 2\ln\left(16 M(\epsilon, \mathcal{F}, \|\cdot\|_\infty)^2 M(\epsilon, \mathcal{G}, \|\cdot\|_\infty)/\delta^2\right) \right],$$

with $M(\cdot)$ denoting the $\|\cdot\|_\infty$ packing number, and $\|f\|_\infty = \sup_{h,x,a} |f^h(x,a)|$. Then

$$\mathbb{E} \sum_{t=2}^{T} [V_*^1(x_t^1) - V_{\pi_t}^1(x_t^1)] \leq \delta T + \sqrt{\mathrm{EC}_Q(\epsilon, \mathcal{F}, T) \left(\epsilon H T + \delta H T^2 + 4 \sum_{t=2}^{T} \beta_{t-1}^2 \right)}.$$

Proof For $t \geq 2$, we have

$$
\begin{aligned}
&V_*^1(x_t^1) - V_{\pi_t}^1(x_t^1) \\
&= V_*^1(x_t) - f_t(x_t^1) + f_t(x_t^1) - V_{\pi_t}^1(x_t^1) \\
&\leq \mathbb{1}(Q_* \notin \mathcal{F}_{t-1}) + [f_t(x_t^1) - V_{\pi_t}^1(x_t^1)] \\
&= \mathbb{1}(Q_* \notin \mathcal{F}_{t-1}) + \mathbb{E}_{(x_t, a_t, r_t) \sim \pi_t | x_t^1} \sum_{h=1}^{H} \mathcal{E}^h(f_t, x_t^h, a_t^h).
\end{aligned}
$$

The inequality used the fact that if $Q_* \in \mathcal{F}_{t-1}$, then $f_t(x_t^1) = \max_{f \in \mathcal{F}_{t-1}} f(x_t^1) \geq V_*^1(x_t^1)$, and if $Q_* \notin \mathcal{F}_{t-1}$, $V_*^1(x_t) - f_t(x_t^1) \leq 1$. The last equation used Theorem 18.11.

Theorem 18.14 implies that $\Pr(Q_* \in \mathcal{F}_{t-1}) \geq 1 - \delta$. We thus have

$$\mathbb{E}[V_*^1(x_t^1) - V_{\pi_t}^1(x_t^1)] \leq \delta + \mathbb{E} \sum_{h=1}^{H} \mathcal{E}^h(f_t, x_t^h, a_t^h).$$

We can now obtain

$$
\begin{aligned}
&\mathbb{E} \sum_{t=2}^{T} [V_*^1(x_t^1) - V_{\pi_t}^1(x_t^1)] \\
&\leq \mathbb{E} \sum_{t=2}^{T} \sum_{h=1}^{H} \mathcal{E}^h(f_t, x_t^h, a_t^h) + \delta T \\
&\leq \delta T + \sqrt{\mathrm{EC}_Q(\epsilon, \mathcal{F}, T) \mathbb{E} \sum_{t=2}^{T} \sum_{h=1}^{H} \left(\epsilon + \sum_{s=1}^{t-1} \mathcal{E}^h(f_t, x_s^h, a_s^h)^2 \right)} \\
&\leq \delta T + \sqrt{\mathrm{EC}_Q(\epsilon, \mathcal{F}, T) \left(\epsilon H T + \delta H T^2 + 4 \sum_{t=2}^{T} \beta_{t-1}^2 \right)}.
\end{aligned}
$$

The second inequality used Definition 18.19. The last inequality used the fact that for each t, Theorem 18.14 holds with probability $1 - \delta$, and otherwise, $\mathcal{E}^h(f_t, x_s^h, a_s^h)^2 \leq 1$. $\qquad \square$

To interpret the theorem, we still consider the d-dimensional linear MDP with bounded $\mathcal{F}$ and $\mathcal{G}$. If the model coefficients at different step h are different, then the metric entropy can be bounded (ignoring log factors) as $\tilde{O}(H \ln(M_{\mathcal{F}} M_{\mathcal{G}})) = \tilde{O}(Hd)$, and hence with $\epsilon = \delta = O(1/T^2)$, we have

$$\beta_t^2 = \tilde{O}(H \ln(M_{\mathcal{F}} M_{\mathcal{G}})) = \tilde{O}(Hd).$$

Since $\text{EC}_Q(\epsilon, \mathcal{F}, T) = \tilde{O}(dH)$, we obtain a regret of

$$\mathbb{E}\sum_{t=2}^{T}[V_*^1(x_t^1) - V_{\pi_t}^1(x_t^1)] = \tilde{O}\left(H\sqrt{dT\ln(M_{\mathcal{F}}M_{\mathcal{G}})}\right) = \tilde{O}\left(Hd\sqrt{T}\right). \quad (18.8)$$

If a Q function at different steps h shares the same model coefficient, then we have $\beta_t^2 = \tilde{O}(\ln(M_{\mathcal{F}}M_{\mathcal{G}})) = \tilde{O}(d)$, which is independent of H. In this case the regret becomes

$$\mathbb{E}\sum_{t=2}^{T}[V_*^1(x_t^1) - V_{\pi_t}^1(x_t^1)] = \tilde{O}\left(\sqrt{dHT\ln(M_{\mathcal{F}}M_{\mathcal{G}})}\right) = \tilde{O}(d\sqrt{HT}).$$

The resulting regret bound is optimal in its dependence on d and T (see Theorem 17.13), but suboptimal in the dependence on H. The H dependency can be improved using weighted regression, where the weight is inversely proportional to an upper bound of the variance. The resulting procedure is more complex, and thus we will not consider it here.

18.3 Least Squares Value Iteration

It was shown in Theorem 18.21 that the UCB method in Algorithm 18.1 can handle linear MDP with Q-type Bellman eluder coefficients. However, it requires solving a minimax formulation with global optimism, which may be difficult computationally. This section shows that a computationally more efficient approach can also be used to solve linear MDP. In this approach, we are restricted to the case that the function class $\mathcal{F}$ can be factored as the product of $\mathcal{F}^h$, and we need to make a stronger assumption of Bellman completeness in (18.9), and a stronger form of Bellman eluder coefficient to control the point-wise confidence interval in (18.10).

Assumption 18.22 Assume that the Q function class $\mathcal{F}$ can be factored as the product of H function classes:

$$\mathcal{F} = \prod_{h=1}^{H}\mathcal{F}^h, \quad \mathcal{F}^h = \{\langle w^h, \phi^h(x^h, a^h)\rangle, w^h \in \mathcal{H}^h\},$$

so that for all $g^{h+1}(x^{h+1}) \in [0, 1]$,

$$(\mathcal{T}^h g^{h+1})(x^h, a^h) \in \mathcal{F}^h. \quad (18.9)$$

Assume for any $\epsilon > 0$, there exists a function class $\mathcal{B}^h(\epsilon)$ so that for any sequence $\{(x_t^h, a_t^h, \hat{f}_t^h) \in \mathcal{X} \times \mathcal{A} \times \mathcal{F}^h : t = 1, \ldots, T\}$, we can construct a sequence of nonnegative bonus functions $b_t^h(\cdot) \in \mathcal{B}^h(\epsilon)$ (each $\hat{f}_t^h$ and b_t^h only depend on the historic observations up to $t-1$) such that

$$b_t^h(x^h, a^h)^2 \geq \sup_{f^h \in \mathcal{F}^h} \frac{|f^h(x^h, a^h) - \hat{f}_t^h(x^h, a^h)|^2}{\epsilon + \sum_{s=1}^{t-1}|f^h(x_s^h, a_s^h) - \hat{f}_t^h(x_s^h, a_s^h)|^2}, \quad (18.10)$$

and the bonus function satisfies the following *uniform eluder condition*:

$$\sup_{\{(x_t^h, a_t^h)\}} \sum_{t=1}^{T} \min(1, b_t^h(x_t^h, a_t^h)^2) \le \dim(T, \mathcal{B}^h(\epsilon)).$$

We note that the uniform eluder condition of Assumption 18.22 is related to the coverage coefficient of Definition 9.42 (also see the conditional versions in Definition 17.35 and Definition 18.30), and the assumption is stronger than Bellman eluder coefficients. However, the following example shows that linear MDP satisfies Assumption 18.22.

Example 18.23 Consider a linear MDP in Definition 18.15 such that

$$\|\theta^h\|_{\mathcal{H}^h} + \int \|\nu^h(x^{h+1})\|_{\mathcal{H}^h} |d\mu^{h+1}(x^{h+1})| \le B^h.$$

If $\mathcal{F}^h$ is any function class that contains

$$\tilde{\mathcal{F}}^h = \{\langle w^h, \phi^h(x^h, a^h)\rangle : \|w^h\|_{\mathcal{H}^h} \le B^h\},$$

then the proof of Proposition 18.18 implies that (18.9) holds. Note that if $r^h \in [0, 1]$, then $(\mathcal{T}^h g^{h+1})(x^h, a^h) \in [0, 2]$. Therefore at any time step t, we may consider a subset of $\mathcal{F}^h$ that satisfies the range constraint on historic observations, and in the meantime, impose the same range constraints in $\tilde{\mathcal{F}}^h$ as

$$\tilde{\mathcal{F}}^h = \{\langle w^h, \phi^h(x^h, a^h)\rangle : \|w^h\|_{\mathcal{H}^h} \le B^h, \ \langle w^h, \phi^h(x_s^h, a_s^h)\rangle \in [0, 2] \,\forall s \in [t-1]\}.$$

If moreover, each $f^h(x^h, a^h) \in \mathcal{F}^h$ can be written as $\langle \tilde{w}^h(f^h), \tilde{\phi}^h(x^h, a^h)\rangle$ so that $\|\tilde{w}^h(f^h) - \tilde{w}^h(\tilde{f}^h)\|_2 \le \tilde{B}^h$ (here we assume that $\tilde{\phi}^h$ may or may not be the same as ϕ^h), then we can take

$$b_t^h(x^h, a^h) = \|\tilde{\phi}^h(x^h, a^h)\|_{(\Sigma_t^h)^{-1}}, \tag{18.11}$$

$$\Sigma_t^h = \frac{\epsilon}{(\tilde{B}^h)^2} I + \sum_{s=1}^{t-1} \tilde{\phi}^h(x^h, a^h)\tilde{\phi}^h(x^h, a^h)^\top,$$

so that (18.10) holds. By using Lemma 13.9, we have

$$\sum_{t=1}^{T} \min\left(1, \|\tilde{\phi}^h(x_t^h, a_t^h)\|_{(\Sigma_t^h)^{-1}}^2\right) \le \sum_{t=1}^{T} \frac{2\|\tilde{\phi}^h(x_t^h, a_t^h)\|_{(\Sigma_t^h)^{-1}}^2}{1 + \|\tilde{\phi}^h(x_t^h, a_t^h)\|_{(\Sigma_t^h)^{-1}}^2}$$

$$\le \ln\left|((\tilde{B}^h)^2/\epsilon)\Sigma_t^h\right|.$$

Using Proposition 15.8, we can set $\dim(T, \mathcal{B}^h(\epsilon)) = \mathrm{entro}(\epsilon/((\tilde{B}^h)^2 T), \tilde{\phi}^h(\cdot))$.

With the stronger assumptions in Assumption 18.22, we can solve the corresponding RL problem using Algorithm 18.2, which is computationally simpler than Algorithm 18.1. At each time step t, the algorithm forms upper confidence bounds of the optimal Q function for $h = H, H-1, \ldots, 1$, and then plays the greedy policy according to the upper confidence bounds. This requires explicit bonus term $b_t^h(\cdot)$. We call this algorithm *least squares value iteration* (with UCB) to be consistent with (Jin et al., 2020). However, the algorithm is also referred to as *fitted Q-learning* in the literature.

Algorithm 18.2 Least Squares Value Iteration with UCB (LSVI-UCB)

Input: $\epsilon > 0$, T, $\{\mathcal{F}^h\}$, $\{\mathcal{B}^h(\epsilon)\}$

1 **for** $t = 1, 2, \ldots, T$ **do**
2   Let $f_t^{H+1} = 0$
3   **for** $h = H, H-1, \ldots, 1$ **do**
4   Let $y_s^h = r_s^h + f_t^{h+1}(x_s^{h+1})$, where $f_t^{h+1}(x_s^{h+1}) = \max_a f_t^{h+1}(x_s^{h+1}, a)$
5   Let

$$\hat{f}_t^h = \arg\min_{f^h \in \mathcal{F}^h} \sum_{s=1}^{t-1} (f^h(x_s^h, a_s^h) - y_s^h)^2.$$

       Find $\beta_t^h > 0$ and bonus function $b_t^h(\cdot)$ that satisfies (18.10)
6   Let $f_t^h(x^h, a^h) = \min(1, \max(0, \hat{f}_t^h(x^h, a^h) + \beta_t^h b_t^h(x^h, a^h)))$
7   Let π_t be the greedy policy of f_t^h for each step $h \in [H]$
8   Play policy π_t and observe trajectory (x_t, a_t, r_t)
9 **return** randomly chosen π_t from $t = 1$ to $t = T$

Lemma 18.24 *Consider Algorithm 18.2 under Assumption 18.22. Assume also that $Q_*^h \in \mathcal{F}^h$, $Q_*^h \in [0,1]$, $r^h \in [0,1]$, $f^h \in [0,2]$ for $h \in [H]$, and $f^h \in \mathcal{F}^h$. Given any $t > 0$, let $\beta_t^{H+1} = \beta^{H+1}(\epsilon, \delta) = 0$, and for $h = H, H-1, \ldots, 1$,*

$$\beta_t^h = \beta^h(\epsilon, \delta) \geq 4(1 + \beta^{h+1})\frac{\epsilon}{\sqrt{T}} + \sqrt{\epsilon}$$

$$+ \sqrt{24(1 + \beta^{h+1}(\delta))\epsilon + 12 \ln \frac{2H \, M_T^h(\epsilon)}{\delta}},$$

where (with $\|f\|_\infty = \sup_{x,a,h} f^h(x, a)$)

$$M_T^h(\epsilon) = M(\epsilon/T, \mathcal{F}^h, \|\cdot\|_\infty) M(\epsilon/T, \mathcal{F}^{h+1}, \|\cdot\|_\infty) M(\epsilon/T, \mathcal{B}^{h+1}(\epsilon), \|\cdot\|_\infty).$$

Then with probability at least $1 - \delta$, for all $h \in [H]$, and $(x^h, a^h) \in \mathcal{X} \times \mathcal{A}$,

$$Q_*^h(x^h, a^h) \leq f_t^h(x^h, a^h),$$
$$|f_t^h(x^h, a^h) - (\mathcal{T}^h f_t^{h+1})(x^h, a^h)| \leq 2\beta^h(\epsilon, \delta) b^h(x^h, a^h).$$

Proof Let $\mathcal{F}_\epsilon^{h+1}$ be an $(\epsilon/T) \|\cdot\|_\infty$ packing of $\mathcal{F}^{h+1}$, and $\mathcal{B}_\epsilon^{h+1}$ be an $(\epsilon/T) \|\cdot\|_\infty$ packing of $\mathcal{B}^{h+1}(\epsilon)$. Then

$$\bar{\mathcal{F}}_\epsilon^{h+1} = \mathcal{F}_\epsilon^{h+1} \oplus \beta^{h+1} \mathcal{B}_\epsilon^{h+1}$$

is a $(1 + \beta^{h+1})(\epsilon/T) \|\cdot\|_\infty$ cover of $\{f_t^{h+1}(\cdot)\}$.

Given f_t^{h+1}, let $\bar{f}_t^{h+1} \in \bar{\mathcal{F}}_\epsilon^{h+1}$ so that $\|\bar{f}_t^{h+1} - f_t^{h+1}\|_\infty \leq \bar{\epsilon} = (1 + \beta^{h+1})(\epsilon/T)$. Let $\bar{y}_s^h = r_s^h + \bar{f}_t^{h+1}(x_s^{h+1})$, and

$$\tilde{f}_t^h = \arg\min_{f^h \in \mathcal{F}^h} \sum_{s=1}^{t-1} (f^h(x_s^h, a_s^h) - \bar{y}_s^h)^2.$$

Then we have

$$\left(\sum_{s=1}^{t-1} (\hat{f}_t^h(x_s^h, a_s^h) - \bar{y}_s^h)^2\right)^{1/2} \le \left(\sum_{s=1}^{t-1} (\hat{f}_t^h(x_s^h, a_s^h) - y_s^h)^2\right)^{1/2} + \sqrt{t}\bar{\epsilon}$$

$$\le \left(\sum_{s=1}^{t-1} (\tilde{f}_t^h(x_s^h, a_s^h) - y_s^h)^2\right)^{1/2} + \sqrt{t}\bar{\epsilon}$$

$$\le \left(\sum_{s=1}^{t-1} (\tilde{f}_t^h(x_s^h, a_s^h) - \bar{y}_s^h)^2\right)^{1/2} + 2\sqrt{t}\bar{\epsilon}.$$

The first and the third inequalities used triangle inequalities. The second inequality used the fact that $\hat{f}$ is the ERM solution of the least squares problem. We can apply Theorem 13.15 to $\bar{y}_s^h$, with f_* in Theorem 13.15 replaced by $\mathbb{E}[\bar{y}_s^h | x_s^h, a_s^h] = (\mathcal{T}^h \bar{f}_t^{h+1})(x_s^h, a_s^h)$ and $\epsilon' = 2\bar{\epsilon}$ and $\sigma = 1$. By taking a union bound over $\bar{f}_t^{h+1} \in \bar{\mathcal{F}}_\epsilon^{h+1}$ and $h \in [H]$, we obtain with probability at least $1 - \delta$;

$$\left(\sum_{s=1}^{t-1} \left(\hat{f}_t^h(x_s^h, a_s^h) - (\mathcal{T}^h f_t^{h+1})(x_s^h, a_s^h)\right)^2 + \epsilon\right)^{1/2}$$

$$\le \left(\sum_{s=1}^{t-1} \left(\hat{f}_t^h(x_s^h, a_s^h) - (\mathcal{T}^h \bar{f}_t^{h+1})(x_s^h, a_s^h)\right)^2\right)^{1/2} + \sqrt{t}\bar{\epsilon} + \sqrt{\epsilon}$$

$$\le \sqrt{t}\bar{\epsilon} + \sqrt{\epsilon} + \sqrt{8t\left(\frac{\epsilon}{T} + 2\bar{\epsilon}\right)\left(1 + \frac{2\epsilon}{T} + 4\bar{\epsilon}\right) + 12\ln\frac{2HM_T^h(\epsilon)}{\delta}} \le \beta_t^h.$$

The first inequality used the triangle inequality. The second inequality used Theorem 13.15 with $\epsilon' = 2\bar{\epsilon}$ (and union bound over $\bar{f}_t^{h+1}$ and $h \in [H]$). The last inequality is algebra.

Now by using the definition of $b_t^h(\cdot)$, we obtain

$$|\hat{f}_t^h(x^h, a^h) - (\mathcal{T}^h f_t^{h+1})(x^h, a^h)| \le \beta_t^h b_t^h(x^h, a^h).$$

Therefore the definition of f_t^h in the algorithm implies that

$$0 \le f_t^h(x^h, a^h) - (\mathcal{T}^h f_t^{h+1})(x^h, a^h) \le 2\beta_t^h b_t^h(x^h, a^h). \tag{18.12}$$

This proves the second desired bound. By using induction from $h = H, H - 1, \ldots, 1$, with $Q_*^{H+1} = f_t^{H+1} = 0$, we obtain that when $f_t^{h+1}(\cdot) \ge Q_*^{h+1}(\cdot)$,

$$f_t^h(x^h, a^h) - Q_*^h(x^h, a^h) \ge (\mathcal{T}^h f_t^{h+1})(x^h, a^h) - Q_*^h(x^h, a^h)$$

$$= \mathbb{E}\left[f_t^{h+1}(x^{h+1}) - Q_*^{h+1}(x^{h+1}) | x^h, a^h\right] \ge 0.$$

The first inequality used (18.12). The next equality used the Bellman equation for Q_*. The last inequality used the induction hypothesis at $h + 1$. This proves the first desired inequality. □

We are now ready to prove the following regret bound for Algorithm 18.2. We state the result in expectation. A slight modification of the proof also leads to a high-probability result (see Exercise 18.4).

Theorem 18.25 *Consider Algorithm 18.2, and assume that all conditions of Lemma 18.24 hold. Then*

$$\mathbb{E}\sum_{t=1}^{T}[V_*^1(x_t^1) - V_{\pi_t}^1(x_t^1)] \le \delta T + 2\sqrt{dHT\sum_{h=1}^{H}\beta^h(\epsilon,\delta)^2} + 2Hd,$$

where $d = H^{-1}\sum_{h=1}^{H}\dim(T, \mathcal{B}^h(\epsilon))$.

Proof From Lemma 18.24, we know that for each t, with probability at least $1-\delta$ over the observations $\{(x_s, a_s, r_s) : s = 1, \ldots, t-1\}$, the two inequalities of the lemma hold (which we denote as event E_t). It implies that under event E_t, f_t^h satisfies the following inequalities for all $h \in [H]$:

$$\mathbb{E}_{x_t^1}V_*^1(x_t^1) \le \mathbb{E}_{x_t^1}f_t^1(x_t^1), \tag{18.13}$$

$$\mathbb{E}_{x_t^h, a_t^h}|\mathcal{E}^h(f_t, x_t^h, a_t^h)| \le 2\mathbb{E}_{x_t^h, a_t^h}\beta^h(\epsilon,\delta)b^h(x_t^h, a_t^h). \tag{18.14}$$

We thus obtain

$$\mathbb{E}\sum_{t=1}^{T}[V_*^1(x_t^1) - V_{\pi_t}^1(x_t^1)] \le \delta T + \mathbb{E}\sum_{t=1}^{T}[f_t^1(x_t^1) - V_{\pi_t}^1(x_t^1)]\mathbb{1}(E_t)$$

$$= \delta T + \sum_{t=1}^{T}\mathbb{E}\sum_{h=1}^{H}\mathcal{E}^h(f_t, x_t^h, a_t^h)\mathbb{1}(E_t)$$

$$\le \delta T + 2\sum_{t=1}^{T}\mathbb{E}\sum_{h=1}^{H}\left[\beta^h(\epsilon,\delta)\min(1, b^h(x_t^h, a_t^h)) + \min(1, b^h(x_t^h, a_t^h))^2\right]$$

$$\le \delta T + 2\sqrt{\sum_{t=1}^{T}\sum_{h=1}^{H}\beta^h(\epsilon,\delta)^2}\sqrt{\mathbb{E}\sum_{t=1}^{T}\sum_{h=1}^{H}\min(1, b^h(x_t^h, a_t^h))^2}$$

$$+ 2\mathbb{E}\sum_{t=1}^{T}\sum_{h=1}^{H}\min(1, b^h(x_t^h, a_t^h))^2$$

$$\le \delta T + 2\sqrt{T\sum_{h=1}^{H}\beta^h(\epsilon,\delta)^2}\sqrt{\sum_{h=1}^{H}\dim(T, \mathcal{B}^h(\epsilon))} + 2\sum_{h=1}^{H}\dim(T, \mathcal{B}^h(\epsilon)).$$

The first inequality used (18.13). The first equality used Theorem 18.11. The second inequality used (18.14) and $|\mathcal{E}^h(f_t, x_t^h, a_t^h)| \le 2$. The third inequality used the Cauchy–Schwarz inequality. This proves the desired bound. □

Example 18.26 Consider the linear MDP example in Example 18.23, where we assume feature $\phi^h(\cdot) = \tilde{\phi}^h(\cdot)$ is known and is d-dimensional for all h. We have $\ln N(\epsilon/T, \mathcal{F}^h, \|\cdot\|_\infty) = \tilde{O}(d)$. Moreover, since the bonus function of (18.11) can be regarded as a function class with the $d \times d$ matrix Σ_t^h as its parameter, we know from Theorem 5.3 that

$$\ln N(\epsilon/T, \mathcal{B}^{h+1}(\epsilon), \| \cdot \|_\infty) = \tilde{O}(d^2). \tag{18.15}$$

This means that in Theorem 18.25, we have $\beta^h = \tilde{O}(d^2)$. Moreover $\dim(T, \mathcal{B}^h(\epsilon)) = \tilde{O}(d)$ from Example 18.23 and Proposition 15.8. It follows from Theorem 18.25 that for Algorithm 18.2, we have a regret bound of

$$\tilde{O}(Hd^{3/2}\sqrt{T}).$$

Compared to (18.8), the bound is inferior by a factor of $\sqrt{d}$. This suboptimality is caused by the entropy number of the bonus function class $\mathcal{B}^{h+1}(\epsilon)$ in (18.15), which is $\tilde{O}(d^2)$ due to the d^2 parameters in Σ_t^h. In comparison, the Q-function class $\mathcal{F}^h$ has d parameters, and the entropy number is $\tilde{O}(d)$.

18.4 Bellman Factorization and V-type Bellman Eluder Coefficient

In linear MDP, we assume that the Q function class is a linear model. Although moderate nonlinear generalization can be handled by eluder coefficient, it still requires a near-linear Q-function class. In particular, one condition to ensure small eluder coefficient is to assume that the Q function lies in the linear space spanned by the feature maps $\{\phi^h(\cdot)\}$ of the underlying MDP. It is however, desirable to allow the Q function class to contain functions outside $\{\phi^h(\cdot)\}$. The resulting algorithm will be able to allow more nonlinearity in the Q function class, similar to the case of contextual bandits of Section 17.4 and Section 17.5.

We first state the following structural assumption of the MDP, in terms of eluder coefficient, which we refer to as the V-type Bellman eluder coefficient.

Definition 18.27 (V-type Bellman Eluder Coefficient)   Given a candidate Q function class $\mathcal{F}$, its V-type Bellman eluder coefficient $\mathrm{EC}_V^h(\epsilon, \mathcal{F}, T)$ at step $h \geq 1$ is the smallest number d so that for any filtered sequence $\{f_t, (x_t, r_t, a_t) \sim \pi_{f_t}\}_{t=1}^T$,

$$\mathbb{E}\sum_{t=2}^T \mathcal{E}^h(f_t, x_t^h, a_t^h) \leq \sqrt{d\mathbb{E}\sum_{t=2}^T \left(\epsilon + \sum_{s=1}^{t-1} \mathbb{E}_{\tilde{x}\sim\pi_{f_s}}\mathcal{E}^h(f_t, \tilde{x}^h, \pi_{f_t}(\tilde{x}^h))^2\right)}.$$

In order to bound the Q-type Bellman eluder coefficient, we need to assume in Proposition 18.20 that the Q-function class can be embedded in a linear vector space. This is not necessary for the V-type Bellman eluder coefficient, which allows general nonlinear Q-function class.

We note that for linear MDP, from the proof of Proposition 18.18, we know that for any $h \geq 2$, there exists $u^{h-1}(f) \in \mathcal{H}^{h-1}$ so that

$$\mathbb{E}_{x^h|x^{h-1},a^{h-1}}\mathcal{E}^h(f, x^h, \pi_f(x^h)) = \langle u^{h-1}(f), \phi^{h-1}(x^{h-1}, a^{h-1})\rangle.$$

If moreover, we assume that $(x^{h-1}, a^{h-1}) \sim \pi'$, where π' is referred to as a *roll-in policy*, then we have the following decomposition,

$$\mathbb{E}_{x^h\sim\pi'}\mathcal{E}^h(f, x^h, \pi_f(x^h)) = \langle u^{h-1}(f), \phi^{h-1}(\pi')\rangle,$$

where $\phi^{h-1}(\pi') = \mathbb{E}_{x^{h-1},a^{h-1}\sim\pi'}\phi^{h-1}(x^{h-1},a^{h-1})$.

One may expand this property and define Bellman factorizable MDPs as follows, which includes linear MDP as a special case.

Definition 18.28 (Bellman Factorization) Let $\mathcal{H} = \{\mathcal{H}^h\}$ be a sequence of vector spaces, with dimensions (Bellman ranks) $\dim(\mathcal{H}^h)$ for $h = 1,\ldots,H$. We allow $\dim(\mathcal{H}^h) = \infty$. An MDP has a Bellman factorization with respect to $\mathcal{H}$ if the following condition holds. There exists $u^{h-1}(f) \in \mathcal{H}^{h-1}$ for all $h \geq 2$ and Q-function $f \in \mathcal{F}$; there exists $\phi^{h-1}(\pi') \in \mathcal{H}^{h-1}$ for all policy π', so that the following factorization is valid:

$$\mathbb{E}_{x^h\sim\pi'}\mathcal{E}^h(f,x^h,\pi_f(x^h)) = \langle u^{h-1}(f),\phi^{h-1}(\pi')\rangle.$$

Note that in general, the feature $\phi^{h-1}(\pi')$ is neither known nor used by the RL algorithms. The concept is a structural condition of the MDP that is needed only for bounding the V-type Bellman eluder coefficient. Specifically, the following result presents such a bound.

Proposition 18.29 *Consider an MDP that has a Bellman factorization with respect to $\mathcal{H}$ as in Definition 18.28. Assume that x_t^1 are iid samples drawn from the same underlying distribution, and for $h \geq 2$, $\sup_{f\in\mathcal{F}}\|u^{h-1}(f)\|_{\mathcal{H}^{h-1}} \leq B$. Assume that $|\mathcal{E}^h(f,x^h,a^h)| \in [0,1]$, then*

$$\mathrm{EC}_V^1(0,\mathcal{F},T) \leq 1 + \ln T,$$
$$\mathrm{EC}_V^h(1,\mathcal{F},T) \leq 2\mathrm{entro}(1/(B^2 T),\phi^{h-1}(\cdot)), \quad (h \geq 2),$$

where $\mathrm{entro}(\cdot)$ *is defined in Proposition 15.8. In particular, if $\{\mathcal{H}^h\}$ are finite dimensional, and let $B' = \sup_{h\geq 2}\sup_{\pi}\|\phi^{h-1}(\pi)\|_{\mathcal{H}^{h-1}}$, then for $h \geq 2$,*

$$\mathrm{EC}_V^h(1,\mathcal{F},T) \leq \dim(\mathcal{H}^{h-1})\ln(1 + T(BB')^2).$$

Proof For $h = 1$, we have

$$\mathbb{E}\sum_{t=2}^T \mathcal{E}^1(f_t,x_t^1,a_t^1)$$

$$\leq \mathbb{E}\sqrt{\sum_{t=2}^T \frac{1}{t-1}}\sqrt{\sum_{t=2}^T (t-1)\mathcal{E}^1(f_t,x_t^1,a_t^1)^2} \quad \text{(Cauchy–Schwarz inequality)}$$

$$\leq \sqrt{\sum_{t=2}^T \frac{1}{t-1}}\sqrt{\mathbb{E}\sum_{t=2}^T (t-1)\mathbb{E}_{x_t^1}\mathcal{E}^1(f_t,x_t^1,\pi_{f_t}(x_t^1))^2}$$

$$\leq \sqrt{1+\ln T}\sqrt{\mathbb{E}\sum_{t=2}^T\sum_{s=1}^{t-1} \mathbb{E}_{x_s^1}\mathcal{E}^1(f_t,x_s^1,\pi_{f_t}(x_s^1))^2}.$$

The second inequality used the Jensen inequality and concavity of $\sqrt{\cdot}$, and $a_t = \pi_{f_t}(x_t^1)$. The third inequality used the fact that x_s^1 has the same distribution as x_t^1, and $\sum_{t=2}^T 1/(t-1) \leq 1 + \ln T$.

For $h \geq 2$, we let $\mathrm{EC}_V^h = 2\mathrm{entro}(1/(B^2 T), \phi^{h-1}(\cdot))$, then

$$\mathbb{E} \sum_{t=2}^{T} \mathcal{E}^h(f_t, x_t^h, a_t^h) = \mathbb{E} \sum_{t=2}^{T} \langle u^{h-1}(f_t), \phi^{h-1}(\pi_{f_t}) \rangle$$

$$\leq \sqrt{\mathrm{EC}_V^h \mathbb{E} \sum_{t=2}^{T} \left(1 + \sum_{s=1}^{t-1} (\langle u^{h-1}(f_t), \phi^{h-1}(\pi_{f_s}) \rangle)^2 \right)}$$

$$= \sqrt{\mathrm{EC}_V^h \mathbb{E} \sum_{t=2}^{T} \left(1 + \sum_{s=1}^{t-1} \mathbb{E}_{\tilde{x} \sim \pi_s} \mathcal{E}^h(f_t, \tilde{x}^h, \pi_{f_t}(\tilde{x}^h))^2 \right)}.$$

The inequality follows from (17.10). □

Compared with the Q-type Bellman eluder coefficient, the V-type Bellman eluder coefficient employs the optimal action π_{f_t} on the historic data without using the historic action a_t. It is necessary to draw random actions according a fixed exploration policy $\tilde{\pi}$ by using the techniques of Section 17.5. For finite actions, we can simply draw the actions uniformly at random. Otherwise, we have to design a policy $\tilde{\pi}$ for the purpose. The resulting algorithm is given in Algorithm 18.3.

Algorithm 18.3 V-type Bellman Error UCB Algorithm

Input: λ, T, $\mathcal{F}$, $\mathcal{G}$, $\tilde{\pi}$

1 Let $\mathcal{F}_0 = \{f_0\}$
2 Let $\beta_0 = 0$
3 **for** $t = 1, 2, \ldots, T$ **do**
4   Observe x_t^1
5   Let $f_t \in \arg\max_{f \in \mathcal{F}_{t-1}} f(x_t^1)$
6   Let $\pi_t = \pi_{f_t}$
7   Draw $h_t \sim [H]$ uniformly at random
8   Play policy π_t and observe trajectory (x_t, a_t, r_t) up to $x_t^{h_t}$
9   Play random policy $a_t^{h_t} \sim \tilde{\pi}^{h_t}(\cdot | x_t^{h_t})$, and observe $(r_t^{h_t}, x_t^{h_t+1})$
10   Let

$$\mathcal{F}_t = \left\{ f \in \mathcal{F} : \sup_{g \in \mathcal{G}} \sum_{s=1}^{t} L^{h_s}(f, g, x_s^{h_s}, a_s^{h_s}, r_s^{h_s}, x_s^{h_s+1}) \leq \beta_t^2 \right\}$$

    with appropriately chosen β_t, where $L^h(\cdot)$ is defined according to (18.3).

11 **return** randomly chosen π_t from $t = 1$ to $t = T$

If we compare Algorithm 18.3 to Algorithm 18.1, there are two major differences. One difference is that at each time t, it stops at a randomly chosen h_t. Another difference is that a one-step exploration using a predefined policy $\tilde{\pi}$ is needed. The policy is designed so that the optimal action π_{f_t} for any f_t is well covered, so that we can bound the Bellman error with π_{f_t} by $a_s \sim \tilde{\pi}$. We may use Definition 17.35, which we adapt to the RL problem as follows.

Definition 18.30   The coverage coefficient $\mathrm{CC}^h(\epsilon, \tilde{\pi}, \mathcal{F})$ (for $\epsilon > 0$) of a random policy $\tilde{\pi}$ at step h is defined as

$$\mathrm{CC}^h(\epsilon, \tilde{\pi}, \mathcal{F}) = \sup_{f \in \mathcal{F}, x^h \in \mathcal{X}} \frac{\mathcal{E}^h(f, x^h, \pi_f(x^h))^2}{\epsilon + \mathbb{E}_{a^h \sim \tilde{\pi}(\cdot|x^h)} \mathcal{E}^h(f, x^h, a^h)^2}.$$

We note that Definition 18.30 is consistent with Definition 17.35, which can be regarded as a conditional version of Definition 9.42. Therefore we may employ a conditional G-optimal design $\tilde{\pi}^h(a^h|x^h)$ by conditioning on x^h. The following result shows that if Bellman error is linearly embeddable (with possibly unknown feature map), then good coverage coefficients can be obtained using nonlinear G-optimal design. It is a direct consequence of Theorem 9.44.

Proposition 18.31   *Assume that $\mathcal{F}$ is complete with respect to $\mathcal{G}$, then for each $h \in [H]$,*

$$\{\mathcal{E}^h(f, x^h, a^h) : f \in \mathcal{F}\} \subset \mathcal{F}^h \ominus \mathcal{G}^h = \{f^h - g^h : f^h \in \mathcal{F}^h, g^h \in \mathcal{G}^h\}.$$

If $\mathcal{F}^h \ominus \mathcal{G}^h$ is linearly embeddable in $\mathcal{H}^h$, with a decomposition $u^h(x^h, a^h) = f^h(x^h, a^h) - g^h(x^h, a^h) = \langle w^h(u^h, x^h), \psi^h(x^h, a^h) \rangle$ for some unknown embedding functions $w^h(\cdot)$ and $\psi^h(\cdot)$ (see Definition 17.24). Let $B = \sup_{x^h, u^h, \tilde{u}^h} \| w^h(u^h, x^h) - w^h(\tilde{u}^h, x^h) \|_{\mathcal{H}^h}$, and for all x^h, let $\{\tilde{\pi}^h(\cdot|x^h)\}$ be the solution of the conditional G-optimal design problem

$$\min_{\pi(\cdot|x^h)} \sup_{x^h, a^h} \sup_{u^h, \tilde{u}^h \in \mathcal{F}^h \ominus \mathcal{G}^h} \frac{|u^h(x^h, a^h) - \tilde{u}^h(x^h, a^h)|^2}{\epsilon + \mathbb{E}_{\tilde{a}^h \sim \pi(\cdot|x^h)}(u^h(\tilde{x}^h, a^h) - \tilde{u}^h(\tilde{x}^h, a^h))^2}.$$

Then

$$\mathrm{CC}^h(\epsilon, \tilde{\pi}, \mathcal{F}) \leq \dim(\epsilon/B^2, \psi^h(\cdot)),$$

where $\dim(\cdot)$ is the effective dimension in Proposition 9.36.

The linear embedding condition allows the Q-function class to be nonlinear and it does not need to be contained in the linear space spanned by the feature maps of the underlying MDP (which is needed for the analysis of the Q-type problems). The analogy for the bandit case has been discussed in Section 17.4. For example, if the number of actions is finite, then any nonlinear function classes $\mathcal{F}$ is linearly embeddable.

Example 18.32   If the number of actions K is finite, then one may use encoding $\psi^h(x^h, a^h) = e_{a^h} \in \mathbb{R}^K$, and the corresponding G-optimal design is uniform $\tilde{\pi}$ over the actions. Using this result, we obtain $\mathrm{CC}^h(0, \tilde{\pi}, \mathcal{F}) \leq K$.

By combining Proposition 18.29 and Proposition 18.31, we know that both eluder and covering coefficients can be bounded without the need to know either the linear embedding feature maps or the Bellman factorization. The overall complexity is stated as follows.

Proposition 18.33 *In Algorithm 18.3, we let*

$$\tilde{d} = \sum_{h=1}^{H} \mathrm{EC}_V^h(\epsilon, \mathcal{F}, T) \max(1, \mathrm{CC}^h(\epsilon', \tilde{\pi}, \mathcal{F})),$$

then

$$\mathbb{E} \sum_{h=1}^{H} \sum_{t=2}^{T} \mathcal{E}^h(f_t, x_t^h, a_t^h) \leq \sqrt{\tilde{d}\mathbb{E} \sum_{t=2}^{T} \left(\epsilon H + \epsilon' HT + \sum_{s=1}^{t-1} \sum_{h=1}^{H} \bar{\mathcal{E}}^h(f_t, \pi_{f_s}, \tilde{\pi})^2 \right)},$$

where

$$\bar{\mathcal{E}}^h(f, \pi, \tilde{\pi})^2 = \mathbb{E}_{\tilde{x}^h \sim \pi} \mathbb{E}_{a^h \sim \tilde{\pi}(\cdot|x^h)} \mathcal{E}^h(f_t, x^h, a^h)^2.$$

Proof Let $d_1^h = \mathrm{EC}_V^h(\epsilon, \mathcal{F}, T)$, and $d_2^h = \mathrm{CC}^h(\epsilon', \tilde{\pi}, \mathcal{F})$. We obtain

$$\mathbb{E} \sum_{h=1}^{H} \sum_{t=2}^{T} \mathcal{E}^h(f_t, x_t^h, a_t^h) \leq \sum_{h=1}^{H} \sqrt{d_1^h \mathbb{E} \sum_{t=2}^{T} \left(\epsilon + \sum_{s=1}^{t-1} \mathbb{E}_{\tilde{x} \sim \pi_{f_s}} \mathcal{E}^h(f_t, \tilde{x}^h, \pi_{f_t}(\tilde{x}^h))^2 \right)}$$

$$\leq \sum_{h=1}^{H} \sqrt{d_1^h \mathbb{E} \sum_{t=2}^{T} \left(\epsilon + d_2^h \sum_{s=1}^{t-1} \left(\epsilon' + \bar{\mathcal{E}}^h(f_t, \pi_{f_s}, \tilde{\pi})^2 \right) \right)}$$

$$\leq \sum_{h=1}^{H} \sqrt{d_1^h \max(1, d_2^h) \mathbb{E} \sum_{t=2}^{T} \left(\epsilon + \epsilon' T + \sum_{s=1}^{t-1} \bar{\mathcal{E}}^h(f_t, \pi_{f_s}, \tilde{\pi})^2 \right)}.$$

The first inequality used Definition 18.27. The second inequality used Definition 18.30. We then used the Cauchy–Schwarz inequality to obtain the result. $\quad\square$

Using Proposition 18.33, we can reduce regret to in-sample prediction error on historic data. This allows us to prove the following result for Algorithm 18.3, which is similar to Theorem 18.21.

Theorem 18.34 *Assume that Assumption 18.12 holds, $\mathcal{F}$ is complete with respect to $\mathcal{G}$, and $g^h(\cdot) \in [0,1]$ for all $g \in \mathcal{G}$. If we set β_t in Algorithm 18.3 as*

$$\beta_t^2 \geq \inf_{\epsilon > 0} \left[4\epsilon t(4 + \epsilon) + 2.4 \ln \left(16 M(\epsilon, \mathcal{F}, \|\cdot\|_\infty)^2 M(\epsilon, \mathcal{G}, \|\cdot\|_\infty)/\delta^2) \right) \right],$$

where $M(\cdot)$ denotes the $\|\cdot\|_\infty$ packing number, and $\|f\|_\infty = \sup_{h,x,a} |f^h(x,a)|$, then we have

$$\mathbb{E} \sum_{t=2}^{T} [V_*^1(x_t^1) - V_{\pi_t}^1(x_t^1)] \leq \delta T + \sqrt{\tilde{d} H \left(\epsilon T + \epsilon' T^2 + \delta T^2 + 4 \sum_{t=2}^{T} \beta_{t-1}^2 \right)},$$

where $\tilde{d} = \sum_{h=1}^{H} \mathrm{EC}_V^h(\epsilon, \mathcal{F}, T) \max(1, \mathrm{CC}^h(\epsilon', \tilde{\pi}, \mathcal{F}))$.

Proof Sketch First, we would like to prove an analogy of Theorem 18.14 for β_t by using the same notations in its proof. Using the same sub-Gaussian logarithmic moment generating function, we obtain the following counterpart of (18.4) from

Theorem 13.11 by taking conditional expectation with respect to each trajectory. With probability at least $1 - \delta/2$, for all $f_\epsilon \in \mathcal{F}_\epsilon$, $g_\epsilon \in \mathcal{G}_\epsilon$ and $t \geq 0$,

$$\underbrace{\left| \sum_{s=1}^{t} \Delta_s^{h_s}(f_\epsilon, g_\epsilon) \epsilon_s^{h_s}(f_\epsilon) \right|}_{A} \leq \frac{1}{\lambda} \sum_{s=1}^{t} \ln \mathbb{E}_{h^s} \mathbb{E}_{x_s^{h_s}, a_s^{h_s}} \exp\left(\frac{\lambda^2 \Delta_s^{h_s}(f_\epsilon, g_\epsilon)^2}{8} \right)$$

$$+ \frac{\ln(4M_1 M_2/\delta)}{\lambda},$$

where we choose $\lambda = 0.9$. Let $\xi = \lambda^2 \Delta_s^{h_s}(f_\epsilon, g_\epsilon)^2/8$, then $\xi \leq 0.9^2/8 \leq 0.102$, and thus

$$\frac{1}{\lambda} \ln \mathbb{E} \exp(\xi) \leq \frac{1}{\lambda}[\mathbb{E} \exp(\xi) - 1] \leq \frac{\exp(0.102)}{\lambda} \mathbb{E}\xi.$$

By combining the previous two inequalities, and using $\exp(0.102)\lambda \leq 1$, and $1/\lambda \leq 1.2$, we obtain

$$A \leq \sum_{s=1}^{t} \frac{1}{H} \sum_{h=1}^{H} \mathbb{E}_{x_s^h \sim \pi_s, a_s^h \sim \tilde{\pi}(\cdot|x_s^h)} \frac{\Delta_s^h(f_\epsilon, g_\epsilon)^2}{8} + 1.2 \ln(4M_1 M_2/\delta).$$

This inequality can replace (18.4) in the proof of Theorem 18.14. The same argument leads to the following inequalities as counterparts of (18.5) and (18.6). With probability at least $1 - \delta$, for all $f \in \mathcal{F}$, $g \in \mathcal{G}$, and $t \geq 0$,

$$\left| \sum_{s=1}^{t} \Delta_s^{h_s}(f, g) \epsilon_s^{h_s}(f) \right| \leq \frac{1}{4H} \sum_{s=1}^{t} \sum_{h=1}^{H} \mathbb{E}_{x_s^h \sim \pi_s, a_s^h \sim \tilde{\pi}(\cdot|x_s^h)} \Delta_s^h(f, g)^2$$

$$+ \epsilon t(4 + \epsilon) + 1.2 \ln\left(4M_1 M_2/\delta \right),$$

$$\left| \sum_{s=1}^{t} \Delta_s^{h_s}(f, f) \epsilon_s^{h_s}(f) \right| \leq \frac{1}{4H} \sum_{s=1}^{t} \sum_{h=1}^{H} \mathbb{E}_{x_s^h \sim \pi_s, a_s^h \sim \tilde{\pi}(\cdot|x_s^h)} \Delta_s^h(f, f)^2$$

$$+ \epsilon t(4 + \epsilon) + 1.2 \ln\left(4M_1/\delta \right).$$

We can set

$$0.5\beta_t^2 \geq [\epsilon t(4 + \epsilon) + 1.2 \ln\left(4M_1 M_2/\delta \right)] + [\epsilon t(4 + \epsilon) + 1.2 \ln\left(4M_1/\delta \right)]$$

as in the proof of Theorem 18.14, and obtain $Q_* \in \mathcal{F}_t$, and

$$\frac{1}{H} \sum_{s=1}^{t} \sum_{h=1}^{H} \bar{\mathcal{E}}^h(f, \pi_s \tilde{\pi})^2 \leq 4\beta_t^2,$$

where $\bar{\mathcal{E}}^h$ is defined in Proposition 18.33. The result now follows directly from Proposition 18.33 and the same derivation of Theorem 18.21. $\square$

It is worth pointing out that while Algorithm 18.3 returns a policy π_t with good average regret, the online algorithm itself does not achieve such a regret, because the algorithm needs to employ a one-step pure exploration policy $\tilde{\pi}$ that is different from π_t. The purpose of this policy is to cover all possible actions equally well (e.g. by using nonlinear G-optimal design). It is similar to pure exploration in contextual bandit of Section 17.5, which also employs nonlinear G-optimal design. Nevertheless, the algorithm can solve the low-Bellman-rank MDP problem with a nonlinear Q-function class, and without knowing the underlying Bellman factorization. If we consider linear MDP with d-dimensional unknown feature maps, and assume that we have finite K actions, with $\mathcal{F}$ containing $M_{\mathcal{F}}$ members and $\mathcal{G}$ containing $M_{\mathcal{G}}$ members, then $\tilde{d} = \tilde{O}(HdK)$, $\beta_t^2 = \tilde{O}(\ln(M_{\mathcal{F}}M_{\mathcal{G}}))$. Therefore the regret of π_t return by Algorithm 18.3 satisfies

$$\mathbb{E}[V_*^1(x_t^1) - V_{\pi_t}^1(x_t^1)] = \tilde{O}\left(H\sqrt{dK\ln(M_{\mathcal{F}}M_{\mathcal{G}})}\right).$$

Compared to that of Theorem 18.21, this result is worse by a factor of $\sqrt{HK}$. The $\sqrt{H}$ factor is due to the random h_t choice, which does not efficiently use all data in a trajectory. The $\sqrt{K}$ factor is due to pure exploration with a nonlinear Q-function class without knowing the feature maps of the underlying Bellman factorization.

18.5 Model-Based Reinforcement Learning

In linear MDP, the version space UCB algorithm does not need to know or to learn the transition probability $P^h(x^{h+1}|x^h, a^h)$. Such an algorithm is referred to as *model free* in reinforcement learning. On the other hand, if the learning algorithm estimates and employs the transition probability $P^h(x^{h+1}|x^h, a^h)$ information, then the corresponding method is referred to as *model based*. Instead of looking at Q-function class, in model-based RL, we consider a class of MDP models and explicitly estimate the transition probabilities.

Definition 18.35 In a model-based RL problem, we are given an MDP model class $\mathcal{M}$. Each $M \in \mathcal{M}$ includes explicit transition probability

$$P_M^h(x^{h+1}|x^h, a^h),$$

and expected reward

$$R_M^h(x^h, a^h) = \mathbb{E}_M\left[r^h|x^h, a^h\right].$$

We use $\mathbb{E}_M[\cdot]$ to denote the expectation with respect to model M's transition dynamics P_M. Given any f^{h+1} on $\mathcal{X}$, we define the model Bellman operator

$$(\mathcal{T}_M^h f)(x^h, a^h) = R_M^h(x^n, a^h) + \mathbb{E}_M[f^{h+1}(x^{h+1})|x^h, a^h].$$

We use $f_M = \{f_M^h(x^h, a^h)\}_{h=1}^H$ to denote the Q function of model M, and use $\pi_M = \pi_{f_M}$ to denote the corresponding optimal policy under model M.

We will also impose the following assumption for model-based RL.

Assumption 18.36 Let $\mathcal{M}$ be a class of MDP models. We assume that the correct model $M_* \in \mathcal{M}$: the true transition probability is given by $P_{M_*}^h(x^{h+1}|x^h, a^h)$, and the true expected reward is given by

$$\mathbb{E}_{M_*}\left[r^h|x^h, a^h\right] = R_{M_*}^h(x^h, a^h).$$

We assume that $r^h + f_M^h(x^h, a^h) \in [0, 1]$ and $f_M^1(x^1) \in [0, 1]$. We also assume that there is a *planning oracle* that solves the optimal policy π_M and Q-function $f_M^h(x^h, a^h)$ for any given model $M \in \mathcal{M}$.

One advantage of model-based RL is that the completeness assumption is not required if the model Bellman operator $(\mathcal{T}_M^h f)(x^h, a^h)$ can be evaluated efficiently. In this case, we may simply compare the model value to $r^h + f^{h+1}(x^{h+1})$, which is an unbiased estimate of the true Bellman operator $(\mathcal{T}_{M_*}^h f)(x^h, a^h)$. Using this observation, one may define the following loss function

$$L^h(M, M', x^h, a^h, r^h, x^{h+1}) = \left((\mathcal{T}_M^h f_{M'}(x^h, a^h) - r^h - f_{M'}(x^{h+1})\right)^2, \quad (18.16)$$

which we call value-targeted loss to be consistent with Ayoub et al. (2020). It is natural to require that a good model has a value-targeted loss that fits well on historic data. This allows us to define a version space for the models in $\mathcal{M}$. We can then apply the general principle of optimism as in Algorithm 17.4 and Algorithm 18.1. The resulting algorithm is presented in Algorithm 18.4. Since we do not need completeness, the analysis of the algorithm is a direct extension of Algorithm 17.4.

Algorithm 18.4 Value-Targeted Loss UCB Algorithm

Input: $\lambda, T, \mathcal{M}$

1 Let $\mathcal{F}_0 = \{f_0\}$

2 Let $\beta_0 = 0$

3 **for** $t = 1, 2, \ldots, T$ **do**

4   Observe x_t^1

5   Let

$$M_t \in \arg\max_{M \in \mathcal{M}_{t-1}} f_M(x_t^1).$$

    Let $\pi_t = \pi_{M_t}$

6   Play policy π_t and observe trajectory (x_t, a_t, r_t)

7   Let

$$\hat{M}_t = \arg\min_{M \in \mathcal{M}} \sum_{h=1}^H \sum_{s=1}^t L^h(M, M_s, x_s^h, a_s^h, r_s^h, x_s^{h+1}),$$

    where $L^h(\cdot)$ is defined according to (18.16).

8   Define

$$\mathcal{M}_t = \left\{ M \in \mathcal{M} : \sum_{h=1}^H \sum_{s=1}^t ((\mathcal{T}_M^h f_{M_s})(x_s^h, a_s^h) - (\mathcal{T}_{\hat{M}_t}^h f_{M_s})(x_s^h, a_s^h))^2 \le \beta_t^2 \right\}$$

    with appropriately chosen β_t.

9 **return** randomly chosen π_t from $t = 1$ to $t = T$

In order to analyze Algorithm 18.4, we need to introduce the concept of model-based Bellman error for model-based RL problems.

Definition 18.37 (Model-Based Bellman Error) For model-based RL, given a model M and candidate Q-function f, we define the corresponding model-based Bellman error as

$$\mathcal{E}^h(M, f, x^h, a^h) = (\mathcal{T}_M^h f)(x^h, a^h) - (\mathcal{T}_{M_*}^h f)(x^h, a^h)$$
$$= \mathbb{E}_M[r^h + f(x^{h+1})|x^h, a^h] - \mathbb{E}_{M_*}[r^h + f(x^{h+1})|x^h, a^h].$$

We also use the following simplified notation:

$$\mathcal{E}^h(M, x^h, a^h) = \mathcal{E}^h(M, f_M, x^h, a^h).$$

The definition of $\mathcal{E}^h(M, x^h, a^h)$ is consistent with the corresponding model-free Bellman error $\mathcal{E}^h(f_M, x^h, a^h)$ in Definition 18.10:

$$\mathcal{E}^h(M, x^h, a^h) = \mathcal{E}^h(f_M, x^h, a^h). \tag{18.17}$$

This immediately implies the following specialization of Theorem 18.11 for model-based RL. The proof is left to Exercise 18.6.

Theorem 18.38 *Consider a model M with its value function f_M and optimal policy π_M. Then we have*

$$[f_M(x^1) - V_{\pi_M}^1(x^1)] = \mathbb{E}_{(x,a,r)\sim\pi_M|x^1} \sum_{h=1}^{H} \mathcal{E}^h(M, x^h, a^h),$$

where $V_{\pi_M}^1(x^1)$ is the true value function of the true underlying MDP M_*, and $(x, a, r) \sim \pi_M|x^1$ denotes the trajectory of policy π_M under the true MDP M_*.

We can now introduce the definition of Bellman eluder coefficient for model-based RL. Instead of reducing the on-policy Bellman error $\mathcal{E}^h(M_t, x_t^h, a_t^h)$ to squared Bellman error on the historic training data as in Definition 18.19, we can reduce it to different loss functions. Note that similar to Definition 18.19, we define it in expectation for more generality.

Definition 18.39 (Model-Based Bellman Eluder Coefficient) Consider an arbitrary loss function sequence $L = \{L_t^h(M, M_*): \mathcal{M} \times \mathcal{M} \to \mathbb{R}_+, t \in [T], h \in [H]\}$ so that each loss function L_t^h may also depend on (M_t, x_t^h, a_t^h). The L-loss Bellman eluder coefficient $\mathrm{EC}_L(\epsilon, \mathcal{M}, T)$ of a model-based RL problem $\mathcal{M}$ is the smallest d so that for any filtered sequence $\{M_t, (x_t, r_t, a_t) \sim \pi_{M_t}, L_t\}_{t=1}^{T}$,

$$\mathbb{E} \sum_{t=2}^{T} \sum_{h=1}^{H} \mathcal{E}^h(M_t, x_t^h, a_t^h) \leq \sqrt{d\mathbb{E} \sum_{h=1}^{H} \sum_{t=2}^{T} \left(\epsilon + \sum_{s=1}^{t-1} L_s^h(M_t, M_*)\right)}.$$

Definition 18.39 is generic, so can include both V-type and V-type problems. We will only consider Q-type problems in this section. In the following, we introduce several commonly used Q-type loss functions for model-based RL.

Definition 18.40 Consider model-based eluder coefficients in Definition 18.39 with the following Q-type loss functions.

The loss function

$$L_t^h(M, M_*) = \mathcal{E}^h(M, f_{M_t}, x_t^h, a_t^h)^2$$

is referred to as the *value-targeted loss*, and the corresponding Bellman eluder coefficient, denoted by $\mathrm{EC}_{Q-\mathrm{VT}}$, is referred to as the Q-type value-targeted Bellman eluder coefficient.

Given a Q-function class $\mathcal{F}$ that contains $\{f_M \colon M \in \mathcal{M}\}$, assume that $r^h + f^h(x^h, a^h) \in [0, 1]$ for all $f \in \mathcal{F}$ and $h \in [H]$. The loss function

$$L_t^h(M, M_*) = \sup_{f \in \mathcal{F}} \mathcal{E}^h(M, f, x_t^h, a_t^h)^2$$

is referred to as the *witness loss*, and the corresponding Bellman eluder coefficient, denoted by $\mathrm{EC}_{Q-\mathrm{Wit}}$, is referred to as the Q-type witness Bellman eluder coefficient.

The loss function

$$L_t^h(M, M_*) = H(P_M^h(\cdot | x_t^h, a_t^h) \| P_{M_*}^h(\cdot | x_t^h, a_t^h))^2$$

is referred to as the *Hellinger loss*, and the corresponding Bellman eluder coefficient, denoted by $\mathrm{EC}_{Q-\mathrm{Hel}}$, is referred to as the Q-type Hellinger Bellman eluder coefficient.

We have the following result concerning the relationship of different model-based eluder coefficients. The proof is left as an exercise.

Proposition 18.41 *We have*

$$\mathrm{EC}_{Q-\mathrm{Hel}}(\epsilon, \mathcal{M}, T) \leq \mathrm{EC}_{Q-\mathrm{Wit}}(\epsilon, \mathcal{M}, T) \leq \mathrm{EC}_{Q-\mathrm{VT}}(\epsilon, \mathcal{M}, T).$$

With this definition, we can now prove a regret bound for Algorithm 18.4 using the value-targeted eluder coefficient. We first state a result that is an extension of Theorem 13.15. The proof is almost identical to that of Theorem 13.15 (with $\sigma = 0.5$), and thus we leave it as an exercise.

Lemma 18.42 *Assume that Assumption 18.36 holds. Consider function class $\mathcal{F} = \{f^h(M', x^h, a^h) \colon \mathcal{M} \times \mathcal{X} \times \mathcal{A} \to \mathbb{R}\}$ that contains $\{\mathcal{E}^h(M, \cdot, \cdot) \colon M \in \mathcal{M}\}$. Assume that in Algorithm 18.4, we set*

$$\beta_t^2 \geq \inf_{\epsilon > 0} \left[4\epsilon t H(1 + 4\epsilon) + 3 \ln(2N(\epsilon, \mathcal{F}, \| \cdot \|_\infty)/\delta) \right],$$

where $\|f\|_\infty = \sup_{M', h, x^h, a^h} |f^h(M', x^h, a^h)|$. Then with probability at least $1 - \delta$, for all $t \leq T$, $M_* \in \mathcal{M}_t$.

We can now obtain the following regret bound, which is analogous to Theorem 18.21, with a similar proof.

Theorem 18.43 *Assume that Assumption 18.36 holds. Consider function class* $\mathcal{F} = \{f^h(M', x^h, a^h)\colon \mathcal{M} \times \mathcal{X} \times \mathcal{A} \to \mathbb{R}\}$ *that contains* $\{\mathcal{E}^h(M, \cdot, \cdot, \cdot)\colon M \in \mathcal{M}\}$. *Assume that in Algorithm 18.4, we set*

$$\beta_t^2 \geq \inf_{\epsilon > 0}\left[4\epsilon t H(1 + 4\epsilon) + 3\ln(2N(\epsilon, \mathcal{F}, \|\cdot\|_\infty)/\delta)\right],$$

where $\|f\|_\infty = \sup_{M', h, x^h, a^h} |f^h(M', x^h, a^h)|$. *Then*

$$\mathbb{E}\sum_{t=2}^{T}[V_*^1(x_t^1) - V_{\pi_t}^1(x_t^1)] \leq \delta H T + \sqrt{d\left(\epsilon H T + \delta H T^2 + 4\sum_{t=2}^{T}\beta_{t-1}^2\right)},$$

where $V_{\pi_t}^1$ *is the true value function of policy* π_t, *and* $d = \mathrm{EC}_{Q-\mathrm{VT}}(\epsilon, \mathcal{M}, T)$.

Proof   Let $f_t = f_{M_t}$. For $t \geq 2$, we have

$$
\begin{aligned}
&V_*^1(x_t^1) - V_{\pi_t}^1(x_t^1) \\
&= V_*^1(x_t) - f_t(x_t^1) + f_t(x_t^1) - V_{\pi_t}^1(x_t^1) \\
&\leq \mathbb{1}(M_* \notin \mathcal{M}_{t-1}) + f_t(x_t^1) - V_{\pi_t}^1(x_t^1) \\
&= \mathbb{1}(M_* \notin \mathcal{M}_{t-1}) + \mathbb{E}_{(x_t, a_t, r_t) \sim \pi_t | x_t^1} \sum_{h=1}^{H} \mathcal{E}^h(M_t, x_t^h, a_t^h).
\end{aligned}
$$

The inequality used the fact that if $M_* \in \mathcal{M}_{t-1}$, then $f_t(x_t^1) = \max_{M \in \mathcal{M}_{t-1}} f(x_t^1) \geq V_*^1(x_t^1)$; if $M_* \notin \mathcal{M}_{t-1}$, then $V_*^1(x_t) - f_t(x_t^1) \leq 1$. The second equality used Theorem 18.38.

Lemma 18.42 implies that $\Pr(M_* \in \mathcal{M}_{t-1}) \geq 1 - \delta$. We have

$$\mathbb{E}[M_*^1(x_t^1) - V_{\pi_t}^1(x_t^1)] \leq \delta + \mathbb{E}\sum_{h=1}^{H}\mathcal{E}^h(M_t, x_t^h, a_t^h).$$

We can now obtain

$$\mathbb{E}\sum_{t=2}^{T}[V_*^1(x_t^1) - V_{\pi_t}^1(x_t^1)]$$

$$\leq \mathbb{E}\sum_{t=2}^{T}\sum_{h=1}^{H}\mathcal{E}^h(M_t, x_t^h, a_t^h) + \delta T$$

$$\leq \delta b T + \sqrt{\mathrm{EC}_{Q-\mathrm{VT}}(\epsilon, \mathcal{M}, T)\mathbb{E}\sum_{t=2}^{T}\sum_{h=1}^{H}\left(\epsilon + \sum_{s=1}^{t-1}\mathcal{E}^h(M_t, f_{M_s}, x_s^h, a_s^h)^2\right)}$$

$$\leq \delta T + \sqrt{\mathrm{EC}_{Q-\mathrm{VT}}(\epsilon, \mathcal{M}, T)\left(\epsilon H T + \delta H T^2 + 4\sum_{t=2}^{T}\beta_{t-1}^2\right)}.$$

The second inequality used Definition 18.39. The last inequality used the fact that when $\Pr(M_* \notin \mathcal{M}_{t-1}) \leq \delta$, and in this case $\mathcal{E}^h(f_t, x_s^h, a_s^h)^2 \leq 1$; when $M_* \in \mathcal{M}_{t-1}$, we have

$$\sum_{h=1}^{H}\sum_{s=1}^{t-1}\mathcal{E}^h(M_t, f_{M_s}, x_s^h, a_s^h)^2$$

$$= \sum_{h=1}^{H}\sum_{s=1}^{t-1}((\mathcal{T}_{M_t}^h f_{M_s})(x_s^h, a_s^h) - (\mathcal{T}_{M_*}^h f_{M_s})(x_s^h, a_s^h))^2$$

$$\leq 2\sum_{h=1}^{H}\sum_{s=1}^{t-1}\Big[((\mathcal{T}_{M_t}^h f_{M_s})(x_s^h, a_s^h) - (\mathcal{T}_{\hat{M}_{t-1}}^h f_{M_s})(x_s^h, a_s^h))^2$$

$$+ (\mathcal{T}_{M_*}^h f_{M_s})(x_s^h, a_s^h) - (\mathcal{T}_{\hat{M}_{t-1}}^h f_{M_s})(x_s^h, a_s^h))^2\Big] \leq 4\beta_{t-1}^2.$$

The last inequality used $M_t \in \mathcal{M}_{t-1}$ and $M_* \in \mathcal{M}_{t-1}$. $\qquad\square$

One advantage of a model-based approach is that one can use other types of Bellman eluder coefficients in Proposition 18.41 that are weaker than value-targeted Bellman eluder coefficients. We may consider the Hellinger Bellman eluder coefficient, which reduces the on-policy Bellman error to the Hellinger loss on the historic training data. The latter can be bounded using a log-likelihood (KL) loss and posterior sampling, as shown in Corollary 10.26. Therefore a more general approach (with the weaker Bellman eluder coefficient) to model-based RL is to use log-likelihood loss to directly estimate the model parameter M. Given trajectories $S_{t-1} = \{(x_s^h, a_s^h, r_s^h): h = 1, \ldots, H, s = 1, \ldots, t-1\}$, we may define a posterior with optimistic Feel-Good terms as follows

$$p_t(M|x_1^t, S_{t-1}) \propto p_0(M)\exp\left(\lambda\sum_{s=1}^{t-1}f_M(x_s^1) + \sum_{h=1}^{H}\sum_{s=1}^{t-1}L_s^h(M)\right), \qquad (18.18)$$

where

$$L_s^h(M) = -\tilde{\eta}(R_M^h(x_s^h, a_s^h) - r_s^h)^2 + \eta\ln P_M^h(x_s^{h+1} \mid x_s^h, a_s^h).$$

We can then employ posterior sampling as in Algorithm 18.5, which only requires the value $f_M^1(x^1)$ to be calculated. Compared to the value-targeted approach, Algorithm 18.5 replaces the integration of $f_{M_s}^{h+1}(x_s^{h+1})$ for $h \geq 1$ by log-likelihood, which is simpler for many problems. Since the algorithm relies on the weaker Hellinger Bellman eluder coefficient, it can be more effective in exploration. For example, it applies to problems such as model-based linear MDP (which we will discuss later) that cannot be handled by the value-targeted approach.

Although one can derive a general regret analysis for Algorithm 18.18 (see Agarwal and Zhang, 2022a, for example), the general analysis needs to deal with the reward term and the Feel-Good term $f_M^1(x_s^1)$ in addition to the log-likelihood term. In the following, we want to focus on the analysis of the log-likelihood term, and thus we will consider a simplified version as follows. We assume that the expected reward is known, so that $R_M^h(x^h, a^h) = R_{M_*}^h(x^h, a^h)$ for all $M \in \mathcal{M}$. Moreover, we assume that the distribution of x_t^1 is known, so that $f_M = \mathbb{E}_{x^1}f^1(x^1)$ is also given. With these modifications, we can simplify (18.18) as

---

Algorithm 18.5 Q-type Model-Based Posterior Sampling Algorithm

---

Input: λ, η, $\tilde{\eta}$, T, p_0, $\mathcal{M}$

1 **for** $t = 1, 2, \ldots, T$ **do**

2 $\quad$ Observe x_t^1

3 $\quad$ Draw

$$M_t \sim p_t(M|x_t^1, S_{t-1})$$

$\quad$ according to $p_t(M|x_1^t, S_{t-1})$ defined in (18.18)

4 $\quad$ Let $\pi_t = \pi_{M_t}$

5 $\quad$ Play policy π_t and observe trajectory (x_t, a_t, r_t)

$$p_t(M|S_{t-1}) \propto p_0(M) \exp\left(\lambda f_M + \sum_{h=1}^{H} \sum_{s=1}^{t-1} 0.5 \ln P_M^h(x_s^{h+1} \mid x_s^h, a_s^h) \right). \quad (18.19)$$

We introduce the following definition, which plays a role similar to the concept of covering (see Example 17.32).

Definition 18.44 Given a model class $\mathcal{M}$ and true model M_*, we define the KL ball and Hellinger ball around the true model M_* as

$$\mathcal{M}_{\mathrm{KL}}(\epsilon) = \left\{ M \in \mathcal{M} : \sup_{x^h, a^h} \mathrm{KL}(P_{M_*}^h(\cdot|x^h, a^h) \| P_M^h(\cdot|x_s^h, a_s^h)) \le \epsilon^2 \right\},$$

$$\mathcal{M}_H(\epsilon) = \left\{ M \in \mathcal{M} : \sup_{x^h, a^h} H\left(P_{M_*}^h(\cdot|x^h, a^h) \| P_M^h(\cdot|x_s^h, a_s^h)\right)^2 \le \epsilon^2 \right\}.$$

We have the following result, which shows that as long as we avoid negative-infinity model log-likelihood, the Hellinger ball and KL ball are equivalent up to a log-factor specified by ρ.

Lemma 18.45 *Let*

$$\rho = \sup_{M \in \mathcal{M}} \sup_{h \in [H]} \sup_{x^h, a^h, x^{h+1}} \ln \frac{dP_{M_*}(x^{h+1}|x^h, a^h)}{dP_M^h(x^{h+1}|x^h, a^h)}.$$

We have

$$\mathcal{M}_H\left(\epsilon/\sqrt{3+\rho}\right) \subset \mathcal{M}_{\mathrm{KL}}(\epsilon) \subset \mathcal{M}_H(\epsilon).$$

Moreover, for any $M \in \mathcal{M}_H(\epsilon)$, we have

$$|f_{M_*} - f_M| \le H\epsilon.$$

Proof The first two inequalities used $H(P\|Q)^2 \le \mathrm{KL}(P\|Q) \le \rho H(P\|Q)^2$ in Proposition B.11. For the last desired inequality, due to the symmetry between M_* and M, we can assume that $f_{M_*} \le f_M$ without loss of generality. In this case,

$$|f_{M_*} - f_M| \leq \mathbb{E}_{x^1} [f_M^1(x^1) - V_{\pi_M}^1(x^1)]$$

$$= \mathbb{E}_{(x,a,r) \sim \pi_M} \sum_{h=1}^{H} \mathcal{E}^h(M, x^h, a^h)$$

$$\leq \mathbb{E}_{(x,a,r) \sim \pi_M} \sum_{h=1}^{H} \|P_{M_*}^h(\cdot|x^h, a^h) - P_M^h(\cdot|x_s^h, a_s^h)\|_{\mathrm{TV}} \leq H\epsilon.$$

The first inequality used $f_{M_*}^1(x^1) \geq V_{\pi_M}^1(x^1)$. The next equality used Theorem 18.38. The second inequality used the definition of TV-norm and the model-based Bellman error. The last inequality used Theorem B.9. $\qquad\square$

Similar to Corollary 10.26, we have the following lemma.

Lemma 18.46 *The posterior distribution of* (18.19) *satisfies*

$$\mathbb{E}_{\mathcal{S}_{t-1}} \mathbb{E}_{M \sim p_t} \left[\lambda(f_{M_*} - f_M) + \sum_{s=1}^{t-1} \sum_{h=1}^{H} H(P_{M_*}^h(\cdot|x_s^h, a_s^h) \| P_M^h(\cdot|x_s^h, a_s^h))^2 \right]$$

$$\leq \kappa(\lambda, H, t, \mathcal{M}),$$

where

$$\kappa(L(\lambda, H, t, \mathcal{M}) = \inf_{\epsilon > 0} [2(\lambda + \epsilon)Ht\epsilon - 2\ln p_0(\mathcal{M}_{\mathrm{KL}}(\epsilon))].$$

Proof We introduce the short notation $z_s^h = (x_s^h, a_s^h)$, and consider any loss function $\phi^h(M, z_s^h, z_s^{h+1})$. Let

$$\phi_s^h(M) = \phi^h(M, z_s^h, z_s^{h+1}) - \ln \mathbb{E}_{z_s^{h+1}|z_s^h} \exp[\phi^h(M, z_s^h, z_s^{h+1})].$$

The same proof of Theorem 10.18 implies that

$$\mathbb{E}_{\mathcal{S}_{t-1}} \exp \left[\mathbb{E}_{M \sim p_t(M|\mathcal{S}_{t-1})} \sum_{s=1}^{t-1} \sum_{h=1}^{H} \phi_s^h(M) - \mathrm{KL}(p_t\|p_0) \right]$$

$$\leq \mathbb{E}_{\mathcal{S}_{t-1}} \mathbb{E}_{M \sim p_0} \exp \left[\sum_{s=1}^{t-1} \sum_{h=1}^{H} \phi_s^h(M) \right]$$

$$= 1.$$

The first inequality used Proposition 7.16. The last equation used Lemma 13.1. Using Jensen's inequality, we obtain

$$\mathbb{E}_{\mathcal{S}_{t-1}} \left[\mathbb{E}_{M \sim p_t(M|\mathcal{S}_{t-1})} \sum_{s=1}^{t-1} \sum_{h=1}^{H} \phi_s^h(M) - \mathrm{KL}(p_t\|p_0) \right] \leq 0. \qquad (18.20)$$

Now, we can set

$$\phi^h(M, z_s^h, z_s^{h+1}) = -0.5 \ln \frac{P_{M_*}^h(x_s^{h+1}|x_s^h, a_s^h)}{P_M^h(x_s^{h+1}|x_s^h, a_s^h)},$$

$$\Delta \hat{L}_t(M) = \lambda[f_{M_*} - f_M] + 0.5 \sum_{s=1}^{t-1} \sum_{h=1}^{H} \ln \frac{P_{M_*}^h(x_s^{h+1}|x_s^h, a_s^h)}{P_M^h(x_s^{h+1}|x_s^h, a_s^h)},$$

$$\Delta \bar{L}_t(M) = \lambda[f_{M_*} - f_M] + 0.5 \sum_{s=1}^{t-1} \sum_{h=1}^{H} \mathrm{KL}(P_{M_*}^h(\cdot|x_s^h, a_s^h)\|P_M^h(\cdot|x_s^h, a_s^h)),$$

and obtain

$$\mathbb{E}_{\mathcal{S}_{t-1}} \mathbb{E}_{M \sim p_t} \left[2\lambda[f_{M_*} - f_M] + \sum_{s=1}^{t-1} \sum_{h=1}^{H} H(P_{M_*}^h(\cdot|x_s^h, a_s^h)\|P_M^h(\cdot|x_s^h, a_s^h))^2 \right]$$

$$\leq \mathbb{E}_{\mathcal{S}_{t-1}} \mathbb{E}_{M \sim p_t} \left[2\lambda[f_{M_*} - f_M] \right.$$
$$\left. -2 \sum_{s=1}^{t-1} \sum_{h=1}^{H} \ln \mathbb{E}_{x^{h+1}|x_s^h, a_s^h} \exp\left(-0.5 \ln \frac{P_{M_*}^h(x^{h+1}|x_s^h, a_s^h)}{P_M^h(x^{h+1}|x_s^h, a_s^h)} \right) \right]$$

$$\leq 2\mathbb{E}_{\mathcal{S}_{t-1}} \left[\mathbb{E}_{M \sim p_t(M|\mathcal{S}_{t-1})} \Delta \hat{L}_t(M) + \mathrm{KL}(p_t\|p_0) \right]$$

$$= 2\mathbb{E}_{\mathcal{S}_{t-1}} \inf_p \left[\mathbb{E}_{M \sim p} \Delta \hat{L}_t(M) + \mathrm{KL}(p\|p_0) \right]$$

$$\leq 2 \inf_p \mathbb{E}_{\mathcal{S}_{t-1}} \left[\mathbb{E}_{M \sim p} \Delta \bar{L}_t(M) + \mathrm{KL}(p\|p_0) \right].$$

The first inequality used the definition of Hellinger distance and $2 - 2u \leq -2 \ln u$. The second inequality used (18.20). The next equation used Proposition 7.16 and the fact that $p_t(M) \propto p_0(M) \exp(-\Delta \hat{L}_t(M))$. The last inequality can be obtained by moving $\mathbb{E}_{\mathcal{S}_{t-1}}$ inside inf, and then taking conditional probability $x_s^{h+1}|x_s^h, a_s^h$.

By taking $p(M) \propto \tilde{p}_0(M)\mathbb{1}(M \in \mathcal{M}_{\mathrm{KL}}(\epsilon))$, we obtain

$$\mathbb{E}_p \lambda[f_{M_*} - f_M] \leq \lambda H t \epsilon,$$

where the inequality follows from Lemma 18.45. This implies the result. $\square$

We are now ready to prove a regret bound for Algorithm 18.5 using the simplified posterior (18.19).

Theorem 18.47 *Consider Algorithm 18.5 with the simplified posterior (18.19). We have*

$$\mathbb{E} \sum_{t=2}^{T} [V_*^1(x_t^1) - V_{\pi_t}^1(x_t^1)] \leq \frac{T}{\lambda} \kappa(\lambda, H, T, \mathcal{M}), + \frac{\lambda}{4} \mathrm{EC}_{Q-\mathrm{Hel}}(\epsilon, \mathcal{M}, T)$$

$$+ \sqrt{\epsilon H T \mathrm{EC}_{Q-\mathrm{Hel}}(\epsilon, \mathcal{M}, T)}.$$

Proof Let

$$\hat{L}_s^h(M) = H(P_{M_*}^h(\cdot|x_s^h, a_s^h)\|P_M^h(\cdot|x_s^h, a_s^h))^2.$$

We have

$$\mathbb{E} \sum_{t=2}^{T} [V_*^1(x_t^1) - V_{\pi_t}^1(x_t^1)]$$

$$= \mathbb{E} \sum_{t=2}^{T} [f_{M_*} - f_{M_t}] + \mathbb{E} \sum_{t=2}^{T} \sum_{h=1}^{H} \mathcal{E}^h(M_t, x_t^h, a_t^h)$$

$$\leq \mathbb{E} \sum_{t=2}^{T} [f_{M_*} - f_{M_t}] + \sqrt{\mathrm{EC}_{Q-\mathrm{Hel}}(\epsilon, \mathcal{M}, T) \sum_{t=2}^{T} \left(\epsilon H + \mathbb{E} \sum_{s=1}^{t-1} \sum_{h=1}^{H} \hat{L}_s^h(M_t) \right)}$$

$$\leq \mathbb{E} \sum_{t=2}^{T} [f_{M_*} - f_{M_t}] + \frac{1}{\lambda} \mathbb{E} \sum_{s=1}^{t-1} \sum_{h=1}^{H} \hat{L}_s^h(M_t) + \frac{\lambda}{4} \mathrm{EC}_{Q-\mathrm{Hel}}(\epsilon, \mathcal{M}, T)$$

$$+ \sqrt{\epsilon H T \mathrm{EC}_{Q-\mathrm{Hel}}(\epsilon, \mathcal{M}, T)}$$

$$\leq \frac{T}{\lambda} \kappa(\lambda, H, T, \mathcal{M}) + \frac{\lambda}{4} \mathrm{EC}_{Q-\mathrm{Hel}}(\epsilon, \mathcal{M}, T) + \sqrt{\epsilon H T^2 \mathrm{EC}_{Q-\mathrm{Hel}}(\epsilon, \mathcal{M}, T)}.$$

The first equality used Theorem 18.38. The first inequality follows from the definition of Bellman eluder coefficient in Definition 18.39. The second inequality follows from simple algebra. The last inequality follows from Lemma 18.46. $\square$

We note that in Theorem 18.47, κ behaves like the sample complexity caused by covering numbers. By optimizing λ, the resulting regret bound becomes

$$O \left(\sqrt{T \, \mathrm{EC}_{Q-\mathrm{Hel}}(\cdot) \cdot \kappa(\cdot)} \right).$$

This is comparable to the result for the value-targeted approach. However, as we have pointed out, the Hellinger Bellman eluder coefficient is never larger than value-targeted Hellinger Bellman eluder coefficient. Therefore it can be applied to more general settings. We also observe from Lemma 18.45 that instead of using the KL ball to define $\kappa(\cdot)$, we may also use the Hellinger-ball, with a logarithmic penalty in terms of ρ. To achieve this in the general setting, we may simply add a small constant to each conditional probability model to avoid negative infinity model log-likelihood, so that ρ is not large.

18.6 Linear Mixture MDP

As a simple example of model-based reinforcement learning problems, we consider the linear mixture MDP model.

Definition 18.48 Let $\mathcal{H} = \{\mathcal{H}^h\}$ and $\tilde{\mathcal{H}} = \{\tilde{\mathcal{H}}^h\}$ be inner product vector spaces. An MDP $M = \mathrm{MDP}(\mathcal{X}, cA, P)$ is a linear MDP with respect to feature maps $\phi = \{\phi^h(x^h, a^h, x^{h+1}) \colon \mathcal{X} \times \mathcal{A} \times \mathcal{X} \to \mathcal{H}^h\}_{h=1}^{H}$ and $\tilde{\phi} = \{\tilde{\phi}^h(x^h, a^h) \colon \mathcal{X} \times \mathcal{A} \to \tilde{\mathcal{H}}^h\}_{h=1}^{H}$, if for all $h \in [H]$, there is a model-independent measure $d\mu^{h+1}$ on $\mathcal{X}$, and a model-dependent parameter $\theta^h \in \mathcal{H}$ and $\tilde{\theta}^h \in \tilde{\mathcal{H}}$ such that

$$dP_M^h(x^{h+1}|x^h, a^h) = \langle \theta^h(M), \phi^h(x^h, a^h, x^{h+1}) \rangle d\mu^{h+1}(x^{h+1}),$$
$$R_M^h(x^h, a^h) = \langle \tilde{\theta}^h(M), \tilde{\phi}^h(x^h, a^h) \rangle.$$

Note that a linear mixture MDP is not necessarily a linear MDP because the transition matrix may not be low rank. The following are examples of linear mixture MDPs.

Example 18.49 (Tabular MDP) In a tabular MDP, we assume that $|\mathcal{A}| = A$ and $|\mathcal{X}| = S$. Let $d = AS^2$, which encodes the space of $\mathcal{X} \times \mathcal{A} \times \mathcal{X}$ with components indexed by (x, a, x'). Then we can take $\phi^h(x, a, x') = e_{(x,a,x')}$ and w^h be a d-dimensional vector so that its (x, a, x') component is $P^h(x^{h+1} = x'|x^h = x, a^h = a)$. Similarly, let $\tilde{\phi}^h(x, a) = e_{(x,a)}$ be a $d' = AS$-dimensional vector. We can take θ^h as a $d' = AS$-dimensional vector so that $\tilde{\phi}^h(x, a) = e_{(x,a)}$, and its (x, a) component is $\mathbb{E}[r^h|x^h = x, a^h = a]$. Therefore a tabular MDP is a linear mixture MDP.

Example 18.50 (Mixture of Known MDPs) Consider d-base MDPs $M_1, \ldots, M_d$, where each MDP M_j corresponds to a transition distribution $P_{M_j}^h(x^{h+1}|x^h, a^h)$ and an expected reward $R_{M_j}^h(x^h, a^h)$. Consider a model family $\mathcal{M}$, where $M \in \mathcal{M}$ is represented by $w_1, \ldots, w_d \geq 0$ and $\sum_{j=1}^d w_j = 1$. Then we can express

$$P_M^h(x^{h+1}|x^h, a^h) = \sum_{j=1}^d w_j P_{M_j}^h(x^{h+1}|x^h, a^h).$$

One can similarly define $R_M^h(x^h, a^h) = \sum_{j=1}^d w_j R_{M_j}^h(x^h, a^h)$.

Similar to Proposition 18.18, we have the following structural result for linear mixture MDPs.

Proposition 18.51 *Consider a linear mixture MDP in Definition 18.48. There exist $w^h(M) \in \mathcal{H}^h \oplus \tilde{\mathcal{H}}^h$ and $\psi^h(M', x^h, a^h) \in \mathcal{H}^h \oplus \tilde{\mathcal{H}}^h$ such that*

$$(\mathcal{T}_M^h f_{M'}(x^{h+1}))(x^h, a^h) = \langle w^h(M), \psi^h(M', x^h, a^h) \rangle.$$

It implies that

$$\mathcal{E}^h(M, f_{M'}, x^h, a^h) = \langle w^h(M) - w^h(M_*), \psi^h(M', x^h, a^h) \rangle.$$

For linear mixture MDPs, one can employ Proposition 17.20 (and Proposition 15.8) to obtain an estimate of the Q-type value targeted eluder coefficient in Definition 18.39.

Proposition 18.52 *Consider a linear mixture MDP with representation in Proposition 18.51. Assume that $\sup_{M \in \mathcal{M}} \|w^h(M) - w^h(M_*)\|_{\mathcal{H}^h \oplus \tilde{\mathcal{H}}^h} \leq B$, then*

$$\mathrm{EC}_{Q-\mathrm{VT}}(1, \mathcal{M}, T) \leq 2 \sum_{h=1}^H \mathrm{entro}(1/(B^2 T), \psi^h(\mathcal{M} \times \mathcal{X} \times \mathcal{A})).$$

In particular, if $\mathcal{H}^h \oplus \tilde{\mathcal{H}}^h$ are finite for all h, then we have

$$\text{EC}_{Q-\text{VT}}(1, \mathcal{M}, T) \leq 2 \sum_{h=1}^{H} \dim(\mathcal{H}^h \oplus \tilde{\mathcal{H}}^h) \ln(1 + T(BB')^2),$$

where $B' = \sup_h \sup_{M, x^h, a^h} \|\psi^h(M, x^h, a^h)\|_{\mathcal{H}^h \oplus \tilde{\mathcal{H}}^h}$.

We can apply Algorithm 18.4 to solve the linear mixture MDP problem. Assume that $\dim(\mathcal{H}^h \oplus \tilde{\mathcal{H}}^h) = d$ for all h, then $\text{EC}(1, \mathcal{M}, T) = \tilde{O}(Hd)$. If different h-steps do not share feature maps and model coefficients, then we know that the entropy in Theorem 18.43 can be bounded as $\tilde{O}(Hd)$. This implies that $\beta_t^2 = \tilde{O}(Hd)$. We thus obtain the following regret bound:

$$\mathbb{E} \sum_{t=2}^{T} [V_*^1(x_t^1) - V_{\pi_t}^1(x_t^1)] = \tilde{O}(dH\sqrt{T}). \tag{18.21}$$

We note that this regret bound is similar to that for the linear MDP of (18.8). The dependency in d is not improvable because it matches the lower bound for bandit problems. However, the dependency on H can be improved using weighted regression (see Zhou et al., 2021; Zhou and Gu, 2022).

18.7 Q-type Model-Based Linear MDP

Consider linear MDP in Definition 18.15. In a model-based approach, we may assume that that $\nu^h(x^{h+1})$ is parametrized as $\nu^h(M, x^{h+1})$, so that we have a full model for transition probability and for the expected reward.

Definition 18.53 Let $\{\mathcal{H}^h : h \in [H]\}$ be inner product spaces. In Q-type model-based linear MDP, we assume that there exist maps $\nu^h \colon \mathcal{M} \times \mathcal{X} \to \mathcal{H}^h$, $\theta^h \colon \mathcal{M} \to \mathcal{H}^h$, and $\phi^h \colon \mathcal{X} \times \mathcal{A} \to \mathcal{H}^h$, so that model dynamics can be expressed as

$$dP_M^h(x^{h+1}|x^h, a^h) = \langle \nu^h(M, x^{h+1}), \phi^h(x^h, a^h) \rangle d\mu^{h+1}(x^{h+1}),$$
$$R_M^h(x^h, a^h) = \langle \theta^h(M), \phi^h(x^h, a^h) \rangle.$$

Note that although we work with linear MDP, the models for P_M and R_M do not have to be linear functions. However, for the Q-type approaches, we assume that they can be embedded into a linear function space with respect to the true feature map $\phi^h(x^h, a^h)$ of the underlying linear MDP. Proposition 18.18 implies that for model-based linear MDP in Definition 18.53, there exist maps $w^h \colon \mathcal{M} \times \mathcal{F} \to \mathcal{H}^h$ for $h \in [H]$, so that

$$\mathcal{E}^h(M, f, x^h, a^h) = \langle w^h(M, f), \phi^h(x^h, a^h) \rangle. \tag{18.22}$$

This implies that, unlike linear mixture MDP, value-targeted Bellman eluder coefficients (see Definition 18.40) cannot be directly used in model-based linear MDP because the weight vector $w(M_t, f_{M_s})$ (for $s < t$) depends on M_s in the decomposition of (18.22). If we use $w(M_t, f_{M_t})$ instead of $w(M_t, f_{M_s})$, then the resulting method is equivalent to model-free linear MDP, as

$$\mathcal{E}^h(M_t, f_t, x^h, a^h) = \mathcal{E}^h(f_t, x^h, a^h),$$

based on (18.17). This decomposition leads to the same eluder coefficient for model-free linear MDP in Proposition 18.20. However, for model-based problems, we can also replace $L_s^h(M_t, M_*)$ on the right-hand side of Definition 18.39 by any upper bound. Therefore we can use the witness-loss upper bound,

$$\mathcal{E}^h(M_t, f_t, x^h, a^h)^2 \leq \sup_{f \in \mathcal{F}} \mathcal{E}^h(M_t, f, x^h, a^h)^2,$$

to obtain the following result from Proposition 18.20. The proof is left as an exercise.

Proposition 18.54   *Consider the model-based linear MDP in Definition 18.53. Assume that* $\|w^h(M, f_M) - w^h(M_*, f_{M_*})\|_{\mathcal{H}^h} \leq B$, *where* $w^h(M, f_M)$ *is defined in* (18.22), *then*

$$\mathrm{EC}_{Q-\mathrm{Hel}}(1, \mathcal{M}, T) \leq \mathrm{EC}_{Q-\mathrm{Wit}}(1, \mathcal{M}, T) \leq 2 \sum_{h=1}^{H} \mathrm{entro}(1/(B^2 T), \psi^h(\mathcal{X} \times \mathcal{A})).$$

Proposition 18.54 implies that we can apply Algorithm 18.5 to solve the model-based linear MDP problem. Assume that each $\mathcal{H}^h$ is d-dimensional, then

$$\mathrm{EC}_{Q-\mathrm{Hel}}(1, \mathcal{M}, T) = \tilde{O}(Hd),$$

and we obtain the following regret bound from Theorem 18.47 with optimal λ:

$$O\left(\sqrt{T \, H d \kappa(\cdot)}\right).$$

We note that $\kappa(\cdot)$ behaves like an entropy number. For a finite function class of M members, $\kappa(\cdot) \leq \ln M$. For function class with infinite members, similar results can be obtained by choosing a small Hellinger-ball for the model class, with a small constant added to each conditional probability model to avoid negative infinity model log-likelihood.

18.8 Model-Based V-type Bellman Eluder Coefficient

We have shown in Section 18.4 that in the model-free setting, it is possible to learn an MDP that has an unknown Bellman factorization with a nonlinear Q-function class that is linearly embeddable. If we assume that the transition probability is known, then it is also possible to learn similar models using a model-based approach. To motivate this approach, we may consider the model-based approach to linear MDP. In the Q-type approach, we have to assume that the model can be represented linearly with the true linear map of the underlying MDP. In the V-type approach, this is not necessary. Similar to the model-free approach in Definition 18.27, we can introduce the following definition.

Definition 18.55 (Model-Based V-type Bellman Eluder Coefficient)   Consider loss functions $\{L^h(M, M_*, x^h, a^h)\colon \mathcal{M} \times \mathcal{M} \times \mathcal{X} \times \mathcal{A} \to \mathbb{R}_+, h \in [H]\}$. For each $h \in [H]$, the corresponding V-type L-loss Bellman eluder coefficient $\mathrm{EC}_L^h(\epsilon, \mathcal{M}, T)$ of a model-based RL problem $\mathcal{M}$ is the smallest d so that for any filtered sequence $\{M_t, (x_t, r_t, a_t) \sim \pi_{M_t}\}_{t=1}^T$,

$$
\mathbb{E} \sum_{t=2}^T \mathcal{E}^h(f_t, x_t^h, a_t^h) \le \sqrt{d\mathbb{E} \sum_{t=2}^T \left(\epsilon + \sum_{s=1}^{t-1} \mathbb{E}_{\tilde{x}^h \sim \pi_{M_s}} L^h(M_t, M_*, \tilde{x}^h, \pi_{M_t}(\tilde{x}^h)) \right)}.
$$

Although the generic definition in Definition 18.39 can handle V-type problems, we rewrite it in Definition 18.55 to focus on the special structure of V-type problems (and to separate different h instead of taking the sum over h). Specifically, Q-type problems considered in Definition 18.40 assume that the Q-type loss function $L_s^h(M_t, M_*)$ depends on (M_t, M_s, x_s^h, a_s^h). The dependency is replaced by dependency on $(M_t, M_s, \tilde{x}^h, \tilde{a}^h = \pi_{M_t}(\tilde{x}^h))$, with $\tilde{x}^h \sim \pi_{M_s}$ in the V-type definition of Definition 18.55. Similar to model-free RL in Definition 18.27, we require the loss to depend on the action $\tilde{a}^h = \pi_{M_t}(\tilde{x}^h)$ using the current model M_t. We may still consider loss functions in Definition 18.40 for V-type problems.

Definition 18.56   Consider model-based V-type eluder coefficients in Definition 18.55. Given a Q-function class $\mathcal{F}$ that contains $\{f_M : M \in \mathcal{M}\}$, assume that $r^h + f^h(x^h, a^h) \in [0, 1]$ for all $f \in \mathcal{F}$ and $h \in [H]$. The Bellman eluder coefficient corresponding to the following loss

$$
L^h(M, M_*, x^h, a^h) = \sup_{f \in \mathcal{F}} \mathcal{E}^h(M, f, x^h, a^h)^2,
$$

denoted by $\mathrm{EC}_{V-\mathrm{Wit}}(\epsilon, \mathcal{M}, \mathcal{F}, T)$, is referred to as the V-type witness Bellman eluder coefficient.

The Bellman eluder coefficient corresponding to the loss function

$$
L^h(M, M_*, x^h, a^h) = H(P_M^h(\cdot|x^h, a^h)\|P_{M_*}^h(\cdot|x^h, a^h))^2,
$$

denoted by $\mathrm{EC}_{V-\mathrm{Hel}}(\epsilon, \mathcal{M}, T)$, is referred to as the V-type Hellinger Bellman eluder coefficient.

The following result is a counterpart of Proposition 18.41.

Proposition 18.57   *We have*

$$
\mathrm{EC}_{V-\mathrm{Hel}}(\epsilon, \mathcal{M}, T) \le \mathrm{EC}_{V-\mathrm{Wit}}(\epsilon, \mathcal{M}, \mathcal{F}, T).
$$

It was shown in Proposition 18.29 that Bellman factorization in Definition 18.28 can be used to bound the V-type Bellman eluder coefficient for model-free RL. For model-based RL, we can introduce a weaker form of Bellman factorization using the witness loss. To motivate it, we note that the model-free Bellman factorization and (18.17) implies that

$$
\begin{aligned}
|\langle u^{h-1}(f_M), \phi^{h-1}(\pi')\rangle| &= |\mathbb{E}_{\tilde{x}^h \sim \pi'} \mathcal{E}^h(M, f_M, \tilde{x}^h, \pi_M(\tilde{x}^h))| \\
&\le 1 \cdot \mathbb{E}_{\tilde{x}^h \sim \pi'} \sup_{f \in \mathcal{F}} |\mathcal{E}^h(M, f, \tilde{x}^h, \pi_M(\tilde{x}^h))|.
\end{aligned}
$$

We can thus employ an easier-to-satisfy inequality for witness loss to define a factorization assumption. This leads to an inequality-based definition called witness Bellman factorization, which is weaker than the Bellman factorization in Definition 18.28 for model-free RL.

Definition 18.58 (Witness Bellman Factorization) Let $\mathcal{H} = \{\mathcal{H}^h\}$ be a sequence of inner product vector spaces for $h = 1, \ldots, H$. An MDP has a witness Bellman factorization with respect to $\mathcal{H}$ if the following condition holds. For all $h \geq 2$ and model $M \in \mathcal{M}$, there exists $u^{h-1}(M) \in \mathcal{H}^{h-1}$, and for all policy π', there exists $\phi(\pi') \in \mathcal{H}^{h-1}$ such that the following factorization holds:

$$\left| \mathbb{E}_{\tilde{x}^h \sim \pi'} \mathcal{E}^h(M, \tilde{x}^h, \pi_M(\tilde{x}^h)) \right| \leq \left| \langle u^{h-1}(M), \phi^{h-1}(\pi') \rangle \right|$$

$$\leq \kappa \mathbb{E}_{\tilde{x}^h \sim \pi'} \sup_{f \in \mathcal{F}} \left| \mathcal{E}^h(M, f, \tilde{x}^h, \pi_M(\tilde{x}^h)) \right|,$$

where $\kappa \geq 1$ is some constant.

Similar to Proposition 18.29, we have the following result for the witness Bellman eluder coefficient. The proof is left as an exercise.

Proposition 18.59 *Consider an MDP with a witness Bellman factorization in Definition 18.58. Assume that x_t^1 are iid samples drawn from the same underlying distribution, and for $h \geq 2$, $\sup_{f \in \mathcal{F}} \|u^{h-1}(M)\|_{\mathcal{H}^{h-1}} \leq B$. Assume that $r^h + f^{h+1}(x^h, a^h) \in [0, 1]$, then*

$$\mathrm{EC}^1_{V-\mathrm{Wit}}(0, \mathcal{M}, \mathcal{F}, T) \leq 1 + \ln T,$$

$$\mathrm{EC}^h_{V-\mathrm{Wit}}(1, \mathcal{M}, \mathcal{F}, T) \leq 2\kappa^2 \mathrm{entro}(1/(\kappa^2 B^2 T), \phi^{h-1}(\cdot)), \quad (h \geq 2),$$

where $\mathrm{entro}(\cdot)$ *is defined in Proposition 15.8.*

Proposition 18.57 and Proposition 18.59 imply that the V-type Hellinger Bellman eluder coefficient can be bounded using witness Bellman factorization. Therefore a general approach for model-based RL is to employ the Hellinger eluder coefficient, which reduces on-policy Bellman error to Hellinger loss on the training data. The latter can be bounded using the standard likelihood-based criterion. The resulting procedure is given in Algorithm 18.6, which has been analyzed in (Agarwal and Zhang, 2022a) using decoupling coefficients. One can also derive a regret bound for this algorithm comparable to that of Theorem 18.34 by using techniques for analyzing Algorithm 18.5 via Bellman eluder coefficients.

One benefit of a model-based approach over a model-free approach is that exploration is generally easier in a model-based approach. This is a direct implication of the fact that model-based witness eluder coefficients are smaller than model-free eluder coefficients. In fact, it is easy to check that the following result holds.

Proposition 18.60 *Consider model class $\mathcal{M}$ and a candidate Q-function class $\mathcal{F}$ so that $\{f_M : M \in \mathcal{M}\} \subset \mathcal{F}$. Then*

$$\mathrm{EC}_{Q-\mathrm{Wit}}(\epsilon, \mathcal{M}, \mathcal{F}, T) \leq \mathrm{EC}_Q(\epsilon, \mathcal{F}, T),$$

$$\mathrm{EC}^h_{V-\mathrm{Wit}}(\epsilon, \mathcal{M}, \mathcal{F}, T) \leq \mathrm{EC}^h_V(\epsilon, \mathcal{F}, T) \quad (h \geq 2).$$

Algorithm 18.6 V-type Model-Based Posterior Sampling Algorithm

---

Input: $\lambda,\ \eta,\ \tilde{\eta},\ \tilde{\pi},\ T,\ p_0,\ \mathcal{M}$

1 **for** $t = 1, 2, \ldots, T$ **do**

2 $\quad$ Observe x_t^1

3 $\quad$ Draw

$$M_t \sim p_t(M|x_t^1, S_{t-1})$$

$\quad$ according to

$$p_t(M|x_1^t, S_{t-1}) \propto p_0(M) \exp\left(\lambda \sum_{s=1}^{t} f_M(x_s^1) + \sum_{s=1}^{t-1} L_s^{h_s}(M)\right),$$

$\quad$ with $L_s^h(M) = -\tilde{\eta}(R_M^h(x_s^h, a_s^h) - r_s^h)^2 + \eta \ln P_M^h(x_s^{h+1} \mid x_s^h, a_s^h)$.

4 $\quad$ Draw Let $\pi_t = \pi_{M_t}$

5 $\quad$ Play policy π_t and observe trajectory (x_t, a_t, r_t) up to $x_t^{h_t}$ with uniformly random h_t

6 $\quad$ Play random policy $a_t^{h_t} \sim \tilde{\pi}^{h_t}(\cdot|x_t^{h_t})$, and observe $(r_t^{h_t}, x_t^{h_t+1})$

7 **return** randomly chosen π_t from $t = 1$ to $t = T$

Proposition 18.60 shows that in general, model-based RL problems can be easier to solve than model-free problems. In fact, there can be a significant separation between model-free method and model-based method for certain problems such as factored MDPs.

Example 18.61 (Factored MDP (Kearns and Koller, 1999)) Let $d \geq 1$ and let Ω be a small finite set. Define the context space $\mathcal{X} = \Omega^d$, with the natural partition by time. For a state $x^h \in \mathcal{X}$, we use $x^h[i] \subset \Omega$ for $i \in [d]$ to denote ith component of x^h, and for a subset of state variables. For each $i \in [d]$, the parent of i, $\mathrm{pa}_i \subset [d]$ are the subset of state variables that directly influence i. In factored MDPs, the transition probability P factorizes according to

$$P^h(x^{h+1}|x^h, a^h) = \prod_{i=1}^{d} P_{(i)}^h[x^{h+1}[i]|x^h[\mathrm{pa}_i], a^h].$$

It is known that factored MDPs are learnable using a model-based approach in polynomial time, with well-behaved witness Bellman factorization. However any model-free method has a complexity exponential in H (Sun et al., 2019).

18.9 Historical and Bibliographical Remarks

Reinforcement learning (Sutton and Barto, 2018) has a long history, and important algorithms such as Q-learning (Watkins and Dayan, 1992) for value function-based approaches, and policy gradient (REINFORCE) (Williams, 1992) for policy-based approaches were developed in the earlier 1990s. The theoretical analysis considered in this chapter only covers the value function approach. The mathematical foundation of reinforcement learning is closely related to dynamic programming and optimal control (Bertsekas, 2012). While the convergence analysis of Q-learning appeared shortly after the algorithm was introduced (Jaakkola et al., 1993), the earlier theoretical results did not consider exploration, and they studied the simpler tabular setting.

Theoretical analysis of reinforcement learning with exploration has been studied much more recently, and main results have been developed using value function based approaches. This chapter introduced the main technical tools to analyze reinforcement learning that have been developed in recent years. We mainly considered statistical behavior of various algorithms, and did not consider their computational complexity. In fact, many algorithms studied in the chapter may not necessarily be computationally efficient. Earlier results on reinforcement learning that take exploration into consideration studied the tabular case (Kearns and Singh, 2002; Auer et al., 2008; Bartlett and Tewari, 2009; Dann and Brunskill, 2015). In particular, a sharp result matching minimax rate was obtained by Azar et al. (2017).

A Q-learning-style model-free algorithm for tabular problems was considered by Jin et al. (2018), and its extension to linear MDP, referred to as least squares value iteration with UCB (LSVI-UCB), was analyzed in Jin et al. (2020). Algorithm 18.2 can be considered as a variant of LSVI-UCB in Jin et al. (2020). This algorithm is quite similar to practically used Q learning, but with an extra bonus term added into the regression target. The regret bound for this algorithm has a slight suboptimal dependence on d. It is possible to improve the dependency on both H and d in the leading order by using weighted regression, similar to that of Zhou and Gu (2022). While Algorithm 18.2 can handle some nonlinearity, it is more complex than Algorithm 18.1 due to the requirement to explicitly incorporate the bonus function $b_t^h(\cdot)$ in the regression target. This complication can be seen in other variants such as Wang et al. (2020), which proposed a generic procedure for bonus function design.

For linear MDP, a different approach was proposed by Zanette et al. (2020) that improved the d dependency of Jin et al. (2020). The minimax objective used in Zanette et al. (2020) was introduced by Antos et al. (2008). This approach, when generalized to nonlinear Q-function classes, becomes Algorithm 18.1. An advantage of this method over LSVI-UCB is that the nonlinear generalization only requires the Q-function class $\mathcal{F}$ to be complete with respect to another function class $\mathcal{G}$, which is relatively easy to satisfy. The extension presented here using the concept of Bellman eluder coefficient has also been considered by Jin et al. (2021), who employed a similar notion of Bellman eluder dimension. A posterior sampling approach was studied by Dann et al. (2021), in which the concept of Bellman eluder coefficient was introduced.

The idea of Bellman decomposition (and Bellman rank) was introduced by Jiang et al. (2017), and the paper presented a V-type algorithm OLIVE to solve this problem with low Bellman rank. The regret decomposition in Theorem 18.11 was also presented there. An advantage of OLIVE over Algorithm 18.3 is that it does not require the completeness assumption. However, it only works for the case with finite actions (there is no easy way to generalize OLIVE to handle infinite actions), and the resulting bound is inferior in terms of its dependency on various MDP parameters such as d and H. A more generic framework for model-free MDP was considered in Du et al. (2021), which can handle many cases discussed in this chapter. However, their regret bounds may be suboptimal for specific problems. The generalization of V-type results to infinite actions when the linear embedding feature is unknown was obtained by Agarwal and Zhang (2022b), where the idea of employing linear G-optimal design was studied under the assumption that the embedding feature is known.

Algorithm 18.4 is similar to the method of Ayoub et al. (2020). For linear mixture MDP, the H dependency is suboptimal, and was subsequently improved in Zhou et al. (2021) and Zhou and Gu (2022) using variance (and uncertainty) weighted regression, as well as law of total variance used by Azar et al. (2017) to achieve minimax regret for tabular MDPs. The concept of witness rank for V-type problems, and the decomposition in Theorem 18.38 were both introduced by Sun et al. (2019). Other V-type algorithms for learning the underlying representation of the MDP such as Flambe have also been developed Agarwal et al. (2020). The general approach to model-based reinforcement learning presented in Algorithm 18.6 using log-likelihood function was presented and analyzed in Agarwal and Zhang (2022a) using the decoupling coefficient approach of Section 17.4. One may also employ Bellman eluder coefficients as shown in Theorem 18.47.

Exercises

18.1 Prove Proposition 18.7.

18.2 Prove Theorem 18.9.

18.3 Prove a high-probability version of Theorem 18.21, with a modified Bellman Eluder coefficient in Definition 18.19 without the expectation.

18.4 Derive a high-probability version of Theorem 18.25.

- Show that with probability at least $1 - \delta$,

$$\mathbb{E} \sum_{t=1}^{T} \sum_{h=1}^{H} \mathcal{E}^h(f_t, x_t^h, a_t^h) \leq \sum_{t=1}^{T} \sum_{h=1}^{H} \mathcal{E}^h(f_t, x_t^h, a_t^h) + \epsilon_T(\delta)$$

for some $\epsilon_T(\delta)$ using an appropriate martingale tail inequality from Chapter 13.
- Show that $\sum_{t=1}^{T} \sum_{h=1}^{H} \mathcal{E}^h(f_t, x_t^h, a_t^h)$ can be bounded with large probability under the assumptions of Lemma 18.24.
- Derive a high-probability version of Theorem 18.25.

18.5 Fill in details in the proof of Theorem 18.34.

18.6 Show that (18.17) holds, and use this to prove Theorem 18.38.

18.7 Prove Lemma 18.42 using Theorem 13.15.

18.8 Prove Proposition 18.41 and Proposition 18.59.

18.9 Prove Proposition 18.51 and compare the result to Proposition 18.18.

18.10 Prove Proposition 18.54 by using a similar argument to that of Proposition 17.20.

18.11 Prove Proposition 18.59 by using a similar argument to that of Proposition 18.29.

18.12 Prove Proposition 18.60.

Appendix A

Basics of Convex Analysis

We informally review some basic concepts of convex functions used in this book. For readability, we avoid nonessential technical conditions that may be needed for mathematical rigor. A more formal and rigorous treatment of convex analysis can be found in (Rockafellar, 2015).

A.1 Definitions

Definition A.1 A set Ω in a vector space is a convex set if for all $w, w' \in \Omega$ and $\alpha \in [0, 1]$, $\alpha w + (1 - \alpha)w' \in \Omega$. A real-valued function $\phi(w)$ of w is a convex function on a convex set Ω if its epigraph $\{(w, t) \in \Omega \times \mathbb{R} : t \geq \phi(w)\}$ is a convex set.

We also say that a function $\phi(w)$ is concave if $-\phi(w)$ is convex.

Proposition A.2 *Here $\phi(w)$ is a convex function on Ω if and only if for all $\alpha \in (0, 1)$, and $w, w' \in \Omega$,*

$$\phi(\alpha w + (1 - \alpha)w') \leq \alpha \phi(w) + (1 - \alpha)\phi(w').$$

Proposition A.3 *A function $\phi(w)$ is convex on Ω if for all $w \in \Omega$, there exists vector g so that for all $w' \in \Omega$,*

$$\phi(w') \geq \phi(w) + g^\top(w' - w).$$

Here g is referred to as a sub-gradient *in convex analysis, which may not necessarily be unique.*

If a convex function $\phi(w)$ is differentiable at an interior point $w \in \Omega$, then $g = \nabla\phi(w)$ is unique.

Without causing confusion, we will use $\nabla\phi(w)$ to denote an arbitrary sub-gradient of a convex function $\phi(w)$ in this book. An example of nonunique sub-gradient is given by the one-dimensional convex function $\phi(w) = |w|$, for which any $g \in [-1, 1]$ is a sub-gradient at $w = 0$.

Definition A.4 Given $\lambda > 0$, a function $\phi(w)$ is λ-strongly convex in w if for all $w, w' \in \Omega$,

$$\phi(w') \geq \phi(w) + \nabla\phi(w)^\top(w' - w) + \frac{\lambda}{2}\|w - w'\|_2^2.$$

A strongly convex function may not be differentiable. An example is the one-dimensional function $\phi(w) = |w| + 0.5w^2$, which is $\lambda = 1$ strongly convex, but not differentiable at $w = 0$. The following definition is frequently used in theoretical analysis. It can be applied even for nonconvex functions.

Definition A.5 A function $\phi(w)$ (which may not necessarily be convex) on Ω is L-smooth if it is differentiable and for all $w, w' \in \Omega$,

$$\|\nabla\phi(w') - \nabla\phi(w)\|_2 \le L\|w - w'\|_2.$$

We say $\phi(w)$ is G-Lipschitz if for all $w \in \Omega$,

$$\|\nabla\phi(w)\|_2 \le G.$$

Proposition A.6 *If $\phi(w)$ is L-smooth, then for any $w, w' \in \Omega$,*

$$\nabla\phi(w') \le \phi(w) + \nabla\phi(w)^\top(w' - w) + \frac{L}{2}\|w - w'\|_2^2,$$

and $\|\nabla^2\phi(w)\|_2 \le L$.
  If ϕ is G-Lipschitz, then for any $w, w' \in \Omega$,

$$|\phi(w) - \phi(w')| \le G\|w - w'\|_2.$$

A.2 Basic Properties

We list some results for convex functions that are useful in the analysis of this book.

Proposition A.7 *If $\phi(w)$ is L-smooth on $\mathbb{R}^d$, then for all $w, w' \in \mathbb{R}^d$,*

$$\|\nabla\phi(w') - \nabla\phi(w)\|_2^2 \le 2L\left[\phi(w) - \phi(w') - \nabla\phi(w')^\top(w - w')\right].$$

Proof Let

$$\tilde{\phi}(w) = \phi(w) - \phi(w') - \nabla\phi(w')^\top(w - w').$$

Then $\tilde{\phi}(w)$ is L-smooth, and $\tilde{\phi}(w) \ge 0$ due to convexity. Let $\eta = 1/L$, then

$$0 \le \tilde{\phi}(w - \eta\nabla\tilde{\phi}(w))$$

$$\le \tilde{\phi}(w) - \eta\nabla\tilde{\phi}(w)^\top\nabla\tilde{\phi}(w) + \frac{\eta^2 L}{2}\|\nabla\tilde{\phi}(w)\|_2^2$$

$$= \tilde{\phi}(w) - \frac{1}{2L}\nabla\tilde{\phi}(w)^\top\nabla\tilde{\phi}(w).$$

The second inequality used Proposition A.6. This implies the desired bound. $\square$

Proposition A.8 *If $\phi(w)$ is convex on a closed convex set Ω and*

$$w_* = \arg\min_{w\in\Omega} \phi(w).$$

Then there exists a subgradient $\nabla\phi(w_*)$ such that for all $w \in \Omega$,

$$\nabla\phi(w_*)^\top (w - w_*) \geq 0.$$

Moreover, if $\phi(w)$ is λ-strongly convex, and there exists a real number $g \geq 0$ such that

$$\nabla\phi(w)^\top (w_* - w) \geq -g\|w - w_*\|_2,$$

then $\|w_* - w\|_2 \leq g/\lambda$.

Proof The first result follows from the theory of convex optimization (Boyd and Vandenberghe, 2004; Rockafellar, 2015), which says that w_* is a minimizer of $\phi(w)$ on Ω if there exists a sub-gradient $\nabla\phi(w_*)$ such that

$$\forall w \in \Omega: \nabla\phi(w_*)^\top (w - w_*) \geq 0.$$

Using the definition of strong convexity, we obtain

$$\phi(w_*) \geq \phi(w) + \nabla\phi(w)^\top (w_* - w) + \frac{\lambda}{2}\|w_* - w\|_2^2,$$

$$\phi(w) \geq \phi(w_*) + \nabla\phi(w_*)^\top (w - w_*) + \frac{\lambda}{2}\|w_* - w\|_2^2 \geq \phi(w_*) + \frac{\lambda}{2}\|w_* - w\|_2^2.$$

Summing up the two inequalities, we obtain

$$0 \geq \nabla\phi(w)^\top (w_* - w) + \lambda\|w - w_*\|_2^2 \geq -g\|w - w_*\|_2 + \lambda\|w - w_*\|_2^2.$$

This implies the second bound. □

We also use the following result regularly in the book.

Proposition A.9 (Jensen's Inequality) *Assume that $\phi(w)$ is a convex function on Ω. Consider $w_1, \ldots, w_m \in \Omega$, and nonnegative numbers $\alpha_1, \ldots, \alpha_m \in \mathbb{R}$ so that $\sum_{i=1}^m \alpha_i = 1$. Then*

$$\phi\left(\sum_{i=1}^m \alpha_i w_i\right) \leq \sum_{i=1}^m \alpha_i \phi(w_i).$$

More generally, let p be a probability measure on Ω, then $\phi(\mathbb{E}_{w \sim p} w) \leq \mathbb{E}_{w \sim p}\phi(w)$.

Proof Let $w = \sum_{i=1}^m \alpha_i w_i$. Using convexity, we know that for each i,

$$\phi(w_i) \geq \phi(w) + \nabla\phi(w)^\top (w_i - w),$$

where $\nabla\phi(w)$ is a sub-gradient of ϕ. Multiply by α_i and sum over i, we obtain

$$\sum_{i=1}^m \alpha_i \phi(w_i) \geq \phi(w) + \nabla\phi(w)^\top \sum_{i=1}^m \alpha_i (w_i - w) = \phi(w).$$

This finishes the proof. The more general inequality can be proved similarly. □

Proposition A.10 (Cauchy–Schwarz inequality)   *Let $\langle \cdot, \cdot \rangle$ be an inner product, and $\|u\| = \sqrt{\langle u, u \rangle}$, then*

$$\langle u, v \rangle \le \|u\| \|v\| \le \frac{1}{2} \|u\|^2 + \frac{1}{2} \|v\|^2.$$

Proposition A.11 (Hölder's Inequality)   *Let $p, q \ge 1$ such that $1/p + 1/q = 1$. Then for any $u, v \in \mathbb{R}^d$,*

$$|u^\top v| \le \|u\|_p \|v\|_q \le \frac{1}{p} \|u\|_p^p + \frac{1}{q} \|v\|_q^q.$$

A.3 Common Convex Functions

The following functions are convex:

- $\phi(w) = |w|^p \colon \mathbb{R} \to \mathbb{R}$ for $p \ge 1$.
- $\phi(w) = -w^p \colon \mathbb{R}_+ \to \mathbb{R}$ for $p \in (0, 1)$.
- $\phi(w) = w^p \colon \mathbb{R}_+ \to \mathbb{R}$ for $p < 0$.
- $\phi(w) = -\ln w \colon \mathbb{R}_+ \to \mathbb{R}$.
- $\phi(w) = w \ln w \colon \mathbb{R}_+ \to \mathbb{R}$.
- $\phi(w) = \ln(1 + \exp(w)) \colon \mathbb{R} \to \mathbb{R}$.
- $\phi(w) = \|w\| \colon \mathbb{R}^d \to \mathbb{R}$, where $\|\cdot\|$ is any norm.
- $\phi(w) = \ln \sum_{i=1}^{d} p_i \exp(w_i) \colon \mathbb{R}^d \to \mathbb{R}$ $(p_i \ge 0)$.
- $\phi(w) = \ln \mathbb{E}_{\xi \sim p} \exp(w(\xi))$ as a function of $w(\cdot)$, where p is a probability distribution of ξ.

The following results are useful for constructing convex functions.

Proposition A.12   *Let $\phi_1(w)$ and $\phi_2(w)$ be two convex functions, and $a_1, a_2 \ge 0$, then*

$$a_1 \phi_1(w) + a_2 \phi_2(w)$$

is a convex function.

Proposition A.13   *If $\phi_1(z)$ is a nondecreasing convex function on $\mathbb{R}$ and $\phi_2(w)$ is a convex function on $\mathbb{R}^d$, then*

$$\phi_1(\phi_2(w))$$

is a convex function on $\mathbb{R}^d$.

Proposition A.14   *Assume that for each $\theta \in \Theta$, $\phi(\theta, w)$ is a convex function of w, then*

$$\sup_{\theta \in \Theta} \phi(\theta, w)$$

is a convex function of w.

This result implies that the hinge loss

$$\phi(w) = \sup_y \max[0, b_y - x_y^\top w]$$

is convex on $\mathbb{R}^d$, where $(x_y, b_y) \in \mathbb{R}^d \times \mathbb{R}$.

Proposition A.15 *Let $\phi(z)$ be a convex function on $\mathbb{R}^q$, and let A be a $q \times d$ matrix. Then*

$$\phi(Aw)$$

is a convex function on $\mathbb{R}^d$.

Proposition A.16 *If $\phi(z)$ is convex on Ω, then $t\phi(z/t)$ is convex on $\{(z/t, t) \in \Omega \times \mathbb{R}_+\}$.*

Proof We have

$$(\alpha t + (1-\alpha)t')\phi\left(\frac{\alpha z + (1-\alpha)z'}{\alpha t + (1-\alpha)t'}\right)$$

$$= (\alpha t + (1-\alpha)t')\phi\left(\frac{\alpha t(z/t) + (1-\alpha)t'(z'/t')}{\alpha t + (1-\alpha)t'}\right)$$

$$\le \alpha t\phi(z/t) + (1-\alpha)t'\phi(z'/t'). \qquad \text{(Jensen's inequality)}$$

This proves the convexity of $t\phi(z/t)$. $\qquad\qquad\qquad\qquad\square$

A.4 Matrix Trace Functions

We can also directly form convex functions for symmetric matrices.

Definition A.17 Let $f(z)$ be a real-valued function. For a symmetric matrix W with decomposition $W = U^\top \Lambda U$, where $\Lambda = \mathrm{diag}(\lambda_1, \ldots, \lambda_d)$ is a diagonal matrix, and U orthogonal matrix, we define

$$f(W) = U^\top f(\Lambda)U,$$

where $f(\Lambda) = \mathrm{diag}(f(\lambda_1), \ldots, f(\lambda_d))$.

If $f(z)$ is differentiable with derivative $f'(z)$, then it is not difficult to check that

$$\frac{d}{dt}\mathrm{trace}(f(W + t\Delta W))\Big|_{t=0} = \mathrm{trace}(f'(W)\Delta W).$$

The following result is useful in some of the theoretical analysis in the book.

Theorem A.18 *Let $S_{[a,b]}^d$ be the set of $d \times d$ symmetric matrices with eigenvalues in $[a, b]$. If $f(z): [a, b] \to \mathbb{R}$ is a convex function, then*

$$\mathrm{trace}(f(W))$$

is a convex function on $S_{[a,b]}^d$. This implies that for $W, W' \in S_{[a,b]}^d$,

$$\mathrm{trace}(f(W')) \ge \mathrm{trace}(f(W)) + \mathrm{trace}(f'(W)(W' - W)),$$

where $f'(z)$ is the derivative of $f(z)$.

Proof Consider $\alpha \in (0,1)$ and $W = \alpha W' + (1 - \alpha)W''$, with $W', W'' \in S_{[a,b]}^d$. Let $u_1, \ldots, u_d$ be an orthonormal basis corresponding to eigenvalues of W. Let $u'_1, \ldots, u'_d$ be an orthonormal basis corresponding to eigenvalues of W', with eigenvalues $\lambda'_i = {u'_i}^\top W' u'_i$, then

$$\sum_{j=1}^d f(u_j^\top W' u_j) = \sum_{j=1}^d f\left(\sum_{i=1}^d \lambda'_i (u_j^\top u'_i)^2\right)$$

$$\overset{(a)}{\leq} \sum_{j=1}^d \sum_{i=1}^d (u_j^\top u'_i)^2 f(\lambda'_i)$$

$$\overset{(b)}{=} \sum_{i=1}^d f(\lambda'_i) = \text{trace}(f(W')).$$

The inequality in (a) used Jensen's inequality, with $\sum_{i=1}^d (u_j^\top u'_i)^2 = \|u_j\|_2^2 = 1$. The equation in (b) used $\sum_{j=1}^d (u_j^\top u'_i)^2 = \|u'_i\|_2^2 = 1$. Similarly, we have

$$\sum_{j=1}^d f(u_j^\top W'' u_j) \leq \text{trace}(f(W'')).$$

It follows that

$$\text{trace}(f(W)) = \sum_{j=1}^d f(u_j^\top W u_j)$$

$$\leq \alpha \sum_{j=1}^d f(u_j^\top W' u_j) + (1 - \alpha) \sum_{j=1}^d f(u_j^\top W'' u_j)$$

$$\leq \alpha \text{trace}(f(W')) + (1 - \alpha)\text{trace}(f(W'')).$$

The first inequality used the fact that $f(z)$ is a convex function on $[a, b]$. This proves the convexity. $\square$

Theorem A.18 implies that both

$$\ln |W| = \text{trace}(\ln W)$$

and

$$\text{trace}(W^p)$$

for $p \in (0, 1)$ are concave functions of a symmetric positive definite matrix W.

Appendix B

f-divergence of Probability Measures

Consider a probability space Ω, with a properly defined σ-algebra. Consider two probability measures P and Q that are absolutely continuous with respect to a reference measure μ with density p and q:

$$dP = pd\mu, \qquad dQ = qd\mu.$$

We have the following definition of f-divergence.

Definition B.1 Given a convex function $f(t)$ defined on $\mathbb{R}_+$ such that $f(1) = 0$, the f-divergence of P and Q is defined as

$$D_f(P\|Q) = \int_\Omega f\left(\frac{p(z)}{q(z)}\right) q(z) d\mu(z) = \mathbb{E}_{z\sim Q} f\left(\frac{p(z)}{q(z)}\right).$$

Let W and Z be two random variables, with probability measures P and Q respectively. We also write

$$D_f(W\|Z) = D_f(P\|Q).$$

Note that the condition of absolute continuity is stated for notation convenience. For certain f-divergence that are always bounded, absolute continuity is not required.

B.1 Basic Properties of f-divergence

Due to the convexity of f, f-divergence is always nonnegative.

Proposition B.2 *We have*

$$D_f(P\|Q) \geq 0.$$

Moreover, if $f(t)$ is strictly convex at 1, that is, there exists a sub-gradient g of f at 1 so that

$$f(t) > f(1) + g(t - 1),$$

then $D_f(P\|Q) = 0$ only when $P = Q$.

Proof Using Jensen's inequality, we obtain

$$D_f(P\|Q) = \mathbb{E}_{z\sim Q} f(p(z)/q(z)) \geq f\left(\mathbb{E}_{z\sim Q} \frac{p(z)}{q(z)}\right) = f(1) = 0.$$

This proves the first desired result. For the second result, we note that

$$D_f(P\|Q) = \mathbb{E}_{z\sim Q}\left[f\left(\frac{p(z)}{q(z)}\right) - f(1) - g\left(\frac{p(z)}{q(z)} - 1\right)\right],$$

which is zero only when $p(z)/q(z) = 1$ almost everywhere.   □

The following result shows that f-divergence is jointly convex in P and Q.

Proposition B.3   *Given any* $\alpha \in [0, 1]$, *probability measures* P, P', Q, Q', *we have*

$$D_f(\alpha P + (1 - \alpha)P'\|\alpha Q + (1 - \alpha)Q') \leq \alpha D_f(P\|Q) + (1 - \alpha)D_f(P'\|Q').$$

Proof   This is a direct consequence of the fact that the function $qf(p/q)$ is jointly convex in $[p, q] \in \mathbb{R}_+ \times \mathbb{R}_+$ (see Proposition A.16).   □

The following data-processing inequality of f-divergence is very useful for establishing lower bounds for statistical estimation.

Theorem B.4 (Data Processing Inequality)   *Let* W *and* Z *be two random variables on* Ω. *Let* $h\colon \Omega \to \Omega'$ *be a data processing map which can be a random function. Then*

$$D_f(h(W)\|h(Z)) \leq D_f(W\|Z).$$

Proof   Let W and Z be distributed according to probability measures $P(W)d\mu$ and $Q(Z)d\mu$ respectively. Let $W' = h(W)$ and $Z' = h(Z)$. Let $P(W, W')$ and $Q(Z, Z')$ be the joint distributions of $[W, W']$ and $[Z, Z']$. By the definition of data processing, the conditional distribution satisfies

$$Q(Z' = x'|Z = x) = P(W' = x'|W = x).$$

Therefore

$$\frac{P(X)}{Q(X)} = \frac{P(X'|X)P(X)}{Q(X'|X)Q(X)} = \frac{P(X, X')}{Q(X, X')}. \tag{B.1}$$

Moreover, we have

$$\frac{P(X')}{Q(X')} = \mathbb{E}_{X\sim P(X|X')}\frac{P(X')}{Q(X')} = \mathbb{E}_{X\sim Q(\cdot|X')}\frac{P(X|X')P(X')}{Q(X|X')Q(X')}$$

$$= \mathbb{E}_{X\sim Q(\cdot|X')}\frac{P(X, X')}{Q(X, X')}. \tag{B.2}$$

It follows that

$$
D_f(h(W)||h(Z)) = \mathbb{E}_{X' \sim Q} f\left(\frac{P(X')}{Q(X')}\right)
$$

$$
\overset{(a)}{=} \mathbb{E}_{X' \sim Q} f\left(\mathbb{E}_{X \sim Q(\cdot|X')} \frac{P(X, X')}{Q(X, X')}\right)
$$

$$
\overset{(b)}{\leq} \mathbb{E}_{X' \sim Q}\mathbb{E}_{X \sim Q(\cdot|X')} f\left(\frac{P(X, X')}{Q(X, X')}\right)
$$

$$
\overset{(c)}{=} \mathbb{E}_{X' \sim Q}\mathbb{E}_{X \sim Q(\cdot|X')} f\left(\frac{P(X)}{Q(X)}\right)
$$

$$
= \mathbb{E}_{[X, X'] \sim Q} f\left(\frac{P(X)}{Q(X)}\right) = D_f(W||Z).
$$

Note that (B.2) implies (a); (b) follows from Jensen's inequality, and (c) can be obtained from (B.1). □

B.2 Examples of *f*-divergence

In the following, we list useful examples of *f*-divergence encountered in the main text. However, it is worth noting that different $f(t)$ can lead to the same divergence, as shown by the following simple fact.

Proposition B.5 *The f-divergence with $f(t)$ is the same as the f-divergence with $\tilde{f}(t) = f(t) + \beta(1 - t)$ for any $\beta \in \mathbb{R}$.*

We will choose only one $f(t)$ for each divergence in the example, although one can choose different $f(t)$ for convenience. The examples are all strictly convex at $z = 1$, and thus $D_f(P||Q) = 0$ if and only if $P = Q$.

KL-divergence

With $f(t) = t \ln t$, we obtain the KL-divergence (Kullback–Leibler divergence) as follows

$$
\text{KL}(P||Q) = \int_\Omega \ln\left(\frac{p(z)}{q(z)}\right) p(z) d\mu(z).
$$

KL-divergence can be unbounded.

Given random variables $[X, X']$, with probability measure P, their mutual information is defined as

$$
I(X, X') = \text{KL}(P(X, X')||P(X)P(X')).
$$

Mutual information is often used to measure the independence of the random variables X and X'. If the random variables are independent, then the mutual information is zero. In the general case, mutual information can be unbounded.

χ^2-*divergence*

With $f(t) = (t-1)^2$, we obtain χ^2-divergence as follows:

$$\chi^2(P||Q) = \int_\Omega \left(\frac{p(z) - q(z)}{q(z)}\right)^2 q(z)d\mu(z) = \int_\Omega \left(\frac{p(z)}{q(z)}\right)^2 q(z)d\mu(z) - 1.$$

The χ^2-divergence can be unbounded.

Squared Hellinger distance

With $f(t) = (1 - \sqrt{t})^2$, we obtain squared Hellinger distance as follows:

$$H(P||Q)^2 = \int_\Omega \left(\sqrt{p(z)} - \sqrt{q(z)}\right)^2 d\mu(z) = 2 - 2\int_\Omega \sqrt{p(z)q(z)}d\mu(z).$$

Hellinger distance is always between $[0, 2]$.

α-*divergence*

KL-divergence, χ^2-divergence, and Hellinger divergence all belong to the more general family of α-divergence for $\alpha \geq 0$. It is defined with $f(t) = (1-\alpha)^{-1}(t - t^\alpha)$ for $\alpha > 0$:

$$D_\alpha(P||Q) = \frac{1}{1-\alpha}\left(1 - \int_\Omega \left(\frac{p(z)}{q(z)}\right)^\alpha q(z)d\mu(z)\right). \tag{B.3}$$

We have

- $D_1(P||Q) = \mathrm{KL}(P||Q)$: when $\alpha \to 1$, we have $f(t) \to t\ln t$.
- $D_2(P||Q) = \chi^2(P||Q)$.
- $D_{0.5}(P||Q) = H(P||Q)^2$.

When $\alpha < 1$, α-divergence is bounded, and when $\alpha \geq 1$, α-divergence is unbounded.

We can also write α-divergence differently as follows:

$$D_\alpha^{\mathrm{R\acute{e}}}(P||Q) = \frac{1}{\alpha - 1}\ln[1 + (\alpha - 1)D_\alpha(P||Q)]$$

$$= \frac{1}{\alpha - 1}\ln \int_\Omega \left(\frac{p(z)}{q(z)}\right)^{\alpha-1} p(z)d\mu(z).$$

The quantity $D_\alpha^{\mathrm{R\acute{e}}}(\cdot)$ is often referred to as Rényi entropy, which is also nonnegative. When $\alpha = 1$, we use the convention that

$$D_1^{\mathrm{R\acute{e}}}(P||Q) = \lim_{\alpha \to 1} D_\alpha^{\mathrm{R\acute{e}}}(P||Q) = \mathrm{KL}(P||Q). \tag{B.4}$$

One important property of α-divergence is that it is convenient to estimate the α-divergence of product distributions. This property can be used to obtain lower bounds for statistical estimation.

Theorem B.6 *Let P^n and Q^n be the product distribution of n iid samples from P and Q respectively. Then*

$$D_\alpha^{R\acute{e}}(P^n||Q^n) = n \cdot D_\alpha^{R\acute{e}}(P||Q).$$

For $\alpha = 1$, this becomes

$$\mathrm{KL}(P^n||Q^n)) = n \cdot \mathrm{KL}(P||Q)).$$

L_1 *norm and TV-norm*

With $f(t) = |z - 1|$, we obtain the L_1 norm between two measures as

$$\|P - Q\|_1 = \int_\Omega |p(z) - q(z)|d\mu(z).$$

The quantity is always bounded between $[0, 2]$. We can also define the TV-norm between two measures as

$$\|P - Q\|_{\mathrm{TV}} = \frac{1}{2}\|P - Q\|_1 = 1 - \int_\Omega \min(p(z), q(z))d\mu(z),$$

which is always between $[0, 1]$.

The TV-norm can also be defined equivalently as follows.

Proposition B.7

$$\|P - Q\|_{\mathrm{TV}} = \sup_A |P(A) - Q(A)| = \frac{1}{2} \sup_{g\,:\,\|g\|_\infty \leq 1} [\mathbb{E}_{Z \sim P} g(Z) - \mathbb{E}_{Z \sim Q} g(Z)],$$

where A is over all measurable sets, and g is over all measurable functions with bounded L_∞ norm.

B.3 Basic Inequalities

Many *f*-divergence inequalities can be found in Sason and Verdú (2016). In the following, we will only present some of the inequalities that are used in the book.

In many applications, it is useful to bound the TV-norm of two distributions in terms of other divergences. The following inequality is a straightforward application of data-processing inequality.

Lemma B.8 *We have*

$$\|P - Q\|_{\mathrm{TV}}^2 \leq \frac{1}{c_f} D_f(P||Q),$$

where c_f is defined below with $p(s) = (1 - s)q + sp$:

$$c_f = \min_{p,q \in [0,1]} \int_0^1 \left[\frac{1}{q}f''\left(\frac{p(s)}{q}\right) + \frac{1}{1-q}f''\left(\frac{1-p(s)}{1-q}\right)\right](1-s)ds.$$

Proof Given any measurable set A, let $p = P(A)$ and $q = Q(A)$. By the data processing inequality, with $h(z) = \mathbf{1}(z \in A)$, we have

$$D_f(P\|Q) \geq qf\left(\frac{p}{q}\right) + (1-q)f\left(\frac{1-p}{1-q}\right)$$

$$= \underbrace{qf\left(1 + s\frac{p-q}{q}\right) + (1-q)f\left(1 + s\frac{q-p}{1-q}\right)}_{g(s)}\bigg|_{s=1}$$

$$= g(0) + g'(0) + \int_0^1 g''(s)(1-s)ds$$

$$= (p-q)^2 \int_0^1 \left[\frac{1}{q}f''\left(\frac{p(s)}{q}\right) + \frac{1}{1-q}f''\left(\frac{1-p(s)}{1-q}\right)\right](1-s)ds$$

$$\geq c_f(p-q)^2,$$

where we have used Taylor expansion, and $g(0) = g'(0) = 0$. Therefore,

$$\frac{1}{c_f}D_f(P\|Q) \geq \sup_A (P(A) - Q(A))^2 = \|P - Q\|_{\mathrm{TV}}^2.$$

This proves the desired bound. □

This result implies the following inequalities. The bound of TV-norm in KL-divergence is often referred to as Pinsker's inequality.

Theorem B.9 *We have*

$$\|P - Q\|_{\mathrm{TV}}^2 \leq \frac{1}{4}\chi^2(P\|Q),$$

$$\|P - Q\|_{\mathrm{TV}}^2 \leq \frac{1}{2}\mathrm{KL}(P\|Q),$$

$$\|P - Q\|_{\mathrm{TV}}^2 \leq H(P\|Q)^2.$$

Proof Consider α-divergence with $\alpha = 1, 2$. Let $f(t) = (1-\alpha)^{-1}(t - t^\alpha)$, and $f''(t) = \alpha t^{\alpha-2}$. Let

$$c(p,q) = \int_0^1 [q^{1-\alpha}p(s)^{\alpha-2} + (1-q)^{1-\alpha}(1 - p(s))^{\alpha-2}](1-s)ds.$$

There exists $p_0 \in (0, 1)$ such that (for $\alpha = 1, 2$)

$$c(p,q) = \frac{1}{2}[q^{1-\alpha}p_0^{\alpha-2} + (1-q)^{1-\alpha}(1-p_0)^{\alpha-2}] \geq 2.$$

We can now apply Lemma B.8 with $c_f = \alpha \min_{p,q}$ and $c(p,q) \geq 2\alpha$ to obtain the result. This implies the first two inequalities of the theorem. For the third inequality, we may still estimate a lower bound of $c(p,q)$ as defined. However, the following derivation is more direct:

$$\|P - Q\|_{\text{TV}}^2 = \left[\frac{1}{2} \int \big| p(z) - q(z) \big| d\mu(z) \right]^2$$

$$= \frac{1}{4} \left[\int \big| \sqrt{p(z)} - \sqrt{q(z)} \big| \cdot \big| \sqrt{p(z)} + \sqrt{q(z)} \big| d\mu(z) \right]^2$$

$$\leq \frac{1}{4} \int \big| \sqrt{p(z)} - \sqrt{q(z)} \big|^2 d\mu(z) \cdot \int \big| \sqrt{p(z)} + \sqrt{q(z)} \big|^2 d\mu(z)$$

$$\leq \frac{1}{4} \int \big| \sqrt{p(z)} - \sqrt{q(z)} \big|^2 d\mu(z) \cdot \int 2 \left[p(z) + q(z) \right] d\mu(z)$$

$$= \int \big| \sqrt{p(z)} - \sqrt{q(z)} \big|^2 d\mu(z) = H(P\|Q)^2.$$

The first inequality used the Cauchy–Schwarz inequality. The second inequality used $(\sqrt{a} + \sqrt{b})^2 \leq 2(a + b)$. The last two equations used the definition of Hellinger distance and the fact that each density $p(z)$ and $q(z)$ integrates to 1. □

We can also derive an upper bound of Hellinger distance by the square root of TV norm. However, in general, this bound is not tight when the norms are small.

Proposition B.10   *We have*

$$H(P\|Q)^2 \leq 2\|P - Q\|_{\text{TV}}.$$

Proof   We note that

$$H(P\|Q)^2 = \int_\Omega \big| \sqrt{p(z)} - \sqrt{q(z)} \big|^2 d\mu(z)$$

$$\leq \int_\Omega \big| \sqrt{p(z)} - \sqrt{q(z)} \big| \cdot \big| \sqrt{p(z)} + \sqrt{q(z)} \big| d\mu(z)$$

$$= \int_\Omega |p(z) - q(z)| \, d\mu(z).$$

This implies the result. □

The following result is also useful.

Proposition B.11   *Let $\rho = \sup_z \ln(p(z)/q(z))$. Then*

$$H(P\|Q)^2 \leq \text{KL}(P\|Q) \leq (3 + \rho) H(P\|Q)^2.$$

Proof   The first desired inequality used Proposition B.12 and $-2 \ln z \geq 2(1 - z)$:

$$H(P\|Q)^2 \leq D_{0.5}^{\text{Ré}}(P\|Q) \leq D_1^{\text{Ré}}(P\|Q) = \text{KL}(P\|Q).$$

Now let $f_{\text{KL}}(t) = t \ln t - t + 1$ and $f_H(t) = (\sqrt{t} - 1)^2$. Let

$$\kappa = \sup_{0 \leq t \leq \exp(\rho)} \frac{f_{\text{KL}}(t)}{f_H(t)},$$

then by using the fact that $f_{KL}(t)/f_H(t)$ is an increasing function of $t \in [0, \infty)$, we obtain $\kappa \leq f_{KL}(\exp(\rho))/f_H(\exp(\rho))$.

Moreover we know that for ratio of distributions $\rho \geq 0$, and when $\rho \in (0, \infty)$, we have $\kappa \leq f_{KL}(\exp(\rho))/f_H(\exp(\rho)) \leq 2.5 + \rho$. We now have

$$\mathrm{KL}(P||Q) = \mathbb{E}_{Z \sim Q} f_{KL}(p(z)/q(z)) \leq \kappa \mathbb{E}_{Z \sim Q} f_H(p(z)/q(z)) = \kappa H(P||Q)^2,$$

which implies the desired bounds. $\square$

It is also relatively easy to obtain bounds of α-divergences for different values of α. In general, if $\alpha < \alpha'$, then we can bound α-divergence by α'-divergence as follows. It is a direct consequence of Jensen's inequality.

Proposition B.12 *If $0 < \alpha < \alpha'$, then*

$$D_\alpha^{R\acute{e}}(P||Q) \leq D_{\alpha'}^{R\acute{e}}(P||Q),$$

where the convention of (B.4) is adopted for $\alpha = 1$ or $\alpha' = 1$.

Proof We consider the case of $1 < \alpha \leq \alpha'$. Then Jensen's inequality implies that

$$\left[\int_\Omega \left(\frac{p(z)}{q(z)} \right)^{\alpha-1} p(z) d\mu(z) \right]^{(\alpha'-1)/(\alpha-1)} \leq \int_\Omega \left(\frac{p(z)}{q(z)} \right)^{\alpha'-1} p(z) d\mu(z).$$

By taking the logarithm and dividing each side by $\alpha' - 1$, we obtain the desired bound. Similarly, we can prove the case of $0 < \alpha \leq \alpha' < 1$. By combining the two cases, and taking limit at $\alpha \to 1$ or $\alpha' \to 1$, we obtain the desired inequality for all $0 < \alpha \leq \alpha'$. $\square$

Theorem B.9 is useful to bound the product distributions for TV-norm via α-divergence. Due to Proposition B.12, it is beneficial to use $\alpha < 1$. In particular, we have the following result using Hellinger distance.

Theorem B.13 *Let P^n and Q^n be the product distribution of n iid samples from P and Q respectively. We have*

$$\|P^n - Q^n\|_{\mathrm{TV}}^2 \leq H(P^n||Q^n)^2 = 2 - 2(1 - 0.5H(P||Q)^2)^n.$$

Proof From Theorem B.6 with $\alpha = 0.5$, we obtain

$$\ln(1 - 0.5H(P^n||Q^n)^2) = n \ln(1 - 0.5H(P||Q)^2).$$

It follows that

$$H(P^n||Q^n)^2 = 2 - 2(1 - 0.5H(P||Q)^2)^n.$$

Together with Theorem B.9, we obtain the desired bound. $\square$

References

Abadi, Martin, Chu, Andy, Goodfellow, Ian et al. 2016. Deep learning with differential privacy. *Proceedings of the 2016 ACM SIGSAC Conference on Computer and Communications Security.* Association for Computing Machinery, pp. 308–318.

Abbasi-Yadkori, Yasin, Pál, Dávid, and Szepesvári, Csaba. 2011. Improved algorithms for linear stochastic bandits. *Advances in Neural Information Processing Systems*, 24. Curran Associates. https://proceedings.neurips.cc/paper/2011/file/e1d5be1c7f2f456670de3d53c7b54f4a-Paper.pdf

Agarwal, Alekh, and Zhang, Tong. 2022a. Model-based RL with optimistic posterior sampling: Structural conditions and sample complexity. *Advances in Neural Information Processing Systems*, 35. https://proceedings.neurips.cc/paperfiles/paper/2022/file/e536e43b01a4387a2282c2b04103c802-Paper-Conference.pdf

Agarwal, Alekh, and Zhang, Tong. 2022. Non-linear reinforcement learning in large action spaces: Structural conditions and sample-efficiency of posterior sampling. *Conference on Learning Theory*, PMLR, pp. 2776–2814.

Agarwal, Alekh, Wainwright, Martin J., Bartlett, Peter, and Ravikumar, Pradeep. 2009. Information-theoretic lower bounds on the oracle complexity of convex optimization. *Advances in Neural Information Processing Systems*, 22. Curran Associates. https://proceedings.neurips.cc/paper/2009/file/2387337ba1e0b0249ba90f55b2ba2521-Paper.pdf

Agarwal, Alekh, Dudík, Miroslav, Kale, Satyen, Langford, John, and Schapie, Robert. 2012. Contextual bandit learning with predictable rewards. This is a conference, also called AISTAT see http://aistats.org/aistats2023/

Agarwal, Alekh, Hsu, Daniel, Kale, Satyen et al. 2014. Taming the monster: A fast and simple algorithm for contextual bandits. *Proceedings of the 31st International Conference on Machine Learning*, PMLR **32**(2), 1638–1646.

Agarwal, Alekh, Kakade, Sham, Krishnamurthy, Akshay, and Sun, Wen. 2020. FLAMBE: Structural complexity and representation learning of low rank MDPs *Advances in Neural Information Processing Systems*, 33. Curran Associates. https://proceedings.neurips.cc/paper/2020/file/e894d787e2fd6c133af47140aa156f00-Paper.pdf

Agrawal, Rajeev. 1995. Sample mean based index policies with $O(\log n)$ regret for the multi-armed bandit problem. *Advances in Applied Probability*, **27**, 1054–1078.

Agrawal, Shipra, and Goyal, Navin. 2012. Analysis of Thompson sampling for the multi-armed bandit problem. *Conference on Learning Theory*, also referred to as COLT, is an annual peer reviewed conference organized by https://learningtheory.org

Agrawal, Shipra, and Goyal, Navin. 2013a. Further optimal regret bounds for Thompson sampling. *Artificial Intelligence and Statistics*, **31**, 99–107.

Agrawal, Shipra, and Goyal, Navin. 2013b. Thompson sampling for contextual bandits with linear payoffs. *Proceedings of the 30th International Conference on Machine Learning*, 28, 3, 127–135. https://proceedings.mlr.press/v28/agrawal13.html

Akaike, Hirotugu. 1974. A new look at the statistical model identification. *IEEE Transactions on Automatic Control*, **19**(6), 716–723.

Allen-Zhu, Zeyuan, Li, Yuanzhi, and Liang, Yingyu. 2019a. Learning and generalization in overparameterized neural networks, going beyond two layers. *Advances in Neural Information Processing Systems*, 32. Curran Associates, pp. 9244–9255, https://proceedings.neurips.cc/paperfiles/paper/2019/file/62dad6e273d32235ae02b7d321578 ee8-Paper.pdf

Allen-Zhu, Zeyuan, Li, Yuanzhi, and Song, Zhao. 2019b. A convergence theory for deep learning via over-parameterization. *Proceedings of the 30th International Conference on Machine Learning*, 97, 242–252. https://proceedings.mlr.press/v97/allen-zhu19a.html

Alvarez, Mauricio A., Rosasco, Lorenzo, and Lawrence, Neil D. 2012. Kernels for vector-valued functions: A review. *Foundations and Trends in Machine Learning*, **4**(3), 195–266.

Antos, András, Szepesvári, Csaba, and Munos, Rémi. 2008. Learning near-optimal policies with Bellman-residual minimization based fitted policy iteration and a single sample path. *Machine Learning*, **71**(1), 89–129.

Aronszajn, Nachman. 1950. Theory of reproducing kernels. *Transactions of the American Mathematical Society*, **68**(3), 337–404.

Assouad, Patrice. 1983. Deux remarques sur l'estimation. *Comptes rendus des séances de l'Académie des sciences. Série 1, Mathématique*, **296**(23), 1021–1024.

Audibert, Jean-Yves. 2007. Progressive mixture rules are deviation suboptimal. *Advances in Neural Information Processing Systems*, 20. Curran Associates, pp. 41–48.

Audibert, Jean-Yves. 2009. Fast learning rates in statistical inference through aggregation. *The Annals of Statistics*, **37**(4), 1591–1646.

Audibert, Jean-Yves, and Bubeck, Sébastien. 2009. Minimax policies for adversarial and stochastic bandits. In *Conference on Learning Theory*, Montreal, Quebec, June 18–21, 2009. www.cs.mcgill.ca/colt2009/proceedings.html

Auer, Peter. 2002. Using confidence bounds for exploitation-exploration trade-offs. *Journal of Machine Learning Research*, **3**(Nov), 397–422.

Auer, Peter, Cesa-Bianchi, Nicolo, and Fischer, Paul. 2002a. Finite-time analysis of the multiarmed bandit problem. *Machine Learning*, **47**(2–3), 235–256.

Auer, Peter, Cesa-Bianchi, Nicolo, Freund, Yoav, and Schapire, Robert E. 2002b. The nonstochastic multiarmed bandit problem. *SIAM Journal on Computing*, **32**(1), 48–77.

Auer, Peter, Jaksch, Thomas, and Ortner, Ronald. 2008. Near-optimal regret bounds for reinforcement learning. *Advances in Neural Information Processing Systems*, 21, 89-96 https://www.jmlr.org/papers/volume11/jaksch10a/jaksch10a.pdf

Ayoub, Alex, Jia, Zeyu, Szepesvari, Csaba, Wang, Mengdi, and Yang, Lin. 2020. Model-based reinforcement learning with value-targeted regression. *Proceedings of the 30th International Conference on Machine Learning*, 119, 463–474. https://proceedings.mlr.press /v119/ayoub20a.html

Azar, Mohammad Gheshlaghi, Osband, Ian, and Munos, Rémi. 2017. Minimax regret bounds for reinforcement learning. *Proceedings of the 34th International Conference on Machine Learning*, 70, 263–272. https://proceedings.mlr.press/v70/azar17a.html

Azuma, Kazuoki. 1967. Weighted sums of certain dependent random variables. *Tohoku Mathematical Journal (2)*, **19**(3), 357–367.

Bai, Zhidong, and Silverstein, Jack W. 2010. *Spectral Analysis of Large Dimensional Random Matrices*, vol. 20 of Springer Series in Statistics. Springer.

Bakry, Dominique, and Émery, Michel. 1985. Diffusions hypercontractives. *Seminaire de probabilités XIX 1983/84*. Springer, pp. 177–206.

Barron, Andrew, Rissanen, Jorma, and Yu, Bin. 1998. The minimum description length principle in coding and modeling. *IEEE Transactions on Information Theory*, **44**(6), 2743–2760.

Barron, Andrew R. 1993. Universal approximation bounds for superpositions of a sigmoidal function. *IEEE Transactions on Information Theory*, **39**(3), 930–945.

Barron, Andrew R., Cohen, Albert, Dahmen, Wolfgang, and DeVore, Ronald A. 2008. Approximation and learning by greedy algorithms. *The Annals of Statistics*, **36**(1), 64–94.

Bartlett, Peter L., and Mendelson, Shahar. 2002. Rademacher and Gaussian complexities: Risk bounds and structural results. *Journal of Machine Learning Research*, **3**(Nov), 463–482.

Bartlett, Peter L., and Tewari, Ambuj. 2009. REGAL: A regularization based algorithm for reinforcement learning in weakly communicating MDPs. *Proceedings of the 25th Conference on Uncertainty in Artificial Intelligence*. Arlington, VA: AUAI Press, pp. 35–42.

Bartlett, Peter L., Long, Philip M., and Williamson, Robert C. 1996. Fat-shattering and the learnability of real-valued functions. *Journal of Computer and System Sciences*, **52**(3), 434–452.

Bartlett, Peter L., Bousquet, Olivier, and Mendelson, Shahar. 2005. Local Rademacher complexities. *The Annals of Statistics*, **33**(4), 1497–1537.

Bartlett, Peter L., Long, Philip M., Lugosi, Gábor, and Tsigler, Alexander. 2020. Benign overfitting in linear regression. *Proceedings of the National Academy of Sciences*, **117**(48), 30063–30070.

Bassily, Raef, Feldman, Vitaly, Guzmán, Cristóbal, and Talwar, Kunal. 2020. Stability of stochastic gradient descent on nonsmooth convex losses. *Conference on Neural Information Processing Systems* arXiv abs/2006.06914.

Belkin, Mikhail, Hsu, Daniel, Ma, Siyuan, and Mandal, Soumik. 2019. Reconciling modern machine-learning practice and the classical bias–variance trade-off. *Proceedings of the National Academy of Sciences*, **116**(32), 15849–15854.

Belkin, Mikhail, Hsu, Daniel, and Xu, Ji. 2020. Two models of double descent for weak features. *SIAM Journal on Mathematics of Data Science*, **2**(4), 1167–1180.

Bennett, George. 1962. Probability inequalities for the sum of independent random variables. *Journal of the American Statistical Association*, **57**(297), 33–45.

Bergman, Stefan. 1970. *The Kernel Function and Conformal Mapping*, vol. 5 of Mathematical Surveys and Monographs. American Mathematical Society.

Bergstra, James, Bardenet, Rémi, Bengio, Yoshua, and Kégl, Balázs. 2011. Algorithms for hyperparameter optimization. *Advances in Neural Information Processing Systems*, 24, Curran Associates, pp. 2546–2554.

Bernstein, Sergei. 1924. On a modification of Chebyshev's inequality and of the error formula of Laplace. *Ann. Sci. Inst. Sav. Ukraine, Sect. Math*, **1**(4), 38–49.

Bertsekas, Dimitri. 2012. *Dynamic Programming and Optimal Control*, vol 1. Athena Scientific.

Bickel, Peter J. 1982. On adaptive estimation. *The Annals of Statistics*, **10**, 647–671.

Bickel, Peter J., Ritov, Yaacov, and Tsybakov, Alexandre. 2009. Simultaneous analysis of Lasso and Dantzig selector. *The Annals of Statistics*, **37**(4), 1705–1732.

Birgé, Lucien. 1986. On estimating a density using Hellinger distance and some other strange facts. *Probability Theory and Related Fields*, **71**(2), 271–291.

Birgé, Lucien, and Massart, Pascal. 1993. Rates of convergence for minimum contrast estimators. *Probability Theory and Related Fields*, **97**(1–2), 113–150.

Birgé, Lucien, and Massart, Pascal. 1997. From model selection to adaptive estimation. *Festschrift for Lucien LeCam*. Springer, pp. 55–87.

Birgé, Lucien, and Massart, Pascal. 1998. Minimum contrast estimators on sieves: Exponential bounds and rates of convergence. *Bernoulli*, **4**(3), 329–375.

Blumer, Anselm, Ehrenfeucht, Andrzej, Haussler, David, and Warmuth, Manfred K. 1989. Learnability and the Vapnik–Chervonenkis dimension. *Journal of the ACM*, **36**(4), 929–965.

Boser, Bernhard E., Guyon, Isabelle M., and Vapnik, Vladimir N. 1992. A training algorithm for optimal margin classifiers. *Proceedings of the Fifth Annual Workshop on Computational Learning Theory*. Association for Computing Machinery, pp. 144–152. https://doi.org/10.1145/130385.130401

Boucheron, Stéphane, Lugosi, Gábor, and Massart, Pascal. 2000. A sharp concentration inequality with applications. *Random Structures & Algorithms*, **16**(3), 277–292.

Boucheron, Stéphane, Lugosi, Gábor, and Massart, Pascal. 2003. Concentration inequalities using the entropy method. *The Annals of Probability*, **31**(3), 1583–1614.

Boucheron, Stéphane, Lugosi, Gábor, and Massart, Pascal. 2013. *Concentration Inequalities: A Nonasymptotic Theory of Independence*. Oxford University Press.

Bousquet, Olivier. 2002. A Bennett concentration inequality and its application to suprema of empirical processes. *Comptes Rendus Mathematique*, **334**(6), 495–500.

Bousquet, Olivier, and Elisseeff, André. 2002. Stability and generalization. *The Journal of Machine Learning Research*, **2**, 499–526.

Bousquet, Olivier, Klochkov, Yegor, and Zhivotovskiy, Nikita. 2020. Sharper bounds for uniformly stable algorithms. *Proceedings of 33rd Conference on Learning Theory*, 125, 610–626. https://proceedings.mlr.press/v125/bousquet20b.html

Boyd, Stephen, and Vandenberghe, Lieven. 2004. *Convex Optimization*. Cambridge University Press.

Buja, Andreas, Hastie, Trevor, and Tibshirani, Robert. 1989. Linear smoothers and additive models. *The Annals of Statistics*, **17**, 453–510.

Candes, Emmanuel J., and Tao, Terence. 2005. Decoding by linear programming. *IEEE Transactions on Information Theory*, **51**, 4203–4215.

Cantelli, Francesco Paolo. 1933. Sulla determinazione empirica delle leggi di probabilita. *Giornale dell'Istituto Italiano degli Attauri*, **4**, 421–424.

Carl, Bernd. 1997. Metric entropy of convex hulls in Hilbert spaces. *Bulletin of the London Mathematical Society*, **29**(4), 452–458.

Chapelle, Olivier, and Li, Lihong. 2011. An empirical evaluation of Thompson sampling. *Advances in Neural Information Processing Systems*. Curran Associates, pp. 2249–2257.

Chen, Scott Shaobing, Donoho, David L., and Saunders, Michael A. 2001. Atomic decomposition by basis pursuit. *SIAM Review*, **43**(1), 129–159.

Chen, Zixiang, Cao, Yuan, Gu, Quanquan, and Zhang, Tong. 2020. A generalized neural tangent kernel analysis for two-layer neural networks. *Thirty-fourth Conference on Neural Information Processing Systems* (NeurIPS). Vancouver, BC.

Cheng, Chen, Duchi, John, and Kuditipudi, Rohith. 2022. Memorize to generalize: On the necessity of interpolation in high dimensional linear regression. *Proceedings of 35th Conference on Learning Theory*, 178, 5528–2260. https://proceedings.mlr.press/v178/cheng22a.html

Chentsov, Nikolai N. 1956. Weak convergence of stochastic processes whose trajectories have no discontinuities of the second kind and the "heuristic" approach to the Kolmogorov–Smirnov tests. *Theory of Probability & Its Applications*, **1**(1), 140–144.

Chernoff, Herman. 1952. A measure of asymptotic efficiency for tests of a hypothesis based on the sum of observations. *The Annals of Mathematical Statistics*, **23**(4), 493–507.

Chizat, Lenaic, and Bach, Francis. 2018. On the global convergence of gradient descent for over-parameterized models using optimal transport. *Advances in Neural Information Processing Systems*. Curran Associates, pp. 3036–3046. https://proceedings.neurips.cc/paper/2018/file/a1afc58c6ca9540d057299ec3016d726-Paper.pdf

Chizat, Lenaic, and Bach, Francis. 2020. Implicit bias of gradient descent for wide two-layer neural networks trained with the logistic loss. *Annual Conference on Learning Theory*, 125, 1305–1338. https://proceedings.mlr.press/v125/chizat20a.html

Chizat, Lenaic, Oyallon, Edouard, and Bach, Francis. 2019. On lazy training in differentiable programming. *Advances in Neural Information Processing Systems*, 32. Curran Associates. https://papers.nips.cc/paper_files/paper/2019/hash/ae614c557843b1df326cb29c57225459-Abstract.html

Chu, Wei, Li, Lihong, Reyzin, Lev, and Schapire, Robert. 2011. Contextual bandits with linear payoff functions. *Proceedings of the Fourteenth International Conference on Artificial Intelligence and Statistics*, 15, 208–214. https://proceedings.mlr.press/v15/chu11a.html

Clarkson, Kenneth L. 2010. Coresets, sparse greedy approximation, and the Frank–Wolfe algorithm. *ACM Transactions on Algorithms (TALG)*, **6**(4), 1–30.

Collins, Michael. 2002. Discriminative training methods for hidden Markov models: Theory and experiments with perceptron algorithms. *Proceedings of the 2002 Conference on Empirical Methods in Natural Language Processing (EMNLP 2002)*. Association for Computational Linguisticspp. 1–8. https://aclanthology.org/W02-1001

Cortes, Corinna, and Vapnik, Vladimir. 1995. Support-vector networks. *Machine Learning*, **20**(3), 273–297.

Cramér, Harald. 1938. Sur un nouveau théoreme-limite de la théorie des probabilités. *Actual. Sci. Ind.*, **736**, 5–23.

Cramér, Harald. 2016. *Mathematical Methods of Statistics (PMS-9)* Princeton University Press.

Craven, Peter, and Wahba, Grace. 1978. Smoothing noisy data with spline functions. *Numerische Mathematik*, **31**(4), 377–403.

Cristianini, Nello, and Shawe-Taylor, John. 2000. *An Introduction to Support Vector Machines and Other Kernel-Based Learning Methods*. Cambridge University Press.

Cucker, Felipe, and Smale, Steve. 2002. On the mathematical foundations of learning. *American Mathematical Society*, **39**(1), 1–49.

Dai, Dong, Rigollet, Philippe, and Zhang, Tong. 2012. Deviation optimal learning using greedy Q-aggregation. *The Annals of Statistics*, **40**(3), 1878–1905.

Dalalyan, Arnak S., and Tsybakov, Alexandre B. 2007. Aggregation by exponential weighting and sharp oracle inequalities. *International Conference on Computational Learning Theory* Springer, pp. 97–111.

Dani, Varsha, Hayes, Thomas P., and Kakade, Sham M. 2008. Stochastic linear optimization under bandit feedback. *Conference on Learning Theory*. http://colt2008.cs.helsinki.fi

Dann, Christoph, and Brunskill, Emma. 2015. Sample complexity of episodic fixed-horizon reinforcement learning. *Advances in Neural Information Processing Systems*, 28. Curran Associates. https://proceedings.neurips.cc/paper/2015/file/309fee4e541e51de2e41f21bebb342aa-Paper.pdf

Dann, Christoph, Mohri, Mehryar, Zhang, Tong, and Zimmert, Julian. 2021. A provably efficient model-free posterior sampling method for episodic reinforcement learning. *Advances in Neural Information Processing Systems*, 34, 12040–12051.

Deuschel, Jean-Dominique, and Stroock, Daniel W. 2001. *Large Deviations* American Mathematical Society.

Donoho, David L. 2006. Compressed sensing. *IEEE Transactions on Information Theory*, **52**(4), 1289–1306.

Donsker, Monroe D. 1952. Justification and extension of Doob's heuristic approach to the Kolmogorov–Smirnov theorems. *The Annals of Mathematical Statistics*, **23**(2), 277–281.

Doob, Joseph L. 1953. *Stochastic Processes*, vol. 7 of Wiley Classic Library. Wiley New York.

Du, Simon, Kakade, Sham, Lee, Jason et al. 2021. Bilinear classes: A structural framework for provable generalization in rl. *Proceedings of the 38th International Conference on Machine Learning*, 139, 2826–2836. https://proceedings.mlr.press/v139/du21a.html

Du, Simon S., Lee, Jason D., Li, Haochuan, Wang, Liwei, and Zhai, Xiyu. 2019. Gradient descent finds global minima of deep neural networks. *Proceedings of the 36th International Conference on Machine Learning*, 97, 1675–1685. https://proceedings.mlr.press/v97/du19c.html

Duchi, John, Hazan, Elad, and Singer, Yoram. 2011. Adaptive subgradient methods for online learning and stochastic optimization. *Journal of Machine Learning Research*, **12**(61), 2121-2159

Dudik, Miroslav, Hsu, Daniel, Kale, Satyen et al. 2011. Efficient optimal learning for contextual bandits. *Conference on Uncertainty in Artificial Intelligence, Proceedings of the Twenty-Seventh* 169–178. https://dl.acm.org/doi/proceedings/10.5555/3020548

Dudley, Richard M. 1967. The sizes of compact subsets of Hilbert space and continuity of Gaussian processes. *Journal of Functional Analysis*, **1**(3), 290–330.

Dudley, Richard M. 1978. Central limit theorems for empirical measures. *The Annals of Probability*, **6**(6), 899–929.

Dudley, Richard M. 1984. A course on empirical processes. *Ecole d'été de Probabilités de Saint-Flour XII-1982*. Springer, pp. 1–142.

Edmunds, Fang, Cong, Lee, Jason. *Function Spaces, Entropy Numbers, Differential Operators*. Cambridge University Press.

Efron, Bradley, and Stein, Charles. 1981. The jackknife estimate of variance. *The Annals of Statistics*, **9**(3), 586–596.

Engel, Andreas, and Van den Broeck, Christian. 2001. *Statistical Mechanics of Learning*. Cambridge University Press.

Fan, Jianqing, and Li, Runze. 2001. Variable selection via nonconcave penalized likelihood and its oracle properties. *Journal of the American Statistical Association*, **96**(456), 1348–1360.

Fang, Cong, Lee, Jason D., Yang, Pengkun, and Zhang, Tong. 2021. Modeling from features: A meanfield framework for over-parameterized deep neural networks. *Proceedings of 34th Conference on Learning Theory*, 134, 1887–1936. https://proceedings.mlr.press/v134/fang21a.html

Fang, Cong, Gu, Yihong, Zhang, Weizhong, and Zhang, Tong. 2022. Convex formulation of overparameterized deep neural networks. *IEEE Transactions on Information Theory*, 68(8), 5340–5352.

Fano, Robert M. 1961. Transmission of information: A statistical theory of communications. *American Journal of Physics*, **29**(11), 793–794.

Fedorov, Valerii Vadimovich. 2013. *Theory Of Optimal Experiments*. Elsevier Science.

Feldman, Vitaly, and Vondrak, Jan. 2019. High probability generalization bounds for uniformly stable algorithms with nearly optimal rate. *Proceedings of the Thirty-Second Conference on Learning Theory*, 99, 1270–1279. https://proceedings.mlr.press/v99/feldman19a.html

Foster, Dylan, and Rakhlin, Alexander. 2020. Beyond UCB: Optimal and efficient contextual bandits with regression oracles. *Proceedings of Machine Learning Research*, 119, 3199–3210. https://proceedings.mlr.press/v119/foster20a.html

Frank, Marguerite, and Wolfe, Philip. 1956. An algorithm for quadratic programming. *Naval Research Logistics Quarterly*, **3**(1–2), 95–110.

Freedman, David A. 1975. On tail probabilities for martingales. *The Annals of Probability*, **3**(1), 100–118.

Freund, Yoav, and Schapire, Robert E. 1997. A decision-theoretic generalization of on-line learning and an application to boosting. *Journal of Computer and System Sciences*, **55**(1), 119–139.

Friedman, Jerome, Hastie, Trevor, and Tibshirani, Robert. 2000. Additive logistic regression: A statistical view of boosting (with discussion and a rejoinder by the authors). *The Annals of Statistics*, **28**(2), 337–407.

Friedman, Jerome H. 2001. Greedy function approximation: A gradient boosting machine. *The Annals of Statistics*, **29**(5), 1189–1232.

Friedman, Jerome H., and Stuetzle, Werner. 1981. Projection pursuit regression. *Journal of the American Statistical Association*, **76**(376), 817–823.

Garivier, Aurélien, and Cappé, Olivier. 2011. The KL-UCB algorithm for bounded stochastic bandits and beyond. *Proceedings of the 24th Annual Conference on Machine Learning Research*, 19, 359–376. https://proceedings.mlr.press/v19/garivier11a.html

Geman, Stuart, and Hwang, Chii-Ruey. 1982. Nonparametric maximum likelihood estimation by the method of sieves. *The Annals of Statistics*, **10**(2), 401–414.

Gibbs, Josiah Willard. 1902. *Elementary Principles in Statistical Mechanics*. C. Scribner's Sons.

Glivenko, Valery. 1933. Sulla determinazione empirica delle leggi di probabilita. *Giornale dell'Istituto Italiano degli Attauri*, **4**, 92–99.

Grenander, Ulf. 1981. *Abstract Inference*. Wiley.

Grünwald, Peter D. 2007. *The Minimum Description Length Principle*. MIT Press.

Gu, Yihong, Zhang, Weizhong, Fang, Cong, Lee, Jason, and Zhang, Tong. 2020. How to characterize the landscape of overparameterized convolutional neural networks. *Advances in Neural Information Processing Systems*, 33. Curran Associates, pp. 3797–3807.

Guo, Ying, Bartlett, Peter L., Shawe-Taylor, John, and Williamson, Robert C. 1999. Covering numbers for support vector machines. *Proceedings of the 12th Annual Conference on Computational Learning Theory.* ACM Press, pp. 267–277.

Hanin, Boris. 2019. Universal function approximation by deep neural nets with bounded width and ReLU activations. *Mathematics,* **7**(10), 992. https://www.mdpi.com/2227-7390/7/10/992

Hardt, Moritz, Recht, Ben, and Singer, Yoram. 2016. Train faster, generalize better: Stability of stochastic gradient descent. *Proceedings of The 33rd International Conference on Machine Learning,* 48, 1225–1234. https://proceedings.mlr.press/v48/hardt16.html

Hastie, Trevor, Montanari, Andrea, Rosset, Saharon, and Tibshirani, Ryan J. 2022. Surprises in high-dimensional ridgeless least squares interpolation. *The Annals of Statistics.* **50**(2), 949–986.

Haugeland, John. 1989. *Artificial Intelligence: The Very Idea.* MIT Press.

Haussler, David. 1992. Decision theoretic generalizations of the PAC model for neural net and other learning applications. *Information and Computation,* **100**(1), 78–150.

Haussler, David. 1995. Sphere packing numbers for subsets of the Boolean n-cube with bounded Vapnik–Chervonenkis dimension. *Journal of Combinatorial Theory, Series A,* **69**(2), 217–232.

Hazan, Elad, Agarwal, Amit, and Kale, Satyen. 2007. Logarithmic regret algorithms for online convex optimization. *Machine Learning,* **69**(2–3), 169–192.

Hoeffding, W. 1963. Probability inequalities for sums of bounded random variables. *Journal of the American Statistical Association,* **58**(301), 13–30.

Holley, Richard, and Stroock, Daniel W. 1987. Logarithmic Sobolev inequalities and stochastic Ising models. *Journal of Statistical Physics,* **46**, 1159–1194.

Hsu, Daniel, Kakade, Sham M., and Zhang, Tong. 2012a. Random design analysis of ridge regression. *Proceedings of the 25th Annual Conference on Learning Theory,* 23, 9.1–9.24. https://proceedings.mlr.press/v23/hsu12.htmls

Hsu, Daniel, Kakade, Sham M., and Zhang, Tong. 2012b. A tail inequality for quadratic forms of subgaussian random vectors. *Electronic Communications in Probability,* **17**, article 52.

Huang, Guang-Bin, Zhu, Qin-Yu, and Siew, Chee-Kheong. 2006. Extreme learning machine: theory and applications. *Neurocomputing,* **70**(1–3), 489–501.

Huber, Peter J. 1985. Projection pursuit. *The Annals of Statistics,* **13**(2), 435–475.

Jaakkola, Tommi, Jordan, Michael, and Singh, Satinder. 1993. Convergence of stochastic iterative dynamic programming algorithms. *Advances in Neural Information Processing Systems,* 6. Morgan-Kaufmann. https://proceedings.neurips.cc/paper/1993/file/5807a685d1a9ab3b599035bc566ce2b9-Paper.pdf

Jacot, Arthur, Gabriel, Franck, and Hongler, Clément. 2018. Neural tangent kernel: Convergence and generalization in neural networks. *Advances in Neural Information Processing Systems,* 31. Curran Associates. https://proceedings.neurips.cc/paper_files/paper/2018/hash/5a4be1fa34e62bb8a6ec6b91d2462f5a-Abstract.html

Jiang, Nan, Krishnamurthy, Akshay, Agarwal, Alekh, Langford, John, and Schapire, Robert E. 2017. Contextual decision processes with low Bellman rank are PAC-learnable. *Proceedings of the 34th International Conference on Machine Learning,* 70, 263–272. https://proceedings.mlr.press/v70/azar17a.html

Jin, Chi, Allen-Zhu, Zeyuan, Bubeck, Sebastien, and Jordan, Michael I. 2018. Is Q-learning provably efficient? *Advances in Neural Information Processing Systems,* 31. https://proceedings.neurips.cc/paper/2018/file/d3b1fb02964aa64e257f9f26a31f72cf-Pap-er.pdf

Jin, Chi, Yang, Zhuoran, Wang, Zhaoran, and Jordan, Michael I. 2020. Provably efficient reinforcement learning with linear function approximation. *Proceedings of 33rd Conference on Learning Theory,* 125, 2137–2143. https://proceedings.mlr.press/v125/jin20a.html

Jin, Chi, Liu, Qinghua, and Miryoosefi, Sobhan. 2021. Bellman eluder dimension: New rich classes of RL problems, and sample-efficient algorithms. *Advances in Neural Information Processing Systems,* 34, 13406–13418. Curran Associates. https://proceedings.neurips.cc/paper/2021/file/6f5e4e86a87220e5d361ad82f1ebc335-Paper.pdf

Joag-Dev, Kumar, Perlman, Michael D., and Pitt, Loren D. 1983. Association of normal random variables and Slepian's inequality. *The Annals of Probability*, **11**(2), 451–455.

Jones, Lee K. 1992. A simple lemma on greedy approximation in Hilbert space and convergence rates for projection pursuit regression and neural network training. *The Annals of Statistics*, **20**(1), 608–613.

Kaufmann, Emilie, Korda, Nathaniel, and Munos, Rémi. 2012. Thompson sampling: An asymptotically optimal finite-time analysis. *International Conference on Algorithmic Learning Theory*. Springer, pp. 199–213. https://link.springer.com/book/10.1007/978-3-642-34106-9

Kearns, Michael, and Koller, Daphne. 1999. Efficient reinforcement learning in factored MDPs. *International Joint Conference on Artificial Intelligence*, 16, 740–747.

Kearns, Michael, and Singh, Satinder. 2002. Near-optimal reinforcement learning in polynomial time. *Machine Learning*, **49**(2), 209–232.

Kearns, Michael J., and Schapire, Robert E. 1994. Efficient distribution-free learning of probabilistic concepts. *Journal of Computer and System Sciences*, **48**(3), 464–497.

Kiefer, Jack, and Wolfowitz, Jacob. 1960. The equivalence of two extremum problems. *Canadian Journal of Mathematics*, **12**, 363–366.

Kingma, Diederik P., and Ba, Jimmy. 2015. Adam: A method for stochastic optimization. *The International Conference on Learning Representations*, San Diego, CA. `www/doku.php%3Fid=iclr2015:main.html`

Kivinen, Jyrki, and Warmuth, Manfred K. 1999. Averaging expert predictions. *European Conference on Computational Learning Theory*. Springer, pp. 153–167. https://dl.acm.org/doi/proceedings/10.5555/646945

Kleinberg, Robert, Slivkins, Aleksandrs, and Upfal, Eli. 2008. Multi-armed bandits in metric spaces. *Proceedings of the 40th Annual ACM Symposium on Theory of computing*. Association for Computing Machinery, pp. 681–690.

Kolmogorov, Andrei Nikolaevich, and Tikhomirov, Vladimir Mikhailovich. 1959. ε-entropy and ε-capacity of sets in function spaces. *Uspekhi Matematicheskikh Nauk*, **14**(2), 3–86.

Koltchinskii, Vladimir. 2001. Rademacher penalties and structural risk minimization. *IEEE Transactions on Information Theory*, **47**(5), 1902–1914.

Koltchinskii, Vladimir, and Panchenko, Dmitry. 2002. Empirical margin distributions and bounding the generalization error of combined classifiers. *The Annals of Statistics*, **30**(1), 1–50.

Krige, Daniel G. 1951. A statistical approach to some basic mine valuation problems on the Witwatersrand. *Journal of the Southern African Institute of Mining and Metallurgy*, **52**(6), 119–139.

Kühn, Thomas. 2011. Covering numbers of Gaussian reproducing kernel Hilbert spaces. *Journal of Complexity*, **27**(5), 489–499.

Lai, Tze Leung, and Robbins, Herbert. 1985. Asymptotically efficient adaptive allocation rules. *Advances in Applied Mathematics*, **6**(1), 4–22.

Langford, John, and Zhang, Tong. 2007. The epoch-greedy algorithm for multi-armed bandits with side information. *Advances in Neural Information Processing Systems*, 20. Curran Associates. https://proceedings.neurips.cc/paper/2007/file/4b04a686b0ad13dce35fa99fa4161c65-Paper.pdf

Lattimore, Tor, and Szepesvári, Csaba. 2020. *Bandit Algorithms*. Cambridge University Press.

Laurent, Béatrice, and Massart, Pascal 2000. Adaptive estimation of a quadratic functional by model selection. *The Annals of Statistics*, **28**(5), 1302–1338.

Le, Quoc, Sarlós, Tamás, and Smola, Alex. 2013. Fastfood-approximating kernel expansions in loglinear time. *Proceedings of the 30th International Conference on Machine Learning*, 28(3), 224–252. https://proceedings.mlr.press/v28/le13.html

LeCam, Lucien. 1973. Convergence of estimates under dimensionality restrictions. *The Annals of Statistics*, **1**(1), 38–53.

Lecué, Guillaume. 2007. Suboptimality of penalized empirical risk minimization in classification. *International Conference on Computational Learning Theory*. Springer, pp. 142–156.

Lecué, Guillaume, and Rigollet, Philippe. 2014. Optimal learning with Q-aggregation. *The Annals of Statistics*, **42**(1), 211–224.

Ledoux, Michel. 1997. On Talagrand's deviation inequalities for product measures. *ESAIM: Probability and Statistics*, **1**, 63–87.

Ledoux, Michel, and Talagrand, Michel. 2013. *Probability in Banach Spaces: Isoperimetry and Processes*. Springer Science & Business Media.

Leshno, Moshe, Lin, Vladimir Ya, Pinkus, Allan, and Schocken, Shimon. 1993. Multilayer feed-forward networks with a nonpolynomial activation function can approximate any function. *Neural Networks*, **6**(6), 861–867.

Li, Jonathan, and Barron, Andrew. 1999. Mixture density estimation. *Advances in Neural Information Processing Systems*, 12. MIT Press. https://proceedings.neurips .cc/paper/1999/file/a0f3601dc682036423013a5d965db9aa-Paper.pdf

Li, Yuanzhi, and Liang, Yingyu. 2018. Learning overparameterized neural networks via stochastic gradient descent on structured data. *Advances in Neural Information Processing Systems*, 13. https://proceedings.neurips.cc/paper/2018/file/54fe976ba170c19ebae453679b362263-Paper.pdf

Li, Jian, Luo, Xuanyuan, and Qiao, Mingda. 2020. On generalization error bounds of noisy gradient methods for non-convex learning. *The International Conference on Learning Representations*. https://dblp.org/rec/conf/iclr/LiLQ20.html

Liang, Shiyu, and Srikant, Rayadurgam. 2017. Why deep neural networks for function approximation? *Fifth International Conference on Learning Representations*, ICLR 2017, Toulon, France, April 24–26.

Liang, Tengyuan, Rakhlin, Alexander, and Sridharan, Karthik. 2015. Learning with square loss: Localization through offset Rademacher complexity. *Proceedings of The 28th Conference on Learning Theory*, 40, 1260–1285. https://proceedings.mlr.press/v40/Liang15.html

Littlestone, Nick. 1988. Learning quickly when irrelevant attributes abound: A new linear-threshold algorithm. *Machine Learning*, **2**(4), 285–318.

Littlestone, Nick, and Warmuth, Manfred K. 1994. The weighted majority algorithm. *Information and Computation*, **108**(2), 212–261.

Lorentz, G. G. 1966. Metric entropy and approximation. *Bulletin of the American Mathematical Society*, **72**(6), 903–937.

Lu, Zhou, Pu, Hongming, Wang, Feicheng, Hu, Zhiqiang, and Wang, Liwei. 2017. The expressive power of neural networks: A view from the width. *Advances in Neural Information Processing Systems*, 30. Curran Associates. https://proceedings.neurips.cc /paper/2017/file/32cbf687880eb1674a07bf717761dd3a-Paper.pdf

Maillard, Odalric-Ambrym, Munos, Rémi, and Stoltz, Gilles. 2011. A finite-time analysis of multi-armed bandits problems with Kullback–Leibler divergences. *Proceedings of the 24th Annual Conference on Learning Theory*, 19, 497–514.

Mallat, Stéphane G., and Zhang, Zhifeng. 1993. Matching pursuits with time-frequency dictionaries. *IEEE Transactions on Signal Processing*, **41**(12), 3397–3415.

Mallows, Colin L. 2000. Some comments on C_p. *Technometrics*, **42**(1), 87–94.

Mammen, Enno, and Tsybakov, Alexandre B. 1999. Smooth discrimination analysis. *Annals of Statistics*, **27**(6), 1808–1829.

Massart, Pascal. 2000. About the constants in Talagrand's concentration inequalities for empirical processes. *The Annals of Probability*, **28**(2), 863–884.

Matheron, Georges. 1965. *Les variables régionalisées et leur estimation: une application de la théorie de fonctions aléatoires aux sciences de la nature*. Masson et CIE.

McAllester, David. 1999. PAC-Bayesian model averaging. *International Conference on Computational Learning Theory*. ACM, pp. 164–170. https://dl.acm.org/doi/proceedings /10.1145/307400

McCarthy, John, Minsky, Marvin L., Rochester, Nathaniel, and Shannon, Claude E. 2006. A proposal for the Dartmouth summer research project on artificial intelligence, August 31, 1955. *AI Magazine*, **27**(4), 12–12.

McCulloch, Warren S., and Pitts, Walter. 1943. A logical calculus of the ideas immanent in nervous activity. *The Bulletin of Mathematical Biophysics*, **5**(4), 115–133.

McDiarmid, Colin. 1989. On the method of bounded differences. *Surveys in Combinatorics*, **141**(1), 148–188.

Mei, Song, and Montanari, Andrea. 2022. The generalization error of random features regression: Precise asymptotics and the double descent curve. *Communications on Pure and Applied Mathematics*, **75**(4), 667–766.

Mei, Song, Montanari, Andrea, and Nguyen, Phan-Minh. 2018. A mean field view of the landscape of two-layer neural networks. *Proceedings of the National Academy of Sciences*, **115**(33), E7665–E7671.

Mei, Song, Misiakiewicz, Theodor, and Montanari, Andrea. 2019. Mean-field theory of two-layers neural networks: Dimension-free bounds and kernel limit. *Proceedings of the 32nd Conference on Learning Theory*, 99, 2388–2464. https://proceedings.mlr.press/v99/mei19a.html

Meir, Ron, and Zhang, Tong. 2003. Generalization error bounds for Bayesian mixture algorithms. *Journal of Machine Learning Research*, **4**(Oct), 839–860.

Mercer, James. 1909. Functions of positive and negative type and their connection with the theory of integral equations. *Philosophical Transactions of the Royal Society of London, Series A*, **209**, 4–415.

Micchelli, Charles A., and Pontil, Massimiliano. 2005. On learning vector-valued functions. *Neural Computation*, **17**(1), 177–204.

Micchelli, Charles A., Xu, Yuesheng, and Zhang, Haizhang. 2006. Universal kernels. *Journal of Machine Learning Research*, **7**(12), 2651–2667.

Minsky, Marvin, and Papert, Seymour. 1969. *Perceptrons: An introduction to computational geometry*. MIT Press.

Mou, Wenlong, Wang, Liwei, Zhai, Xiyu, and Zheng, Kai. 2018. Generalization bounds of SGLD for non-convex learning: Two theoretical viewpoints. *Proceedings of the 31st Conference on Learning Theory*, 75, PMLR, pp. 605–638.

Nakkiran, Preetum, Kaplun, Gal, Bansal, Yamini et al. 2021. Deep double descent: Where bigger models and more data hurt. *Journal of Statistical Mechanics: Theory and Experiment*, **2021**(12), 124003.

Natarajan, Balas Kausik. 1995. Sparse approximate solutions to linear systems. *SIAM Journal on Computing*, **24**(2), 227–234.

Neal, Radford. 1995. *Bayesian learning for neural networks*. Ph.D. thesis, Department of Computer Science, University of Toronto.

Neal, Radford. M. 1999. Regression and classification using Gaussian process priors. *Bayesian Statistics 6*. Oxford University Press, pp. 475–501.

Nesterov, Yurii. 2014. *Introductory Lectures on Convex Optimization: A Basic Course*, vol. 87 of Applied Optimization. Springer.

Nickl, Richard, and Pötscher, Benedikt M. 2007. Bracketing metric entropy rates and empirical central limit theorems for function classes of Besov- and Sobolev-type. *Journal of Theoretical Probability*, **20**(2), 177–199.

Novikoff, Albert B. 1963. *On Convergence Proofs for Perceptrons*. Tech. rept. Stanford Research Institute, Menlo Park, CA.

Park, Jooyoung, and Sandberg, Irwin W. 1991. Universal approximation using radial-basis-function networks. *Neural Computation*, **3**(2), 246–257.

Pavliotis, Grigorios A. 2014. *Stochastic Processes and Applications: Diffusion Processes, the Fokker-Planck and Langevin Equations*, vol. 60 of Texts in Applied Mathematics. Springer.

Pisier, Gilles 1980–1. Remarques sur un resultat non publié de B. Maurey. *Séminaire d'Analyse Fonctionelle*, vol. 1.

Pisier, Gilles. 1999. *The Volume of Convex Bodies and Banach Space Geometry*, vol. 94 of Cambridge Tracts in Mathematics. Cambridge University Press.

Pollard, David. 1984. *Convergence of Stochastic Processes*. Springer.

Raftery, Adrian E. 1995. Bayesian model selection in social research. *Sociological Methodology*, **25**, 111–163.

Raftery, Adrian E., Madigan, David, and Hoeting, Jennifer A. 1997. Bayesian model averaging for linear regression models. *Journal of the American Statistical Association*, **92**(437), 179–191.

Rahimi, Ali, and Recht, Benjamin. 2007. Random features for large-scale kernel machines. *Advances in Neural Information Processing Systems*, **20**. https://proceedings.neurips.cc/paper_files/paper/2007/hash/013a006f03dbc5392effeb8f18fda755-Abstract.html

Rahimi, Ali, and Recht, Benjamin. 2009. Weighted sums of random kitchen sinks: Replacing minimization with randomization in learning. *Advances in Neural Information Processing Systems*, 20. Curran Associates. https://proceedings.neurips.cc/paper/2007/file/013a006f03dbc5392effeb8f18fda755-Paper.pdf

Rakhlin, Alexander, Shamir, Ohad, and Sridharan, Karthik. 2012. Making gradient descent optimal for strongly convex stochastic optimization. *International Conference on Machine Learning*. https://dl.acm.org/doi/proceedings/10.5555/3042573

Rao, C. Radhakrishna. 1992. Information and the accuracy attainable in the estimation of statistical parameters. *Breakthroughs in Statistics*. Springer, pp. 235–247.

Rasmussen, Carl Edward. 2003. Gaussian processes in machine learning. *Summer School on Machine Learning*. Springer, pp. 63–71.

Ravikumar, Pradeep, Lafferty, John, Liu, Han, and Wasserman, Larry. 2009. Sparse additive models. *Journal of the Royal Statistical Society: Series B (Statistical Methodology)*, **71**(5), 1009–1030.

Rigollet, Philippe, and Tsybakov, Alexander B. 2007. Linear and convex aggregation of density estimators. *Mathematical Methods of Statistics*, **16**(3), 260–280.

Rissanen, Jorma. 1978. Modeling by shortest data description. *Automatica*, **14**(5), 465–471.

Robbins, Herbert. 1952. Some aspects of the sequential design of experiments. *Bulletin of the American Mathematical Society*, **58**(5), 527–535.

Robert, Christian P. 2007. *The Bayesian Choice: From Decision-Theoretic Foundations to Computational Implementation*. Springer.

Rockafellar, Ralph Tyrell. 2015. *Convex Analysis*. Princeton University Press.

Rosenblatt, Frank. 1957. *The Perceptron, a Perceiving and Recognizing Automaton Project Para*. Cornell Aeronautical Laboratory.

Rosenblatt, Frank. 1962. *Principles of Neurodynamics: Perceptrons and the Theory of Brain Mechanisms*. Spartan.

Rudelson, Mark, and Vershynin, Roman. 2010. Non-asymptotic theory of random matrices: extreme singular values. *Proceedings of the International Congress of Mathematicians 2010 (ICM 2010) (In 4 Volumes) Vol. I: Plenary Lectures and Ceremonies Vols. II–IV: Invited Lectures*. World Scientific, pp. 1576–1602.

Rudin, Walter. 2017. *Fourier Analysis on Groups*. Courier Dover Publications.

Rumelhart, David E., Hinton, Geoffrey E., and Williams, Ronald J. 1986. Learning representations by back-propagating errors. *Nature*, **323**(6088), 533–536.

Russo, Daniel, and Van Roy, Benjamin. 2013. Eluder dimension and the sample complexity of optimistic exploration. *Advances in Neural Information Processing Systems*, 26. Curran Associates. https://proceedings.neurips.cc/paper/2013/file/41bfd20a38bb1b0bec75acf0845530a7-Paper.pdf

Russo, Daniel, and Van Roy, Benjamin. 2016. An information-theoretic analysis of Thompson sampling. *The Journal of Machine Learning Research*, **17**(1), 2442–2471.

Russo, Daniel, and Zou, James. 2016. Controlling bias in adaptive data analysis using information theory. *Proceedings of the 19th International Conference on Artificial Intelligence and Statistics*, 51, 1232–1240. https://proceedings.mlr.press/v51/russo16.html

Russo, Daniel, and Zou, James. 2019. How much does your data exploration overfit? Controlling bias via information usage. *IEEE Transactions on Information Theory*, **66**(1), 302–323.

Samuel, Arthur Lee. 1959. Some studies in machine learning using the game of checkers. *IBM Journal of Research and Development*, **3**(3), 210–229.

Sason, Igal, and Verdú, Sergio. 2016. f-divergence inequalities. *IEEE Transactions on Information Theory*, **62**(11), 5973–6006.

Sauer, Norbert. 1972. On the density of families of sets. *Journal of Combinatorial Theory, Series A*, **13**(1), 145–147.

Schapire, R. E., Freund, Y., Bartlett, P. L., and Lee, W. S. 1998. Boosting the margin: A new explanation for the effectiveness of voting methods. *The Annals of Statistics*, **26**(5), 1651–1686.

Schölkopf, Bernhard, Herbrich, Ralf, and Smola, Alex J. 2001. A generalized representer theorem. *International Conference on Computational Learning Theory*. Springer, pp. 416–426.

Schölkopf, Bernhard, Smola, Alexander J., and Bach, Francis. 2018. *Learning with Kernels: Support Vector Machines, Regularization, Optimization, and Beyond*. MIT Press.

Schwarz, Gideon. 1978. Estimating the dimension of a model. *The Annals of Statistics*, **6**(2), 461–464.

Shalev-Shwartz, Shai, Srebro, Nathan, and Zhang, Tong. 2010. Trading accuracy for sparsity in optimization problems with sparsity constraints. *SIAM Journal on Optimization*, **20**, 2807–2832.

Shalev-Shwartz, Shai, Singer, Yoram, Srebro, Nathan, and Cotter, Andrew. 2011. Pegasos: Primal estimated sub-gradient solver for SVM. *Mathematical Programming*, **127**(1), 3–30.

Shamir, Ohad, and Zhang, Tong. 2013. Stochastic gradient descent for non-smooth optimization: Convergence results and optimal averaging schemes. *Proceedings of the 30th International Conference on Machine Learning*, 28, PMLR, pp. 71–79. https://proceedings.mlr.press/v28/shamir13.html

Simchi-Levi, David, and Xu, Yunzong. 2021. Bypassing the monster: A faster and simpler optimal algorithm for contextual bandits under realizability. *Mathematics of Operations Research*, **47**(3), 1904–1931.

Slepian, David. 1962. The one-sided barrier problem for Gaussian noise. *Bell System Technical Journal*, **41**(2), 463–501.

Steele, J. Michael. 1986. An Efron–Stein inequality for nonsymmetric statistics. *The Annals of Statistics*, **14**(2), 753–758.

Steinwart, Ingo. 2001. On the influence of the kernel on the consistency of support vector machines. *Journal of Machine Learning Research*, **2**(Nov), 67–93.

Stone, Charles J. 1982. Optimal global rates of convergence for nonparametric regression. *The Annals of Statistics*, **10**(4), 1040–1053.

Stone, Charles J. 1985. Additive regression and other nonparametric models. *The Annals of Statistics*, **13**(2), 689–705.

Studer, Rudi, Benjamins, V. Richard, and Fensel, Dieter. 1998. Knowledge engineering: Principles and methods. *Data & Knowledge Engineering*, **25**(1–2), 161–197.

Sudakov, Vladimir N. 1969. Gaussian measures, Cauchy measures and ε-entropy. *Soviet mathematics. Doklady*, **10**, 310–313.

Sun, Wen, Jiang, Nan, Krishnamurthy, Akshay, Agarwal, Alekh, and Langford, John. 2019. Model-based RL in contextual decision processes: PAC bounds and exponential improvements over model-free approaches. *Proceedings of the 32nd Conference on Learning Theory*, 99, 2898–2933. https://proceedings.mlr.press/v99/sun19a.html

Sutton, Richard S., and Barto, Andrew G. 2018. *Reinforcement Learning: An Introduction*. MIT Press.

Talagrand, Michel. 1995. Concentration of measure and isoperimetric inequalities in product spaces. *Publications Mathématiques de l'Institut des Hautes Etudes Scientifiques*, **81**(1), 73–205.

Talagrand, Michel. 1996a. Majorizing measures: The generic chaining. *The Annals of Probability*, **24**(3), 1049–1103.

Talagrand, Michel. 1996b. New concentration inequalities in product spaces. *Inventiones mathematicae*, **126**(3), 505–563.

Tan, Mingxing, and Le, Quoc V. 2019. Efficientnet: Rethinking model scaling for convolutional neural networks. *Proceedings of the 30th International Conference on Machine Learning*, 97, 6105–6114. https://proceedings.mlr.press/v97/tan19a.html

Telgarsky, Matus. 2016. Benefits of depth in neural networks. *29th Annual Conference on Learning Theory*, 49, PMLR, pp. 1517–1539. https://proceedings.mlr.press/v49/telgarsky16.html

Thompson, William R. 1933. On the likelihood that one unknown probability exceeds another in view of the evidence of two samples. *Biometrika*, **25**(3/4), 285–294.

Tibshirani, Robert. 1996. Regression shrinkage and selection via the Lasso. *Journal of the Royal Statistical Society: Series B (Methodological)*, **58**(1), 267–288.

Tropp, Joel A. 2004. Greed is good: Algorithmic results for sparse approximation. *IEEE Transactions on Information Theory*, **50**(10), 2231–2242.

Tropp, Joel A. 2006. Just relax: Convex programming methods for identifying sparse signals in noise. *IEEE Transactions on Information Theory*, **52**(3), 1030–1051.

Tropp, Joel A. 2015. *An Introduction to Matrix Concentration Inequalities*. Now Foundations and Trends.

Tsigler, Alexander, and Bartlett, Peter L. 2020. Benign overfitting in ridge regression. arXiv preprint arXiv:2009.14286.

Tsochantaridis, Ioannis, Joachims, Thorsten, Hofmann, Thomas, and Altun, Yasemin. 2005. Large margin methods for structured and interdependent output variables. *Journal of Machine Learning Research*, **6**(Sep), 1453–1484.

Tsybakov, Alexandre B. 2003. Optimal rates of aggregation. *Learning Theory and Kernel Machines*. Springer, pp. 303–313.

Tsybakov, Alexandre B. 2004. Optimal aggregation of classifiers in statistical learning. *The Annals of Statistics*, **32**(1), 135–166.

Valiant, Leslie G. 1984. A theory of the learnable. *Communications of the ACM*, **27**(11), 1134–1142.

van de Geer, Sara. 1993. Hellinger-consistency of certain nonparametric maximum likelihood estimators. *The Annals of Statistics*, **21**(1), 14–44.

van de Geer, Sara. 2000. *Empirical Processes in M-estimation*, vol. 6. of Cambridge Series in Statistical and Probabilistic Mathematics. Cambridge University Press.

van der Vaart, Aad. 1994. Bracketing smooth functions. *Stochastic Processes and their Applications*, **52**(1), 93–105.

van der Vaart, Aad W., and Wellner, Jon A. 1996. *Weak Convergence and Empirical Processes with Application to Statistics*. Springer.

Vapnik, Vladimir. 2013. *The Nature of Statistical Learning Theory*. Springer Science & Business Media.

Vapnik, Vladimir N. 1999. An overview of statistical learning theory. *IEEE Transactions on Neural Networks*, **10**(5), 988–999.

Vapnik, Vladimir Naumovich, and Chervonenkis, Aleksei Yakovlevich. 1968. The uniform convergence of frequencies of the appearance of events to their probabilities. *Doklady Akademii Nauk*, **181**(4), 781–783

Vapnik, V. N., and Chervonenkis, A. J. 1971. On the uniform convergence of relative frequencies of events to their probabilities. *Theory of Probability and Applications*, **16**, 264–280.

Vardi, Gal, Yehudai, Gilad, and Shamir, Ohad. 2022. Width is less important than depth in ReLU neural networks. *Proceedings of 35th Conference on Learning Theory*, 178, 1249–1281. https://proceedings.mlr.press/v178/vardi22a.html

Vovk, Volodimir G. 1990. Aggregating strategies. *Proceedings of Computational Learning Theory, 1990*. https://dl.acm.org/doi/proceedings/10.5555/92571

Vovk, Volodya. 2001. Competitive on-line statistics. *International Statistical Review*, **69**(2), 213–248.

Wahba, Grace. 1990. *Spline Models for Observational Data*. SIAM.

Wainwright, Martin J. 2009. Sharp thresholds for high-dimensional and noisy sparsity recovery using ℓ_1-constrained quadratic programming (Lasso). *IEEE Transactions on Information Theory*, **55**(5), 2183–2202.

Wainwright, Martin J. 2019. *High-Dimensional Statistics: A Non-Asymptotic Viewpoint*, vol. 48 of Cambridge Series in Statistical and Probabilistic Mathematics. Cambridge University Press.

Wand, Matt P., and Jones, M. Chris. 1994. *Kernel Smoothing*. CRC Press.

Wang, Ruosong, Salakhutdinov, Russ R., and Yang, Lin. 2020. Reinforcement learning with general value function approximation: Provably efficient approach via bounded eluder dimension. *Advances in Neural Information Processing Systems*, **33**, 6123–6135.

Wasserman, Larry. 2000. Bayesian model selection and model averaging. *Journal of Mathematical Psychology*, **44**(1), 92–107.

Watkins, Christopher J. C. H., and Dayan, Peter. 1992. Q-learning. *Machine Learning*, **8**(3), 279–292.

Welling, Max, and Teh, Yee W. 2011. Bayesian learning via stochastic gradient Langevin dynamics. *Proceedings of the 28th International Conference on Machine Learning (ICML-11)* Omnipress, pp. 681–688. https://dl.acm.org/doi/proceedings/10.5555/3104482

Williams, Christopher K.I. 1997. Computing with infinite networks. *Advances in Neural Information Processing Systems*, 9. MIT Press. https://proceedings.neurips.cc /paper/1996/file/ae5e3ce40e0404a45ecacaaf05e5f735-Paper.pdf

Williams, Ronald J. 1992. Simple statistical gradient-following algorithms for connectionist reinforcement learning. *Machine Learning*, **8**(3), 229–256.

Wong, Wing Hung, and Shen, Xiaotong. 1995. Probability inequalities for likelihood ratios and convergence rates of sieve MLEs. *The Annals of Statistics*, **23**(2), 339–362.

Xu, Aolin, and Raginsky, Maxim. 2017. Information-theoretic analysis of generalization capability of learning algorithms. *Advances in Neural Information Processing Systems*, **30**. Curran Associates. https://proceedings.neurips.cc /paper/2017/file/ad71c82b22f4f65b9398f76d8be4c615-Paper.pdf

Yang, Yuhong. 1999. Minimax nonparametric classification. I. Rates of convergence. *IEEE Transactions on Information Theory*, **45**(7), 2271–2284.

Yang, Yuhong, and Barron, Andrew. 1999. Information-theoretic determination of minimax rates of convergence. *The Annals of Statistics*, **27**(5), 1564–1599.

Yu, Bin. 1997. Assouad, Fano and LeCam. *Festschrift for Lucien LeCam*. Springer, pp. 423–435.

Zanette, Andrea, Lazaric, Alessandro, Kochenderfer, Mykel, and Brunskill, Emma. 2020. Learning near optimal policies with low inherent Bellman error. *Proceedings of the 37th International Conference on Machine Learning*, 119, 10978–10989. https://proceedings.mlr.press/v119/zanette20a.html

Zhang, Chiyuan, Bengio, Samy, Hardt, Moritz, Recht, Benjamin, and Vinyals, Oriol. 2017. Understanding deep learning requires rethinking generalization. *5th International Conference on Learning Representations*. Palais des Congrès Neptune, Toulon, France, April 24–26.

Zhang, Cun-Hui. 2010. Nearly unbiased variable selection under minimax concave penalty. *The Annals of Statistics*, **38**(2), 894–942.

Zhang, Cun-Hui, and Zhang, Tong. 2012. A general theory of concave regularization for high-dimensional sparse estimation problems. *Statistical Science*, **27**(4), 576–593.

Zhang, Tong. 2002. Covering number bounds of certain regularized linear function classes. *Journal of Machine Learning Research*, **2**, 527–550.

Zhang, Tong. 2003a. Leave-one-out bounds for kernel methods. *Neural Computation*, **15**, 1397–1437.

Zhang, Tong. 2003b. Sequential greedy approximation for certain convex optimization problems. *IEEE Transaction on Information Theory*, **49**, 682–691.

Zhang, Tong. 2004a. Solving large scale linear prediction problems using stochastic gradient descent algorithms. *Proceedings of the 21st International Conference on Machine Learning*. Association for Computing Machinery.

Zhang, Tong. 2004b. Statistical behavior and consistency of classification methods based on convex risk minimization. *The Annals of Statistics*, **32**(1), 56–85.

Zhang, Tong. 2005. Data dependent concentration bounds for sequential prediction algorithms. *Learning Theory: 18th Annual Conference on Learning Theory*. Springer, pp. 173–187.

Zhang, Tong. 2006. Information theoretical upper and lower bounds for statistical estimation. *IEEE Transactions of Information Theory*, **52**, 1307–1321.

Zhang, Tong. 2009a. On the consistency of feature selection using greedy least squares regression. *Journal of Machine Learning Research*, **10**, 555–568.

Zhang, Tong. 2009b. Some sharp performance bounds for least squares regression with $L1$ regularization. *The Annals of Statistics*, **37**(5A), 2109–2144.

Zhang, Tong. 2011. Sparse recovery with orthogonal matching pursuit under RIP. *IEEE Transactions on Information Theory*, **57**, 6215–6221.

Zhang, Tong. 2022. Feel-Good Thompson sampling for Contextual Bandits and Reinforcement Learning. *SIAM Journal on Mathematics of Data Science*, **4**(2), 834–857. https://doi.org/10.1137/21M140924X

Zhang, Tong, and Yu, Bin. 2005. Boosting with early stopping: convergence and consistency. *The Annals of Statistics*, **33**, 1538–1579.

Zhang, Tong, Damerau, Fred, and Johnson, David. 2002. Text chunking based on a generalization of Winnow. *Journal of Machine Learning Research*, **2**(4), 615–637.

Zhao, Peng, and Yu, Bin. 2006. On model selection consistency of Lasso. *Journal of Machine Learning Research*, **7**, 2541–2567.

Zhou, Ding-Xuan. 2002. The covering number in learning theory. *Journal of Complexity*, **18**(3), 739–767.

Zhou, Ding-Xuan. 2003. Capacity of reproducing kernel spaces in learning theory. *IEEE Transactions on Information Theory*, **49**(7), 1743–1752.

Zhou, Dongruo, and Gu, Quanquan. 2022. Computationally efficient horizon-free reinforcement learning for linear mixture MDPs. In *Conference on Neural Information Processing Systems*, vol. 35. arXiv preprint arXiv:2205.11507.

Zhou, Dongruo, Gu, Quanquan, and Szepesvari, Csaba. 2021. Nearly minimax optimal reinforcement learning for linear mixture Markov decision processes. *Proceedings of 34th Conference on Learning Theory*, 134, 4532–4576. https://proceedings.mlr.press/v134/zhou21a.html

Zinkevich, Martin. 2003. Online convex programming and generalized infinitesimal gradient ascent. *ICML'03: Proceedings of the Twentieth International Conference on International Conference on Machine Learning*. AAAI Press, pp. 928–936.

Zou, Difan, and Gu, Quanquan. 2019. An improved analysis of training over-parameterized deep neural networks. *Advances in Neural Information Processing Systems*, 32. Curran Associates. https://proceedings.neurips.cc/paper/2019/file/6a61d423d02a1c56250dc23ae7ff12f3-Paper.pdf

Zou, Difan, Cao, Yuan, Zhou, Dongruo, and Gu, Quanquan. 2020. Stochastic gradient descent optimizes over-parameterized deep ReLU networks. *Machine Learning*, **109**(3), 467–492.

Zou, Difan, Wu, Jingfeng, Braverman, Vladimir, Gu, Quanquan, and Kakade, Sham. 2021. Benign overfitting of constant-stepsize SGD for linear regression. *Proceedings of 34th Conference on Learning Theory*, 134, 4633–4635. https://proceedings.mlr.press/v134/zou21a.html

Author Index

Subject Index

Printed in the USA
CPSIA information can be obtained
at www.ICGtesting.com
LVHW080925030923
757096LV00006B/15